Félix Fénéon

Félix Fénéon in 1886. Photograph, Paulhan archives, Paris.

Félix Fénéon
Aesthete & Anarchist in Fin-de-Siècle Paris

JOAN UNGERSMA HALPERIN

FOREWORD BY *Germaine Brée*

YALE UNIVERSITY PRESS
New Haven & London

Publication of this book has been aided by a grant from The Millard Meiss Publication Fund of the College Art Association of America.

MM

Designed by Susan P. Fillion and set in Garamond 3 type by The Composing Room of Michigan, Inc. Printed in the United States of America by Arcata Graphics/Halliday.

Library of Congress Cataloging-in-Publication Data
Halperin, Joan U.
Félix Fénéon, aesthete and anarchist in fin-de-siècle Paris / Joan Ungersma Halperin ; with a foreword by Germaine Brée.
p. cm.
Bibliography: p.
Includes index.
ISBN 0-300-04300-7 (alk. paper)
1. Fénéon, Félix, 1861–1944. 2. Art critics—France—Biography. 3. Art critics—France—Political activity. 4. Arts, French—France—Paris. 5. Arts, Modern—19th century—France—Paris. 6. Arts, Modern—20th century—France—Paris. I. Title.
NX640.5.F46H35 1988
700′.92′4—dc19
[B] 88-9649

The paper in this book meets the guidelines for permanence and durability of the Committee on Production Guidelines for Book Longevity of the Council on Library Resources.

10 9 8 7 6 5 4 3 2 1

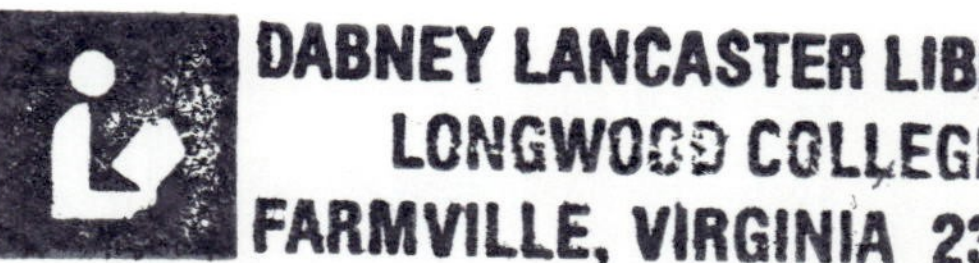

to Matthew, Ilana,
and to Mary and Aaron

Contents

PART FOUR. *Iris-In on Anarchism: 1891–1894*

PART FIVE. *And After . . . 1894–1910*

Foreword

"I have said that we need to know everything about Fénéon and that we know very little. There is less continuity in his life than there are discontinuities. He shows himself to us, fully, but only briefly, then disappears. We don't see him again for a long time." So wrote Jean Paulhan in his introduction to the collection of Félix Fénéon's writing which he published in 1948. Four years earlier Fénéon, at age eighty-three, had disappeared for the last time—almost completely, too, until a young scholar from California, Joan Ungersma, intrigued by Fénéon's "Nouvelles en trois lignes" (three-line "fillers" on trivial daily events sent to the press), set out to investigate the man known essentially as *the* outstanding art critic of the turn of the century.

Today, we know a great deal more about Fénéon than did even Jean Paulhan, one of his friends and admirers. We know more because of the exemplary work of Joan Ungersma Halperin, and a few others who aided her search. Her research led her in unexpected directions, including the Police Archives of Paris where she was most courteously received, but where she had to deal with the work of *real* bookworms, who had eaten their way undisturbed through important documents. Her task required patience, humor, an understanding of very different people's ways, and a total commitment to the researcher's goal during the twenty-five years of work which culminate in the present biography. In 1970, Halperin's prize-winning publication of Fénéon's *Oeuvres plus que complètes* (undertaken under the aegis of Paulhan, who had come to trust the young scholar), followed in 1980 by a brilliant and well-illustrated essay on *Félix Fénéon and the Language of Art Criticism,* brought back into public view the critic who had successfully carried out a "disappearing act" throughout his long life. Now Joan Halperin's biography does much to fill in the gaps remarked by Paulhan, to explore and situate the "discontinuities" in a life Fénéon had always carefully guarded from public view, and part of which he concealed even from his friends.

It must have been a great temptation, in presenting so complex a figure, to take the bits of information collected fifteen to thirty years after his death (and up to eighty years after his most active period) and shape or unify them for the sake of coherence, adjusting facts to suit a theory. This Halperin never does. Wisely, she presents Fénéon in all his roles, still complex, still enigmatic, but more human, fallible, and interesting. The biography brings us many new documents: hitherto unpublished letters, some intimate, highlighting facets of Fénéon's private life.

Halperin discovered, through circumstantial evidence and the corroboration of one of Fénéon's friends, that it was he who bombed the elegant Foyot restaurant at the apogee of the anarchist protest against social injustice and suffering at the end of the nineteenth century. One may well wonder at the thoughts and feelings of a man who could listen with perfect self-control to the testimony of the poet Mallarmé, who vouched with touching sincerity that Fénéon was a gentle person incapable of any such act of violence as he had in fact perpetrated. There is nothing Dostoevskian about Fénéon. It is, however, one of Halperin's strengths that she makes no attempt to psychoanalyze him, leaving it to the reader to confront the facts in the data she has so scrupulously collected, and Fénéon's essential mystery.

Her main problem was to bring into focus materials from disparate areas of activity. Fénéon's life refused to be told as a story centered in a personality, developing along chronological lines. The task was made yet more complex by the fact that there was nothing flamboyant or "romantic" about the man. Quite the contrary. Adept at hiding his several selves, he was simultaneously: a champion of new art and literature; an editor and critic; a member of the anarchist movement; a far-from-orthodox but devoted lover and friend; a loving son to his mother.

Among the many aspects of Fénéon's work were several that place him among the early modernists: most clearly, the fragmentation of his work, which was paralleled in his life, a life as fragmented as the literary coteries of the time. What distinguished him as a critic, Halperin notes, was his uncanny knack of recognizing from the start those beginners who were destined for lasting fame. Yet she follows his lead in speaking also of the lesser known artists and writers he praised who also made their mark, influencing others. Thus the story of his life restores fragments missing from the scenarios of grander figures.

Fénéon's combination of intuitive judgment and indifference to personal prestige, of involvement, individual loyalties and cool, ironic detachment, all crisscross in unexpected ways. Thus the format Halperin has chosen: a sequence of time frames, presenting the major activities of each period, focusing on a "specific field" in order to "see it in depth," then refocusing on a different field in the same time span. The method explains her use of terms borrowed from cinematography such as focus, refocus, and "iris-in": a shot, Halperin explains, that "opens from darkness in an expanding circle of light." From segment to segment that circle slowly expands as she writes, to illuminate all the zones of activity of Fénéon's life successively highlighted. Throughout, Halperin also etches the unchanging marks of the critic's personality, his *style,* and his *morality.*

Using Fénéon as ubiquitous guide, she also recreates the Paris scene, chaotic, fragmented. She avoids stressing the primacy of Fénéon in that scene, the biographer's temptation and an overriding concern in our Western culture, preoccupied mainly by the individual. What she does rather is to adumbrate certain underlying forces of malaise and refusal in French society which Fénéon somehow reflected and acted upon.

Thus, her book is more than a biography of Fénéon, although it is indeed that. As it brings to life the struggles of the post-impressionists and the symbolists, it also sketches, in some depth, the underlying turmoil beneath the brilliant facade of "La Belle Epoque." Terrorism has, of course, its own history. But the motivation of the individual terrorist is not all of a piece. Since Fénéon gives no clue to his internal life, one can only surmise that—vividly aware as he was of the deep perturbations in the realm of the creative arts—he found unbearable the complacency of a class as blind to the plight of the working classes as was the European "grande bourgeoisie" of La Belle Epoque. This was all the more unbearable, perhaps, because of the high visibility of the arts in that milieu, and the political impotence of that triple outsider, the intellectual artist-critic-anarchist Fénéon was. Only the most skillful and sympathetic researcher could have brought this complex man and his era so clearly into focus for us.

Germaine Brée

Preface

Félix Fénéon developed a new style of art criticism, ably defended Seurat and other post-impressionists, and then stopped writing. His silence disturbed other writers; the symbolist critic, Remy de Gourmont, exclaimed his distress: "Having written and shown a superior talent in exposing new ideas, and then suddenly to fall silent? . . . If M. Fénéon thinks we have too many good writers at this time, he is mistaken!"[1]

Yet Fénéon, who did not always sign his work, wrote more than his contemporaries knew. Scattered in many little reviews, a fair number of his articles were gathered and published four years after his death by Jean Paulhan (*Oeuvres,* 1948); Françoise Cachin later chose and presented a brilliant selection of his art criticism (*Au-delà de l'impressionnisme,* 1966). Invited by Jean Paulhan in 1962 to look for Fénéon's "lost works," I searched out many more pieces and published his "More Than Complete Works" in 1970, choosing this title for its fin-de-siècle flavor and, more pertinently, because Fénéon adamantly refused any offer during his lifetime to collect his writings in book form. I wished to defer posthumously to his feeling that such an edition would be "more than" he wanted and to warn the reader that I may have included by mistake some anonymous piece actually written by another.

As editor of more than a dozen little magazines between 1883 and 1903, Fénéon printed new and significant works, including the poet Rimbaud's *Illuminations* and the novelist André Gide's *Paludes.* He preferred, he said, to "work indirectly" and, more particularly, to work invisibly. His influence in this capacity was so wide that he became known as the éminence grise of the Paris literary and art worlds, the shadowy "hidden power" whose decisions helped form the taste and values of a whole generation. He continued to ferret out and support interesting new artists and writers throughout his long life (1861–1944), but he crowded his most significant work into his first forty-five years, the period covered in this biography.

From the mid-1880s until the turn of the century, he was intimately involved in three great movements for artistic and social change: symbolist literature, post-impressionist art, and anarchist agitation for workers' rights. His influence in these areas helped to shape the modern age. For the sake of clarity, this study treats the three fields separately, whereas in fact Fénéon easily combined all spheres at once and served as a link between them.

It has taken years of detective work to thread together the life of this secretive man. He never spoke about himself. He wrote no memoirs, no diary, no autobiographical fiction. But he left an impact on his friends, who spoke about him, and his correspondence with them reveals some of the intimate side of his personality. His style and sense of humor also betray his private concerns. Thus through stylistic analysis I was able to gain a sense of the man while I was searching out his anonymous writings. Interviewing more than twenty people who had known him and tracing evidence in various archives gave me plenty of facts to work with. What I found sometimes surprised even his closest friends, whose testimonies were often contradictory.

"He never laughed," remarked the orientalist Solange Lemaître, "Smile, yes, often—but laugh? Never."

"Laugh?" said the painter Emile Compard. "He had a great Ho! Ho! that would wake up the dead if they still loved life." More than a puzzle, the elusive F. F. became something like a Moebius strip for me: self-contained and continually evolving.

Beyond tracing the man, there was the delicate problem of his prose: "Translating Fénéon would be tantamount to rendering a Sung landscape in department-store plastic," the art historian Robert L. Herbert has said.[2] With this caution in mind, I have nevertheless undertaken to render the many quotations from Fénéon and his contemporaries into English. I hope the reader will get some sense of F. F.'s wit and lapidary language and enjoy the peculiar blend of austerity and arabesque that the symbolists used to express themselves in the 1880s and 1890s.

Taking a cue from the critic himself, who liberally quoted from the authors he was reviewing and even invented stylistic devices that would allow a work of art to speak for itself, I have let the "characters" talk as much as possible in their own words. Most of the letters quoted here were unpublished when I collected them in the 1960s; almost all are still unavailable to the public, even in France.

Here is a brief cast of characters to situate the main figure and his family among the many others in this book:

Félix Fénéon, b. 29 June 1861 (Turin, Italy), d. 29 Feb. 1944 (La-Vallée-aux-Loups, Châtenay-Malabry, Hauts-de-Seine, France). As a young man, he was called "Elie" by his friends; throughout his adult life he was known as "F.F."

Marie-Louise Fénéon, née Jacquin, b. 1836 (Saint-Maurice, Switzerland), d. 1906 (Paris), mother of Félix.

Jules Fénéon, b. 6 Aug. 1824 (Bellevesve, in Burgundy), d. 11 Feb. 1894 (Paris), father of Félix.

Fanny (Stéphanie) Fénéon, née Goubaux, b. 2 Aug. 1868 (Louhans, in Burgundy), d. 19 April 1946 (Plessis-Trévise, Seine-et-Oise). Married Félix Fénéon on 17 June 1897.

Camille Platteel, b. 3 Nov. 1854, (Brussels), d. 23 March 1943 (La Vallée-aux-Loups, Châtenay-Malabry, France). Professor of French literature at the Daschbeck School in Brussels. Met and fell in love with F.F. around 1887. Moved to Paris in 1897 (the year of his marriage to Fanny) and remained his "other wife" the rest of her life.

Acknowledgments

This book would have been less good if I had spent less time on it, and yet twenty-five years seems very long. Long, too, is the list of those who helped me along the way. My gratitude to each is enormous.

Most of the people who first aided me and who knew Fénéon are no longer alive. Their names appear at the beginning of his *Oeuvres plus que complètes*. Others to whom I am particularly indebted are the late Gina Signac and the late Jean Sutter; Pierre Angrand, Françoise Cachin, Gina Doveil, Jean Bouin-Luce, Christopher Lloyd, Jacqueline F. Paulhan, François Sullerot, and Anne Thorold.

I also owe much to Robert L. Herbert, John Rewald, and Martha Ward for helping me bridge the gap between the worlds of letters and art, and to Paul Avrich and the late Arhne Thorne for enriching my understanding of anarchism.

Maureen Wesolowski was untiring in reading for errors in my translations. Before the days of word processors, Esther Davis cheerfully typed and kept my spirits up. Cerinda Survant helped me shape and prune the raw material for the book, while Sandra Grayson must be thanked for her graceful, judicious editing of the final manuscript. Victoria Ungersma was generous in helping obtain the illustrations, and Ute Saine in checking the final copy. "Burning the Effigy" owes much to John Sklute, while Janice Doane, Sandra Grayson, Brenda Hillman, Carol Lashof, Katherine Roper, Phyllis Stowell, and Mary Springer raised important issues that made the last revisions most exciting. My parents Mary and Aaron Ungersma outlived several incarnations of F. F. and helped me read Alexander Cohen's memoirs in the Dutch.

My research began in Paris under an A. B. Johnson Traveling Fellowship from the University of California at Berkeley during 1961–63. The scope of the research was broadened thanks to a fellowship from the American Council of Learned Societies in 1975–76. In 1984–85, a fellowship from the National Endowment for the Humanities allowed me to take time from teaching to finish writing the biography. In March

1986, the manuscript was awarded the Gilbert Chinard Literary Prize for unpublished manuscripts (Institut français de Washington, D.C.). I am also indebted to the Saint Mary's College Alumni Faculty Relations Committee and to the Committee on Faculty and Curriculum Development for grants for illustrations.

Documents for this biography were found in the Bibliothèque Nationale, Paris; the Fondation Jacques Doucet, Universités de Paris, Bibliothèque d'Art et d'Archéologie, and the Bibliothèque Littéraire, whose curator, Monsieur François Chapon, I wish particularly to thank; the Bibliothèque Royale, Brussels; the Ashmolean Museum, Oxford; the Museum and Archives of the Préfecture de Police, Paris; the Galerie Bernheim-Jeune, Paris; the libraries of Yale University and the University of California, Berkeley. In addition, my gratitude goes to the many individuals who opened their archives to me or who responded to my requests for information.

I should like to thank Judy Metro, Judith Calvert, and others at Yale University Press who with sense and style produced this book.

Among my special friends and mentors I wish to name Simone Balayé, Charles Muscatine, Claire Guichard, and most of all: David J. Halperin.

PART ONE

Beginnings 1861–1886

Preview

One spring evening in Paris in 1894, an elegant young man was strolling alone near the Luxembourg Gardens. The sun had set, extinguishing the blooming candelabra of the chestnut trees. Café lights were up and the Latin Quarter stirred with its usual throngs, especially near the Odéon, where the Prince of Wales was expected that night at a performance of the Comédie française. It was the dinner hour for those who ate fashionably late at the Foyot restaurant, across from the Senate on the rue de Vaugirard. The young man had not dined, nor was it his custom to enter establishments like the Foyot, where senators and wealthy foreigners ate leisurely meals served in the grand old style. He passed it by, glancing in at the window, and lit a cigarette. In the crook of his other arm he carried, somewhat incongruously, a flowerpot with a tender young shoot of hyacinth in it—a gift, perhaps, for his lady friend or for his recently widowed mother, to whom he was devoted.

He walked under the trees again and smoked a second cigarette with an air of detachment that was habitual to him. Then he turned and with long strides went down the little street behind the Foyot, stopped for a moment to light a third cigarette, and set the flowerpot on the windowsill of the stately back room of the restaurant. He glanced at his watch, seemed suddenly to realize that he was late for an appointment, and stepped smartly off in the direction of the omnibus that stopped at Odéon square and went in the direction of Montmartre. He jumped on the platform of a departing bus and climbed to the top open deck. He had just sat down, arranging the folds of his Inverness cape, when an explosion rocked the street. The horses bolted and the omnibus went careening down the boulevard Saint-Germain, while the passengers craned their necks to look back at the site of the noise.

"Another bomb," someone said, "after Ravachol, Vaillant, and that young one, Emile Henry! Vermin keep spawning!"

The thin lips of the elegant young man lifted slightly in a smile.

"It's the Odéon!" someone else exclaimed, "just like Barcelona, the anarchists had to hit the theater! What a shame! All those lovely ladies!"

"Indeed?," said the young man, and stood, bracing himself on his long legs, peering back at the thin column of smoke reflecting orange in the light of the street lamps. "No, I believe it is the Foyot," he said, and sat down again. He closed his eyes and felt a wave of satisfaction. The orange smoke shimmered in his memory like a fragile enlarged afterimage of the blue hyacinth. Then it was gone and he erased it from his thoughts.

M. Fénéon was, of course, correct. It was the Foyot restaurant that was devastated by the bomb.[1] The crime was never solved.

> Anarchism was born of a moral revolt against social injustice. When men were to be found who felt as if suffocated by the social climate in which they were obliged to live; who felt the pain of others as if it were their own; who were also convinced that a large part of human suffering is not the inevitable consequence of inexorable natural or supernatural laws, but instead stems from social realities depending on human will and can be eliminated through human effort—the way was open that had to lead to anarchism.
>
> *Errico Malatesta*[2]

CHAPTER 1

Burning the Effigy

Who was this Félix Fénéon, who could slip away unnoticed from committing an act of war on his fellow citizens and escape public accusation for that crime? A man so active in the Paris literary and art worlds of the 1880s and 1890s that every major account of the period names him as a pivotal figure; "He had an instinct," John Rewald said, "for singling out among hundreds of budding talents the two or three which promised genius."[1] Yet he remained intentionally obscure, unknown.

Félix Fénéon was an enigma to his contemporaries. He was a dandy and an anarchist; a model functionary at the War Office and an enemy of the State; a loyal comrade to ordinary people and an aesthete man of letters. "He is perhaps the only critic we have had in the last one hundred years," said Jean Paulhan.[2] In spite of this acclaim, he very nearly succeeded in disappearing from the pages of history.

He was equally a man of letters and a man of action. Mallarmé spoke up for Fénéon when he was arrested in 1894 on suspicion of conspiracy and the possession of explosives: "[He] is one of our most distinguished young writers. . . . Certainly, for Fénéon, there were no better detonators than his articles!"[3] Although ignorant of the fact that Fénéon was the source of the Foyot bomb, Mallarmé was right. The explosion at the Foyot was soon forgotten, but Fénéon's writing still shakes his readers into a new awareness. And yet his willingness to take action where others only talked or posed "shines brighter and higher than many a ruddy page of writing," claimed the symbolist critic, Remy de Gourmont.[4]

Intellectuals like Paul Valéry and Jean Paulhan valued their friendship with him. Valéry said one day, "F. F. is one of the most intelligent men I have ever met. He is just, pitiless, and gentle."[5] Paulhan evoked his paradoxical nature by speaking of Félix Fénéon in the same breath as Buffalo Bill, whose Wild West Show Paulhan had seen when he was a boy, angry and amazed that the enemy of Indians should also be their friend.[6] Just so, Fénéon embodies contradictions that disorient the rest of us, who choose to be something specific (critic or artist, republican or anarchist, cowboy or Indian). Any attempt to circumscribe Fénéon ends in deception, said Paulhan, because he escapes the usual categories.

Fénéon wrote superbly, created a style both eloquent and specific, and then fell silent. He recognized and championed artists destined for lasting fame (Seurat, Rimbaud, Laforgue), but refused credit for the critical role he played in shaping the values of his own and future generations. What led this gifted and successful critic to step away from the limelight? The source of our confusion, Paulhan suggests, is that Fénéon made a choice that few people consider. While working as editor, critic, War Office functionary, art gallery director, newspaperman or publisher, he chose to be—or rather to become—himself, a man freely exploring his own nature.

The paradoxes others saw in him were in fact different segments of a complex whole, carefully kept from view. Behind a mask of impassivity, he was free to explore a fuller range of human possibilities. His decorous manner kept others at a distance and created the kind of privacy that allowed him to discover his own ambivalences and inner contradictions. If something threatened to pin him down, he responded with the unexpected. "I am a Burgundian born in Turin," he said to those who wanted to know where he was from. Yet he had no romantic mission to "startle the bourgeois." It was enough, simply, to preserve his own individuality—the flash of wit in an unattended turn of thought, his anarchist choice for freedom in all regards. Or a touch of irony, stating the opposite of what he intended, a chance for others to fill in and judge for themselves, to reclaim their own freedom. To maintain this liberty without arousing shock and opposition, style was of the essence—style seen not only as a way of speaking, painting, writing, but as a way of being.

Out of the many conflicting aspects of his life and character, he built his own persona. His style, how he spoke, dressed, joked, wrote, made love, was the fruit of his individual imagination. Everything from his anarchism to his syntax was shaped deliberately. His style of writing was as contrived and composed as his top-hatted appearance; often difficult to decipher, sometimes crystalline and always terse, "cuneiform." Because of a consummate sense of style, he was able to conduct a double or triple existence with "absolute integrity." He "always had two wives," said Jean Paulhan; he convinced the Assize Court of the Seine that he was innocent of wrongdoing, whereas he had participated in anarchist propaganda not only by writing, but by planting a terrorist bomb.

Certain facets of his own identity were drawn from the contradictions in the world around him. After the debacle of the Second Empire and the repression of the Commune, conflicting impulses tore at French society: monarchist and proletarian claims on a bourgeois Republic (the third attempted since the Revolution); isolationist policy and the drive for imperial conquests; "decadence" in the arts and industrial progress; eroticism and decorum; unbearable suffering of workers amid the pleasures of the "Belle Epoque . . . ." How can one live a philosophy of integrity in a tumultuous, evolving society? Fénéon took a bipolar or even tripolar stance, a logical emblem of the multivalent, modern world, where people live with complex and even contradictory value systems.

In order to be himself, Fénéon wore a variety of masks. His physical mask is apparent in every portrait and description of him. Tall, angular, with a long face, small pale gold-flecked eyes, wide thin lips, and a big straight nose, he chose to complete a certain resemblance to the figure of Uncle Sam by shaving beard and mustache (in a time when only priest or actor went clean-shaven), leaving only a handful of blond strands *under* his chin. This goatee, which the French saw mainly in caricatures of Yankees or in Jules Verne novels, became his hallmark. "Monsieur Félix Fénéon is a satyr born in Brooklyn (U.S.A.)," quipped Alfred Jarry, speaking as Monsieur Ubu; Guillaume Apollinaire referred to Fénéon in 1914 as a "false Yankee" selling avant-garde paintings.

His speech and manner, and particularly his deadpan humor, impressed his contemporaries as Anglo-Saxon. He was, according to them, immutably phlegmatic.

> Félix Fénéon has such a distinctive way of talking, that when one thinks of him, one hears him first of all. He hesitates slightly when speaking, as if he were deciphering a rather difficult text. The word he finds in his mind is always the rarest one, but also the most accurate . . . This chosen thought comes to you slowly, through a high pitched voice with no modulation, ritualistic and extremely gentle, relating so little to his tall, solidly built frame that at first it makes you think of a hoax—but one gets used to it quickly.[7]

His hands made only slight, infrequent motions, different from the gesticulation of his more volatile compatriots. While talking, he often went to get a book that illustrated his idea, or to the Littré dictionary, which he owned in a multivolume edition. "He liked to savor the absolute density of a word," one of his painter friends remarked.[8]

Fénéon claimed that he wrote as he spoke—slowly, and without facility. Willy called him *Le père Laconique* (Old Man Laconic) and Jarry, *Celui qui silence* (The Silent One).* Although spare, Fénéon's words carried far. "Ce fut un bel adolescent," he quipped of Jean Cocteau. Samples of his barbed wit can be found in the *Petit bottin des lettres et des arts* (Little Who's Who of Arts and Letters) that he wrote with comrades and published anonymously in 1886:

> LEMAITRE (Jules). Belongs to that category of professors—the most dangerous—who pretend to understand something.
>
> LOTI (Pierre). In a pale style, he paints in pale blue, pale green, pale rose, and pale black—the sea, tropical blossoms, the faces of good mariners, and the breasts of little dark-skinned girls.

Or in his book reviews (1888):

> DOSTOYEVSKY: *The Brothers Karamazov.* A lot of characters; for each a lot of cucumbers, quantities of mysterious sufferings, and adventures in abundance (2 volumes). Interesting milieux for curious Westerners: convents, courtrooms, etc.

*Jarry's verb, *silence,* is a neologism, meaning not at all "to cause to be silent," as in English, but the act itself of silence; it also contains a pun incorporating a hidden antithesis: *Celui qui s'y lance* (He who plunges ahead).

JEAN LARROQUE: *Pen and Sword in the Seventeenth Century.* It was not without tedium that M. Larroque was able to read—and how conscientiously!—every work produced in one century. He thought he should not have to suffer this tedium alone.

Reporting on an exhibition (1888):

Jules MACHARD. Over shoulders, arms, bosoms, M. Machard maneuvres.

John-Lewis BROWN. Horses, jockeys, society for the betterment of the equine species, bois de Boulogne, etc. M. Edgar Degas found twenty paintings there, and M. Brown the way to make a single one a hundred times over.

Finally, reporting the news in three lines (1906):

—Silot, a valet in Neuilly, installs a lady of
pleasure during his master's absence, then disappears,
taking everything—except her.
—Finding his daughter (aged 19) lacking in austerity,
watchmaker Jallot of Saint-Etienne killed her. True,
he still has eleven other children.

This kind of wit, call it "black humor" or "yellow laughter," later flourished among writers Fénéon liked, from Jarry and Oscar Wilde to Max Jacob. It was just as pervasive in the work of his favorite painter, Seurat: enigmatic yet open to the viewer's cast of thought.

Fénéon cultivated a style which he called "icy Anglo-American comic."[9] He was expert at telling the most scabrous of stories with a perfectly bland expression. Those who knew only his genteel side have expressed total disbelief at hearing these tales. When asked for his opinion about certain obscene drawings on the walls of public toilets, he responded: "These graffiti are the work of unsung artists who lack means of expression and are the victims of circumstance."[10]

Fénéon's mask assumed, for different people, different proportions. Toulouse-Lautrec, one of his most acute observers, used to call him "le Bouddha," evoking the inner calm and intensity beneath Fénéon's inscrutable exterior. But when Lautrec portrayed Fénéon in the foreground of his painting for the dancer La Goulue, he gave the critic a satanic air, his head and goatee painted entirely in yellow (pl. 19). Other observers, such as Remy de Gourmont, remarked that Fénéon often "took on the airs of an American Mephistopheles." More than once, in fact, Fénéon drew self-portraits suggesting a likeness between his features and those of Goethe's demon as traditionally depicted for Parisians, complete with wispy goatee, in popular productions of Gounod's opera, *Faust,* and Berlioz's *Damnation of Faust.*

Beyond the physical mask, Fénéon evoked the moral stance of Mephistopheles, a wholehearted skeptic who, unlike Satan, suffers no "divine discontent." One of his self-portraits, probably done while awaiting trial in 1894, shows his head hanging from a hook nailed to the wall, and the face, with its intent gaze, questioning frown, and goatee, is Mephistophelean. He had given a similar drawing to the English poet John Gray, who wrote in 1890, "Please send me another picture of you! I had the misfortune to lose that self-portrait of noble Mephistopheles."[11] The pose Fénéon struck for a photographer after his release from prison again mirrors the fierce, eerie gaze of Faust's devil.

However, he did not reflect Mephistopheles' wordiness. Many of Fénéon's acquaintances were piqued, in fact, by his diabolic reserve. They were suspicious of being fooled, or even of *being fools,* in his presence:

> What was Fénéon thinking, exactly? Nobody could have known. I think that deep down he had the greatest contempt for his contemporaries . . .[12]

"At bottom, he's not thinking anything, he doesn't care a fig!" exclaimed his close friend Paul Adam and added: "a loud clear burst of laughter, like the laugh of an English Miss, breaks his impenetrable calm from time to time."[13]

Fénéon's enthusiasm for what appeared to others as outlandish—such as Poictevin's prose, the *vers libre,* Rimbaud's *Illuminations,* and Seurat's painting—was sometimes felt by even his close associates to be a hoax. During a gathering at the *Revue indépendante* in 1888, where a group of writers and artists were speaking, gesticulating, revealing their fears and aspirations, Fénéon, "who seemed the most original, whose hide we would have particularly liked to peel off, sat in silence, looking, listening, and apparently judging. Perhaps he was in fact judging, and the approval he gave to outrageous effects was simply persiflage, and he was laughing to himself."[14] People who knew Fénéon often felt cheated. They also felt vulnerable in the face of his wit.

As soon as he had established his reputation as a critic, Fénéon began indulging in a series of mystifying pseudonyms: Gil de Bache, for example, the name of a pirate from the seventeenth century who reportedly robbed his victims of their finery and set them ashore to continue their journey in their stocking feet. He encouraged his friends to use the name Elie, a euphonic improvement over the rather ordinary and absurd name Félix ("lucky"). In fact, Elie was the last of Fénéon's five baptismal names, and the most unusual.

He was also "Porphyre," borrowed from Porfiry Petrovitch, the examining magistrate in Dostoyevsky's *Crime and Punishment,* whose role bears some resemblance to Félix Fénéon vis-à-vis the painters and poets whose works he criticized.[15] Both are masters of irony, recognizing a hollowness in their elevated status as critic or judge. To protect their deep and direct intuitions, they are each bent upon an exact and mathematical presentation of evidence. "I should like to make a chain of evidence such as twice two are four!" exclaims Porfiry Petrovitch.[16] In a similar vein, Félix Fénéon once wrote, after a dry enumeration of bad paintings:

> Enough verdicts without sanction. Henceforth, with Charles Henry's Aesthetic Protractor and Triple-decimeter in hand and with a serene soul, the critic can record without bombast the rhythm and measurement of colorations, angles, lines, can write a name, a title and a few figures.

Although he spoke seriously elsewhere of Charles Henry's scientific investigation of color and form, Fénéon continued here, tongue in cheek:

> The reader can verify if the numbers that symbolize a certain work of art have the form 2^n or are the prime numbers of the form $2^n + 1$, or are products of one or more numbers of this form by a power of 2.[17]

Above, ***Félix Fénéon in 1894.*** Photograph by ALFRED NATANSON. Courtesy Annette Vaillant, Paris.

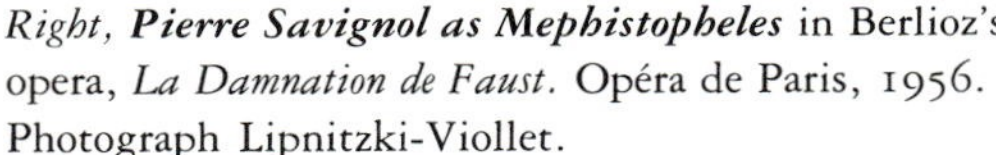

Right, ***Pierre Savignol as Mephistopheles*** in Berlioz's opera, *La Damnation de Faust.* Opéra de Paris, 1956. Photograph Lipnitzki-Viollet.

Certainly some insight into Fénéon is implicit in his metamorphizing his own name into "Elie Manéon," "Ottocar Phellion," and even "Outagawafénéon,"[18] most of them erotic and decipherable only by the symbolist in-group.* He seemed cold and impenetrable, yet Willy once replied to him: "How many kind things you say to me,

*"Manéon" is suggestive of *Manon,* Massenet's opera (1884) based on Prévost's novel, and also of *Manette Salomon* (1867), a novel of artist life by the Goncourt brothers. Manon and Manette are women of extraordinary wiles. Fénéon, however, may simply have borrowed "Man" from English, as he did for "Ottocar" (*autocar*—which did not become a French word until about 1907).

Phellion appears in Balzac's novel *Les Employés,* a minor civil servant in a public ministry who works hard and "looks for the right word," like Fénéon, but is unaware of his own ridiculousness.

"Outagawa" is a play on *Uta*maro I, also known as Kita*gawa,* an eighteenth-century Japanese artist known for his representation of wanton women and illustrations for erotica.

FÉLIX FÉNÉON. ***Self Portrait.*** Drawing reportedly done during the Trial of the Thirty, August 1894. Words on the hook and nail: ANTRURIA RIDULARIUM.

scoffing, in your gentle way, dear and nearly impassive F. F."[19] Willy was in many ways a disreputable character, and yet he enjoyed Fénéon's affection. Not everyone felt so lucky. When Jean Paulhan published a collection of Fénéon's writings three years after his death, André Breton said:

> Although I got to know him, was amazed by him, admired and loved him, I never understood him as you have. With no little chagrin and sadness I mull over the fact that I did not know how to see him and that it is too late. Besides, his outer shell was rough, and slippery . . .[20]

Fénéon himself recognized the unusual degree of formality he kept in social relations. He admitted to a woman he loved in later years, "I must really have a cross-grained character! Just now I was writing Gustave Kahn that the death of his wife grieves me, and I realized he is the only man in the world to whom I say *tu.*"[21]

Fénéon's extreme courtesy, more than his wit, raised a barrier between him and others. "Hating—or fearing—any display of emotion, Fénéon accepted being labeled 'enigmatic' by his friends, who thus admitted their regret that they could give only esteem to one they would have liked to love."[22]

Did he keep the same distance with his women friends, his wife, and lovers? Presumably not. Those very elements—correct behavior and sensitivity—that created a barrier between him and other men were those which gave him access to womens' thoughts and desires. He had a strongly sensual nature and he was not bound by conventional morality. Yet his cool impassivity convinced most of his male associates that he was not vulnerable to what they would have called female wiles. Heroines in novels where he is depicted (P. Veber's *Passade,* P. Adam's *Coeurs utiles,* and A. Charpentier's *Roman d'un singe,* for example) tend to sigh in amazement, "Why doesn't he respond to my charms?" When the fictional Félix is happily coupled (*Roman d'un singe*), it is with a young woman whose intellect is so developed that she is characterized as having a "male soul," albeit in a virginal, Gibson-girl body. The unrelenting sexism in these novels is reflected in their salacious subject matter.

Fénéon was not exempt from the misogyny that prevailed in late nineteenth-century France, particularly among the symbolists, whose quest to find and express man's unconscious feelings led them to state their distrust and scorn for the female sex without ever coming to grips with their hidden fears and their belief that women were of an evil or inferior "animal" nature. Although one can hardly say that Fénéon held himself aloof from women, it is clear that he did not think of them as equals, at least throughout his early manhood; and the novelists who portrayed Fénéon obviously believed he was above loving an ordinary woman.

In fact, Fénéon was an ardent lover of common working women as well as women privileged with more education and status. It was not unusual in Fénéon's time for men to seek a mistress among dancers and laundresses; both worked in public places, with arms, shoulders, bosoms bared. Yet when my research turned up evidence of Fénéon's lusty, long-lived love affairs, most of his male friends were shocked and disbelieving. The women who shared in his affection and the rare others who knew of these relationships were respectful of his self-imposed laws of secrecy and loyalty, which also protected them. "He did not escape complications in his love life," said one of his women biographers, "but he always arranged things so as to cause the least possible hurt. He was sensible, and perhaps his vulnerability was elsewhere?"[23]

His marriage at age thirty-six was in a sense conventional, since his mother picked the bride, Fanny Goubaux, a divorced woman, the daughter of a friend. But this choice was motivated by compassion rather than the self-interest of traditional bourgeois matches which sought to maintain or increase family status and fortune, for Madame Goubaux was in difficult social and financial circumstances because of her divorce.

Throughout his marriage, with his wife's knowledge, he maintained a relationship with a Belgian woman he had met several years before, Camile Platteel, with whom he also shared his intellectual and artistic interests; an unusual ménage à trois, which lasted forty-six years, until Platteel's death at age eighty-eight.

The complexity of Fénéon's attitude towards women—a mélange of daring, repression, rage, and insight—pertains to the way he defined himself. His pseudonyms include a series of female names: Félicie, Luce, Thérèse, Denise, Agathe. He sometimes signed the name of a woman in his love letters and even in messages to men friends involved in symbolist publications. He admitted using a female pseudonym for some of his published articles. Was this simply a playful game of hidden identities, meant to celebrate some muse in symbolist circles? (Waitresses called Thérèse and Denise are named in a contemporary account of literary gatherings in a Latin Quarter café.) Or rather, given that Fénéon shared the prevailing opinion that a woman's creative endeavors were best conceived as minor or "modest," did he harbor some obscure desire to belittle his own work? This recurrent wish to "become female," which continued through Fénéon's old age, was not a simple matter. When he discovered that Stendhal had experienced the same wish, he wrote to Paul Signac: "It is not at all insignificant to know that the friends of H. B. [Henri *Beyle,* real name of Stendhal] sometimes called him *Belle*—or, supposing H. B. is fooling us, that he would have liked to have been called that."[24]

Fénéon's mistrust of his own feminine sensibilities may help explain why he chose progressively not to write for publication. He had strong emotions, yet hated any effusiveness, any freely expressed enthusiasm—feminine traits. Good writing he found to be controlled, "virile," and he judged himself harshly as a writer. While enjoying, in his imagination, what it would be like to be a woman, he may have despised his own feminine other.

But his playfulness in seeming to be a woman, assuming an identity basically opposite to his own, was also a way of becoming most energetically himself. When Fénéon was well past middle age, a young co-worker noted the integration he had achieved of opposing traits: "simultaneously calm and passionate, nonchalant and hard working, skeptical and fervent, unsentimental and overflowing with lyrical feelings."[25]

Even as a young man, he was nurturing. His friends, one of whom spoke of his "motherly care," knew they could count on him in every sort of circumstance. He identified with outcasts and served as their liaison with conventional society. The poet Henri de Régnier told Edmond de Goncourt that Fénéon was an outlandish fellow who shocked people with odd phrases and surprising ideas and at the same time was "a great-hearted man, good, sensitive, who gives himself totally to eccentric individuals, to the downtrodden, to the very poor."[28] His salary rarely arrived home intact. On the last day of the month, people who were counting on his help were lying in wait for him after he left the cashier's window. Walking quickly, he doled out cash "with his arm stretched out behind him, to avoid any expression of gratitude."[27]

His friends discovered in him a curious indifference to food. Although Count Curnonsky, Paris's official "Prince of Gastronomes," was a close acquaintance, Fénéon himself took no particular interest in the culinary art (except, perhaps, from a sculptural point of view—see "La Plastique culinaire," F, 429). For dinner, which he sometimes took at his desk in the office, he was easily satisfied with a piece of chocolate or Swiss cheese, and a glass of *vin ordinaire.*

He was insensitive to music, except for a brief flirtation in his youth with the work of Wagner, an enthusiasm that was obligatory among the symbolists. After they had attended a concert featuring the music of Francis Poulenc, Fénéon murmured to his mistress, "I prefer the drum." Although he chose Debussy in 1901 to write the music criticism for the *Revue blanche* and published the scores of Darius Milhaud and other composers when editor of the Sirène publishing house in 1920, his musician friends were unanimous in agreeing that F. F. was totally ignorant of the subject.

As for the spiritual side of life, which also enjoyed a great vogue among different groups of artists and writers at the end of the nineteenth century, "no one was further from any preoccupation of the metaphysical sort than Fénéon. No 'agony,' no religious or philosophical question ever disturbed the rare and astonishing equilibrium of his mind."[28] He enjoyed telling how Mallarmé took God out of a poem, replacing that word with another one. Fénéon refused all idolatries, including that of the intellect. Much as he loved Valéry the poet, he had no patience with the Valéry who embodied "intelligence incarnate."[29] He did not yearn for immortality. He admitted he awaited death as one awaits sleep: "a black lake where one is lost, with no return."[30] These were his words when an old man. But what about when he was young, just thirty-three, and facing a possible death penalty as an accused anarchist? A young woman once asked him, and he replied that life had revealed itself sufficiently disillusioning that death seemed no penalty at all.

But he was not wholly imperturbable, and perceptive friends were aware of his intense emotions. "I have seen his face flush with pleasure in front of a canvas," said Emile Verhaeren.[31] His emotions were not only aesthetic. If anyone raised the subject of Emile Henry, his young anarchist friend who was guillotined in 1894, tears filled Fénéon's eyes. Those who knew him found him guilty of imprudence—jumping on a moving train, for instance, or busily correcting proof when he had a high fever.

He cut his wrist once when he pressed too hard on a window that wouldn't open, and answered his mistress who reproached him for his rashness, "She (*la* fenêtre) was resisting me."* He was capable of great indignation, and expressed it, however politely, in an incident that his wife liked to recount: one day they were entertaining a friend at home, when their guest named a woman "with whom I am," he said, "on intimate terms." Fénéon rose and went to his room. After a time his wife went after him, saying that her husband must not be feeling well. She found him placidly reading. Never again did Fénéon receive this guest nor recognize him anywhere, such was his disdain for the behavior of a cad.

He strode out of the cabaret where Aristide Bruant was singing his songs about

*A sardonic reference, perhaps, to a line from a popular play by Alexandre Dumas *fils:* "elle me résistait, je l'ai assassinée" (*Antony*).

Portrait of Solange Lemaître, student of oriental art and friend of F. Fénéon, ca. 1910. Photograph courtesy of Madame Bernard Lemaître.

the poor and the downtrodden and told a young companion: "The money that fellow used to collect in one evening during his heyday would have guaranteed a year's work to one of our people."[32] When displeased Fénéon was not vicious, he was eloquently absent.

"If he seemed made of contradictions," said Solange Lemaître, "it was, I believe, because he became mature very young":

> He looked at the world with a sorrowing eye. The suffering he observed gave him a kind of rancor. . . . Oh, yes, when he was young, perhaps, he enjoyed playing the role of *mystificateur.* Later, the people he gulled never really understood, and he never treated us that way. He had developed a certain gravity, a certain . . . yes, I can say agony over the human condition. As for him, he believed in beauty: beauty in art, in literature, and moral beauty. The ugliness, the pettiness of man revolted him. 'There is a flow inside of humanity,' he would say, as of a flawed gem.[33]

Thus he was like Oscar Wilde, who said, "Aesthetics are higher than ethics. They belong to a more spiritual sphere."[34] René Tavernier confirmed, "Ethics were for him Aesthetics, which explains his extreme attention to beauty—and even his fastidiousness in dress."[35]

Fénéon's passion for beauty, his cool intellect and ardent heart are very like the metaphysical portrait of the *dandy* that Baudelaire drew in his essay, *The Painter of Modern Life.* Barbey d'Aurevilly and especially Mallarmé exemplified the dandy ethic for Fénéon's generation. In fact, people often think of the dandy as having an effeminate taste for dress and material elegance. Fénéon was always impeccably attired. In 1886, he regularly appeared in silk top hat, puce-colored suit, dark red gloves and patent leather shoes. He carried a cane—and a debt of some forty francs to various shoemakers.

"But a dandy does not aspire to money as to something essential . . .," said Baudelaire. "He would be perfectly content with a limitless credit at the bank."[36] While pursued by creditors, Fénéon willingly paid printers' deficits for little magazines and helped many a comrade in need. Only the Yankee goatee struck a defiant note in his carefully groomed appearance. To a dandy's eyes, "which are in love with *distinction* above all things," as Baudelaire noted, "the perfection of his toilet will consist in absolute simplicity."[37]

Although perhaps born of a burning desire for originality, the dandy's persona is not flamboyant, but self-contained, Buddha-like. "The distinguishing characteristic of the dandy's beauty consists above all in an air of coldness which comes from an unshakeable determination not to be moved; you might call it a latent fire which hints at itself, and which could, but chooses not to burst into flame."[38] This self-possession is a kind of pride, pride in self-knowledge and in world-knowledge, and the consequent refusal to participate in vulgarity and trivialities, the will to pursue instead the difficult truths of individual consciousness.

A dandy might commit a crime, said Baudelaire, but never in some trivial cause. When Fénéon was arrested in 1894, the evidence clearly showed that his behavior was criminal in the eyes of the law; his acquittal* was largely due to the perfection of his dandyism.

There seems to be a contradiction between the dandy's cult of the self and Fénéon's anarchist commitment to improve the lot of the ignorant, the poor, and the oppressed, even at the risk of losing his own freedom. Dandyism, however, can be seen as a leveler of old class distinctions, since it is up to the individual to create his or her own "class": "Who ever heard of George B.'s father?" said George "Beau" Brummel, the archetypical dandy.[39] For Fénéon, the perfecting of his own person was contingent upon the anarchist ideal that all people should have the means to enjoy maximum moral and material development. Without ever abandoning his dandyism, he put himself increasingly at the service of others, finding his own pleasure in their achievements. This progressive self-effacement, which began with his youthful series of pseudonyms, resulted finally in a nearly total invisibility.

He signed his first articles with his full name, joined by a hyphen, FELIX-FENEON. Later he kept only his initials, F. F., more often f. f., and this became his ordinary signature, used also in personal correspondence, where he would often draw them in a comic or Fescennine paraph (see letter to Suzanne, p. 20). As time passed, he simply left his articles unsigned, with rare exceptions. If supreme elegance consists in utmost simplicity, supreme pride manifests itself in complete modesty. The initials,

*The trial and acquittal are discussed in chap. 14.

the anonymity of Fénéon are on the one hand signs of modesty, on the other the marks of an aesthete's pride.[40]

Because of his untrammeled self-esteem, Fénéon was able to enjoy the work of others with complete openness. He believed that criticism should be a viaduct between the artist and the public:

> The critic must be a discriminating and inclusive intellect, penetrating the soul of the artist, seizing his aesthetic personality, considering the work of art both from the point of view of the author and from the point of view of the public—a channel for the one and for the other.

At the same time he has to retain a kind of naiveté:

> Anyone can err, especially a critic. But to express without frivolity or insincerity what one feels—I admire that![41]

To understand F. F., one has to accept a statement of opposites, a series of refusals and assents—modesty, pride, enthusiasm, restraint, withdrawal, involvement. "In short," wrote Jean Paulhan, "the most opposite qualities unite in him to form a rather mellow blend. And yet each quality is so extreme that one can't help thinking that Fénéon was a composite of quite a few men, each of whom would have left a tremendous work, if he had not been thwarted by all the others at the same time."[42]

The most interesting of Fénéon's signatures is the simplest, found on two early pieces, one a text on Diderot, the other contesting religious education in the schools, both signed with a star. The star, in kabala, is "man." It frequently appears later in the century in anarchist journals. In 1884, Fénéon had not yet developed his multiple pseudonyms. "Man," or, as another article is signed, "Hombre," sufficed.[43] Arthur Cravan, the poet-athlete and nephew of Oscar Wilde, addressed a letter to Félix Fénéon in 1916, "Cher Homme";[44] not "Cher Monsieur," not "Cher Maître," but simply, "Dear Man."

The mask Fénéon wore, the stilted pose he struck were not impediments to those who loved him and who saw in him the subversion of old dichotomies: real/unreal, wrong/right, cowboy/Indian. Under the guise of a false Yankee, F. F. could give free rein to his own contradictions and so rethink reality, which was then altered, in the reciprocal conversion that Oscar Wilde noted: "Life always imitates Art."

"In F. F. there was neither familiarity, nor distance, but the complete contact that comes from a personality that has achieved its own truth," said one of his young friends.[45] Oscar Wilde stated this was the very purpose of the critic:

> The influence of the critic will be the mere fact of his own existence. He will represent the flawless type. In him the culture of the century will see itself realised. You must not ask of him to have any aim other than the perfecting of himself.[46]

Fénéon was not flawless, as his friends may have wanted to believe, but he did come close to Wilde's ideal. By his taste, the likes and dislikes that distinguished him from others, he influenced his world and represented those facts of his existence with clarity and wit.

Tes grandes lettres te font étrangement présentes à moi. Elles reflètent tes hésitations et tes enthousiasmes, tes sévérités pour l'Elohim des Elohim (que Voltaire appelait Monsieur de l'Etre) et tes indulgences pour ses créatures, tes froncements de sourcil et tes sourires. Telle quelle, vous me plaisez, Fanny, et je suis votre

FELIX

et je voudrais sauter autour de vous, dans le soleil, quand vous grimpez vers les rochers jardins de [illegible].

Je te réexpédie "Regards" du 4 mai. Puisse-t-il te rejoindre! Le président n'y a pas réussi, m'a-t-on dit.

Last Page of a Letter from Fénéon to His Wife Fanny. ca. 1934. Courtesy Gina Doveil.

Your long letters bring you strangely close to me.
They reflect your hesitations and your enthusiasms, your
harsh judgment of the God of Gods (whom Voltaire used to call
Monsieur de l'Etre)* and your indulgences toward his creatures,
your frowns and your smiles. Just as you are, you
please me, Fanny, and I am your

Félix (as a dog)**

and I would like to jump
around you, in the sun, when
you climb up towards the
gardens on the rock.

I am sending you back "Regards" of May 4. I hope it finds you! You said the previous one did not.

*Pun. *Monsieur de l'Être/de lettres* (Master of Being/man of letters)

**Picturing an expression of affection he used in other letters: *ton grand chien.*

Dimanche

Ma chère Suzanne si jolie,

Le télégraphe a-t-il fonctionné hier? Sachez du moins que, de la gare même, j'ai envoyé une dépêche au Dr. de l'Alhambra Taverne et une dépêche à vous. Votre absence fait ici un vide qui m'est douloureux, votre sourire me manque et j'envie les pires malades de Vichy. Ayez dans cette ville des journées agréables et des soirées applaudies. Si ces gens sont sensibles aux belles formes et aux mouvements harmonieux ils vous fêteront.

Baisers sur vos yeux clairs

f

Letter from Fénéon to Suzanne Alazet Des Meules, *dancer for the Toulon Opera,* ca. 1934.

Sunday

My dear Suzanne so lovely,

Did the telegraph function yesterday? Know at least that I sent a wire right off from the station to the Dr. of the Alhambra Taverne and another one to you. Your absence leaves a painful emptiness here for me. I miss your smile and I envy the sickest patients at Vichy. Pass pleasant days in that city and evenings full of success. If those people are sensitive to beautiful forms and harmonious movements, they will applaud and celebrate you.

Kisses upon your clear eyes,

f

(phallic f)

CHAPTER 2

Genesis of an Anarchist 1861–1882

Fénéon was born in Turin, the capital of Piedmont in northern Italy, a center of political resistance to foreign rule ever since the Risorgimento took hold in 1848. His father, Jules Fénéon, a traveling salesman from a village in Burgundy, had gone there to seek his fortune, for commerce flourished alongside revolution as diplomats, foreign troops, and carbonari came and went before the king of Piedmont, Victor Emmanuel II, soon to be king of a reunited Italy.

Jules Fénéon found success not in business but in romance. He met a young Swiss woman, Marie-Louise Jacquin, who had come from the border town of Saint-Maurice to work in the city. She was pretty, small, and sturdy, and at age twenty-four, twelve years his junior; but she had the quiet gentility and resourcefulness of mountain folk used to dealing with strangers. They were married, and on June 29, 1861—just as Italy emerged as a unified nation-state—their son was born. In October, they baptized him and registered his given names: Louis-Félix-Jules-Alexandre-Elie.[1] Soon after, the couple returned to the husband's home in Burgundy, a region called the Charolais, where the Fénéon family can be traced to an artisan of the seventeenth century.

Little exceptional can be seen in this family of merchants, ribbon manufacturers, peasants, and civil servants, with an occasional religious vocation for a daughter inevitably named "Félicie." Fénéon's grandfather was a doctor and therefore the "notable" of his village, Gueugnon, where he also was mayor.[2] He may have had an influence on young Félix's scientific and anticlerical thinking. Fénéon's father tried out a number of occupations besides that of traveling salesman, and he was known as a copyist, homme de lettres, railway employee, and agent for alcoholic beverages. One can only wonder what "man of letters" signified; he left no trace of his writings, and Félix never enlarged on his father's literary activities, although he allowed, with a smile, that his father had wielded the pen.[3] Fénéon was meticulous, however, in correcting a newspaper report on his own arrest in 1894 that named his father as having been receipt-boy at the Bank of France. He penciled in the margin, "Neither receipt-boy nor, according to other news bulletins, office-boy—his father, beginning at the Bank after he had passed the age of retirement, was simply employed as an aide in keeping records."[4] Jules, who never earned enough to support his family, was described by another reporter as "a very decent sort, peaceable and calm, who did not in the least understand his son's ideas, and was often appalled by them."[5] His death shortly before his son's arrest spared him the publicity which the Trial of the Thirty gave the name of Fénéon.

Marie-Louise Fénéon was quite another sort of person. She not only understood but shared the ideas of Felix. "The mother, on the contrary, seems to admire without reservation everything that Félix Fénéon does," the reporter observed. In her quiet way, she nurtured in her only son a fervent love of freedom and a compassionate heart. He unconsciously imitated her lilting, unhurried Swiss intonation (the "strange" manner of speech people later noticed). She understood personal worth and independence, perhaps because her people came from a region that for centuries had resisted assimilation by Switzerland, Piedmont, and France. She realized early in her marriage that she would have to supplement Jules's irregular earnings. She obtained a position in the Post Office, one of the first institutions to open white-collar jobs to women, and was soon named superintendent of the post in Montpont-en-Bresse, where Félix spent his early childhood. When they later moved to Lugny to be closer to a secondary school for Félix, she held the same job there.

Today Montpont-en-Bresse and Lugny are suburbs for people who work elsewhere or who live in Lyons and keep a country house for weekends. But when Fénéon was a child, village life was much as it had been over the centuries, slow, regular, and calm. People lived by the dictum: *bien penser, bien faire, et laisser dire* (Think right, do right, and let people talk). They took pride in their local history, their local celebrities—it was the country of Lamartine, and of Marshal MacMahon, the old soldier who crushed the Parisian defense during the Commune and became, although a royalist, the second president of the Republic. This occurred during the adolescence of Félix, whose opinion of MacMahon differed from that of most Burgundians.

The surrounding countryside, along the Saône river, was mostly marshland, a perfect place for a boy who liked to swim in mist-shrouded ponds and explore the waterways in a canoe, watching the light filter through the willows. He grew quickly and was strong and taller than average. He was famous among his schoolmates for the astounding leaps he could take, and he liked to amuse them, a poker-faced clown. He read voraciously and was very bright. His mother saved so that he could attend a lycée.

When Félix was fifteen, an uncle offered to help pay the tuition at the exclusive Ecole Normale Spéciale at Cluny, and so the boy was enrolled along with the son of his benefactor. The director wrote the uncle concerning Félix: "He is very intelligent, well-mannered. and we shall make of him, I hope, an excellent fellow."[6] Within the secularized halls of the old Benedictine abbey, Fénéon completed two years of upper division studies and was awarded a number of academic prizes in the regional competition, placing first in history and geography. But Félix's uncle found the financial strain of subsidizing two educations too great. Thus for his last year of school Félix attended the public lycée Lamartine in Mâcon where, although closer to his family in Lugny, he

Cluny College, where F. F. went to school in 1878.

was enrolled during the week as a boarder. That year (1879) he again received the first prize in history and geography, and also passed his *baccalauréat,* one of about 7,200 in France, out of twice as many candidates. This degree, awarded after rigorous examinations, gave access to the university, but Fénéon, like most *bacheliers* of his generation, did not plan any further studies.

Politics existed at Lamartine. In July 1879, the school band refused to take part in a religious event, the Corpus Christi parade. Under the new minister of education, Jules Ferry, who wanted to rid state schools of the influence of the Church, anticlericalism was in vogue. But headmaster Bourciez of Lamartine was not of the same mind and was not to be bullied by his students. Because of their "detestable spirit," he declared the lycée's brass band to be dissolved.[7]

Five years later, in one of his first known articles, Fénéon railed against the inescapable presence of religion in the schools:

> We have all been marked, as children, by the official stamp of religion . . . Even the son of an atheist is raised in the respect of religion and contaminated with mysticism. His father watches this outrage quite calmly, knowing that his son will soon forget those lessons. All right, he will forget them; at least, he will think he has forgotten them: but dogma will have made him dull-witted; his thinking will always just stagger along; used to giving in to the absurd authority of an imaginary deity, he will no longer have any conception of the majesty of man; the feeling of liberty will have been obliterated in him; he will be ripe for all kinds of subservience.[8]

This bitter denunciation of "spiritual education" came from a young man who was nonetheless full of hope that *materialism*—positivism without the sham of pantheism—would free future generations to reach their full potential.

Although Jules Ferry, who had read John Stuart Mill, had begun to talk of universal free education for all Frenchmen (and women), secondary schools in Fénéon's time, and for some time to come, were neither free nor compulsory and, of course, were segregated by sex. In fact, there had been no lycées for girls until 1867, since it was considered that women could be educated properly only by the Church. It was not until 1880 that the state established a regular system of secondary education for girls, providing courses more superficial than the boys', and not culminating in the baccalauréat.

As for boys' lycées, they could hardly be considered cradles of liberty. School buildings give a good reflection of how humans conceive of their social organization. Fénéon's lycée was built like a prison, with an inner courtyard, and long straight corridors that a warden at each end could supervise at a glance. Locked doors, and classes regulated by the drum. In such barracks, built to last, the elite of the nineteenth century learned conformity, order, and discipline, so that the best among them could serve a hierarchical, centralized state, where exactness was prized over imagination.[9] It follows, then, that Fénéon, who excelled at school, became a model civil servant. Yet, according to a friend, his professors long remembered his thoughtful answers, and most of all his questions, "which often made them, as Rabelais says, *tressuer d'ahan*" (sweat and grunt with the effort).[10]

His attitude toward women was shaped in part by the French educational system, in which real instruction was for boys and men only. Even though increasing numbers of middle-class women were joining the work force, women were not taken seriously outside the home. As Pierre-Joseph Proudhon, the father of French anarchism, saw it, "a woman can only be a housewife or a whore."[11] Male-dominated society reacted to feminist movements in the mid-nineteenth century with a social theory to justify denying women the rights and opportunities of men: "separate spheres." Male "producers" were to occupy the market place, politics, and the arts, (and have exclusive rights to sexual promiscuity), while the female "consumers" were to maintain the private, personal, and chaste world of the home. The schools prepared boys and girls for their respective, mutually exclusive roles. Women writers, hampered by their inferior schooling and lack of access to the public domain of culture, were barely tolerated if they were not wholly excluded from contemporary literary movements. Artists faced worse strictures because of the aura of immorality attached to the training of an artist: female students were barred from art academies to prevent them from studying the nude as male students did.

During his young manhood, the period of his activity as a critic, Fénéon usually belittled or ignored women writers and painters. His sexism was largely unconscious. This, however, is curious, inasmuch as he really loved women, "loved them *seriously,*" a close friend remarked, and also consciously explored, as we have seen, the feminine in his own nature. One cannot tell whether he was being satiric or sexist when he reported in 1888, on the "Seventh Annual Exhibition of Women Painters and Sculptresses":

> Contrary to all expectations, this sex predestined by nature to needlepoint and the decoration of porcelain is exhibiting here several lively, delicate, well conceived and well executed paintings, even though mesdames Berthe Morisot, Mary Cassatt, Charlotte Besnard and Louise Breslau are absent.

His attitude is clear, however, as he reviewed the efforts of a few hardy souls who exhibited regularly in the prestigious Salon, and added a sexist jibe to his customary scorn for establishment art: "One prefers the naive, varicolored chirping of one hundred fifty young girls to the peevish, pedantic maxims of these experienced painteresses."[12] According to F. F., not only women's art, but women themselves should be primarily "decorative."

His antifeminism was mild compared to that of other symbolists, whose ideas can be seen most clearly in the seductive vampires and androgynous angels of the Rose † Cross movement in the arts. Fénéon mocked a critic who saw satanic activity in women writers and painters (F, 781). Later, he may have been influenced by the egalitarian ideals of his anarchist friends, and by the poet Jules Laforgue who commented in some unpublished notes that Fénéon printed posthumously in the *Revue anarchiste:*

> We say: humans, and that we are all brothers! No, woman is not our brother; our laziness and corruption have made her into a creature apart, an outsider, with no other arm than her sex . . . not a frank companion . . . but one who is forced to use all the ruse of an eternal little slave. . . . Up until now we have played doll with Woman. Well, that's been going on too long.[13]

As Fénéon's view of women were shaped by his time, so too were his political views—a product of the social unrest and governmental turmoil engendered by the coming industrial age, wars, insurrections, and the repeated restoration of a monarchy. Fénéon grew up in a century that had seen Napoleon, Waterloo, the Bourbon Restoration and July Monarchy, two revolutions (1830 and 1848), a president turned dictator (Napoleon III), and now, in 1870, national disaster.

He was nine, turning ten, when France, led by Napoleon III, suffered crushing defeat in the Franco-Prussian War. Bismarck's troops surrounded Paris (September 23), but the city and its National Guard resisted the siege, in spite of the threat of starvation and epidemic. In January 1871 an armistice was arranged, but the citizens of Paris would not accept the national government's acquiescence to Prussian terms for ending the war. Shortly after a peace treaty was negotiated, the new French government removed to Versailles, to avoid public pressures in Paris. But Paris and several other major cities repudiated the authority of the Versailles government. Negotiations between Versailles and Bismarck soon resulted in the French laying siege to Paris in place of the Prussians.

In Paris, the National Guard held elections creating the Commune (18 March to 28 May 1871), supported by men as disparate as Gustave Courbet, Henri Rochefort, Jules Méline, and Clemenceau.[14] The Commune, a term used since the Middle Ages for town governments in France—and in Paris during the 1792 Reign of Terror—was a bid for self-determination as well as a social revolution. Paris had had no mayor and no municipal powers, and the Commune was predominantly intended to give her the same degree of self-government enjoyed by other French cities.

Some members of the Commune, inspired by the ideas of P.-J. Proudhon and the Workers' International, conceived of a new kind of state, or antistate, made up of autonomous communities. These independent communes did spring up, momentarily. There was quite a stir in Mâcon, the chief town in the department where young Fénéon lived, and he was bitterly disappointed at age ten when the forces of order put down a workers' demonstration in favor of the "revolutionary federation of communes." In nearby Lyons, a commune was proclaimed eight hours before that of Paris. The communes of Narbonne, Marseilles, Toulouse, Saint-Etienne, and Limoges also had their brief history. But the Paris Commune has eclipsed the others, because of its vitality—and the brutal regression that followed it.

Young Félix soon heard with horror how the regular troops, reinforced by 300 thousand French prisoners of war released for the purpose by Bismarck, crushed the Parisians' resistance and massacred them during what became known as Bloody Week. Between 25 thousand and 35 thousand men, women, and children were summarily executed, their bodies burned in piles or tossed into mass graves. There were more executions in this week than in the three-year Reign of Terror during the French Revolution. Thousands of others were arrested, imprisoned, executed, or deported to New Caledonia and French Guiana. Although Clemenceau and Méline were untouched, Rochefort was deported and Courbet condemned to prison for six months, then fined so heavily that he was obliged to seek refuge in Switzerland. But it was mostly the workers of Paris who did the fighting and dying—the Commune had held out the promise of improving their miserable lives—and it was with them that young Fénéon identified.

When Fénéon moved to Paris at age nineteen, many people he came to know had lived through these events. Jean Ajalbert, poet, lawyer, and anarchist, was a child of seven the year of the siege, the Commune, and the repression. He remembered most vividly the famine (to which he attributed his ensuing poor health as well as the early death of his father) and the horror:

> The Commune is, for me—when I hear "Revolution," hear of civil war always happening, in Russia, in Spain—the ineradicable image of a red night when I am screaming in horror, terrorized; soldiers in front of my bed, pushing my mother, dressed only in petticoat and camisole, her legs naked, jabbing a bayonet into my mattress by the light of stable lamps.[15]

They were looking for his father (who had fled in time, the child later learned); a peasant from Auvergne with a modest wine business and some livestock, he had been obliged by the Commune to slaughter his animals to help feed the people, which made him a collaborator in the eyes of the Versailles government.

Robert Caze, a young writer of eighteen, had embraced the Commune enthusiastically. Given a minor role in the "delegation" of Foreign Affairs, he immediately offered the post of Ambassador to London to Anatole France. "He did it in all sim-

WALTER CRANE. ***To the Memory of the Paris Commune.*** Print placed at the head of the dossier that Marie-Louise Fénéon kept on the Trial of the Thirty. Paris, Bibliothèque littéraire Jacques Doucet.

plicity," the eminent author later wrote, "on his calling card which he left at my bookseller's; I must say that we were not on speaking terms at the moment."[16] For such activities young Caze was exiled. His years of isolation only increased his enthusiasm for new ideas, and after his return to Paris, in the amnesty of 1880, his home became one of the places where Fénéon used to meet with painters and other young writers.

Paul Bourget, who like Fénéon grew up in the provinces, described how the war and its aftermath affected the psychology of the young. "That Terrible Year [1870–71] mutilated not only the map of our dear country," he said, referring to the loss of Alsace, "gutted not only the monuments of our dear city, but deposited something of that destruction in us, in all of us, like an incipient poisoning that left us deprived, less capable of fighting off the intellectual sickness of the society where we had to grow up."[17] Bourget later fell victim to the "intellectual sickness" of reactionary royalism and an insatiable thirst for revenge on Germany.

The Terrible Year left other youth of '75 open to extremism of the left or, as in the case of Arthur Rimbaud, cynical about all politics and politicians. Just seventeen in the year after the war, Rimbaud wrote of "Baron Goatfart," member of the Constituent Assembly at Versailles, corresponding with his secretary at the castle of Saint MyGlory:

> We have reorganized an army, bombarded Paris, crushed the insurrection, shot all the rebels, condemned their leaders, established duly constituted authority, hoodwinked the Republic, prepared a monarchist government and passed a few laws that will be rewritten sooner or later.—We didn't come to Versailles to make laws! We are men, Anatole, before being legislators. We didn't make our pile before, at least we've got to rake it in now.[18]

This biting satire reveals the political climate of Fénéon's adolescence.

But his response was idealistic. At age twelve, he founded the *Société de la mort facile,* which members could join only by swearing they were already willing to die. This was not a case of mere schoolboy bravado; it was one of the few events of his childhood Fénéon referred to in later years.[19]

The Paris Commune, seen as a rare attempt to live by the ideals of 1789, helped mold Fénéon as an anarchist-communist. "To the Memory of the Paris Commune, 1871," a drawing by Walter Crane, was placed by Fénéon's mother at the head of a dossier she kept on the Trial of the Thirty in 1894, when her son was accused of taking part in an anarchist conspiracy. In 1897, to commemorate the twenty-sixth anniversary of the establishment of the Commune, Fénéon published in the *Revue blanche* a series of interviews with those who had participated in the Commune and some who had opposed it (though most opponents, Fénéon noted, chose to remain silent).[20] When Fénéon was seventy-four, although he called himself a Communist sympathizer, he reaffirmed his hope for a socialist union when he raised on the rooftop of his apartment the red flag to celebrate the establishment of Léon Blum's Popular Front.[21]

The decade that began bitterly with the victory of the Prussians and the repression of the Commune ended benignly with Jules Grévy as head of the Third Republic. During the revolution of 1848 Grévy had proposed that there should be no president; in 1879 he was chosen as the next best thing to nothing. This was the year Fénéon finished his studies in Mâcon and embarked on a precarious career as journalist in that town.

None of his early writings has been identified. It is difficult to imagine him contributing to any of the known Mâcon newspapers. The *Journal de Saône-et-Loire* exclaimed concerning *libertaires** publicists in Paris, "Is there no longer any repression against these public poisoners?" Perhaps F. F. was such a "poisoner" in Mâcon. He met

**Libertaire* in French is virtually synonymous with *anarchiste* and has little in common with the English term *libertarian.*

LA COMMUNE

A l'occasion de l'anniversaire du 18 Mars, nous avons adressé à toutes les personnes qui nous paraissaient qualifiées le questionnaire suivant:

I. Quel a été votre rôle du 18 mars à la fin de mai 1871?

II. Quelle est votre opinion sur le mouvement insurrectionnel de la Commune et que pensez-vous, notamment, de son organisation: parlementaire? militaire? financière? administrative?

III. Quelle a pu être, à votre avis, l'influence de la Commune, alors et depuis, sur les événements et sur les idées?

Opening Remarks of Fénéon's Survey of Opinion on the Paris Commune, with a woodcut by **FÉLIX VALLOTTON.** *Revue blanche* 12:91 (15 March 1897): 249.

another aspiring writer, Georges Lecomte (future editor of the symbolist review in Paris, the *Cravache*), who shared the same floor at his lodgings. They both worked as apprentice reporters, without bylines. In any event, Félix was regarded as a "man of letters" by various branches of the Fénéon family, who were not happy about this development. "He was always broke," complained the cousin who had attended Cluny with him, and this cousin, now a hard-working pharmacist, soon tired of doling out loans and broke off relations. He knew that some of his money was being passed on to the down-and-out of Mâcon by the subtle hand of his disreputable cousin.

That same year, 1879, the eleven-year-old Fanny Goubaux met and remembered a tall, unusual fellow from the lycée Lamartine, Félix Fénéon. Her mother was acquainted with Marie-Louise Fénéon. Eighteen years later, in Paris, Fanny would become F. F.'s bride.

In 1880 Fénéon entered his period of compulsory military service. Since 1872, when the Third Republic, in imitation of victorious Germany, reorganized the army on

Fanny Goubaux before Her Marriage to F. Fénéon. Courtesy Gina Doveil.

the principle of universal conscription, the bourgeois were no longer exempt from military duty. They normally served five years, but the privileged could reduce this term to twelve months if they passed an examination and paid 1,500 francs (about $500, then a large sum). This shorter term, euphemistically called the *volontariat,* was what Fénéon obtained. He served as an infantryman, eating mess hall food and enduring fatigue duty with an amused smile. His military career was undistinguished. Except for one account, it passed without a trace; but, "the lubricity of Fénéon," said an anonymous report, "is legendary in the annals of the *volontariat.*"[22]

Toward the end of his year of army duty, F. F. noticed an announcement of a competitive examination in Paris for jobs in the War Office. Seizing the opportunity for a three-day pass to the capital, Fénéon sat for the exam and placed first. His livelihood thereby assured, he moved to Paris at the end of his military service in March 1881 and took a position as a junior clerk in the recruiting office, where he was considered a model employee.

Paris, whose working class had been decimated in the repression of the Commune, was still struggling to reestablish its industries. In a few years, a nationwide economic depression would affect all the French. At the same time Paris had become once again a center of creativity in the letters and the arts. The impressionists held their sixth and seventh exhibitions in 1881 and 1882, and Fénéon eagerly inspected the works of these painters Zola had so valiantly defended. He found that he loved painting, more than women perhaps, and certainly more than food, and he frequently went without his midday meal to visit a gallery or one of the museums.

He briefly rented a room on the Left Bank not far from the War Office, and then found more elegant lodgings, still modestly priced, on the rue de Lille at the corner of Bellechasse—the same rooms that Stendhal had occupied in 1799 when he was a provincial on his first visit to Paris. Fénéon was unaware at the time of this "honorable coincidence," he later told Paul Signac.[23]

Fénéon soon lost any resemblance to a country boy or ex-army recruit. Personal grooming became a fetish. He kept his military haircut, a close-cropped brush—it was the most elegant, recent style. But he shaved his cheeks and upper lip clean of the traditional beard and mustache; his facial hair was light-colored and made a poor showing, he thought. He left only the blond tuft that seemed to flourish naturally under his chin. He used pumice stone on his elbows and knees and manicured the nails of his long fingers, "hands molded as if by Michelangelo."[24] His skin was fresh and smelled faintly of cuir de Russie, his favored perfume. And he dressed soberly, as elegantly as he could, with never a discordant note: no stickpin in his tie, no square of white linen in his breast pocket. He had just turned twenty, but had left callow youth behind.

At the War Office he worked quietly at his desk by the tall windows on the first floor, overlooking the boulevard Saint-Germain, where horsedrawn cabs and omnibuses clattered along over the paving stones. His immediate superior remarked that he was "sensitive to marks of approval, even more sensitive to criticism, an excellent writer, rather uncommunicative."[25] His main fault was an irregularity in keeping office hours—a lifelong habit—but no one could blame him for work left undone. To his office mates' delight, he often wrote up their delinquent reports in perfect administrative jargon. It was an odd literary genre, he said, that relaxed him. His work, in preference to others', was placed under the eyes of the minister. Indeed, he was one of those rare civil servants who are so efficient that they cannot be promoted without detriment to the system. After thirteen years, he was still in the recruiting section, one of the head clerks "in the bureau of military exemptions, so it seems to us," said a newspaper of the times,[26] which was, in fact, mistaken; but he had helped so many people get exemptions that the mistake was a natural one.

Some of the information that passed across Fénéon's desk also appeared, anonymously, in anarchist reviews to which he contributed. He compared the "profits" of ordinary thieves to those of French soldiers involved in the conquest of Indochina:

> *Spoils of war.*
>
> To discourage unlicensed killing, they published, after Allarto's recent arrest, the amount of money that crimes committed by civilians have brought in to these gentlemen in the past ten years. Miserable sums, averaging about 4.75 francs.
>
> For advertising purposes, to show that the profession is more lucrative when practised in uniform, the military has divulged a similar statistic. To each corporal or infantryman, Nam-Dinh provides 168.44; Phu-Moy, 137.79. Okay, but those windfalls are rare. For Bac-Ninh, you only get 4.34. Hoang-Hoâ is paid off by 0.38, and Tayn Guyen isn't worth three *sous*. The chiefs of the gang, offs and petty-offs, pocket more dough, without really getting rich. . . .
>
> If not money, at least glory . . . [27]

As for Fénéon's estimation of his colleages at the ministry and civil servants in general, no lesson could be clearer than this parable:

> M. Chincholle has just published a little collection of short, synthetic sentences. It would be better to quote all of them, but we will have to be satisfied with one for today:
>
> *The tortoise's dream is to fly.*
>
> How prettily said, and such meaning in these simple words. A whole quintessence. The tortoise's dream is to fly!
>
> So it is not only by their sluggishness that civil servants resemble tortoises.[28]

Not all at the War Office, however, were tortoiselike. Two young poets, Louis Denise and Zénon Fière, and a middle-aged critic, Jules Christophe, introduced Fénéon in literary circles. He met Zola, Verlaine, and a friend of Victor Hugo, Fabre des Essarts, whose writings included a chronicle of the French colonization of Pondicherry, which Fénéon, the ex-laureate in geography, illustrated with a map of India.[29] Fabre des Essarts admired Fénéon's "curious inquiry into human behavior," but he was disconcerted by the young man's taste for the new in art: "I met him shortly after he entered the War Office. He was already very enamoured of art, but of subtle art, of oddities and bizarre conceptions. In painting, his gods were Manet and Puvis de Chavannes; in poetry, Paul Verlaine, Mallarmé, Raymbaud [*sic*], the author of that famous sonnet called *Voyelles,* which good-hearted Fénéon used to recite to all and sundry with melodramatic emphasis . . . "[30]

The confusing variety of interests that perplexed Fénéon's companion was but a symptom of the proliferation of new art forms and theories at the end of the century. The rush of conflicting ideas is shown by the numerous little reviews that sprang up in Paris between 1880 and 1900. Each of these reviews followed a similar pattern: an article or two by a well-known author, and then the works of a band of "jeunes" seeking to replace existing forms—Zola's naturalism, Parnassian poetry—with "an art more subtle and more true."[31] The life span of these little magazines varied between a few weeks and several years, longevity depending more on finances than on quality.

In a twelve-year period (1883–95), Fénéon published in more than twenty-one different reviews, most of them symbolist, others devoted to the anarchist cause. Although he usually signed his art criticism, many of his literary reviews and all of his anarchist writings were either anonymous or published under pseudonyms.

Still anonymously, he edited texts of other writers, translated foreign works, and wrote articles for journalists like Willy who were chronically short on time, or Zo d'Axa, exiled for political reasons. He did this work in his spare time, and without pay: "remunerating its writers was not among the customs of the symbolist press," he once explained.

Just as the novel had been the main literary focus from Balzac to Zola, the little magazine dominated the late 1800s. Its contributors were labeled *décadents, harmonistes,* or *symbolistes* (depending on whether they cited Verlaine, Wagner, or Baudelaire), and they faced a common enemy, the uncomprehending public. Never before, not even in the era of romanticism, had society so ostracized the artist.[32] Political corruption and social injustices contributed further to the alienation of young writers and painters, and they frequently came to associate their lot with that of the workers, under the ideologies of anarchism and socialism.

Elegant young Fénéon associated easily with the proletariat. He often ate in a simple bistro and spoke as naturally with a charwoman as with a high official at the ministry, only more openly. He loved to roam across Paris at night and to the Halles during the early morning unloading of farm wagons. He explored every part of the capital—the underworld, for example, with Oscar Méténier, a writer who was an ideal guide because of his position as secretary to the chief of police. These forays taught Fénéon to speak slang with gusto.

Paris was not all glitter and gaslight, art exhibitions and literary gatherings. Fénéon saw it from all sides, like the poet Jules Laforgue who, at age eighteen, wrote notes on Paris that Fénéon salvaged and published after the poet's early death:

> Near the Variétés, a café streaming with gaslight. A prostitute dressed all in red going from beer to beer. On the second floor, all shadowy and quiet, a few lamps, tables with heads bent over them—a reading-room. On the third floor, adazzle with gas, all the windows open, flowers, perfumes, a dance in progress. One can't hear the music for the din of the street swarming with cabs and people, with the alleys devouring and vomiting people incessantly, and the hawking of programs in front of the Variétés.—But one can see, gliding past in front of these ten windows, men in black tails with white shirt fronts, revolving to the music, holding ladies, blue, pink, lilac, white, holding them ever so lightly, so correctly, one can see them pass, to and fro, with serious, unsmiling faces. . . .

With a single upward sweep of his eyes, Laforgue observed the strata of classes in the city and how they inhabited the same space but did not mix (pl. 1). Penniless himself and far from home, he felt the misery and degradation of the poor.

> Several pimps wander by; one says to the other: "She made ten francs, pal. . . ." A crowd swarms out of the Variétés during intermission; and the hell of the boulevard continues, the cabs, the cafés, the gaslight, the shopwindows, more and more pedestrians—more prostitutes filing by under the harsh lights of the cafés. Near

> me a newspaper stall and two women chatting; one says: "She certainly won't last the night, that one, and to think my kid caught scabies from hers!" Buses filled with members of both sexes, each with his or her own feelings, troubles, vices.
>
> And above it all, the gentle, eternal stars.

For Fénéon, there was no time to sit and muse over the myriad colors of the capital, its garrulous poor and vapid rich; and if he looked at the stars it was not a fraternal glance at eternity, but a gaze that questioned the nature of those distant entities. But he was more aware than most of what this poet saw, because Laforgue described the Paris Fénéon lived in. His word pictures, like Baudelaire's, reveal the soul of the city, expanding unceremoniously to accomodate the new flood of working-class people:

> Boulevard Bourdon—along the canal spilling through a black, choked-up subterranean hole into the swarming Seine. . . . facing the empty horizon and the endless building sites with their stacks of logs, a huge billboard—red fresco on wash-water blue—displays an enormous fierce moronic musketeer hugging in one arm a bottle of Vicat insecticide and with the other working a bellows exuding a tangible stream that slays lice, bed bugs and fleas, enlarged as if by a microscope. . . .
>
> I have just won a bet. In the heart of Paris I have spent three days alone, without addressing a word to my fellow man, without opening my mouth. Try it, you'll be surprised what it's like.[33]

Fénéon the laconic, *celui qui silence,* might have played such a game, had he been an outsider like Laforgue. But his days and nights were full of busy exchanges. Even as he worked in the War Office, he sent out a constant flow of *petits bleus,* the little express letters on blue paper that served so well to communicate with one's friends in Paris before, and indeed after, the installation of telephones. Notes in his elegant hand would advise a lady that he would be a half-hour late for their rendezvous, or remind a connoisseur that his paintings were waiting at the Bon Bock. He responded to all kinds of requests from friends, and reported on things he had seen or heard concerning their work. Friends also came to the War Office to talk with him, leaving their calling cards with sardonic notes when he was too busy to visit. Two of them filled out an official Request-Response form in the Waiting Room:

> M *Henri de Régnier and Paul Adam*
> begs M *Félix Fénéon*
> to *come scatter a few flowers of eloquence*[34]

Ministère de la Guerre.

Salle d'attente.

Demande. Réponse.

Paris, le 18..

M Henri de Régnier et Paul Adam
prie M Félix Fénéon
de venir épandre quelques
fleurs d'éloquence

Adresse du visiteur.

PAUL ADAM and **HENRI DE RÉGNIER.** ***Note on the French Ministry of War "Waiting Room Request Form."*** Paris, Paulhan archives.

CHAPTER 3

Young Editor and Critic 1883–1885

Within two years of his arrival in Paris Fénéon helped create one of the first little magazines serving the new generation, the *Libre revue,* whose very title stressed the ideal of freedom. It was conceived in a noisy, newly established cabaret in Montmartre, the Chat Noir, where art students and a group of writers called the Hydropathes entertained one another by singing songs and reciting poetry to the sound of a tinny piano. Fénéon found willing contributors among its clientele. Along with a poet from the Midi, Martial Moulin, he produced a rather attractive review, with large clear print on royal paper. The illustrations reflected the Beaux-Arts taste of the art students, the cover sporting a winged Muse, one breast and leg exposed, resting in clouds and jotting casually on a large folio.

To launch the publication Fénéon solicited contributions from some well-known people, including the photographer Nadar, aged sixty-three, who had lent his studio in 1874 for the first impressionist exhibition. Fénéon wrote him at the end of July 1883:

> Dear and merry Master,
>
> On the first of October a new bi-monthly publication of 24 pages *in octavo* will appear—under the title of *La Libre revue,*—which would be most happy to count you among its contributors.
>
> Paul Bourget, Paul Verlaine, Soulary, Henri de Lacretelle, Leconte de Lisle, Fabre des Essarts, J. Barbey d'Aurevilly, A. Daudet, Marie Krysinska (of the Chat Noir), Coppée, Rollinat, Hughes, etc. have already promised us their regular assistance. You would thus find yourself, at the Libre revue, among those you have rendered in photographs and caricatures, your peers and your friends.
>
> La Libre revue would be beside itself with joy if you contributed a few unpublished lines from time to time. It must be added that it will not be able to pay its contributors, in the beginning. So I have the honor of asking a sacrifice of you . . .[1]

Apparently Nadar did not feel up to the sacrifice. Nor did all the promised names appear in the review. But Fénéon's letter shows his own enthusiasm for the project. He knew Nadar was not only a fine artist but a good writer; fourteen years later he asked the old man for his impressions of the Commune and received an answer which he used to conclude his "Inquiry on the Commune" for the *Revue blanche.*

Fénéon was chief editor and critic of the *Libre revue,* signing with his initials or his full name joined by a hyphen. The hyphen, he felt, individualized the name; he later suggested its use to other young writers and artists—Henri-Matisse, for example, who before he became known was confused with another Matisse who sold seascapes in quantity. Besides literary and art criticism, F.-F. contributed two short stories and the teasing outline of a pseudonovel.

It is not surprising that Fénéon should have tried his hand at writing fiction; at twenty-two he had not realized his peculiar talents—and limitations. The two short stories reveal the latter. "Bellies," a story where the "haves" triumph over the "have-nots," is written in the naturalist tradition and shows Fénéon's concern for man's inhumanity to man. But neither it nor "The Suit of Armor," about a scholarly cuckold, adds any glitter to Fénéon's fame as a writer. Was Fénéon mocking himself or the general trend of post-Goncourt fiction when he announced his own forthcoming "psychological novel," *La Muselée* (The Muzzled Woman)? Here is the outline in full:

> 1st part: *Uh!* 2d part: *Two purplish butterflies alight on Jacqueline's zygomatic muscle.* 3d part: *Paul's Sa's bed.* 4th part: *The menacing eye of the lewd druggist.*[2]

No expanded version ever appeared. Throughout the fall and winter of 1885–86, however, F. F. labored over a more serious novel called *Au Port,* but this, too, remained unpublished. Remy de Gourmont later compared F. F. to M. Th. . . , the man of genius who planned to write a single book and never got it done. But Fénéon himself had already developed enough critical acumen to see that, try as he might, he was no novelist. His was a style founded in concision and allusive accuracy. While Stendhal, whom Fénéon greatly admired, could elaborate the newspaper account of a shooting into two volumes (*The Red and the Black*), Fénéon's most popular success resided in his ability to reduce such an event to a narration of three lines:

> Marie Jandeau, a handsome girl well known to many
> gentlemen of Toulon, suffocated in her room last
> night, on purpose. (News in brief, 1906)

Fénéon abandoned the writing of fiction, except for two sardonic vignettes that he wrote in 1896 to accompany the stark black and white woodcuts of his friend Félix Vallotton, portraying life in Paris; but the vignettes suggest art criticism as much as fiction.

In the *Libre revue,* Fénéon's first book reviews show a sureness of taste and a pungent style. His language often suggests visual sensations. For example, to describe Verhaeren's *Contes de Minuit* (Midnight Stories): "Too solid, too rich in red pigment to make one feel the lambent light of the supernatural, these tales—illustrated with

JEAN-JACQUES HENNER. *Andromeda.* 1879. Two studies for the painting Fénéon saw at the Salon of 1883, whose present location is unknown. *Left,* Oil on wood, 26 x 17 cm. *Right,* Conté crayon on tracing paper, 28.5 x 17.5. Paris, Musée national J.-J. Henner.

highly evocative drawings by Théo van Rysselberghe—are nonetheless a source of delight."[3]

The early art criticism of Fénéon surprises the reader accustomed to the myth of F. F. the infallible critic. His first article, "Exhibition nationale des Beaux-Arts," was carefully pruned sixty-two years later by Jean Paulhan in his edition of Félix Fénéon's writings. The deletions reveal that in 1883 Fénéon's judgment was not only fallible but immature. His writing lacks the punch of his literary criticism, and his praise, in contrast to his later writing, appears not only misplaced but foolish and vague:

> The *Andromeda* of Jean-Jacques Henner is a masterful page, an enthusiastic hymn to the splendor of form.

In a later context, one would think Fénéon was joking. But no, he was touched by the lily-white nude (Henner's specialty) chained to the dark rock. He was struck by the emotional nature of the subject and extrapolated a story from the canvas, much as Diderot and Baudelaire had done for painters they preferred.

> Superb in the tragic shroud of her hair of burnished gold, shivering from the salty vapors brought to her by the sea, Andromeda, her bosom offered up, anxiously questions the impassive skies.[4]

Fénéon later developed an acute antipathy for any literary effect in painting. He never again indulged in the anecdotal—except for a humorous effect. But he did have, as the critic Pascal Pia pointed out, the natural enthusiasm of youth.[5] He savored this "epidermis, where little trails of light are playing . . . "

Fénéon gave his first piece of art criticism no specific line of argument except, briefly, a political one. He mocked the very idea of an official state exhibition (organized by premier Jules Ferry, anxious to govern the arts as well as the state) and found it even more surprising that artists suffered "this scandalous meddling" in their autonomy. "Of course," Fénéon concluded, "one can look in vain for a single impressionist painting at this 'National' Exhibition." In the sculpture section, looking at the profusion of Cupids, Psyches, and Chloës, and at number 978 entitled *Bébé, soyez sage!* (Baby, Be Good), Fénéon exclaimed, "For whom, then, are guillotines made?"

Faced with rooms of uninspired art, Fénéon was also hampered by outmoded criteria. He looked for "solidity" in painting, for "modeling," for the play of perspective, all concepts based on the ideal of verisimilitude, the standard that ever since the Renaissance had seen painting as the rendering of three-dimensional objects in a two-dimensional space. He offered no systematic evaluation of these works done in the style of sentimental realism so popular under the Third Republic. He did not compare them to the new concepts and techniques of the impressionists who, in 1883, had become well enough known that regular Salon artists were imitating their style, superficially at least. Fénéon even expressed an outdated romanticism when he lamented that Meissonier, a most successful painter, had never "placed a frankly human, moving, thrilling note on canvas."

Fénéon paid attention to technique, but instead of finding a new way to describe a particular effect, as he would do later, he used traditional jargon: *un faire énergique* (energetic execution), *un ragoût admirable* (savory tones; literally, "stew," a word used by French artists and critics for centuries to indicate bold, pleasing color). However, he expressed a distinct dislike for impasto, as used, for example, by Jules Dupré, painter of pastoral scenes:

> Dupré puts an enormous layer of color on his canvas—not laid on with the palette knife, but placed like little pellets—so that his paintings seem to have undergone acupuncture.[6]

Again, three years later, he raised a similar objection when he saw that among the group of young painters rallying around Seurat, Charles Angrand had not succeeded in adopting the new "impersonal and as it were abstract treatment" of the neo-impressionists. Angrand's brush, quipped Fénéon, "ingeniously works and rubs a thick, plastic layer of paint, molds it in relief, scores it, scrapes, guilloches and cockles it."[7] Fénéon's language here mimes Angrand's use of paint; in the original French, the reader fairly has to masticate the words, they are so thick and juicy:

> *Sa brosse, d'une violence rusée, travaille et triture ingénieusement une pâte épaisse et plastique, la configure en reliefs, l'érafle, l'écorche, la guilloche et la papelonne.**

*Fénéon created a verb, *papelonner*, from the heraldic term *papelonné* (shell-shaped semi-circle); *quillocher* = to decorate with interlaced lines making a pattern of locked circles.

Despite the general laxity of Fénéon's thinking and style in this first article, his observations on the work of two artists, Jean-François Millet and Pierre Puvis de Chavannes, give evidence of his early discernment and personal taste. His choices paralleled the development of his yet unknown contemporary, the painter Georges Seurat, who was attracted to the architectural balance and control in the work of both Puvis and Millet.

In his review, Fénéon criticized some harvesting scenes by Léon Lhermitte, who was often compared to Millet:

> Millet—need one say so?—has a much greater breadth in the conception of his subjects. His peasants have, in their brutishness, a kind of sacred, hieratic grandeur not dreamt of by the peasants of Lhermitte. It is evident that the latter will never create a painting that could be placed without sacrilege next to the *Angelus*.[8]

Unlike Baudelaire and Huysmans before him, who had excoriated Millet's scenes of rural poverty and humble devotion,[9] Fénéon saw that Millet's peasants were archetypes, set in a highly conceptualized environment. He would admire this sort of "hieratic grandeur" three years later in the work of Georges Seurat.

Fénéon liked even more the work of Millet's near contemporary, Puvis de Chavannes, and singled out this artist for praise:

> It is in good taste these days to jeer at Puvis de Chavannes . . .
> Let us not ask this artist for what he has deliberately set aside—I mean photographic exactitude and chronologic specialization. He envisages painting as a great decorative art. His quiet color scales, discordant in an easel painting, harmonize perfectly with the architectural lines of buildings. Puvis is the master of frescoes; walls at Marseilles, Poitiers, Amiens give irrefragable proof of that. His work—hermetic and symbolic, intelligible only to thinking people, painted in a superbly simple style that connects with the tradition of the great primitives Buffalmacco, Benozzo Gozzoli, and Gaddo Gaddi—will be one of the glories of this century.[10]

Most of Fénéon's contemporaries were insensitive to the art of Puvis. André de Fontainas later explained, "We felt blocked in the presence of Puvis de Chavannes; we needed time for the slow, sweet charm of his grave allegories to penetrate us."[11] Painting that Fénéon significantly called "hermetic and symbolic" would come to be admired by the poets Moréas and Laforgue, by painters who called themselves the Nabis (prophets), and by other symbolist artists. But in 1880 the poet Verhaeren wrote to a friend, "What do you think of Puvis de Chavannes' painting? It seems false to me."[12] In 1883 Huysmans claimed he was annoyed by Puvis's "pretentious simplicity," and in 1887 he called him on "old rigadoon* trying to be a requiem."[13] Yet Fénéon

*Rigadoon: a dance with a peculiar jump step, popular in the sixteenth and seventeenth centuries, or the music for this dance. Huysmans's image evokes, in burlesque, the simple scenes of life in Gaul or Old France painted by Puvis.

Opposite, PIERRE PUVIS DE CHAVANNES. ***Ave Picardia Nutrix: The River.*** 1864–65. Photograph Bulloz. Fresco, ca. 400 x 760 cm. Amiens, grand stairwell, Musée de Picardie.

IX

immediately grasped the importance of this individualistic painter, whose roots, like Seurat's, were in neoclassical ground.

Fénéon's style and judgment developed rapidly, as can be seen in his report on the first Manet retrospective in January 1884. "Manet dead, the public is willing to admire," he remarked. He carefully described the evolution of Manet's technique and mentioned here, for the first time, the "optical mixture" of colors.[14] His seven or eight earlier pieces, moreover, show that he was developing distinct criteria, discarding vague epithets and unconsidered reactions for a more consistent view and a deeper understanding of the artist's conception. His primary concern was that a painter work toward self-fulfillment, constantly "lightening the useless baggage of conventional formulas and augmenting the stock of documents he has wrested from living reality."[15] Fénéon recognized that this was a question of integrity and courage as well as technique: the painter's eye must be "quick, precise, and capable of synthesizing,—his hand bold."[16]

He endorsed Baudelaire's dogma of modernity, urging the public not to gape in belated admiration at Manet but to seek out young painters working in new directions. The term *realism* appeared from time to time under his pen (Fénéon was an admirer of Duranty, who in his short-lived review, *Réalisme,* had exhorted painters in 1856, "Create what you see! Not Greek visions, Roman visions, medieval visions . . . "). Realism for Fénéon meant not only authenticity on the part of the artist, but also the choice of subject matter—contemporary, and especially humble scenes from life. It meant loyal rendering of whatever the painter saw, and Fénéon managed to apply it to the frothy lyricism of Fragonard and Watteau: "The eighteenth century had, in art, its own originality and its own character . . . These artificial painters of an artificial time were *realists.* We can admire them."[17]

Photographic realism was not at all what he had in mind. He remarked tongue-in-cheek on the slick representation of the politician Gambetta's deathbed by the successful artist Jean-Charles Cazin:

> My colleagues of the daily news have all admired "the emotion that M. Cazin was able to get into this little canvas." We don't quite understand. Once or twice we have flipped through illustrated catalogues of furniture salesmen and have never sobbed at the sight; cabinet work has no effect on our heart.[18]

It is significant that from 1883 to 1886 Fénéon did not speak of the impressionists, except for an occasional mention of their names. They were a generation older—F. F. was a provincial schoolboy of thirteen at the time of their first exhibition in Paris. In 1883, he visited the one-man shows that Durand-Ruel set up for Pissarro, Monet, Renoir, and Sisley, but he did not report on them; he knew they were ably defended by such writers as Zola, Duranty, Théodore Duret, and Huysmans, whose book, *L'Art moderne,* appeared that year. Soon, F. F. would outdistance all these writers in describing Degas, for example, or Monet, but in 1883 he considered himself strictly an amateur.

Early in 1884, Fénéon left the *Libre revue* to found a publication of far greater impact, the *Revue indépendante,* which he edited from May 1884 to May 1885. Fénéon's

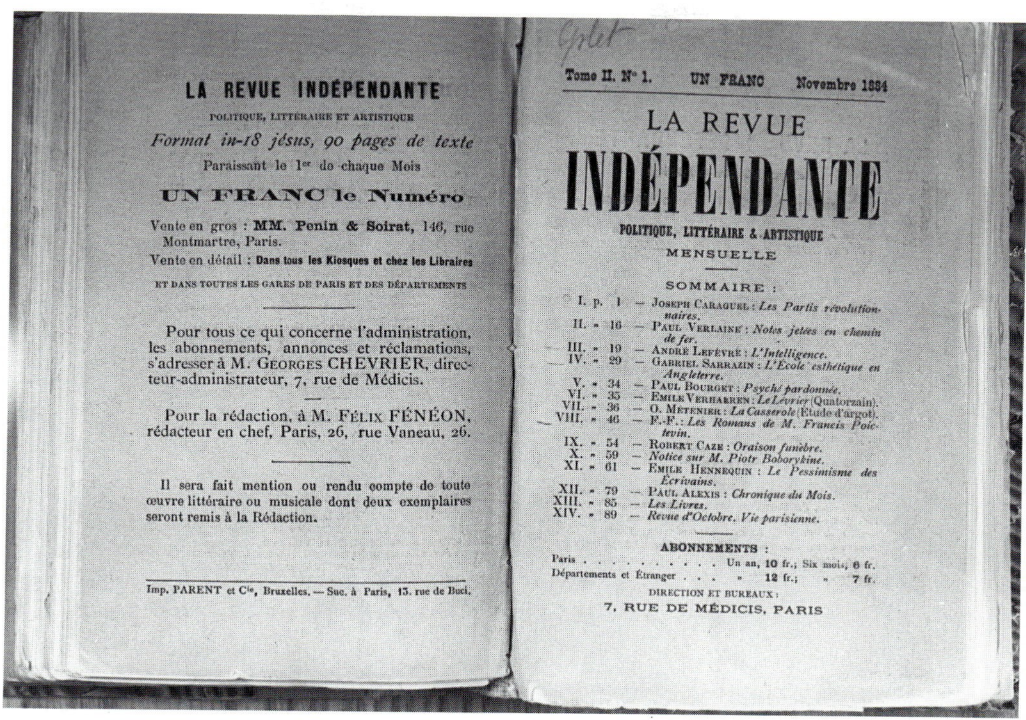

LA REVUE INDÉPENDANTE

POLITIQUE, LITTÉRAIRE ET ARTISTIQUE

Format in-18 jésus, 90 pages de texte

Paraissant le 1er de chaque Mois

UN FRANC le Numéro

Vente en gros : **MM. Penin & Soirat,** 146, rue Montmartre, Paris.

Vente en détail : **Dans tous les Kiosques et chez les Libraires**

ET DANS TOUTES LES GARES DE PARIS ET DES DÉPARTEMENTS

Pour tous ce qui concerne l'administration, les abonnements, annonces et réclamations, s'adresser à M. Georges CHEVRIER, directeur-administrateur, 7, rue de Médicis.

Pour la rédaction, à M. Félix FÉNÉON, rédacteur en chef, Paris, 26, rue Vaneau, 26.

Il sera fait mention ou rendu compte de toute œuvre littéraire ou musicale dont deux exemplaires seront remis à la Rédaction.

Imp. PARENT et Cie, Bruxelles. — Suc. à Paris, 13. rue de Buci.

Tome II. No 1. UN FRANC Novembre 1884

LA REVUE

INDÉPENDANTE

POLITIQUE, LITTÉRAIRE & ARTISTIQUE

MENSUELLE

SOMMAIRE :

I. p. 1 — Joseph Caraguel : *Les Partis révolutionnaires.*
II. » 16 — Paul Verlaine : *Notes jetées en chemin de fer.*
III. » 19 — André Lefèvre : *L'Intelligence.*
IV. » 29 — Gabriel Sarrazin : *L'École esthétique en Angleterre.*
V. » 34 — Paul Bourget : *Psyché pardonnée.*
VI. » 35 — Emile Verhaeren : *Le Lévrier* (Quatorzain).
VII. » 36 — O. Metenier : *La Casserole* (Étude d'argot).
VIII. » 46 — F.-F. : *Les Romans de M. Francis Poictevin.*
IX. » 54 — Robert Caze : *Oraison funèbre.*
X. » 59 — *Notice sur M. Piotr Boborykine.*
XI. » 61 — Emile Hennequin : *Le Pessimisme des Écrivains.*
XII. » 79 — Paul Alexis : *Chronique du Mois.*
XIII. » 85 — *Les Livres.*
XIV. » 89 — *Revue d'Octobre. Vie parisienne.*

ABONNEMENTS :

Paris . . . . Un an, 10 fr.; Six mois, 6 fr.
Départements et Étranger . . . » 12 fr.; » 7 fr.

DIRECTION ET BUREAUX :

7, RUE DE MÉDICIS, PARIS

Title Page of *La Revue indépendante,* November 1884, and the back cover of preceding issue.

journal has often been confused with a second series started by Edouard Dujardin. F. F. set the record straight sixty years later in response to a researcher's letter:

> With a friend from school, Georges Chevrier, who was its director and financial backer, I founded in 1884 the *Revue Indépendante,* where declining naturalism and rising symbolism grouped the signatures of Goncourt, Céard, Alexis, Caze, Huysmans, Mallarmé (Prose pour des Esseintes), Verlaine, Moréas, Vignier, Poictevin, Emile Hennequin, Paul Adam, Caraguel along with those of some professors from the School of Anthropology . . . The review died in the spring of 1886 [*sic* for 1885]. Since then I have not seen a trace of the life or activities of Georges Chevrier.
>
> In autumn of 1886 a review of the same name and aspect appeared. Dujardin was its initiator and he directed it for a year or two. Contributors to this review were Teodor de Wyzewa, J.-E. Blanche, Jules Laforgue, George Moore, Mallarmé, Villiers de l'Isle-Adam . . . In January 1888 it was in the hands of Kahn and that year I contributed regularly to it. In the beginning of 1889 its fate rested with François de Nion. It declined, disappeared.[19]

This summary, written shortly before Fénéon's death in 1944, leaves out a few important names, such as the novelists Zola and Paul Bourget, and the poet Emile Verhaeren, but it shows the high tenor of the review he created. The professors from the School of Anthropology were two men in their fifties, Charles Letourneau, physician, anarchist, and confirmed evolutionist, and André Lefèvre, a proponent of materialism.

J.-K. Huysmans's short stories were a mainstay of the review, and he became quite fond of Fénéon, who enjoyed visiting the older writer and browsing in his library of esoteric books. F. F. liked less well the affection of Huysmans's cat, who, sensing Fénéon's distaste for him, persistently leapt into his lap or, when the young dandy would not sit, circled fondly round his legs and left a knee-high felt of yellow fur on the carefully creased dark trousers.

A note of Huysmans to Fénéon reveals both his bearish disposition and his affection for the younger man:

> I am back in Paris, in the midst of this heat when we should be dumping wagonloads of ashes on that excremental sun.
>
> You can always find me in the morning for sure—very probably Monday evening—but I don't dare promise you because I have to go out on business often these days—Wednesday for sure.
>
> My God! but this abominable heat is hard on my nervous system. See you again soon, my dear friend, and until then a hearty handshake.[20]

The review was not exclusively literary, as its full title reveals: *Revue indépendante, politique, littéraire et artistique.* The emphasis, in fact, was on political philosophy. Each issue contained an analysis of some aspect of society from a materialist or socialist point of view. The lead article in the first issue, "Materialism," rejected the positivism of Auguste Comte that had influenced Renan, Taine, and a whole generation of writers. Since positivism had become "simply a decent name for materialism" and had led to a political and religious sectarianism of its own, it was no longer acceptable to the young editors of the *Revue indépendante.* They elected to shock their readers with "the terrible word, *materialism*" which they traced to the ancients, Anaximander, Epicurus, and Lucretius, but preferred to associate with the eighteenth-century thinkers Diderot, d'Holbach, Condorcet, and La Mettrie; with Goethe; with the transformism of Lamarck; and with Darwin's theory of evolution.

Materialism, for them, meant faith in progress, to be achieved by the application of experimental science to all the mysterious phenomena of life. Recent discoveries in physiology, chemistry, cosmology and, above all, the work of Darwin on the origin of species furnished proof that humans were in charge of their own lot and capable of improving it. The *Revue indépendante* pushed its thinking even further: "The materialist treats with an exquisite lack of deference Honor, Country, Family, Convictions; he has the cult of his five senses and even the sixth; egoism is the core of the doctrine."[21]

The editors cited over a dozen contemporary scientists and thinkers but, interestingly, not Marx or Engels. Marxism had come to France in the preceding decade, with the publication of *Das Kapital* in French; and in 1883, a year before the birth of the *Revue indépendante,* French militants Jules Guesde and Paul Lafargue founded the *Parti ouvrier* on an orthodox Marxist program. But just as the French worker was slow to turn to syndicalism or Marxism, radical French intellectuals preferred to follow in the paths of anarchist Proudhon, socialist Blanqui, or the exiled Russian anarchists Bakunin and Prince Kropotkin, familiar figures in France. Indeed, Marx's bitter struggle against Bakunin for control over the Workers' International left Fénéon distrustful of this new form of authoritarianism under the guise of revolution. It was only after the turn of the century, when the anarchist movement had run its course, that Fénéon, along with the painter Paul Signac and others, joined forces with the Marxists.

Defending his materialist position, Fénéon wrote an article attacking religion in the schools, a burning issue in the 1880s. For many Frenchmen in Fénéon's time—Clemenceau, for example—anticlericalism was a matter of fervent belief. Fénéon was consistently, even devoutly, anti-Catholic. As for the Protestants, he regretted that they "had kept the Church from reverting to paganism."[22] He ridiculed positivist premier Jules Ferry's attempt to control the Church by turning teaching brothers and nuns into civil servants, for Fénéon felt that the religious teaching they would continue was antisocial. "Isn't it asking too much of a man who believes in the beyond to accept the struggle for life, the fervent, thoughtful search for earthly happiness, the effort?" Logically, he said spiritual teaching should lead to total detachment, but since most people dilute it prudently with skepticism, it only leads to "an unhealthy fear of the unknown, hesitation in face of life, anxiety in face of death."[23]

Fénéon turned from attacking spiritualism in education to attacking patriotism in public life. His article, "Patrie," was controversial among a population that had just invented the word "chauvinism"* and recovered some degree of self-respect after the defeat in the Franco-Prussian War.

> Because the "Fatherland" is just one more entity, an empty, hollow entity, like God, like Society, like the State, like Nature, like Virtue, like Morality, etc. It is possible that the mass of citizens still believe in it, it is possible that this last idol will be longer and harder to break than the others, but it is only an idol . . .
>
> We protest with all our strength against this barbarian and Roman prejudice by virtue of which a man is an enemy—worse, a ferocious beast—because he happens to have been born on the other side of the river, the mountain or the emblazoned barrier planted on the road one fine day by a baker's dozen of diplomats![24]

This is the first written manifestation of Fénéon's lifelong aversion to nationalism, his mockery of governments that find glory in chopping up "the enemy," and his scorn and pity for those who let themselves be so used in the name of the Fatherland. This article was signed symbolically, and prudently, "Hombre." Five years later Remy de Gourmont had the misfortune of losing his job at the Bibliothèque nationale because he published a much more innocuous article, "Le Joujou patriotisme" (That Plaything, Patriotism) under his own name at the *Mercure de France.*

In March of 1885 editors Chevrier and Fénéon presented their public a "Practical Program"—a fifteen-point outline for total revision of the Third Republic and, to some extent, the world. The Republic paid no heed, in spite of the evident concern and youthful enthusiasm of the writers:

> We are living in strange times. The people have lost their incentive, enthusiasm is snuffed out, hope is gone. A kind of deadening torpor, weariness or cowardice, weighs on public opinion, which seems no longer to exist . . . [25]

*Chauvinism implied a sincere though blind love of country and did not have the wholly negative sense it has today; from Chauvin, a fictional soldier under the First Empire whose patriotism was depicted in a play (*La Cocarde Tricolore,* 1831, frères Cogniard) and in Charlet's lithographs.

In the face of such public indifference, the *Revue indépendante* criticized French policies specifically and forcefully. For example, it pointed out the foolishness of France's involvement in Indochina, *des tonkineries sans issue* (dead-end Tonkineries):

> We do not consider our questionable action in Tonkin a strictly external affair, since it could cause serious problems in domestic security if it continued to develop as a distant ruinous war . . . [26]

And it reported on the corruption and recklessness of France's internal affairs, which were leading to bankruptcy.[27]

It was at least theoretically possible that this call for reform would reach influential ears. Antonin Proust (Minister of Fine Arts under Gambetta), Waldeck-Rousseau, and other figures in the Union Republican party frequented the Chat Noir cabaret, trying to make contact with young radical intellectuals. In 1881, Gambetta's short-lived cabinet had discussed the nationalization of railroads, savings insurance, sickness and disability insurance—all items on the agenda of the *Revue indépendante.* But in 1885, business interests controlled the Opportunists* in government, and the government not only gave up its right to build and own railroads, for example, but guaranteed large companies profits on the construction of new lines. Undaunted, the editors of the *Revue indépendante* proposed their program specifically to the socialists lurking in the ranks of parliament and apologized to the "real revolutionaries" for their practical approach.

Chevrier wanted to make the review almost exclusively political and objected to Fénéon's literary interests.[28] However, the *Revue indépendante* was known chiefly for its literary content. As editor in chief, F. F. secured manuscripts from the best of the naturalists: Zola, Léon Hennique, Edmond de Goncourt, and Huysmans. At the same time, he afforded a forum for the writers who would later be known as symbolists: Mallarmé, Verlaine, Moréas, Verhaeren, Francis Poictevin, Charles Morice, and Paul Adam. The chronicle of monthly events was written at first by Zola's disciples Paul Alexis and Henry Céard, and later by Maurice Barrès, Laurent Tailhade, and once by Oscar Wilde,[29] whom F. F. met at Mallarmé's. Literary criticism was written generally by Emile Hennequin, who was working out new ideas on the basis of Taine's scientific criticism.[30] Fénéon, remembering Auguste Comte's dream of a progressive cosmopolitan paper, published résumés of new foreign reviews, invited the Russian critic Boborykin to write on Turgenev, and published reports on contemporary literature in Italy, Holland, and Belgium.

He refrained from signing much in the *Indépendante.* He wrote, anonymously, a remarkable article on Diderot that reveals how much of Fénéon's thinking can be traced to this eighteenth-century *philosophe.* Fénéon called Diderot an apostle of materialism,

*The new crop of politicians that sprouted at the end of the Second Empire and the beginning of the Third Republic, for whom republicanism was "both a panacea and a living, an ideal of equality and a source of supremacy" (Theodore Zeldin, *France, 1848–1945,* vol. 1 [Oxford, 1973], p. 605).

far ahead of his time in affirming that mathematics and empirical science were superior to rationalism. Diderot observed that philosophy based on reasoning weighs possibilities, makes a pronouncement, and stops short, stating boldly: "light cannot be decomposed." The experimental philosophers, on the other hand, do not know what will come of their work, but they work without respite for centuries. Then they produce the prism, and say: "light is decomposed." Fénéon found Diderot completely modern in his position on ethics, laughing at the idea of "eternal and universal laws" governing human behavior. In contrast to Voltaire who "scoffed at the rabble," Diderot had so much faith in the common people that he thought the way to get philosophy to advance was to include the masses in the search for liberty and truth.

Fénéon admired Diderot's *Salons*. "As an art critic, Diderot reconstitutes in its action, its preliminaries and its developments, the painted scene. His ink translates every effect of color." This capacity to see and speak of colors was a quality Fénéon missed in most art critics. But he also found that Diderot's exuberance invaded everything and that he indulged in the unscientific habit of remonstrating with the artist and redoing the painting, instead of "scrutinizing it, taking it apart, showing what makes it work."

Writing on the centenary of Diderot's death, Fénéon quoted the Goncourt brothers:

> Voltaire is immortal, Diderot is only famous. Why? Voltaire buried the epic poem, the short story, incidental verse, and tragedy. Diderot inaugurated the modern novel, modern drama, and art criticism. One is the last thinker of Old France; the other is the first genius of New France.

Fénéon concluded: "When we say that Diderot is our contemporary, we are giving undue praise to the nineteenth century. The twentieth—if then!—might allow itself this hyperbole."[31]

Fénéon initialed a few book reviews for the *Revue indépendante,* including a penetrating essay on Dostoyevsky, but the only article he signed with his whole name, ostensible sign of his allegiance, was one he wrote on the novelist Francis Poictevin, a man who has almost disappeared from literary history. Fénéon discovered in his earliest novels, *La Robe du Moine, Ludine,* and *Songes* (1882–84), what would later be recognized by Verlaine, Barrès, and Régnier as the finest symbolist prose.[32] Today one wonders if Nathalie Sarraute, Michel Butor, Claude Simon, and other inventors of the *nouveau roman* were aware of Poictevin's work. The surrealists were familiar with it: Aragon wrote that while working on a sort of antinovel (which he later destroyed) he was led to quote "a classic" as his authority. "I mean," said Aragon, "Francis Poictevin, who was for us (at least for Eluard, Breton and myself) a predecessor."[33]

Like the naturalists, but more consistently, Poictevin eschewed narrational portraiture and let his characters emerge little by little from the book, "with a sharpness that is always rigorously proportionate to their importance, some outlined without smudges, others with imprecise contours, in faded tones." Fénéon noted how Poictevin observed with documentary precision the awakening consciousness of the child, a topic recently opened by Taine and contemporary physiologists. Poictevin's style, according

FRÉDÉRIC-AUGUSTE CAZALS. ***Portrait of Francis Poictevin.*** Reprinted from *Entretiens politiques et littéraires* 2:12 (March 1891).

to Fénéon, was "characterized by a conciseness that, if it were less clear, could be called Mallarméan by the boldness of the ellipses, the absence of conjunctions and relative pronouns, the obstinate return to etymological meanings, the abhorrence of ready-made phrases."[34]

Friends of Fénéon saw an affinity between him and Poictevin's characters (who were known simply as *he* and *she* in the later novels). In 1886, Fénéon appeared "très Ludine" to a group of fellow writers meeting at a café to discuss their work; Ludine was a character who "dreaded attention. One was not supposed to touch her, examine her . . . What she sought, without being aware of it, was, if one can say so, to slip out of her own skin."[35]

Fénéon's article on Poictevin marked a turning point in the *Revue indépendante* away from "declining naturalism" and toward "rising symbolism." The naturalist Henry Céard wrote angrily to Zola in November 1884:

> I don't know what the *Revue indépendante* is thinking about, but the last issue strikes me as totally extravagant. One could call it a fairyland pantomime: the kingdom of gibberish, and one awaits the ballet of mistakes in French grammar and neologisms. Really it's inconceivable that the present day movement is wasting its time with these childish tricks, that literature is taking on the tortuous shape of the neck of a violin. It sets my nerves on edge.[36]

Although it had its detractors, the review had its powerful admirers as well. A new star had risen over the twenty-three-year-old critic. Mallarmé was quite taken with the *Revue indépendante,* "once the naturalists' grip had been shaken off," and soon Fénéon found himself at the poet's famous Tuesday gatherings. Mallarmé's conversation during these evenings profoundly impressed the young writers and artists who came to his little apartment on the rue de Rome. Mallarmé was for them not a master or the leader of a school, but a source of inspiration—a priest, some said, of the new literature. "We came diligently to the rue de Rome to dispel a blindness," one of them later said: "We were raised up, those evenings, beyond ourselves; we were no longer absent from ourselves."[37]

An anonymous sketch of "Elie-Félix-Fénéon" in 1886 shows him introducing "Swedes, Bulgarians, painters and mute characters" at Mallarmé's, and "responding according to the ritual."[38] He was said to combine qualities of the poet's venerable British friend, John Payne, and the Giaour (demon) in Beckford's "Arabic tale," *Vathek,* which Mallarmé had published some years before. Even in the home of the high priest of poetry, F. F. managed to be both decorous and devilish.

Mallarmé liked Fénéon and thought highly of him as a critic and as a man, and Fénéon had the deepest admiration and affection for the poet, as can be seen in letters they exchanged over the years. Their correspondence dealt mainly with the externals of printing and publishing, but the tone reveals their mutual friendship and confidence. For the New Year 1885 Mallarmé, who had written no poetry for more than six years, presented Fénéon with a new poem, "Prose (pour des Esseintes)," to print in the *Revue indépendante.* The event brought unexpected fame to the poet and unleashed a fury of insults and contradictory interpretations. The title itself was enigmatic—what sort of "prose" was this, written in rhyming octosyllables? The allusion to des Esseintes was recognizable at least to the initiate: he was the eccentric hero of Huysmans's novel *A Rebours,* a "decadent soul" who reveled in Mallarmé's poetry.

Mallarmé paid young Fénéon a singular compliment by choosing him to publish this poem, the first of his deliberately hermetic works. Other people had been pressing Mallarmé for new poems, to no avail. In 1882 Huysmans had asked for material to use in *A Rebours.* Verlaine, preparing his *Poètes maudits,* requested "something unpublished, quickly, quickly!" In 1883 Mallarmé answered Charles Morice who had also been entreating him: "I would need to talk for ten minutes to explain to you that I have no new unpublished verse . . . "[39] For several years Mallarmé had been constructing the framework in prose of an essential new poetry. Finally the time was ripe. Two months after "Prose pour des Esseintes," he gave two more new poems to the *Revue indépendante,* the beautiful and now famous sonnet about the swan on the frozen lake, "Le vierge, le vivace et le bel aujourd'hui" (The vibrant, shining, and virginal today), and a second sonnet, the erotic love poem "Quelle soie aux baumes de temps" (Such silk on balms of time). Like F. F., this poet celebrated both the ethereal and the earthy.

That summer he invited Fénéon to visit him at Valvins in the autumn, and F. F. was delighted to spend a few days in this little country town near Fontainebleau, rowing on the streams and talking with the poet he admired above all others. He was a

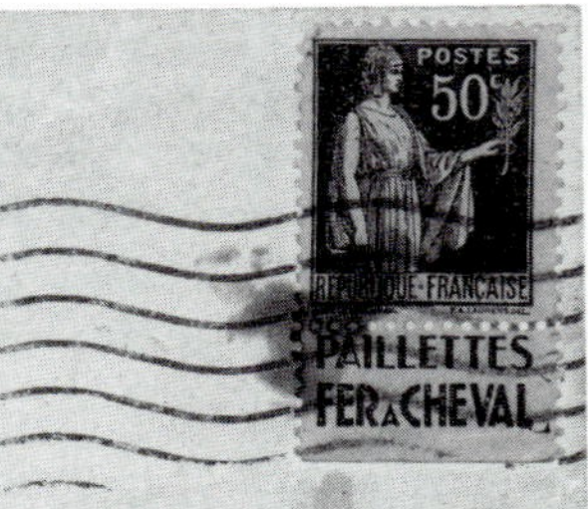

Dans la rue où Perrin Sollier inscrit son nom,
A Marseille, cent-deux, zèbre postal, arrête!
Car c'est là que sourit, dame de haut renom,
Suzanne Alazet dont la tête
Se nimbe d'un nuage blond.

RAID FEMININ AUTO
PARIS-ST RAPHAEL

RAID FEMININ AUTO
PARIS-ST RAPHAEL

Fais fuir l'espace sous tes skys,
Facteur exquis;
Stoppe au vingt-quatre, Bonne Brise,
Fortin de Montredon; puis brise
Le heurtoir, d'un coup sûr, car c'est
Là que Notre Dame Alazet
Avec la grâce et sans l'aiguillon d'une abeille
Hume l'air capiteux de l'illustre Marseille.

En sifflotant un air de Ganne
Rends-toi, courbé sur ta bécane,
A Lozère (par Palaiseau)
En Seine-et-Oise et remets au
Subtil Charles Saunier
Mon encre et mon papier.

×
× ×

Non, il ne sied pas que l'on erre!
A travers Seine-et-Oise, rue-
Toi, fils d'Atalante, à Lozère,
Près de Palaiseau, 15, rue
Béranger, et livre ma lettre
A Charles Saunier, ès-arts maître.

×
× ×

Pourvu qu'obsèques, ni mariage, ni crue,
Ni barricade, ni dragon n'obstruent la rue
Béranger, à Lozère, auprès de Palaiseau,
Puisque c'est là, numéro 15, en plein réseau
D'Orléans, qui avec cent fils nuancés tu brodes
Tes jours, Saunier, quand tu n'es pas aux antipodes

×
× ×

Above, ***Rhymes*** written by FÉNÉON for envelopes addressed to the art critic Charles Saunier. Courtesy of the late Joseph Jolinon.

favorite with Madame Mallarmé and Geneviève, the daughter, who liked his reserve and gentle gallantry. Fénéon was among the few disciples who had the sense not to ask for her hand, and she was grateful to him for that. Her father, she knew, did not want to let her go. They all laughed delightedly one morning when Fénéon appeared with some

Opposite, FÉLIX FÉNÉON. ***Rhymed Addresses*** on envelopes annotated by the P. T. T., 11 May 1936 and 30 March 1939.

addresses he had written out in verse—imitating Mallarmé. "Those are quite good!" the poet said, "You should send them out that way. I've got no copyright on this literary genre!" Thereafter Fénéon's friends received their mail, somewhat miraculously, with their name and address buried in verses such as these:

Facteur, ne mets sous le boisseau
Ni ne confie aux vents ma lettre
Ainsi, par ta grâce, ce pli
Pourra résoudre par un oui
Le dilemme "être ou ne pas être"

(Postman, don't put my letter under a bushel
Or send it flying to the winds.
By your grace, this message
can say yes
To the problem "to be or not to be")

Quand danseuse à la riche envergure, Suzanne
. . . apparaît, le tympanon ahanne
Et les cuivres royaux se mettent à rugir

(When the dancer of the rich wingspan, Suzanne
. . . appears, the dulcimer pants and moans
And the royal brass begins to roar.)[40]

Verlaine, the other "spiritual father" of the symbolists, had also become a familiar of Fénéon, who often went to visit him in his home. It was the storage room of a wine shop in an old courtyard under the elevated train running from the Bastille to Vincennes ("between two keeps," his young friends joked, thinking of the poems he had written years before in his Belgian prison room after shooting his difficult lover Rimbaud in the wrist). In his way, the "drunken Manchu joker" was just as hospitable as Mallarmé and made his friends comfortable at a table among dusty wine bottles or had them sit in his tiny alcove while he looked for his glasses and then read his "ineffably fine verses" to them in a beautiful, soft voice,[41] drowned out intermittently by the rumble of a train. Fénéon was very fond of Verlaine and liked the odd dignity the poet kept in the midst of his squalor—at least when not drunk and repentant. Later on, toward the end of Verlaine's life, Fénéon sometimes brought him home to dinner, and Madame F. was delighted to receive the man her son's friends called the Prince of Poets, in spite of his gruff manner and tattered clothes. One time another guest arrived late and was astonished to hear idyllic verses roll out from under the table, where the well-seasoned poet lay, his arms round his hostess's ankles:

Ici les rosiers nains qu'un goût docte effila
Plus loin des ifs taillés en triangle. La lune
D'un soir d'été sur tout cela. . .

(Here the dwarf rosebushes that a learned hand has tapered into points. / Further off yew trees pruned to triangles. The moon / Of a summer eve shining down on all that . . .)

Verlaine broke off and smiled out at the newcomer, enjoying his discomfiture, while Fénéon's mother extricated herself and laughed.[42]

Fénéon liked the fact that Verlaine was not doctrinaire, any more than Mallarmé, in spite of the younger generation's desire to venerate each of them as a master. Both sought only to find the essence of poetry, its design, and the dreams it evokes. But while Verlaine tended toward piquant simplicity and artful clarity, Mallarmé sought to capture the essence of sensation and being in the web of a new discourse. His rigorous effort in this pursuit came to be the yardstick against which Fénéon measured all art.

The subtitle of the *Revue indépendante* mentioned "art" last, and even then Fénéon's partner Chevrier begrudged the meager space allotted it. Whereas F. F. had written a quantity of art criticism for the *Libre revue,* this year he published none, except for a brief, unsigned chronicle in the last issue of the *Indépendante:* "From the show of Eugène Delacroix, filling the School of Fine Arts with a thundering red storm, to that of Bastien-Lepage, Opportunist of painting . . ." (F, 25). Just as he was founding his review, however, a much more significant event had occurred which was to affect both Fénéon and the history of art.

From May 15 to July 1, 1884, the first Salon des Artistes Indépendants was held, a showing for those painters scorned by the jury of the official Salon. In a temporary post-office building on the site of the former Tuileries Palace (burnt down by retreating Communards when MacMahon's army recaptured Paris in 1871), 402 artists displayed their work. "Here they are," wrote a reporter for *Gil Blas,* "all of them, row upon row, the rejected, the misunderstood, the bewildered, the incoherent, the anemic, the unheard-of, the frauds and fops of painting."[43] Among them, unknown to one another, were Odilon Redon and the future neo-impressionists, Dubois-Pillet, Charles Angrand, Henri-Edmond Cross, Paul Signac, and Georges Seurat. Seurat's single entry, *Une Baignade, Asnières* (Bathing at Asnières, pl. 2), was hung near the refreshment bar. The Independents' hanging committee must have thought it either too unwieldy (201 × 301.5 cm) or too unusual for the exhibition walls proper. Forty-two years later, Fénéon wrote:

> Was the committee of the enterprise ashamed of this canvas? Did they consider it improper, when one cannot paint, to spread one's infirmity over six square meters? The fact is that the *Baignade* was kept out of the exhibition rooms and modestly relegated to the buffet. Only a few drinkers whose attention strayed from their beer noticed that a new way to cipher reality had just appeared and that a valid convention had been added to the repertory of the no less valid but perhaps worn-out conventions that painting depended on.[44]

Fénéon was one who noticed.

The initial impact on a poet-critic of "his" painter is unmistakable. "It was as if a boxer hit me in the belly," said Léopold Senghor, when confronted with Pierre Soulages's work.[45] The same had happened to Baudelaire with Delacroix, to Huysmans with Degas, and now to Fénéon with Seurat, as he explained in 1940 to John Rewald:

> Seurat's art was revealed to me by "Bathing (Asnières)" . . . Although I did not express myself in writing, I was deeply struck by the importance of this painting: the masterpieces which were its logical consequences followed one after the other; but, much as I delighted in them, the initial spice of surprise was never repeated."[46]

Projecting the intense heat of a summer day, the painting shared the impressionist celebration of the out-of-doors. But gone were the fleeting impressions of sunlight on water, on grass, on bared skin. Seurat had made the figures, the Seine, the embankment, the industrial smokestacks on the skyline take on ideal proportions, with a geometric balance recalling the monumental calm of ancient bas-reliefs.

Seurat, aged twenty-four (a year and a half older than Fénéon), had created a masterpiece that blended two traditions: the impressionists' use of light, bright colors, and their modern portrayal of ordinary people, and the classicizing art of Poussin, Millet, and Puvis de Chavannes where forms are idealized by pure lines and given statuesque solidity and balance. Fénéon's own appreciation of these artists and his predilection for clarity and control sparked his instant emotional response to *Bathing at Asnières*.

With its rigorous use of light and line, the painting also spoke of contemporary life, for it showed men and boys resting on a treeless riverbank or playing solemnly in the water—water fouled, as T. J. Clark has pointed out, by the great collector sewer nearby.[47] A new dialectic between labor and leisure, freedom and control, industry and nature, pulsed in the calm of the picture. It is hardly surprising, therefore, that at the first major public sale of Seurat's works in 1900, Fénéon purchased *Bathing at Asnières* for his personal collection.

Yet it was not until he met Seurat, two years after he saw the painting, that Fénéon became Seurat's champion. Thus it cannot be said that he was the first publicly to "discover" Seurat. The exhibition of the Indépendants in spring of 1884 had not aroused much public interest, but several commentaries appeared in print. Although most scoffed at the artists who had been rejected by the establishment, a few were friendly, and *Bathing at Asnières* drew one or two favorable comments. Later that year the Société des Artistes Indépendants was founded and opened its first official exhibition in December. This show aroused even less interest than the exhibition of the previous spring. Perhaps Fénéon did not attend it, for he later admitted that he could not bring Seurat's contribution to mind.[48] It was a significant one: a study for a great new painting (a small landscape of the island called *La Grande Jatte*) and several of his preparatory "croquetons" in oils. "All this is done," reported the critic Roger Marx, "in a sincere and candid style and reveals a depth of conviction which one regrets not to find among certain other 'converts to impressionism'."[49]

The main concerns of Fénéon in 1884–85 were editing and promoting symbolist writers and theorists of social or scientific thought. The same issue of the *Indépendante* that practically ignored the exhibition of the Artistes Indépendants in December 1884 gave a report on Charles Henry's work in progress, *Expression des Lignes,* showing mathematically how certain colors and lines have definite emotional significance. Eventually Fénéon would bring Charles Henry and Georges Seurat together.

This was not an easy time for F. F. He was threatened with losing his job at the War Office in January 1885; I do not know why. Perhaps he showed some of his personal antipathy to the war business; more likely he spent too many hours in and out of the office working on copy for the *Revue indépendante,* which published "Prose pour des Esseintes" that same month. The only evidence of Fénéon's dilemma is a letter from Teodor de Wyzewa to Edouard Dujardin, both members of Mallarmé's entourage and founders of the influential *Revue wagnérienne:*

> But if, around eleven o'clock, you would consent to come see me, we could tell each other remarkable things; Fénéon would accompany you back home, Fénéon who, just yesterday, underwent, very amiably, a stern talking-to and who, today, is dragging himself along the muddy pavement, looking for a job from shop to shop. . . .[50]

Jobs were hard to find in 1885, and Fénéon was doubtless relieved to be able to stay on at the War Office.

He needed his salary not only to pay deficits at the review and to attire himself with discreet dandy elegance; his parents also required his support. His father wanted to end his precarious career as a traveling salesman, and his mother was ready to give up her job at the post office.* They told him they would like to join him in Paris, and he agreed it would be best for them to reunite as a family. He found an apartment at 26 rue Vaneau, a pleasant extension of the rue de Bellechasse where he had been living. The flat was small but adequate: two bedrooms, a dining room that also served as the parlor, and a minuscule kitchen. It was in a block of buildings set back from the narrow roadway to make room for a clump of trees in front; Madame Fénéon was quite pleased with the choice her son had made.

After Fénéon's *Revue indépendante* died out in May 1885, the family apartment served as an informal meeting place for young writers. Georges Lecomte dedicated his book on Pissarro:

> *To my first friend of the literary life,*
>
> FELIX FENEON
>
> in remembrance of the evenings spent at rue Vaneau where, in the presence of his charming mother, above the tall, quivering trees, together we read Baudelaire, Verlaine, Mallarmé, Jules Laforgue, Jean Moréas.[51]

This brief description reveals more than Fénéon ever did about his family life. His father, aged sixty-three, having little sympathy with Félix's artist friends, secluded himself in his room. Marie-Louise Fénéon was the kindly hostess. The apartment was one of the cheaper ones in the building since it was on a top floor; rent came down radically as one climbed up, without aid of an elevator. But it was pleasant and cheerful, looking out on the greenery. The young men read aloud—Fénéon often recited by heart, while pretending to read—from the works of their favorite poets.

*Although the French Postal Service employed women clerks in the countryside, only men were hired in urban centers until the 1890s (Bachrach, "The Feminization of the French Postal Service").

Poetry, however, was not the only preoccupation of Fénéon. The economic crisis that lasted from 1883 to 1887 was making life more and more hopeless for the working classes. Unlike the governments of Great Britain and Germany, where social legislation was being introduced, the French Chamber of Deputies did little but gesticulate. The only action was a law passed in 1884 providing freedom of association: trade unions would be legal *if* they published their officers' names. Since union members had no protection against being fired and blacklisted by employers, unionism naturally did not flourish under this law.

French workers, driven by hunger, overwork, and wretched living conditions, resorted more and more to wildcat strikes. Zola's novel, *Germinal,* conceived and written in 1885, was based on his observation of a fifty-six-day strike in the mines of Anzin in northern France. Earlier strikes in Monceau-les-Mines had resulted in riots and dynamiting, followed by brutal retaliation on the part of the authorities.

Prince Peter Kropotkin, the genial Russian scientist and anarchist, whose writings F. F., Georges Lecomte, and Paul Adam also avidly read and discussed, was suspected of having influenced the miners. Arrested and brought to trial in Lyons with sixty-five other anarchist sympathizers, Kropotkin was found guilty of affiliation with the Workers' International—which even the prosecution conceded was no longer in existence—and sentenced to five years in prison. The large number of the accused and the charge of belonging to a nonexistent organization were harbingers of elements in the Trial of the Thirty, in which Fénéon would be a defendant eleven years later.

The last issues of the *Revue indépendante* had reflected the growing social concern of Fénéon and his associates. In February and March 1885 they noted that while a new union called "Oeuvre de la Presse" was trying to raise funds for jobless workers in Paris by operating a lottery of 20 million francs and organizing gala benefits at the Opéra, the Chamber of Deputies had refused to vote an emergency credit of 25 million francs for the destitute families of the unemployed throughout France.

The review also reported that the War Office had a new minister, General Lewal, "who is sending new troops to the Far East, in the intention of decimating and pillaging the Chinese—who have all our good wishes."[52]

Defending a young novelist condemned for "outrage to good morals," Fénéon commented:

> Are good morals outraged? That is the only question. The intrinsic value of the book is beside the point.
>
> But perhaps one could purely and simply abolish all laws against the press, and at the same time most of the other laws.

He added. "The purpose of all government should be to make government unnecessary."[53]

Fénéon had lost all faith in the socialist reforms proposed in the *Revue indépendante* of earlier months. Henceforth, he would look to anarchism for real reform.

CHAPTER 4

Midwife of Symbolism 1886

In 1886 a coalition of young talents, including Fénéon, created a symbolist manifesto and a host of innovative publications. Much of this activity was carried on in a spirit of good fun.

One of the numerous groups F. F. attended was called *La Courte Echelle* (A Leg Up), which met every Monday night from nine to midnight at the café Voltaire, place de l'Odéon, to read poetry or discuss some aspect of the new literature. Armand Charpentier, one of the group's chief organizers, recalled that from thirty to fifty people would be present, and that one of the most entertaining was "the aesthete Félix Fénéon, Prince of Irony, whose voice, by turns melodic or thundering, would hammer out Rimbaud's sonnet, *Voyelles,* or intone, as if it were a long poem, the only line of verse that he ever consented to give to modern anthologies: *Un laquais en laque est sur le quai Malaquais* . . . " (A lacquer lackey is on quai Malaquais . . .).[1]

From the beginnings of the symbolist movement, Fénéon was perceived its eminence grise or hidden power. He was also its factotum, or lackey: his friends relied on him for all sorts of things. Charles Henry, away from Paris on vacation, sent Fénéon proofs of one of his numerous erudite editions to correct. Then he added, "You know I have to move . . . " and made it clear that he expected F. F. to find reputable movers, fix the price, including the tips, "and that is not all. My table," wrote Henry, "cannot be moved in one piece into my new apartment." Fénéon was to hire a carpenter and "not let this intruder alone in my rooms. Watch over my papers with all the maternal devotion that I know is yours."[2] This was in October 1886, when Fénéon, besides his daily work at the War Office, published important work of his own and edited two different symbolist reviews.

One of his favorite places to talk with other writers was the relatively tranquil Brasserie Gambrinus in the Latin Quarter, across from the Odéon theatre on the avenue de Médicis that cut through a corner of the Luxembourg Garden. The literary crowd there was described by Jules Christophe, critic and fellow bureaucrat from the War Office:

> Every evening you could see . . . this "budding" literature, shaded by elms: Gustave Kahn, a refined Semite; Papadiamantopoulos, a blue-bearded Athenian (alias Jean Moréas); Joseph Caraguel, a read-bearded Narbonnian; Félix Fénéon, a Yankee-looking Burgundian born in Turin; Charles Vignier, an elegant Swiss; Paul Adam, a Parisian with very starched white collars . . . .

Kahn's friend Jules Laforgue also used to appear, when he was in town, and Charles Henry, "the dynamist of art, future author of an experimental, mathematic aesthetics." The group also included the Italian doctor, Barbavara, a student of the brilliant neurologist Charcot, the teacher of Freud.

It had become quite fashionable, under the bourgeois Republic, to drink beer attended by women. "Under the calm gaze of mighty Madame Mansuy," three Muses served this cosmopolitan crowd: "Valentine, a wraithlike brunette, Hélène, an adorable Fragonard-type beauty, and Denise, a delicate blond with sky-blue eyes."

Thus, at the Brasserie Gambrinus, Christophe affirmed:

> Symbolism was born, explorer of souls, of fragile nuances, of sensational phrasing, of fugitive and—sometimes—quite painful and intense impressions; an esoteric art, necessarily aristocratic, something of a bluff, if you like, where one can see a certain desire to mystify in order to revolt against universal foolishness, an art claiming kinship with both Science and dreams . . . [3]

Falling into the category of "bluff" was a highly articulate book of criticism, the *Petit bottin des lettres et des arts,* which appeared anonymously early in 1886. Engendered by witty discussions at the Brasserie Gambrinus, it was scribbled off in three evenings at one of the tables by Fénéon, Jean Moréas, Paul Adam, and Oscar Méténier (who, Fénéon said, died years later thinking he was Louis XIV).[4] The *Petit bottin* deftly characterized subjects as diverse as "The Swiss" and "The May Queen of Asnières" alongside Whistler and Mallarmé. In spite of the speed with which it was composed, the overall style and the meticulous form of the book show a shaping hand; that of Fénéon, its editor. With tongue in cheek, he cross-referenced certain entries, such as one, for example, on an eminent drama critic: "SARCEY (Francisque). See: Ugalde (Marguerite)." Under the *U*'s, one finds: "UGALDE (Marguerite). 'In the diction of Mlle Ugalde, one finds the hand of her mother.'—Francisque Sarcey." Fifty-five years later, Fénéon identified the authorship of various entries. Here are some of his own.

> DEGAS. A thigh, a flower, a chignon, ballerinas convoluted in the flurry of the tutu; the nose of a tippler; race horses and jockeys turning on the green; the hand of a milliner amidst a fluttering of feathers and ribbons; painted waxworks that live. Unerring kinematics. The tricks of artificial lights taken by surprise. The expression of Modernity.
>
> TAINE (Hippolyte). Applies to literary history the techniques of agronomy. For any given country studies soil chemistry, topography, and climate, then treats a generation of artists like a crop of mushrooms, beets, sycamores and Brussels sprouts.

Jean Moréas

Paul Verlaine

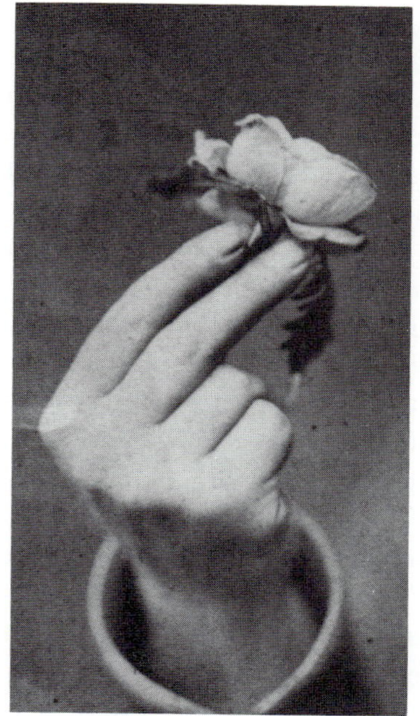

Laurent Tailhade

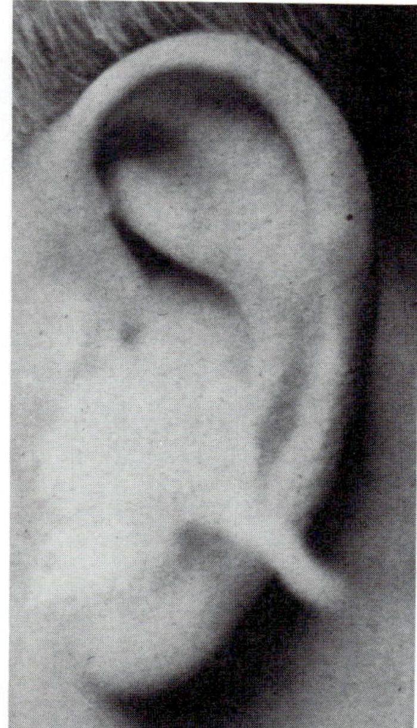

Léon Cladel

EMILE COHL. ***Photographs for Têtes de Pipes,*** by L. G. Mestrailler, Paris, 1885. Courtesy Rev. Noel Richard.

WHISTLER (James). Remote, mysterious creatures emerge with serpentine grace from symphonies of shadow.

VERLAINE. From his very beginnings, the fatality of his own name drew him toward all Rimbauds: hence, conjugal and judicial misadventures, into which we are initiated by his prose and poems. Stirs guile, hocus-pocus, and candor into mixtures, according to complex formulae; fragile, nostalgic aromas float off this mixture, smothered at times in nasty whiffs of blood . . . .

Verlaine was once a Maratist, an atheist, and a Communard. Contemplative life has transformed him: on a friendly footing with the most influential of lady saints, he is becoming pickled in popery. . . .

His magnificent shaggy poll of a drunken Manchu joker has sniffed the air of numerous lands, jails, churches, taverns and steamers. Of late he lived in the forest of Ardennes, like Rosalind. His lodgings now are near the Place de la Roquette, where he will doubtless perish, and thereby outdo even François Villon.[5]

There was no limit to the fond disrespect with which the *Petit bottin* treated its notables. Mallarmé was defined simply as "born of the teratological love affairs of Mlle Sangalli, Father Didon and the illustrious Sapeck" (a woman obliterated from history, a Dominican priest who publicly defended striking workers, and a humorist popular at the Chat Noir for his outrageous spoofs). Symbolism in France has often been accused of taking itself too seriously, printing manifestoes, definitions, positions, and counter-positions. The *Petit bottin,* like the better known *Déliquescences d'Adoré Floupette,* reveals the fun and whimsy that also prevailed. Eight years after its publication, Paul Adam proposed to F. F. that they bring out a sequel to the *Bottin,* made of notes they had already written, but Fénéon declined; times had changed, and he was never one to look backward.

The young generation reveled in using new or unusual words, a revolutionary venture in a country whose language had been regimented for two hundred and fifty years by the Académie française. (The French "half" of an English-French dictionary is markedly thinner than the English half, because of the winnowing of French Academicians throughout the years.) The symbolists did not create neologisms so much as go back and ferret out words that had fallen out of usage or had been deemed unworthy of the Dictionnaire de l'Académie française. Fénéon did this, though with more restraint than most of his contemporaries.

F. F. had two languages, Jean Paulhan pointed out. The one contains no difficult words and is epitomized in his "News in three lines." One can imagine his using this correct, concise, and clear language in his reports for the War Office. The other he developed between 1884 and 1886 to describe the painters and poets of his choice. Many of Fénéon's "inventions" appeared in an ephemeral paper which he rescued briefly from extinction, the *Revue moderniste.*[6] Late in 1885 the stationery of the *Revue moderniste* bore Fénéon's address at 26 rue Vaneau and the notation, "the only administration is here." Besides running the affair, F. F. wrote the unsigned book reviews. Some of his expressions printed there made history in the annals of symbolism and were later published as examples of neologisms in the *Petit glossaire pour servir à l'intelligence des*

EMILE COHL. ***Caricature of Paul Verlaine,*** with "ANARCHY" inscribed in Greek on his forehead. Cover for *Les Hommes d'aujourd'hui,* no. 144. Photograph courtesy Rev. Noël Richard.

auteurs décadents et symbolistes (Little Dictionary to Help in the Understanding of Symbolist and Decadent Authors), compiled by Paul Adam in 1888 (under the pseudonym of a one-armed robber, Jacques Plowert). Since Fénéon decided which words to send in to the *Petit glossaire,* they give us some idea of what he defined as new. One was *beylisme* (etymol. Henri Beyle, real name of Stendhal), which can be found in the *Petit Larousse* today. Others, less obvious, are also dictionary words:

> Quelques pages *aptères* (wingless, as *apterous insect,* but also an art term, as in Wingless Victory; F, 665).

Fénéon borrowed terms from technical vocabularies, botany, medicine, heraldry, costume, mathematics, and architecture. Sometimes he revived words from Old French, particularly verbs, for example, *enger* (to encumber), *délinquer* (to fail, as in "the light is failing"), *nuer* (to blend or harmonize colors). Less often he made up new words, mostly humorous, and always specific:

> Neuf nouvelles *pelviennes* (nine pelvic tales; F, 666).

Fénéon's language is difficult at times but it is never outlandish. Recourse to a dictionary will clarify one's reading of F. F., whereas dictionaries are of little avail, for example, in the following passage from Jean Moréas:

> The lists were wild with excitement at the sound of orthios and epinicia; Biblical beggar-women with atramantled flesh, tintalorized Abrahams, Jesuses wearing bearded masks from the drugstore . . . halbrened Titans, napaious Venuses, latitant Nymphs, suburban Napoleons, all the Shrovetide revelers of quai Malaquais, daubers of Prussian blue and Bitumen and raw Sienna . . . left the arena. In spite of the stupid bleating of the public and the curses of morosophers nailed to clichés, the innovators won the day.[7]

This was Moréas's review of Fénéon's *Impressionnistes en 1886*. He meant, simply, that the new kind of painting had kicked out the old; that impressionism was better than Salon art—traditional figures from the Bible, Greek mythology, and French history painted in traditional dark colors. Moréas was aiming for specific effects, but he overshot his goal. A reporter for *France* found this language inappropriate for a report on Fénéon "who," he said, "writes simply enough and whose style resembles that of the decadents only by a few incongruities that he lets fall here and there on purpose." To which the symbolists sardonically responded, "There's a commendation that is not kind to our fellow-worker [Fénéon]."[8]

The symbolist movement was officially announced in September 1886 when Jean Moréas convinced the *Figaro* to let him publish a manifesto in grandiose style on the new kind of writing. Three months earlier, Fénéon had set the stage for this event in a monograph on Moréas for *Hommes d'aujourd'hui,* where he placed the new poetry in an historical context—remarks that were repeated word for word in Moréas's manifesto.[9] Fénéon drew an admiring, seriocomic picture of the young immigrant from Greece who by reason of his audacity—and because of Fénéon's early support—became the titular head of the latest literary movement: "A rose in his lapel, his blue-black hair spilling over his forehead; a cigar and the black bars of his mustache with twisted ends pasted against his dark, even complexion; his right eye masked by a monocle . . . " F. F. went on to praise his comrade's work:

> Skillful and forbidding poems, controlled by a precise echometry, colored with mineral tints . . . And always, a well-determined syntax, bold and supple, a vocabulary of a mathematic, essential precision, a sonorous music, highlighted by hoarse diphthongs and plausible appeals thrown out by alliterative assonances.[10]

While Moréas's symbolist manifesto meant to establish a philosophical basis for the new literature, Fénéon concentrated on the technical aspects of the writing itself.

EMILE COHL. ***Drawing of Jean Moréas.*** Cover for *Les Hommes d'aujourd'hui,* no. 268 [1886]. Text by F. Fénéon. Photograph G. Roche.

Much of the symbolists' theorizing, which he passed over, was but ill-digested fare from Schopenhauer, stirred over the coals of a platonic fire. For example, in Moréas manifesto: "Symbolic poetry seeks to clothe the Idea in perceptible form." It is not clear whether "Idea" indicates a transcendental truth, or simply the essence of a human experience.

Symbolist poetry, as Henri de Régnier explained, was intrinsically obscure:

> Its meaning is not obvious but carried secretly within it, in the same way that a tree carries in its seed the fruit that will grow from it. A symbol is, as a matter of fact, a comparison and an identification of the abstract with the concrete, a comparison where *one of the terms remains implicit.*[11] (Italics added.)

This explanation, limited to a technical detail, was one Fénéon would have endorsed. A symbol is not the substitution of one object for another, as when Victor Hugo speaks of a *child* as a "barely opened flower." It is, rather, a concrete image that represents an emotion or an abstract idea. The concrete image, the symbol, stands alone, inviting the reader to make out the unstated comparison. This is the poet's gamble, for readers must draw on their own experiences in life, quickened by the life in the poem. Poetry is then a participatory act that jolts readers into a closer intimacy with themselves and the rest of the world. If a reader is not ready or willing to reach both out and inwards, or if the poem does not make him want to, then the symbol remains locked, and the poem senseless.

This sort of art may be elitist, since it requires effort on the part of the reader, but the game is known to any human being, since speech itself plays with symbol (the "*root* of the problem," the "*march* of time"). Symbolist poetry asks, in effect, that we assume—and enjoy—our humanity to the utmost. Mallarmé, again, said it best:

> Poetry is the expression, through human language reduced to its essential rhythm, of the mysterious meaning in life's appearances: in this way, it gives our life on earth authenticity and constitutes the sole spiritual task.[12]

Fénéon echoed this as he concisely described the symbolists: "Aesthetes [who] rejected rhetorical verbosity, summoned all the resources of music to give their work a supreme efficacy, and behind the superficial appearance of things, evoked their mysterious meaning."[13]

Early in 1886, Fénéon joined Gustave Kahn, Charles Henry, and Jules Laforgue in creating one of the most brilliant symbolist reviews, *La Vogue.* It was the brainchild of the poet Kahn, who had recently returned to Paris after four years' military duty in North Africa. He lost no time in recruiting the most gifted people he knew, a scientist, a poet, and a critic, who shared his love for new ideas. Kahn had been the first literary person to befriend Laforgue, and while he was off in Africa, Laforgue sorely missed his "diabolic banter" from when they used to "roam the throbbing streets."[14] Now Laforgue was living in Germany, earning his livelihood as French reader to Empress Augusta, and he sent his copy for *Vogue* through the mail. Henry was full of ideas, but not very practical. Kahn soon realized he would need a good editor, and asked Fénéon, who was glad to lend his services to this talented triumvirate.

Kahn put F. F. in charge of the art criticism of *Vogue,* and it was here that Fénéon's first articles on the impressionists and neo-impressionists appeared. But the critic played another role behind the scenes. Thanks to Fénéon, and thanks only to him, Kahn later confessed, the review came out regularly and on time, since F. F. went at night to the printer's in the working-class "zone" outside Paris to supervise production and correct last-minute typos so that the review could arrive back in Paris in time for the Sunday sales.[15]

Kahn was a warm, outgoing man, and F. F. was soon on a first-name basis with him. He admired Kahn's keen intelligence and his efforts at developing "a new science of language." They became close friends. "He has very fine dark gold eyes," Fénéon later wrote in another issue of *Hommes d'aujourd'hui,* "and his conversation is full of rapid, bright antics and wide-ranging ideas. In daily life, as in the contemplative one, he is a fighter, and an experimenter."[16]

Fénéon had known Charles Henry since 1884. He met Laforgue the following summer in Henry's apartment, where Laforgue stayed during his annual vacation from the Imperial German court. Fénéon was immediately taken by the unassuming young poet and his ironic sense of humor. He was very fond of all three men, the strangest of whom was Henry, who, having served as a laboratory assistant to Claude Bernard, was now delving into odd manuscripts at the Sorbonne, where he worked as librarian.

Henry's interests turned in many directions, but the most stimulating to his comrades was his investigation into the relatively new field of the physiology of sensation. Neurobiology, then in its infancy, held out fascinating ideas for Fénéon, Kahn, and Henry, who understood that the functioning of the mind and body could be analyzed in terms of reflexes, instincts, reactions, and interactions of nerve and brain cells. Ever since Descartes, there had been a gradual movement away from the religious or metaphysical explanation of human behavior toward a psychological and physiological one, accelerated in the nineteenth century by scientists like Claude Bernard and Henry Maudsley. Fénéon and his friends saw that this was a way not only to counteract superstitions and prejudices embedded in religious and moral codes, but also to understand and explore new literary and art forms. Laforgue found similar indications in Eduard von Hartmann's writings on the unconscious. Fénéon later analyzed both Kahn's and Laforgue's poems with these ideas in mind, for in fact such theories played a role in the formation of the poems themselves.

Henry was not a scientist in the strict sense of the term, although he carried out laboratory studies and was later named head of the Sorbonne's new laboratory of experimental psychology. He was, rather, an extremely inventive and well-informed dilettante. He was his friends' closest link with the world of science, but they thought of him as a poet.

In the *Petit bottin,* Fénéon defined HENRY (Charles):

> Measures the power of a metaphor of Mallarmé on the dynamograph, analyzes the verses of Jules Laforgue on the blackboard, makes charts of illnesses, reduces the paintings of Degas to equations . . . . (F, 542)

More than a decade later, Signac recorded in his diary, "Visit from Charles Henry, becoming more and more poetic. From a specific scientific datum he will draw the most delightfully whimsical conclusions that he strives to prove mathematically."[17]

Henry's nature was independent, but not aloof. When Fénéon told him that a young nihilist from Narbonne, Joseph Caraguel, wanted to organize a group to meet regularly at a reserved table in a nearby restaurant, Henry responded:

> Why chain ourselves down? We could just as easily meet at my apartment and drink the rum of brotherhood. Then no one need feel obliged to excuse himself if he

> couldn't come; there would be no empty chair, no angry restaurant-owner. . . . So, if you would like to come as a group regularly to smoke and discuss ideas, just let me know! Even people who *haven't done anything* could come.[18]

But it was the more creative individuals who sought the hospitality of Charles Henry, as another note to Fénéon reveals: "Tuesday night you will come, won't you? Nine o'clock at the quai d'Anjou. Laforgue, Kahn, Moréas, Ysaÿe will be here. Would you be good enough to pass this invitation on to Barrès, since I don't have his address?" More often, however, Henry would ask Fénéon to come over and watch some experiment he was carrying out. Or he wanted to know what Fénéon was doing: "When will you bring me a manuscript, large or small, for my delight? Some evening soon, won't you? Just let me know in the morning because I often go out roaming in the evening. And you can leave your frigid serenity behind somewhere, all right?"

Like Félix Fénéon, Charles Henry formed a link between artists and writers in his generation. Also like Fénéon, he was sympathetic to those in need, finding texts for impecunious young writers to translate. He once appealed to Fénéon at the War Office, addressing him "My dear Elie," and asking him to help a retired noncommissioned officer who was trying to get into the gendarmerie. The old soldier's request had become bogged down in red tape and Henry exclaimed, "I am afflicted by this kind of trouble as if I had done something to cause it. Give me a hand, Elie. . . ."[19]

La Vogue only lasted from April through December 1886, but in that time it published Laforgue's *Concile féerique,* his translations of Walt Whitman, and some of his tales called *Moralités légendaires;* various studies by Charles Henry, such as one on Rameau's musical theory; translations of letters of Dostoyevsky and Keats' *Hyperion;* and Fénéon's *Impressionnistes en 1886.* Many more texts of prime interest appeared there, but the most important was Rimbaud's *Illuminations.*

Fénéon was given the charge of publishing *Les Illuminations.* Rimbaud, whose poems the symbolists knew only through Verlaine, had left his literary pursuits far behind and chosen a life of adventure and business in the British protectorate of Aden. He had become something of a legend; it was even rumored he had died. Gustave Kahn told Verlaine that he wanted to publish Rimbaud's works, but the problem was finding the manuscript of *Les Illuminations.* Verlaine had lent it out so that it would circulate, and circulate it did. "Luckily," Kahn said, "Fénéon remembered that the manuscript had been in the hands of Zénon Fière, a co-worker at the War Office. . . . We got it that very evening, read it, put it in order, and published it without delay."[20] It was Fénéon who arranged the order of the pages (loose-leaf in the manuscript), corrected the proofs, and made various adjustments in the text. In 1939 Henri Bouillane de Lacoste, the author of a critical edition of *Les Illuminations,* began a lengthy correspondence with Fénéon, who explained:

> Unofficially, and without any supervision by Kahn, our lenient director, or anyone else, I prepared *Les Illuminations* not only for their publication in the review, but for their reprinting as a booklet. If, between these two operations the order of the poems was changed, this modification, however untoward and unfortunate it might be, can only be attributed to me. Persuaded rightly or wrongly that the loose pages delivered

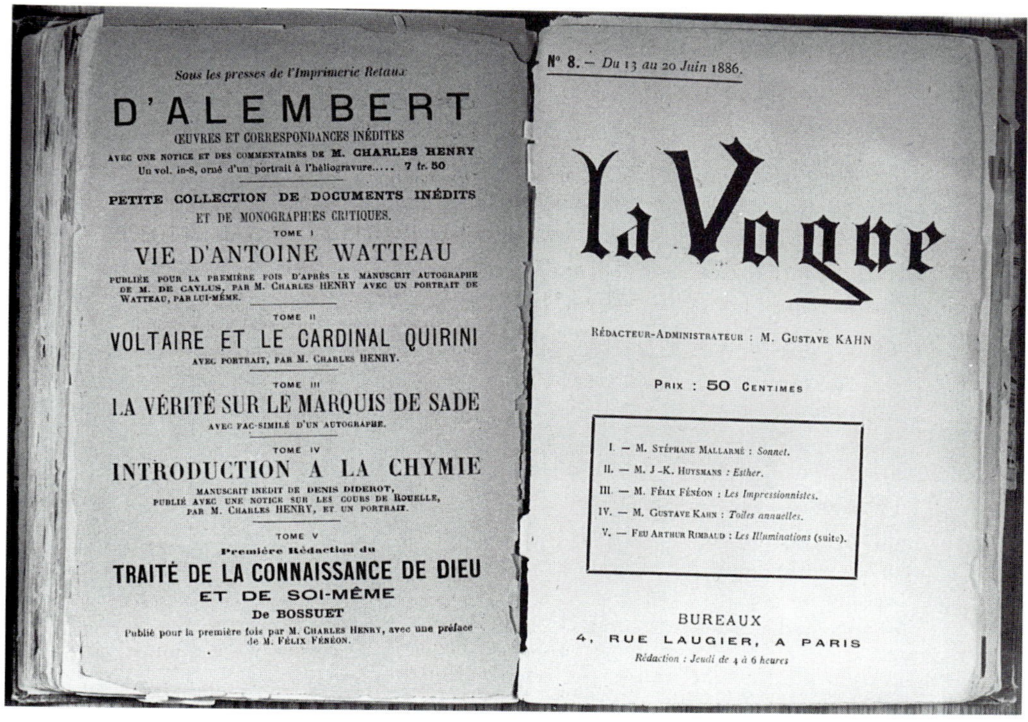

Sous les presses de l'Imprimerie Retaux

D'ALEMBERT

ŒUVRES ET CORRESPONDANCES INÉDITES

AVEC UNE NOTICE ET DES COMMENTAIRES DE M. CHARLES HENRY

Un vol. in-8, orné d'un portrait à l'héliogravure..... 7 fr. 50

PETITE COLLECTION DE DOCUMENTS INÉDITS

ET DE MONOGRAPHIES CRITIQUES.

TOME I

VIE D'ANTOINE WATTEAU

PUBLIÉE POUR LA PREMIÈRE FOIS D'APRÈS LE MANUSCRIT AUTOGRAPHE DE M. DE CAYLUS, PAR M. CHARLES HENRY AVEC UN PORTRAIT DE WATTEAU, PAR LUI-MÊME.

TOME II

VOLTAIRE ET LE CARDINAL QUIRINI

AVEC PORTRAIT, PAR M. CHARLES HENRY.

TOME III

LA VÉRITÉ SUR LE MARQUIS DE SADE

AVEC FAC-SIMILÉ D'UN AUTOGRAPHE.

TOME IV

INTRODUCTION A LA CHYMIE

MANUSCRIT INÉDIT DE DENIS DIDEROT, PUBLIÉ AVEC UNE NOTICE SUR LES COURS DE ROUELLE, PAR M. CHARLES HENRY, ET UN PORTRAIT.

TOME V

Première Rédaction du

TRAITÉ DE LA CONNAISSANCE DE DIEU

ET DE SOI-MÊME

De BOSSUET

Publié pour la première fois par M. CHARLES HENRY, avec une préface de M. FÉLIX FÉNÉON.

N° 8. — *Du 13 au 20 Juin 1886.*

La Vogue

RÉDACTEUR-ADMINISTRATEUR : M. GUSTAVE KAHN

PRIX : 50 CENTIMES

I. — M. STÉPHANE MALLARMÉ : *Sonnet.*
II. — M. J.-K. HUYSMANS : *Esther.*
III. — M. FÉLIX FÉNÉON : *Les Impressionnistes.*
IV. — M. GUSTAVE KAHN : *Toiles annuelles.*
V. — FEU ARTHUR RIMBAUD : *Les Illuminations* (suite).

BUREAUX

4, RUE LAUGIER, A PARIS

Rédaction : Jeudi de 4 à 6 heures

Title Page of *La Vogue* 1:8 (13–20 June 1886), listing *Les Illuminations* by "the late" Arthur Rimbaud and *Les Impressionnistes,* by Fénéon; on the back cover of the preceding issue, announcement of an edition by Charles Henry of Bossuet's *Knowledge of God and One's Self,* with a preface by Fénéon, apparently never published.

> to me had already been shuffled around due to all the handling they had received, why should I have had any qualms about arranging as I pleased such a chance pack of cards?[21]

Fénéon also made occasional changes in spelling or punctuation. He corrected Rimbaud's spelling of the Greek name for the Fates, *Erinyes,* and substituted a simpler typography for some unusual effects, "since we were not yet in the presence of a sacred text." His letters to Lacoste show that he could enjoy a laugh at his own expense and that in spite of his interest in Rimbaud, he did not always understand his imagery. For example, regarding a line in "Vagabonds,"

> . . . *and we wandered, sustained by the wine of caverns* . . .

Fénéon wrote:

> By what sleight of hand did I end up with *Pavermes* in the separate edition, leaving the *cavernes* of *la Vogue* far behind and starting on the path to the *Palermes* of Vanier's edition? At least *Palermes* is amusing through its illogical geography [Palermo, in Sicily]. Though less picturesque, *cavernes* is hardly less absurd. If you had not decreed

> that there is "no other rule than scrupulous fidelity," I would ask you if it were not all right to infringe upon the manuscript and put, quite simply, *tavernes*.[22]

Evidently, F. F. did not see that the wanderers had no wine at all, but water, the "wine of caverns."

When Fénéon's separate edition of *Les Illuminations* first came out, only one buyer came around to get a copy: Laforgue's close friend Paul Bourget. So F. F. wrote an article, "Arthur Rimbaud," which had a resounding effect. Anatole France exclaimed upon reading it, "Symbolism has found its Pascal!"[23] Fénéon gave some documentary information before launching into a description of the poems:

> While his work, which is finally in print, terrifies some people and enthralls others, the man himself is becoming indistinct. His life is already in dispute, and Rimbaud floats over the symbolists like a mythical shadow. Yet, people saw him, around 1870. Portraits perpetuate his memory. M. Verlaine remembers one by M. Fantin showing him at a "table corner" and says he can find another one by M. J.-L. Forain. Photography even captured him . . . Verlaine considers that it is the face of an angel; but it is the face of a murderous peasant. To conclude this iconography, a hitherto unknown line drawing of him by Edouard Manet is posted on the wall of the *Revue wagnérienne:* a shifty-eyed ephebe, standing against a table where you can see a tumbler of wine and a drunkard's head.[24]

Fénéon then journeyed through the poems, quoting liberally from them. Finally, he described how he had tried, as editor, to set the loose-leaf pages in a certain "logical order:"

> First, cosmic revolutions, and his exultant joy frolics, leaping, to the riots, to the fires. Then monstrous cities, where haggard humanity is creating a tinsel-land out of crime and insanity. A single person escapes from the crowd and the bustle: raptures of passion, soon sourish and acrid, deflect into high-pitched erotic convulsions. Lypothemia prostrates him. He craves a vegetative life; shadowy forms of a few humble creatures wander past, little gardens in a Belgian suburb display their faintly tinted blossoms in a kind of plaintive dreariness.
>
> The early sinewy prose, bright colored and supple, has been supplanted by murmuring labile songs, fading into engulfing waves of sleep, babbling in benign imbecility, or whimpering. Abrupt, then, an awakening full of hate, sudden jolts, a call for social upheaval yelped in an alcoholic's voice, an insult shouted at this military and utilitarian Democracy, a final and ironic "Forward march!"
>
> In short, this is poetry beyond—and probably superior to—all literature.[25]

The reaction of Anatole France was somewhat equivocal: was Fénéon or Rimbaud the "Pascal of symbolism"? France quoted Fénéon's last words and said: "As for me, I am going to conclude in turn, if I may, with a quotation from Rousseau: 'There are, so to speak, contagious states of mind that are transmitted from one person to the next like an epidemic,' " which amounts to saying that Fénéon was the *Illuminé*.

Fénéon's concluding statement on *Les Illuminations* was prophetic, but he was not as enthralled by Rimbaud as Anatole France believed. When *Vogue* decided to reprint *A*

Season in Hell, Fénéon did not assist in its publication. He later explained, "As a simple lover of letters—therefore without obligations to them—I did not find it necessary to spoil for their austere benefit my pleasure in the *Illuminations* by getting on intimate terms with *A Season in Hell,* which put me off a bit by its frenzy."[26] One imagines also that the Don Quixote in F. F. was finding other causes to fight for. Rimbaud no longer had need of him.

PART TWO

Focus on Neo-Impressionism 1886–1892

CHAPTER 5

Catching up with Seurat and the Impressionists in 1886

There is no record of where or when Fénéon met Georges Seurat. From Fénéon's point of view, their relationship dated from 1884, when he saw *Bathing at Asnières* at the Indépendants. Yet it was only after Fénéon came to know and talk with the painter that he began writing about the impressionists and their successors and became Seurat's foremost advocate.

Tradition has it that they first saw one another in front of Seurat's large painting, *A Sunday Afternoon on the Island of the Grande Jatte,* at the eighth impressionist exhibition held in the spring of 1886. But they may have met earlier. Seurat, along with two other artists from the Indépendants who became his associates, Paul Signac and Albert Dubois-Pillet, attended literary gatherings held by the former Communard, Robert Caze, in his home on rue Condorcet. Fénéon was frequently there.[1] These meetings ended suddenly when Caze was fatally wounded in a duel on February 15, 1886. This was three months before the impressionist exhibition opened, and longer yet before Fénéon wrote anything about Seurat. The circumstances surrounding Caze's duel, however, indicate a likely connection between F. F. and painters close to Seurat: Caze's seconds were Paul Adam, a friend of Fénéon's, and Dubois-Pillet, Seurat's follower.

The duel, typical of the times, started with a quarrel between Caze and another journalist who exchanged insults and a few blows in the *café Américain.* Caze got the worst of it, but he was furious when Charles Vignier, a young Swiss writer who desired entry into symbolist circles, went about saying that the other writer had "thrashed M. Caze." Caze challenged Vignier, and they met: swords at dawn in Meudon, beyond the eyes of the law. Caze again proved he was not a fighter. At the en garde, he became overexcited, thinking of his wife and children, and rushed on his adversary, literally skewering himself on Vignier's rapier.[2] For six weeks he lay in agony, with his friends helplessly watching each day the progress of peritonitis until Caze's death on March 31. The young men were bitter over this turn of events. To them Caze had been not only an

6e volume. N° 300. — 10 c. Un an : 6 fr.

LES HOMMES D'AUJOURD'HUI

DESSIN DE M. REYMOND

TEXTE DE FÉLIX FÉNÉON

Bureaux : Librairie Vanier, 19, quai Saint-Michel, à Paris.

CHARLES VIGNIER

M. REYMOND. ***Portrait of Charles Vignier.*** Cover for *Les Hommes d'aujourd'hui,* no. 300 [1887]. Photograph G. Roche.

affable host but a kind of hero because of his youthful dedication to the Paris Commune and his subsequent years of exile. Many of them, including the painter Paul Signac, had witnessed the duel. No one thought of blaming the practice of dueling or the hotheadedness of Caze. Instead, they saw Vignier as a villain; most of the symbolists shunned him. Fénéon, however, invited him to do translations for *La Vogue* and later did a portrait study of him for *Les Hommes d'aujourd'hui.*

After the duel, during the long vigil over the dying man, Paul Adam had frequent opportunities to talk with Dubois-Pillet. This painter was a genial fellow approaching forty, who managed to pursue his true vocation outside his hours of duty as an officer of the Republican Guard. He was also one of the chief organizers of the Society of

Independent Artists, which was just then taking shape. Adam soon gained an appreciation for Dubois-Pillet's newest paintings, which he must have seen in the artist's studio. He depicted several of them in detail in his novel, *Soi* (Oneself), where he meant to show "by impressionist touches" the latest developments in music, poetry, and art. He ascribed Dubois's works to a fictional painter "Vibrac," to whom he also gave traits inspired by the robust and ebullient Signac.[3]

Fénéon apparently accompanied Adam on at least one visit to Dubois-Pillet's studio, for later, in his review of the impressionist exhibition, he included several of this painter's "limpid landscapes"—even though Dubois-Pillet was not in the show. He was excluded because Degas and Eugène Manet (speaking for his wife, the painter Berthe Morisot) had declared that they would not participate if yet another of Seurat's "workers in petit point" was invited. Fénéon argued that Dubois-Pillet should have been included: "He is," along with Seurat, Signac, Lucien and Camille Pissarro, "in the avant-garde of impressionism."[4]

This was Fénéon's way of emphasizing the importance of Seurat's new style; his followers, the critic implied, should be accepted as colleagues by the older impressionists. But it was also a way for the critic to thank the artist who in all probability first invited him into his study to see and discuss the new art.

It is likely that Dubois-Pillet introduced Fénéon to Seurat. But the traditional version may be correct: since Seurat was not as gregarious as the others, it may well be that F. F. did not actually have a chance to talk with him until the exhibition opened, or shortly before, during the hanging of the pictures. In any event, it is clear that once they met, Seurat discussed his large new painting with the critic in great detail.

La Grande Jatte hung in the last room of the exhibition, in a space reserved for Signac, Seurat, and Lucien and Camille Pissarro. Flanked by smaller canvases, the painting seemed immense, ten feet long and almost seven feet high. Much more complex than *Bathing at Asnières* as Fénéon remembered it, the new painting also appeared to vibrate or to scintillate with its own light (pl. 3).

The critic silently took it in: a tranquil wooded island, now stirring with the life of people young and old, fishing in the sun, sitting in the shade, or stiffly promenading. The woman in the absurd bustle was oddly dignified; the painter had somehow idealized the very exaggeration of line in the current fashion. This was a modern scene: the unmarried girls, the boatman resting on his back oblivious of the stylish lady, most probably a *cocotte* ("kept woman"), on the arm of her gentleman, holding on a leash not a dog but a monkey—an atavistic glimpse of humanity, perhaps, or a symbol of lasciviousness. Seurat had slyly depicted the mores of the middle class at this isolated pleasure spot in the middle of the Seine, which sat directly opposite the plain denuded shore used by the men (workers?) he had painted in *Bathing at Asnières*. Did he mean, in choosing these two sites for his first large canvases, to create a contemporary diptych reflecting a polarized society? Most of the bathers face right, the direction of the island, and most of the figures in the *Grande Jatte* face left, toward the bathers' shore.[5] Fénéon never commented on this intentional or unintentional confrontation. The art itself was revolutionary and there was nothing anecdotal in the picture. Its modernity was paradoxically contained in a classic or even hieratic schema.

The critic's gaze followed the geometric contours of the trees, the sails, the spiraled tails of dog and monkey, and even the outlines of the human figures, as vertical as gnomons with their oblique, sundial shadows.[6] But above all he was moved by the vibrant life in the color itself. He asked Seurat to explain. Fénéon knew something—quite a bit, in fact—of "optical mixture," but this painting was a complete, new paradigm.

Seurat spoke in a calm, slightly pedantic manner, keeping his eyes fixed on the other man, watching for his least reaction.[7] He explained that his art was built on a harmony of opposites and that his use of color was informed by recent studies such as those by the British scientist James Clerk Maxwell and the American Ogden Rood. These scientists had shown that the traditional complementaries—red and green, orange and blue, yellow and violet—are opposites of *matter* which, when mixed, result in muddy hues. Seurat was seeking rather to express opposites observed in rays of *light:* that is, for red or orange, cyan-blue (a greenish blue); for green, purple; for emerald green, a red purple; and so on, according to a chart Rood had drawn up.[8] Complementaries in colored rays of light, when combined, produced white light. Thus the *optical mixture* the painters were striving for was a "move towards brightness." By careful observation and scientific control, they could place flecks of color so as to enhance luminosity.

F. F. understood that such juxtapositions gave the painting its extraordinary vibrancy. And just as the painting touched his aesthetic sense, the scientific basis for the method appealed to his materialist convictions: the wedding of physicists' knowledge to the intuition of artists provided a way to discover the very mechanism by which Nature produces color. Seurat explained how certain variables directed the choice of color contrasts in the *Jatte:* "for a plot of lawn in the shade, the majority of strokes give the local color of the grass, permeated with bits of purple—the complementary of green—and sparked with thinly scattered elements of pale orange—to express the scarcely felt action of the sun." But for the stretch of grass in full sunlight, "two elements only converge": orange interspersed in the green, where the orange presents the solar light which is "so direct that it wipes out all other reactions to the green of the grass."[9]

This information, which Fénéon later used in his review, did not reveal all of Seurat's procedure, his underlayers of color applied in broader strokes, for example, or his concern with geometric structure. But it informed the critic of the basic dynamics in Seurat's optical mixture. Fénéon's detailed description has permanent value: it allows us to construct in our mind's eye Seurat's vibrantly contrasting oranges and greens. Six years after the painting was completed, these colors had radically altered, for in the final stages of his canvas, Seurat had used unstable pigments—unfortunately suggested to him by Pissarro.[10]

The newborn *Grande Jatte* offered Fénéon, through its "harmony of contrasts," the end of his own inward search for a style. He read the French translation of Rood's *Modern Chromatics* and studied other aspects of Seurat's work before attempting to review it. He offered to introduce the painter to Charles Henry, explaining that Henry had written "a work full of numbers and imagination" on the way different elements of the spectrum affect the nervous system: some, which he called cool or sad, inhibiting it, and others, hot or gay, generating energy.

Fénéon soon learned that, unlike Signac and other artists in the group, Seurat rarely discussed anything other than painting. He seemed to live for and in his work, with the deep intensity of a reformer. With his tall stature, somber clothes and quiet, forceful presence, he reminded F. F. of an austere Huguenot at the time of the Reformation.

A large number of visitors, most of them unsympathetic, attended the opening of this Eighth Exhibition of Painting upstairs from a well-known restaurant, the Maison Dorée, on May 15, 1886. Degas had insisted, not without reason, that "impressionist" be dropped from the title. Cézanne was again absent; he had not exhibited with the group since 1877. Monet, Renoir, Sisley, and Caillebotte had declined to take part, fearful that the presence of the young painters sponsored by Pissarro (Seurat, Signac, and his own son Lucien), and several others promoted by Degas, would diminish the exhibition's quality. Four years had elapsed since the impressionists' last exhibition, and twelve since they had first banded together in 1874. As it turned out, this was to be their last group endeavor. On opening day, the fashionable painter and former friend of Manet, Alfred Stevens, amused himself by shuttling back and forth between the Maison Dorée and a café on the nearby boulevard des Italiens, recruiting sophisticates there to come and witness the "horrors" that Degas had allowed into the show.[11] He did not mean the chrysanthemums and troweled nudes of Tillot, Schuffenecker, Zandomeneghi, Marie Bracquemond, and other protégés of Degas; the butt of the joke was Seurat's *Grand Jatte* and "identical confettisms" by Camille and Lucien Pissarro and Signac.

The disarray among the older impressionists, along with the presence of this group of young "upstarts" supported by the anarchist Pissarro, made impressionism even harder to define. Most critics lumped the new painters in with the old, although some saw a difference of degree between the latter and the "young intransigents" or "madmen" of painting. The few who spoke favorably made little or no distinction among divergent styles and concepts, calling all the exhibitors "impressionist." Fénéon alone put the exhibition in a clear historical perspective.

He divided his review into three separate sections, each headed by a major figure: Degas, Gauguin, and Seurat. Gone were the "heroic days" of impressionism, heralded by Manet and carried by the "luminists": Pissarro, Renoir, Degas, and above all Claude Monet. Today, Degas was exhibiting characteristic works, conceived differently from the spontaneous manner of his peers. Gauguin, Guillaumin, and Madame Morisot represented impressionism as it had appeared in previous exhibitions. Pissarro, Seurat, and Signac were breaking new ground.

Degas was showing a series of pastels of women bathing, drying off, or combing their hair. Most reviewers found these unidealized figures repulsive or obscene. Huysmans praised Degas for "vilifying that constantly coddled idol of our times, woman" by showing her as she actually looked, squatting naked at her "intimate

EDGAR DEGAS. ***Woman Bathing in a Shallow Tub.*** 1885. Pastel on paper, 80 x 55 cm. New York, The Metropolitan Museum of Art. Bequest of Mrs. H. O. Havemeyer, 1929. *An angular backbone stretches out; breasts ripe as Virgoulée pears hang free as arms plunge vertically between the legs.* (F, 30)

tasks."[12] Fénéon's studied word picture of the Degas nudes is a classic example of his style: *Des femmes emplissent de leur accroupissement cucurbitant la coque des tubs . . .*

> Women crouching fill the hull of tubs with swollen melon shapes: this one, chin on breast, scrapes at the nape of her neck; another, twisting in a spiral, arm stuck to her back, works a frothing sponge on coccyx regions. An angular backbone stretches out;

> breasts ripe as Virgoulée pears hang free as arms plunge vertically between the legs. . . .

Evoking fruits and vegetables, Fénéon has his reader visualize first of all the shapes and colors in the pastels. The pear he names—*virgouleuse* in French—is a very juicy, "pear-shaped" pear. F. F. employs a common metaphor for breasts (Are they apples, pears, or melons?), but his botanical term evokes further associations in the reader's mind: *virgule, goule, virer, vir* . . . (a comma's shape, a throat or "gullet," veering, and the Latin root for man, virility, and so on).[13] Degas's nudes have become delectables for the devouring gaze of the viewer—who is understood to be male.

He also takes the scientific name for the gourd or melon family (Cucurbitaceae) and makes up a word that is both recondite and obscene, as one hears *cu(l), cu(l)* and sees the piling up of *c*'s in a typographical mime of buttocks. This is echoed further on in a second neologism (*coccygiennes*) based on the anatomical term for tailbone, suggesting again the animal nature of the bathers.

He breaks and reshapes syntax—with inversions such as the verb *fall* in the next extract—in order to "elucidate the lines of this cruel and astute observer."

> Crushing into one another, fall hair on shoulders, bust on hips, belly on thighs, limbs on joints, and this trollop viewed from the ceiling, standing beside her bed, hands pressed to her buttocks, is a series of slightly swollen nested cylinders.

Finally, F. F. puts his readers in touch with the humanity of the models by evoking their lives and surroundings:

> It is in dim furnished rooms and wretched hovels that these bodies with their rich patinas, bodies bruised and shaped by whoring, child-bearing, and illnesses, husk their skins and stretch their limbs.[14]

The word translated here as "whoring" is, in the original, *noces,* a subtler term that can mean either of two things: (1) nuptials or (2) carousing. Fénéon has the two meanings mingle their values for a more potent ambiguity. At first he calls the models "women," but toward the end says "trollop" and "whore" (*maritorne, fille*). He makes it clear that Degas's models are the poorest of prostitutes, the "edibles" society can partake of and then toss on the refuse heap. But in spite of his social concerns, he does not dwell on this injustice. It was not his style to preach. Moreover, while he may have seen the exploitation of women in a society geared toward men's pleasures, and even unmasked it through his eloquent choice of words, he also remained ambivalent, both enjoying and resisting the feast.

His chief interest in the pictures is aesthetic. Thus Fénéon's commentary veers away from the models in their wretched rooms, back to the pastels, which he describes with metaphorical words: *talés* (bruised) and *décortiquer* (to peel). These words in French refer normally only to fruits and vegetables, not human flesh or skin. Fénéon uses them brilliantly to bring to life the rich colors and contours Degas achieved in layering on his "patina" of pastels (pl. 4).

Fénéon chose Gauguin as the second principal artist of the exhibition. He drew

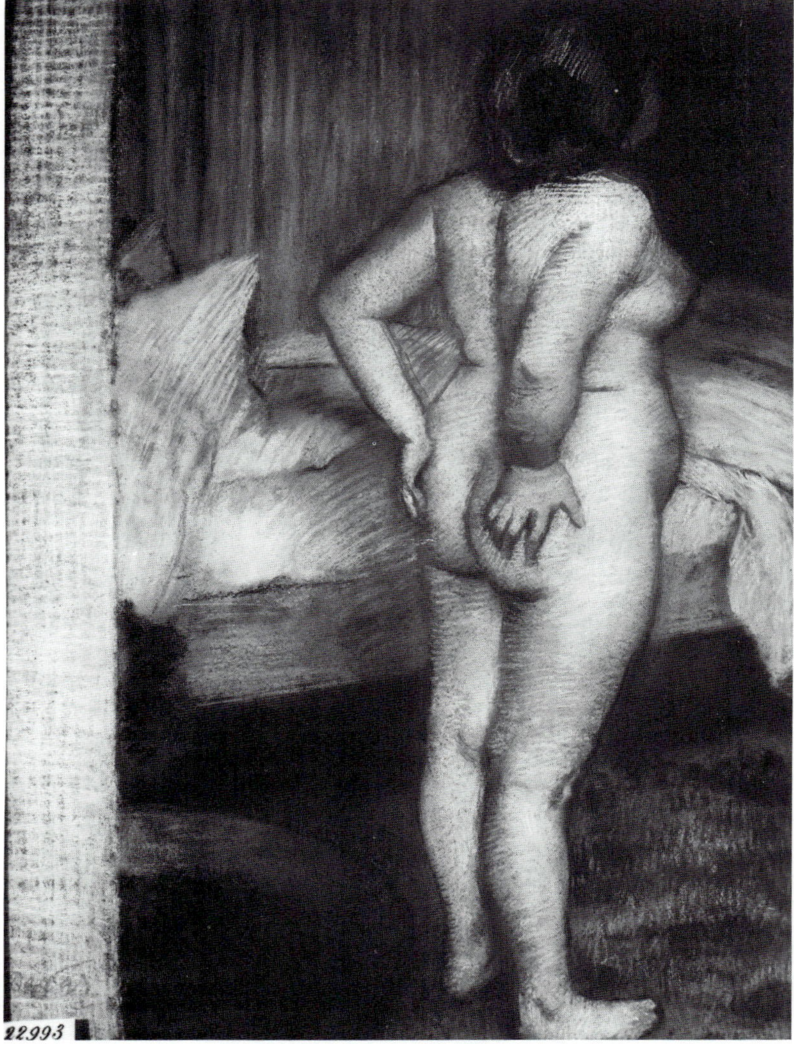

EDGAR DEGAS. From ***Suite of Nudes,*** now known as ***La Boulangère (The Baker's Wife).*** ca. 1886. Pastel on paper, 67 x 52.1 cm. Private collection. *Crushing into one another, fall hair on shoulders, bust on hips, belly on thighs, limbs on joints, and this trollop viewed from the ceiling, standing beside her bed, hands pressed to her buttocks, is a series of slightly swollen nested cylindres.* (F, 30)

attention to Gauguin's originality in carving and painting wood sculpture and then pointed out unique traits in his painting (pl. 5):

> That muffled harmony in M. Paul Gauguin's paintings flows from the close-set tones he uses. Dense trees gush from rich, humid, lush soil, overflowing the frame, banishing the sky. A heavy air. A glimpse of bricks suggests a nearby house; hides stretch, muzzles part the brushwood—cows.[15]

In the space of a dash, Fénéon stills the uncanny motion of the hides, the muzzles, and retrieves the inertia of the painting. He sees the cows not as subject matter but as elements of the painting, and his fragmented sentence perfectly translates the eye's discovery. "He attains the unreal and substantial plane on which the crystal of time dehisces," said the poet André Du Bouchet.[16]

Gauguin's nineteen paintings—most of them rural scenes from the Normandy countryside—hung in the room just preceding the *Grande Jatte.* Without making comparisons, Fénéon pointed up Gauguin's muted tones, the shapes and heavy sensuousness that set his work apart. Only one other writer, Fénéon's friend, Paul Adam, had seized the significance of Gauguin's new canvases, concentrating on the feelings emanating from them. In his first piece of art criticism, which appeared two or three weeks before Fénéon's celebrated review in *La Vogue,* Adam wrote that Gauguin's landscapes revealed "the self-centered sadness of vegetation, its unfathomable life that has its own being and seems to brood."[17] Similarities in their thinking and their language indicate that the two friends influenced one another and that Félix benefited from the exchange.

The last section of Fénéon's review was devoted to Seurat and his group. Before focusing on the newcomers' work, he reviewed all that the impressionists had brought to painting: choosing subjects from modern life, and painting directly from nature; abandoning "tenebrous sauces concocted on the palette," and using separate strokes of pigment to capture fugitive effects of atmosphere and light. This color division, however, had been arbitrary and relied on happy accident: "a brush dragged over a green landscape gave the sensation of red." But since 1884, 1885, and 1886, a new path had been opened. "Georges Seurat, Camille and Lucien Pissarro, Dubois-Pillet, and Paul Signac divide color values in a conscious and scientific manner."

Fénéon then plunged into a minute description of the colors in a few square inches of "uniform tone" in Seurat's *Grande Jatte.* "You will find on each centimeter of this surface, in a whirling host of tiny spots, all the elements that make up the tone." He brought these elements of color to life, endowing them with movement: "A cyan-blue, brought out by the proximity of a plot of grass in the sunlight, accumulates its siftings towards the line of demarcation, and progressively grows thinner away from this line. . . . Black being a non-light, the black dog is colored by reactions to the grass; its dominant color is therefore deep purple; but it is also attacked by the dark blue arising from neighboring spaces of light." The critic's faith in Seurat and in science is such that he believes, and wants us to believe, that the painter very nearly duplicates the mysterious processes of nature. He goes on to say that the colors, "isolated on the canvas, recombine on the retina: a mixture not made of pigments but of differently colored rays of light." Although this is something of an overstatement, it tells what Seurat and his followers believed, and Fénéon lays out the scientific evidence:

> Need one be reminded that even when the colors are the same, mixed pigments do not necessarily produce the same results as mixed rays of light? It is also generally understood that the luminosity of optical mixture is always much greater than that of

> pigmentary mixture, as is shown by the numerous equations worked out by Mr. Rood. For carmine violet and Prussian blue, which produce a blue-gray:
>
> 50 C + 50 B = 47 C + 49 B + 4 black;
> *mixture of pigments* — *mixture of light*
>
> for carmine and green:
>
> 50 C + 50 G = 50 C + 24 G + 26 black.
>
> We can understand why the impressionists, in striving to express a maximum of luminosity—as occasionally Delacroix before them—would want to substitute optical mixture for mixing pigments on the palette.
>
> Georges Seurat is the first to have presented a complete and systematic paradigm of this new technique.[18]

This kind of criticism, like the art it represents, strikes an entirely new note. Neither Huysmans nor Théodore Duret, whose writing on the impressionists Fénéon cited, nor any other critic, had taken such pains to translate and explain the work of a recent avant-garde artist. One cannot say that such criticism is inspired, in the manner of Baudelaire, nor enthusiastic, in the manner of Diderot—two critics much admired by Fénéon. But it was surely faithful to the intentions of the artist. And it was largely due to Fénéon that *La Grande Jatte* became what Signac called the "manifesto-painting" of the movement.

By furnishing his readers with scientific authority, Fénéon was inviting them to believe in the new art. It seemed as if he were giving away arcane secrets by quoting one of Seurat's technical sources. This made the informed viewers feel superior to the uninitiated, and fortified them against their own discomfort in face of the unknown. Oddly enough, the complicity between a painter and those reviewers who share his secret can create the sort of publicity needed for something really new to catch hold. Fénéon quite legitimately utilized the elitist appeal of science and mathematics to promote Seurat's painting.

At the same time, Fénéon knew that a work of art is "irreducible in our consciousness."[19] No amount of equations and no analysis, however brilliant, can unwind its vital rhythms. And so the cryptic formulae in his text are both explication and mystification. The dandy in him, adept at masking intimate reality and cognizant of Seurat's own need to keep his art aloof, used the language of science as a crystal to clarify the gaze of the "happy few" and to deflect the derision of the vulgar herd.

Writing in *La Vogue* for an elite audience of symbolists and their friends, Fénéon assumed that his reader was acquainted with Rood's work, which had been translated into French in 1881; but there is a certain snobbery in his remarks, "Need one be reminded that . . . . It is also generally understood that . . . . " In fact, the theory of optical mixture was not generally understood and, as Fénéon noted, *La Grande Jatte* was its first methodical application in painting. Yet he did not explain the experiments behind them, where Rood, following the lead of the Scottish physicist Maxwell, had demonstrated the superiority of optical mingling of color over a mixture of pigments. This involved painting two disks with two different colors, for instance, one in vermilion and the other in ultramarine-blue, and then combining the disks (which had a radial slit) so that each color formed one half of a circle. Then a smaller disk was painted with a mixture of equal parts of the same colors and placed in the center of the combined disks. The whole thing was then rotated at high speed. The larger disk became red-purple while the one in the center seemed dull and grayish in comparison (it was actually a darker violet-purple). In order to match the duller tone of the pigment mix, Rood had to add a sector of black to the Maxwell disks.[20] That is the "black" in the equations quoted by Fénéon, who telescoped the terms of the experiment by saying, "mixture of light," rather than "mixture by rotation," as did Rood. Fénéon's elitism and love of concision made him reduce the scientific evidence to brief formulae, hermetically sealing the secrets of the new art in apparently crystalline terms. ("One does not only wish to be understood when one writes; one wishes just as surely *not* to be understood."—Nietzsche, *The Gay Science,* no. 381.)

Fénéon then explored the advantages of the "monotonous, patient" brushstroke in Seurat's "myriad-speckled tapestry":

> Here in truth fancy brushwork is futile, tricks of the trade impossible; there is no room for bravura—let the hand be numb, but the eye quick, shrewd, and knowing. Whether the subject is an ostrich plume, a bundle of straw, a wave, or a rock, the handling of the brush remains the same. And if it is possible to give "virtuoso painting" points for slashing and scumbling, say, rough weeds, waving branches, fluffy fur, at least "la peinture au point"[21] is exactly right for rendering smooth surfaces, and more particularly the nude, to which it has not yet been applied.

That last remark may have inspired Seurat to do a painting of the nude; in any event, he began his studies for *The Models* a few months later, after a summer of work at the seashore.

The seriousness of Fénéon's criticism is all the more evident when set against the contemporary reaction to Seurat's *Grande Jatte.* When Pissarro told Degas that this painting was very interesting, Degas replied with a bit of his customary sarcasm: "Oh, I would have noted that myself, Pissarro, except that the painting is so large!"[22] The writer George Moore reported that the major attraction in Seurat's work was the monkey in the foreground, "with a tail three yards long."[23] Some forty years later, Fénéon remembered the scene:

> There must have been something aggressively odd in this canvas, for it reduced the visitor to paroxysms of rage as soon as he entered the room reserved for Seurat and Signac and saw it occupying almost all of the back wall. Soon the intruder's anger, at first scattered over the forty figures on the scene, became localized . . . on the monkey held on a leash by the lady in the foreground and particularly on its spiraled tail. It seemed as if that little beast . . . and that tail were there to insult personally anyone who crossed the threshold.[24]

In his first account of the exhibition, Fénéon paid no heed to the hilarity of the crowd. After discussing Seurat's technique, he briefly evoked the subject of the painting, seen not as an anecdote but as a formal structure:

> The subject: beneath a sultry sky, at four o'clock, the island, boats slipping past its flank, stirring with a casual Sunday crowd enjoying the fresh air among the

GEORGES-PIERRE SEURAT. ***Monkeys,*** study for *La Grande Jatte.* 1884–85. Conté crayon, 30.2 x 23.3 cm. Paris, Musée d'Orsay, bequest of Camille Pissarro. Photograph courtesy Bernheim-Jeune Galleries, Paris. *It seemed as if that little beast and that tail—an atavistic glimpse?—were there to insult personally anyone who crossed the threshold.* (F, 488)

trees; and these forty or so figures are endowed with a succinct, hieratic line, rigorously drawn in full-face or in profile or from the back, some seated at right angles, others stretched out horizontally, others standing rigidly; as though by a modernizing Puvis.

The atmosphere is transparent and uncommonly vibrant; the surface seems to flicker or glimmer. Perhaps this sensation, which is experienced in front of certain other paintings in the same room, can be explained by the theory of Dove:[25] the retina, expecting distinct rays of light to act on it, perceives in very rapid alternation both the disassociated colored elements and their resultant.[26]

Thus, without elaborating further on the figures—for the subject is "the island . . . stirring"—Fénéon returns to the visual nature of the picture whose vibrant, transparent quality is due to the multiplicity of colored units, interpreted by the visual system as a rapid succession of alternating impulses: the "vibration" that Chevreul and Rood had described in their scientific studies. Fénéon's description of this effect, "The surface seems to flicker or glimmer" (*la surface semble vaciller*), is identical to the French translation of Rood.[27]

This is more accurate than saying that the colors actually recombine on the retina. "Take two steps away, and all these versicolored spots melt into undulating, luminous masses," said Fénéon.[28] As the receptors on the human retina, fatigued by a hue, emphasize its complementary, the eye experiences a lustrous flickering from these alternating perceptions of the separate colored particles; "an effect," Rood concludes, "that no doubt arises from a fainter perception from time to time of [the] constituents. This communicates a soft and peculiar brilliancy to the surface, and gives it a certain appearance of transparency; we seem to see into it and below it."[29]

Seurat and his comrades were pleased with Fénéon's explanations. Of all the critics, Paul Signac remarked, "only the infallible F. Fénéon gave a pertinent analysis of the painter's technical achievement."[30] Others concurred: "He is the first to have discovered scientific criticism of painting," said Paul Adam.[31]

After the first few days, the number of visitors to the Maison Dorée lessened drastically, and the exhibition was far from a success. The very fact that it had happened, however, was a cause for rejoicing among the artists. It was agreed among them to celebrate with a dinner and to invite some of the young writers who had expressed enthusiasm over their work, Gustave Kahn, Paul Adam, and Félix Fénéon. Gauguin suggested the spot: not the usual locale of the impressionists, but lake Saint-Fargeau in Belleville, a working-class suburb.[32] It would be good to get out of the city and into some greenery among the common folk. Camille Pissarro agreed, and he arranged for everyone to meet at Arts et Métiers to catch the omnibus to Belleville.

They all rode out together on the top deck, the writers and Gauguin, Seurat, Signac, Guillaumin, Lucien Pissarro and his father Camille. They sat at a long table in the best pavilion, watching young couples promenade by, the girls looking like Renoir's models in their white and pink cotton frocks. (Renoir himself was not there; he had refused to join the exhibition, fearful that association with the newcomers and "the [anarchist] Jew Pissarro" would damage his sales.[33]) The table conversation centered mostly around Seurat's new method of painting. Although Gauguin admired Seurat's theoretical approach, it seemed to him that the young painter had usurped a role he believed should rightfully have been his, that of a new Messiah leading away from impressionism. He resented the enthusiasm of Kahn and Fénéon for Seurat's new method and the parallel they drew between color division and the symbolist "theory of discontinuity," where words regain their autonomy and achieve new interactions.

On June 15, the exhibition ended, and a new impressionist show opened in the fashionable gallery of Georges Petit, including those artists who had declined to take part in the Maison Dorée exhibition. Fénéon went to review them, and found that Renoir had nothing interesting to show. "He must have left his best paintings home," he said. In fact, the "radiant painter of sea-green eyes" was in a period of transition; two years later Fénéon would remark on a new linear strength in his work, although the faces of his nudes still wore the same "snubnosed mask of a Parisian shopgirl, ennobled by his brush."[34]

Monet, Fénéon commented, is a painter "whose eye instantaneously catches all aspects of a scene and spontaneously divides up the tones." Just as he did for Degas, the critic invented terms and phrases to create word pictures that are practically untranslatable. But whereas he applied an orderly, logical syntax to Degas's well thought-out work, he employed an elliptical style for Monet, making language correspond intimately to the nature of the painting under view.

> These waters, viewed by gazing vertically down, cover the whole enframed space; but the sky, though invisible, is sensed: its changing moods are betrayed by the restless play of light on water. . . .
> *The Needle-Rock at Etretat*—the rock and, sails blued a bit, breasting boats crudely invert in this expanse of violet, shading here and there into icy greens, forerunners of hesitant blues and furtive reds. *Rainy weather:* the rocks, the needle dissolve in that fog, where delicate harmonies of gray are frolicking. . . . *The View from Cape Martin:* a faintly green sky with Etesian winds scudding over; on the flank of a cliff, an ocher path; in the distance, far off, Alps of shimmering amethyst.[35]

This juxtaposition of various sense perceptions in short choppy phrases mirrors Monet's poetic rendering of spontaneous impressions—the solid rocks dissolving in the mist, the boats inverted (rather than "reflected") in the greening violet sea. To evoke another seascape, Fénéon used a single word, a technical term meaning "inner arch," descriptive of a certain rock formation off the coast of Normandy that Monet liked to paint: "The intrados of the *Manne-Porte.*" The statement stands with no more structure than that, without a predicate. So looms the shape in Monet.

These two exhibitions in spring 1886 marked a turning point for Fénéon. Whereas he had previously written art criticism in a casual way, giving only lip service to the importance of the impressionists, his dedication to the new art of Seurat involved him as well in a critical re-reading of the older generation. His two articles in *La Vogue* made him, in the eyes of his colleagues, the chief interpreter of contemporary art.

Not everyone was happy, however, with Fénéon's report on the Maison Dorée exhibition. Some were annoyed that he spent a full paragraph on a little known Swiss artist, David Estoppey, whose name had not even been listed in the catalogue. Fénéon defended himself: it mattered to give support to a young unknown, who gave proof of a supple talent and an eagerness to move in new directions; besides, he confessed, Estoppey had just done a portrait of Jean Moréas and was in the process of doing one of him, Félix; what better way to repay him, he chuckled, than to speak of him in the same breath as Guillaumin, Gauguin, and Madame Morisot? A more serious objection arose over the paragraph that Fénéon had devoted to Dubois-Pillet, even though his work had not been shown at the Maison Dorée. Fénéon felt he was justified in this

CLAUDE MONET. ***The Manneporte, Etretat II.*** 1886. Oil on Canvas, 81.3 x 65.4 cm. New York, The Metropolitan Museum of Art. Bequest of Lizzie P. Bliss, 1931.

choice; it was clear that Dubois-Pillet's adoption of Seurat's method not only gave his own work validity but added strength to the whole group.

Gauguin got his friend Guillaumin worked up over the matter. It seemed that young Fénéon was creating a chapel for Seurat and adding invisible converts. Who was this Dubois-Pillet?—*du bois pilé* (sawdust) "good for pointillism" according to Degas.[36] Why should Fénéon want to name *that* in the "avant-garde of impressionism!" Guillaumin found Seurat at Vetzel's one evening and launched into a diatribe against Fénéon, who was not there. Seurat later described the incident in a letter to Signac:

> Having read Fénéon incorrectly, Guillaumin said to me: "Dubois-Pillet is no more in the avant-garde *than you and Signac.*"

> I kept my trap shut and stuck my nose in the newspaper. Apparently age is the yardstick. Evidently Guillaumin had just been wound up by Gauguin, who has a special key.[37]

Gauguin's jealousy and wounded pride were soon exacerbated in another misunderstanding. Paul Signac was leaving Paris for a sojourn in Les Andelys and told Gauguin he could use his studio. Seurat, who sometimes worked with Signac and had a key to his place, was unaware of the offer to Gauguin, who, penniless, had no proper studio. After Signac's departure, Seurat closed Signac's flat and told the concierge not to allow anyone in. When Gauguin arrived and learned he was barred from the studio, he was furious. Rather than seeking a logical explanation, he refused to listen to Seurat and Signac when he saw them later at the Nouvelles Athènes and stormed out, refusing to speak even to his old friend Pissarro. This incident and Gauguin's hostility toward their scientific style created a more or less permanent feud between Gauguin and Seurat's group. Although Fénéon was not personally involved in the quarrel and continued to write appreciative reviews of Gauguin, the painter thereafter considered him a captain in the other camp.

Through his writing and his personal allegiances, Fénéon was intimately involved in the post-impressionist divisions among the painters. Not a little of his choice depended on his anarchist leanings. The social consciousness of Pissarro and Signac, their openness and generosity, appealed deeply to him. Seurat's new method, which tapped both the poetic and the scientific spheres, corresponded to his ideal of developing humanity's full potential. Subjects frequently chosen by these painters, laboring peasants, workers at rest, industrial sites, were significant images of a society in transition. Fénéon had remarked on such an image by Paul Signac at the Maison Dorée exhibition (pl. 6):

> *Gas Tanks at Clichy* . . . with its picket fences laden with work trousers and jackets set out to dry, the desolation of its peeling walls, its scorched grass and its incandescent roofs in an atmosphere that asserts itself and darkens as it rises, hollowing out an abyss of blinding blue.[38]

When asked half a century later if Georges Seurat shared the anarchist views of his comrades, Fénéon replied:

> He did not air his opinions. But in that time when it was not yet stylish for young people to be fed up with everything, his literary and artistic friends and those who supported his work in the press belonged to anarchist circles; and if Seurat's opinions had differed radically from theirs, if he had been influenced by his father [who collected pious images of saints], the fact would have been noticed.

As for the man himself, Fénéon said, a poem by Henri de Régnier "gave, to my mind, the most faithful portrait of Seurat. I do not see any trait I can add to it":[39]

> Seurat, you had a noble, ardent soul . . .
> I remember. You were calm, grave and gentle,

Taciturn, knowing how much of ourselves is
Wasted in the frivolous noise of talk.
You used to listen without answering, in silence;
A deliberate silence contradicted by your eyes
But if your art was the subject of discussion
Your rebellious gaze took fire,
For you conceived within yourself,
Seurat, in due deliberation, the obstinacy of an
Innovator, beside which nothing can prevail or
even exist . . . [40]

The rather Homeric terms used to portray Seurat in this poem suggest the distance that was kept between him and even those who admired him most. Yet all who knew him felt the force of his personality. Not only artists in his entourage but painters as different as Vincent van Gogh and Emile Bernard were attracted to him and tried out his style.

It is tempting to think that Fénéon's perception of Seurat's method was the product of a uniquely close relationship. But in fact no special friendship developed between them, although they frequently saw one another in the months following the Maison Dorée exhibition. That summer, Seurat moved into a studio on the boulevard Clichy, not far from Signac's spacious place in the impasse Hélène, and became somewhat more gregarious. In the winter, Dubois-Pillet invited Fénéon, Pissarro, Seurat and Signac to Sunday dinner at his bachelor apartment on the quai Saint-Michel, where they enjoyed a leisurely afternoon of talk, brandy, and tobacco while the rain glinted grey off the Seine outside. When the weather became fair, Fénéon joined the painters on Sunday outings for a moderately priced meal at Asnières or Levallois-Perret, near the recreational sites depicted by Seurat in *Bathing at Asnières* and *La Grande Jatte.* They also met less intimately during the week at their favorite cafés.

Seurat and Signac soon made a habit of dropping by the offices of reviews where Fénéon worked in the late afternoon and evening. The cramped, untidy premises became distilleries of ideas among the painters, writers like Wyzewa and Kahn, and the scientist Charles Henry. In the heated discussions, Seurat said little, and Fénéon even less. But when they spoke, others listened attentively. Seurat was always serious, decorous as a notary, Degas remarked. Fénéon, on the other hand, sometimes broke in with a remark that set the others howling with laughter; the kind of remark, one of them later said, "that would have made the Baron d'Ange blush."

Although their relations were cordial, Seurat must have felt that Fénéon had revealed too much about his art, for he never again spoke with him as openly as he did that first time in front of *La Grande Jatte.* Instead, he fed the critic lateral information, such as some notes, "Remembrances concerning Corot," which he dictated to Fénéon from a letter he had from an old friend of the painter. Or he gave Fénéon a copy of what is now known as "Gauguin's paper" (actually an eighteenth-century Turkish or Persian treatise on crafts), which Gauguin had lent Seurat some time before. Fénéon printed a shortened version of it with an introductory note indicating how Seurat's work exemplified one of the precepts: "Each of your figures ought to be in a static position."[41]

Left, GEORGES SEURAT. ***Félix Fénéon.*** ca. 1886. Conté crayon, 23.5 x 30 cm. Geneva, Galerie Jan Krugier. Photograph Claude Mercier.

Right, GEORGES SEURAT. ***The Artist in his Studio.*** ca. 1884. Conté crayon, 30.8 x 22.8 cm. Philadelphia Museum of Art, A. E. Gallatin Collection.

So Fénéon utilized every grain that fell his way, but did not press the wary artist further.

Seurat once sketched a little drawing of Fénéon, seen, significantly, with his back turned. The critic never posed for Seurat, as he did for Signac and other painters in the group, and Seurat doubtless did this sketch without Fénéon's knowledge. The face shows only in "lost profile" view, and if it were not for the little *f* scrolled to one side following the curve of the jacket, one would be hard put to say if this were not another dandy in top hat and coat. However, it is F. F., seen by Seurat on a tangent and not face to face. The painter later gave Fénéon the drawing, done on the back of an earlier one, and the critic lightly added the notation, "f, by Seurat."

In some ways Seurat's character, enigmatic and private, was similar to Fénéon's. He was, wrote Jules Christophe, "silent, obstinate, and pure,"[42] a statement that brings to mind Paul Valéry's description of Fénéon as "just, pitiless, and gentle."[43] The enigma projected by Félix's physical appearance is also present in the figures painted by Seurat in *La Grande Jatte* and other works. In Fénéon's writing, as in Seurat's painting, an attitude of indifference or restraint is jostled by passion and penetrating analysis. However, Seurat had more staying power, more "obstinacy" in developing his gifts. While Fénéon found self-fulfillment in working for and with others, Seurat was almost completely self-contained. Although he was always loyal to his commitments, Seurat held himself basically aloof. "He never so much as glanced at the comrades struggling along beside him," remarked Emile Verhaeren.[44] This was a trait which would ultimately dampen Fénéon's enthusiasm for Seurat. But, for the next three years—more than half his career as art critic—he remained this artist's most dedicated spokesman.

Fénéon was different from other critics, said the twentieth-century artist Emile Compard: "He did not thrust himself upon you. First of all, he knew how to listen—which is very rare. But at the same time he was both transmitter and receiver, so to speak. He asked questions, and between his questions and the painter's answers, there was a discovery of the painting itself. Even more, there was a kind of mimesis between Fénéon and the artist."[45]

This receptive reciprocity explains that special quality in Fénéon's writing, which assumes a different shape for different painters. To deal with Degas, who thought out his works in advance, Fénéon used expository language that revealed the coherence of his compositions. When writing on Monet's spontaneous art, he dropped logical connectors, relations of cause and effect, and frequently the verb itself. For Seurat, he had recourse to the scientific treatises that the painter had consulted, and he went so far as to print mathematical equations to initiate the public. Overall his criticism was the scientific, poetic, and logical presentation of data, suffused with his own response to the work.

As it turned out, Fénéon would be most perceptive in his remarks about Monet, Gauguin, and Seurat—the three most influential painters of his time (Cézanne was not yet exhibiting regularly in Paris). He also pointed out the weaknesses in their work. Second- or even third-rate artists passed unscathed, as long as they pursued their own intent and personal vision with integrity. Imitators, or those captivated by easy formulae, he ridiculed. "Eugène d'Argence, de l'herbe" (grass) was all he had to say of a would-be Monet.[46] Hard criticism, the honest confrontation of the work unfolding, he reserved for those who proved to be the elect of the century.

CHAPTER 6

Inventing Neo-Impressionism

Fénéon did not use the word *néo-impressionniste* in his first article on Seurat and his followers. To distinguish them from the impressionist clan and from Degas and his group, he called them *novateurs* or *dissidents* from impressionism. He repeatedly used the word "reform" to indicate that the new art was building consciously on the discoveries made intuitively by the impressionists.

The Society of Independent Artists held their second exhibition in late August and September 1886. Some four hundred works were displayed in the same Tuileries barracks used in 1884. This time Seurat, Signac, Cross, Angrand, Lucien Pissarro and Dubois-Pillet managed to reserve a whole room to themselves in order to present a united front. Public reaction can be gauged by this report in the *Figaro*:

> Not very interesting, really, this exhibition, from the point of view of art, but very useful if you are bored by life; we advise those of our friends who like a good laugh to see this show. The room reserved for the "intransigents" of painting is especially priceless.[1]

Fénéon seized the occasion to write again of the innovating painters and sent a long article to *L'Art moderne* of Brussels, which had just engaged him to replace Huysmans as its Paris correspondent.

Entitled "L'Impressionnisme aux Tuileries," Fénéon's review appeared on 19 September 1886; the following day in Paris *La Vogue* printed extracts from it. It was here that the term "neo-impressionist" appeared for the first time. Fénéon spoke of "the neo-impressionist method"—not yet an *-ism,* but a method of painting separate and distinct from that of Monet, Renoir, Morisot, and Sisley. The young painters themselves were considering the term "chromo-luminarist."[2] But color and light had also been the essential quest of the impressionists. The word "neo-impressionist" both underlined the debt of the new art to the old and indicated a progressive change.

As he had done before, Fénéon began by describing the virtues of the "traditional" impressionists, but then he dwelt on what he considered their failings: impasting so that their canvases looked like relief maps, improvising on the spur of the moment, accepting any result that looked good. Fénéon did concede that those results were captivating.

He focused, though, on the reform brought about by Seurat and his followers, briefly evoking individual styles. "No playfulness in Seurat's color, no brag in his brush, but a certain salty savor and a biting austerity" (pl. 7). Paul Signac's colors "provoke each other to wild chromatic escalades, exult, and shout" (pl. 8). In both cases, Fénéon evokes one sensation (taste or sound) to depict another (sight), as well as emotion (restraint in Seurat, joy in Signac) and character (calm or combative). Thus in a glance the reader/spectator gets to know something of both the work and the artist. In fewer words than other symbolist critics, F. F. expressed the Wagnerian ideal of an art touching the soul through all the senses, noting that in these new works, "colorations interpenetrate like circles of waves, and the painting gives out a unified, synthesized harmonic sensation."[3]

His explanation of scientific theory was less technical than in his article on the last impressionist exhibition. He would have liked to discuss certain questions with Seurat, but the artist had become wary of divulging details of his technique to so clear-sighted a spokesman, and so Fénéon turned to Camille Pissarro to correct and confirm the data he had prepared for his review. Great-hearted and conscientious, the old impressionist found himself in a quandary. "It's not easy," he later said to Paul Signac, "not wanting on the one hand to tear away too much of the mysterious veil and yet not being able to refuse M. Fénéon who, all things considered, has been very good to us."[4] He returned Fénéon's manuscript with the comment:

> I am sorry I cannot reply in more detail. Please excuse me if it's not very clear . . . I would have to have been in front of the paintings to ascertain the colors produced either by reflected light or by simultaneous contrast, and even local color.[5]

Pissarro, who was in Paris, could very well have observed the paintings in the light of Fénéon's remarks, but he declared that he would have needed more time; he still had to clarify certain things for himself before he could assert definite opinions. The principal thing, he said, was to name Seurat as the leader of the group.

Fénéon's article named the elder Pissarro several times, even though he was not exhibiting at the Tuileries, having decided to leave the field open to the younger generation. Fénéon paid tribute to him in his concluding sentence: "As for new recruits to impressionism, they will turn not towards Claude Monet but towards the analyst Camille Pissarro."

He even made a comparison unfavorable to Seurat in discussing a point that was "not yet clarified" in the neo-impressionist method: judging from Pissarro's paintings, he noted, a colored surface not only throws its complementary on neighboring surfaces, but reflects some of its own color on them. "The opinion of M. Seurat and M. Signac," wrote Fénéon, "seems less positive. And, for example, the woman in the foreground of *A Sunday at la Grande Jatte* is standing in the grass and yet not one spot of green contributes to the formation of the tone of her dress."[6] Robert Herbert has pointed out something that Fénéon did not realize at the time, that Pissarro "remained an impressionist at heart even when using much of the neo-impressionist technique . . . He sought the harmony of similar tones, not opposites . . . [and] usually showered one area with the local color of the adjacent area, not its complementary. As a result, he tended to blend two areas together, instead of separating them as did Seurat and Signac."[7] What Fénéon had perceived as an unexplicated area was indeed a problem for Pissarro, who was to work out his basic incompatibility with neo-impressionism three or four years later.

The critic touched on various technical problems. For example, the small, separate strokes of the neo-impressionists dried evenly and thus did not crack. The painters put glass over their canvases to prevent colors from dulling, without adding the brownish yellow left by even the purest varnish. They used white frames because gold destroys the quality of orange tones on the canvas. Technical counsel given by Camille Pissarro is evident particularly in a discussion of the chemical problem of pigments that change and deteriorate with time—the old problem of Leonardo, still unsolved. These and other points were so well elucidated that Camille Pissarro wrote to his son Lucien:

> I am afraid that these questions are only too well explained and that [other] painters will take advantage of us. I would have liked [Fénéon] to discuss this with Seurat, but that is impossible.[8]

Pissarro was referring to Seurat's pride as an innovator and to his increasing fear that his territory was being invaded. A few months later, Pissarro wrote Lucien that he was afraid Seurat would object to exhibiting in Brussels with the Belgian avant-garde, *Les XX,* who were interested in Seurat's new method. "His prudence is so extreme. But we—I, rather,—see no objection, since I recognize no *secret* in painting other than one's own artistic feeling, which is not easily swiped!"[9]

Fénéon, too, had made it clear that all the science in the world would not make a work of art if the painter lacked the temperament of a real artist. Nor could a common scientific technique deprive authentic artists of their individuality:

> That is mistaking calligraphy for style. . . . "A recent Pissarro, a Seurat, a Signac, all look alike," proclaim the critics. Critics have always made, with pride, the most embarrassing confessions.—Finally, these painters are accused of subordinating art to science. But they are simply using scientific data to direct and perfect the education of their eye and to control the accuracy of their vision. . . . Mr. X can read treatises on optics for all eternity, but he will never paint *La Grande Jatte.* . . . This kind of painting is only for *painters.* The studio jugglers will have to go back to card tricks and their cup-and-balls.[10]

Urged by his friends, Fénéon decided to make a separate edition of his articles on the impressionists and their successors that year: the two done in June for *La Vogue* on exhibitions at the Maison Dorée and the Georges Petit gallery, and this last one on the Indépendants in September, from which he took only short extracts. The result was

Fénéon's only book—booklet, rather: *Les Impressionnistes en 1886.* He arranged it with care and rigorously revised his writing, although his articles had already been subject to several drafts. Striving for concision, he struck any remark that appeared to give a personal opinion. In the following passage, for example, he eliminated the first sentence:

> (M. Signac, moreover, paints alluring seascapes.) Seas froth up under flaming skies. (F, 37 and 49)

He simplified language so that it did not detract from the painting; thus, of a Pissarro:

> A limitless space and, very high, (blue skies are) the blue is dappled with light clouds. (F, 37 and 49)

He also strove for historical accuracy and asked Camille Pissarro for the dates of earlier impressionist exhibitions and the names of all the participants. He had only an inadequate chronology compiled for his first article, where he had omitted, out of ignorance, the year of the first impressionist exhibition. Pissarro immediately sent back an eight-page letter from his home in Eragny, and he promised to bring old catalogues and discuss further questions with him two days later in Paris.[11] F. F. encapsulated all this information in a one-page note.

The forty-three pages of *Les Impressionnistes en 1886* were elegantly ordered, with a title page for each of the three exhibitions in 1886. The names of the artists were set in large type over each section, in the manner of Diderot's *Salons,* an arrangement Baudelaire also copied in his first *Salon* (1845).

The booklet meant a great deal to Fénéon; it was his first purely personal creation. Every detail had to meet his image of that creation, even the paper on which it was printed. In August, the printer sent him a perplexed note:

> We see on the instructions for printing the
> *Impressionnistes*: 199 on Saint-Omer
> 1, unnumbered, on pumicif
> What kind of paper is Saint-Omer? And what is
> this "pumicif"?[12]

Fénéon took a dandy's delight in providing exactly the right materials, and soon *La Vogue* announced that book was on sale, one copy *sur pumicif* (for 100 francs), six copies *sur Japon* (ten francs), twenty-one *sur Hollande* (four francs), and 199 *sur Saint-Omer* (1.25 francs, or about thirty cents). Before it came out, Fénéon wrote to Gustave Kahn, director of *La Vogue,* which was publishing the brochure:

> Dubois-Pillet's exhibition [Salon des Indépendants] is being prolonged for eight days. If I received the final proofs of the *Impressionnistes* the order could be placed right away and the brochure put on sale one or two days before the closing and while the paintings are being taken down.[13]

However, *Les Impressionnistes en 1886* did not come off the printer's press until the following month, at the end of October. It went unnoticed for a month or two, until Fénéon thought of sending courtesy copies to the artists and their literary friends. Then it caught on as the manifesto of the latest art movement and sold out quickly. Fénéon never allowed a second edition. Today a collector's item, it was not considered very important at the Bibliothèque nationale, where it was bound with other pamphlets published in 1886: *Catalogue of the Collection of Tobacco Pipes; Classification of 160 Vegetable Oils, Followed by a Classification of 95 Animal Oils; The Petticoat,* and more.[14]

Fénéon reached his maturity as a writer in this work. No longer would he be inclined to write, as in some of his earlier art criticism: *c'est d'une gracilité exquise. . . . d'un large dessin* (it is done with exquisite fragility and grace. . . . amply drawn).[15] Not only were generalities and hackneyed phrases banished from his criticism, but also his own identity. The "I" or "we" which had found its way from time to time into Fénéon's writing was definitively eliminated. Indeed, the absence of *je* became one of the hallmarks of his style. "He banished *je* and *argent* (*I* and *money*) from his conversation," reported one of his friends.[16] This was not an affectation of modesty, for F. F. was not a humble man. Rather, it was the critic's aesthetic ideal to put the work of art forward, to keep his own personality "latent, like that of Flaubert in his books."[17] This apparent objectivity, craftmanship, and inner intensity were also what attracted him to the work of Seurat and the other neo-impressionists.

"Inert words," he said, can only crudely approximate a painting,[18] and yet he strove to make language assume shapes that would awaken a creative response in the reader. A painting is not a story and so, unlike many critics, Fénéon did not resort to anecdote to describe it. Because of his ideal of detachment, he refused to pass judgment. His anarchist thinking kept him from laying down a system of rules by which to make or measure art; the only laws or precepts he quoted were those that the artists themselves had chosen.

His aim as a critic was to serve as a conduit between the work of art and the public, and he chose to do this in such a way that the paintings appeared to speak for themselves.

> The seascapes of M. Seurat extend calm and melancholic, and right up to the distant drop of the sky, monotonously, are lapping. A rock oppresses them,—"The Bec du Hoc"; a series of sails are stated as scalene triangles,—"Boats off Grandcamp."[19]

In the original French, the seascapes extend or "spread themselves out" (*s'épandent*), and the sails "state themselves" (*s'y affirment*) as uneven triangles. Fénéon often exploited the semi-animate quality of verbs used with a reflexive pronoun to form a sort of middle voice, neither active nor passive, where the subject and the object of the action are the same. Thus the critic leads his reader to accept the paintings as having their own objective existence. Although these works were in fact highly charged personal events for F. F., his artful and meticulous style makes it appear that he absents himself—and even the painter—from the scene.

Upon reading *Les Impressionnistes en 1886,* Teodor de Wyzewa complained of Félix's "grammatical hylozoism" (the doctrine that all matter has life): "Why must he see the sky incurving itself, the brushstrokes scattering THEMSELVES, the little boats inverting their own image in the water?"[20] Yet Fénéon's style was not as unusual as Wyzewa thought it; the reflexive verb was exploited by many symbolist writers.

Fénéon uses it together with active verbs in the same sentence, and thus leads the reader inside the painting: "Les marines s'épandent . . . et *clapotent*. Un roc les *opprime*." We hear as well as see the waves lapping, and feel the domination of the rock.

At other times, Fénéon creates a noun structure that takes over the work of the verb. We see not boats sailing by, but a "series of sails," not the river flowing past, but a "shimmering stretch of river," not branches hanging down, but "overhangings of foliage," and finally, the untranslatable *chutes du ciel* which implies a falling movement of the sky as in a waterfall. These nouns are in fact solidified verbs. Descriptive of form rather than motion, they nonetheless inject life into the form.

He displaced words to help in the visualization of a picture, often postponing the subject in order to evoke the total context:

> In front view and silhouetted in black against the great green rectangle of the window, a young woman . . .
>
> Indistinctly, from a background blurred by the brightness of the foreground arrive crowds . . .[21]

These inversions keep the reader from imagining the "contents" of the painting at the expense of the actual configuration. Finally, the postponed verb in a sentence describing a work by Dubois-Pillet, reaches out to the reader:

> A young woman, fragile in her grace, by a pond with water inset in foliage turning gold, then purple, changing—dreams.[22]

Figure and surroundings are caught in a permanent fixed relation, and it is not altogether clear in the French whether "changing, dreams," refers to the water or to the girl: *Une gracile jeune femme, au bord d'un étang dont l'eau encastrée dans des feuillages, se dore, se pourpre, changeante, rêve.* Forced to supply the intervals and to interpret the values, the spectator-reader is mobilized into a personal reading of the painting.

In preparing *Les Impressionnistes en 1886* for publication, Fénéon not only revised stylistically, he also tried to repair certain broken fences by taking the paragraph on Dubois-Pillet out of the section on the eighth impressionist exhibition and putting it in the one on the Indépendants, where it belonged. There is no evidence, however, that Gauguin was mollified by this adjustment. Fénéon also made a bow in the direction of Paul Adam by quoting his description of Dubois-Pillet and the neo-impressionist technique in the novel *Soi,* which preceded any of Fénéon's writing on the subject.[23]

Some contemporaries admired *Les Impressionnistes en 1886* as much for the poetic precision of its language as for the prophetic accuracy of its statements. Remy de Gourmont said of Fénéon: "He has all the qualities of an art critic: the eye, the analytical mind, the style which makes visible what the eye has seen and intelligible what the mind has understood."[24] Fellow symbolists appreciated particularly his idiosyncratic style. "Far from the banal," said Paul Adam, "toward the precise term that fixes and paints and provokes, the concise style of M. Fénéon never ceases to strive."[25] According to Jean Moréas, the self-appointed captain of the current linguistic revolution, Fénéon literally talked painting, "now elliptical, now loquacious, with strings of words or trap-door sayings, orbicular or dagger-sharp . . ."[26]

Other contemporaries were less admiring. Teodor de Wyzewa, predictably, further criticized Fénéon for revealing, "under an apparent impassivity, an excess of enthusiasm" for the neo-impressionists, "who he thinks are innovators and who are only continuing the work of their predecessors, at the risk of ruining it."[27] The critic Arsène Alexandre enjoyed laughing at Fénéon's "decadent" vocabulary: "I bet you never suspected that Degas' nudes had breasts like *virgouleuses* . . . Lord! the critic's job is to explain the work of art; does he need to have a commentary himself? . . . He finds that M. Raffaëlli's composition is 'sometimes spoiled by literature' . . . Does he mean that a painting by Raffaëlli can contain a whole little novel about neurosis, poverty and labor, a story that would take pages and pages to write? I refuse to take that for a defect!" The painters defended by Fénéon, Alexandre said, were currently under attack. "There is perhaps a little place for them. Our decadent critic predicts that it will be considerable. But will the decadents live long enough to see that?"[28]

Emile Hennequin, a friend of Fénéon's who was writing an ambitious art-critical work called *La Critique scientifique,* wrote to thank Fénéon for sending a copy of *Les Impressionnistes en 1886*:

> The accuracy of your descriptions make it an excellent record. I notice however that we differ on two points. The impressionist paintings do not seem to have struck you as they have me by their total lack of emotional content and their lack of realism through uglification. Then again, you defend the technical innovations of Seurat for reasons that do not seem valid to me and—in spite of the quotation from Rood—not very accurate scientifically. I heartily enjoy the sterling qualities of your writing, your concision and rare vocables—except "mastoid" which is off-color.[29]

It was not for nothing that Charles Henry called Hennequin "the pure, the rigid."[30] Fénéon used "mastoid" simply to describe the lumpy terrain of Parisian suburbs painted by David Estoppey. He borrowed terms from medicine and other sciences not, as Huysmans had, for emotional effect, but to describe form, often with humor. As is evident from his letter, Hennequin was attuned neither to Fénéon's style nor to the painting he described, although, like Wyzewa, Hennequin subsequently became an advocate of Seurat.

As for Seurat himself, he was quite satisfied with what Fénéon had written. Two years later he wrote to Paul Signac: "I still consider Fénéon's brochure as the expression of my ideas on painting."[31] Fénéon defended Seurat and his group with clocklike regularity between 1886 and 1890, writing in various symbolist reviews in Paris and in *L'Art moderne* of Brussels.

At the invitation of a certain Dr. Ferroul, an ardent socialist and lover of letters from the southern town of Narbonne, he also wrote for a local left-wing journal, *L'Emancipation sociale.* In its pages, we see another side of Fénéon, writing about events and people, rather than books, paintings and ideas, for readers who were quite removed from the atmosphere of the capital and the small world of the avant-garde existing within it.

In 1887, the Indépendants exhibited not in the Tuileries barracks but in a sort of covered garden, the Paris Pavilion, built for the Universal Exhibition of 1878. The use of this elegant, multicolored structure had been obtained through the good offices of Dubois-Pillet who, dressed in uniform and red plumes flying, had argued the Indépendants' case before the city officials. Fénéon painted a picture for his provincials in Narbonne:

> Red and blue banners, colors of the city of Paris, float over the *Society of Independent Artists* on the Champs-Elysées, lashed by squalls of rain and sun on this 25th day of March. The Pavilion of the city of Paris itself is polychrome.
>
> Tomorrow the exhibition opens. Today, the dress rehearsal—Varnishing Day. Not the usual dusty turmoil of the yearly Salons on varnishing day, with its shuffling mob recruited from every milieu. Here we have a select group of invited guests: pretty women, artists and gentlemen. From the entrance, guarded by a kind of hairy haiduk in livery, you can see an animated scene against a background of paintings, tapestries and plants: flowery gowns, heads bowed sharply in greeting, hands gesturing towards the walls, groups that soon break up and as soon form anew. . . .
>
> On the untiring arm of Labruyère, the heroine of the day appears, Séverine, the Théroigne of the *Cri du peuple,* with her slightly massive grace, jaunty elegance, and high coiffure. She passes by and smiles.[32]

Subscribers to *L'Emancipation sociale* were familiar with the writings of Séverine, director of the *Cri du peuple* since the death of Jules Vallès in 1885; Fénéon compared her to Théroigne de Méricourt, known as the "Amazon of Liberty" during the French Revolution. Séverine later wrote vehemently in defense of Fénéon when he was arrested as an anarchist.

Fénéon then introduced his readers to the young clan of neo-impressionists: "Paul Signac, alert and voluble, Dubois-Pillet, with his full cravat and monocled bright eye blinking, Lucien Pissarro, looking like a Sudra in Indian picture-books, Georges Seurat, with the austere features of a sixteenth-century Calvinist. And with them all, a batch of symbolist poets. Common tendencies and the foolish criticism of journalists bleating like Panurge's sheep have united these poets and painters." The journalist critics, he remarked, could not tell a Velázquez from a pair of boots. But he could name a number of authentic writers, from Mallarmé to Paul Alexis, who ably wrote on contemporary art.[33]

Just as he had done in his first review of the impressionists, Fénéon was careful to identify different elements within the evolving movement. "The impressionist school is a school of colorists," he explained to his Narbonne readers. "Thus it was wrong to include under the label of Impressionism painters like M. Degas, M. Forain, M. Raffaëlli who are interested particularly in movement, anecdote and character."[34] He outlined point by point how the technique of the neo-impressionists differed from that of the impressionists and proclaimed the superiority of the later, more conscious and scientific style. "How right Fénéon was to lay down categories!" Camille Pissarro later exclaimed,[35] although he also worried that Fénéon's enthusiasm would exacerbate the rising tension between the old and new impressionists.

F. F. began to praise neo-impressionism in increasingly exultant tones, and his criticism of the older group turned at times to mockery. To his eye, impressionist works "had an appearance of improvisation; their landscapes were views of nature seen at a glance, as if a shutter had been quickly opened and closed: it was hasty and approximate."[36] The impressionists felt they had to capture a landscape in a single sitting, and so they had "a propensity for making nature grimace," he said, "to prove that the moment was unique and would never be seen again." In contrast, he emphasized the neo-impressionists' "distance from the accidental and the transitory" and their desire to synthesize a landscape or human figures "in a permanent pose that perpetuates the sensation they give."[37] Camille Pissarro found these remarks "too aggressive towards the old masters of Impressionism who," he said, "will obviously take them as evidence of ill-will."[38]

From Fénéon's viewpoint, however, these statements were simply a foil for his defense of the *new* impressionism, which he now defined.

> Among the mobs of mechanical copyists of externals, these four or five artists impose the sensation of life itself. For them objective reality is simply a theme for the creation of a higher, sublimated reality, suffused with their own personality.[39]

This focus on a sublimated reality, superior to what is seen as the "real world," was central to the symbolist aesthetic. Not at all mystical, Fénéon took his image from the chemical laboratory, where matter can be distilled (sublimated) into a vapor state to rid it of impurities and then condensed into a solid again.

The "mobs of mechanical copyists" that Fénéon opposed to the neo-impressionists were not the old guard impressionists, but the commercially successful artists of the time who "believed in the reality of things, adored the mannequin of truth, and prided themselves on their photographic realism."[40] Hardly better were those artists, "the hordes of Gauguin,"[41] Fénéon later said, who looked for phantasmagoric images of truth. The neo-impressionist remained in joyous contact with ordinary reality, with nature and with his own humanity, and, as Mallarmé had done with words, distilled his experience into a refined form. What mattered was the quality and nature of the "still," that is, the temperament of the artist and the technique with which the process was carried out.

"More than any other," Fénéon said, "the neo-impressionist process allows the painter to objectify his sensations in all their complexity and to translate his innermost originality with legitimate force. But . . . it is full of unexpected obstacles and requires a certain amount of genius."[42] These statements, more than his technical discussions, reveal how much the art of the neo-impressionists met the needs of Fénéon and other members of the symbolist generation. Coming out of an era dominated by naturalism in literature and impressionism in painting, during a period of continuing political disillusionment and economic distress, the younger generation wished to disassociate itself from humdrum existence on the one hand and the exaltation of fleeting sensations on the other. Their needs are expressed in terms Fénéon used to contrast neo-impressionism with impressionism in an 1890 monograph on Paul Signac:

> Exemplary specimens of a highly developed decorative art, which sacrifices anecdote to arabesque, nomenclature to synthesis, fugitive to permanent and . . . confers on Nature—weary at last of its precarious reality—an authentic Reality.[43]

Fénéon had predicted in 1886 that a "compromise" would unite the technique of the impressionists with that of the "dissidents."[44] Pissarro, too, thought that Monet would have no recourse but to join the new movement, "since he must feel the need to achieve what the impressionists lacked—great purity of design."[45] Two years later, Fénéon realized this hope was vain, and his criticism became suddenly virulent:

> The old soldiers of impressionism, except Pissarro (certainly the most gifted of them), persist in practising at random their raving purple passages, spouting onomatopoeias that will never agglutinate as sentences.[46]

Evoking a primitive, mimicking sort of utterance, the word *onomatopoeia* here emphasizes the impressionists' facile, emphatic "casting" of paint, as Martha Ward has pointed out.[47] Monet, the impressionist par excellence, was Fénéon's chief target.

F. F. felt curiously ambivalent toward Monet. He berated him for the "excessive bravura of his execution" and the "lyric banality" of his works, but his descriptions of the paintings themselves are among his most inventive and poetic. Clearly he enjoyed Monet's painting more than he cared to admit. Yet he diagnosed a problem that haunted the painter all his life: how to reconcile devotion to the *motif* and fleeting phenomena with the demands of an expressive, intelligible, and consistent technique:

> Flowering gardens of Vétheuil, blazing checkerboards of tulips in Holland, haggard apparitions of locomotives leaving the station, spangled camouflages of Paris on Bastille Day, ice floes on the Seine, magic configurations of Antibes amethyst hills, parasol pines and olive trees, the Norman coast, the Breton coast—such a variety of paintings is a matter of geography and the calendar. Nowhere the quiddity of a scene surveyed and plotted in an unexpected or fervent manner: everywhere the joy of "a fine painter" before colors to transfer from nature to the canvas.[48]

The neo-impressionists, in contrast, sought to make their "analytical technique serve a grand synthesis. Their visual philosophy and their technique did not necessarily derive from each other," declared Fénéon, but "became mutually stimulating as soon as they were both consciously recognized." This was the sixth time he had written in favor of the new impressionism, and now, in 1888, he chose to retract some of the scientific paraphernalia in his criticism and even to suggest that some of his previous arguments had been deceptive:

> To confuse other painters and to amuse the onlooker, somebody chose to envelop the neo-impressionists in barbarous trappings; but however useful these notions of science were to them in the beginning, it would be wrong to imagine these painters manipulating color wheels (generally inaccurate) and consulting the reports of physicists (not very revealing) about the way complementary colors really lust after one another.[49]

Straight-faced as ever, the arch-dandy critic executed this 175° turn without so much as a beg-your-pardon.

While Pissarro, Signac, Seurat, and the other neo-impressionists thought of their technique as the means to an end, most critics and several imitating artists saw the technique, particularly the dot, as the end in itself, and gave it much attention.

Huysmans spoke of thumbtacking one's colors; the prestigious press thought of confetti (which had come into recent use for mock battles on Mardi Gras)—or smallpox. The style soon became known as pointillism, although the artists themselves did not accept this label. Fénéon never said *pointillisme* or even *le point* to describe the dot, although he used the verb *pointiller* once or twice to mock lesser adepts of divisionism: "A few other neophytes . . . dot indefatigably: let us not disturb their exercises."[50] Instead, he invented many different expressions to render the luminous, pulsating effect of the neo-impressionist brushstroke: "versicolored droplets; a seeding of tiny coloring strokes; markings" [as spots on bird wings or leopard skin]; "a whirling host of minute spots; a speckling of blue; a scattering of orange; tiny pullulating stroke; a swarming of prismatic spangles in vital competition for a harmony of the whole."[51] That series, taken out of context, sounds extravagant; but Fénéon explained the rationale behind the technique:

> This seeding of coloring spots is extremely sensitive because its constituent elements can be continuously varied. . . . So the painters chose this uniform stroke, but the spot itself had no more reality than the stitch in tapestry; it was like substituting a neutral typography—to the benefit of the text—for an affected and immoderate handwriting.[52]

This seemingly impersonal and "as it were abstract execution," said Fénéon, only enhanced the originality of each artist.[53] By "abstract" he naturally did not mean nonrepresentational art but rather that distillation or synthesis of form and color that he prized in neo-impressionism. The very qualities that Fénéon identified, however, would soon furnish the basis for twentieth-century fauvism (wild color) and abstraction in art.

One of the extremes, if not excesses, of the first neo-impressionists came in their search for a suitable frame. Here, Fénéon retained an amused objectivity. Of Dubois-Pillet's first effort to create the perfect frame, Fénéon asked: "Is it colored to enhance the painting, or vice-versa?"[54] He found Seurat's solution more legitimate, with certain reservations: when Seurat dotted his frame with blue or solar orange to indicate whether the sun was behind or before the observer, the frame took on "an absurd reality." The following year Seurat abandoned that concept and modified his treatment, painting a border on the canvas itself so as to continue the play of optical contrast of colors while attenuating the brusque interruption of the frame. Fénéon, who documented all these developments, complimented the painter on this evolution.

No detail was too small for his attention. Noting that Seurat signed his name not on the picture but in pale letters on the painted border, Fénéon invited him to "substitute a monogram for a still too literary signature."[55] This was a tradition Fénéon had observed in the Japanese woodcuts recently "discovered" by the Paris art world. Although Seurat stuck to his signature, other neo-impressionists found the monogram to their liking: Lucien Pissarro had used one since 1886, a modern touch that differentiated him from his father. Among *Les XX* in Belgium, Henri van de Velde designed a floral monogram and Théo van Rysselberghe signed with a stylized TVR almost exclusively after 1889, the year Fénéon made the suggestion to Seurat.

There were just six or seven painters, besides Seurat and Signac, whom Fénéon strongly supported during the formative years of neo-impressionism. Most of these men were his friends or close associates: Albert Dubois-Pillet; Camille Pissarro and his son Lucien; Maximilien Luce; Charles Angrand; Henri-Edmond Cross; and, to a lesser extent, the Belgian Théo van Rysselberghe.

His selectivity resembled that of other writers in the nineteenth century—Baudelaire and Zola for example—who limited their criticism to artists with whom they had an affinity based on a shared aesthetic, and on friendship. Their narrowness of choice has led art historians to regret that these gifted writers had "blind spots." Fénéon's blind spot, for example, was Picasso. But where he was not blind, he was brilliant in his responses. He took pains to distinguish the styles, problems, and issues of his chosen few.

"Just as they cannot tell a bird by Nōsan from a bird by Hokusai, or a woman by Eishi from a woman by Utamaro, the public does not distinguish a Seurat from a Pissarro or a Signac," said Fénéon at the Fifth Exhibition of Independent Artists (September 1889).[56] It was his role to point out individual differences. The previous year he had remarked on Dubois-Pillet (pl. 9):

> His paintings are not orchestrated with as much breadth and complexity as neighboring paintings: the play of complementary colors is hesitant; the modification of local colors by solar light overrides other effects, and these tones then have elective affinities and blend into a melodic movement. An unforeseen detail or an odd arrangement make his subjects unique: in all, a rather whimsical sense of taste, always exquisite, a feeling for ornamental design, and a personal way of looking at things.[57]

Fénéon liked this "witty, well-read, cordial man." Although not rich, the officer/artist was generous and kind to painters less fortunate than he. Even Pissarro had occasion to be grateful for his discreet and thoughtful aid. And of course the Indépendants owed much to his judgment and leadership.

Late in 1889 Dubois-Pillet was ordered by the National Guard to command a garrison at Puy-en-Velay in a mountainous region to the south of Auvergne. He did not complain of this exile from Paris and set about studying his surroundings for new subjects to paint—red earth, vertical villages, lacemakers at work. But he died of smallpox in August 1890 when an epidemic struck the garrison town. In a brief obituary for *L'Art moderne,* Fénéon put his work in a rather negative light, saying that Dubois-Pillet had often "adulterated the purity" of the new technique and that in spite of his sincerity, his paintings had a somewhat too "rigid elegance."[58]

A loss of a different sort was sustained when Camille Pissarro found he could no longer accommodate his temperament and art to Seurat's method. The time-consuming process of letting the separate strokes dry before applying new ones, so as not to muddy the colors, was inhibiting his creativity. He had given a small one-man show early in 1889, and Fénéon had once more cited him as the most prestigious convert to the new style. Signac alerted Fénéon to the older man's change of heart: the violent

Left, ALBERT DUBOIS-PILLET. ***Self-portrait.*** 1890. Pen drawing published on the cover of *Les Hommes d'aujourd'hui,* no. 370. [1890]. *Dubois-Pillet, with his . . . full cravat and monocled bright eye blinking.* (F, 64)

Below, ALBERT DUBOIS-PILLET. ***The Steam Crane.*** Pen drawing, published in the *Catalogue des XX,* 1888, Brussels. *Towards the end of last year, M. Paul Signac and M. Dubois-Pillet had the idea of drawing in ink without hatching or outlines, expressing the subject by dots, dense in places and elsewhere scattered.* (F, 75, 1 May 1887)

CAMILLE PISSARRO. ***River—Early Morning, Isle Lacroix.*** 1888. Oil on canvas, 44 x 55 cm. Philadelphia Museum of Art. John G. Johnson Collection. *Still more youthful strength in the latest works of Camille Pissarro: the Seine under a hazy mist . . . scenes he used to render austerely he now idealizes in gentle splendor.* (F, 118)

contrast of tints inherent to divisionism "hurts his eye," he said. Pissarro was searching for more delicate harmonies and applying what he called "passages" to lessen the contrasts. Fénéon immediately wrote Pissarro asking for clarification, since he was planning a second brochure on the impressionists and their successors. The painter replied:

> I have just received from Eragny your letter asking me to give you some technical information on "passage." It would be difficult to say anything about this; I am trying at this very moment to master the technique which ties me down and stifles the spontaneity of impressions on the canvas. It would be better to say nothing about it, nothing definite yet.[59]

Respectful of Pissarro's request, Feneon remained silent and eventually abandoned his idea of a second brochure. In the fall of that year, the elder Pissarro exhibited with the Indépendants, and Fénéon reported:

Above and opposite, **CAMILLE PISSARRO.** Drawings from the album ***Turpitudes sociales.*** 1890. Pen and brown ink over brief indications in pencil on glazed paper, 31.5 x 24.5 cm. Reprinted from the facsimile edition of Albert Skira, Geneva, 1972. ***Title Page,*** with "Anarchy" spelled out in the rays of the sun.

For Camille Pissarro, it has become impossible to continue to try to reach an unstrained accommodation between his art, already established by so many masterpieces in his long life, and the demanding technique he adopted in 1886. Having augmented his clarity of analysis through this experience, he has now come back, with some modification, to his former rough-rendering of inextricable strokes.[60]

The St.-Honoré Prison.

Even though the painter abandoned Seurat's method and often had harsh words for what he remembered as a coldly demanding manner of execution, Fénéon never lost affection and esteem for this "elder statesman" of neo-impressionism. Pissarro, for his part, considered Fénéon the best possible critic. Remarking on the cowardice of Albert Wolff, the influential critic of the *Figaro,* Pissarro exclaimed, "Come on now. Wolff is too old for our time, what we need is a Félix Fénéon. But that wouldn't suit the schemers."[61]

Camille and Lucien Pissarro were becoming increasingly dedicated to the anarchist cause, contributing drawings and lithographs to anarchist reviews such as *La Révolte* and *Le Père peinard,* depicting the hard life of the working poor, the complacency and greed of their "betters," or, conversely, calm strong scenes of a harmonious,

Ruth gleaneth in Boaz' field.
Go not to glean in another field, neither go from hence, but abide here fast by my maidens:
IX Let thine eyes be on the field that they do reap, & go thou after them: have I not charged the
x young

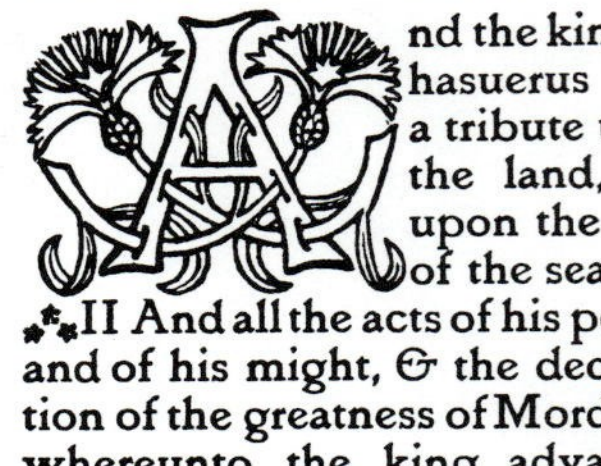

The Book of Esther.
CHAPTER THE TENTH.
i Ahasuerus his greatness. iii Mordecai's advancement.
nd the king Ahasuerus laid a tribute upon the land, and upon the isles of the sea.
II And all the acts of his power and of his might, & the declaration of the greatness of Mordecai, whereunto the king advanced him, are they not written in the book of the chronicles of the kings of Media and Persia?
III For Mordecai the Jew was next unto king Ahasuerus, and great among the Jews, & accepted of the multitude of his brethren, seeking the wealth of his people, & speaking peace to all his seed.
End of the book of Esther.
lxxxii

LUCIEN PISSARRO. Illustrations for ***The Book of Ruth*** (*left*) and ***The Book of Esther*** (*right*). Woodcuts, 7.5 x 6.5 cm. Epping, Eragny Press, 1896. Courtesy Book Arts Collection, Sacramento Public Library.

agrarian society. Their anarchist beliefs reinforced Fénéon's growing commitment to a renewed, freer and fairer society. F. F. made a typical anarchist remark in his review of Pissarro's one-man show in 1889: "Anything really new, to be accepted, requires that many fools die. We heartily wish this to happen as soon as possible." This attitude endeared him to Pissarro: "We need the shouts and dry laughter of Fénéon," he told a friend, using the title of Fénéon's anonymous anarchist column (*Hourras, tollés et rires maigres*), ". . . but perhaps serious folk wouldn't appreciate these caprices? Too bad; I should nevertheless so enjoy laughing at the expense of the bourgeois."[62]

Pissarro was in dire financial straits during this period, obliged to run around Paris trying to sell his paintings and trifles, such as fans he had decorated, for enough cash to feed his large family. He sometimes turned to Fénéon for help, not for himself, but for Lucien, who was trying to establish himself as a printmaker and book illustrator. Fénéon always spoke admiringly of Lucien's prints and also served as mentor when the young artist tried writing his own stories. "Despite the fog and cold," Camille reported to his son in January 1887, "I went last evening to the 'Taverne anglaise,' where the young collaborators in *La Vogue* hold forth; I was hoping to see Fénéon, and he was there.—I asked him to look over your fairy tale; delighted to be of service to you, he took the manuscript remarking, 'the title is quite perfect.' I will have it back in two or three days."[63] Soon Lucien, bent on settling in England, went to London furnished with a letter from Fénéon introducing him to artists in the Aesthetic Movement, a connection that was to influence his whole career.

Paris
111 rue St Lazare

11 Dec 96

Mon cher Fénéon
J'ai à vous parler d'affaires concernant Lucien, pourriez vous me donner un rendez-vous à l'Hôtel soit à déjeuner ou à dîner le jour qui vous conviendra, je suis à Paris pour deux ou trois jours?
Le plus tôt possible.
amicalement votre
C. Pissarro.

Mon cher Fénéon
Recevez je vous prie une page de mon album en souvenir du grand soulagement que vous me procurez –
Lucien Pissarro.
Nous serons enchantés de prendre le thé avec vous demain, mais excusez nous si nous sommes un peu en retard. Nous déjeunons à Houilles chez ma sœur –

Letter from Camille Pissarro to F. Fénéon, Paris, 11 December 1896, soliciting help for his son Lucien, and an undated letter of thanks from Lucien Pissarro to Fénéon. Paris, Paulhan archives.

When Fénéon learned that Lucien's younger brother Georges was also an artist, he wrote Camille: "May I already speak of your second son? I have not seen a single work of his yet; what sort of thing would be suitable to say in anticipation?"[64] Camille cautioned Fénéon to wait; he wanted his sons to develop their own artistic temperaments and not be known simply as little Pissarros. F. F. was enthusiastic about anything coming out of this household. He was in Signac's studio one day when a painting by Dubois-Pillet arrived from Pissarro's home in Eragny. Camille had sent it for the dead painter's retrospective, packing it in some cardboard on which his nine-year-old daughter Jeanne, known as Cocotte, had been drawing and where Georges had also made a pastel of geese. Fénéon seized the cardboard with delight. "He thought the

CAMILLE PISSARRO. ***Peasant Women Planting Pea Sticks,*** design for a fan. 1890. Gouache with traces of black chalk on grey-brown paper, 39 x 60.2 cm. Oxford, The Ashmolean Museum. See also pl. 10.

geese were mine," the proud father told Lucien, "and as for Cocotte's second symbolic drawing, he was totally enthused . . . there's Cocotte launched into symbolist art without knowing it—what will Gauguin think of this unexpected competitor!"[65]

But it was not Gauguin, thought Fénéon, but the neo-impressionists and Camille Pissarro who were the most authentic artists of the symbolist era. When Pissarro had passed his sixtieth year, Fénéon wrote:

> This painter objectifies with increasing mastery his youthful capacity for fresh impressions. . . .[66]
>
> After accumulating many rich observations directly from Reality . . . he stops painting outdoors and treats Nature as a repertory of decorative motifs . . . Then you have *Girl Tending Geese,* 1890, and its heroic, astonished movement towards the mystery of the infinite water; and his *Peasant Women Planting Pea Sticks,* 1891, where gestures and colors form a garland for Botticellian spring festivals . . . [pl. 10]. And the *Cowherdess* . . . holding on a snaking tether a cow seen from the front, two-legged, a neck of cameline cloth, muzzle creeping in the grass. And if Durand-Ruel is amazed at this cow, unforeseen by photographers, the good-hearted old man says: "But it's not a cow, it's an ornament." . . . It is this Camille Pissarro, the very recent one, who must be praised.[67]

Although the old master had returned to a style that was more akin to that of the impressionists, Fénéon never accused him, as he had Renoir and Monet, of monotony

CAMILLE PISSARRO. *The Cowherdess.* 1892. Oil on canvas, 73 x 51 cm. Present location unknown. Photograph courtesy of the Photography Archives, National Gallery of Art, Washington, D.C.

and a too facile use of his talent. Fénéon wrote, "All creatures, all forms are glorified by Pissarro, who gives them style and intense life without deforming them, simply through his personal vision of them and the expressive way he synthesizes that vision."[68] F. F. did not write so positively about the more abstract compositions in Seurat's last works.

Neo-impressionism gained more adherents than it suffered losses in the late 1880s. One of the first to join was a young Parisian called Maximilien Luce. Fénéon noticed his contributions to the third Indépendants in 1887:

> M. Maximilien Luce. A newcomer, a tough, loyal fellow with a primitive, muscular talent. In garrets without women, a bare-chested worker scrubs himself, another dunks his crust of bread in a bowl. He chooses to paint scenes of the delapidated areas around the fortifications on the outskirts of Paris (*View of la Glacière, Corner of a Garden in la Glacière*).[69]

Luce was a member of the working class himself, and Fénéon felt an immediate attraction to the independent nature of this self-taught man, an anarchist who earned his living as a wood engraver. He became a steadfast comrade of the elite neo-impressionist clan—even Seurat trusted him—but he continued to live as a member of the proletariat. Fénéon was a civil servant; Signac had an independent income; Seurat's family was quite wealthy; Pissarro, though struggling financially, was well schooled and came from a merchant family. Their anarchism had intellectual roots: loss of faith in the republican process and despair over a corrupt, stratified society that did not recognize the efforts of innovating artists any more than it did the suffering of the workers. Luce came to his anarchism from a direct experience of oppression. His political consciousness had been awakened at age thirteen by the Commune and its repression, when, walking home from school, he witnessed a mass murder of men and women lined up against a wall. He later put his talent to the service of his beliefs and, like Signac and the Pissarros, but on a much broader basis, provided countless illustrations for anarchist and syndicalist publications.

Luce was a regular visitor at Fénéon's apartment. When other friends came to call, there would be Luce, quietly sitting at table with his workman's liter of *vin ordinaire,* reading *La Révolte* or another anarchist paper. His manners and his way of dressing were the opposite of his host's. He rarely removed a shapeless felt hat from his head, and his trousers looked as if they had never been pressed. To those who did not know him he seemed surly, for he rarely spoke, and when he did, it was briefly and coarsely.

In spite of appearances, he and his aesthete friend F. F. had much in common. They both had little use for fame or money but they valued beauty, human dignity, and their own internal freedom. The friendship continued into the next generation, for when Luce's son Frédéric was a lad, apprenticed like his father to a trade, he took his dinner often in Fénéon's home.[70]

Although Luce exhibited with the neo-impressionists and adopted their system, Fénéon immediately noticed basic discrepancies: "If one thinks of the symphonic charm emanating from the work of M. Signac or M. Seurat, who today seem admirably normal, the art of M. Luce will seem ill-balanced, ultra-nervous. But it is the uneasy unique personality present in his paintings that demands they be examined on a par with more perfect works (pl. 11)." There were "authentic images" such as the *Fireman* thrusting his clinker bar into the white-hot coal, and the *Ragpickers* at rest. "And again, under wide, sad skies, many an aspect of Paris looms up real."

MAXIMILIEN LUCE. ***Workman Washing Up.*** 1886. Oil on canvas, 92 x 73 cm. Geneva, Musée du petit palais. Oscar Ghez Collection.

From Montmartre and surging over kilometers the panorama of Paris extends, and to show the receding perspective M. Luce does not resort to the naive subterfuge of staggered towers and domes of decreasing height; a great ray of sunlight falls obliquely through piles of polychrome clouds and covers the distances of the city with a fine powder of light.

MAXIMILIEN LUCE. ***Outskirts of Montmartre.*** 1887. Oil on canvas, 45.5 x 81 cm. Otterlo, Kröller-Müller Museum.

Luce also painted the outskirts of Paris, which was expanding to meet the needs of the industrial age:

> In a new, outlying district, he shows the long, unbroken facade of a row of houses rising in front of a rectangle of land with fences enclosing cows in summer and painted with signs bearing the address of a real estate agent and a cost estimate of floor space. . . .

Fénéon remarked on Luce's technique: "If you step back, the aggressive medley of colors on these canvases tones down to spacious harmonies of violet."[71] But soon he expressed reservations. Luce was not "restraining his mettle by the prescribed discipline; he applies new pigment to underlayers of paint before letting them dry and so falls again into the disadvantage of pigmentary puddings."[72]

Finally, in 1889, Fénéon saw earth tones—the old earth tones that the impressionists had tossed out—back on the palette of Luce, giving "a heavy, aeruginous [rusty] look to his paintings—in spite of their violets." And while Seurat's work brought to mind Mallarmé's newborn language, Luce reminded him of an old-style orator and hero of revolutionary thought, Jules Vallès:

> In spite of his unbridled vigor, wild tone, and the new process, M. Luce is, as was Vallès, a strictly classic artist . . . and the creators, the revolutionaries are those patient, serene and limpid painters that were named earlier [Signac, Dubois-Pillet, Seurat].[73]

In the end, what F. F. prized most in Luce was the way he portrayed contemporary life without need for grandiloquence or sentimentality. In his series on the Black

Country in Belgium, where van Gogh had earlier tried to live as an apostle among the poor, Luce never exploited the flaming inferno of the ironworks or dramatized the hideous smokestacks and slag heaps: "he doesn't need bombast to stamp such spectacles with his own originality." The paintings spoke plainly and directly:

> No literary effect falsifies the very real emotion that they arouse. Luce never gambled on an uncommon motif, contrived lighting, or an unusual angle. It is under other brushes that the fluctuations of the moment, the heathland, the mist, the moon and Christian humility conspire to overwhelm those who pride themselves on their sensitivity.[74]

This praise of Luce was in fact an indirect attack on both the old impressionists and the new symbolist school of Gauguin, who denigrated the "crass realism" and "limited vision" of the neo-impressionists.

Another addition to neo-impressionism in 1887 was Charles Angrand, an entirely different sort of fellow from Maximilien Luce, who was his close friend. Fénéon was hard at first on this convert from impressionism, who still relied on imitative "niceties" in brushwork. Worse, it appeared he did not use the neo-impressionist method to advantage: "The emotion from the fervor of his recent conversion has left him a bit anemic: his landscapes suffer sadly from decoloration . . ." Fénéon chose not to describe these landscapes, farm scenes which Angrand was particularly good at observing, but spoke rather about his portrayal of a Paris street scene at night, *An Accident,* and its problems (pl. 12):

> Lit by the gasjets of street lamps and pharmacy globes, a crowd is gathering on the sidewalk. The lines have gone stiff and the colors are out of joint. To give a canvas the sensation of artificial light when it will in fact be viewed in natural light is an interesting but intricately hard experiment. The spectator, plunged into the yellow gaslight, assumes that it is white and so adopts an inaccurate term of reference for all the other colors; he becomes practically color-blind. And so many other difficulties. . . .[75]

Seurat probably took into account Fénéon's remarks when he painted his gaslit scene at night, *The Side-Show.* When this painting was exhibited the following year, however, Fénéon was remarkably laconic, noting only that it was "interesting in so far as it applies to a night piece a method that has been used mainly for effects of daylight."[76] Perhaps his judgment was colored by Angrand's unsuccessful attempt, or perhaps he himself was "color-blind" to this development in neo-impressionism.

Charles Henry and his theories on the psychophysics of lines were an obvious influence on the painters at this point, and Fénéon did not really like the results, which he felt were too contrived. His objection to the "stiffness" of the drawing in *An Accident* ("*le dessin s'ankylose*") was repeated two years later when he found that the figures in Seurat's *Port-en-Bessin* also suffered from "ankylosis."[77]

If Fénéon spoke critically of Angrand's work, it was because he knew this artist was, like Seurat, a thinker and a searcher. In fact, Charles Angrand was one of the rare intimates of Seurat, who felt at ease exchanging ideas with this taciturn man from Normandy, so dedicated to his art.

In January 1889, Fénéon reported that Angrand's work was no longer anemic and had gained in "exactitude, transparency, and luminosity." He was in control at last of the new technique "and not at all superstitious of reality," declared his critic friend. Fénéon took delight in describing a painting Angrand had done of the *Grande-Jatte* island:

> Contrasting with the reflecting, shimmering stretch of river, a stretch of lawn turns blue in spots from the shade of trees; overhangings of slightly uneven foliage restrict the sky which grows pink around their contour; the other bank is cross-ruled with red houses, white houses; two sailboats slide by. The skill with which M. Angrand chooses and arranges his themes is very evident in this *A la Grande-Jatte* and in the accompanying canvases.[78]

Details in this passage reveal Fénéon's own creative response to Angrand's work. He suggests the dynamics of composition through unusual expressions: the opposite bank "squares itself off," for example, and the branches "restrain the sky." The optical contrast of colors is revealed in two recently coined verbs (*se bleuter, rosir*) which render the blueing of the grass in shadow and the rose-haloing of the sky around the foliage. Thus, without becoming bogged down in scientific theory, the reader can visualize the painting in all its intensity.

Soon, though, the antagonistic play of colors "became too noisy for Angrand, as was Paris,"[79] Fénéon remarked, and the painter left to live in his native province of Caux and work exclusively in black and white. He continued to send his work to the Indépendants, and in 1893 Fénéon included him in one of his last art-critical reviews, written for the anarchist *Père peinard*—entirely in slang:

> Hey, here's a prolo! Working his tail off in front of a furnace hot enough to fry the Mont-Blanc in five minutes. That's part of a series of drawings in black pencil, by Charles Angrand. In these drawings, better not look for details: our comrade only bothered with the total effect and they're damn full of poetry and mystery without asshole tricks and weaseling.[80]

The vulgar language of this report seems ill suited to the quiet gentility of Angrand, whom Seurat portrayed as the sober spectator in elegant top hat and coat behind the tumbling clown in *The Circus.* Angrand, however, shared the proletarian concerns of Fénéon, Luce, and Signac, and enjoyed the game Félix had played in successfully adapting the speech of the "populo" to his art criticism.

In the spring of 1891, Fénéon was intensely moved by a painter who was to be a main force in solidifying the permanent contribution of neo-impressionism to modern art. "Cross, ah! Cross!" he cried, at the exhibition of the Indépendants, "These clusters

Opposite, MAXIMILIEN LUCE. *A Slag Heap Near Marchiennes.* 1898. Oil on canvas. 54.6 x 73 cm. Copyright © Indianapolis Museum of Art. Gift of Mr. and Mrs. B. Gerald Cantor.

CHARLES ANGRAND. ***Maximilien Luce at Work.*** ca. 1896. Conté crayon, 31 x 23 cm. France, private collection. The work represented in the background is an enlarged version of Luce's lithograph, *The Incendiary,* 1896.

Opposite, above, HENRI-EDMOND CROSS. ***Portrait of Mme Cross.*** 1891. Oil on canvas, 207 x 150 cm. Paris, Musée national d'art moderne. Photograph © Musées nationaux.

Opposite, below, HENRI-EDMOND CROSS. ***Rocky Shore near Antibes.*** 1891–92. Oil on canvas, 65.1 x 92.3 cm. Washington, D.C., National Gallery of Art. John Hay Whitney Collection.

of flowers that prepare one for the woman undulating beyond them."[81] In this painting, a portrait of his future wife, Henri-Edmond Cross attained the decorative ideal that Fénéon cherished. Born Delacroix, Cross, who anglicized his name when he became known as a painter, was a latecomer to neo-impressionism, although he had long been friendly with Seurat and his group.

In 1891, Cross moved to southern France, settling in Saint-Clair, not far from the newly adopted home of Signac in Saint-Tropez. Later on, Fénéon spent most of his holidays with these friends in their southern retreat. In his last formal report on the Indépendants in April 1892, Fénéon briefly referred to Cross's new work, among that of other Neos: "The landscapes of Charles Angrand are bathed in mysterious, taciturn calm; those of Luce luxuriate in active atmospheres; those of Henri-Edmond Cross expressively translate a pebbly Midi."[82] Cross was in Paris at the time, and he sent Fénéon an acknowledgment:

> I am very happy for the space you give me in your article for the "Chat Noir" in spite of the evident mediocrity of my work. I thank you very sincerely. I am going back to the Midi at the end of this month. I hope to acquire one day the state of mind of the pure artist.[83]

This was no false modesty on the part of Cross. He felt the significance of even the slightest notice by Fénéon, whose critical acumen had already become legendary.

Over the years Fénéon acquired many of Cross's paintings, both oils and watercolors, and during his first year at the Galerie Bernheim-Jeune in 1907, he organized what turned out to be the last one-man show for Cross, who died shortly thereafter. On display were thirty-four recent canvases done in brilliant color applied with large, mosaic-like strokes, the second phase of neo-impressionism which Cross and Signac had developed and which strongly influenced Matisse, Derain, Delaunay, Kandinsky, and others. After Cross's premature death, Fénéon went to Saint-Clair to help his widow and Paul Signac make a proper inventory of his work. There he found and later published the last of the painter's notebooks, revealing the immense charm and culture of his friend, and the intensity with which he had pursued his craft.[84]

Fénéon was very much interested in the work of the Belgian neo-impressionists, but he recognized Octave Maus and Emile Verhaeren as the premier critics of the *XX* and limited his public attention to those artists in Paris with whom he was personally associated.

One Belgian neo-impressionist, Théo van Rysselberghe, was a special friend of Fénéon's. He lived much of the time in Paris or in the south of France—for a time at Saint-Clair near Cross—and he was an important link between the literary and art circles of Paris and Brussels. When Fénéon went to Brussels to see an exhibition or visit friends, he stayed at Théo's house. It was there that he met a woman, a professor in a progressive school for young women, Camille Platteel, who would later become his lifelong companion. Van Rysselberghe, who had married one of her former students (Maria Monnom, interesting in her own right), was a handsome, good-hearted fellow, "brawny," Fénéon once remarked of him, "and romantic—even Sardanapalesque."[85]

THÉO VAN RYSSELBERGHE. *The Reading.* 1903. Oil on canvas, 181 x 240 cm. *Left to right*: Félix Le Dantec, Emile Verhaeren (reading), Francis Vielé-Griffin, Henri-Edmond Cross (back turned), Félix Fénéon (standing), André Gide, Henri Ghéon (standing), Maurice Maeterlinck. Ghent, Musée des Beaux-Arts. Photograph copyright A.C.L.-Brussels.

He once fantasized an anarchist bohemian lifestyle, telling Fénéon in 1891 that he had a plan of living in a gypsy caravan, stopping in villages to give exhibitions for one or two *sous.* In the end he would have painted a great many important works, plotted and schemed and acquired a sudden reputation. Then, when enthusiasm was at its height, he would set fire to the lot, punishing the indifference of people during earlier years, and as for him, he would have had the joy of painting. This fantasy did not materialize, so his paintings remain.

One of his best known paintings, *Reading,* composed in Paris in 1903, shows a group in Emile Verhaeren's study, listening to this poet read from a manuscript. Fénéon is there, leaning against the mantelpiece and smoking a cigarette in a debonair fashion. Around the table one can see Henri-Edmond Cross next to Verhaeren, and then Francis Vielé-Griffin, Maeterlinck, Henri Ghéon, Félix Le Dantec, and André Gide: a French neo-impressionist, a Belgian poet, a poet of American origin, a Belgian dramatist, a French biologist, a French doctor, a French novelist, plus Fénéon—more than enough to provide a stimulating interchange.

In 1921, Fénéon named three neo-impressionists who had brought most to modern art's "understanding and control of what we might call the 'primary matter' of painting"—Seurat, Cross, and Signac.[86] Still later, when Jean Paulhan was preparing "F. F. ou le Critique," he told Fénéon that he liked Cross best among the neo-impressionists and asked to illustrate his essay with a study of the *Bather* by Cross from Fénéon's collection. Fénéon did not disagree with Paulhan's choice: "I am very pleased that you prefer Cross. But how unjust . . . how harshly Signac has been treated! Thinking of Seurat, whom we will call Poussin, I would give Signac the importance of Claude Lorrain."[87]

These few painters—Seurat, Signac, Camille and Lucien Pissarro, Dubois-Pillet, Maximilien Luce, Charles Angrand, and Henri-Edmond Cross—formed the core of the group that Fénéon spoke for during the formative years of neo-impressionism. There were many others,[88] but Fénéon mentioned them only in passing, or not at all if they joined the movement after 1893 when he gave up are criticism. It is also significant that the painters he chose to stand by were all committed, in varying degrees of intensity, to the anarchist protest against an exploitive, capitalist society and to a positive vision of a more just and harmonious world.

Presumably even Seurat was committed to anarchism. His work is such a rich commentary on the ambiguities of modern life, its economic stresses, dreams and delusions, that a century later, the figures in *La Grande Jatte* have peopled the cover of a textbook in psychology, *Playboy* magazine, and a Broadway stage.[89]

The reasons for Fénéon's choosing silence after 1893 are complex and stem essentially from his nature and his anarchist convictions. A certain disillusionment, however, seems to hover in the end over his claim that neo-impressionism was the only legitimate modern art. This can be understood in part by looking more closely at his relations with Seurat and Signac, and at their interest in the science of lines, fostered by Charles Henry's studies in aesthetics.

CHAPTER 7

Lines and Loyalties

"Dear Elie," wrote Charles Henry to Fénéon in early May 1889, "I would like us to do a study together of lines and their rhythms. So try to find three or four types of Japanese prints . . . all by illustrious artists. If Japanese art doesn't seem right to you, look for different drawings of an identical subject by Raphael, Michelangelo or Leonardo."[1]

Just as he had with colors, Henry was applying his principles of a "scientific aesthetics," based on mathematical formulae, to discover how lines and their rhythms affect the viewer. Fénéon was his obliging helper, intrigued by this psychological exploration, which would incorporate neurophysiological research, art, and mathematics. Georges Seurat followed Henry's research with interest, since it developed certain notions he already had about "gay," "calm," or "sad" lines. He did not work directly with Henry, but Paul Signac and Fénéon regularly collaborated with the scientist in measuring sensory reactions to form, color, sound, and even taste, odor, and touch, for Henry wanted to develop a general psychophysical aesthetics.

In response to Henry's summons to find prints or drawings for his study, Fénéon chose a single Japanese wood engraving, printed twice in different colors. When he and Henry copied the engraving freehand, their drawings of the two versions were quite different. They concluded that this was because the hand and eye were influenced by the colors in the two prints. They also measured the angles of lines in a series of lithographs done by a contemporary artist after Degas's pastels of dancers. Fénéon reported only vaguely on the ensuing results, saying simply that one print "left . . . some particularly complex and delectable residues."[2] He did not explain what he meant by "residues," mathematically or otherwise.

Henry taught that the only "rhythmic" or "harmonic" angles were those formed by lines which, radiating from the center of a circle, divided its circumference into equal parts—a formula the ancient Greeks had exploited. This return to ancient ideas of harmony, which appealed to Seurat's classicizing mind, was Henry's way of creating a "modern" aesthetics for a newly industrialized society, which could produce multiple mechanized forms while neglecting principles of beautiful proportions. Using a theorem proved by the German mathematician Carl Friedrich Gauss, Henry worked out a list of harmonic angles and printed them on an ordinary protractor, which anyone could use to measure or lay out "rhythmic" lines. This practical program was complemented by Henry's terminology, which subjected principles of Elucidean geometry to newly found concepts of psychophysiology: a line was not a line but a "direction," an angle was a "change in direction," a circle was a "cycle," and so on. Lines going up or to the right were "dynamogenous" or energy-releasing and pleasurable. Those going down or to the left were "inhibitory" or displeasing.

Fénéon's attitude toward these ideas is difficult to determine. He reported on Henry's work using Henry's vocabulary, but he did not explain it. He sometimes spoke with tongue in cheek, and it is clear that he enjoyed teasing the public, or repelling it, with Henry's esoteric formulae. Just as with Rood's equations for pigment mixtures, he played upon the scientific appeal of numbers, but in an even more mystifying way. He referred to Gauss's theorem whenever he spoke of Henry's work (and even in his obituary), but he always misquoted it. Fénéon's customary clarity deserted him, or he abandoned it deliberately.

For example, when Henry published his "Chromatic Circle," along with an explanation of his general theory, F. F. wrote an article, "A Scientific Aesthetics," to promote Henry's work. He quoted Gauss's "beautiful theorem" twice, leaving out a critical element each time.[3] Oddly enough, Henry read Fénéon's manuscript and made various suggestions, but he did not correct this mistake. Fénéon went on to apply Gauss's theorem, listing the first two hundred possible numbers. Mathematically minded readers have just about decided that Fénéon is serious, when they read: "Do you want the third hundred? . . . M. Bronislas Zebrowski has followed the list out up to 8,589,934,590." A figure might be constructed with over eight trillion rhythmic angles, but those angles would hardly be distinguishable one from another.

Henry refers to angles as "changes of direction," as we have noted, and views them as "determined by the arc of a circle intercepted by the [angle's] edges, the center of which is the vertex of the angle." Here is a sketch as illustration:

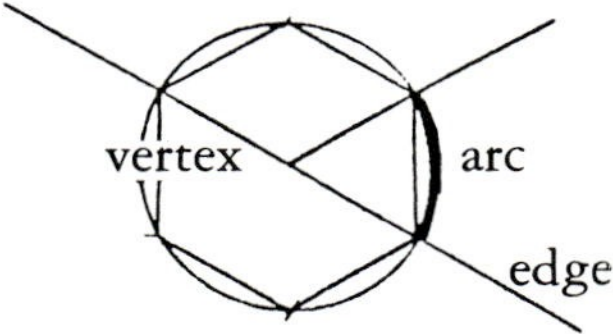

Henry then uses Gauss's theorem to define those angles which are harmonious:

> We shall thus define rhythm: *a change of direction determined* [by an arc] *on the circumference* [of a circle] *whose center is the center of change* [i.e., vertex of the angle] *such that the arc is geometrically constructable, that is to say a division* [of the circumference] *into*

> *M* [equal] *parts, where M may be 2, 2^n or a prime number of the form $2^n + 1$ or the product of a power of 2 by one or several different numbers of this form.* For example, among the first hundred, only the following values of *M* will be rhythmic: 2, 3, 4, 5, 6, 8, 10, 12, 15, 16, 17, 20, 24, 30, 32, 34, 40, 48, 51, 60, 64, 68, 80, 85, 96.[4]

The rhythmic angles corresponding to the values given above are 180°, 120°, 90°, 72°, 60°, and so on, created by dividing a circle (360°) into *M* equal parts. Though no one seems to have noticed it, Henry's definition of rhythm puts strange limits on the artist's choice, allowing for an infinite number of acute angles, but only one obtuse angle (120°).

It was not Gauss's theorem, but Henry's versatile application of it that attracted his artist and poet friends, for he used it to investigate not only energizing angles and the harmony of sections in a straight line, but rhythm in poetry. His influence, Fénéon later noted, "was perhaps critical in the formation of two poets, the closest friends of his youth, Jules Laforgue and Gustave Kahn, and on two painters, Seurat and Signac."[5]

F. F. also appreciated Henry's desire to broaden the base of aesthetics and make it available to ordinary workers and artisans. "These experiments justify particular efforts of our scientific age," he said, to provide practical applications for ". . . a general theory to perfect forms in typography, clothing, architecture, love, furniture—indeed, all the industrial arts."[6] Fénéon was not just joking when he classified love as an industrial art. Henry's work included investigating the physiology of what "literature and current language understand by the word 'love',"[7] measuring genital reactions to electromagnetic stimuli (colors, sounds, and odors).

Given Fénéon's awareness of these efforts to establish a "scientific aesthetics," it seems odd that he did not express much interest in the way Seurat's new paintings began to exemplify Henry's ideas on the "dynamogeny" of lines as well as colors. Fénéon was obviously not insensitive to the structural lines of composition. For example, he remarked on the lines in a Monet: "Trees are shaking on slopes whose thalweg gives an axis to the picture."[8] Using the geological term *thalweg* (a line of maximum continuous descent, cutting all contours at right angles), Fénéon is precise. He also used the language of geometry to portray, for example, how a figure in a Forain painting was *inscribed* inside another (drawn, that is, so as to touch as many points of the perimeter as possible): "A fortyish lady in a heavy, red dress pours a flow of words on the apex of a triangle in which her daughter, dressed in sea-green tulle, is inscribed."[9]

Much of Henry's theory involved the emotional or "psychophysical" effect of colors and lines, which he mapped out on his chromatic circle. Fénéon thought that these relationships could not be dictated by anything other than the individual artist's sensibility. However, he did use Henry's theory to point out a problem in Lucien Pissarro's portrait of his sister Jeanne, which Fénéon thought suffered from the wrong psychological effect: "The blue curtain wants to drown out the dress; and the folds of this curtain follow the general direction of the composition, and thus make it gloomy."[10] Mindful of this remark, Lucien painted out the folds of the curtain and attenuated the blue of the background to Jeanne's portrait, which he did not want to "sadden."

After Charles Henry's *Esthétique scientifique* appeared in 1889, Fénéon mentioned his friend's work in relation to certain paintings: "The landscapes of M. Signac, with their diagonal direction, frequent intersections of straight lines, and acute angles, should offer good opportunities for a Charles Henry to make his measurements."[11] But he did not elaborate, and he implied that the paintings served Henry's theories more than the reverse. While Gustave Kahn and other symbolists applied many of Henry's theories to the interpretation of Seurat's work, Fénéon maintained a curious silence. It was not until after Seurat's death that Fénéon noted that the painter had known Henry's writings and that he "chose to draw up a philosophy of harmonies between the characteristics of color tones (dark, light . . .), hues (cold, warm . . .), lines (falling, rising . . .)—And," Fénéon concluded, "his theories were always submissive to the finest artistic genius."[12]

In 1889, however, he was less positive about Seurat's work; instead, he singled out Paul Signac's painting as exemplifying the "dynamogeny" of lines. And he remarked that it was more intuition than principle that led Signac to structure his compositions according to a dominant direction, accentuated by secondary lines. Naturally, said F. F., Signac knows all about Henry's theories.

> But he is not a slave to these charming mathematics; he is well aware that a work of art is *inextricable.* Besides, Henry has never claimed to furnish artists with a means to create (or even to analyze) systematically a thing of beauty that was the least bit complex; he has said: "Every direction is symbolic." Even without any scientific accompaniment, this simple idea has been fruitful if all it did was destroy M. Signac's faith in chance and fortify him in a lucid empiricism, on the threshold of his own consciousness.[13] [Italics added.]

The following year Fénéon wrote articles dealing exclusively with Signac, not only out of friendship but because he enjoyed the real qualities of Signac's art: "Under his brush a lusty spurt of colors takes fire and sparkles," he said in 1887.[14] He noted how Signac began numbering his works like a composer, Opus 156, Opus 157, and so on, and how he covered the official red walls of exhibitions with gray paper in the room where his paintings hung and even removed the cardboard labels the organizers had inserted between the canvas and the frame, because they interfered with the picture. "Minute details," reported F. F., "prove his faith in his work, his need for the absolute in creating his artistic project."[15]

Although Fénéon spoke of "reading" a painting like an oriental text, from top to bottom, or deciphering it like a musical score, he did not let the science of lines override his intuitive response to the work. Indeed, for him, the "primary matter" of painting was pigment, and so he continued to study and quote physicists' work on optics and color.[16] Other critics, though, and the painters themselves, began to talk

Opposite, above, GEORGES SEURAT. ***Le Chahut.*** ca. 1889–90. Oil on canvas, 169 x 139 cm. Otterlo, Kröller-Müller Museum.

Opposite, below, GEORGES SEURAT. ***Invitation to the Side Show (La Parade).*** 1888. Oil on canvas, 100 x 150 cm. New York, The Metropolitan Museum of Art. Bequest of Stephen C. Clark, 1960.

overtly about the power of lines. Henry van de Velde, one of the neo-impressionists among the Belgian *XX,* wrote of Seurat's painting of cancan dancers, *Chahut*:

> The intention, through a sustained direction of lines, is to create a feeling of gaiety. Hence all these lines rising from the right towards the left, shooting forth from one corner of the frame and bursting into fireworks on the other side. For, soon, the meaning of lines will be revealed to us. Seurat indicates the gay ones, fixed for all time, according to him. Straight ones—*austere,* because devoid of rhythm. Can one not also see heartbroken ones, letting themselves slip *below the ground plane;* and insinuating ones?[17]

Somewhat tongue-in-cheek, van de Velde enjoyed the new line-value theory "fixed for all time" by Seurat.

Fénéon was plainly less convinced. He never wrote a word about *Chahut,* which must have struck him as a painting to prove a thesis rather than one with real emotion. Did Seurat really feel impelled to express a feeling of gaiety? The painting resembled a corseted version of the laughing forms in a Chéret poster. For Gustave Kahn, who soon bought it, the picture epitomized the female essence (and brain),[18] while for Fénéon it teetered on the edge of caricature. In fact, he disliked any serious artistic work that schematized or deformed the human face and figure—Gauguin's self portraits, for example, and, later on, Picasso's work. ("You should stick to caricature," Fénéon said to Picasso when Apollinaire took him to see *Les Demoiselles d'Avignon* at the Bateau-Lavoir in 1907.[19])

Fénéon also never wrote about Seurat's portrait of his mistress, *Young Woman Powdering Herself,* and barely mentioned *The Side Show* or *The Circus,* which, along with *Chahut,* were the last of Seurat's seven larger canvases. He might have been expected to comment on these new works of Seurat; but his silence speaks of an increasing estrangement from the painter and his work. The rift was caused by personality problems and attitudes rather than by any objective aesthetic judgment. Fénéon thought of himself as an interpreter, a "channel" between the artist and the public. But Seurat distrusted the force of such a channel and, as we have seen, avoided speaking in any depth about his painting with Fénéon. By 1888, he had become so touchy over his "paternity rights" to neo-impressionism that he quarrelled with even his old comrade Signac on the subject. Further, Seurat's apparent egoism and disregard for his comrades' feelings rankled Fénéon, who felt that appreciation for genius need not exclude notions of solidarity and mutual support.

The painter, never sociable, withdrew yet further in the beginning of 1889, when a young woman from Belgium, Madeleine Knobloch, began living with him. He kept this liaison a secret from his family and from all but two of his closest friends, Charles Angrand and Paul Signac. He was devoted to her and broke off his summer stint of painting in the port of Crotoy when he learned she was pregnant. To avoid inquiries by friends and neighbors, he moved with her to a small secluded studio in a courtyard off a little street near place Pigalle.

Fénéon was unaware of the relationship between Seurat and the model represented in *Young Woman Powdering Herself.* He found her opulent flesh and primping pose a

GEORGES SEURAT. ***Young Woman Powdering Herself.*** ca. 1889–90. Oil on canvas, 94.2 x 79.5 cm. Formerly Félix Fénéon. London, Courtauld Institute Galleries. Courtauld Collection.

rather unworthy subject for the sensitive and refined Seurat. He far preferred the model Seurat had used in his great painting of nudes, a small woman with a mature and serious face and a lithe, almost childlike body.

This work, *The Models,* first shown along with *The Side Show* in 1888, was the last important painting by Seurat that Fénéon described in any detail. He had been enthralled the previous year at the Indépendants by a delicately modulated preparatory painting of the model in front view: "A study for a nude, *Poseuse,*" wrote Fénéon, "which would glorify the haughtiest museums (pl. 13)."[20] Fénéon hailed Seurat's final composition showing the nude model in three stances—front, side, and back—posing in the artist's studio next to *La Grande Jatte:* "a spacious painting, with a supreme, smiling serenity . . . the most ambitious endeavor of the new art." He described the figures lovingly and concluded: "The ground swell of a glorious and tranquil rhythm

GEORGES SEURAT. *The Models.* 1886–88. Oil on canvas, 200 x 250 cm. The Barnes Foundation. Photograph © copyright (1988) The Barnes Foundation.

gives enhanced life to both color and form, and this work puts to shame any memory of nudes in galleries and legends."[21] Fénéon still liked nudes, but he now preferred them more modern than Henner's *Andromeda.* He responded to classical proportions, but not those in the drawing Seurat made of his voluptuous mistress, "the big lump lying down," Fénéon privately said, "which gives a false and offensive idea of Seurat."[22]

He appreciated the fact that *The Models* dealt lightly with current concerns about the meaning of colors and lines: "By a piece of pseudoscientific fantasy, the red parasol, the straw-colored parasol, and the green stocking are oriented in the directions adopted by red, yellow and green on Henry's chromatic circle." On the other hand, he barely mentioned Seurat's other painting, *The Side Show,* noting only that its coloration as a night scene was interesting, and passing over its geometric straight lines that followed the classic proportions of the "golden section" revived in Henry's writings (the ancient ratio where a finite line segment is divided so that the shorter part is to the longer as the longer part is to the whole).

In 1887 and 1888, Fénéon had expressed unreserved praise for Seurat's smaller canvases executed at the seaside, pointing out that the predominance of horizontal lines helped to establish a feeling of serenity and wonder.[23] Reporting on the Indépendants of 1889, he noted that Seurat was utilizing the "measurable abstract value" of a line, and that the forms in his landscapes were governed by one or two basic directions, paired off with the picture's dominant colors. But then he cautioned that this linear structure was at times too evident:

> Notice in *Le Crotoy (Afternoon)* the strip of sand streaming up from the corners towards the seaboard, and the cloud shaped like a mushroom or a jelly-fish, dropping its vertical filaments towards the horizon line: these are obvious contrasts made of right angles, the kind that M. Chéret uses so freely. Perhaps that is what makes his posters so effective.[24]

F. F. was keenly aware of Seurat's attraction to Chéret. He told John Rewald in 1940 that the only "permanent ornament" in Seurat's studio near place Pigalle was a poster by Jules Chéret for some fancy goods store. Seurat liked to remark, said Fénéon, that Chéret broke his lines almost always at 90°.[25] In 1889, however, Fénéon found the influence all too obvious. "M. Seurat's art is so innately straightforward that it hardly thinks of concealing such techniques. The plausibility of these scenes suffers from this:"

> The conchoid clouds of *Le Crotoy (Morning)* are not very convincing. One wishes that the figures moving about the quay of *Port-en-Bessin* were a little less ossified: if the stance of the wandering baby is charming and lifelike, the vague customs officer and the woman carrying wood or seaweed remain quite improbable. We met this customs officer two years ago: he was the impresario in the *Side Show* by the same M. Seurat.

Seurat's schematizing of forms, particularly human forms, conflicted with Fénéon's notions of a complex reality and his attachment to a more traditional realism. The critic's bantering tone, moreover, betrayed a lack of deference toward Seurat's leadership role and no doubt deepened the rift that had been created earlier by the painter's pride and remoteness.

Fénéon needed an open dialogue with an artist in order to remain in tune with his work. Rather than air his disillusionment further, he simply stopped writing about Seurat. His commitment to the other neo-impressionists remained firm, and he felt it was time to put the movement in a certain historical perspective with monographs on each painter. He convinced Léon Vanier, the publisher of *Les Hommes d'aujourd'hui,* which had previously treated only literary figures, to open a series on painters. He suggested that they begin with Camille Pissarro, Seurat, Signac, Luce, Dubois-Pillet, and then continue with Cézanne, van Gogh, and Gauguin. Vanier agreed and put Fénéon in charge of coordinating the series. The critic Jules Christophe, a senior colleague of Fénéon's at the War Office, wrote the biographies of Seurat, Luce, and Dubois-Pillet, while Fénéon chose Signac. Since Georges Lecomte had expressed a desire to write about Pissarro, Fénéon arranged to have him meet the artist. Charles Morice later presented himself as Gauguin's biographer, and Emile Bernard wrote of Cézanne and van Gogh. As usual, Fénéon took care of all the editorial work and suggested appropriate portraits for the cover page. But he left complete freedom to the authors as to content, suggesting only that they interview their subjects directly whenever possible.

GEORGES SEURAT. ***Signac.*** Conté crayon. Cover of *Les Hommes d'aujourd'hui,* no. 373, [1890]. Photograph G. Roche.

Fénéon began preparing his monograph on Signac with great care in the spring of 1890, sending copies of his draft to the artist, who was in Brittany, and also to Charles Henry for comment on the technical parts. Henry was the first to reply, sending back supplementary notes on such things as the saturation of tints and the absorption of light by pigments. He found Fénéon's "synopsis" of technique dispensable and not very clear,[26] though Seurat later called it superb. Fénéon forwarded Henry's remarks to Signac and asked for his "opinion in detail," saying he would change the text in certain

Opposite, above, GEORGES SEURAT. ***Le Crotoy, Downstream (Le Crotoy, Afternoon).*** 1889. Oil on canvas, 70.2 x 86.3 cm. Private collection.

Opposite, below, GEORGES SEURAT. ***The Bridge and the Quays, Port-en-Bessin.*** 1888. Oil on canvas, 67 x 84.3 cm. The Minneapolis Institute of Arts.

regards; "but H[enry]'s demands as to terminology seem excessive to me. We are in a studio, not a laboratory . . ." Just the same, he strove for accuracy, asking Signac for verification step by step, after a first revision:

> Do you think the first lines [of that paragraph] are enough? I took out all comparisons. The not very philosophically minded reader will still be able to see the correspondence between the optical mixture in your paintings and the mixture on the [rotating] disks of Musschenbroek. But will he see its correspondence with two superimposed portions of the spectrum?[27]

Signac made notes on Fénéon's manuscript, but in general his response was more enthusiastic than technical:

> Oh, how pleased I am with your text! It's a perfect statement of our technique, written with incomparable charm and precision. Don't worry too much about the criticism of our Henry: he is not much concerned with the play of complementaries, which he finds quite barbarous.[28]

Fénéon was persistent. He sent Signac his rewritten version of his text with several more questions and the remark: "Although I revel in those of your last letter, please don't send any compliments this time, but give me suggestions for strong modifications in my text."[29] The three friends, signing their letters F. F., P. S., and C. H., hammered out the details of the text, which included a long paragraph on Signac's collaboration with Henry in experiments measuring the "rhythmic proportions" of various objects—part of Henry's research for the education of workers in industrial art.

F. F. ended the biography with a symbolist flourish, describing the books in Signac's library: Leonardo da Vinci bound in silvery blue; Rimbaud and Mallarmé in white parchment and gold; Baudelaire, violet; Kahn, blue and orange; Tolstoy, purple and black; Paul Adam, glazed rose . . . and the boats Signac owned, a regular "flotilla at the service of his painting: a jiggersail sloop for the ocean, *The Magus,* (a 7 tonner, 10 meters from stem to stern and 2.80 meters at the midship beam); for the Seine, a catboat, the *Tub,* and a Norwegian round-stemmed rowing boat, the *Valkyrie.*" F. F. clearly enjoyed his friend's love of life, color, sailing and seafaring language, along with his sense of humor about current trends and intoxications among the symbolists. He associated Signac with one of Henry's close friends, the poet Jules Laforgue, writing that the hero of one of Laforgue's *Moralités Légendaires,* the tetrarch Emerald-Archetypas, would appoint Signac the official landscape artist of the Esoteric White Iles, should he ever sail by.[30]

As a further little in-joke, Fénéon printed an enigmatic, speckled circle of black marks at the end of his monograph. He had planned to use a circular lithograph Signac had done to illustrate a book of poems by their friend Jean Ajalbert, picturing a solitary bench on the old fortifications where Ajalbert had played as a boy. But Signac did not have a photograph of it to send him, so Fénéon used this mysterious circle, "a seductive work," he explained to Signac, "due to the collaboration of Henry and the bottom of a saucepan."[31]

Signac stayed on in Brittany in the spring of 1890, inviting Félix to come out and conduit une théorie générale de la dynamogénie et des expériences patientes, M. Signac lui apporta son concours: son analyse du profil (anses déployées) des vases de Cnide, de Thasos et de Rhodes et leurs définitions par indicateurs d'écart, de dynamogénie, d'inhibition, de contraste, d'acuité, de diversité, de variété et de complication sont un type très pur de critique scientifique (1) En 90 sera publiée l'Éducation du Sens des formes (2) dont il a établi les vingt planches et les chiffres. Dans la première partie il opère sur des échantillons, longuement choisis, de coupes grecques, vases persans,

(1) Pages 20-31 d' Application | de | nouveaux instruments de précision | (cercle chromatique, | rapporteur et triple décimètre esthétiques) | à l'archéologie | par | M. Charles Henry | Paris | Ernest Leroux, éditeur | 28, rue Bonaparte, 28 | 1890

(2) avec préface de M. Charles Henry.

FÉLIX FÉNÉON. ***Page from the Final Manuscript of "Signac,"*** for *Les Hommes d'aujourd'hui,* no. 373, [1890). Photograph courtesy of the late Solange Lemaître, Paris.

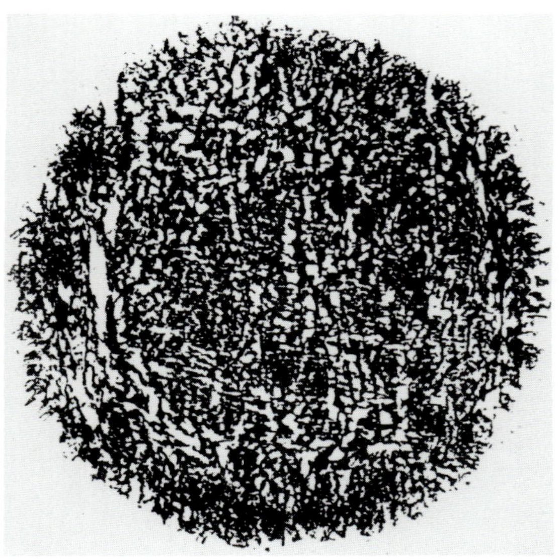

CHARLES HENRY. ***Imprint from the Bottom of a Saucepan.*** Published by Fénéon at the end of his monograph on Signac, *Les Hommes d'aujourd'hui,* [1890].

sail with him. But the young critic's precarious finances would not allow for the expense of even a modest room in a Breton inn, and so he wrote back, "Everything you say is so gracious. I would love to go sailing on the Magus, but it is very probable I shall have the joy of seeing you only when you return to Paris."[32] When the Indépendants opened, Fénéon reported to Signac: "You are obviously the winner in this Salon. The opinion of people whose opinion might interest you: Paul Adam, Vielé-Griffin, Retté, Ajalbert, Edmond Cousturier, Henri de Régnier . . . was absolutely unanimous on varnishing day and afterwards." Fénéon especially praised the vigorous form and delicate colorations of two paintings of Cassis and one of the Seine at Herblay.[33] Signac wrote back to say how sorry he was that those canvases no longer belonged to him. "But what other painting," he asked, "might fill a hole in the gallery of my friend Fénéon?" F. F. laughed in reply, for he had known that the canvases were taken:

> That is why I allowed myself to praise them so indiscreetly, for I have hardly ever dared tell you, good Paul Signac, that I like this or that painting of yours. In any case, I am very fond of the new and the old P. S. which annul my walls; and quite truly they are an element of joy in my life more important than you could believe.[34]

When Seurat read Fénéon's monograph on Signac, the fourth of the new *Hommes d'aujourd'hui* concerning painters, he seethed with anger: this superb statement on neo-impressionism failed to mention him even once, and it was not the first time that he had been slighted or ignored in this series directed by Fénéon. Georges Lecomte had written in his biography of Camille Pissarro, that "a friend of M. Henry, the painter Georges Seurat" had explained the rules of optical painting to the older painter. Lecomte had meant to indicate that Seurat's explanations of Henry's mathematical terms had helped Pissarro understand the new method, but to Seurat it seemed that Lecomte had put the cart before the horse. Then, too, Jules Christophe, who had elected to do Seurat's biography, had published some inaccuracies that were minor but nonetheless irritating. Now Seurat felt himself betrayed by Fénéon who (for the first time) failed to name him as leader of the neo-impressionists. One detail in particular rankled him. "It matters not that the old Impressionists did not embrace optical painting," Fénéon wrote, "It appealed to several young painters of a more philosophical bent of mind. This happened around 1885." It was inconceivable to Seurat that Fénéon should say this without naming him as the instigator of divisionism. This hurt all the more since it was followed by one of the most beautiful statements on the new art:

> And so, M. PAUL SIGNAC was enabled to create exemplary specimens of a highly developed decorative art, which sacrifices anecdote to arabesque, nomenclature to synthesis, fugitive to permanent, and in its celebrations and its magic, confers on Nature—weary at last of its precarious reality—an authentic Reality.[35]

Seurat "hardly ever wrote," Fénéon once explained, and then "always laconically, with difficulty, as can be seen by his schoolboy's handwriting."[36] But in his anxiety Seurat scribbled off a letter to Fénéon which is one of the rare documents that have survived showing the relationship between the two men. In fact, several rough drafts of it exist; it is hard to say which was the final version, since all contain crossed-out words, unfinished sentences and little punctuation. Scholars have appreciated this letter for the information it contains on the painter's development. But it also reveals much of the man.

Paris, 20 June 1890

My dear Fénéon

Allow me to point out a mistake in the biography of
Signac
—or rather to remove any doubt allow me to specify
—"It [optical painting] appealed—around 1885," p.
2, par. 4 Begun ~~in~~ the evolution of Pissarro and
Signac was slower I protest and I re-establish to
within a fortnight the following dates:
The purity of the spectral element being the keystone
of ~~my~~ the technique—~~and being~~ which was first
consecrated by You
Seeking as long as I have held a brush an optical
formula on this basis 1876–1884
[*Seurat here names the authors and painters*
who had influenced his thinking]

I must insist on establishing the following dates

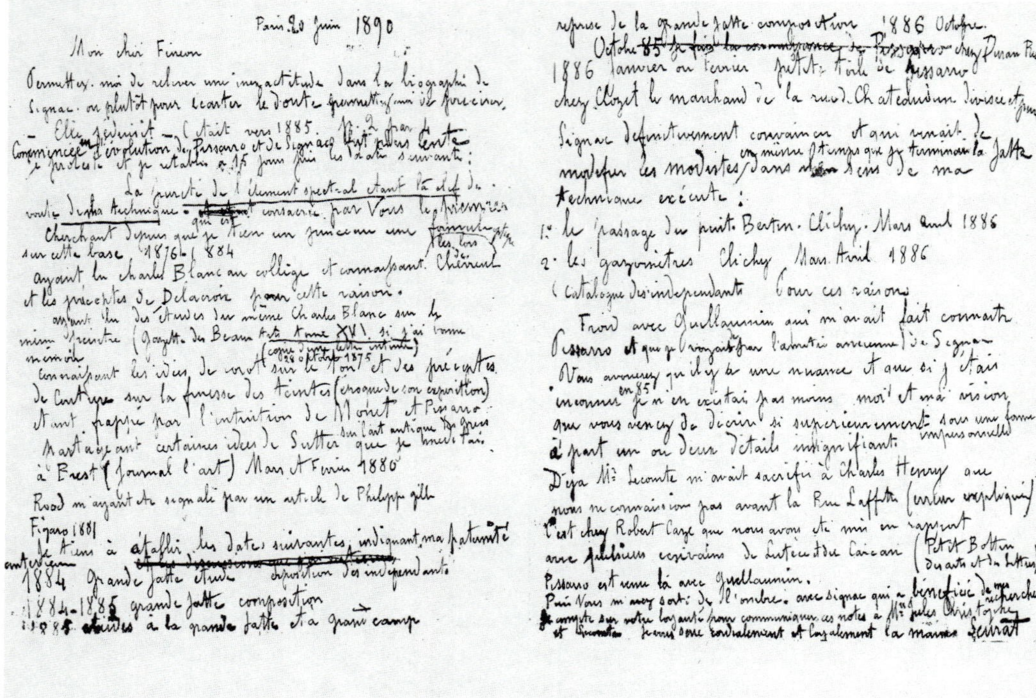

GEORGES SEURAT. ***Draft of a Letter to Félix Fénéon.*** ca. 20 June 1890. New York, Pierpont Morgan Library. Gift of John Rewald. This is a different (earlier?) draft than the one printed in the text.

> indicating my earlier paternity
>
> 1884 Grande Jatte study exhibition of indépendants
>
> ~~and the discussions that I had~~
>
> 1884–1885 Grande Jatte composition
>
> 1885 studies at the grand Jatte and at Grand-camp
>
> resumption of la Grande Jatte composition 1886 October
>
> October ~~85 I meet Pissarro~~ at Durand-Ruel's
>
> 1886 January or February little canvas of Pissarro at Clozet dealer on rue Châteaudun divided and pure
>
> Signac finally convinced and who had just modified [his painting] the milliners—while I was finishing la Jatte—painted in ~~my~~ accordance with my technique
>
> 1. passage du puits Bertin-Clichy, March–April 1886
>
> 2. les gazomètres Clichy, March–April 1886
>
> (catalogue of the indépendants For these reasons coolness with Guillaumin who had introduced me to Pissarro and whom I saw because of Signac's long-standing friendship. You have to admit that there is a difference and that if I was unknown in 85 I was none the less alive, I and my vision which you have just described so superbly under an impersonal form apart from one or two insignificant details.

Seurat was referring to the "synopsis" of technique that Fénéon had published in his biography of Signac. Finally, after citing yet more names and dates to justify his claim that in 1885 he was virtually alone on the path to optical painting, Seurat concluded his letter:

> Then You brought me out of eclipse, with Signac who benefited from my research. I am counting on your loyalty to communicate these notes to M. Jules Christophe and Lecomte.
>
> I shake your hand cordially and loyally —Seurat[37]

Two days later Fénéon sent his reply:

> Your little chronological account, so heavily documented, my dear Seurat, did not teach me anything essential: I know very well that the technique of optical painting was established by you, and, as you graciously remember, I printed it long ago.
>
> If I had been given the honor of writing your biography I, like Jules Christophe, would have printed it again.
>
> I do not need to re-read my article to ~~know~~ be sure that ~~neither directly nor by way of the sort of insinuation of which I would be incapable~~ it contains nothing ~~that might~~ likely to mislead the public on the origin of this technique that the old impressionists did not greet at all kindly and which appealed to more recent painters, in 1885.
>
> I simply, and deliberately, dispensed with informing the reader about this, judging that it was not the place ~~to do it~~ for such a disclosure.
>
> As you requested, your letter of the 20th was communicated to Messieurs Christophe and Lecomte: to the former on the 21st; to the latter on the 22nd. On the same 22nd, at 5:29 I presented myself at your studio with M. Lecomte, marking with

23 juin

Votre petit historique, si fortement documenté, mon cher Seurat, ne m'a rien appris d'essentiel : je sais bien que la technique de la peinture optique a été établie par vous, et, comme vous avez la gracieuseté de vous le rappeler, je l'ai imprimé il y a longtemps.

Si j'avais eu l'honneur de vous biographier, je l'aurais, comme Jules Christophe, réimprimé de nouveau.

Je n'ai pas besoin de relire mon article pour être sûr qu'il ne contient rien à nature à tromper le public sur l'origine de cette technique que les vieux impressionnistes accueillirent mal et qui séduisit des peintres plus récents, en 1885.

Je me suis simplement, et de parti pris, dispensé de renseigner le lecteur à ce sujet, jugeant que ce n'était pas le lieu d'[illegible] cette considération.

Comme vous en avez exprimé le désir, MM. Christophe et Lecomte ont reçu communication de votre lettre du 20 : celui-là, le 21 ; celui-ci, le 22. Le même 22 à 5 h. 25, je me présentais à votre atelier, avec M. Lecomte, marquant par une carte l'inutilité de ma visite. Ne sachant quand je pourrai aller vous voir ni si vous ne quittez pas bientôt Paris, je vous écris, — ce qui me permet de vous offrir mes plus cordiaux compliments et de dissiper, mon cher Seurat, votre inquiétude.

Félix Fénéon

Félix Fénéon to Georges Seurat, 23 June 1890. Facsimile published by C. M. de Hauke and Paul Brame, *Seurat et son oeuvre,* Paris, 1961.

a card the futility of my visit. Not knowing when I can go to see you nor if you will soon be leaving Paris, I am writing you—which permits me, ~~my dear Seurat~~ to ~~send~~ offer you my most cordial ~~respects~~ regards and to dispel, my dear Seurat, your anxiety.

félix fénéon[38]

Both men strove in vain to hide their feelings behind "statements of fact." Fénéon's emotion is betrayed by the controlled irony of his reply and the numerous blacked-out words, which did not often mar his correspondence. His pride and sense of justice were obviously offended. He had been writing reviews stressing the priority of Seurat for the past four years, and the painter had responded only with increasing distrust. Control overrode emotion, though, sending him in search of expressions that would soothe Seurat's feelings without falsifying his own position. Always the attentive critic, he preserved Seurat's letter and, two years later (a year after the painter's untimely death), published the information Seurat had furnished on his development.[39]

Seurat's anxiety is evident in the broken phrases of his writing, which cannot be attributed solely to a lack of aptitude. He clearly thought of Fénéon as his primary interpreter: "You brought me out of eclipse . . ." He felt not only betrayed but abandoned by the critic. Jules Christophe, in his biography of Seurat, had named all his friends—including Fénéon. It seemed to Seurat that Fénéon had obviously meant to slight him by omitting his name entirely from the biography of Signac. Others had also noticed the insult; Angrand had expressed an offensive sympathy for him on the subject.

In late afternoon, the proper time to call, Fénéon and Lecomte had presented themselves at Seurat's door to make amends. Seurat refused, however, to see them. Fénéon makes this clear in his letter by noting both the hour and the minute of their call (as if to say, "You know and I know you were home") and the likely futility of future visits. He did not know that the artist had a personal reason for not admitting visitors to his studio. Madeleine Knobloch had given birth in February and Seurat had legally recognized his son. But he avoided any conflict with his devout, bourgeois family by continuing to keep his mistress and child a secret. None of his friends knew about the baby, either. By moving to the new studio and not receiving anyone there, he had meant to convey the idea that, like Delacroix, he considered his atelier private. Therefore it was doubly offensive that the two critics had sought him out in his refuge and tried to violate that privacy. His behavior was incomprehensible to Fénéon, who could attribute this wariness and hostility only to an unreasonable fear that he or another comrade would spy out the "secret" of the painter's art. The day after he received Fénéon's reply, Seurat wrote again. Rather than an answer, this letter is a continuation of his first, with no acknowledgment of Fénéon's response or his visit.

Tuesday 24 June 1890

My dear Fénéon out of 30 articles referring to me
as innovator I count you 6 times so that is not what
made me write.

> If you had done my biography and if you had asked for
> my opinion I would have asked you not to lay any stress
> on technique. That's what I did with respect to Mr.
> Christophe ....
> Signac must be suffering as much as I from technical
> popularization
> He was of my opinion two months ago.
> People who have read you feel sorry for me they no
> doubt do not understand very well if very
> offensive condolences for me there. They believe I
> have been wronged. That is the reason why I am taking
> a very open stand and why I am telling you what I think
> without any kind of bitterness.
> In 1885 since you want to move things up several months
> it appealed to an old master Pissarro and a young man
> Signac. I therefore do not find it in its place, and I
> am saying so because I am hurt.
>
> *Your friend Seurat*
>
> I am going to the département du Nord around Calais?[40]

The "it" in the last two sentences is the same "it" quoted in Seurat's first letter, from Fénéon's remark in his monograph that *it* (optical painting) *appealed to several young painters around 1885*. Fénéon's efforts to correct the misunderstanding had had no effect whatsoever on Seurat. Indeed, the painter expressed yet another complaint: whereas in his first letter he complimented the critic on his synopsis of technique, he now implied that Fénéon had laid too much stress on it and that he and Signac were both suffering from this "popularization" of their method.

One can hardly accept Seurat's statement that he is speaking "without any kind of bitterness," and yet there is a kind of pathos in his immense hurt. From Seurat's viewpoint, Fénéon should have been able to understand the tremendous risk he, the artist, was taking each day, putting himself on the line, creating his works and then exposing them, his life's blood, for writers to criticize and lesser artists to imitate. He had opened himself to Fénéon in 1886 and revealed all, perhaps too much. And the critic's brochure of that year was still the best, the only description faithful to his art. Nothing should intervene between him and his chosen defender. It cut deeply that Fénéon had been, in Seurat's eyes, unfaithful or, at best, uncaring.

He wanted Fénéon to understand how much he still counted on him. Presumably at this time, he sent the critic the small study of the standing model that he had exhibited in 1888, which Fénéon had said "would glorify the haughtiest museums." Fénéon was overwhelmed. The little painting (26 × 17.2 cm) became his most cherished possession. He had a black velvet cover made for it, as he did for its two pendants, *Seated Model, Profile,* and *Seated Model, Back,* which he acquired some time after Seurat's death (pls. 14 and 15). Slipping them into his inner coat pockets, he took them with him whenever he left Paris on business or vacation. Their "fullness, serenity and distinction" brought even the plainest hotel room to life. They were acquired by the Louvre in 1947 when Fénéon's collection was dispersed, fulfilling the remark he

1. MAXIMILIEN LUCE. ***Paris Street.*** 1905. Oil on paper with canvas support, 48 x 37 cm. U. S. A., private collection. *The hell of the boulevard continues, the cabs, the cafés, the gaslight, the shopwindows, more and more pedestrians—more prostitutes filing by under the harsh lights.* —Jules Laforgue

Seurat.

4. **Edgar Degas.** ***The Tub.*** 1886. Pastel on board, 60 x 83 cm. Paris, Musée d'Orsay. Photograph © Musées nationaux. *Women crouching fill the hull of tubs with swollen melon shapes. . . .* (F, 30)

2. **GEORGES SEURAT.** ***Bathing at Asnières.*** 1883–84 (retouched 1887). Oil on canvas, 201 x 301.5 cm. Formerly Félix Fénéon. London, The National Gallery. *Seurat's art was revealed to me by "Bathing, Asnières . . ."* (Félix Fénéon to John Rewald, 8 May 1940)

3. **GEORGES SEURAT.** ***A Sunday Afternoon on the Island of La Grande Jatte.*** Oil on canvas, 225 x 340 cm. Chicago, The Art Institute of Chicago. Helen Birch Bartlett Collection. *Beneath a sultry sky, at four o'clock, the island, boats slipping past its flank, stirring with a casual Sunday crowd enjoying the fresh air among the trees; and these forty or so figures are endowed with a succinct, hieratic line. . . . The atmosphere is transparent and uncommonly vibrant; the surface seems to flicker or glimmer.* (F, 37)

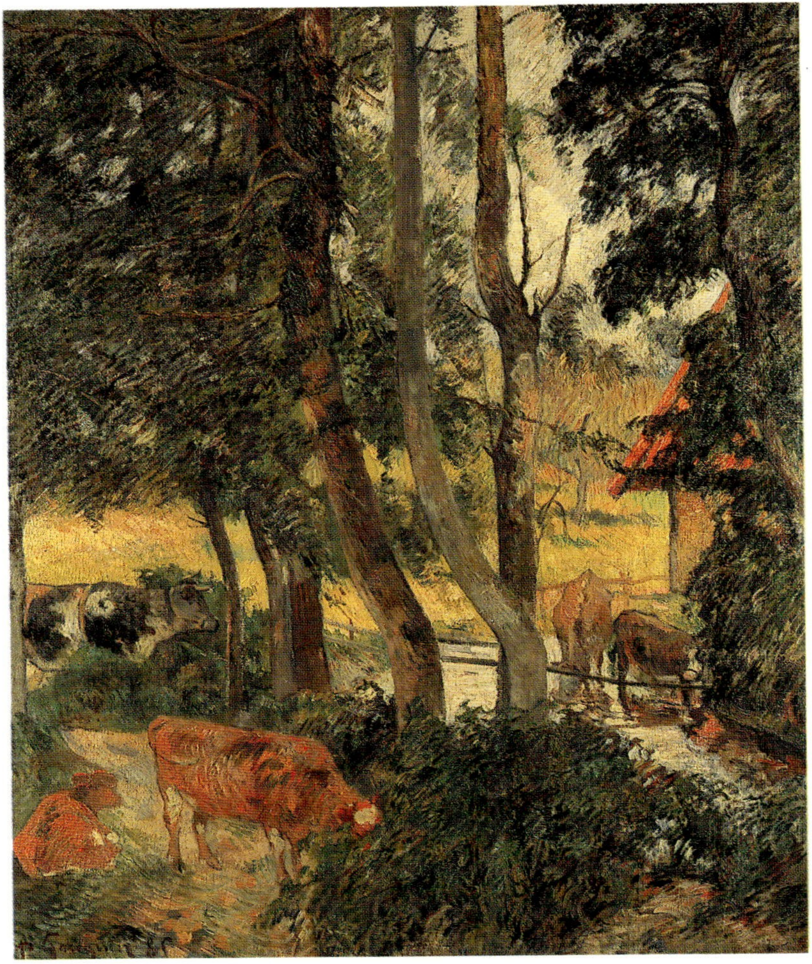

5. PAUL GAUGUIN. ***Edge of the Pond.*** 1885. Oil on canvas, 81 x 65 cm. Milan, Civica Galleria d'Arte Moderna, Raccolta Grassi. Photograph Saporetti. *Dense trees gush from rich, humid, lush soil, overflowing the frame, banishing the sky. A heavy air. A glimpse of bricks suggests a nearby house; hides stretch, muzzles part the brushwood—cows.* (F, 33)

6. PAUL SIGNAC. ***The Gas Tanks at Clichy.*** 1886. Oil on canvas, 65 x 81 cm. Felton Bequest, 1948. Reproduced by permission of the National Gallery of Victoria, Melbourne. Gas Tanks at Clichy . . . *with its picket fences laden with work trousers and jackets set out to dry, the desolation of its peeling walls, its scorched grass and its incandescent roofs in an atmosphere that asserts itself and darkens as it rises, hollowing out an abyss of blinding blue.* (F, 37)

7. GEORGES SEURAT. ***La Rade de Grandcamp, Bateaux*** (*The Roadstead at Grandcamp*). 1885. Oil on canvas, 65 x 81.2 cm. Private collection. *Sails stated as scalene triangles. . . . No playfulness in Seurat's color, no brag in his brush, but a certain salty savor and a biting austerity.* (F, 56)

P. Signac

8. PAUL SIGNAC. ***Parisian Sunday.*** 1889–90. Oil on canvas, 150 x 150 cm. France, private collection. *Except for Gustave Caillebotte, indoor scenes rarely tempted the impressionists. Paul Signac is reinstating them in broad, savory pages. . . . And under his brush, close-set spurts of color ignite and sparkle.* (F, 75–76)

9. ALBERT DUBOIS-PILLET. ***River's Edge in Winter.*** ca. 1889. Oil on canvas, 37.7 x 49.9 cm. New York, Mr. and Mrs. Arthur G. Altschul. *A somewhat blond vision gives his oil paintings the powdery, velvet softness of pastels. . . . Under the citrine siftings of sunlight, the blue of the sky is altered.* (F, 44)

10. CAMILLE PISSARRO, ***Peasant Women Planting Pea Sticks.*** 1891. Oil on canvas, 55 x 46 cm. England, private collection. *After accumulating many rich observations directly from Reality . . . he stops painting outdoors and treats Nature as a repertory of decorative motifs.* Peasant Women Planting Pea Sticks, *where gestures and colors form a garland for Botticellion spring festivals.* (F, 209)

11. MAXIMILIEN LUCE. ***Landscape of Saint-Tropez.*** 1893. Oil on canvas, 46 x 55 cm. Langer Collection. *If you step back, the aggressive medley of colors on these canvases tones down to spacious harmonies of violet.* (F, 82–83)

12. CHARLES ANGRAND. ***An Accident.*** 1887. Oil on canvas, 50.6 x 64 cm. Josefowitz Collection. *Lit by the gasjets of street lamps and pharmacy globes, a crowd is gathering on the sidewalk. The lines have gone stiff and the colors are out of joint. . . . The spectator, plunged into the yellow gaslight, assumes that it is white and so adopts an inaccurate term of reference for all the other colors.* (F, 75)

13. **GEORGES SEURAT.** Study for ***Les Poseuses: Model from the Front.*** ca. 1887. Oil on panel, 26 x 17 cm. Formerly F. Fénéon. Paris, Musée d'Orsay. Photograph © Musées nationaux. *A study for a nude,* Poseuse, *which would glorify the haughtiest museums.* (F, 75)

14. **GEORGES SEURAT.** Study for ***Les Poseuses: Model from Behind.*** ca. 1887–88. Oil on panel, 24.4 x 15.7 cm. Formerly F. Fénéon. Paris, Musée d'Orsay. Photograph © Musées nationaux.

15. GEORGES SEURAT. Study for *Les Poseuses: Model in Profile.* ca. 1887–88. Oil on panel, 24 x 14.6 cm. Former F. Fénéon. Paris, Musée d'Orsay. Photograph © Musées nationaux.

16. PAUL SIGNAC. ***Against the Enamel of a Background Rhythmic with Measures and Angles, Tones and Hues, the Portrait of M. Félix Fénéon in 1890, Opus 217.*** Oil on canvas, 74 x 95 cm. Private collection. *It would not be a commonplace portrait at all, but a carefully composed picture, with very carefully arranged colors and lines. A rhythmic and angular pose. A decorative Félix, entering with his hat or a flower in his hand. . . .* (Signac to Fénéon, Saint Briac, 21 July [1890], Cachin-Signac archives, Paris)

P. Signac

8. **PAUL SIGNAC.** ***Parisian Sunday.*** 1889–90. Oil on canvas, 150 x 150 cm. France, private collection. *Except for Gustave Caillebotte, indoor scenes rarely tempted the impressionists. Paul Signac is reinstating them in broad, savory pages. . . . And under his brush, close-set spurts of color ignite and sparkle.* (F, 75–76)

T-L
Application du Cercle Chromatique de Mr Ch. Henry.
P. Signac
Lith. EUGENE VERNEAU, 108, Rue de la Folie Méricourt. Paris.

17. PAUL SIGNAC. ***Application du cercle chromatique de Mr. Ch. Henry.*** 1888. Color lithograph, 16 x 18.6 cm. The design celebrates both Charles Henry's book, *Le Cercle chromatique,* and Antoine's Théâtre Libre (T-L) with a spectator's head enshrined in the circle. Program for productions on 10 December 1888. Photograph courtesy André Vasseur, Paris.

18. PAUL GAUGUIN. ***The Woman in the Waves.*** 1889. Shown at the Volpini café during the World's Fair. Oil on canvas, 92 x 72 cm. Cleveland Museum of Art. Gift of Mr. and Mrs. William Powell Jones. *He . . . accentuates lines, limits their number, makes them hieratic; and in each of the spacious cantons formed by their interlacing design, an opulent and sultry color sits in bleak glory.* (F, 158)

19. HENRI DE TOULOUSE-LAUTREC. ***The Moorish Dance.*** Decoration for the booth of the dancer, La Goulue. 1895. Oil on canvas, 285 x 307.5 cm. Paris, Musée d'Orsay. Photograph © Musées nationaux. *That is I . . . elbow to elbow with Wilde in the foreground, among the idlers gaping at la Goulue.* (Fénéon to M. Saint-Clair, ca. 1943.)

20. EDOUARD VUILLARD. ***At the Revue Blanche (Portrait of Félix Fénéon).*** 1901. Oil on board, 46.4 x 57.5 cm. New York, Solomon R. Guggenheim Museum. Photograph David Heald.

had made sixty years before. But in 1890 Seurat could not feel confident of Fénéon's devotion and understanding; and his lack of trust prevented any nurturing of the kind of friendship that Fénéon enjoyed with other artists.

Paul Signac had decided to do a portrait of Fénéon as his next major work. It would be a stylized effigy, implementing the latest ideas of Henry on the rhythms of hues and lines, and a sort of tribute to their work in common. He wrote Fénéon from Brittany asking if he would agree to sit. Fénéon replied on June 25 (the day after Seurat's last letter, which he naturally did not mention). He treated the idea as a joke:

> Your idea of a portrait, Oh! my dear Paul, I am only too willing to be your accomplice. If one of these winters my performance is fairly satisfactory, I would rather like for it to be immortalized for the cymae of future art galleries, whose catalogue would say:
> Paul Signac (1863–1963):
> Portrait of a Young Man.
> H. 2.30 m.—L. 1.15 m.
> Have you already thought of the pose, the costume and the décor? and can I keep the monocle that you haven't yet seen on my right eye? But I am afraid that this project will not be feasible, due to the difficulty in reconciling Painting and War, both diurnal. Oh, well, you can do a portrait in pen and ink as big as my hand, and I will be delighted.[41]

Signac was not put off by Fénéon's affectation of modesty, and wrote back:

> It would not be a commonplace portrait at all, but a carefully composed picture, with very carefully arranged colors and lines. A rhythmic and angular pose. A decorative Félix, entering with his hat or a flower in his hand, on a very high, very narrow canvas. A well-defined background composed of two complementary colors, and a suit blending with them: let's work it out together and we will find the right combination. Do you have any wishes or ideas? Moreover you won't have to put up with much posing: just long enough to make a panel and a sketch from which—a painting.[42]

The painter already had a very definite image of the portrait he would execute later that year and call *Sur l'émail d'un fond rhythmique de mesures et d'angles, de tons et de teintes, portrait de M. Félix Fénéon en 1890, Opus 217*. ("Against the Enamel of a Background Rhythmic with Measures and Angles, Tones and Hues, the Portrait of M. Félix Fénéon in 1890, Opus 217.") Somewhat tongue in cheek, Signac was evoking the great synthesis of sensation, sound, music, motion, lines, light, and color that was the subject of Charles Henry's scientific inquiry and the current topic of concern to symbolists desirous of carrying Wagnerian theories to the ultimate.

Signac's letter convinced Fénéon that the proposed portrait was not simply a friendly gesture but a serious project, and he replied affirmatively, with some reservations:

> If I were a painter, doing a large portrait of anyone masculine would appall me. So do not expect me, as you wished, to submit any ideas on the subject: any pose or

> costume that I think up immediately strikes me as absurd, but whatever they may be, your brush, as it paints them, will, I am sure, make them a necessary part of the whole. You have outlined a project that has my entire approval. I will express only one opinion: effigy absolutely full-face—do you agree?[43]

If Fénéon thought his profile unsuitable, this was not the opinion of Signac, nor later of Toulouse-Lautrec, Vuillard, Vallotton, and van Dongen, who all chose to represent him in side view. The sittings began in late fall of 1890 in Signac's spacious studio on the impasse Hélène, not far from Seurat's hideaway in Montmartre. On 25 November Fénéon wrote to his friend Gustave Kahn:

> Sunday our Signac made some sketches for my portrait: it was the first sitting. I already look like some poor fool who has been dipped in the dyers' vat, shooting at a target with an iris. I feel like asking for a palmbranch instead. But, except for me, I think it will be very fine, and it will carry on the scandalous tradition of the cow with the snout by Caillebotte and the monkey in the *Jatte.*[44]

Signac must have kept his promise that Fénéon would not have to spend much time posing. Today the only known study for the portrait is a small, expressive black chalk drawing of Fénéon's face in profile—about the size of the palm of his hand, as a matter of fact.

The final composition turned out very much as Signac had described it five months earlier to Fénéon (pl. 16): a profile view of Félix entering from the right as if crossing a stage, carrying his top hat, cane and gloves stiffly in his left hand, while the right reaches out to offer a flower to an unseen recipient—perhaps a woman, or a painter or poet? In any case, his gaze is set upon the other, the one he celebrates. The critic's impassive expression contrasts oddly with the precious elegance of his gesture, and his straight stiff body is antithetical to the bold rhythmic background, which looks like a giant pinwheel in motion, each of its eight segments painted in patterns of opposed colors: blue and orange, red and green, yellow and purple—the "enamel" of jewel-like tones evoked in the title. With this astounding backdrop, the portrait was as Signac had wanted it, "rhythmic and angular."

One of the more exotic elements of the portrait was recently identified by Signac's granddaughter Françoise Cachin. Leafing through the painter's collection of Japanese prints, she discovered the inspiration for the swirling ground of the painting in a page of an album of colored designs—probably kimono textile patterns.[45] This hidden reference to oriental design was appropriate to "Utagawafénéon" and the delight he took in the unashamed eroticism and poetry of Japanese prints. Fénéon doubtless helped to pick it out, as Signac had suggested they "find the right combination together." The painter rearranged the pattern to suit his needs, inserting an odd arabesque in one segment and painting five-pointed stars in another to symbolize Fénéon's mannered style and bizarrely cultivated resemblance to Uncle Sam. The kimono pattern provided the proportions for the canvas. Not the tall, narrow one Signac originally thought of, but a canvas more wide than high, where the gesture of a truly "decorative Félix" could evolve.

The inordinately long title Signac gave the painting shows that he meant it to be

PAUL SIGNAC. ***Profile of Félix Fénéon.*** Study for the painting, *Against the enamel . . .* 1890. Black chalk on grayish paper, 10 x 7 cm (irregular). New York, John Rewald Collection.

both a significant portrait and a joyous spoof. In nearly every detail, the picture is a rigorous and flamboyant application of Charles Henry's theories on the dynamogeny of lines and colors. The title quotes Henry's own terms, "measures and angles . . ." and specifies the year as if to commemorate the time when the scientist, the critic, and the painter all collaborated in the research and illustration of works such as Henry's *Education du sens des formes.*

Angles in the "Rhythmic Background" of the portrait, when one measures the sweep between major segments of the pinwheel, are generally harmonic, for example 15°, 72°, 60°.* Signac, in fact, altered the proportions of the Japanese pattern so that the segments formed a variety of angles closer to the rhythmic angles prescribed by Henry. In contrast, the obtuse angle formed by Fénéon's extended right arm is nonhar-

*That is, they correspond to those which can be constructed according to Gauss's theorem, dividing a circle (360°) into *M* equal parts:

M	angle		
2 =	180°	12 =	30°
3 =	120°	15 =	24°
4 =	90°	16 =	22.5°
5 =	72°	17 =	21.1765°
6 =	60°	20 =	18°
8 =	45°	24 =	15°
10 =	36°	etc.	

monic: 130° (not in the list of "possibles"). Very likely this was because Signac meant to establish a contrast between an "angular" or inhibitory Félix and the dynamic backdrop. Fénéon's left arm, however, forms a readily visible 90° "harmonic" angle which, completed by the opposing upper arm, outlines a perfect golden rectangle. Thus, both "pleasing" and "displeasing" angles are given to the critic, while the background spins dynamically in harmony.

So as to divide his canvas according to the rule of the golden segment, Signac moved the center of the "pinwheel" up from the picture center. The more arresting patterns, such as the waves of red and green and the convoluted arabesque of gold on violet, are on the left or "inhibitory" side, while the more easily flowing designs move to the right. Within one segment the red climbs in "gay" patterns and the green falls in cool or sad ones. A ray of blue streaks from the center and grows darker as it moves out, flecked always with its opposite, orange. Even the choice of the flower was significant. Beyond its visible association with decadent refinement in a time when Fénéon's friend Oscar Wilde walked around Paris carrying a carnation dyed green, there was its name. It could have been an orchid, but Signac and Fénéon said no, it was a blown-up cyclamen, which, coming from the Greek word for circle, is redolent of Henry's *Cercle chromatique,* and of his theory of lines as *directions* (cycles, not circles).

José Arguëlles believes that the cycle pattern and the cyclamen in the painting signify a mystical concept of Henry's that all life is cyclical, existing in "continual autogenesis".[46] If that is so, then Paul Signac's reference to such a concept, especially in a portrait of Fénéon, would be part of the spoof or mystification played out by these young men (aged twenty-seven and twenty-nine). It is likely that certain elements in the painting were meant not to tease Henry but rather to mock the current rage for the occult and a pseudoreligious mysticism that was increasingly in fashion among the symbolists and painters like Gauguin and the Nabis. The yellow stars on a dark blue ground could evoke not only Uncle Sam, but the stars of astrologers like the Magi, especially as the adjacent segment sports astral globes on its field. All of this was a playful, serio-comic evocation of the esoteric taste of the times. One of Signac's sailboats was named *The Magus,* since knowledge of the stars is useful to a navigator, but there was a laugh in this name, just as there was in his rowboat the *Valkyrie,* making sport of the current intoxication with Wagner.

The painting also looked forward in certain ways, revealing the rising interest in textile patterns and the rhythmic designs that would develop in art nouveau. And although it struck nearly all observers, including artists like Pissarro, as absurdly strong in color and pattern, it later proved to be an inspiration for the twentieth-century painter Robert Delaunay.[47]

Friends of Fénéon found the likeness too cold and dry. Emile Verhaeren said that only the detail of the flower suggested the subject's real qualities of grace and gentility.[48] Maria van Rysselberghe exclaimed:

> What a pity that the portrait Signac left us of [Fénéon] is not at all beautiful. It might have been. It should have been. Despite a rather grim and disagreeable aspect,

> it is nonetheless deeply meaningful. Homage be rendered to Signac, since he chose to paint him that way. . . .
>
> On the whole it is rather like him; everything is there: testimony in favor of a new art, humorous indifference towards the outsider, the precious affectation of the pose, the rarity of the gift—yes, everything, except for grace and charm which cannot be congealed.[49]

There is certainly humor in Signac's portrait, as there was in almost all of Seurat's paintings of people (though not in his drawings). And it is precisely the deadpan humor of F. F. Showing him paradoxically rigid against a profusion of forms, it is an authentic portrait, revealing something of his rich inner nature under the perfected shell of his appearance.

However, Fénéon did not like the portrait. He thought that both "portraitist and portrayed had done one another a cruel disservice."[50] Although it was still in his possession at the end of his life, Fénéon wrote Jean Paulhan in 1943:

> The portrait, my dear Jean, that you are enquiring after—why?—is not allowed to see the light of day, being the least successful work painted by Signac (in 1890 he did not yet know me well enough).[51]

Perhaps this was an expression of modesty on Fénéon's part; or, more likely, a residue of vanity. The tight-lipped, strong-boned, big-nosed profile painted by Signac definitely fulfills Fénéon's apprehensions about a male portrait and is certainly less flattering than the elegant preliminary drawing. Perhaps also, after a half century of mellowing time, Fénéon could no longer identify with the young man and his affected pose. The application of Henry's theories was all too obvious, he thought, as was the portrayal of his own studied impassivity. The portrait Georges Seurat had done of the young woman primping in front of her mirror had seemed a gross burlesque of the female form, and now his own portrait looked rather like a caricature of the contemporary male. Nonetheless, he took it graciously and hung it on his wall—until Signac's death in 1935.

His comment that Signac did not yet know him well enough in 1890 could only have been written from the vantage point of 1943. By 1890, Fénéon and Signac were companions sharing fun, painting, and politics. Although he did not manage to go sailing on *The Magus,* Fénéon often joined the painter for trips on a new boat, *The Olympia,* that Signac bought in 1891 and later took to the Mediterranean (via inland waterways). The two friends sometimes joined one another in outings with young women friends. Fénéon's usual discretion did not prevent him from speaking of a certain Hélène in a letter he wrote Signac in summer of 1891:

> In remembrance of you we went rowing on the lake of the Bois de Boulogne, awhile ago, at night. Swans around us. We almost sank under the downpour of a little cascade. We were able to put back into our home port, opposite Azaïs, without being obliged to tuck up skirts and trousers and pull the boat along behind us. Hélène loves seeing all the boats on the park lakes, the Seine, even in the

> newspapers—reading about the French fleet at Kronstadt; she delights in memories of the "Olympia" and her sailors. One evening around 10 o'clock, from Rue Lafayette to the dock at La Villette, we followed the achingly slow voyage, broken by locks, of a barge being towed along the canal by three men.
>
> My beautiful walking stick, imagine, was drowned! It was the end you would have chosen for it. And yet I was grieved, grieved. It fell into the Seine. I had never known such a beautiful walking stick. Just a night or two before, I had had the pleasure of cracking it over the back of a professional gymnast. A troop of those people passed like a hurricane over a sidewalk where we were standing. It was, as you can imagine, the week of Bastille Day.[52]

The walking stick eulogized by Fénéon was doubtless the one in the portrait Signac had painted a few months earlier. One gathers from the letter that it had been given Fénéon by Signac. Other letters Fénéon wrote the painter around this time bore the double signature, "Hélène d'Orchidée" next to his "Félix d'Iris"—echo or origin of the flower in the picture.

Fénéon committed himself to the neo-impressionists for personal reasons, because he was enthralled by their art and because he liked the artists themselves. But he did not consider himself their only interpreter. It was time, he thought, to make room for new voices. His comrade Georges Lecomte had become keen on neo-impressionism. In 1890 Fénéon offered him his post as Paris correspondent for *L'Art moderne de Bruxelles* and stopped reporting regularly on the Indépendants, although for a while he continued to contribute art criticism to different reviews, picking artists like Toulouse-Lautrec and Bonnard out of the new generation and writing occasional pieces about his old friends, until about a year before his arrest in 1894. In essence, however, he felt he had already said all that he had to say about the *new* impressionists.

Did he lack perseverance? Gauguin's star seemed to be rising, and Seurat's falling. Or was he nothing but a dilettante, who cut deep, but did not stay deep? Fénéon supported artists and writers throughout his life in different ways; but writing criticism was not a vocation for him, or a posture he felt necessary to maintain. Given the critic's rapport with a certain kind of painting, and his indebtedness to that vision, he found it difficult, if not impertinent, to write at length about new and different works, works which he recognized as good, but which failed to set up the same resonance in him.*

Paul Signac remained one of Fénéon's closest friends throughout his life, and they shared many interests, not the least of them an enthusiasm for contemporary literature. During the time that Fénéon was involved with neo-impressionism (1886–91), he was

*Fénéon made one exception to his own rule not to write about twentieth-century artists: Emile Compard. The two prefaces he wrote for Compard's exhibitions in 1927 and 1930 are among his finest pieces of art criticism and have often been quoted to show his understanding of modern art. Fénéon's ideas, however, evolved from talking with Compard, whom he rated on a par with Bonnard, Kandinsky, and Braque.

also very active as editor and critic of the symbolists. All that he did and wrote in relation to the neo-impressionists was interwoven with his interest in the symbolist movement in literature and, in Fénéon's eyes, its unfortunate stepdaughter, symbolist painting.

PART THREE

Refocus on Symbolism 1886–1892

CHAPTER 8

Working Behind the Scenes 1886–1892

By the middle of 1886, when he had just turned twenty-five, Fénéon had become France's leading exponent of neo-impressionism, a guiding light behind several symbolist reviews, and the creator of a new style of criticism. He devoted great energy to what he called *les travaux indirects*—promoting and editing the work of others.

He was a familiar figure on the boulevards, striding along to some meeting with poets, to a *vernissage,* or to visit a friend. A contemporary sketched him:

> With the controlled, circumspect gestures of an adroit diplomat, Félix Fénéon hurries along the boulevards. His tall figure is dominated by his cold, linear, rather angular Yankee face. The pockets of his fashionable clothes conceal articles, biographies, galley proofs, an extensive correspondence from foreign lands, and newspapers in every language. For a long while he maintained in unique splendor the innovating periodical, the *Revue indépendante,* which shaped the present movement. . . .[1]

The "splendor" of Fénéon's review (May 1884–April 1885) was such that Edouard Dujardin decided to start a second series. Dujardin spent the better part of the year planning his review and enlisted the aid of F. F., who was then editor of both *Le Moderniste* and *La Vogue.*

Dujardin wanted a much more stable publication than most symbolist reviews, as he explained to F. F.:

> It must be a monthly review with a very limited number of contributors, who will be paid, and *very* organized: a *mixed liability company limited by shares,* with a capital, say, of 12,000 francs in 12 shares of 1,000 francs.

He urged the critic to sell shares to the owners of the *Moderniste* and to create a merger under Dujardin's directorship. "Now, my dear Fénéon," he concluded, "if I am writing you about these things which we have already discussed, it is not just for your entertainment . . . First of all, we really want you to be our editor in chief, really, absolutely!"[2] In March 1886, when the *Moderniste* concluded its brief but independent existence, F. F. wrote Dujardin and Wyzewa that all of his evenings, with the exception of a few poses for his portrait by the painter David Estoppey, would "be governed by your will, which has become mine."[3]

Fénéon and Dujardin had known one another since meeting at Mallarmé's in 1885. Dujardin regularly sent F. F. free copies of his *Revue wagnérienne,* and the critic gave him in turn information on such relevant material as Charles Henry's study of the psychological effect of rhythm in Wagner. In 1886, communication between Dujardin and Fénéon changed. Whereas previously F. F.'s notes began, "Dear Sir and colleague," and ended with the usual fixed phrases of French correspondence, they suddenly became more intimate and inventive. This new warmth was due in part to the partnership Dujardin had with the cosmopolitan Teodor de Wyzewa, whom Fénéon had come to know and like.

Fénéon addressed his letters to both men at once, since Dujardin and Wyzewa shared lodgings in Montmartre, at 79 rue Blanche, headquarters of the *Revue wagnérienne* and the new review being planned. The two partners formed a curious contrast. Poet and novelist Dujardin was a tall, bearded, silken-haired dandy—"your beauty in trousers striped as dark as they are longitudinal," Fénéon once addressed him. He was considered the "businessman" of the symbolist generation, but he also enjoyed a reputation as its Don Juan. Teodor de Wyzewa, a Pole educated in Paris, looked a gamin, with his hair fringing his forehead, wide ears sticking out, and no beard to lengthen his heart-shaped face, which was broken by the circumflex of a thick mustache. Gifted in transposing ideas from Slavic literature and Wagnerian music into French terms, he was an influential theorist. F. F. found Wyzewa's writing "somewhat specious" at times,[4]—not surprisingly, since at the very moment Fénéon was extolling Seurat, Wyzewa proclaimed that his art lacked life and sincerity. But this difference of opinion did not impinge upon the cordial relations between Fénéon and the young expatriate, who used to join F. F. in long strolls across Paris at night, somewhat breathlessly trying to keep pace. Once he was worn out, and Fénéon apologized in a note the next day: "Remorse for having wearied you, already somewhat ill, on those roads, has ruined our rare evening for me. You are really a gentle soul, of whom I am very fond."[5]

Fénéon enjoyed the confidence of both Wyzewa and Dujardin who (according to Dujardin's second wife) were lovers for a time. F. F. amused them by sending one of his rhymed envelopes through the mail, calling attention to a phallic monument and the graphic inversion "69":

Non, certes, au 69, puisque
la rue a l'épithète: Blanche
chez Wyzewa que l'obélisque
de Luxor et M. Ballanche
n'égalent pas, Granet, va mettre
au 79 ma lettre.[6]

> (Certainly not at 69, since the street is called [virginal] White, but to Wyzewa, whom even Luxor's obelisk and M. Ballanche cannot equal, go deliver my letter, Granet, to No. 79.)

The postman (Mr. Granet, presumably) must have enjoyed deciphering this, since it arrived at destination.

F. F. regaled Dujardin-Wyzewa not only with his rhymed envelopes but with a series of facetious signatures, beginning with the old favorites *Elie* and *Porphyre* and going on to *fille Elisa, Ophélix, félix Tubal,* and *Félix dolichocéphale*—the last referring to his "long head," one of the types just established by the criminologist Bertillon in the first scientific method of identifying people. Just as he would sometimes sign amorous notes to women with a female name, his inventions here were lusty games, but more salacious and more literary: *La Fille Elisa* was a novel about a prostitute by Edmond de Goncourt; and while Laforgue and other symbolists seriously identified with Hamlet, F. F. preferred to play Ophélix, in jest (Oh! Félix!).

Between joking addresses and signatures, the business of creating a review was carried on, and Fénéon served once again as the obliging midwife. First, as for any progeny, there was the problem of its name. The title "Moderniste" no longer boded well after the death of that review. Dujardin then thought of the "New" review; Fénéon responded by telegram:

> My dear Edward*
>
> Everyone acts appalled by the title Revue *Neuve:* Bloy, Huysmans, everyone without exception. They see in it an imitation of boulevard Poissonnière. Caresses to Fedor. Cordial respects to you, Sir,
>
> *from this Lucy*[7]

Dujardin then toyed with the idea of "Revue Cosmopolite" before friends convinced him he would do well to revive Fénéon's *Revue indépendante.*

Fénéon labored tirelessly for Dujardin's review, but he also sometimes imposed on his friend's generosity: "I come here with a wretched friend who, despite his outstanding qualities, asks me for five francs. He needs them badly and I do not have them. And you? . . . P.S. I will pass by again after going to [Theo] van Gogh's gallery."[8] In June 1886 he made a more substantial request, withholding, as usual, the identity of the needy person:

> I need 40 francs today. Do you have ready money, and can you take such a sum from it?
>
> I did not say anything to you about this yesterday: our lofty ratiocinations prevented it, and, besides, I thought I had other resources.
>
> I cannot wait for our usual meeting tomorrow: given the urgency of the situation, I shall even ask you either to notify me of impossibility by telegraph, or to get these louis to me before 5 o'clock.[9]

*Fénéon used the English version of Dujardin's name. Boulevard Poissonnière was the location of a big newspaper.

JULES LAFORGUE. ***Drawings of Skeletons on his Manuscripts.*** Reprinted from François Ruchon, *Jules Laforgue, sa vie, son oeuvre,* Geneva, 1924.

Forty francs (about 90 francs today, or $20) does not seem a large amount now, but it was a sizable sum in 1886. Fénéon owed a comparable amount that same year to various shoemakers, who brought suit against him and succeeded in having his pay docked at the War Office.

But F. F. was not asking his friend to pay for shoes. The sum was needed by a young poet whom Dujardin, as it happened, had met in Berlin just two months earlier, Jules Laforgue. Impecunious as ever, Laforgue was considering marriage to an young English woman he had met in Berlin, and in any event he wanted to leave his post "in exile" as Reader to Empress Augusta. He made a hurried trip to Paris in June to start arrangements for his return, and found himself in financial straits. His friends were worried for him and, typically, Fénéon came up with a practical solution. He not only garnered some cash but obtained 330 francs from a moneylender. Before leaving, Laforgue wrote Wyzewa, "Thank you for having taken my predicament to heart. Luckily it only lasted one day and a night. Fénéon arrived on the scene, looming up, cold as ever, like the statue of the Commandant (may the name forever be his!)"[10] Laforgue's macabre association of his benefactor with the Commandant who led Don Juan to his death was, in black Pierrot style, a piece of pathetic clairvoyance. Still, he had another year to live, and Fénéon recruited him to write a regular "Chronique parisienne" in Dujardin's new review.

Not least of Fénéon's duties was lining up prospective contributors, and Dujardin wanted most of them to be recognizable names. He wrote peremptorily in June 1886: "Do not forget the requests for contributions in your charge, Félix Fénéon," and reminded him to secure, among others, Verlaine, Moréas, and Zola. "*Most important is Zola*: if you have not written him, write him, Félix Fénéon."[11] Zola had led off Fénéon's *Revue indépendante* in 1884. Now he answered Fénéon again in the affirmative; but no article of his appeared in the Dujardin series. Paul Bourget, however, lent his support. He had been asked for a poem to enter in the first issue, but Fénéon reported to Dujardin a few days before the deadline:

> Noble friend,
>
> M. Bourget writes me: "This October is really too soon. I could not give you anything that would be worthy of the *Revue*. . . . Put my short story in now and reserve a dozen pages in the second issue [for a poem]. . . it will be better Bourget."

Fénéon advised, "Wouldn't it be best to appeal immediately to Laforgue, finally settled in Paris this week?"[12] So Laforgue's poem, "Sur une défunte" (For a Dead Woman) appeared in November 1886, the first issue of the *Revue indépendante*.

It had taken the better part of a year to get the new *Indépendante* under sail—more than the whole life span of *Vogue*, which began in mid-April and expired on December 27, 1886, dead but not forgotten. Forty years later, Fénéon recalled with humor how a bit of its mystique continued to exist in the language of some peasants in the south of France. A friend of his, "jovial Dr. Ferroul," socialist mayor of Narbonne, managed to get subscriptions from many of his patients and political supporters in that town. "So *Vogue* had a double public: a small number of elitist readers scattered throughout Europe, and bizarrely, in a corner of Languedoc, a dense conscription of vintners and coopers who could not understand a word of it." Leading off the June 13 issue had been an erotic sonnet by Mallarmé, the one beginning "M'introduire dans ton histoire" (To get myself into your tale), and ending "Du seul vespéral de mes chars" (Of the only twilight cart I own).* Now the good people of Narbonne were considerably intrigued by this poem:

> That evening, the café was humming with talk of it. The last line was straight away etched in their memory. Thereafter, when something unusual happened, they never said, "C'est épatant" (It's terrific), but "C'est très vespéral de mes chars" (It's very twilight of my carts). *Vogue* ceased to exist. The origin of the saying was lost in the fogs of time. And still the saying lived on, condensed in a group of ritual syllables; and even today, when they hear of something astounding, peasants, dockers, and

*The word *char* in this poem is usually translated "chariot"—that is, chariot of the sun, as inferred from the "dying red wheel" in the preceding line. I used "cart" since that is the way the peasants of Narbonne probably understood it (*char à foin; char de vendange*). The first line is translated with a double-entendre not up to the calibre of Mallarmé, but which catches enough of the flavor of the original to suggest why the café in Narbonne was "humming with talk."

N° 8. — *Du 13 au 20 Juin 1886*

LA VOGUE

SONNET

M'introduire dans ton histoire
C'est en héros effarouché
S'il a du talon nu touché
Quelque gazon de territoire

A des glaciers attentatoire
Je ne sais le naïf péché
Que tu n'auras pas empêché
De rire très haut sa victoire

Dis si je ne suis pas joyeux
Tonnerre et rubis aux moyeux
De voir en l'air que ce feu troue

Avec des royaumes épars
Comme mourir pourpre la roue
Du seul vespéral de mes chars

STÉPHANE MALLARMÉ

STÉPHANE MALLARMÉ. ***"M'introduire dans ton histoire,"*** published in *La Vogue,* 13 June 1886. *If Mallarmé only knew that . . . a new word, foreign to the language . . . had actually been achieved in his honor by common folk*! (F, 484)

> sailors of Cuxac, Ginestas, Capendu, Marcorignan, Capestang or La Nouvelle slap their thighs and bellow, "Spéraldeméchar!"

"Thus, concluded Fénéon, "was *refabricated out of several old words a total, new word, foreign to the language and as it were incantatory* . . . If Mallarmé only knew that this phenomenon which he defined so well had actually been achieved in his honor by common folk!"[13]

Unlike *Vogue,* Dujardin's "independent" review steered a relatively conservative course and announced that it would be "as independent from vain decadent agitations as from academic traditions." Camille Pissarro reacted immediately and wrote to his son Lucien concerning Dujardin, "The publisher, as pusillanimous as ever, tries to conciliate the hare and the hounds.—A colorless review."[14] In fact, trying to achieve "class," Dujardin wanted to avoid the "extreme avant-gardism" of *Vogue.* He also wanted to placate the burghers who financed his venture and so aimed for a digestible mixture of writers on the verge of recognition: Mallarmé, Huysmans, Anatole France, and Théodore de Banville appeared alongside young writers. For its founding patrons the review published luxury editions illustrated by Whistler, Renoir, J.-F. Raffaëlli, Helleu, Redon, and Albert Besnard (of whom Degas said, "he flies with our wings").

After two issues the masthead no longer designated Félix Fénéon as Editor-in-Chief. When a financial backer asked why the critic was no longer with the review, Dujardin explained: "He was pushing towards decadence."[15] Gustave Kahn gave a similar account, but from a different viewpoint: "Weary of not being able to introduce young writers to this review, which appeared reactionary in its first issues and spoke, in the style of big newspapers, of 'vain decadent agitations,' Fénéon left."[16] There was no ill feeling on the part of Fénéon, as can be seen in his letter of resignation to Dujardin-Wyzewa, written in a hasty hand at midnight, December 16, 1886:

> My good friends,
>
> Here is the address requested by Dujardin, M. Ch. Cabrillac: Ambert (Puy-de-Dome).
>
> Kindly, then, do not put my name on page 3 of volume II of the *Revue Indépendante* and on page 2 of the cover. That is to say, I pray you accept my resignation. But once I am no longer editor in chief of this review, let me have the honor of contributing to it (should I ever write some fine story) and be a regular visitor.
>
> I cannot go tonight to Asnières, which I regret; but tomorrow I shall go help you correct proofs.[17]

Fénéon continued to work invisibly for the review, correcting proof, but declined to publish in it, as can be seen in this letter dated 10 August 1887.

> My dear Dujardin,
>
> Such graciousness is yours: you ask me when I shall send you some work of mine.—Never,—too unworthy to collaborate in such a noble review. I shall offer you better: I present M. Armand Charpentier to you—and you will thank me for this swap![18]

Charpentier was a lightweight naturalist writer, and although Fénéon might have sincerely wanted to help him, he probably did not consider him a true "independent." Fénéon remained faithful, however, to Dujardin, reading each of his new books with interest. Half a century later, he responded with candor to a young scholar's inquiry about Dujardin's role in the symbolist movement:

> Dear Sir, since nothing marked him out for a career as writer or dandy, the naive heroism with which he threw himself into these forbidden paths, the way he persevered (and finally succeeded) makes Dujardin the most photogenic figure in symbolism.[19]

FÉLIX VALLOTTON. ***Portraits*** in Remy de Gourmont, *IIe Livre des Masques,* Paris, 1898. Woodcuts. *Left,* ***Félix Fénéon.*** *Right,* ***Edouard Dujardin.***

Fénéon was sympathetic to the problems of Dujardin as director of a financially solvent review. He himself had never taken on this responsibility, with good reason. He once gave the "life-cycle" of such a director:

> Before launching a review, the director is quite determined to disturb the peace of the contemporary scene of Letters, never to compromise with the public, and to allow his contributors the most anarchic liberty, even to stimulate their daring, and to conquer his subscribers through sheer terror. He has a healthy complexion and moves with energy. But as soon as his first issue has gone to press, he is another man. Fear and trepidation assail him; at the sight of an unusual epithet, he sees a subscription fade away; the only ideas that can circulate around him are those that have been duly licensed; he loses his color and becomes anxious. Among his financial cares, his concern for the subscriber and the ironic sympathy of his contributors, he moves in a ghostly fashion—and he would die himself if his review did not hasten to do so first.[20]

The briefest of all these ephemeral reviews was created in the fall of 1886 by Gustave Kahn, Moréas, Laforgue, and Paul Adam—the *Symboliste,* a weekly priced at 2 sous "to be accessible to small pocketbooks." It lasted four weeks (7–30 October). The first issue contained Fénéon's analysis of Rimbaud's *Illuminations,* and the second a droll report of a visit he made to the Musée du Luxembourg, Paris's current museum of "modern art," where he looked in vain for works of Degas, Camille Pissarro, Manet, Puvis de Chavannes, and found just one Gustave Moreau, dating from 1865. So he concluded:

> We would applaud a fire cleansing the Luxembourgian stables except for the fact that they are accumulating a collection of documents indispensable for future monographs on the stupidity of the XIX century.[21]

This remark has been seen as an anarchist's incitement to terrorism; in fact, it is a variant of one made some twenty years earlier by the critic Duranty, defending the impressionists. The *Symboliste* announced a third article by Fénéon on circuses, and many more glories to come, but the review "hastened to die," leaving, one supposes, its director in good health.

In January 1888 Edouard Dujardin, weary of managing everything at the *Indépendante,* asked Gustave Kahn to become editor in chief. Fénéon became once again a visible member of the staff and wrote a monthly "Calendar" of events: art, books, and theatre. These pages are among the best of his criticism and form a poetic index to the life of the times. He also continued his anonymous editorial work, helping Jean Ajalbert who was officially in charge of proof. While Dujardin continued to handle the budget and was the nominal director, the review became markedly more modern. The luxury edition, for example, contained prints by the neo-impressionists Signac, Maximilien Luce, Camille and Lucien Pissarro. Fénéon took his work at the review most seriously, especially his regular column. Concerning his first "Calendar," he wrote Dujardin:

> Here are the proofs which I received this morning. I earnestly beseech you, entreat you, to have all my corrections made. They were not done for the pleasure of putting ink on paper. They deal especially with repetitions of words; with unbalanced, discreditable sentences.
>
> The changes at the beginning of the Circus paragraph are as necessary as all the others. The end of the text about Mr. C. Pissarro's engravings was not sent to me. I have written a new text: this is the one to be printed; the other contains *errors.*
>
> Make sure there are not any interpolations in my reports on exhibitions. There were some in the proofs.
>
> Really don't make me suffer these delays. The other contributors received their proofs yesterday, I this morning.[22]

Fénéon's "Calendar" ran seventeen pages—so much for "celui qui silence." He reported on anything that took his fancy, not just organized exhibitions, but paintings seen "in merchants' windows" (Gauguin at Theo van Gogh's shop) and "in the street" (posters by Chéret). He gave up some of his social life to devour countless books and write—always with difficulty, he said—serious or comic reviews of them. He was conscientious about attending even minor exhibitions of his friends. Prevented from entering an exhibit of Willette's illustrations, he wrote this note on his calling card and sent it to the organizer of the show:

> FELIX FENEON
>
> was denied entrance to the Willette exhibition on the pretext that the groom of the turnstile did not have change for a louis; nor was he able to enter upon simply presenting his calling card. He nevertheless must give the Review an article on Mr. W. this evening.[23]

This ploy must have been successful, since his report was published in the next issue.

Dujardin had supplemented his review by creating a bookstore in a little shop he bought at 11 Chaussée d'Antin near the Vaudeville. Fénéon named the bookstore

"Librairie de l'Art Indépendante" and set up a series of exhibitions there of the impressionists and their successors. Here Armand Guillaumin and Maximilien Luce had their first one-man shows. The paintings of Pissarro, Seurat, Signac, Angrand, Besnard, Morisot, Rafaëlli, Anquetin, and van Gogh, and sculptures by Rodin and Henry Cros were displayed in a monthly rotating exhibition. Manet's unknown sketches, pastels, etchings, and watercolors were shown. It is difficult to imagine how Fénéon, in his spare time, could organize such a series in less than a year; simply convincing Luce to exhibit was a major undertaking. But he did it as naturally as he brought the works of Seurat and Signac to the foyer of Antoine's Théâtre Libre.

The bookstore became the regular office of the review, and Paul Alexis, writing in slang under the pseudonym, "Trublot," described a visit there in April 1888. Between five and seven o'clock in the afternoon, he said, one could see "the white beard of Pissarro, the silence of Seurat, and the gently sloping profile of Paul Adam." Jacques-Emile Blanche introduced a note of fashionable brilliance, countered by the exuberant Signac. Antoine appeared, followed by Luce and a bevy of writers. The perplexing inventor, Charles Henry, stopped by to see if Fénéon had finished editing his articles. At last Fénéon himself appeared:

> Looks around as coolly as a diplomat, and tells a story that would have made the Baron d'Ange blush; remarks in a soft, celestial sing-song voice how "tiresome it is to deal with scribblings."[24]

Alexis ended his report with a prediction that the *Indépendante* would be called to "high destinies." But 1888 marked its apogee. It went bankrupt early in 1889. Fénéon helped in a last-ditch attempt to muster new subscribers, reporting back to Dujardin on December 12, 1888:

> Yesterday, around 3:30, I was at Le Havre. And the little count from whom I wanted two hundred [francs] gave me one hundred. He knew all about your projects. He did not seem in the least disposed to become a shareholder, fearing he would have to furnish a few thousand francs every year.[25]

Wise little count. A small publisher, Albert Savine, bought the review; it soon turned royalist and "declined, disappeared . . ." as F. F. put it.

These were lean times for Fénéon, and although he did not expect to be paid for his editorial work on the *Indépendante,* he, like Mallarmé and other contributors, had often badgered Dujardin for the regular fee (50 francs) due him for the articles he wrote. Some time in 1887 he and his parents were obliged to move from the pleasant little apartment on rue Vaneau. At first Félix had to accept the hospitality of his friend Victor Barrucand, who set up partitions in his room near Montmartre cemetery. Félix and his parents spent more than a year looking for new lodgings, moving from spot to spot, possibly running from creditors. His income as clerk in the War Office was obviously not sufficient to support his family and others in need whom he chose to help, as well as indulge his own tastes as a dandy and amateur of art. He asked Charles Henry to help him find an editing job for which he might be paid, and Henry wrote to the vice-chancellor of the university and other public officials, to no avail. Fénéon beseeched

Dujardin again for money that was due him: "I am being dangerously persecuted by several process servers and am quite worried for various reasons."[26] But at last he was able to settle his family in a working class quarter, at 85 rue Lecourbe, where they stayed five years until they moved to Montmartre, 72 rue Lepic, which was then an outlying district undergoing urban development. Whatever the reasons for Fénéon's financial problems, he did not reveal any details. Apologizing to Dujardin for not having sent him some requested back copies of symbolist reviews, Fénéon said laconically: "I have had several moves which have slowed everything up."[27]

Jules Laforgue died just as Fénéon entered this difficult period. After returning to Paris with his English bride, Leah Lee, Laforgue had no earnings except what his writing brought in—small sums from the *Revue indépendante* and other journalistic commissions. He had contracted tuberculosis, and soon not only his failing health but the opium pills prescribed to calm coughing prevented him from working. Too late, his friends tried to arrange for him to move to the climate of Algiers. He died in August 1887, just four days after his twenty-seventh birthday. Fénéon described the meagerly attended funeral:

> At Bagneux cemetery . . . no more than nine persons, besides two or three women, accompanied him. For future biographers, they were: MM. Georges Seurat, Jean Moréas, Gustave Kahn, Paul Adam, Emile Laforgue, Paul Bourget, Ysaÿe, and two strangers.[28]

The names of these mourners, the critic knew, would also have their place in history, and they were a fitting tribute to the dead poet. Seurat had come at Fénéon's invitation, for he, too, admired how Laforgue assimilated the most advanced scientific and philosophic ideas and tempered his spirit with hard work and explorations in technique. Laforgue's word-pictures, transposing the language of ordinary people into a poetic schema, bore some analogy to his own work. Fénéon was the strangely split, hidden identity behind the "two strangers." He considered his own name, like those of the women, of little interest to posterity. Ysaÿe was a gifted pianist Laforgue had met in Berlin; Emile Laforgue was the poet's elder brother. To "future biographers" it seems odd that Fénéon passed over the presence of the young widow; but it was not his manner to dwell on the pathos of the scene, to mention, as did other witnesses, the hysterical laughter coming from Leah Laforgue's cab when a carpenter fashioning a plain wooden marker asked if that was "his customer" arriving.

As he would do less than four years later at the sudden death of Seurat, Fénéon simply published a list of the man's works for an obituary.[29] He afterwards characterized Laforgue's poetry as centering around the refrain:

> To love and to be loved. That woman should be at last man's brother and not a being apart, a midge with a chignon: this overwhelming desire, expressed by turns in desperate or impertinent tones, flows throughout a work that is uniquely beautiful due to the sacred, virgin variety found in a single human being. And the death that interrupted this heroic, provocative work was not premature, but rather longanimous: for Jules Laforgue, when he died (after six months' marriage with frail Miss Lee) at age twenty-seven, 20 August 1887, had written the *Complaintes, l'Imitation de Notre-*

> *Dame la Lune, le Concile féerique, Moralités légendaires, Des Fleurs de bonne volonté,* and some last poems free of all prosodic fetters and supremely autumnal.[30]

By concentrating on Laforgue's accomplishments, Fénéon negated the general assumption that the poet's work was unfinished. With Edouard Dujardin, he set about publishing those last poems in an unparalleled edition, *Derniers Vers,* which they planned to have privately printed. Dujardin took care of the finances, obtaining subscriptions among writers, artists, and one or two interested booksellers, while Fénéon did the actual editing, carefully recording all the variants he found in the original manuscripts. As he had with Rimbaud's *Illuminations,* Fénéon established the order of the poems, this time, however, according to some indications left by the author, and scrupulously respectful of the text. Better than editorial comment, he thought, was to offer the reader every available aspect of the poet's creation. He insisted that it was important to indicate even the size of the original papers, as he explained to Dujardin:

> I see you are opposed to giving the measurements of the 4 series of mss. I believe that these indications must be given, in case other manuscripts are discovered in the future. Consult Dr. Bertillon on the subject. And from a literary point of view, an editorial note in concert with vague abstraction is quite excellent.[31]

The elegant, cream-colored book finally appeared in November 1890, just fifty-seven copies, reserved for subscribers. Fénéon had asked Dujardin for "six copies at least. . . . Truly, not less than Six. Less would make me sad instead of happy."[32] He received five, in fact, and gave all but one to other friends of the poet. The edition was much admired by the "happy few." Emile Verhaeren said in his review of it, "We recognize the precise, meticulous hand of Fénéon in this admiring and scrupulous work of fraternal homage."[33]

Except for one study, which he wrote right after the poet's death, and a briefer one for an anthology called "Portraits of the Next Century," Fénéon did not write about Laforgue. It was a question, simply, of keeping the poet's work before the public (the elite symbolist public) and letting posterity judge. Along with Charles Henry, he convinced the editors of the Belgian review, *L'Art moderne,* to publish some interesting extracts of Laforgue's letters to Henry. Fénéon planned to do a little edition of them, "with a violet cover," as he wrote to Octave Maus, quoting Laforgue who said his "local color" was the violet of deep mourning.[34] But in 1887–88 the readers of *L'Art moderne* were hardly acquainted with Laforgue's poetry and took little interest in his letters, so the project was discontinued.

Laforgue's unpublished manuscripts were dispersed among several friends after his widow died, also of tuberculosis, in June 1888. For the next decade Fénéon continued to print as many of Laforgue's papers as came his way, publishing them in the various reviews on which he worked—*Cravache, Entretiens politiques et littéraires, Revue anarchiste,* and *Revue blanche.* While he sometimes made omissions to protect the identities of persons or to suit a certain audience, whenever possible he presented the manuscripts just as they were, with words scratched out or added in the margin, upside-down, sideways, however they appeared. His only comment, typically, was a factual description of the manuscripts themselves. For example, concerning a packet of papers found in a blue envelope with the title written in carmine-colored ink:

> BAUDELAIRE—ETC—
> CORBIERE—ETC—
>
> Thirty-two unpaginated leaves. The notes on Baudelaire make up nineteen, which we have arranged in a more or less arbitrary order. Leaf 1: black ink on blue glossy laid paper (127 mm. × 203 mm.). Leaves 2 and 3: lead pencil on pale yellow paper (108 × 170). Leaves 4, 5, and 6: black ink on white paper (155 × 200). From 7 to 12: same paper, lead pencil. From 13 to 19: lead pencil on pale yellow paper (141 × 225). On leaf 8: pencil drawing of a young man's head. On leaf 12: a figure reading.[35]

What seems a mania for precision was an aesthetic delight in the physical properties of the manuscripts. And, as his letter to Dujardin shows, Fénéon thought it was important to identify the papers he was editing in case similar papers were found in the future.

It was a matter of pride with him to remain totally anonymous: the editor, he thought, should not interfere with the reader's appreciation of Laforgue. But the director of *Entretiens* counteracted Fénéon's self-effacement by announcing:

> To those individuals who are interested in this publication . . . M. Félix Fénéon is effortlessly deciphering illegible manuscripts of Jules Laforgue transmitted to him by Mr. T. de Wyzewa.[36]

It was not entirely "effortless" for Fénéon. He contacted editors of several reviews in order to establish an accurate bibliography, and he wrote many letters to people in Berlin and elsewhere for information that would elucidate various passages in Laforgue's correspondence.

Even Laforgue's physical remains were entrusted to his care: he must have paid for the lease on the burial plot, since the keeper of Bagneux Cemetery wrote him in January 1891:

> The five-year lease issued in August 1887 for the interment of the body of Mr. Félix [*sic*] Laforgue, will terminate in the month of January 1893.
>
> There is a wooden marker on this tomb, which is not kept up.[37]

F. F. penciled out the name "Félix" and wrote "Jules" in the margin. Then he set about finding a more permanent residence for Jules's bones. He spoke to the directors of *Entretiens politiques et littéraires* and the *Mercure de France,* who asked their subscribers to make donations for a perpetual lease and a tombstone for Jules Laforgue. This was accomplished before the day when his remains were due to be tossed into the common ossuary at Bagneux, and the City of Paris granted him a "grave in perpetuity." It was all done without fanfare. As Laforgue had said:

> *Les morts,*
> *c'est discret;*
> *Ça dort*
> *Bien au frais.*[38]
>
> (The dead are discreet; they sleep just as well out in the cold.)

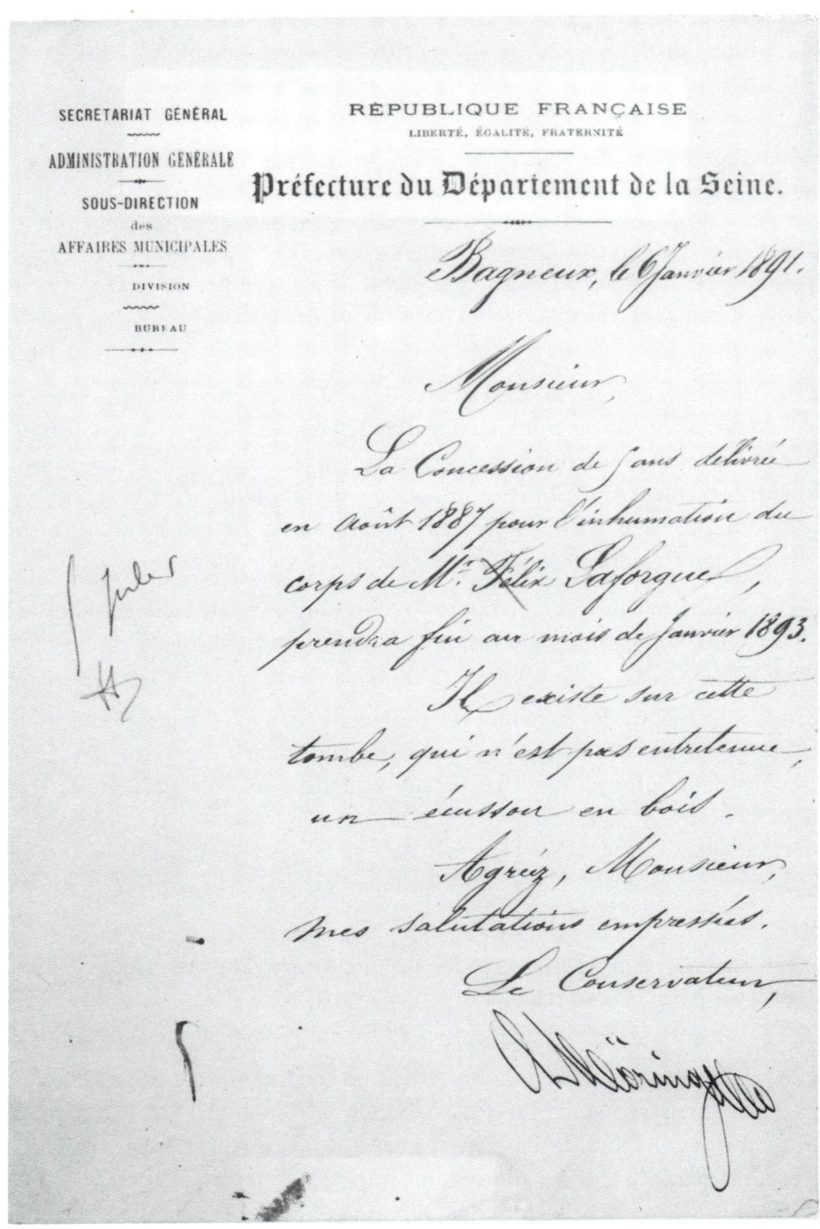

SECRETARIAT GÉNÉRAL

ADMINISTRATION GÉNÉRALE

SOUS-DIRECTION des AFFAIRES MUNICIPALES

DIVISION

BUREAU

RÉPUBLIQUE FRANÇAISE

LIBERTÉ, ÉGALITÉ, FRATERNITÉ

Préfecture du Département de la Seine.

Bagneux, le 6 Janvier 1891.

Monsieur,

La Concession de 5 ans délivrée en Août 1887 pour l'inhumation du corps de Mr. ~~Félix~~ [Jules] Laforgue, prendra fin au mois de Janvier 1893.

Il existe sur cette tombe, qui n'est pas entretenue, un écusson en bois.

Agréez, Monsieur, mes salutations empressées.

Le Conservateur,

Letter from the Keeper of Bagneux Cemetery to F. Fénéon, 6 January 1891, regarding the lease for Jules Laforgue's grave. Paris, Paulhan archives.

Of the young symbolists, Laforgue had the most influence on poets of the twentieth century, but most people who make the pilgrimage to see the fine granite stone that marks his place at Bagneux are unaware that it exists through the common effort of his friends who knew "he was the best among us."

A few years later, the *Mercure de France* decided to publish a multivolume edition of the "Complete Works" of Laforgue, and Fénéon was invited to bring what material he had to a dinner at Vielé-Griffin's, along with Dujardin, Emile Laforgue, and several young writers who had known the poet very little, if at all. One of the latter, Camille Mauclair, the *Mercure's* influential critic, took on the task of editing Laforgue, and Fénéon bowed out of the circle; Mauclair, he later explained to a friend, was an "old numbskull."[39] A very incomplete *Oeuvres complètes* was produced from the papers left with Mauclair, who decided to abandon the project after three undistinguished volumes. In 1922, Fénéon was director of a small publishing house, La Sirène, and engaged the scholar G. Jean-Aubry to edit the book Laforgue had tried to publish in 1887, *Berlin, la cour et la ville,* which appeared in accordance with the high standards of F. F. The following year Jean-Aubry undertook to publish Laforgue's correspondence, which he annotated with the help of Fénéon and Camille Platteel. As for Laforgue's poetry, it was not until late in the twentieth century that Pascal Pia decided it was "necessary to follow the example given us in the remarkable edition established in 1890 by Félix Fénéon of the *Derniers Vers*" and produced *Poésies complètes,* with variants and many unpublished pieces—a tribute to Fénéon's "indirect work."[40]

In the spring after Laforgue's death, life continued to "move on, losing only twenty-four hours each day," as the poet had said. Fénéon helped Georges Lecomte make a symbolist review out of a satirical weekly, *La Cravache parisienne* (Parisian Riding Whip), that had enjoyed good sales because it included the stock market reports. Lecomte talked the owner, a modest printer in the Cour des Miracles, into letting him edit all but the market news and devote the other pages to contemporary literature. "You can't object to having your newspaper well written rather than badly. You won't gain anything, but you won't lose anything either, so put me in charge."[41]

Fénéon sent in a regular "Chronique d'art," reporting on the impressionists and other artists, but not the group of Seurat, which he reserved for his series in *L'Art moderne.* He published his most extensive reviews of Charles Henry's work in *Cravache,* including the poster Paul Signac painted to illustrate Henry's chromatic circle. He signed his description of the poster with the name, "Thérèse," and when Signac wrote *Cravache* to thank "unknown Thérèse for the kind review," Fénéon answered with a humorous note, signing "Thérèse = Félix Fénéon."[42] He signed other articles as Gil de Bache, the name of a pirate who figured in a seventeenth-century travelogue Henry had published.[43]

His own name appeared at the bottom of his review of Mallarmé's translations of Edgar Allan Poe, the only article he ever wrote on Mallarmé. Before attempting to analyze this work, he borrowed four volumes of Poe in English from Mallarmé and studied them carefully. His conclusion:

> Read either the original or Mallarmé's version of Poe's *Ulalume, To Helen, The Sleeper;* the sensation will be the same. (Compared to these marvels *The Raven,* doomed

> by their publication, will seem puny, suffering from a slavish and yet mystifying analysis.) The shifting currents of thought, different degrees of transparency, repetitions in form, vibrations at the end of certain stanzas—all are in M. Mallarmé. . . . [who] has captured the prismatic magic of the original verse. The only revealing marks of his presence: a certain hieratic character and the more full-toned music of his prose version.[44]

When Mallarmé read the review, he wrote his young friend:

> My dear Fénéon,
>
> If I had had my Poe prefaced, I would have wanted it done by a few precise, definitive words like yours. What a lapidary critic you are, and a friend.[45]

In spite of all the verve and inventiveness put to use at *Cravache,* the paper did not gain many adherents. "We had only one subscriber," said Adolphe Retté, "obtained by Félix Fénéon. Besides, we had totally neglected the matter of sales."[46] Nonetheless, the review survived under symbolist rule for more than a year (19 May 1888 to 6 July 1889), "until the printer grew weary of our verses and made a coup d'état, replacing Lecomte by a writer who signed Flic-Flac," recounted Gustave Kahn.[47] Nothing daunted, the staff announced that they would continue their campaign "more systematically" in a new series of *Vogue,* which was briefly resurrected (three issues, July–September 1889). Fénéon was once more its art critic, writing on the encaustic painting of the Egyptians, Claude Monet, and the fifth Indépendants. A luxury edition was planned, to be illustrated by Camille Pissarro and the young neo-impressionists, but the review disappeared before this plan was carried out.

Fénéon's indirect work also included service as an invisible partner or ghost writer for various friends. At the end of 1888, he collaborated with Fabre des Essarts in producing a book about a trial involving the former chief of police, Louis Andrieux, whom Fénéon had always admired for his independent spirit and the elegance with which he handled sordid affairs. F. F. not only helped write the book but obtained some of the documentation, asking Edouard Dujardin to furnish him a portrait of the examining magistrate, a fellow Wagner enthusiast. Fénéon told Dujardin, "We have to fill up 300 pages, which authorizes all kinds of digressions."[48] When the book appeared, with des Essarts as sole author, Fénéon reported: "Chapters full of luxurious, picturesque polemic form a mosaic on the strict documentary background of this work" (F, 804).

A series of letters, or rather, scribbled notes, from Henry Gauthier-Villars to F. F. from 1889 through 1892 reveal that Fénéon was one of the many ghost writers who served this strange *homme de lettres,* better known as Willy, who was terrified of writing. Henry G.-V. is thought of today as a rather shady character who married Colette and exploited her writing talents until she separated from him and began publishing under her own name. Fénéon knew him as a fancy-free bachelor, enthralled by all that was bawdy or beautiful, although mourning the death of a mistress in childbirth and harassed by an elder brother who expected him to work at the family's publishing house, devoted exclusively to scientific and mathematical works. Essentially a misfit, his character had a curious charm made of wit, sensuality, deceit, and candor. But he

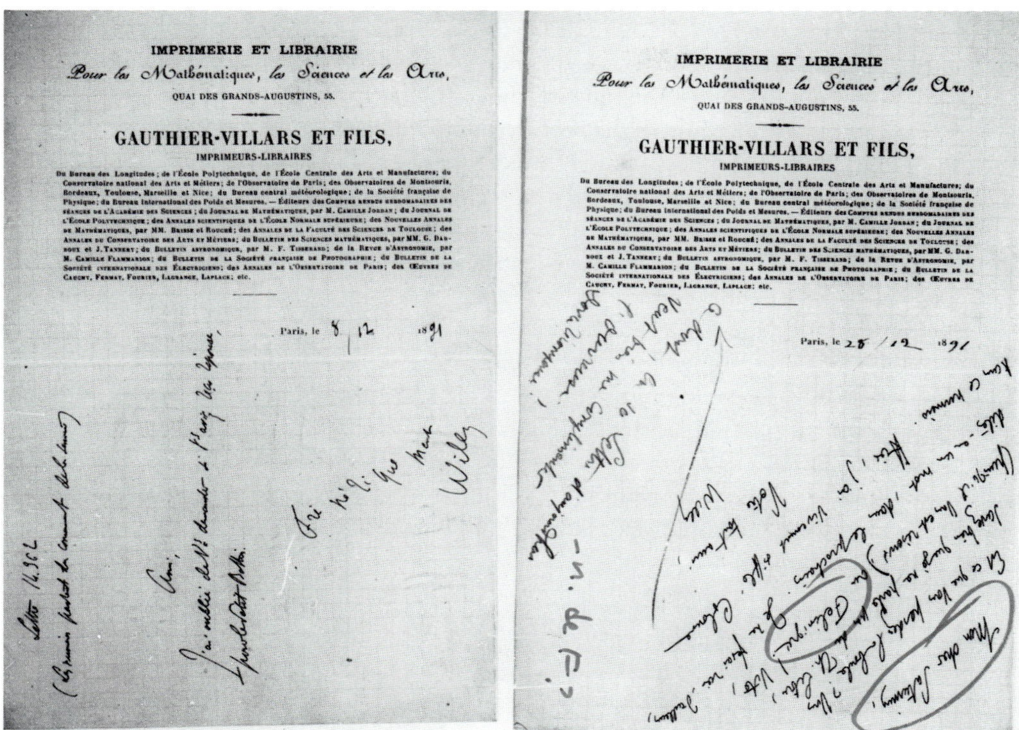

IMPRIMERIE ET LIBRAIRIE
Pour les Mathématiques, les Sciences et les Arts,
QUAI DES GRANDS-AUGUSTINS, 55.

GAUTHIER-VILLARS ET FILS,
IMPRIMEURS-LIBRAIRES

Du Bureau des Longitudes; de l'École Polytechnique, de l'École Centrale des Arts et Manufactures; du Conservatoire national des Arts et Métiers; de l'Observatoire de Paris; des Observatoires de Montsouris, Bordeaux, Toulouse, Marseille et Nice; du Bureau central météorologique; de la Société française de Physique; du Bureau international des Poids et Mesures. — Éditeurs des Comptes rendus hebdomadaires des séances de l'Académie des Sciences; du Journal de Mathématiques, par M. Camille Jordan; du Journal de l'École Polytechnique; des Annales scientifiques de l'École Normale supérieure; des Nouvelles Annales de Mathématiques, par MM. Brisse et Rouché; des Annales de la Faculté des Sciences de Toulouse; des Annales du Conservatoire des Arts et Métiers; du Bulletin des Sciences mathématiques, par MM. G. Darboux et J. Tannery; du Bulletin astronomique, par M. F. Tisserand; de la Revue d'Astronomie, par M. Camille Flammarion; du Bulletin de la Société française de Photographie; du Bulletin de la Société internationale des Électriciens; des Annales de l'Observatoire de Paris; des Œuvres de Cauchy, Fermat, Fourier, Lagrange, Laplace; etc.

Paris, le 8 / 12 1891

IMPRIMERIE ET LIBRAIRIE
Pour les Mathématiques, les Sciences et les Arts,
QUAI DES GRANDS-AUGUSTINS, 55.

GAUTHIER-VILLARS ET FILS,
IMPRIMEURS-LIBRAIRES

Du Bureau des Longitudes; de l'École Polytechnique, de l'École Centrale des Arts et Manufactures; du Conservatoire national des Arts et Métiers; de l'Observatoire de Paris; des Observatoires de Montsouris, Bordeaux, Toulouse, Marseille et Nice; du Bureau central météorologique; de la Société française de Physique; du Bureau international des Poids et Mesures. — Éditeurs des Comptes rendus hebdomadaires des séances de l'Académie des Sciences; du Journal de Mathématiques, par M. Camille Jordan; du Journal de l'École Polytechnique; des Annales scientifiques de l'École Normale supérieure; des Nouvelles Annales de Mathématiques, par MM. Brisse et Rouché; des Annales de la Faculté des Sciences de Toulouse; des Annales du Conservatoire des Arts et Métiers; du Bulletin des Sciences mathématiques, par MM. G. Darboux et J. Tannery; du Bulletin astronomique, par M. F. Tisserand; de la Revue d'Astronomie, par M. Camille Flammarion; du Bulletin de la Société française de Photographie; du Bulletin de la Société internationale des Électriciens; des Annales de l'Observatoire de Paris; des Œuvres de Cauchy, Fermat, Fourier, Lagrange, Laplace; etc.

Paris, le 28 / 12 1891

Two messages from Henry Gauthier-Villars to Fénéon, 8 and 28 December 1891. Paris, Paulhan archives. *Friend, I forgot to ask you if you received the answer about the Petit Bottin, Frantically yours, Willy.* And (upside down): *My dear Saturnine, have you gone dotty? You know very well that I do not report on the Théâtre Libre in the Felinigre* [Chat noir] *(since it is reserved for You)! Quick, a word about it, in the next issue. . . . Totally yours, Willy.* Penciled in by Fénéon: *In her 'Letter' for today, the 'Usherette'* [Willy] *complimented* [my] *theatre review—sweet recompense!*

never tried to deceive Fénéon, because F. F. accepted him and liked him as he was. Although Willy frequently rewrote the material furnished him by his writers or had another ghost writer change the original beyond recognition, he printed Fénéon's remarks word for word, as can be seen in this note relative to a report on the Théâtre d'Art in December 1891:

> I am using your dear notes for *la Paix* (and they will appear also in *l'Avenir*). When I say I am using them! I am simply copying them.[49]

This collaboration ended with Willy's marriage in 1893. Did he fear, perhaps, that F. F. would attract his young and impressionable bride?

Fénéon's influence extended beyond his own country. He served as a link with the Aesthetic Movement in England when John Gray, an aspiring young poet, sought him out in the summer of 1890. Connected with the literary circle around Oscar Wilde, Gray was also a friend of the artists Charles Ricketts, Charles Shannon, and Aubrey

Beardsley, with whom he shared the fin-de-siècle cult of beauty. When Wilde published *The Picture of Dorian Gray* in 1891, it was widely surmised that the real-life hero of the book was John Gray. Wilde had in fact a brief affair with Gray, whom he called "my hero, Dorian," and although Gray later broke with Wilde and threatened to sue a newspaper for naming him as the prototype for *Dorian Gray,* recent biographies of him indicate that he was indeed Wilde's model for the fictional character.[50]

Gray's first visit to Paris, when he met Fénéon, preceded the Dorian controversy by three or four years. He was most anxious to become better acquainted with French symbolist poetry, which he and his friends had discovered in some copies of *Vogue* that had reached them in London. He asked at Léon Vanier's bookstore how he might contact Félix Fénéon, who received him at the War Office and invited him for a more leisurely talk and dinner at home. Fénéon also gave him introductions to all the "notables" of symbolism, and sent him to visit Verlaine in hospital. Since the young Englishman, also a civil servant, had only a few days to spend abroad, Fénéon prepared a package of books and reviews for Gray to take home. At Gray's request, Fénéon also gave him a lithograph he had done of himself—one of his self-portraits resembling Mephistopheles. Gray was very taken with F. F. and later wrote a poem, "Complaint," dedicated to him:

> Men, women, call thee so or so;
> I do not know.
> Thou hast no name
> For me, but in my heart a flame
> Burns tireless . . .[51]

While the sentiments expressed here seem to indicate that Gray felt an erotic attraction to Fénéon, there is no evidence that Fénéon shared these feelings or that their relationship developed into anything other than friendship. Indeed, Gray could keep his feelings very private. He had converted to Catholicism the previous summer, but hardly anyone was aware of this or of the depth of his convictions until he went to Rome in 1895 and began to study for the priesthood.

The contact with John Gray gave Fénéon his first opportunity to visit London. Soon after returning home, Gray wrote that Charles Ricketts insisted Fénéon come stay with him and Shannon in a charming old house that had once belonged to Whistler and where they now lived and worked. Fénéon replied that he could not come that year, but would certainly appear in 1891, and Gray enthusiastically made plans:

> We shall go find everything there is to be seen in London; we shall seek out drawings by a fellow named Siméon Solomon, a pre-Raphaelite, but also something else—somewhat like Verlaine, if what they say is true. People no longer speak of him, except in whispers, but he was one of the great artists of that School (sometimes)—we shall go to Hampton Court, all the art galleries, and see London from one end to the other. Ricketts will decorate a room for you in Whistler's old house with mystical, sweet arabesques and decadent colours, the faint glimmer of gems on a tray of jade.[52]

This letter, which reads like a pale imitation of *A rebours,* may have been just that; Gray was writing in French, in a manner, he himself admitted, that was less than adequate.

Letter from John Gray to Félix Fénéon, [Rome], 15 June 1895, interpreting a passage in Jane Austen's *Northanger Abbey* and announcing (by a drawing) that he would soon be taking holy orders. Paris, Paulhan archives.

ÉDITIONS DE LA SIRÈNE

12, Rue La Boëtie, PARIS-VIIIe — Téléphone : Élysées, 33-94

DERNIERES NOUVEAUTÉS

GASPARD de LA NUIT

Un volume in-8° tellière (12 × 18) de 229 pages, sur papier vergé des manufactures d'Inverness, entièrement tiré en bleu et noir et décoré d'une centaine de gravures et d'ornements d'après Rembrandt et Callot .. .. 20 fr.

IL A ÉTÉ TIRÉ DE CET OUVRAGE :

15 Exemplaires sur vieux papier à la forme du Japon (numérotés I à XV) .. .. .. *(Épuisés)*

200 Exemplaires sur papier vergé des manufactures de Voiron (numérotés 1 à 200). .. 40 fr.

MAX JACOB

CINÉMATOMA

1.200 Exemplaires in-16 raisin de 320 pages sur bel alfa vergé (n°s 46 à 1245) .. .. 10 fr.

45 Exemplaires sur papier de Corée (n°s 1 à 45).. .. .. 40 fr.

COMTE de LAUTRÉAMONT

LES CHANTS de MALDOROR

1.250 Exemplaires in-8° couronne de 320 pages, sur bel alfa vergé (n°s 81 à 1330) .. .. 12 fr.

30 Exemplaires sur papier vergé bleu (n°s 1331 à 3600).. .. .. 25 fr.

80 Exemplaires sur papier Van Gelder (n°s 1 à 80) .. .. 30 fr.

Brochure announcing a new edition of Lautréamont's *Chants de Maldoror.* Editions de la Sirène, 1920, where Fénéon was director.

Fénéon was nonetheless tempted by the invitation. In April 1891 Lucien Pissarro announced that Fénéon, accompanied by Georges Lecomte, would soon spend a few days in London. Although there is no record of this visit, there is no reason to believe it did not take place.

Through his contact with F. F., John Gray introduced symbolist authors to British readers, translating the French poets and placing articles on them in English journals. He sent Fénéon lithographs by Whistler and Charles Ricketts for publication in French reviews, while Fénéon furnished him with notes on symbolist works and recommended illustrations by Lucien Pissarro and other neo-impressionists.

It is quite possible that Fénéon gave John Gray the manuscript of Lautréamont's *Chants de Maldoror,* now considered lost. At the end of 1890, Fénéon produced the first generally circulated edition of this unusual masterpiece, working not only from the version privately printed by the author in 1868 but from the original manuscript.[53] Shortly thereafter, on January 2, 1891, John Gray wrote Fénéon thanking him effusively for having sent him, as a New Year's gift, the manuscript of a work "by a poet who died of hunger."[54] Perhaps F. F.'s letters to Gray (said to have been sold to a private collector sometime in the 1960s) would reveal if this mysterious gift was the manuscript Fénéon had just finished editing. Lautréamont (Isadore Ducasse) died during the siege of Paris in 1870 and, although some writers attach mystery to his death, Fénéon undoubtedly would have told Gray that starvation was the lot of many at that time who were poorer or had distant families. He may have thought that, in the

7e volume. N° 326. — 10 c. Un an : 6 fr.

LES HOMMES D'AUJOURD'HUI

DESSIN DE LUQUE

TEXTE DE PIERRE ET PAUL

Bureaux : Librairie Vanier, 19, quai Saint-Michel, à Paris

FRANCIS VIELÉ-GRIFFIN

MANUEL LUQUE. ***Caricature of Francis Vielé-Griffin.*** Cover for *Les Hommes d'aujourd'hui,* no. 326. Photograph courtesy Rev. Noël Richard.

absence of any legal or literary heir to Ducasse, the manuscript would be well placed in the hands of this scrupulous and intelligent man, Gray. But, whatever the fate of the manuscript, the *Chants de Maldoror* gained a growing readership through Fénéon's edition. He published it again in 1920, in time for the birth of the surrealist movement,[55] supplementing its only other publication, a Dutch translation.

F. F. truly had a gift for seconding extraordinary individuals and works of art that without support might have fallen by the wayside. In a different vein, he also served as second for more than one friend who had been challenged to a duel. Caze's death in 1886 had caused considerable grief and anger among the symbolists, but it did not

Above and opposite, ***Literary People and Bicyclists.*** 1890s. Photographs from the Félix Potin Collection. Courtesy Rev. Noël Richard.

HENRI ROCHEFORT

DUBOIS
CYCLISME

ALPHONSE ALLAIS
HOMME DE LETTRES

Comte DE NION
HOMME DE LETTRES

POULAIN
CYCLISME

BRUANT

ANATOLE FRANCE

GORKI
HOMME DE LETTRES

TRISTAN BERNARD
HOMME DE LETTRES

dampen their enthusiasm for duels. Although outlawed—or perhaps because it was outlawed—dueling was a fashionable thing, and only rarely ended in tragedy. Edouard Dujardin (under the name Ferréus, "Steely") took the trouble of compiling an *Annuaire du duel, 1880–1889,* numbering some two thousand encounters, not all of them between literati, although those were the most picturesque. In 1891, Fénéon stood as second for Francis Vielé-Griffin in a duel with Catulle Mendès. The latter, among other things a Parnassian poet and playwright, was noted among the symbolist generation more for his dueling than his writing, once characterized by F. F. as "needlework of flowers and feathers." Mendès felt insulted by some remark Vielé-Griffin had made concerning Huret's *Inquiry on the Evolution of Literature,* and demanded that the younger poet publish the statement, "Catulle Mendès est un honnête homme" (is a gentleman). Vielé-Griffin responded from his country retreat, where he liked to write peaceably, far from the turmoil of the Latin Quarter: "I do not know M. Mendès. I therefore cannot say if he is or is not 'a gentleman' . . . ," then waited for his seconds, Fénéon and Paul Adam, to tell him of the time and place.

On the dueling ground, in the cold morning air of September, Mendès stood with his open shirt baring his chest, sword in hand, waiting for the "en garde!" and smoking a cigar. He was no novice. Opposite him, slender Vielé-Griffin, born in Norfolk, Virginia, of French and English descent, said exquisitely, "Allow me . . ." and went to the nearby tree where his coat hung, took out his pipe, filled it and began calmly to smoke. A few seconds later the duel was over, with a serious but not fatal wound for Griffin.

Fénéon saw nothing wrong with dueling; he found it superior to the practice of warfare. In 1895, nearly ten years after Robert Caze's death, a second man of letters succumbed; Fénéon wrote:

> M. Harry Alis has been killed by the thrust of a sword. The columnists suddenly notice that a duel is a ridiculous thing. One man dead; but how many bellicose instincts . . . extinguished.[56]

The symbolists had, however, less belligerent ways of entertaining themselves. Esoteric soirées were much in favor and Fénéon, often in the company of Signac, would go by special invitation to a private presentation of an exotic dancer, a gifted guitarist, or famed hypnotist. Sometimes the unknown dancer would prove to be their favorite café muse, or the Spanish guitarist their neo-impressionist friend Dario de Regoyos, and the mesmerist "Star d'Harmandys" none other than the young novelist, Armand Charpentier. But it did not matter so much who they were in real life as how well they played their roles, and according to Fénéon's reports, he was well entertained. There was always a bit of new poetry to hear while some stranger sat strumming the zither. And the pleasure was in the hoax.

Fénéon was a catalyst for the evolving symbolist movement not only through his "indirect work" as editor and friend of fellow writers, but more specifically through his critical appraisal of contemporary prose, poetry, and drama. His role in literature as in art was to direct attention to works that revealed a new consciousness and new forms of expression, as I will show in the next chapter.

CHAPTER 9

New Consciousness and New Voices in Poetry, the Novel, and Drama

"In the field of literature, Fénéon had an absolutely extraordinary track record," better even than in art, according to André Berne-Joffroy, director of Paris's *Musée d'art moderne.* This was because he "grappled with his own likes and dislikes (not easy for anyone) and tried to reconcile his tastes with his ideas," said Berne-Joffroy, who knew Fénéon well in his later years.[1] But F. F. did not build a system of ideas and try to fit the works into that system. If there was a conflict between idea and instinctive taste, he chose to stay where his pleasure lay, and so his choices lead us on a very personal itinerary.

Fénéon came naturally to literary criticism through his work as founder and editor of little magazines. He wrote much of it in haste, reviewing as many as thirty books and several plays in a month, although a manuscript copy of his study on Kahn for *Les Hommes d'aujourd'hui* shows that he lavished as much care on it as on his articles concerning the neo-impressionists.[2]

More descriptive than analytic, his criticism reflects the individual character of a work. He let Goncourt congratulate himself (F, 646), Zola explain himself (F, 647), and the poets Rimbaud, Laforgue, Moréas, Kahn, and Vielé-Griffin express themselves (passim). His concise bibliographies were so up to date that he sometimes described a work-in-progress that never appeared in published form. Fénéon had a bias in favor of first attempts, no matter how faltering; he encouraged a poet's try at prose (F, 665), and he always favored a painter's writing. He gave acute attention to the physical aspect of a book, noting the quality, kind, and number of illustrations. Always the aesthete, he even described the kind of paper and color of the cover, if interesting. On one occasion he mocked his own style, reporting on the *Revue contemporaine:*

> Its cover is yellow; its frequency of issue, monthly; its offices, 2 rue de Tournon in Paris; volume of each of its installments, 367 cubic centimeters. (F, 652.)

He was always glad to report on a work of erotica done with style, like those printed by the Belgian publisher, Henry Kistemaeckers; and he was pleased to review anticlerical books—or books that tended to be anticlerical because of their scientific basis, such as the first medical history of the famous "Possédées de Loudun," the community of Ursuline nuns in the seventeenth century who were thought possessed of the devil (F, 638). Most anticlerical works, Fénéon thought, overshot their mark. For example, in a book called *Blasphemies,* the poet Jean Richepin had been carried away in his war on the gods; after cleaning the sky of their presence, he kept throwing huge blocks of verse into the empyrean void. "A certain amount of calm befits a negator," remarked F. F. "Logically, to blaspheme, you have to believe. One cannot insult *Nothing-at-all*" (F, 640).

Although he never codified them into a general theory, Fénéon had definite criteria for judging the work of his contemporaries. Most important, the work should be *novateur* (innovating), and his preferences went to the most original writers: Poictevin, Rimbaud, Laforgue. He certainly considered Mallarmé the greatest writer of his time, but he wrote hardly anything on him, for Mallarmé was a generation older. His task, as he saw it, was to report on the strictly contemporary or on writers who might otherwise remain unnoticed.

Novateur meant that the work presented aspects that were new, original, even unforeseen (*imprévu*). It was a pleasure for him to find a publication *féconde en surprises.* The innovating writer would naturally revitalize language to correspond to new modes of feeling and thinking, sometimes creating neologisms, more often creating new relationships between words and enriching their meaning by using them in their etymological sense. The most authentic neologist was Laforgue, who used "no archaic turns of phrase and resorted very little to etymology" but created whole new words—verbs from nouns, for example:

> Dans les soirs
> *Feu-d'artificeront* envers vous mes sens encensoirs!
>
> (In the evenings, my incenseful senses will *firework* their way to you.—*Complaint of the poor Knight-Errant.*)

Fénéon particularly liked the way Laforgue's bold but frustrated little Elsa encourages a lukewarm Lohengrin:

> Aime-moi à petit feu, inventorie-moi, massacre-moi,
> *massacrilège*-moi!
>
> (Love me inch by inch, inventory me, massacre me,
> massacrilege me!—*Lohengrin, son of Parsifal.*)

This soldering together of two words to make a third, "mingles their values and gives them a new ambiguity" (F, 584).

To satisfy Fénéon's feeling for modernity, a writer should not so much display his knowledge of philosophers then in vogue (Schopenhauer, Hartmann) as reveal an intimate acquaintance with recent developments in the plastic arts: glass sculpture by Henry Cros, a piece of pottery by Gauguin, a nude by Degas, a chair by Gallé. Most important, he should have a real understanding of current scientific discoveries about the nature of the psyche and the human nervous system. Fénéon admired Francis Poictevin's novels for using totally new concepts of the development of consciousness in the portrayal of character, concepts corroborated, he said, by contemporary clinical studies.

Newness, however, was not to be achieved at the expense of authenticity. Fénéon often attacked an author for a lack of sincerity. Even Poictevin came in for disapproval when he self-consciously began to "improve" on his personal style and when he felt he had to be modern by applying the aesthetic principles of Charles Henry to his descriptions: "One sometimes thinks," said Fénéon, "that one is reading the moral lesson in some paradoxical fable where the rays of the chromatic circle have replaced the classic weasel and dung-beetle."[3] When one takes into account the fact that Fénéon himself encouraged the dissemination of Henry's ideas among poets and painters, this criticism does not seem quite fair!

Unlike modern critics, Fénéon did not shrink from using the word "sincere" to define a work. The highest compliment he could offer a writer on his style was that it was *personnel,* that is, distinct, individual, relating directly to the author's experience. Although his reviews concentrated on the work, Fénéon commented also on the writer's personality: Jules Laforgue, "exquisite poet" is also "a charming soul." But whenever an author showed self-satisfaction or narcissism, Fénéon lost interest. "One cannot take them seriously," he said of the poets René Ghil and the "Sâr" Péladan. He chided Edmond de Goncourt for publishing new prefaces to books he and his brother had written so as to ensure their lasting reputation. Fénéon found this self-defense "inopportune. Does monsieur de Goncourt not know that of the older generation he is the only one whose influence is fervently sustained?" (F, 795). Later he quipped that de Goncourt, like the alexandrine on stage and Bismarck, did not know when to give up (F, 831).

Along with self-satisfaction, Fénéon despised *l'emphase:* bombast, turgidity, or exaggeration. Fénéon admired Léon Bloy, a fervent Catholic, for his lucid criticism of the Church, but "he uses the same cudgel with equal fury to club down a fly or a mammoth; he heaps voluminous words on top of ideas that really need air and delicate treatment."[4] In contrast, he commended Marie Krysinska for her low-key virtuosity and because her subject matter "perfectly fit the efficiency of her means of expression" (F, 853).

Fénéon's personal preference for understatement led him to mock as generous a trait as *l'enthousiasme.* The enthusiasm of one writer, he found, was "noisy. Like that of a spectator paid to clap" (F, 752). Sustained enthusiasm, particularly, bored him:

> *Belgium,* where M. Camille Lemonnier, in 764 red pages on the Rubens and the Jordaens of museums, ineffably palliative at Bruges, grandiloquent at Antwerp, tumultuous at Putte, modifies from province to province the manifestations of his permanent enthusiasm. (F, 718).

Diderot's "exuberance" marred his otherwise brilliant art criticism, according to F. F. (F, 564), since it led him to substitute his own ideas and personality for the artist's. But if exuberance and enthusiasm are not advisable, neither at the other extreme are caution and indecision. Fénéon found Diderot's contemporary, d'Alembert, hindered in his thinking by too much prudence: "His mathematics are really pusillanimous" (F, 738).

What, then, did Fénéon single out for praise? His compliments are much more numerous than his words of blame. More often than not, he presented the evidence directly. For every page of commentary on Laforgue, Moréas, Kahn, and Rimbaud, there are two or three pages of quotations, implying, "These poems stand by themselves." It was also Fénéon's laconic method to let an author condemn himself:

> Baron Ernouf: *Famous Composers.* Studies on the life and work of Beethoven, that Prometheus of music. Rossini, the prolific and inspired author, Meyerbeer—men like that should never die—Mendelssohn, that skilled, charming and prolific composer, Schumann, that powerful and original genius. (F, 756.)

The lack of quotation marks only makes the series of clichés more vacuous.

Bold, vigorous, venturesome are words that come back under Fénéon's pen when a work pleased him. And with these, *supple.* He liked Moréas's "bold, skillful and supple syntax," and Diderot's style, "supple, firm, robust, always concrete." Other complimentary terms used by Fénéon, which seem pejorative out of context, are *rêche* (harsh, rough) and *âpre* (rough to touch or tart to the taste). The critic Jules Christophe had a "harsh, new style, adhering well to the idea." Fénéon enjoyed the "pungent mirth" (*gaieté âpre*) in the first novel of a young writer. The terms of Fénéon's criticism make clear that the symbolists meant to write in a harsh or acrid manner. They wanted to awaken the sensibilities of a public used to the ready-made phrases of Baron Ernouf. A negative term in Fénéon's vocabulary is "soothing, palliative" (*lénitif*). The reader did not need to be lulled into further complacency.

He was the enemy of anything that was *lâche, cotonneux, neutre:* slipshod, woolly, neutral. The occultist strain in symbolism gave him this sense of fuzziness. Remy de Gourmont's drama, *Théodat,* was, according to Fénéon, "neither blasphemous, nor erotic, but rather, woolly" (F, 835). Fénéon favored one of his own characteristics, *précision,* and he sometimes used mathematical terms to describe it. He saw certain sentimental conflicts in Charles Vignier's poems resolved with the precision of a game of chess or a problem in algebra (F, 610). When Edouard Dujardin re-edited some of his early poems, Fénéon found that the metaphors, originally carried to a high exponent, had been "reduced to the second power" (F, 859).

Fénéon did not aspire to be a foremost literary critic and he never collected his remarks into book or essay form. He nonetheless was the primary critic of the symbolists, in a double sense: he both analyzed their work, paying tribute, especially, to an author's *first* book of poems or *first* novel as it appeared; and he wrote in their style. His contemporaries appreciated his writing as much as his critical acumen. In *L'Art symboliste* of 1889, Georges Vanor noted:

> Félix Fénéon expresses himself in a new way: his vocabulary is both rich and concrete, and his sentences have their own personal, rugged rhythms and contours.[5]

Fénéon regretted in 1891 that some warriors of symbolism were not bold enough to carry the battle on. He criticized Dujardin for renouncing the difficult verses he once wrote: "Such fine verses! Now he wants a sentimental poetry, not at all decorative, quite sincere, written in a style open to anyone of good will" (F, 859).

Symbolism for Fénéon was not an esoteric expression of spiritual insights or yearnings. Firmly rooted in the scientific materialism of his youth, F. F. knew that genius, even talent, could not be explained in purely scientific terms, but he was confident that science would eventually be able to elucidate most aspects of human experience. He responded to the neo-impressionists because their art was informed by an inquiring mind. Among the writers of his generation, he preferred those who consciously sought new forms of expression to fit new ways of experiencing life. Symbolism for him was a sensitive, methodical, and knowledgeable striving toward what a human being really is and feels in a constantly changing world.

Shortly after Victor Hugo's death in 1886, Fénéon wrote an article, "Obligatory Fetishism," denouncing his country's adulation of the famous poet. It was fashionable for the sophisticates of Fénéon's generation to vilify Victor Hugo while the general public deified him and the world considered him the personification of French literature. In response to a remark made at the Académie française that the next star discovered by a French astronomer should be called Hugo, Fénéon wrote:

> A star? a little, tiny star, invisible to the naked eye . . . ? That is derogatory to the genius of the Master. The Sun will henceforth be called Victor Hugo. "Victor Hugo is pale today."[6]

For Fénéon, the real luminaries of the nineteenth century were the "autonomous minds," Stendhal, Balzac, Baudelaire, and Flaubert. In this, most of Fénéon's literary friends would have agreed. But his criticism went further than theirs. He had little sympathy for Hugo's years of self-imposed exile during the Second Empire, living with his family, friends, and mistress in relative ease, while hundreds of other political exiles enjoyed no privileges. He disliked the poet's full-blown "rhetorical" style and objected to his reputation as the "source" of all contemporary prose and verse: "Doesn't our novel stem from Balzac, our poetry from Baudelaire?"

Most of all, F. F. blamed Hugo for his ignorance of nineteenth-century science: the transformist explanation of the universe, for example, conceived by Lamarck, Darwin, Haeckel, and Carl Vogt. Hugo, Fénéon believed, was not a thinker. The poet's exploration of the occult in his later years and his search for the mystical meaning of the universe was simply an unreasoned, irresolute mixture of anthropomorphism and pantheism. Even Hugo's humanitarianism was at best based on old-fashioned sentimentality and not in the least revolutionary. "Victor Hugo always remained outside the movement that, in this century, has carried philosophy, socialism and literature toward the exactness and precision of science." The truly modern aspect of the current time lay in its new scientific consciousness. "The Bureau of Longitudes can already announce an eclipse of Victor Hugo for 1900," concluded F. F. (F, 704–5).

It was not at all improbable, Fénéon thought, that scientific thinking should be applied to poetics. Just as Paul Valéry would do several years later, F. F. endorsed Edgar

MAXIMILIEN LUCE. ***Drawing of Gustave Kahn.*** Cover for *Les Hommes d'aujourd'hui*, no. 360. [1890]. Text by F. Fénéon. Photograph G. Roche. *He has very fine dark gold eyes, and his conversation is full of rapid, bright antics and wide-ranging ideas. In daily life, as in the contemplative one, he is a fighter, and an experimenter.* (F, 625)

Allan Poe's suggestion that the exact sciences should form a basis for a correct aesthetics, permitting accurate prediction of the psychological responses of the reader. Poe had said, Fénéon noted, that the question of poetry depended on metaphysics for one-third of its definition, and on mathematics for two-thirds. And while Poe was disheartened because he could not entirely do away with the restrictive rules of versification handed down by tradition, these questions, Fénéon wrote, had since "been thoroughly thought out by a scientific theory soon to be proclaimed" (F, 846). He was referring here to the poetic theories of Gustave Kahn as well as to Charles Henry's "scientific aesthetics."

Kahn was one of those writers who, along with Fénéon, Laforgue, and Charles Vignier, was intrigued by a new branch of science, physiological psychology, or psychophysics, as its founder, Gustav Fechner, had called it, which was rapidly widening man's knowledge of himself. Kahn's quick intelligence absorbed new findings about the human psyche and applied them to his understanding of poetry.

When Fénéon reported in 1887 on Kahn's first book of poems, *Les Palais nomades,* he emphasized the role of what we would call the unconscious and what he termed intuition or instinct:

> Poetry demands that the artist, disregarding all previous teaching, should stop at the living phenomenon that has most interested him, and work, aided by all the resources of his intuition.[7]

In explaining Kahn's poetry, Fénéon alluded to contemporary medical theory:

> Anyone who is well equipped, and who has tried out the counter-irritant power of his nerves in life's struggles, knows that we are subject to our *instincts*; whoever knows, has lived and survived, escaping civilized abysses and misleading problems—has learned to distrust the intellect and logic. [Italics added.]

Quoting medical terminology ("counter-irritant"), Fénéon signaled that he was employing the Darwinian term, "instincts," in its new meaning. According to contemporary physiologists, instincts were not simply inherited determinants of behavior, as Darwin had postulated. Rather they were understood to develop on an individual's cortex, throughout a lifetime, as a complex of association between ideas and emotions, from reactions of the nervous system to stimuli giving pain, pleasure, and so forth.[8]

Poets interested in the nature of the unconscious listened carefully to scientific debates such as the one on hypnosis between Charcot and Janet, whose arguments were fully reported in the press. The latest scientific discourse gave Kahn and Fénéon fresh reasons to trace the source of creative power, not to the poet's reasoning abilities or intellect, but to a deeper area of being, which involved memory and highly charged feelings. Moreover, those who were able to draw upon this complex of emotions and ideas had a life-giving awareness that furnished an antidote to society's notions of civilized human behavior.

> What is the intellect? What previous generations have learned and passed on, the hereditary sequences of compromises with life and its difficulties, hence laws. Official science undertakes to legitimize these laws; innovative science to reform them—but ever so slowly!

The new science, Fénéon admitted, was "extremely recent; it has not yet been able to provide a harmony of the spoken language or a micrography of its rhythm." Since the symbolists were not willing to wait, they would proceed, sure that science would catch up with them in the end:

> Now, a simple piece of common sense: it is impossible to develop new ideas with old formulas. Poetry being that part of literature which must not analyze but synthesize the human moments in a person's life—when he escapes from life and science—it must therefore acquire new formulas.

Kahn, the critic noted, worked to restructure not only the line of verse, but the whole idea of a book of poems. *Les Palais nomades,* Fénéon said, was "the first attempt to make in a very real sense not an anthology or an album, but a book governing the type of verse and legitimizing every rhythm used."

1

Prière à Monsieur Vanier de vouloir bien réserver à l'auteur de la notice deux bonnes épreuves avant la lettre du portrait de M. Kahn par M. Luce

Imprimer aussi recto que la biographie de Huysmans, n° 263.

Deux épreuves, s'il vous plaît

sans précisions

Les épreuves et demander si place manque

Kahn

[Ce poète (1) français est né, le 21 décembre 1859, à Metz.

[En 1881, après avoir publié quelques articles dans la *Revue moderne et naturaliste*, le *Tout-Paris* et l'*Hydropathe* et suivi en curieux les cours de l'École des Chartes et de l'École des Langues orientales, il ~~quitte~~ part pour l'Afrique, où il séjourne quatre ans (Djebel Dissa, Kérouan, Mahares et Gabès).

[En 1885, il est de retour à Paris, — au fort des discussions sur le symbolisme. Avoir mobilisé la césure, écrit des vers de neuf, onze, treize pieds, groupé des rimes masculines, mis quelques sonnets la tête en bas et ~~restauré~~ ressorti de vieux mots : audaces dont on s'enorgueillissait. Le nouveau-venu jugea que c'était peu et reprit, plus systématiquement, ses tentatives de 1880. Aujourd'hui la réforme

(1) Où déjà M. Verlaine.

5

une grosse étoile ★

[« Dans un phénomène moderne, dit M. Gustave Kahn, l'homme qui passe, vit et souffre est un fait d'existence ; le poète qui débarrasse son essence des vêtements et des petits détails modernes et fait parler sa voix en un poème dresse un symbole. » C'est dans ce sens que les *Palais nomades* sont un livre symboliste.

ital.

[*Les Palais nomades* (1) furent écrits en 1886. Ils révélaient un poète libre de toutes traditions, manifestant sans préambule et sans atténuations d'inédites manières de voir et de sentir, et capable de les imposer.

ital.

Le titre s'éplore au recul incessant devant notre marche incessante et nos appels des palais où vont, parmi les polyphonies et l'émoi des banderoles, s'égorger les bêtes, les fleurs fleurir et les ~~parfums~~ encens fumer. Il se fragmente ainsi : Thème et Variations, Mélopées, Intermède, Voix au Parc, Chanson de la Brève démence, Lieds, Mémorial, Finale.

Une sorte d'ouverture où quelques-uns des motifs qui s'exalteront plus tard geignent. Au court passé du héros, du personnage unique, ne se recense encore nulle débâcle et nulle ~~victoire~~ triomphe ; la passion ne l'émeut guère qu'en

(1) *Les Palais Nomades*, Paris, 1887, ~~Tresse et Stock, éditeurs~~ (un vol. in-4° ~~épuisé pour Paris~~ 3.50) chez Vanier.

Opposite and above, **FÉLIX FÉNÉON.** ***Two Pages from the Manuscript for "Kahn,"*** *Hommes d'aujourd'hui,* no. 360. [1890]. Text by F. Fénéon. Photograph courtesy André Vasseur, Paris.

The vehicle Kahn used was *vers libre,* where lines of varying length freely unfold. This was the most celebrated achievement of the symbolist movement, a conquest so decisive that several poets at once claimed priority in using it. Since the early 1600s, when Malherbe annotated and censored the exuberant poetry of the Renaissance, French verse had been codified according to specific rules. Quite deliberately in the spirit of revolt, young poets in the early 1880s, notably Jules Laforgue, Marie Krysinska, and Gustave Kahn, began to write poems that ignored these conventions. Some of Laforgue's lines had the spontaneous feeling of remarks heard in the street, "for there are virtues in the rhythms and idioms of the proletariat," said F. F.,[9] quoting lines from *Les Complaintes*:

> *Je suis-t-il malhûreux!*
> *Tu t'en vas et tu nous laisses,*
> *Tu nous laiss's et tu t'en vas. . . .**

Kahn announced that French as it was actually spoken had more varied rhythms than those allowed by prosody. Other symbolists began to experiment with the rules governing rhyme and the count of syllables, and in 1888 Vielé-Griffin declared in his anthology, *Joies,* "le vers est libre." Thus a name was given to the new kind of verse.

Vers libre became one of the banners of symbolism, but Fénéon did not use this term until some years later. He probably thought it was not distinct enough from the term applied to Verlaine's innovations, *vers libéré* (liberated line), or the older expression, *vers libres* (free verse), used to describe La Fontaine's style in the *Fables.* He first referred to the new poetry as *vers émancipé:* "The emancipated, logical verse that draws its lines from the rhythm of the idea" (F, 586). Considering the shackles from which poetry had just escaped, *vers émancipé* was not a bad description, and *logique* indicated that it was not totally free, but had its own coherence and order.

But the poets picked up the term *vers libre* as soon as it was pronounced, and began to vie for rights to paternity. Jean Moréas said that he had sent a free verse poem to *La Vogue* in 1886 but that Gustave Kahn had delayed publishing it until he had written and printed one of his own. Marie Krysinska belatedly complained she had published free verse poems in the *Chat noir* as early as 1882. Jules Laforgue was not involved, having died the summer before the quarrel began. Shortly thereafter, Fénéon pointed out that Rimbaud had envisaged the new "emancipated, logical verse" as early as 1874 and that it was finally established in 1886 "in a nearly simultaneous, triple effort by Gustave Kahn, Jean Moréas, and our man Laforgue"—all publishing in *Vogue* (F, 586). By 1891, when symbolism had reached a certain maturity and had even been consecrated by a banquet in honor of Moréas, the battle was still raging over who had been the first to write in vers libre.

Marie Krysinska was one of those who had been active since the early 1880s in the

*The street organ complaining, "Ain't I ever outta luck!" and, in the *The Complaint of Pianos Heard in Well-to-do Quarters,* words of children expressing the ennui of boarding school:

> "You're leaving us and you're going away;
> You're goin' away and you're leaving us. . . ."

decadent-symbolist movement, even in the early groups called Hydropathes and Zutistes, and she had helped Fénéon recruit writers for his *Revue indépendante* in 1884. She held a literary salon on Wednesdays and escaped criticism thrown at contemporary "bluestockings" because she maintained a traditionally feminine, submissive attitude. For example, one night at the Chat Noir cabaret she was singing softly at the piano while her fellow poets listened attentively. One of them later wrote:

> Through the cloud of cigarette smoke shimmers the pale profile, like the goddess Isis, as if painted in delicate pastels. . . . Then Verlaine growls, "Krysinska . . . is very fine . . . as for me, I don't like women!" and the Lady with the light hair suddenly, as it were, timidly, vanishes.

Fénéon once quoted some verse in her honor:

> With her beautiful green eyes like green absinth,
> With her beautiful blond hair like a glass of light beer.[10]

—which could have been written by Verlaine, devoted to beer and absinth if not to Krysinska.

When she at last found someone to publish a volume of her works (first a Polish publisher, finally one in Paris), Fénéon reported favorably on them, allowing that the author had not been catalogued among the originators of free verse because she had "exaggerated the discreetness that a feminine name recommends." In an apparent effort to neutralize this handicap, Fénéon used a masculine pronoun to refer to Krysinska throughout his review, but discussed her work in feminine terms; the poet, he wrote, "adorned himself with literature as with a flower or pieces of lace," and "develops a shimmering embroidery on a decorative theme . . ." (F, 852). Fénéon nevertheless analyzed her innovative rhythms, sound patterns, and free stanzaic forms and concluded that her most recent poems, a series evoking Eve, Mary of Nazareth, Adriadne, and Venus, showed real mastery.

Among the *vers libristes,* several Belgians also claimed priority. While Fénéon admired the Belgians for their studious efforts and said they were producing more works of art than Parisians embroiled in publicity, he decided at the end of 1891 that one name should come foremost in the history of French free verse:

> If we disregard 36 lines by the peg-legged poet Arthur Rimbaud (*Mouvement* and *Marine*), an isolated and not very conclusive trial, Laforgue was the first to write (in *La Vogue* of 16 August 1886) poems that were systematically freed of all constraint—let's mark this point in history to annoy Brussels. Since then, even more myriametric verse has been written; but his work . . . presents this unusual phenomenon: a bit of genius.[11]

Fénéon appreciated Laforgue for his independent thinking, the irony that covered the raw edges of his feelings, and the way he could convey emotion authentically by colloquial phrases. The crafted freedom of his last poems convinced Fénéon he was the most gifted poet of his time.

Vers libre, Jean Paulhan said, was the most effective weapon forged by those poets who, like Fénéon, were involved in the anarchist movement. It freed individuals and restored them to their essential task, developing their own mentality. Unlike poets of other literary traditions, English or Italian for example, where blank verse, unrhymed but restricted to syllabic meters, continued to flourish even after Whitman introduced his free-rolling verse,* the French felt they had to dethrone the classic alexandrine to make way for the new order.

In his comments on the new poetry, Fénéon liked occasionally to amuse and shock his readers. When a poet broke the time-honored rule that a feminine rhyme (ending in mute *e*) should alternate with a masculine one, Fénéon called the new rhyme groups lesbian. He spoke of rhyme itself as a clanging gong that interrupted the poem arbitrarily. He criticized some symbolist poets, including Georges Rodenbach and Henri de Régnier, for their faithfulness to the alexandrine: "Isn't the decrepitude of official poetic technique visible to them?" (F, 760).

Fénéon championed vers libre as he did the art of Seurat because, while breaking with "official technique," the artist nonetheless called on all the resources of tradition as well as his own intuition of the new. In his monograph on Jean Moréas, Fénéon pointed out that free verse had its own rigorous logic which he compared with the technique of the neo-impressionists:

> Moréas repudiates any pre-established rule for the composition of his lines, does not want to stake them out with equidistant caesuras. This apparent revolt is only a more faithful submission to the laws of logic that oblige him to calculate for each line a correlation between the position of tonic syllables, the thematic matter, and the intervals. Just like the impressionist masters, who, instead of preparing the tone of a piece on the palette in a grimy mixture of colors, find it on the canvas through the action of pure tones one on another.[12]

Fénéon wrote "impressionist"—this was in 1886, before the term *neo-impressionist* had become current—but it is clear he was thinking as much of Seurat as of Monet. More than once he alluded to the parallel between the neo-impressionists and the symbolists in their search for a valid, new technique, and he thought of both as finding their strength in the certainty of science. Gustave Kahn agreed, and even admitted that the art of Seurat inspired him to work out a similar logic for poetry.[13]

There was no contradiction in the fact that symbolism, the art of "fluidity," allusion, and subjective impressions, found a companion in one of the most controlled and scientific techniques in the history of painting. Fénéon saw Seurat's art as akin to Mallarmé's, both firmly based on the concept that only human creativity, instinct, and intellect combined, can endow life with new significance. Poet and painter were rigorous in refining the tools of their expression, Seurat restricting himself for many months to the exclusive use of black and white drawings until he worked out values he could apply in his painting, while for several years Mallarmé, a born poet, wrote only in prose, in a similar self-disciplining process.

This rigorous reordering of form corresponded to the new consciousness of the

*Whitman, translated by Jules Laforgue in *La Vogue* in 1886, was a source of inspiration to the French symbolists.

age. Fénéon said as much in 1891 to the painter Eugène Carrière, whose "lax and fluid brush" meant to evoke the "symbolic mystery" of a scene:

> A sort of ambiguous charm, uneasiness, and intimacy are thus achieved, that is, by an artificial and not very elevated method. To obtain these effects through harmonies of lines and colors would be an interesting and more arduous process; and if at times a Mallarmé wanted to create a sensation of mystery, it was with crystalline words ruled by a cohesive, sovereign syntax.[14]

The sort of writing Fénéon meant was not accessible to all, he warned. Just as for neo-impressionism, there was no easy recipe for the new poetic technique:

> Not every poet should adopt the musical arabesque called "vers libre." Unless you have a very good ear, it is dangerous to venture out on this supposedly free way of writing poetry, which nonetheless has more pitfalls than any other. In any case, we would *never* counsel a young man to start out with "vers libre" without studying beforehand all combinations of rhythm in the language.

This was in 1891, three years after he chided certain symbolists for sticking with the classic alexandrine verse. Now that vers libre was a viable form, the anarchist in him claimed freedom also for those who wished to remain within the old rules:

> The lively battle that we fought and won for liberty in versification obliges us to claim that same liberty for those who *freely* remain attached to rules when they find they can create new effects with them and an adequate translation of their thought.[15]

Vers libre, just like the optical division of color, was a critical innovation in technique, but it was not the total picture.

Among the new writers, Fénéon was looking for someone to "carry out our dreams of self-contained form, and concise, distilled poetry" (*réaliser nos rêves de forme étanche et de poésie concise et sublimée;* F, 666). This is from an early book review, dating back to 1885, shortly before Fénéon published the first of Mallarmé's hermetic poems. *Etanche* means watertight, or hermetically sealed. This does not imply that the *sense* of the poem is sealed, but that the form embodying the sense is complete in itself, forms a whole, and leaves no gaps. In his expression, *poésie . . . sublimée,* Fénéon takes the word "sublimated"—as Freud would later do*—from its history in chemistry and alchemy, and the Latin *sublimare* (to elevate), to indicate a purifying process of "distillation." I have shown in chapter 6 that Fénéon used this same word, *sublimé,* a year and a half later in his first succinct definition of the work of the neo-impressionists:

> *La réalité objective leur est simple thème à la création d'une réalité supérieure et* sublimée *où leur personnalité se transfuse.*
>
> For them objective reality is simply a theme for the creation of a higher, *sublimated* reality, suffused with their own personality.[16] [Italics added.]

Fénéon's evocative use of this word suggesting purification, subtlety, refinement, illustrates Mallarmé's will to "Give a purer sense to words on every tongue."[17]

*Freud, studying in Paris in 1885–86, was much taken with symbolist writing, according to his own account.

As a critic, Fénéon's primary concern was technical: close analysis of style, the intrinsic indicator of meaning. Although he occasionally used the word *symbole* (without defining it) or *symboliste,* he did not treat the various theories of the symbolists. He referred only fleetingly to the "theory of 'suggested ideas' familiar to poets Mallarmé, Charles Vignier, and Rossetti" (F, 557). Rather, he was more interested in the actual shape and content of the symbolists' works than in their theories. He excelled in giving condensed résumés of even the most complex plots and spiritual itineraries, and he evoked the distinctive style of each writer.

He described the *mot farouche* in Poictevin, the novelist's ability "to track down the elusive, *feral* word that, by its place in the sentence, by its own resonance and the vibration it communicates to neighboring words, even by its graphic appearance, expresses all the qualities of the object it represents."[18] Fénéon's expression, *mot farouche,* though hard to translate (shy/wild/feral word), is, in fact, a self-contained definition of "symbol." When he actually said *symbol,* he let it stand as an invitation to the reader. The philosophy behind Moréas's poems, he said, "is never presented explicitly in a dogmatic way—in symbols, yes, definitive symbols." It was up to the reader to find what they were, although Fénéon indicated the *manner* in which they were presented: "images synthesizing a whole order of sensations, a great expanse punctured here and there by an unexpected reminder of some precise, familiar fact, chosen insidiously"[19]—the sort of thing to trigger an "intuitive" response in the reader.

The graphic force of F. F.'s criticism is evident even in a one- or two-sentence review. Of a collection of poems called *The Death of Hope* he wrote:

> The rather juvenile, naive title impairs only the cover of this little book. The poems, harsh, compact, illuminated by brief copper-toned epithets, march by in slow, imperious formations and create through their symbolic action scenes of legendary, martial Greece. (F, 743)

It is typical that Fénéon scorned the pessimistic title. The fin-de-siècle sense of doom and the world-weary pose some symbolists struck were simply subterfuges, he thought, or juvenile efforts to avoid "male" responsibility and the need to work for a better world. He said he scarcely dared mention the name of Schopenhauer, which had become "the exclusive property" of a few professional pessimists, lugubrious clowns at a sideshow of the Parisian scene (F, 606).

Seeking in art not a vague groping after the otherworldly, but reality "distilled," Fénéon was able to combine an appreciation of symbolist poetry with an admiration for realism and naturalism as they continued to develop in the novel and short story during the 1880s. In this he was unlike many others. Paul Valéry, for example, was unwilling to accept the novel as a legitimate form because he saw it limited by the naturalism he had rejected in his youth. F. F. saw traits in the contemporary novel that would later be identified as elements of an "impressionist" or symbolist trend in fiction, developing out of the naturalists' close observation of human behavior.

The stark realism of Dostoyevsky had a major impact on Fénéon, who reported on the first of his novels to appear in French, *Crime and Punishment* and *The Insulted and Injured:*

> Reading these two books is to know anguish. Dostoyevsky entangles his reader in an instinctive apprehension of what is to come in pages yet unread, suspends him over the edge of precipitous pits and then suddenly pulls him back. You become a gentleman who haunts the streets at night and is going to cross an empty lot knowing full well—with an unfounded and so, ever more gripping conviction—that an ambush lies in wait. . . . At other times, you can feel the tingling of the imminent fall running through your own body. . . .
>
> His characters are not out of the ordinary. If they often take on abnormal shapes, it is because the oblique Dostoyevsky is watching them from an angle that alters their proportions: these deformations are not the result of an error in perception. (F, 568)

Dostoyevsky, he concluded, was in the "realist aesthetic by his implacable investigations and the simplicity of his plots."

Among the French realists who clustered around Zola at Médan, Fénéon most liked Paul Alexis, a jovial soul who befriended the young symbolists and shared their enthusiasm for the neo-impressionists. Fénéon did not write about Zola himself, except in his little parody rebaptizing the sun as Victor Hugo, in which, after claiming the nebula for Mallarmé and Orion for Edmond de Goncourt, he announced that the Mediterranean shore had just been torn apart by a Zola-quake—a reference to the novel *La Terre* (Earth), whose explicit sexual symbology had shocked even Zola's disciples.

Alexis was currently working on a novel about adultery, a popular subject in the nineteenth century. Under the naturalists, said F. F., adultery elicited "fewer plaintive sighs and vows in the moonlight"; now "wash basins and douches make their début into art." Alexis must have consulted F. F. while he was working on the book, for the critic wrote about it three years before it appeared, claiming that Alexis was the only naturalist who had "remained faithful to the cult of exact observation" and that this "strong discipline has allowed him to make some fascinating discoveries" (F, 694–95). But, although Fénéon admired the accurate portrayal of contemporary mores in works such as Alexis's, he objected to prurient novels parading as naturalist works. Of a book called *Entre conjoints!* (Between husband and wife!), he wrote: "These slimy stories told in the style of a police spy on the vice squad, are perhaps thought by Monsieur Gandillot [the author] to be a naturalist study" (F, 765).

Young friends of Fénéon, Oscar Méténier, Louis Desprez, and Paul Adam created a stir with new audacities in their novels, and Fénéon enthusiastically upheld their efforts to depict the commonplace and the derelict in a language inherited from both Zola and the Goncourts. Méténier's particular contribution to literature was spiced by his knowledge of underworld morality and slang. As secretary of the subprefecture of police in Paris, he enjoyed the protection of that body and served in a semi-official capacity as guide for visiting dignitaries curious to know the seedy side of Parisian nightlife. He collaborated with Fénéon in the *Petit Bottin,* where F. F. drew this portrait of him:

> Personal friend of our most fashionable assassins. Can be found with walking stick in hand and a restless eye from midnight to 2:00 A.M. at a table in the back room of bars in the Galande quarter, with diplomats, fly-by-nights, Dominicans, bluestockings, or industrialists whom he is piloting. A Chair of Slang will be installed for him at the Collège de France, as soon as a modernist minister replaces miserable old Goblet. In the meantime, before the official course begins, read *Chair,* churning with characters of all sexes and all levels of society, especially those who bamboozle the bourgeois. . . . (F, 544)

In *Chair* (Flesh), Méténier depicted pimps, cutthroats, black marketeers, eccentric old women, and policemen. Fénéon found that the realism of these tales did not resolve into the usual pessimism: "rather, however nauseous the souls and milieux under scrutiny, the sentence puckers up into an obscenity, as if it were in a jovial mood after carrying out a difficult police search" (F, 664). It is not surprising that, ten years later, Toulouse-Lautrec depicted a scene from one of Méténier's novels of the underworld and named it after the hero, "Alfred la guigne" (Bad Luck Alfred).

The bourgeois Republic was not sympathetic to such work. Louis Desprez, whom Fénéon had known since the first *Revue indépendante,* described a year in the life of a village in *Autour d'un clocher* (Around a Steeple), recounting town council meetings, gossip at the public bathhouse, the amours of the schoolmistress and the priest, and so forth. Fénéon called it one of the best books written about village life in spite of some "tiresome tics in style" (F, 639). Five months after its publication (December 1884), Desprez was indicted for outrage to public morality. At his trial, he quoted Flaubert, thus bringing to mind the famous trial concerning *Madame Bovary* nearly thirty years before. Cleverly, he took Flaubert's platitudinous characters Bouvard and Pecuchet on an imaginary promenade through all the great books, which they, blushing, condemned. Fénéon applauded this brilliant self-defense, but the judges sentenced Desprez to a year's confinement. A chronic invalid, the young man died shortly after his release from prison, whose climate was disastrous for him.

Paul Adam, a close friend of Fénéon, was sentenced to six months in prison for his first novel, *Chair molle* (Soft Flesh), about the life and excruciatingly slow death of a prostitute. Fénéon described Adam at his trial:

> Stands out from his brother writers at the Assize Court by the geometric purity of his clothes, the stiff and formal manners of a plenipotentiary minister, and his high, starched collars surmounted by the twenty-three years of an impassive face, interrupted by the mouth of a whist player. (F, 537)

In symbolist circles, Adam was admired for the nonchalance with which he bore his criminal record. F. F. twitted his friend, a "habitual criminal" who "lived off the prostitution of *Soft Flesh* until the courts intervened" (F, 537). As to *Chair molle* itself, Fénéon wrote:

> Never was a novel more impersonal: everything is told through what Lucie has seen, heard, felt. . . . Not once, in these 250 pages, does M. Adam reveal himself. The style, though nourished on rich vocabularies, is concise, as if it were wrapped in narrow bandages, but not so tightly as to make it go numb. (F, 658)

Later, Adam became a relatively popular and prolific writer, creating simultaneously two kinds of novels, one dealing in political and religious ideas, the other continuing the naturalist or "impressionist" tableaux of contemporary life. This disparity did not dampen Fénéon's enthusiasm. One of the last book reviews he wrote, in the anarchist *Endehors,* said of both series:

> These passions celebrated by M. Paul Adam in his silken, mobile, svelte and compact style—he asks no singultuous [Fénéologism: singular and tumultuous] emotion of them and would not think of treating them in illusionistic perspective: he raises them to the intellectual. (F, 861)

Paul Adam, closely attuned to the innovations of the impressionists and neo-impressionists, saw that the contemporary novel, as well as poetry, could render the "pure phenomenon" much as the painters did the "primary aspect of a visual sensation." "Psychologists," he noted, have "observed the conflict of impulses and ideas that control human behavior." Rather than continue the "pointless plots of the old novel," the new novel would analyze, as if from the inside, the "characters' sensations—down to the simplest elements"[20] These remarks, tucked away in Adam's first piece of art criticism, went generally unnoticed, but they contain the germ of ideas that historians later applied to the "impressionist" or "symbolist" novel.

While championing realism. Fénéon picked out new elements in the novel that corresponded to the symbolist aesthetic. He liked a novel by J.-H. Rosny, *Le Bilatéral* (1887), because it portrayed anarchist circles in Paris—an entirely new subject. But, said Fénéon, the author is also an artist: "his style, barbarously studded with technical words, is of a supple, iridescent, new fabric; neither M. Zola nor M. Huysmans has described the skies and streets of Paris in such suggestive pages" (F, 709). Fénéon applauded writers who focused not so much on plot as on the creation of a mood or state of mind in a central consciousness. He showed how the notion of character was evolving:

> Masters of the contemporary novel eschew full-length portraits of their characters, who must *take shape* by themselves, little by little, as they progressively enter the story; so that at the end of the novel, the secondary characters are still only vague sketches, while the primary roles stand out in full light; the work in this way acquires a kind of perspective—a certain depth, in the pictorial sense of the word. (F, 633, italics Fénéon's)

This kind of writing, like contemporary art, required the reader to participate in deciphering the sense of the work. Thus these novels embodied the symbolist notion that knowledge is relative and depends on both the receiver and the creator to establish meaning.

Fénéon complimented one author for having successfully caught "something of the incoherence of life" by last-minute revelations of unexpected incidents (F, 666). He also praised Edouard Dujardin for his novel, *Les Lauriers sont coupés,* where, "for the first time, the action is limited to the thoughts and actions of a single character during a six-hour span (6 P.M. to midnight)." Earlier attempts to record a monologue, Fénéon said, had "cheated through the use of dreams and memories to establish previous events in the character's life." Thus he highlighted what was later called stream-of-consciousness and which James Joyce acknowledged he had learned from Dujardin's novel.[21]

The most creative novelist of the 1880s in whom Fénéon was interested remained Francis Poictevin, whose writing I discussed earlier in the context of Fénéon's *Revue indépendante*. Poictevin's novels prefigured developments in twentieth-century fiction and cinema, such as the fragmentation of memory.

> Infinitesimal acts jut out; others that were once decisive sink out of sight; then blanks; childhood reminiscences obstinately stuck in the memory, recent incidents obliterated, chronological inversions; threads of events cut, people known on one side and whose other side remains obscure, individuals we have long rubbed shoulders with whose inner mechanisms elude us. . . . (F, 555)

Those novels were symbolist in the sense Mallarmé intended, the evocation of a mood bit by bit, through suggestion, or the extraction of a state of mind from a material object, by a series of decodings.[22] Fénéon called Poictevin the *musical paysagiste de l'insaisissable* (musical painter of the intangible).

> But his characters, however secret their nature, are not absent; simply, in such books—triumphant examples of the theory of "suggested ideas" familiar to the poets Mallarmé, Charles Vignier and Rossetti—the reader has to discover them, and infer from the descriptions of objects around them the psychology of these voracious contemplators, always interesting, for "in the infinitesimal part of a sensation trembles the extreme edge of our joy and pain." (F, 557)

Fénéon characterized the author himself in the *Petit Bottin*: "Paints skies, bonzes, and dream women on Japanese silk, with slender stems for brushes, then rings the gong" (F, 545). Too extreme, too elusive for the common reader, Poictevin remained a novelist best appreciated by poets, in both his and succeeding generations.[23]

New developments in the theater attracted Fénéon's attention as well during these critical years. The theater, and even better, the circus, was a place of entertainment and pleasure precisely because it was artificial, contrived, man-made, and therefore art. But up until 1887, the regular stage was dominated by the "well-made play" or the "right-thinking play" catering to the taste of the bourgeoisie; it had little to attract F. F. Then an obscure employee of the Gas Company who was enamoured of acting, André Antoine, founded the Free Theater, *Le Théâtre Libre.* The first in a series of directors to break with tradition, Antoine believed that Zola's ideas on naturalism in the theater could be carried out even though earlier attempts to dramatize realistic works had failed. Now, in the mid-1880s, when many of the symbolists shared a rising social consciousness with the proletariat, the dramatic portrayal of lower-class life seemed possible. Antoine also intended to revitalize the art of acting. He collected a group of amateur actors like himself and rehearsed in a wine cellar, training them to get into the mood of a play rather than show off their acting abilities in the declamatory style of the "legitimate" theater.

Fénéon was sympathetic to Antoine's aims and became one of the founding patrons of the Théâtre Libre, for Antoine had the foresight to secure sustaining memberships from avant-garde writers and artists. A subscription audience gave him not only financial security but, more important, freedom from official censorship. On opening night, 17 October 1887, Fénéon found himself among "three hundred patron-founders, painters, novelists, critics, impresarios, and varied women," in a small, badly decorated theater, "the most literary in Paris, or anywhere else." There was a double bill that night, two new plays of different styles: one adapted from a novel by the Goncourt brothers, *Sister Philomena,* the other a play by Mallarmé's friend, Villiers de l'Isle-Adam, *The Escape.*

Fénéon reported in detail on the first play, a psychological study in a hospital setting, about the unconscious love of a nursing nun, Philomena, for a young doctor, Barnier, and her vicious, subliminal jealousy of Romaine, a doomed patient, who had once been Barnier's mistress. Fénéon's interpretive remarks were set among numerous quotations from the text, recreating the intense feeling of the play. Since it incorporated the carefully written dialogue of the Goncourts, the stage adaptation, Fénéon concluded, was "far from the conventional brutality familiar to dramatists" and preserved the "refinement and mysterious charm of the original work."

He did not say a word about the play by Villiers de l'Isle-Adam. Perhaps he cut out early that night, as drama critics have been known to do; contrary to custom, however, he did not trump up a report. Jean Ajalbert admitted that *The Escape* was incomprehensible, "a long monologue . . . with a subject beyond the human sphere."[24] It is interesting that seven years later, when Villiers's *Axel* was produced on the stage, it became the symbolist play par excellence. But in 1887, the public and perhaps even the theater were not ready for drama devoid of conflict, of action, of characterization—devoid, it must have seemed, of drama itself.

Fénéon became a regular reporter on the Théâtre Libre, asking Octave Maus, director of the Belgian review *Art moderne,* for the assignment. He also helped Antoine turn the little theater into a picture gallery, with works by Seurat and Signac displayed in the lobby (pl. 17). He sometimes attended the rehearsals, which went on long after midnight. The amateur actors worked hard at obtaining the right "natural" effect, and when they succeeded, there was a kind of "revolutionary thrill" at having overturned old conventions.[25]

"Subject to the obvious reservation that the theater is inherently incapable of creating life," Fénéon liked the "synthesized, raw verism" in new works produced by Antoine (F, 811). He saw both the strengths and weaknesses of naturalism transported to the stage, and laughed at the more outrageous attempts to show a slice of life. Fénéon criticized the opening night performance of Antoine's third season.

> *The Butchers* by M. Fernand Icres (or Crésy) who used to be a poet with rollinatesque, richepinesque and especially cladelian aesthetics. In a butcher's shop with a real side of beef and real mutton carcasses, characters from Ariège in the Pyrenees call each

> other old pal, solemnly declare they are not scoundrels, croon some music, knife one another a bit and drink their own blood. The triumph of paroxysmal verse in an empty and paroxysmal play.[26]

It was not so much the real beef that disgusted Fénéon (although that became the central focus of subsequent critics and historians) as the lack of real poetry, or theater. The aspiring actor Lugné-Poe, who went to learn from Antoine, also commented, "The Free Theater has, in actual fact, lead in its wings."[27]

While reporting on the Théâtre Libre, F. F. also occasionally reviewed a quite different sort of theater, the shadow plays of the illustrator Henri Rivière at the Chat noir cabaret. These were pantomimes created by projecting the shadows of cutout metal figures onto a screen. Fénéon admired the technical developments Rivière made in his shadow theater, where he created the illusion of perspective and then added color. At first Rivière's shows had a literary bent, with, for example, a rendition of Flaubert's *Temptation of Saint Anthony*. Three years later, however, F. F. found that Rivière was catering to the taste of the petite bourgeoisie with his cabaret programs. "The gimmicks of the shadow theater at the Chat noir have made great progress—too much in fact":

> Twenty times in a row, lines and colors are obliterated from the screen only to reappear instantly in new images; and each tableau is further modified by partial maneuvers substituting, from one moment to the next, a Venus for a Hercules armed with his phallic club. . . . The agile and lucid artist who, in 1888, interpreted Flaubert's *Temptations*, will be recognizable, intact, when he chooses once again to let his arabesques perform their evolutions on a solid text. Why not Rimbaud's *Illuminations?* (F, 838)

Why not, indeed? Paul Fort later staged a visualization of Rimbaud's poem, "The Drunken Boat," at the Théâtre d'Art. But Rivière did not take up Fénéon's suggestion.

While programs at the Chat noir had become fatuous, it seemed to Fénéon that Antoine and the Théâtre Libre had begun taking themselves too seriously. The sometimes slender texts they dramatized were given too much importance:

> Five minutes long and funambulesque,* the *Lidoire* by M. Courteline would have been very amusing; but the actors of the Théâtre Libre thought they had to play these drunken soldiers with solemn naturalism and realistic scenery. You would have thought you were at the Meiningers.** (F, 824)

Fénéon also criticized the vulgarity of some "naturalist" plays that, in order to titillate city dwellers, pretended to portray the mores of country folk. After watching one by Marcel Prévost about a village ranged against a wayward widow, Fénéon sighed, quoting Jules Laforgue, "When will we ever show ourselves to be equivalent to the value of phenomena, and live in the right key?"

*From *funambule*, tightrope walker.

**The German troupe which sought to transform the stage into a living historical painting, scrupulously exact in each detail.

HENRI DE TOULOUSE-LAUTREC. ***Au Théâtre Libre: Antoine dans*** **L'Inquiétude.** 1893. André Antoine and Madame Saville in the play "Anxiety," by Jules Perrin and Claude Couturier. Crayon, brush, and spatter lithograph printed in black, 38 x 28 cm. Courtesy Pasquale Iannetti Art Galleries, San Francisco.

In general, however, Fénéon found the sober, intelligent interpretation of Antoine's amateur actors far superior to the "pitiful, fake manner" of professionals in other theaters. The audience of the Théâtre Libre applauded especially Antoine, who, Fénéon reported in January 1888, "neutralizing his voice even more than usual and blurring his whole person, received many bravos for his brief, bleak appearance as 'A Buyer' of chronometers" (F, 812).

These were the heroic years of Antoine's venture, and although he continued to produce plays in the naturalist tradition until 1896, his influence gradually decreased. This decline coincided with Fénéon's increasing withdrawal from literary and art criticism, and his growing activism in the anarchist movement. His last reviews, however, show that he was very sensitive to developments in new theater groups that were opposed to Antoine's naturalism.

In 1890, the poet Paul Fort, aged eighteen, founded the Théâtre d'Art, with the collaboration of the critic Camille Mauclair and the painter Edouard Vuillard. This was to be the first locus for symbolist drama, with the stage, decorated usually by Vuillard and his friends, providing a suitable framework for poetry. Paul Fort's theater, succeeded by Lugné-Poe's Oeuvre, fulfilled to a certain extent the symbolist dream of unifying all the arts.

Fénéon's last reviews for Antoine's Théâtre Libre, doubtless influenced by what he had seen on Paul Fort's stage, show his increasing attention to the total artistic effect of a production. He remarked that the interesting part of a play at the Théâtre Libre, *Un Beau Soir* (A beautiful evening) by Maurice Vaucaire, was the scenery created by Henri Rivière:

> In the distance, dominating a circular landscape, an avenue of lofty trees is ablaze in the dying sunlight. . . . But the lighting painted by M. Rivière should have been confirmed by real red-orange stage lights. M. Maurice Vaucaire's quartet shivers as it is obliged to frolic in an illogically cool late afternoon light. (F, 829)

In another play, he noticed that "the pouncing pattern of the wallpaper—bright green and gold—laps against the wall in waves, then multiplies, fills the stage, and soon it is the Sargasso Sea, where the characters drown and disappear" (F, 830). In a third play, "Princess Olsdorv's face turns pale blue in reaction to her gold costume" (F, 836)—all remarks that show his rediscovery of the laws of painting applied to the stage.

Fénéon did not become a regular reviewer for Paul Fort or Lugné-Poe; he considered his four years of reporting on the Théâtre Libre sufficient service to the drama. However, he once wrote a report on an evening at the Théâtre d'Art: in December 1891, he gave in to the demands of Henry Gauthier-Villars who, signing "Henry the Crampon," begged him to write a review that "Willy" owed to a newspaper. The assignment turned out to be the most complete symbolist production of the season, featuring works by Maeterlinck, Remy de Gourmont, and Jules Laforgue, as well as readings from old French epics and the *Song of Songs.*

Fénéon noticed at once that there were no theater attendants or administrative personnel at the Théâtre d'Art, a state of liberty much appreciated by the *compagnons* from the anarchist publications *Endehors* and *Entretiens* who had come to celebrate symbolism that night. The adaptation of Laforgue's *Concile féerique,* a poem in dialogue form, was the "most legitimate sensation" of the evening:

> The reconciliation of the two Sexes, that is the theme of the *Concile féerique.* When will Woman ever be the Brother of Man? When will they cease sullying their sweet "Stories of mucosa" with the Ideal and live by the grace of the Unconscious? (F, 835)

Not everyone was as enthusiastic as Fénéon over the scenic adaptation of Laforgue's poetry that night. The painter Ibels, who with Vuillard and Sérusier had created the costumes and scenery for the old epic poems in the program, stood up in the balcony and began shouting that Laforgue's modern verse was making his flesh creep.

Several poets, including the dedicated symbolist Saint-Pol-Roux, told Ibels to go to the devil, while the crowd began chanting, "We want a lecture! We want a lecture!" in the direction of the venerable drama critic Francisque Sarcey, who sat as if deaf and dumb in his orchestra stall. Accustomed to such things, the actors went on with the play, and suddenly all was quiet again.[28]

Remy de Gourmont's drama, *Théodat,* Fénéon thought, was pretentious, and notable more for its antipatriotism than its well-worn subject (woman tempts priest).

The third number, *Song of Songs,* carried out the symbolists' dream of union between the arts through synesthesia. Amidst scenery evoking the cedars, temples, and cypresses of Lebanon:

> Vaporizers fit to please Charles Henry, the father of the olfactometer, sprayed the house with incense and the scent of white violets, hyacinth, lilies, acacia, lily of the valley, seringa, orange blossoms and jasmin, while the music of Flamen de Labrély played on. And, under the coalition of these chromatic, auditory and fragrant forces unleashed by M. Paul Roinard, the spectator surrendered to the Word of Solomon. (F, 836)

It is surprising that no one surrendered, rather, to a fit of sneezing.

Fénéon was able to identify all the perfumes used because he had helped plan this part of the program. The year before, he served as a subject for a series of experiments Charles Henry carried out to determine the force and effect of various odors. Fénéon then asked Henry about using fragrance in the theater, and Henry at first responded:

> But you know the problem. To tackle the application of odors to theater, one has to know the rate of diffusion of essences, and that is just about impossible. But one can find out their densities in vapor form. That is the object of my experiments tomorrow; and I hope to submit the results to you soon.[29]

Because of Henry's many duties—he was no longer simply a librarian at the Sorbonne but head of a new laboratory of experimental psychology—it was several weeks before he summoned Fénéon:

> My dear Elie, I finally have something new for you. Would it please your traditional kindness to come on Saturday evening after nine o'clock and react with these instruments?[30]

As it turned out, the Théâtre d'Art could not afford to set up the scientific equipment suggested by Henry. Undaunted, Paul Fort borrowed some perfume atomizers from his wife, and two aides stood in the orchestra pit, solemnly spraying the front rows with the prescribed essences. Spectators beyond the range of the vaporizers began to sniff with all their might, and the reading ended amidst a rippling of laughter.

The "rate of diffusion" was rapid enough so as not to detract from the sobering impact of the final performance of the evening:

> *The Blind Men* by M. Maurice Maeterlinck, twelve of them, sitting in a clearing, at night, await the return of the priest who was leading them, have been waiting for hours, anxious and at last their horrified fingers find among themselves the priest, who had not left them, who was lying there, in their midst, dead. (F, 836)

Fénéon's succinct remark, purely descriptive, nevertheless shows how far Maeterlinck's conception was from conventional notions of drama, with its need for action, crisis, and characterization. His single sentence reveals that in *The Blind Men,* crisis was continuous, spiritual rather than anecdotal, an ever-present truth hanging above everyone, unnoticed. There was no room for action—for the overcoming of obstacles—in the presence of the greatest obstacle, death. The structure of Fénéon's onrunning sentence suggests the single high pitch of intensity that the actors were obliged to maintain, much as in Beckett's plays today, without the aid of dramatic episodes and emotional tirades.

Maeterlinck's plays are now recognized as the most successful symbolist drama. Fénéon, however, either out of loyalty or because he preferred Jules Laforgue's piquant form and frothy despair to Maeterlinck's more somber meditations, ranked Laforgue higher. His allegiances remained with the writers of the earlier decadent-symbolist period rather than the more spiritually inclined writers of the 1890s. For example, although Fénéon noticed the first publication of Paul Claudel, he was less than enthusiastic:

> *Tête d'or,* a drama without an author's name, with several beautiful scenes visibly (perhaps too visibly) inspired from Shakespeare and Aeschylus. We do not understand the rules of rhythm followed by the writer of this poem.[31]

It is amusing to see Fénéon, who had encouraged the use of vers libre by earlier poets, raise an eyebrow over the Claudelian *verset.* But Claudel's "rules of rhythm," inspired by the Bible and Church litany, would not have been familiar to him.

Fénéon's real relationship to the theater increasingly became that of spectator and sometime participant, rather than critic. When Edouard Dujardin's symbolist drama, *Antonia,* was scheduled to open at the Théâtre d'Application in April 1891, Fénéon helped round up partisans to outshout the more traditionally minded theatergoers. He invited Paul Signac, Georges Lecomte, and other friends to the première and attended it himself in the company of the painter Louis Anquetin. When the high-flown language of the drama failed to appeal to the masses, Fénéon drew up to his full height and shouted strident bravos, "like an Indian war-cry or the *You-ou-ou* of an Arab singer," reported Arsène Alexandre, who added, "It was much more entertaining than the play itself."[32] Fénéon did not necessarily believe *Antonia* was a great work of art—he thought Dujardin's less ambitious poems carried better—but he was delighted to play a role in a comrade's effort at creating something new. He enthusiastically attended performances of Lugné-Poe's troupe, as he had those of Paul Fort. At the height of symbolist involvement in the anarchist movement, Fénéon would take part in two plays—outside his own drama in the Trial of the Thirty—that were interpreted as expressive of anarchist ideals. And after his release from prison, he sometimes used the stage doors of the Théâtre de l'Oeuvre to escape from the police escorts that constantly tailed him.

Toward 1890 two main currents within the symbolist movement diverged, the one identifying uniquely with humanity and with its need for freedom and equality, the other immersing itself in religious or mystical ideas removed from "sordid reality." By the time Fénéon met Mallarmé, the poet had evolved from a transcendental symbolism to a purely human one, in his quest to create from the raw material of language a vision, in perfect form. But Fénéon, Kahn, and others such as Jules Laforgue (who abandoned the Catholic faith of his childhood for a highly personal view of the universe) remained outside the mystical current. Other writers entered it, for it offered refuge from the seemingly insurmountable problems of the times: a prolonged economic crisis, unemployment and bloody wildcat strikes, scandals at the highest level of government, increasing terrorist activity, class prejudices, and rising anti-Semitism. Many young painters and writers found it more salutary to turn their backs on all that and involve themselves exclusively in art. For Fénéon and his comrades, however, art was integral to the "struggle for life."

Fénéon's social consciousness was inseparable from his aesthetic and scientific awareness. It tied him radically to reality and to the needs of the community he lived in. He believed that not only the work of scientists but also that of poets and artists could carry humanity forward—a deep-seated optimism stemming from his anarchist ideology. In 1891, shortly before he threw himself wholeheartedly into the workers' agitation for social reform, he stated his faith in younger writers:

> The generation following us has shown, by what they have brought us in the past two years, that they have good, noble concerns that give promise of a future where wrongs will be redressed.

This comment concluded his negative report on a book called *Confiteor* by a theosophic writer, Gabriel Trarieux, who wrote in uninspired alexandrine verse and whom Fénéon quoted as saying:

> "For it is I, the splendor of the World and the glory of Forms!"

"*Splendor* and *glory*, yes," responded F. F. "But not the world or forms."[33]

The symbolist writers Fénéon preferred did not abstract themselves from the world, but strove to understand it and to express their insights in new, significant forms. Beyond the haphazard facts of existence, the poet could achieve a deeper, more permanent reality through a supple reordering of words that translated his own human trajectory. These new forms reached out in solidarity, requiring the viewer or reader to enter the realm of creativity by deciphering them in a participatory act.

A poem by Laforgue or Mallarmé, just like a seascape by Signac or Seurat, gave Fénéon supreme joy: contemplation and involvement in a work of art, evidence of humanity's dominion over death and its own flawed nature. For Fénéon, as later for Malraux, humankind's only knowledge of perfection, and only contact with eternity, lay in feeling and understanding the symbolism inherent in an African fetish, a poem by Valéry, a still life by Cézanne.

CHAPTER 10

Transitions 1889–1891

The Paris literary and art worlds, along with society at large, saw many changes between 1889 and 1891. Paris, with its new dance hall, the Moulin Rouge, and the erection of the Eiffel Tower for the World's Fair, was the center of attraction for a population ready for a "final fling" before the turn of the century. The creative turmoil in the arts and the gay nineties atmosphere contrasted with the severe economic stagnation that had beset France in 1883 and was to continue through 1896. The underlying fears and frustration of the populace were expressed in their adulation of the demogogue Boulanger, whose withdrawal from the public scene, after a crucial electoral victory in the spring of 1889, was followed by a further economic slump.

The financial crisis affected not only the proletariat, farmers, and small businesses, but also struggling artists and the literary reviews that championed them. In another sector, bankers and technicians enjoyed a boom through investments abroad and projects like the Panama Canal. It was a time of exhilaration—and instability. The former camaraderie and free-flowing exchanges among artists and writers turned to schisms and mistrust; old groups became polarized or splintered as they vied for attention from the few dealers and publishers that were interested in their work. Finally, deaths among the painters contributed to the disarray and changes of allegiance in the symbolist press.

The Boulangist movement began in 1886, when Clemenceau and the Radicals succeeded in placing General Georges Boulanger, a dashing, much-decorated officer, as Minister of War. They hoped he would purge the army of its traditional royalist and Catholic elements. Instead, "General Revenge," as the patriots called him, proceeded to ride the rising tide of nationalism in France. Not only the common folk, but many intellectuals were drawn to this man who rode a black charger and who, they thought, could counteract the weakness and corruption of the Third Republic and march forth to

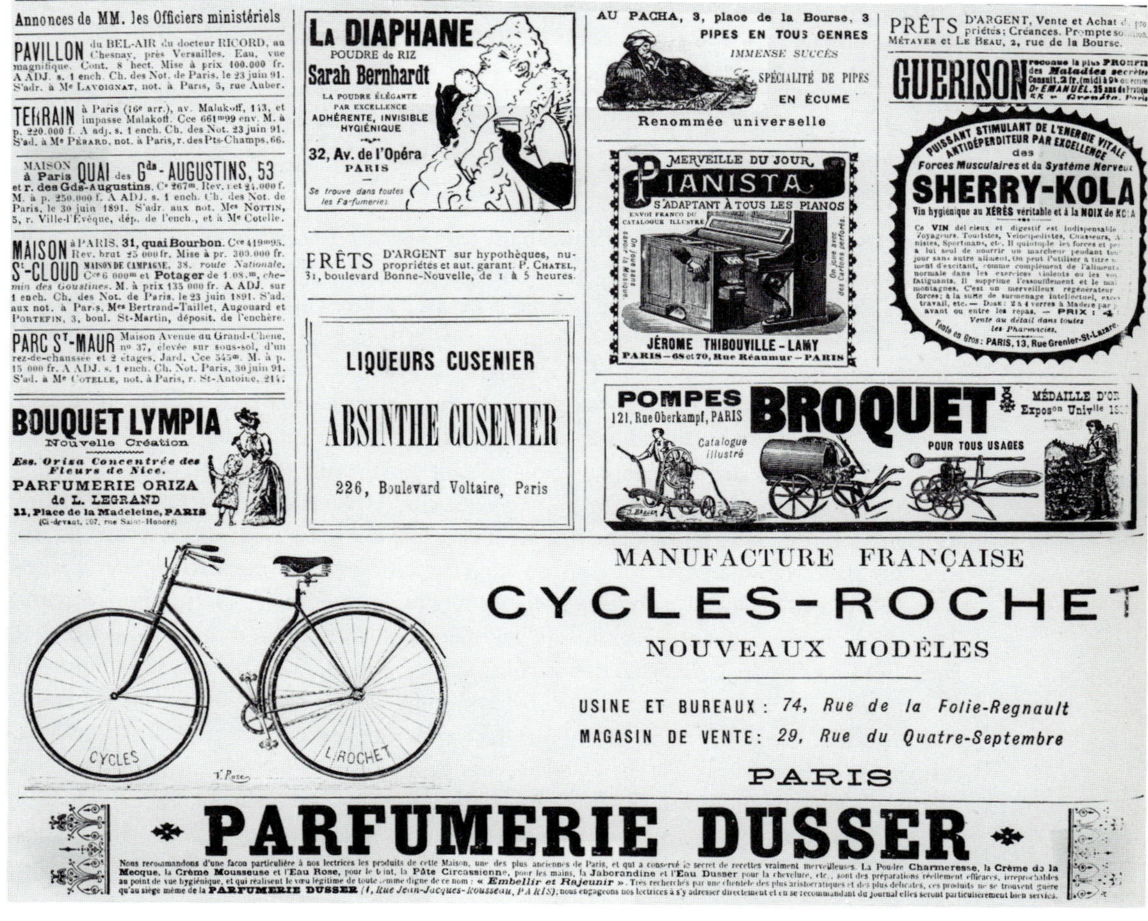

Annonces de MM. les Officiers ministériels

PAVILLON du BEL-AIR du docteur RICORD, au Chesnay, près Versailles. Eau, vue magnifique. Cont. 8 hect. Mise à prix 100.000 fr. A ADJ. s. 1 ench. Ch. des Not. de Paris, le 23 juin 91. S'adr. à Me Lavoignat, not. à Paris, 5, rue Auber.

TERRAIN à Paris (16e arr.), av. Malakoff, 143, et impasse Malakoff. Cce 661m99 env. M. à p. 220.000 f. A adj. s. 1 ench. Ch. des Not. 23 juin 91. S'ad. à Me Pérard, not. à Paris, r. des Pts-Champs, 66.

MAISON à Paris QUAI des Gds-AUGUSTINS, 53 et r. des Gds-Augustins. Ce 267m. Rev. net 24.000 f. M. à p. 250.000 f. A ADJ. s. 1 ench. Ch. des Not. de Paris, le 30 juin 1891. S'adr. aux not. Mes Nottin, 5, r. Ville-l'Évêque, dép. de l'ench., et à Me Cotelle.

MAISON à PARIS, 31, quai Bourbon. Cce 419m95. Rev. brut 25 000 fr. Mise à pr. 300.000 fr. St-CLOUD MAISON DE CAMPAGNE, 38, *route Nationale*. Cce 6 000m et Potager de 1.08.m, *chemin des Goustines*. M. à prix 135 000 fr. A ADJ. sur 1 ench. Ch. des Not. de Paris, le 23 juin 1891. S'ad. aux not. à Paris, Mes Bertrand-Taillet, Augouard et Portefin, 3, boul. St-Martin, déposit. de l'enchère.

PARC St-MAUR Maison Avenue du Grand-Chêne, no 37, élevée sur sous-sol, d'un rez-de-chaussée et 2 étages. Jard. Cce 545m. M. à p. 15 000 fr. A ADJ. s. 1 ench. Ch. Not. Paris, 30 juin 91. S'ad. à Me Cotelle, not. à Paris, r. St-Antoine, 214.

BOUQUET LYMPIA
Nouvelle Création
Ess. Oriza Concentrée des Fleurs de Nice.
PARFUMERIE ORIZA
de L. LEGRAND
11, Place de la Madeleine, PARIS
(Ci-devant, 207, rue Saint-Honoré)

LA DIAPHANE
POUDRE de RIZ
Sarah Bernhardt
LA POUDRE ÉLÉGANTE PAR EXCELLENCE
ADHÉRENTE, INVISIBLE
HYGIÉNIQUE
32, Av. de l'Opéra
PARIS
Se trouve dans toutes les Parfumeries

PRÊTS D'ARGENT sur hypothèques, nu-propriétés et aut. garant. P. Chatel, 31, boulevard Bonne-Nouvelle, de 1 à 5 heures.

LIQUEURS CUSENIER
ABSINTHE CUSENIER
226, Boulevard Voltaire, Paris

AU PACHA, 3, place de la Bourse, 3
PIPES EN TOUS GENRES
IMMENSE SUCCÈS
SPÉCIALITÉ DE PIPES
EN ÉCUME
Renommée universelle

MERVEILLE DU JOUR
PIANISTA
S'ADAPTANT À TOUS LES PIANOS
JÉROME THIBOUVILLE-LAMY
PARIS — 68 et 70, Rue Réaumur — PARIS

PRÊTS D'ARGENT, Vente et Achat de propriétés; Créances. Prompte solution. Métayer et Le Beau, 2, rue de la Bourse.

GUERISON reconnue la plus PROMPTE des *Maladies secrètes* Consult. 2 fr. (midi à 9h ou écrire) Dr EMANUEL. 25 ans de Pratique

PUISSANT STIMULANT DE L'ENERGIE VITALE
ANTIDÉPERDITEUR PAR EXCELLENCE
des
Forces Musculaires et du Système Nerveux
SHERRY-KOLA
Vin hygiénique au XÉRÈS véritable et à la NOIX de KOLA
Ce VIN délicieux et digestif est indispensable aux Voyageurs, Touristes, Vélocipédistes, Chasseurs, Alpinistes, Sportsmans, etc. Il quintuple les forces et permet à lui seul de nourrir un marcheur pendant tout un jour sans autre aliment. On peut l'utiliser à titre seulement d'excitant, comme complément de l'alimentation normale dans les exercices violents ou les voyages fatiguants. Il supprime l'essoufflement et le mal des montagnes. C'est un merveilleux régénérateur des forces; à la suite de surmenage intellectuel, excès de travail, etc. — Dose: 2 à 4 verres à Madère par jour avant ou entre les repas. — PRIX: 4
Vente au détail dans toutes les Pharmacies.
Vente en Gros: PARIS, 13, Rue Grenier-St-Lazare.

POMPES
121, Rue Oberkampf, PARIS
BROQUET
MÉDAILLE D'OR
Exposon Univlle
Catalogue illustré
POUR TOUS USAGES

MANUFACTURE FRANÇAISE
CYCLES-ROCHET
NOUVEAUX MODÈLES
USINE ET BUREAUX: *74, Rue de la Folie-Regnault*
MAGASIN DE VENTE: *29, Rue du Quatre-Septembre*
PARIS

PARFUMERIE DUSSER
Nous recommandons d'une façon particulière à nos lectrices les produits de cette Maison, une des plus anciennes de Paris, et qui a conservé le secret de recettes vraiment merveilleuses. La Poudre **Charmeresse**, la **Crème do la Mecque**, la **Crème Mousseuse** et l'**Eau Rose**, pour le teint, la **Pâte Circassienne**, pour les mains, la **Jaborandine** et l'**Eau Dusser** pour la chevelure, etc., sont des préparations réellement efficaces, irréprochables au point de vue hygiénique, et qui réalisent le vœu légitime de toute femme digne de ce nom: « ***Embellir et Rajeunir*** ». Très recherchés par une clientèle des plus aristocratiques et des plus délicates, ces produits ne se trouvent guère qu'au siège même de la **PARFUMERIE DUSSER** (*1, Rue Jean-Jacques-Rousseau, PARIS*); nous engageons nos lectrices à s'y adresser directement et en se recommandant du journal elles seront particulièrement bien servies.

Page of Advertisements from *Le Chat noir.* 1892. Photograph G. Roche.

crush Bismarck. He rapidly gained the support of the Bonapartists and the monarchists—formerly enemies of each other as well as of the Republic. But while most Parisians turned out joyously to watch his colorful, clattering parades, Fénéon, who had seen him at close quarters in the War Office, thought him a pitiful buffoon. Ironically, Boulanger noted in the margin of one of Fénéon's reports, "One can count on him!"

In 1888 the government, afraid of the monster it had created, retired Boulanger from the army. This had the effect of turning him into a free political animal, and the people welcomed him into the electoral lists for a seat in parliament, where his projected majority, they thought, would allow him to head a new government. While Signac, who shared Fénéon's views, took part in a hoax by furnishing a picture of the general on his deathbed for a pamphlet announcing his "last moments," Maurice Barrès and Paul Adam ran for office as Boulangists. After the election, on January 27, 1889, Edouard Dujardin wrote to his parents, living in Normandy:

> I have been to vote—for *le brav' général,* of course! . . . All of Sunday was superb, and in the evening, after 8 o'clock, when the results began to be known, there was an enthusiasm such as I have *never* seen in Paris: the most beautiful sight you could dream . . .[1]

The mobs begged the military "strongman" to lead them to the Elysée and take over the president's palace. But Boulanger was not as dangerous as the emotions he inspired. If he knew how to lead a parade, he suddenly became aware that he did not know how to lead a nation. He fled an arrest warrant charging him with treason and later took up residence in Belgium with a beloved mistress. She died two years later, and the general shot himself soon thereafter on her grave. Perhaps the planet Mars, Fénéon once said, should be renamed for Boulanger, and the Spica of Virgo for Verlaine.

The effect of the affair was to polarize the government and the people. A reinforced, more authoritarian Right gained over the leftist Radical party that had first supported Boulanger. For others, the opéra-comique events and public scorn for democracy gave the anarchist ideal of no government greater appeal than ever before.

There was renewed activity among elements on the political left as on the right. The 1889 centennial of the Revolution revealed both trends. From May to November, Paris held its fourth Universal Exhibition, spread out on the military showfield, the Champ de Mars, under the newly constructed Eiffel Tower, brave new symbol of France and progress. Many members of the intelligentsia mocked this "spread-legged whore" (Huysmans), but Seurat felt the essence of its geometric shape and painted a luminous study of it even before it was finished. Its open latticework and popular appeal, thought Fénéon, made it a piquant counterpoint to the blind tower of the Bastille, whose destruction it logically commemorated. Over 33 million visitors, enjoying what has been called an orgy of commercialism, went from the Gallery of Machines to the Colonial Exhibition, gawking at wonders as diverse as Edison's new incandescent lamp and Arab belly dancers. Fénéon left no record of having been there, although he made a point of visiting the unofficial exhibition that Gauguin and some fellow painters had set up in a café on the Champ de Mars.

While France was celebrating its place in the world as a leading industrial, imperalist nation, the International Socialist Congress met in Paris in July and decided to institute a universal holiday for workers to publicize demands for more humane working conditions. May 1 was chosen, the anniversary of the 1886 McCormick strike in Chicago, which led to the Haymarket Massacre and the hanging of four strike leaders who were avowed anarchists. The next year the first May Day parades, arrests, and subsequent executions took place, opening a new decade of agitation for workers' rights.

Vogue and the *Indépendante* disappeared early in 1889, while other symbolist publications, associated with cabaret life, prospered. One such was the *Chat noir,* whose editor, the humorist Alphonse Allais, had been pressing Fénéon to write "what you have already done for the *Revue indépendante* (I think)—a kind of artistic diary of events from day to day."[2] And Fénéon complied, sending articles rather regularly for two or three years, picking out new artists such as the Nabis, for example, or Toulouse-Lautrec, whose work captured so many of the ambiguities of the period.

There was also a new symbolist review, *La Plume,* associated with anarchist ideals. Actually quite eclectic in its taste, *La Plume* sponsored beer and poetry parties in the cellar of a café at the foot of boulevard Saint Michel, facing the Seine. One was supposed to present an invitation after going down the stairs at the back of the café, but signing an attendance sheet sufficed. The atmosphere there, said Adophe Retté, was "clearly revolutionary, but with good humor and a light heart."[3] *La Plume* was given to bringing out special issues, and Fénéon wrote an article on Signac for the issue on innovating painters. He was sometimes seen at the crowded, smoke-filled evenings in the café cellar, where piano music alternated with readings by Verlaine, Moréas, Pierre Louÿs, Marie Krysinska, and a host of others. But he preferred quieter surroundings: an art gallery that stayed open late in the evening, allowing its patrons to sit and chat, "far from waiters and tobacco fumes."[4]

This was the beginning of the "Banquet Years," a somewhat misleading term, since it brings to mind crystal, china, and ladies in evening clothes, none of which appeared at these gatherings of men who, over restaurant food, exchanged compliments on work done and ideas for work to come. Such dinners were not an invention of the nineties, for in earlier decades the impressionists had met at table, and Dubois-Pillet organized regular festive meals for the Indépendants—once even in the unheated exhibition rooms, where everyone kept on his coat and muffler. Dujardin had introduced a somewhat more formal note in 1887 when he asked Mallarmé to inaugurate the *Revue indépendante* with a toast at a dinner in his little bookshop (a former tobacconist's) on the rue Chaussée d'Antin. Soon such affairs took on a special importance, meant to mark a day in history, such as the one given for Gauguin in 1891 on the eve of his departure for Tahiti, and another, which F. F. attended with Seurat and Signac, commemorating the birth of symbolism and honoring Moréas.

Fénéon missed the simpler Sunday meals he used to take with Seurat and his friends. One Sunday in the spring of 1889 they decided to spend the day again at Saint-Fargeau, the park in the working-class district of Belleville where Fénéon had joined the painters in celebrating their first exhibition together in May 1886. The Pissarros were not there, but Signac, Seurat, Paul Alexis, Paul Adam, Fénéon, and Jean Ajalbert caught the omnibus together. It was an hour's ride after the horses left the wide boulevards and picked their way along narrow streets lined with tenements toward the lake that today is a reservoir surrounded by a hurricane fence marked "No Entry."[5] It was then known as the "people's Bois de Boulogne"—on the opposite side of Paris—and on Sundays twenty or thirty wedding celebrations took place there. The lake was dotted with couples in canoes, she wearing the white bridal veil, he in his shirt sleeves, paddling, but with the borrowed silk top hat still on his head to mark the solemnity of the occasion. Wedding parties danced and drank in the open-air cafés that surrounded the lake, scenes reminiscent of those painted by Renoir at La Grenouillère and the

Moulin de la Galette, but with only an occasional note of bright color—a soldier's red trousers—among the white and dark blue of the workers in their Sunday best.

Fénéon's party of bachelors had arrived and taken possession of a barrel of wine when a solitary bride passed by, weeping and leaning on the arm of another young woman. Good-hearted Alexis called out solicitously to ask her what was the matter. "The hubby's off drinking, instead of dancing," she replied. "Well, then, come drink with us," offered Alexis; and she ran off, crying, "You men are all the same!" Later, this group of elegant but somewhat impecunious young men were looking for a suitable place to dine, but most of the cafés served greasy food and had their silverware attached to the table; customers ate to the tin music of mechanical pianos and the screeching of violins for hire. As the young men stood contemplating their options, they caught sight of the young bride, now in the midst of her wedding party, anxiously discussing how to pay a musician and rent a dance floor. The symbolists and painters took up a quick collection among themselves and solved the bride's problem—on the condition that she give a kiss to "papa Alexis." She enthusiastically complied, and continued around the circle, giving each a peck on the cheek, until she got to Félix Fénéon, whom she mistook for Valentin le Désossé, the cabaret dancer, later immortalized by the brush of Toulouse-Lautrec: "Toi, je t'ai vu sûrement . . . C'est pas toi qui faisait l'Engliche à Ba-Ta-Clan?" (I've surely seen *you* . . . Wasn't it you who played the Englishman at the café-concert Ba-Ta-Clan?) Fénéon acquiesced with a smile; why abolish the young woman's illusions?

Valentin "le Désossé" (the "deboned," colloquial for acrobat) was in his way as mystifying a personality as F. F. He was a successful businessman who danced for the fun of it, without remuneration, with La Goulue and other immortal creators of the "Chahut," or French cancan. The bride was unaware, when she kissed Seurat, that he was already the most famous man in the group, and that he was engaged that season in painting a new composition called *Chahut.* She was not, however, the only one to mistake Fénéon for Valentin, whose long-limbed body and strong-boned profile bore quite a resemblance to that of F. F. Even some of Fénéon's closest friends thought that Toulouse-Lautrec had painted him when in fact it was Valentin. "We had, it seems," Fénéon later said, "analogies that were flattering for neither one of us."[6]

A waiter who had been attending the bridal group was impressed by the celebrity, Félix/Valentin, and indicated that there was a high class wedding celebration going on at La Chaumière, the best restaurant at the lake, and the only one worthy of the visitor and his companions. They were serving champagne, not beer! Fénéon and his friends moved on to the indicated place and saw through the glass walls of the garden-house restaurant thirty people solemnly sitting at table drinking champagne as fast as they decently could. Fénéon went in, hat in hand, and gravely saluting the bride and groom, delivered a sermon on marriage—union of hearts, salvation of souls, praiseworthy use of the flesh, veneration of cradles—while his companions waited outside and watched the pantomime of this performance through the glass. Finally their ambassador signaled them to enter, and introduced them according to protocol. More champagne was brought, the guests sat down, drank many toasts to the honor of the hosts, and improvised verses far into the night.

HENRI DE TOULOUSE-LAUTREC. ***Moulin Rouge: La Goulue.*** 1891. Poster published in four colors on two sheets, with a strip added at the top, 195 x 122 cm. New York, Collection of Mr. and Mrs. Herbert D. Schimmel. In the foreground, the dancer Valentin "le Désossé," sometimes mistaken for F. F.

They missed the last bus home, and had to sleep in the only hotel they could find, a home for soldiers with a dirt floor and an old madam in clog shoes, who offered her services. "The last circle of Hell," said Jean Ajalbert, who later told the story, "and what Paradise to ride home on the top deck of the first 'bus, in the cool morning air.—What foolishness! you say.—Ah, but you did not see Félix Fénéon that night!"[7]

The following year, on July 27, 1890, just three weeks before Dubois-Pillet's sudden death from smallpox, van Gogh fatally shot himself. Fénéon wrote three days later to Signac, who was in Brittany: "The funeral of Vincent van Gogh took place today at Auvers-sur-Oise. No doubt you have already received the terribly sad news of this death." The next day he wrote Theo van Gogh a letter recently published by Bogomila Welsh-Ovcharov: "Although I never had the honor of knowing Vincent personally, this sad news has grieved me deeply because of you and because of the very great and new talent of your brother. . . . Féliorph Fénéon."[8]

It is somewhat surprising that Vincent never met Fénéon, who often dropped by Theo's gallery and was intimate enough with him to sign his condolence note with one of his fanciful names (evoking Orpheus, the paragon of grief). This lack of contact is the more surprising since Vincent knew Signac and other neo-impressionists. Fénéon wrote very little about van Gogh's work, but it is clear that he held his genius in esteem and was genuinely grieved by his suicide. While abhorring Gauguin's "symbolism with literary intention," Fénéon recognized the power of "the *instinctive* symbolist and colorist" in van Gogh, and later called him *un grand inventeur de formes et d'harmonies.*[9]

While the honor of having recognized the importance of van Gogh goes to Albert Aurier, who published the first critical study of his work six months before the artist's death, Fénéon had remarked the previous year that the *Indépendants* had gained new distinction when they included works by Toulouse Lautrec and van Gogh. He described the two paintings shown by van Gogh:

> His *Irises* shred wild tatters of violet on the thin laths of their leaves. Mr. van Gogh has a droll way of using colors in his eccentric *Starry Night:* upon a rough basket-weave sky cross-ruled with a flat brush, his tubes have squirted little cones of white, pink, yellow—stars; orange colored triangles are engulfed by the river, and baroquely sinister creatures scuttle past boats moored at the wharf.[10]

The violently active verb governing the irises (*déchiquètent,* "slash" or "tear into shreds") conveys not only shape but the feeling given these fragile flowers by the painter. The other canvas, *The Starry Night: The Rhône at Arles,* had been hung in a narrow room and could not be seen from a sufficient distance, according to van Gogh's brother; this explains Fénéon's close-up view of it, down to the little star-squirts of paint. The "baroquely sinister creatures" Fénéon saw in the foreground were, in Vincent's mind, "two colorful little figures of lovers"![11]

"One must fall in love immediately with an unexpected work of art," Fénéon said. "Once it has been elevated to the rank of masterpiece, it can no longer arouse authentic love, but only 'the expression of our heartfelt esteem'."[12] F. F. did not fall in love with van Gogh's painting as he had with Seurat's. Still, he appreciated his work and pitied his anguish, which F. F. believed to be informed by humanitarian concerns.

The spring following their deaths, van Gogh and Dubois-Pillet were honored by their comrades at the *Indépendants* with retrospectives of their work. Seurat showed an unfinished painting, *Le Cirque,* and four canvases from his summer in the port of Gravelines. The sensation of the exhibition, however, was Paul Signac's symbolic portrait of Félix Fénéon, *Sur l'émail d'un fond rythmique . . . ,* showing the critic in the act of bestowing a kind of art nouveau flower upon an invisible recipient. For the second year in a row, Fénéon wrote no review of the *Indépendants,* this time perhaps in order to avoid talking about his own portrait. Willy, however, pressed him for some comments on the exhibition and published them in the *Chat noir,* for once naming his source.

Fénéon barely mentioned the leader of the neo-impressionists: "Seurat, a Circus" is all he seems to have said. This is surprising since the subject of the painting should have pleased Fénéon, who all his life enjoyed the circus, "a place of truth," he called it. He said in 1888 that he hoped one day to see a circus set up according to definite aesthetic principles, where "the artificial lights and tinseled costumes would coalesce in meaningful schemes of color and the movements of clowns and acrobats combine to form a tracery of lines on the arena or in the air." Then the public would be "moved as by a beautiful graphic design and enjoy multiple elements of delight."[13]

Seurat's painting actually embodied the ideal Fénéon dreamed of, yet he passed it by, silent. Nor did he remark on the subtle combination of formal grace and social commentary in *The Circus,* where prim, immobile spectators contrast with acrobats and clowns, alive and lyric in their electric circle. Fénéon's apparent indifference to Seurat's latest achievement can be traced to the ill feelings generated by their misunderstanding and bitter exchange of letters the previous spring (discussed in chapter 7). Although there was no open conflict, they were now wary of one another, each man's pride and sense of fairness wounded still. Fénéon secretly felt that the symbolic strength of this painting made it comparable to the work of da Vinci, but he was not moved to say so at this time.

Seurat had worked desperately hard that winter to finish *The Circus* in time for the *Indépendants.* He had been active in organizing the exhibition and hanging the paintings, a hectic activity which kept the participants working into the small hours for several days. Fénéon came to view the paintings before the official opening and to lend a helping hand, but Seurat did not discuss his work with him. Since it was not like Seurat to show an unfinished painting, there has since been some debate as to whether he considered *The Circus* completed. A letter Fénéon wrote in 1939 revealed his opinion and, incidentally, the lack of communication between himself and Seurat in 1891:

> According to Signac—very emphatic about this point—Seurat did not consider [*The Circus*] finished. I was not acquainted with Seurat's intentions on the subject, but I believe he would have worked more on it, particularly the background (tiers of spectators just barely indicated in blue, with the tip of the brush).[14]

Shortly after the exhibition opened, Seurat came down with a throat infection—diphtheria, probably—and died three days later, on Easter Sunday. The shock of this sudden death reverberated through the community of young artists and writers who knew his work. Fénéon inserted a brief unsigned obituary among his book reviews that week. He expressed no emotion, but only the confidence that Seurat had already achieved greatness.

> Died March 29, aged thirty-one, Seurat: he exhibited at the "Salon" in 1883; with the "Group of Independent Artists" in 1884; at the "Society of Independent Artists" in 1884–85, 1886, 1887, 1888, 1889, 1890 and 1891; at the "Impressionists," rue

> Laffitte, in 1886; in New York in 1885–86; in Nantes in 1886; at the "XX" in Brussels, 1887, 1889 and 1891; with "Black and White," Amsterdam, in 1888. A complete catalogue of his works would include around 170 cigar-box panels, 420 drawings, 6 sketchbooks and some 60 canvases (figures, marines, landscapes) including five measuring several square meters (LA BAIGNADE, UN DIMANCHE A LA GRANDE-JATTE, POSENDER [*sic*], CHAHUT, CIRQUE) and doubtless many a masterpiece.[15]

This starkly objective obituary has a strange impact. It appeared in a series called "Notes et notules," where Fénéon spoke less dispassionately of the yet unknown André Gide. The apparent coldness of his note on Seurat stands out from the reaction of other symbolists. Emile Verhaeren reported at length the disbelief he felt when he heared that Seurat had died:

> Seurat? . . . I had seen him barely ten days before at the opening of the *Indépendants,* in front of his new canvas, *The Circus.* I could still hear the sound of his voice. I kept remembering one of his gestures, his hand moving regularly in a slow, demonstrative manner.[16]

Gustave Kahn wrote several pages for *L'Art moderne* and, while exclaiming over Seurat's accomplishments, insisted his work had been interrupted in mid-course. Jules Christophe, too, lamented his early demise: "I curse Providence and Death!" he cried, several months after the event. Teodor de Wyzewa, whose appreciation of Seurat had been tepid, was moved to write profusely and to conclude that his death meant the end of all hope for contemporary art.[17]

In comparison with these, Fénéon's commentary seems totally lacking in feeling. Most of it was, in fact, a word for word quotation of a list of exhibitions Seurat had sent him the preceding year (before the rift). Dry as it is, it is a fitting tribute to a man who lived for his work. And Fénéon, as usual, was most laconic when most moved. Seurat was gone, and Fénéon did not see fit to wax eloquent over the fact. He did not lament over what might have been; he catalogued what was. He and Signac organized commemorative exhibitions of Seurat for the *Indépendants* and the *XX* in 1892, and larger retrospectives at the *Revue blanche* in 1900, the *Indépendants* in 1905, the Bernheim-Jeune Gallery in 1908–9 and 1920. At the first Bernheim-Jeune exhibition of Seurat, eighteen years after the painter's death, Fénéon reaffirmed:

> If one knows how to look, this exhibition will establish a reputation that has been slowly, quietly and irresistibly growing since 1891. In March of that year, Georges Seurat died. But he had produced definitive works that give the complete measure of his power. A career of seven or eight years, agreed, is a short span: no, for in the history of art there have been a few painters for whom almost as short a time has sufficed.[18]

The painter's father, a devout if somewhat eccentric Catholic, arranged for an elaborate funeral in the imposing church of Saint-Vincent-de-Paul, near the family home, and Fénéon attended along with many other friends. In the midst of their grief, Seurat's family had new cause for concern. Their son's baby boy, whose existence they had not known of until Georges's fatal illness, had the same throat infection. About two weeks later in a note to Edouard Dujardin, Fénéon recorded the death of the child, to whom Seurat had given his own names in reverse order, Pierre-Georges. In the upper righthand corner, instead of the date, Fénéon wrote: "We hardly saw one another at Saint-Vincent-de-Paul. Yesterday they buried the son of the dead painter, Pierre Seurat."[19]

Seurat's family appointed Fénéon, Signac, and Maximilien Luce to classify the contents of his studio and divide it among the heirs. The three friends, assisted by Seurat's brother, made a careful inventory, numbering each work and putting their initials on the back for future identification. Fénéon's little obituary shows that even before Seurat's death he had a precise idea of the extent of his work, for his count of the paintings and drawings is quite close to the total shown in the inventory. Seurat had sold only one of his large paintings (*Chahut,* to Gustave Kahn); very few of the smaller ones had found their way into the homes of friends and informed collectors.

The task of dividing the work was naturally delicate. The family had accepted Madeleine Knobloch, pregnant with a second child by Seurat, as their son's widow. Luce represented her, while Fénéon was asked to serve as chairman of the little committee. Although Fénéon had none too high an opinion of Madeleine Knobloch's intelligence and indeed feared what might happen to the paintings left in her hands, he was scrupulously fair and saw that she shared equally with Seurat's family in the division; he later bought several works from her when she put them up for sale. In a rare indiscretion, however, he detailed his opinion of Madeleine in a letter replying to an inquiry from Gustave Kahn. Kahn was living then in Brussels, where Madeleine, a Belgian. had returned to establish a new life. Kahn's wife "leaked" the contents of Fénéon's letter to her, adding some recriminations to other problems arising from Seurat's death and causing a break between Félix and Gustave that would be healed only after Fénéon's arrest in 1894.

Fénéon's part in cataloguing the contents of Seurat's studio was the beginning of a lifelong preoccupation, keeping track of Seurat's work, tracing various ownerships, compiling auction catalogues, verifying measurements, organizing exhibitions—allowing Seurat's work to speak for itself while public opinion matured to the point of accepting and finally embracing it.

The year 1891 was also a turning point for the symbolist movement, although not as dramatic as the impact on neo-impressionism of Seurat's death: a few months after the banquet in his honor, Moréas did an abrupt about-face, announcing a neo-classicizing school of Romanism in poetry.

At the same time, and up until the Dreyfus Affair, there was a swing away from involvement in contemporary problems, typified by Gauguin's escape to Tahiti. Many symbolists became disillusioned with politics after the Boulanger fiasco, and were further disgusted by government scandals such as that concerning the Panama Canal. Many simply could not believe the unthinkable—the subhuman existence of the workers in the city, which Zola would relentlessly portray in his book, *Paris.* Fénéon had long since lost his youthful hopes that the Republic would attack these very real problems. He became more and more involved in the ideas presented by Proudhon, the father of French anarchism (*What is Property?* "Property is theft!"), and the Russian exiles Bakunin, Alexander Herzen, and Kropotkin. He began publishing regularly, and anonymously, in a series of anarchist reviews.

A fundamental rift among the writers of the first symbolist generation was revealed by an extensive "Inquiry on the Evolution of Literature" carried out in 1891 by a reporter for the *Echo de Paris,* Jules Huret. Huret's interviews showed that some authors felt that their creative impulses were jeopardized by the corrupting influence of an industrialized society and the threat of violence from the dissatisfied classes. Others chose to "note what was going on in the world, and to act according to their conscience. That is when everyone began pulling for himself," Gustave Kahn later explained; "our differences, which we had never hidden . . . became necessarily more visible because we had different ideals."[20] Fénéon did not appear in Huret's inquiry. This was not an oversight on the interviewer's part, for when another reporter pointed out that F. F. had been "piously passed over," Huret responded that it was because of Fénéon's modesty.[21] Actually, regarding the individual's responsibility in society, Fénéon once said, "Only action counts."

Devoting himself more and more to anonymous editing, Fénéon helped Léon Vanier produce a new edition in 1891 of *Les Amours jaunes* by Tristan Corbière, who had died unknown at age thirty in 1875. Fénéon established the texts, including variants and some poems not included in the original edition, and provided Vanier with much of the material in the preface.

Fénéon was also partly responsible for a little edition of Rimbaud's poems, *Reliquaire,* produced in 1891 without the author's knowledge. Rimbaud was then close to death and cloistered with his sister in a Marseilles hospital. Fénéon and other symbolists were aware that he had had his leg amputated upon his return to France from Abyssinia earlier that year, but they remained ignorant of his fate. The month after he died, Fénéon blithely hailed the "peg-legged poet" in a discussion on the origins of vers libre (F, 835), and the editors of *Entretiens politiques et littéraires* announced they had definite information on Rimbaud's "complete recovery" and that he would soon be back in Paris. At the same time, a short announcement of his death and burial appeared in *La Plume* with this remark: "His mother and sister ALONE attended his funeral." This single note of remorse marked the disappearance from the literary scene of a solitary comet, whose brief career had left an indelible mark on the nature of poetry and the nexus between language and the subconscious. Thirty-seven years old when he died, Rimbaud had died to the world of poetry nearly seventeen years earlier, when he renounced all literature in favor of a life of adventure and commerce. Nevertheless, the vagabond Rimbaud had unwittingly ushered in the age of symbolism when his *Illuminations* were published by Fénéon in *La Vogue* of 1886.

Now symbolism was moving beyond the realm of language into painting, a development embraced by many writers and critics. Fénéon, however, doubted the validity of such a venture, which he called "painting for literati."

CHAPTER 11

Speaking of Symbolist Painting

In 1891, when some young painters exhibited together under Gauguin's aegis, Fénéon's reaction was negative. It was a bitter time for him and the movement he had defended: Seurat's death early that spring had caused profound discouragement among the neo-impressionists and there had been several defections from their ranks. The future of Signac, Luce, and other friends of Fénéon seemed uncertain. Meanwhile, Gauguin had been lionized on his departure to Tahiti, and his reputation among symbolist writers was flourishing. Fénéon had been writing penetratingly of Gauguin's work ever since the last impressionist show in 1886, but now his attitude turned sour. He was disappointed in the artist who, Camille Pissarro said, "groveled to get himself elected (that is the word) man of genius."[1] And he was dubious of the value of painting that sought to present an idea or a religious message. Much of so-called symbolist art, he thought, was simply bad painting. Gauguin himself was victimized by his own public relations when his paintings revealed he had become "the prey of littérateurs." And yet, the issues raised by Gauguin and his defenders forced Fénéon to rethink his own understanding of the way artists transform human experience into symbolic works.

Gauguin, now forty-three years old, had long yearned for a position of authority in the avant-garde. He keenly resented the acclaim young Seurat had received as the leader of a new style of painting. In trying so hard to gain recognition, Gauguin never understood or accepted the real admiration Fénéon had for his work. "One really tragic feature of Gauguin's life," Sven Loevgren noted, "was his inability to accept and benefit by Fénéon's dignified and penetrating intellect."[2]

F. F. appreciated particularly "the mysterious, primitive, hostile" air that set Gauguin's canvases apart from surrounding impressionist works. And he saw how the power of his sculpture and pottery prefigured his best work as a painter. Fénéon, however, was never a partisan of Gauguin as he was of Signac or Pissarro. "What really bothered Fénéon," said Jean Paulhan, "was Gauguin's itch for recognition and his fanfaron ways. . . . F. F. preferred more thoughtful and well integrated personalities, without need of pretense."[3] He nonetheless recognized Gauguin's genius and chose him, alongside Degas and Seurat, as a major figure in his *Impressionnistes en 1886.*

Gauguin left Paris after the last impressionist show and went to Brittany, to Panama, to Martinique. When he returned at the end of 1887, F. F. went to see his paintings and pottery pieces, exhibited by Theo van Gogh, and reported on them in the January issue of the *Revue indépendante,* writing that the painter had at last found his own path, separate from the impressionists with whom he had previously been associated. Gauguin's landscapes of Brittany and Martinique, Fénéon said, showed that his style had acquired "a virile eloquence of line," and he pointed out "among the heavy greenery, the red clamour of a roof, as in every genuine Gauguin." In fact, Gauguin once declared he was "in love with red—in search of the perfect vermilion."[4] Fénéon concluded his review with a powerfully worded remark:

> Barbarous and atrabilious in quality, scant of atmosphere, colored by diagonal stains sleeting from right to left, these proud pictures would sum up the work of M. Paul Gauguin, were not this gritty artist chiefly a potter. He cherishes the hard, ill-omened, coarse-grained clay of stoneware, scorned by others: haggard faces with wide glabellae, snub noses and tiny slits for eyes—two vases; a third: the head of an ancient long-lived ruler, some dispossessed Atahualpa, his mouth rent gulflike; two others of an abnormal, gibbous geometry. (F, 91)

Fénéon was the first critic to notice Gauguin's ceramic sculpture and for some time he was the only one to speak favorably of it. The five pieces he saw in 1888 have apparently been lost, but should they ever be found, they will be easy to identify. Evoking Atahualpa—the Inca emperor betrayed and put to death by conquistadores in 1533—Fénéon alluded to the influence on Gauguin of the pre-Columbian pottery he had known since his early childhood in Peru. The critic also hinted at the artist's sense of outrage at the destruction of "primitive" cultures by the "civilized" Western world. To further portray these unusual pieces, Fénéon borrowed from the vocabulary of anatomy, using both a learned word, *glabelle* (the smooth prominence between the eyebrows), and a colloquial one, *gobin* (humpbacked, gibbous). Gauguin once described one of his pots as a "poor devil hunched in upon himself, in order to stand his suffering."[5]

Gauguin did not read Fénéon's article until after he left Paris for Pont-Aven in March 1888, which shows what little contact he had with Fénéon and his friends, for it was customary to pass the word along when a review appeared. He wrote Schuffenecker from Pont-Aven toward the end of the month, saying he had received Fénéon's article, that it was "tolerable" in so far as his art was concerned, but "peculiar" as to his character. "It seems that those gentlemen have been offended by my ways and are little angels themselves. And that is how history is written!"[6]

It was Fénéon's characterizing him as a *grièche artiste* that annoyed Gauguin. While *grièche,* an uncommon word,[7] can mean "irritating," here it is deliberately displaced and takes on the sense of "gritty" from its alliterative association with the nearby word *grès* (stoneware), suggesting both the texture and the rough individualism of Gauguin's work. Unfamiliar with Fénéon's style of criticism, which treated not personalities but art and which reshaped conventional French, Gauguin took the word as a personal insult. In November 1888 he told Schuffenecker that he was declining an invitation to exhibit at Fénéon's rotating show in the offices of the *Revue indépendante,* adding, "At least I shall earn the label of *grièche.*"[8]

Shortly after his January 1888 article appeared, Fénéon noticed that Theo van Gogh had placed a new Gauguin on display, *Deux Baigneuses,* and he wrote a sumptuous word picture of it for the February issue of the *Revue indépendante.* Gauguin probably did not read it; if he did, he would have been annoyed by one particular sentence:

> A slim, smooth, rectilinear trunk, already seen in Cézanne, separates [the bathers] and divides the canvas into two panels. (F, 95)

No matter how laudatory the comparison, Gauguin could not bear anyone's pointing out that he might have learned something from a fellow painter. Foreshadowing twentieth-century artists jockeying for the lead, Gauguin—much like Seurat—needed to "be first" with his vision, just as certain poets claimed priority with the vers libre.

In May 1888, Fénéon called for an exhibition dedicated exclusively to Gauguin in order to show what a powerful, "rye-grained" artist he was (F, 111: *quel artiste puissant et soilé*). Here was another unusual word, *soilé,* used in the Middle Ages to indicate grain mixed with rye. Fénéon definitely needed unusual words to respond to this unusual artist, whose power, he felt, was allied to the grit and grain of the earth itself. He understood that Gauguin's quest was totally different from the neo-impressionists' search for luminosity, epitomized in two Seurats on view at the *Revue indépendante*:

> *Boats off Grandcamp,* a slow procession of triangular sails and another view of the sea where a column of sun is quivering—it makes us stop and wonder, anxious at such infinity. (F, 93)

Here Fénéon's language balances between the seen and the unseen, between motion and immobility, and it touches upon the symbolism of paintings that remind us without rhetoric that we are mortal and will return to dust, while what we can conceive of and look upon partakes of timelessness.

The following year, when Gauguin was not included among the few impressionists invited by the government to exhibit at the Universal Exhibition, he organized a show in a café on the ground floor of the Fine Arts pavilion, the café Volpini. Billed as the "Impressionist and Synthetist Group," he exhibited with seven other painters, including Charles Laval and Emile Bernard who had worked with him at Pont-Aven in Brittany, and Louis Anquetin, whose style Dujardin had recently dubbed *cloisonnisme* (after the flat colors and dark outlining of cloisonné enameling). The café was large, and they managed to hang sixty-four paintings on its claret-colored walls. But the canvases were inaccessible, Fénéon remarked, because of "the counters, beer pumps, tables, the bosom of M. Volpini's cashier, and an orchestra of young lady Moscovites whose violins fill the room with music that has no relation to these polychromatic works" (F, 159). There were many visitors, thirsty from traipsing through the fair, but most of them were more interested in the all-women orchestra of pseudo-Russians than the paintings. Adolphe Retté, in an article called "Bars and Beer-halls at the Fair," briefly described the landscapes of Martinique—he did not mention Gauguin's name—and then launched into a satire of the lady chef d'orchestre.[9] Jules Antoine's criticism was muddled, and Albert Aurier's—it was his first article on Gauguin—desultory.[10] Only Fénéon wrote an intelligent report.

Gauguin liked Fénéon's opening paragraph well enough; he later copied it into a notebook that he made to bequeath to his daughter Aline:

> The mysterious, hostile, and primitive nature of the works of M. PAUL GAUGUIN, painter and sculptor, isolated them from their surroundings at the impressionist exhibitions of 1880, 1881, 1882 and 1886; many details of execution [in his painting], and the fact that he carved his bas-reliefs in wood and colored them showed a distinct tendency towards archaism; the form of his stoneware vases displayed an exotic taste: all characteristics which attain their degree of saturation in his recent canvases. (F, 157)

Fénéon then drew a direct parallel between Gauguin's development and that of Seurat three years earlier: both were intent on creating "an art of synthesis and premeditation," but Gauguin pursued this goal by different means (pl. 18):

> Reality for him was only a pretext for far-reaching creations: he rearranges the materials reality provides, disdains illusionistic effects, even atmospheric ones; accentuates lines, limits their number, makes them hieratic; and in each of the spacious cantons formed by their interlace, an opulent and sultry color sits in bleak glory, without attacking neighboring colors, without yielding its own tone. (F, 157–58)

Here Fénéon defined the essence of Gauguin's art by using terms as precise as they are evocative. Without the trappings of theory, he evoked Gauguin's so-called *cloisonnisme* and his tendency toward symbolism; instead of "-isms," Fénéon used words dear to Mallarmé (*créations lointaines; hiératiser*) and borrowed one from heraldry (*cantons*). It has been said that in this article, Fénéon swept away the literary superstructure of Gauguin's painting;[11] but the literary intention that existed in the painting was implicit in Fénéon's word picture.

Gauguin, however, was once again offended by Fénéon's report. He did not appreciate the parallel Fénéon drew between him and Seurat. He had hoped to push Seurat and his "little dot" thoroughly under by this show; Fénéon understood this, but did not let it prejudice his judgment. In contrast to his appreciation of Gauguin, F. F. derided the other exhibitors, particularly Anquetin, who "speculates on the hypothesis posed by Humboldt about the gentleman abruptly transferred from Senegal to Siberia," and other adventures undermining normal vision. He remarked that Anquetin's use of unbroken contours and flat and intense color "has not been without some influence on M. Paul Gauguin: purely a formal influence, for it is evident that not the least feeling flows through these clever, decorative works" (F, 158). Gauguin was further embittered by this remark and wrote to Emile Bernard: "Fénéon has indeed written that I was imitating *Anquetin,* whom I do not know."[12] He ignored the fact that he had become acquainted with Anquetin's style through Bernard himself. More to the point, Gauguin failed to see that Fénéon placed him clearly above the other exhibitors and had pointed out that despite stylistic similarities, Gauguin's work was too individualistic for his technique to succeed in others' hands.

In September 1889, while reviewing the Indépendants—where Gauguin disdained to show—Fénéon spoke of Gauguin as being the leader of a new group of "dissidents" from impressionism. "Dissident" was the word he had used in 1886 to single out Seurat and his circle, and it was a definite sign of approbation. He blamed Huysmans for being sensitive only to Gauguin's impressionist period:

> He has suppressed the Gauguin that developed after 1887, Gauguin the sculptor and potter who inscribes exotic dreams and innovated forms into the stoneware of 16th and 17th century Takatori ceramists, with strong rich browns enhanced by darkly gleaming runnels of glaze. (F, 172)

Fénéon noticed in the rustic materials chosen by Gauguin a similarity to stoneware pottery from a village in Japan—an influence not remarked by other critics. He was clearly as intrigued by Gauguin's ceramic sculpture as by his painting, and found that some of the contours in his canvases took their shape from a sculptor's hand.

Gauguin's reputation as the leader of the Pont-Aven synthetist painters had grown steadily. He moved back to Paris in December 1890 and began meeting with the writers of the newly reestablished *Mercure de France,* where Albert Aurier was art critic. In their discussions, it seemed that symbolism in literature had found its counterpart in Gauguin's painting, and there was much talk of symbolist painting. The primitive in art, seen in earlier ages of more fervent religious belief, was extolled as the expression of humanity's unspoken ideals. Deliberate distortions were said to reveal that art was not mere imitation of nature, but the intuitive knowledge of inner reality, which only a true artist could grasp. Symbolist painting was therefore conceived as being both subjective and decorative; it was also expected to be enigmatic, spiritual, mysterious, and suggestive.

By the end of 1890, Gauguin had resolved to live in an exotic and primitive land, where his material problems would be solved by a simple life and he could paint freely without the constraints of Western civilization and the jealousy of fellow artists. He mistakenly believed that not only Fénéon but his old mentor Pissarro were undermining his chances for success, and when a friend suggested that he was harming himself by harboring such suspicions, Gauguin explained:

> The people who might be of use to me are not very numerous . . . As to those who can injure me, Pissarro and company, they are more outraged by my talent than by my character. . . . Besides, confound it, one never gets anywhere by courting imbeciles. And I have enough stuff in me to look down on most everyone else.[13]

He set about publicizing his painting to prepare for a sale that would pay for the voyage to Tahiti. He sent reminders to Aurier about a promised article and even furnished him material for it. When the article was not forthcoming, he contacted everyone he could think of that might be useful to him—except Fénéon, "Signac's man," as he called him. He forgot his distrust of Pissarro and begged him to ask his friend Octave Mirbeau for an article in a large newspaper to publicize an auction of his paintings. He asked another friend to approach Mallarmé, but the poet said Mirbeau would do a better job. Mirbeau's long, impassioned article appeared a week before the auction and attracted considerable attention. A short extract suffices to give the tone:

> A strangely cerebral, passionate work, still uneven, yet proud and poignant in its very unevenness. Painful work, for in order to understand it, to feel its impact, one must have suffered pain, oneself—and the irony of pain, which is the pathway to mystery. Sometimes his work rises to the heights of a mystical act of faith; sometimes it grimaces and trembles in the darkness of doubt. And always, the bitter, violent aroma of fleshly poisons arises from it. There is in his work a disquieting and savory mixture of barbaric splendor, of Catholic liturgy, of Hindu reverie, of Gothic imagery, of obscure and subtle symbolism . . .[14]

Fénéon's reaction to this kind of prose was sardonic: "Mirbeau is becoming better and better at pictorial pastiche . . ."

The auction, on February 22, 1891, went well, bringing Gauguin more than 9,000 francs (about 22,500 francs today, or $4,500), a fact which he hid from his wife, who was raising their five children in Copenhagen with what she could earn giving French lessons. Then the March issue of the *Mercure de France* carried Albert Aurier's elaborate manifesto, "Le Symbolisme en peinture: Paul Gauguin," which summed up the aesthetic program Aurier had been meditating for several years and gave a lyrical defense of Gauguin's works, particularly the painting, *Jacob Wrestling with the Angel.*

Aurier assigned five attributes to symbolist painting: it was to be *idéiste, symboliste, synthétique, subjective,* and *décorative.* He further declared that there were two contradictory traditions in the history of art, the one "blind" and the other "clairvoyant": these were realism and ideism (that is, idealism with its realist roots removed). The impressionists belonged in the realist tradition, while Gauguin and his followers were in the "purer, more elevated art that separates matter from idea."[15] Aurier's arguments, couched in such lofty terms, made them an effective pedagogical tool; they are cited still in textbooks on symbolist art. His art criticism, however, was totally different from Fénéon's and spoke little of technique, but much of the aims of art:

> The normal and final goal of painting, I was saying, and for that matter of all the arts, cannot be the direct representation of objects. Its ultimate end is to express Ideas by translating them into a special language.
>
> In the artist's eyes, that is, in the eyes of him who must be the *Enunciator of absolute Beings,* objects (that is, relative beings which are merely a translation proportionate to the relativity of our intellects of those absolute and essential beings—Ideas), objects are valueless simply as objects. They can only appear to him as *signs.* They are the letters of an immense alphabet which only the man of genius can spell out.[16]

PAUL GAUGUIN. ***Agony in the Garden.*** 1889. Oil on canvas, 72.4 x 91.4 cm. West Palm Beach, Norton Gallery and School of Art. Gauguin gave his own features to the figure of Jesus.

Fénéon probably shared the opinion of Camille Pissarro, who sent Aurier's article to his son Lucien with the remark:

> This gentleman thinks we are really naïve. . . . All artists—real artists—agree that the material object is simply a sign that develops the idea we are painting. But the signs must have artistic strength—that's the nub![17]

Pissarro the anarchist also thought that Gauguin was catering to middle class interests by painting religious scenes: "Gauguin is not a seer, he is a schemer who has sensed that the bourgeoisie are moving backwards, recoiling from the great ideas of solidarity which are sprouting among the people."[18] Fénéon concurred: *le bel idéal* was his disdainful comment on some variations by Bernard and Gauguin on the Gethsemane theme (F, 193).

On March 23, a month after the auction, there was the historic banquet in Gauguin's honor. Mallarmé was the first to rise and lift his glass: "Gentlemen, let's get right to the point; let's drink to the return of Paul Gauguin, but not without paying tribute to that superb conscience of his which is driving him into exile at the peak of his talent, to whet his spirit and temper his metal in far-off places."[19] Although Fénéon was listed among the forty invited guests, there is no record of his attendance. The pretension in this fanfare, this *coronation,* nearly, of Gauguin as the king of symbolist painting, aroused his sense of proportion and his ire. Seurat and Signac, however, were at the feast, not begrudging Gauguin his hour of glory.

Six days later: Seurat's death. Another six days: Gauguin's triumphant departure for the South Seas. Fénéon's grief fed his anger. The symbolists had agreed at the banquet to hold another fundraiser for Gauguin, a benefit performance at Paul Fort's new Théâtre d'Art on May 27, with proceeds to be divided between the painter-in-exile and the prince of poets, Verlaine. A week before the performance (which yielded 1,500 francs for the painter), Fénéon published an article revealing that Gauguin was not the original genius he claimed to be.

"The *Cézanne* tradition," he pointedly began, "is now being cultivated, after a long neglect . . ." The critic implied that Gauguin's disciples ("Sérusier, Willumsen, Bernard, Laval, Ibels, Schuffenecker, Filiger, Denis, etc.") had benefited more from Cézanne's early influence on Gauguin than from anything Gauguin himself had to offer. Fénéon went on to trace Gauguin's habit of co-opting the ideas and techniques of other painters and claiming them as his own. "Five years ago, at the Maison Dorée exhibition, his landscapes and bathers suffered somewhat by comparison with the sparkling works of his fellow impressionists and the lucid paintings of some newcomers" (the neo-impressionists). "Was M. Gauguin going to miss his destiny?" No, for he went to Brittany and met a "rather well-informed young painter," Emile Bernard, who was now thought of as Gauguin's pupil but who had been his "initiator."

> M. Bernard was the first to paint those disturbing, distorted Breton peasant women, set in fields of saturated color, lacking atmosphere and contrast, and outlined as in leaded windows. . . . When M. Gauguin came back from Brittany . . . he excelled in those Breton women of M. Bernard, but, being a more experienced painter, he put some logic into their awkwardness, and so his "barbarism," parading as a wild thing, was really quite regimented. . . .
>
> M. Gauguin demands the right to express himself exactly as he pleases. All right. But then, one would expect more hallucinating designs, more quixotic blocks of color—and also, more personality. At the auction-house Drouot, where thirty of his paintings were recently displayed for sale, you could see some Japanese nudes over there, and here landscapes by Monet, or Cézanne's trees, while the canvases from Arles were all van Goghs. (F, 192–93)

Scholars have recently acknowledged that Fénéon was the first critic to point out these relationships, but the article was no erudite analysis of origins; Fénéon was deriding Gauguin and his pretensions. In denying Gauguin's originality, Fénéon did a complete about-face in his own position on the artist: "He is a better potter than painter, and one has to admire his sculpture; but if we continue along this line, we will end up admiring Zapotec funeral jars."

Gauguin had become, in Fénéon's eyes, a profiteer. Pissarro had remarked years before that the former stockbroker had things backward when he expected to make money, quickly, from his painting. In 1891, Fénéon saw that Gauguin wanted to exploit values extraneous to painting: "No doubt he has enriched the contemporary

PAUL GAUGUIN. ***Breton Calvary, The Green Christ.*** 1889. Oil on canvas, 92 x 73 cm. Brussels, Musées Royaux des Beaux-Arts. Photograph copyright A.C.L.-Brussels.

soul. But the asymmetry of his Christs could not have been much help." It was not the visual deformation Fénéon objected to—he had always appreciated Gauguin's formal inventions—but a moral or spiritual deformation: Gauguin exploiting the image of a suffering Messiah to express his own self-pity, and for his self-aggrandizement.

The idea for Gauguin's self-portraits as Christ came from a poem Aurier had written in 1889, identifying the suffering poet with the crucified, misunderstood Master. This use of literary themes and allegories was a new twist in Gauguin, Fénéon noted. Indeed, the critic asserted that until Gauguin met the well-read painter Bernard, he took no interest at all in contemporary writing. But Gauguin, in thinking to exploit this new vein, was in fact exploited himself: "He has become the prey of literary men; the latter have assured him that he has the cure of souls, that he has been entrusted with a mission" (F, 192). Paintings such as "The Loss of Virginity" and "Self-Portrait with Yellow Christ" revealed that the artist had let himself be used by men of letters who capitalized on the symbolism in his art, a symbolism that was false and empty when programmed to please those very writers—authors of art criticism.

Earlier that year Fénéon had received an ironic commentary by Paul Signac on the works exhibited by Gauguin at the Belgian *XX*:

> Be in Love
> Be Mysterious
> Be Symbolist
> Be Boulangist
> Be always well dressed
> Be Grenadine [syrup]
>
> } Trust old Gauguin![20]

Fénéon never lost the distaste he had acquired for Gauguin. "Inauthentic," he firmly said, many years later.[21] He owned no paintings or drawings by Gauguin, not even the pottery he had so admired. It is true that Gauguin placed relatively high prices on the works he sold, and Fénéon was very poor during the 1880s and 1890s. Nor was Gauguin likely to give one of his pieces to a critic whom he considered unfair. But the fact is, Fénéon did not have much personal enthusiasm for Gauguin's painting; for him it lacked structure. "Had Gauguin not chosen exotic subjects, the deficiency of his drawing would have been more apparent," he once remarked.[22]

He nonetheless told the readers of the *Revue anarchiste* to go to Durand-Ruel's and see "the decorative canvases, of a barbaric, opulent and taciturn character, that Paul Gauguin has brought back from Tahiti" (F, 130). And he later helped disentangle the snare Gauguin got himself into as the "prey of littérateurs," for example, when Charles Morice heavily rewrote the painter's impressions of Tahiti, published as *Noa Noa* in 1897: "When I read it in the *Revue blanche,* where it first appeared, it astonished me, but also oppressed me with an ennui that I did not attribute to the painter," Fénéon said to John Rewald, and he firmly suggested that Morice's intervention be made quite clear "to avoid compromising Gauguin in this flux of literature."[23]

The critic did not let his judgment of Gauguin interfere with his appreciation of artists who claimed him as their founding spirit: those painters, for example, in the group calling themselves Nabis (Hebrew for "prophets"), which included Bonnard and Vuillard. However, he enjoyed poking fun at artists who slavishly tried to illustrate Aurier's formula for symbolist art. Visiting the Indépendants in spring of 1891, Fénéon remarked to Willy:

> Look at this etching, a woman about to give birth, watching the growth of a family tree. A caption gives us the explanation: "The old kind of painting had a language that everyone learnt; the new painting has a new language—learn it!"

This "universal language," he said, owed a lot to Paul Gauguin, and it was being spoken in "various dialects by Emile Bernard, Maurice Denis, Louis Roy, and the author of the lady you were just contemplating, the Dane, Jens-Ferdinand Willumsen." But, he concluded, the language was "somewhat arbitrary and its means of expression rather caricatural" (F, 181–82).

So Fénéon satirized the idea expounded by Albert Aurier that symbolist artists had a special hold on a language or "alphabet" of symbols. Fénéon saw that this idiom was "arbitrary"; that is, it relied on coincidences between meaning and form and resulted in caricature or "haphazard allegories."

The theories about symbolist art formulated by Aurier, Charles Morice, and other critics at the *Mercure de France* had an interesting effect on Fénéon, leading him to clarify his own position. He began applying the term "symbolic" more and more to the work of Seurat, Cézanne, and others he preferred, and to express more explicitly the inner feeling and abstract sense of the paintings he described, elements that had always been implicit in his art criticism.

In autumn, some of the same painters exhibited together in Saint-Germain-en-Laye, outside Paris. Fénéon saw the show and used Aurier's newly coined term, "ideist," in the title of his review, "A Few Ideist Painters." But he deliberately set the stage by opening his review with a brief eulogy for neo-impressionism:

> In a milieu subject to the conjugate laws of contrast in tones and valu —a swarm of prismatic spangles in vital competition for a harmony of the whole—thus did the neo-impressionists *conceive* and *objectify* the spectacle of the world. (F, 200, italics added)

In speaking of the need to objectify, F. F. was waving a red flag in front of Aurier and the ideists, who believed that painting should be subjective. He also baited them by praising the syntheses achieved by Signac, Pissarro, and Seurat, in works that "had attracted many other artists." For several years Fénéon had been speaking of synthesis as a primary aim for both neo-impressionist painting and symbolist writing.[24] Recently, however, the term had been claimed by Gauguin and Aurier as the special characteristic of symbolist painting. They thought of it as reducing elements in a painting and simplifying shapes in order to present them more clearly as signs of the ideas they embodied. This was quite different from the concept of Fénéon, who thought of synthesis as the way to integrate the very complexity of human experience into a work whose structure would give meaningful form to reality.

The ideists' striving for simplification was foiled by their predilection for literary scenarios and legends. Looking at the new crop of Tristan-and-Isoldes, Medusas, and Sphinxes, Fénéon wished the artists would understand "that a painter is showing too much humility when he chooses a subject already rich in literary meanings. . . ."

> Three pears on a cloth by Paul Cézanne are moving and sometimes mystical, whereas the entire Wagnerian Valhalla, when painted by them, is as uninteresting as the Chamber of Deputies. (F, 211.)

Fénéon commented positively on the brilliant young theorist of the Nabis, Maurice Denis, who "listened to Gauguin's teaching a bit in 1889, but has since developed his own originality." The anarchist critic had no quarrel with this painter's presenting religious themes in his work; Denis was a more sincere—and humble—

Above, **PAUL CÉZANNE.** ***Still Life with Three Pears.*** 1880–82. Watercolor over pencil, 12.6 x 20.8 cm. Rotterdam, Museum Boymans-van Beuningen. *Three pears on a cloth by Paul Cézanne are moving and sometimes mystical . . .* (F, 211)

MAURICE DENIS. ***Frontispiece*** for *Sagesse* by Paul Verlaine. Drawing cut on the wood by Beltranc. Paris, Amboise Vollard, 1911, facsimile of the 1895 edition. Courtesy Dallas Public Library.

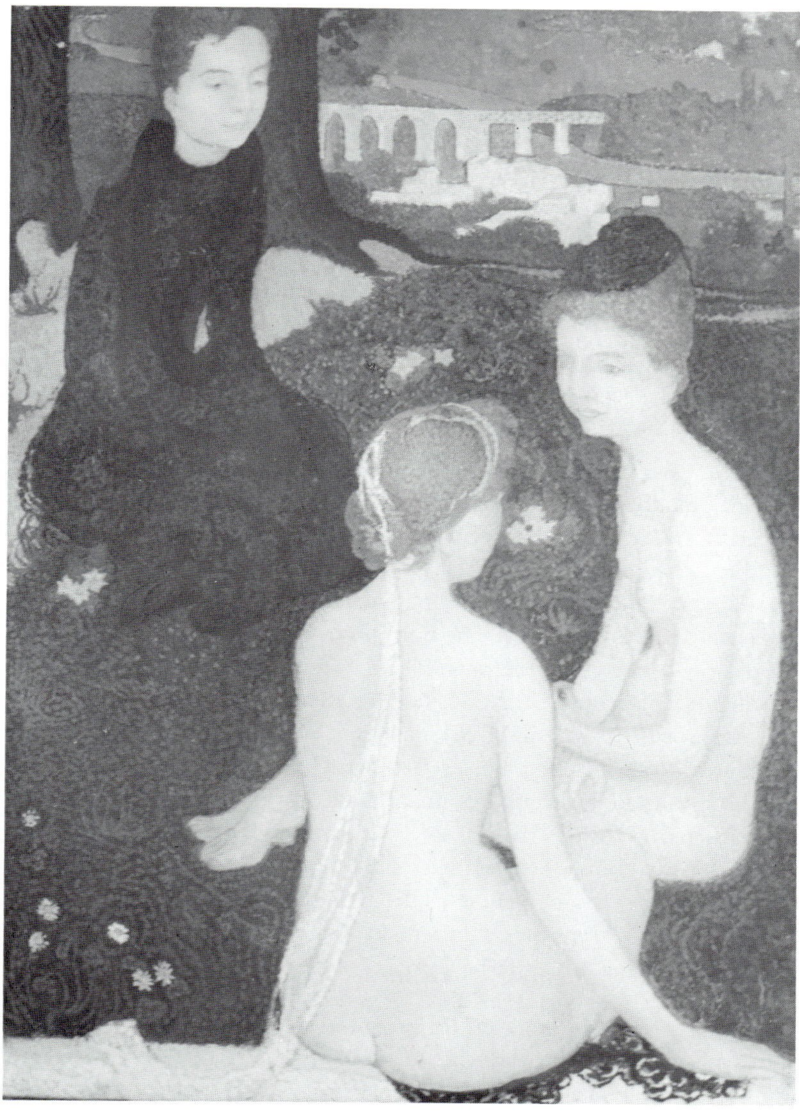

MAURICE DENIS. ***Trinitarian Evening.*** Inspired by a poem of the same name by Adolphe Retté. 1891. Oil on canvas, 102 x 72 cm. Saint-Martin-de-Londres, Collection Mme P. Déjean.

Catholic than Gauguin; and he was not unduly influenced by literature. "If he annotates a poem—from Verlaine's *Sagesse,* for example—he does not dally in visual re-editions of the verbal images, but strives to shape the very emblem of the emotion they engender." As for the form, whether painting or drawing, "he does not care to impose any illusion of depth":

> On a field that is nearly horizontal by definition, his figures rise one above another as it flattened against the flank of a mountain; and he strives to delimit the empty spaces

> between them with a melodic line. His most seductive paintings have a clear tonality; others seem draped in caliginous damask velvet, sprinkled with incongruous sprigs of April color. As for the manner: little dots that he brocades on flat background colors, to add some sort of epidermal life to the painting. (F, 200)

Using the vocabulary of textiles, Fénéon revealed the decorative, tapestry-like effect that Denis and his fellow Nabis were exploring. But at the same time, the critic mocked the dusky atmosphere of certain paintings and a superficial use of the dot, so different from the "prismatic spangles in vital competition for a harmony of the whole" that characterized neo-impressionism.

Turning to Bonnard and the "arabesque" he had painted of the agile modern woman he liked to portray, Fénéon said he was a "possible decorator of furniture, books, costumes, and streets." This seems like a slight, but in fact shows that the critic was aware that Bonnard, like other painters influenced by the applied arts movement in England and Belgium, was interested in designing furniture as well as illustrating books. Fénéon's mention of costumes forecasts the Nabis' activity at Paul Fort's theater later that year, creating costumes and scenery. As for "decorating streets," Fénéon had already noticed and reported on Bonnard's first poster when it went up on the walls in the spring of 1891, advertising a brand of champagne: finally, a superior poster signed by someone other than Chéret or Grasset! The bubbles frothing out of the champagne glass, forming a design like a coral reef and partly hiding the plump body of the waitress, her "spumante" hairdo and eyes squeezed shut in laughter—everything pleased Fénéon, except for the pink and yellow coloring, which he found too mild (F, 195). He looked forward to seeing more posters "of a cruel and serpentine eroticism if, after Chéret and his masks of lyric joy, Bonnard were commissioned to publicize circuses, Elysées, gardens, Moulins" (F, 201).

Fénéon concluded his review of the Ideist Exhibition with a scrutiny of Paul Ranson's painting, "Jésirah—Briah." He consulted the catalogue and inspected the back of the canvas for cabalistic signs planted there: a pentagram, the caduceus, and the word "Nabi" written in Arabic. At last the painting:

> Two monsters with female torsos; one of them, the Intellectual World, wants to contemplate Asia beyond the blue; the other monster, the Material World, looks at the ground. Jésirah is blazoned with a lotus, Briah with an owl. Pigment—pastels that must have been sopped up with a sponge dipped in flour paste. (F, 202).

"But," said Fénéon, "a work of art is eloquent through its internal rhythm—irreducible by our consciousness—and not through its program. An interlaced design by da Vinci touches us deeply. The *Circus* of Seurat is symbolic."

So Fénéon put the lid on further speculation about "Symbolic Painting," which was not to be found in any particular school, but in the inner strength of any well-conceived and executed work, understand not through ideas or doctrines, but through a total response of human consciousness. He could not resist throwing in a final thrust at Gauguin's school of Pont-Aven: "Perhaps the seascapes of Signac can benefit our souls; at least, although Breton, they do not torture our eyes."

PIERRE BONNARD. *France-Champagne.* 1891. Poster from a color lithograph, 78 x 50 cm. New Brunswick, New Jersey, The Jane Voorhees Zimmerli Art Museum, Rutgers—The State University of New Jersey. Gift of Ralph and Barbara Voorhees.

In March 1892, the new *Salon de la Rose † Croix* was created by the novelist Joséphin Péladan. Attracted by the seductive mystery and odd spirituality announced by the program, over one thousand people attended the opening, which included a mass at Saint Germain l'Auxerrois with music from *Parsifal* and a special fanfare composed by Eric Satie. Fénéon was in the crowd and amused himself by reading "The Rule and Admonition" of the Sâr Péladan; he headed his review with these extracts:

> Prohibited: 5) all landscapes, except those done à la Poussin; 7) all seascapes and sailors; 10) all domestic animals or those connected with sports; 11) all still lifes and other trifles that painters usually have the audacity to exhibit. (F, 210)

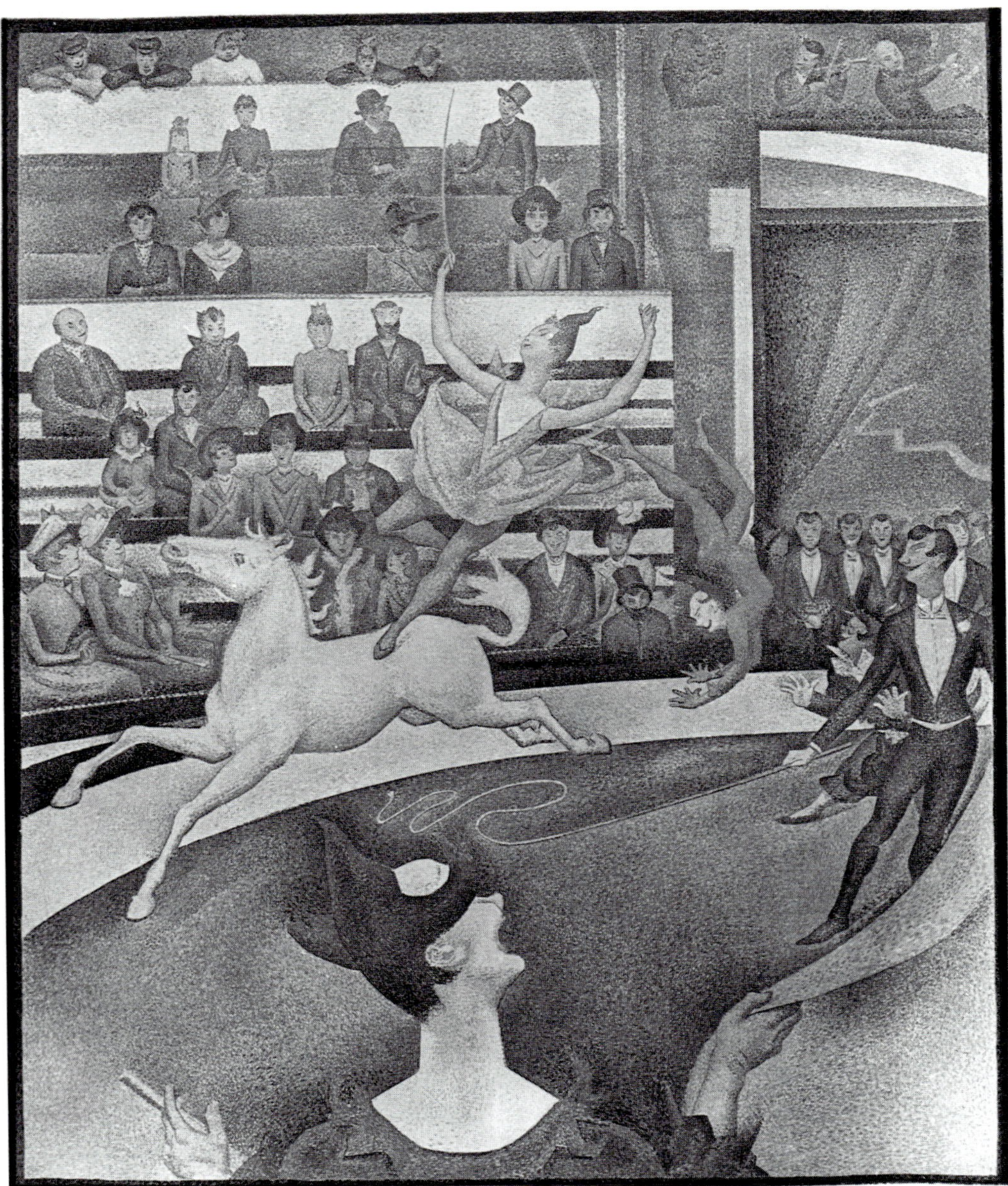

GEORGES SEURAT. ***The Circus.*** 1890–91. Oil on canvas, 185 x 150 cm. Paris, Musée d'Orsay. Photograph © Musées nationaux. *A work of art is eloquent through its internal rhythm . . . An interlaced design by da Vinci touches us deeply. The* Circus *of Seurat is symbolic.* (F 202)

There was also a list of admissable subjects "even though they be imperfectly executed: Myth, Allegory, the Catholic Ideal and Mysticism, the Paraphrase of great poetry and the nude made Sublime." The promise of fun implied in these rules was only partially fulfilled, said Fénéon. He focused an amused eye on the contribution of an erstwhile

PAUL RANSON. ***Christ and Buddha.*** ca. 1890. Oil on canvas, 72.8 x 51.5 cm. Inscription below on the right, *furusiya nabiy* ("Nabi chivalry"). New York, Collection of Mr. and Mrs. Arthur G. Altschul.

pointillist painter who had generously financed the Rose † Croix Salon, Antoine de La Rochefoucauld. He presented the "Angel of the Rose † Croix":

> Snowy peaks, vehement scenery, fresh and flexible mosaic of impressionist strokes. And, leaning on a huge cruciform sword, the Angel regards but does not even see a monster that, in the form of a rather hideous orthopteron named Praying Mantis, sweetly symbolizes all of us. (F, 210.)

Count de La Rochefoucauld withdrew his support from the Rose † Croix Salon before it closed, hastening to return to the neo-impressionist fold.

The incoherent aesthetics and reactionary politics of Péladan's organization should have been anathema to Fénéon. But the bizarre iconography, somewhat kinky eroticism, fierce antimaterialism, and underlying irrationality of this "symbolist" art amused him. He had been called the midwife of symbolism, but here he was more a bemused bystander at a stillbirth. In a curiously counterproductive way, symbolist literature and theory had led artists down a blind alley when they chose to put self-conscious ideas foremost. Symbolism, according to Fénéon, was part of the total creative endeavor and functioned best at the unconscious level while the artist struggled to achieve the form of his work. Thus Pissarro, he said, "Master of forms. . . . treats Nature as a great repertory of signs, frees it from the accidental . . . and attains high unconscious symbolizations" (F, 209).

There were four or five artists among the ideists or Nabis whom Fénéon came to appreciate more and more. Bonnard would one day become a close friend, and the critic was also on very good terms with Vuillard, K.-X. Roussel, and Félix Vallotton. His collection contained many works of theirs, as well as two by Maurice Denis—landscapes with no religious message, in a classicizing style. Except for some hilarious remarks in the slang of the anarchist review, *Le Père peinard,* he wrote nothing on them, for he had abandoned art criticism by this time. It is nevertheless interesting to see how Fénéon viewed not only Gauguin and Cézanne but Japanese art and other common roots of this group that flowered, like art nouveau, at the end of the century.

Models whom the Nabis claimed as their own, Puvis de Chavannes and Odilon Redon, had long been familiar to F. F. In his first piece of art criticism in 1883, Fénéon had foretold that Puvis would one day be recognized as one of the glories of the nineteenth century, and he also called attention to the "great unknown artist, Odilon Redon." At the Maison Dorée in 1886, he saw Seurat as a "modernizing Puvis," and pointed out Redon's work which hung in a corridor, "fifteen badly chosen drawings which nevertheless awaken anxiety in the souls of those who are prepared . . ." (F, 32). Although Fénéon generally disliked Allegory ("that old hag") he found that Puvis's genius triumphed over it, for example, in the "veiled emotional symphony" of figures for the Sorbonne amphitheatre (F, 78–79). His pastels, which other critics found understated, were, he thought, beautifully fresh and modern. The language Fénéon used to describe them reveals what the Nabis would later emulate:

> Through the closely conjugated rhythms of colors and lines, his pastels realize an art of reverie, silence, slow movement, serene beauty. (F, 108)

While his admiration for Puvis remained constant, Fénéon's initial enthusiasm for Redon was tempered over the years. In 1892, when Aurier proclaimed that this long ignored artist was one of the true masters of symbolist painting, Fénéon saw his work

Left, ODILON REDON. ***The Wing.*** 1893. Lithograph printed in black, 31.7 x 24.44 cm. New York, Museum of Modern Art, Lillie P. Bliss Collection. *Of M. Redon we can applaud—obviously—the shield of light made by the horse's chest in the lithograph* THE WING. . . . *But {his} nightmares have become familiar to us.* (F, 220–21)

Right, ODILON REDON. ***Cyclops Smiling and Horrible.*** Plate 3 from *Les Origines.* Paris, L. Dumont, 1883. Lithograph printed in black, 21.3 x 19.84 cm. New York, Museum of Modern Art. Gift of Victor S. Riesenfeld.

with a jaundiced eye. His pastels were done in "indifferent coloring" while his prints and drawings contained odd paraphrases from literature:

> A *Maleine* surprised to see sun on the walls again; a finicky, greedy, comical *Little Prelate;* a sinister *Saint Teresa,* with eyes that no longer know how to look about her; and twenty other plates where a niggardly amount of light creeps in among the inhabited shadows (F, 216).

It was too late to be entranced by this artist, Fénéon thought. His "nightmares have become familiar to us," he said in 1893, "and the time has long since passed when one could come across good people in life (or on their way to the sea) who had been sigillated for having inspected his printed plates" (F, 221). In magic or astrology, a sigil is a sign or image having mysterious power, but in popular French usage *sigillés* can mean people who think they had a mystical experience or look as though they did. "People in life or on their way to the sea" is suggestive of Maeterlinck's *Pelléas et Mélisande,* produced at the Oeuvre earlier that year: another jibe at the literary pretensions and vague mysticism endemic to the symbolist art movement.

Redon's contemporary, Eugène Carrière, was also claimed by Charles Morice and other writers at the *Mercure de France* as a symbolist painter. Fénéon had always noticed, with some approval, the rare appearances of Carrière's work and rated him highly for the "personal" quality of his art; but in May 1891, when the Boussod and Valadon gallery exhibited fifty examples of his domestic scenes, featuring especially "Mother and Child," Fénéon found that the "gracious, doleful, touching smile of this kind of painting turns into simpering and becomes a commercial trademark when repeated so many times" (F, 189). He compared Carrière's easy effects—figures emerging from haze and darkness painted with large silken strokes in toneless greys—with the rigor of Mallarmé and Cézanne who for him were the genuine authors of mystery. "Even when Cézanne does a still-life that is nearly a *grisaille,* his greys carry all the feeling of the hues they envelop, while those of M. Carrière remain neutral."

It is interesting that Fénéon contrasted Carrière's works in blacks and greys not with Seurat's dark drawings in conté crayon but with Cézanne's painting. This may have been because Fénéon wished to compare two effects in the same medium: Carrière's use of oils merely resulted in a silken sheen, he said, while Cézanne's explored the essential nature of painting. But the comparison also came up because the painter of Aix-en-Provence had finally come into his own and was being claimed as a model by the Nabis and other modernizing artists. Fénéon remarked that the Dutch member of the Nabi group, Jan Verkade, had painted two still lifes in Cézanne's manner, but "naturally without the morbid reworking that moves one so in examining a Cézanne" (F, 201). F. F. never devoted an article to Cézanne during the painter's lifetime. True, he had had only occasionally the chance to view his painting on display in the dimly lit back room of Père Tanguy's paint shop; Cézanne had not participated in a Paris exhibition since 1877, three years before Fénéon's arrival, and was not to be given a general show until 1895, after Fénéon had stopped writing art criticism. Some time after the painter's death in 1906, and probably at the request of a young student of art history, Solange Lemaître, Fénéon wrote a cogent piece on Cézanne, which he never bothered to publish (see F, 309). Nonetheless, his rare remarks on Cézanne in the early 1890s show how carefully he looked at the paintings he saw and how keenly he felt their influence.

Perhaps the most decisive influence on the Nabis and other painters of the period, though, was the art of Japan. "Bonnard, très japonard," was all F. F. said of this painter's showing at the Indépendants of 1892.[25] Paul Ranson, who liked to give nicknames to his fellow Nabis, was later credited with having given Bonnard the title of "Nabi très japonard," but he had in fact jovially copied it from Fénéon.

For several years Fénéon had taken a very keen interest in the oriental prints that were the delight of Signac and Seurat. He was planning, in fact, to write a book about eighteenth-century Japanese prints, a project that he eventually abandoned. But several of his published articles reveal how seriously he studied these prints and the techniques involved. Whereas most Western observers tended to lump these artists together, Fénéon carefully pointed out their differences.

> Harunobu always shows young lovers with tapering fingers and affected gestures teasing one another, exchanging a chrysanthemum or a poem. The horizon, eliminated. Scenery, a wall, a strip of grass, a vase, a cat, or nothing at all. Soft

EUGÈNE CARRIÈRE. ***Nativité.*** 1900–1905? Oil on canvas, 50 x 61 cm. New York, Private collection. Photograph courtesy Galerie Patrice Trigano, Paris.

> modulations of soot black or brown control the coloring. The imprint of a sinuous shape here and there. —No relation between this insipid artist and one like Hokusai, hot-headed, quick, farcical, earthy, interested in the life of the common people, in clouds, hurricanes, rutting, mobs, in the Gods, animals, flowers, and all the while changing his style as easily as he changed his name. (F, 121)

In a few words, Fénéon could evoke the world of Japanese prints as precisely as he could the pastels of Degas or the seascapes of Monet. His syntax espouses the form of the art before him: *Fuji-Yama au coucher du soleil: le ciel, la cime, simplement; la cime calcinée de rouge sur le froid ciel blanc et bleu* (Fuji-Yama at sunset: the sky, the peak, simply; the peak seared in red on the cold white and blue sky). Verbs are eliminated, the picture "simply" stands outside time; yet the volcano erupts, the lava is charred on the cold sky; but without the color of charcoal, red.

With humor, Fénéon told the delight of sketches showing creatures in movement:

> A barred ellipse circumscribing a zig-zag, there we have more than enough elements for Hokusai to show us a tortoise. But the ultimate simplifications can be admired in

MARY CASSATT. ***The Coiffure.*** 1891. Color print in drypoint, soft-ground etching, and aquatint. New York, The Metropolitan Museum of Art. Gift of Paul J. Sachs.

> Kitao: Kitao lets his brush fall—and there's a duck splashing about; there's a swan, gobbling up a fish; there's a crane, flying off; and not just any crane, fish, swan and duck, no!—they have their own personality and perhaps their own states of mind. (F, 121–22)

The chattering tone of this passage, full of verbs and movement, reflects the style of the artist. No doubt Fénéon appreciated Bonnard's little sketches of dogs, birds, Negroes, and nudes that he later printed in the pages of the *Revue blanche,* as animated and as amusing in their way as was Kitao's work.

Fénéon enjoyed Japanese influence on French art, but was somewhat ambivalent

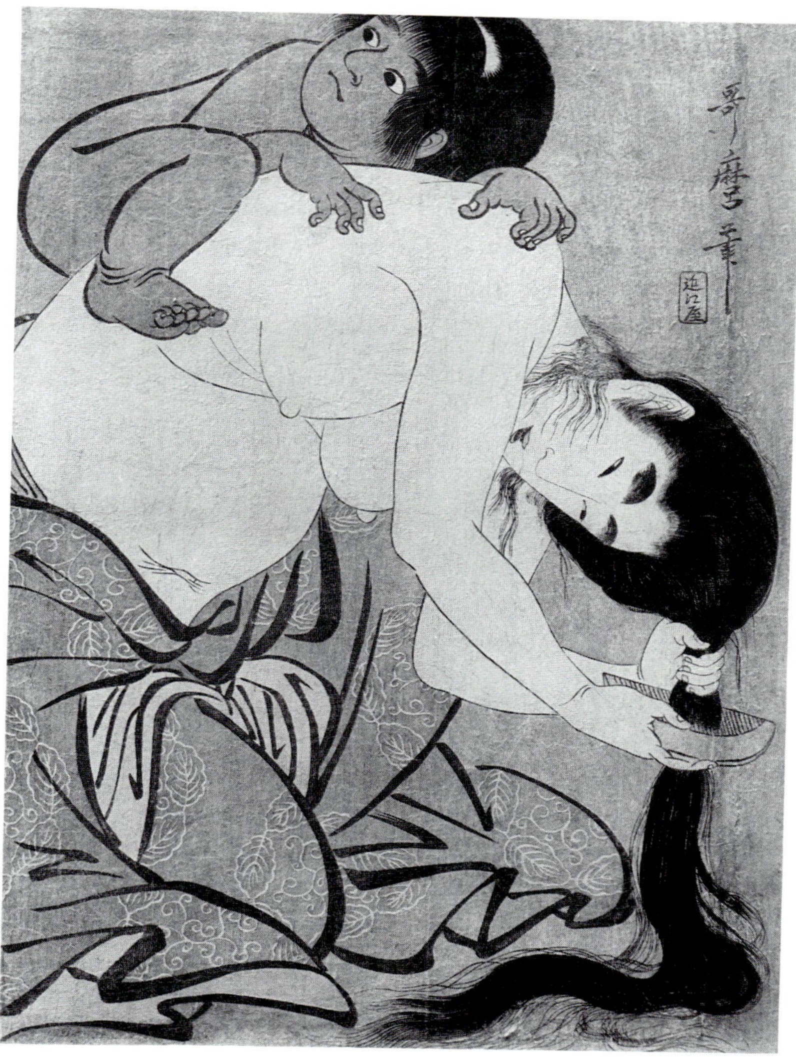

KITAGAWA UTAMARO (1754–1806). ***Yama Uba Combing Her Hair, with the Infant Kintoki on Her Back.*** Color woodcut. New York, The Metropolitan Museum of Art. Gift of Samuel Isham. 1914.

when Mary Cassatt, a skilled printmaker, decided to do an imitation of the Japanese Print:

> She may take what she likes from that tradition provided she keeps her originality intact. . . . She should generalize her interest, rather than emulate a single artist: today, the way she makes a network of the arms, shoulders, and generally all the lines of the nude remind one too much of dear Utamaro, except that the lines here are fuller than in Utamaro and so show the influence of those chubby necks in Kiyonaga—although without the latter's facile, somewhat vulgar naturalism.(F 184.)

This attention to detail shows how closely Fénéon followed Cassatt's interest in Japanese prints, while his admonishing tone and name-dropping suggest his fondness for elitism and possibly a need to feel superior to a woman artist.[26]

Printmaking was an art that had interested Fénéon for some time and which gave him a keen appreciation of the Nabis' lithographs, prints, and illustration of books. Fénéon had been initiated into the applied arts movement earlier by the former neo-impressionist Henry van de Velde, the Pissarros, who had their own press for awhile, and the British artists Shannon and Ricketts. Whenever Fénéon reported on an exhibition of prints, he revealed a precise and intimate understanding of the processes involved. Camille Pissarro, who in this matter had not needed to worry about Seurat's jealous protection of "author's rights," was happy to explain things to him, and F. F.'s inquisitive, methodical mind was satisfied by the intricacies of the techniques he observed.[27]

In 1898, Remy de Gourmont declared: "Since the new era we have had only two art critics, Aurier and Fénéon: one is dead, the other is silent. What a pity! For either one would have been able to bring into line a certain school (the pseudosymbolists) who, for one Maurice Denis or one Filiger, gave us a whole gang of blundering imitators."[28]

The "new era" de Gourmont meant was, presumably, the symbolist one, replacing realism or naturalism, and the "blundering imitators" those artists who continued throughout the 1890s to exhibit under the eclectic banner of symbolist art. It is odd that he should pick Aurier, among the many symbolists who wrote art criticism, to couple with Fénéon. He may have lumped them together because they were both "gone from the scene" and could thus be eulogized. Aurier had died unexpectedly at age twenty-seven in March 1892, and Fénéon stopped writing criticism the following year. More curious yet is the expectation that Fénéon, had he continued to write, would have labored to "bring into line" the new school of symbolist painting, which romanticized a mystic or psychological withdrawal from the world and its problems. Indeed, perhaps one of the reasons F. F. abandoned art criticism in favor of a more direct involvement in the anarchist movement was that the new art related so little to what he felt was important. However, Aurier was for the 1890s what Fénéon had been in the 1880s, an authentic spokesman for a new vision in art. Even posthumously, Aurier's writings, collected in a large volume by the *Mercure de France,* became the preferred sourcebook for art theory, better known than Fénéon's articles, scattered in various defunct literary reviews.

The two critics were almost diametrically opposed, both in their thinking and their style. Aurier found any kind of materialist or positivist thinking antipathetic and retrograde. For him science was anathema and the enemy of art. He cited Swedenborg, rather than Rood or Charles Henry, and took his inspiration from Schopenhauer's notion that objects are not independent entities but symbols of the idea we perceive in them. Rather than espousing the anarchists' ideal of commitment to others and society as a whole, Aurier found contemporary society "putrified" and preached that the pure artist must be "isolated" from crass reality, like Christ in Gethsemane. In almost every respect, spiritual, political, and philosophical, Aurier's thinking was at odds with Fénéon's.

The difference between the two critics is most evident in their styles of writing. Fénéon selected, so to speak, precious stones to set into an exacting mosaic, while Aurier picked up what pearls fell his way and strung them in baroque triple strands. Aurier was inclined to see the man through the paintings, or rather, a mythological version of the man: Renoir was for him "the eternal child" playing in a "universe of toys"; Monet was a modern priest of Baal, a sunworshiper. Fénéon limited himself to a view of the paintings—and revealed more of the painter. Their differences can be seen quite easily in their respective criticism of the same artist—Monet, for example. Here is a brief extract from Aurier's "Claude Monet" dated March 1892:

> . . . One should certainly not ask this lover of divine light anything more than his love of divine light. This voluptuous passion that enthralls him, the ineffable sensations he feels, absolve him from dreaming, thinking, and practically from living. Ideas, creatures, and things no longer live a separate existence for him, but are dissolved in the flaming breath of Baal. . . . Is he not well aware that, with the complicity of his god, nothingness itself would be illuminated, would become a temple of joy and extravagant delights? Therefore, not without a certain unacknowledged coyness, he chooses insignificant pretexts, everyday subjects, in order to metamorphize these trifles into radiant poems, fairyland visions: a haystack in a field, a gully of the Creuse, a few waves of the Mediterranean, some poplars on the bank of the Epte—he simply bathes them in the divine dazzlements that fill his own eyes and fingers and transmutes this contemptible reality into a delightful paradise strewn with gems and smiles.[29]

In contrast, here is a report by Fénéon, "Recent Works of Claude Monet," in May 1891:

> Two haystacks in a field and the play of the seasons and hours upon them in 1890–91. Fifteen different paintings on this motif, rendered differently each time. When the painter is M. Monet, what a glowing commentary on the first phase of impressionism: working amidst the whirling metamorphoses of nature and painting directly from life, to immobilize some transitory effect, forever unique. But nature is not quite so mobile, she does not reel; perhaps we would prefer painters who, less eager to serve her caprices, coordinate her disparate appearance, recreate her in a stable form, and endow her with permanence. Two haystacks . . . see how M. Monet empowers them with his shrewd sight and polychrome intentions. When have colors fused in a more sparkling harmony of clamorous tones? Especially in the evening sun the Haystacks gloried; in summer, sparks of dark red flickering haloed them; in winter, they streamed their phosphescent shadows to the ground, and against a sky first rosy-hued then gold, they glinted, enameled blue by a sudden frost. (F, 191)

It is a question, again, of style. Surely F. F. had his limitations, but he knew how to look and when to say nothing, and that is what makes him the more eloquent critic.

It had been six years since Moréas's symbolist manifesto and Fénéon's *Impressionnistes en 1886*. A half dozen years seems a meager span of time compared to the careers of most critics; but Fénéon had said enough. He had done speaking of symbolism, in literature or in art. The winds of change were rising, he was moving on.

PART FOUR

Iris-in on Anarchism 1891–1894

CHAPTER 12

Move Toward End Game: Anarchism in Print

After 1890, for three and a half years, F. F. was involved in clandestine activity for the anarchist movement. It culminated in his arrest at the War Office in April 1894 and a spectacular trial, in which a group of thirty anarchist workers and intellectuals were accused of belonging to an international conspiracy. Anarchism was indeed an international movement, akin to and born around the same time as Marxism and socialism. But unlike the other ideologies, it strove to remain apolitical. It found adherents throughout newly industrialized Europe and America, but also in Russia and Spain. It was strongest in areas like France, where industrial development was slow and uneven and the labor movement weak.

In France, as elsewhere, anarchists were diverse, with no consistent political program or ideology. They shared a utopian ideal, based on two assumptions: (1) a truly free individual is essentially good, and will cooperate with others in a way beneficial to all; (2) humankind will be better off without a ruler (*an-archos* in Greek) and without any form of government (*an-archê*). To most minds, "anarchy" suggests chaos and unruliness; but Fénéon and his friends envisaged a world of harmony and balance, freed from arbitrarily imposed boundaries and rules. Fénéon recognized that others questioned this vision, as he pointed out in response to the French Marxist, Jules Guesde:

> We would have thought that anarchist civilization—without laws, without bosses—being favorable by its very nature to the development of all individuals, would yield a full flowering complexity.
>
> Not at all. In the entertaining interview published by the *Figaro,* M. Guesde takes the anarchists to task for "their absurd dream of a SIMPLISTIC society"!
>
> No more need be said. It is well known that the goal of our Marxist functionaries would be a society where each citizen will bear a serial number. They prefer the complexity of a clock to that of a living body. (F, 898–99.)

The anarchists did not believe with Engels that the State, once organized along collectivist lines, would evolve and finally wither away. On the contrary, Fénéon observed that collectivist communities multiplied laws and increased central control. The statutes of a utopian colony in Australia, he noted, were full of the folly of servitude:

> "Obedience to the supremacy of laws. . . . The director, elected by a two-thirds vote, is the only executive authority, assisted by the council of superintendents. . . . Superintendents elected by. . . ." And that goes on for column after column. Happy colony; life there is pure pleasure—you vote and obey all the time. (F, 932.)

Only the spontaneous action of truly free individuals could give form to the ideal of nonrule, said Fénéon, and that form would necessarily change constantly (F, 937). This vision, which replaced faith in laws and authority with a deep trust in one's own individuality and a corresponding regard for the individuality of others, appealed to many creative artists and writers. Much has been written about this alliance between anarchism and the arts at the end of the nineteenth century.[1] Fénéon did not analyze it; his commentaries simply attest to it.

In columns called "Facts" and "Agitation" in the *Revue anarchiste* and the *Revue libertaire,* he reported on books, paintings, workers' strikes, and anarchist bombs with equal interest. He objected when the *Revue blanche* classified the painter Luna San Pedro among the impressionists; not only was the work of this "irascible artist" totally uninspired, his reactionary ideas were not in tune with the impressionists "who have almost all adhered to anarchism and put its ideas into practice" (F, 905). The news of Gustave Moreau's election to the Académie des Beaux-Arts was upsetting. Were they trying to disguise the fundamental foolishness of this institution by nominating authentic artists? Fénéon was reassured at the next election, which appointed several well-known nonentities (F, 896). As for the red ribbon of the Légion d'honneur, it evoked nothing but contempt in Fénéon. When he saw Huysmans's name appear on the official list of ribbon wearers, Fénéon said:

> This nasty trick played on the author of *A Rebours, En Rade, Là-Bas* cannot be as bad for him as his dismissal [from his post as clerk in the Ministry of the Interior] which would have followed his refusal to join the herd. Let's pity him! (F, 916)

Fénéon's anarchism did not require that art or literature be shaped to serve as "instruments of the revolution" as was suggested, for example, by Kropotkin.[2] Those who would promote anarchism could use more direct and effective means, while real art, new art, was revolutionary in itself. *La Révolte* accused Francis Vielé-Griffin of writing "bourgeois" poems unrelated to the social struggle,[3] but Fénéon said that the poet of *La Chevauchée d'Yeldis* had created a new level of human consciouness and revealed the depth of his anarchist convictions in a poem about a twelve-year-old laborer who committed suicide—one of the many who chose that alternative to starvation (F, 866). Anarchist ideas did not excuse bad writing; when Georges Lecomte wrote a turgid novel, *The Mill,* showing how an excessively materialist bourgeoisie crushed its most vile members in the social mill, Fénéon said:

> Good is born out of an excess of evil; did not this philanthropic idea lead M. Lecomte to write *La Meule?* We would prefer dynamite: quicker and cleaner.[4]

Dynamite was a possibility: eleven anarchist bombs exploded in Paris between 1892 and 1894. Nine people were killed, fewer than the number of strikers and Labor Day marchers shot by government troops; but the anarchist bombs, touching the sensibilities of the establishment and the popular imagination, received far greater attention. The vast majority of anarchists opposed violence, but the explosions made anarchism virtually synonymous with terrorism. Fénéon was among the very few who believed that "Propaganda by Deed" was just as effective as "Propaganda by Word," or more so. Yet he was involved primarily in propaganda by word. His pithy remarks were written not for posterity but to spur on his readers, from day to day, in the unending struggle for freedom.

During his three and a half years of clandestine activity, Fénéon wrote almost exclusively for anarchist publications. His signature disappeared from the pages of all reviews, except for an occasional piece of art criticism. His literary criticism was sparsely scattered among his notes of social commentary, yet he continued to pick out new writers of unusual talent. In April 1891 he noticed a book that had just appeared anonymously:

> *The Notebooks of André Walter.* . . . If someone put a megaphone in our hands, we still would not shout "Buy this!" to the crowd; it has its purveyors of mercenary romances. . . . But for those, at least, who live according to some kind of nobility, we might say: *read this book, it is for you.*[5]

It was the first novel of André Gide, whom Fénéon would later come to know and publish.

He wrote these remarks for the relatively new review, *Les Entretiens politiques et littéraires* ("Political and literary topics of conversation"), founded by Francis Vielé-Griffin in April 1980. It lasted until December 1893 and became more and more a voice for anarchist thought while continuing to publish writers not directly involved with anarchism, such as Mallarmé and Valéry.

Fénéon remained out of the limelight in *Entretiens.* He established his friendship with Edmond Cousturier there, but he still objected to any public intrusion on his private life. One autumn, *Entretiens* published a chronicle on the travels of its notables: Pissarro had just returned from England, Toulouse-Lautrec was in Arcachon, Signac had been sailing with Luce and a "boatload of literati," when "The Tub" sank to the bottom—all lives, if not feelings, spared. Fénéon was not on holiday but he was included just the same in the report:

> M. Félix Fénéon, that fine, expressive stylist, that guardian of modern techniques, dreams of great art and noble literature, walks around Paris with the supple step of a

> thoroughbred greyhound, and goes to feast his eyes on the splendors in M. Edmond Cousturier's home. (*Entretiens*, no. 7, 1 October 1890, p. 239.)

The next issue carried this item:

> N. B.—M. F. Asks us to advise you that one must not read his name in number 7 of *Entretiens*, p. 239, line 15: any other name—fine.[6]

These exchanges, building upon the mask and mythology of Fénéon the aesthete, obscure the fact that he was one of the most direct and radical adherents of the rising anarchist movement.

The Third Republic was especially fertile soil for anarchism. It was profoundly bourgeois, controlled by a recently empowered middle class which opposed the demands of the proletariat as much as it distrusted innovations in the arts. Albert Camus later spoke of the hypocrisy of this "mediocre and grasping society:"

> The freedom of which Monsieur Thiers dreamed was the freedom of privilege consolidated by the police; the family, extolled by the conservative newspapers, was supported by social conditions in which men and women were sent down into the mines, half-naked, attached to a communal rope; morality prospered on the prostitution of the working classes.[7]

The famous aphorism of P.-J. Proudhon, "Property is theft," took on a new pungency during the era of injustice that arose from the industrial capitalist system, when private ownership of the means of production turned the producers, the workers, into slaves, or worse: unseen, mechanical cogs in the production chain.

Today, one hardly thinks of the Gay Nineties as a time of repression and terrorism. But the *Belle Epoque* was far from "beautiful" for most of the people. It was not uncommon for a man, woman, or child to work a "long day"—that is, eighteen hours. Those who refused were laid off. A cleaning woman labored all day for six *sous* (less than a third of one franc). But she was regarded as a parasite by the laundress, who worked longer and harder for less pay. "Nobody forces them to," was the attitude of the bourgeois. Wages were calculated by what *one* person needed to eat; a man therefore could not feed his family, and the wages of his wife and children were cut according to their gender and size. Fénéon quoted *La Plume* to the effect that, over the preceding fifty years, an average of some two thousand persons died of hunger each year in France. More than one thousand per year, driven by poverty, committed suicide, including entire families (F, 920).

If the workplace was frequently unsanitary or unsafe, urban tenements were even worse, with little or no supervision for small children, because siblings as well as mothers were forced to work. Conditions that we would now consider intolerable were the rule, and there was no legal way to change them. One could perhaps join a trade union, but employers had the right to fire and blacklist union members, and regularly did so. In parliament, the official representatives of labor (members of the socialist parties) failed during this time to initiate legislative reforms.

Compounding injustice, the decade between 1884 and 1894 had more than its share of corruption. One third of parliament was involved in the Panama Canal scam (1884–92), approving legislation for Canal bonds, while aware that the company was nearly bankrupt and the project was foundering. While legislators and journalists accepted bribes from the company to advance its affairs, many little people who invested in those bonds lost their savings. In 1887 another scandal broke; Daniel Wilson, a member of the Chamber of Deputies, was caught selling government honors. This was not an unusual practice, but he became an example because he was President Grévy's son-in-law and more successful in graft than rival politicians. When he was reelected in 1893, Fénéon said, "He will be the most honest in the whole gang!" (F, 917). Besides these in-house scandals, there was the "pacification" of Indochina, Madagascar, and chunks of Africa; antisemitism fed by the publication of Drumont's *France Juive* and his periodical, *La Libre Parole;* the Dreyfus conviction.

The anarchists were moved not so much by these sensational events as by the very existence of what Fénéon called the mendacious Republic, represented on coins by a bounteous woman sowing grain in the sunrise. Not content simply to mouth the slogan stamped on the reverse of the coin, the anarchists wanted to rouse the populace from its weary indifference and to live out the words "Liberté, Egalité, Fraternité." On 1 May 1891, French workers again celebrated the day chosen by the International Socialist Congress in 1889 to draw attention to demands for an eight-hour workday. Many workers took the day off—a one-day strike, as the government saw it. On the outskirts of Paris, a small group of anarchists walked from Levallois to Clichy and had a run-in with the police, who had seen their posters signed "some poverty-stricken rebels." The anarchists' trial and conviction led to events that culminated in a series of bombs aimed successively at the military, the judiciary, the parliament, and finally the electorate, bombings for which the arrested anarchists Ravochol, Vaillant, and F. F.'s friend, Emile Henry, claimed responsibility.

Fénéon did not contribute to the main organ of anarchist discussion, Jean Grave's *La Révolte.* Grave was as serious as his name, and he was sometimes called, behind his back, the pope of rue Mouffetard. Fénéon maintained cordial relations with him for many years, but he preferred to work with more idiosyncratic Zo d'Axa, who created the anarchist paper *L'Endehors.* With his red beard trimmed to a point, Zo d'Axa looked like a gentleman buccaneer. He used to go to prison, quipped Jules Renard, as one goes to the telephone, when called.

Zo d'Axa started *L'Endehors* shortly after the 1891 May Day confrontation between workers and police. The journal's title,* "On the Outside," epitomized his own life-style and character. Zo d'Axa attracted a number of first-rate writers to his review, which Jules Huret characterized in the *Figaro:*

> A weekly that publishes—with unbridled violence—anarchist writing and ultramodern literary criticism. It offers sanctuary to rebels like Georges Darien and to pure

*Unlike the adverb *en dehors,* the journal's title is properly written in one word, "without a space or hyphen—on purpose," F. F. explained to Jean Paulhan (letter, 6 May 1943, Paulhan archives, Paris).

T. A. STEINLEN. ***Poster for La Feuille,*** anarchist paper by Zo d'Axa. ca. 1898. Lithograph printed in black and red, 27.4 x 36.2 cm.

> poets like Henri de Régnier and Saint-Pol-Roux. The director, Zo d'Axa, is a gallant and courageous spirit.[8]

Fénéon became acquainted with Zo d'Axa in August 1891 through a young novelist, as he explained in a letter to Signac:

> My dear Paul,
>
> You didn't know who was sending you those free copies of *l'Endehors:* it was Gallo (is that the spelling?),* who used to be a schoolmate of yours and now goes by the name of Zo d'Axa. We just recently met, thanks to Georges Darien, whom I see and rather like a lot, although I haven't yet read his novels. Have you? Tonight I am going to read *Bas les coeurs.* Darien and Zo are at a meeting right now, a joust among three priests (Father Jouet is one) and three comrades: Sébastian Faure, Leboucher and Martinet.[9]

Darien had recently gained notoriety for two antimilitary novels that he wrote after experiencing life as a rebellious recruit in a disciplinary company on the Sahara.

*Gallaud (pronounced Gallo) was Zo d'Axa's real name, although historians have recorded it *Galland,* copying a newspaper misprint.

According to Lucien Descaves, another antimilitary novelist, Darien was tough: "the play of muscles under the taut skin of his jaws, his intense gaze and thin lips beneath a mustache that twitched like an orange cat's whiskers—said he was not one to mess with. Underneath it all was a fine artistic temperament."[10]

Fénéon used to meet with Darien and Zo d'Axa in the basement of a building on a little street called rue Bochart-de-Saron, off boulevard de Rochechouart. There, around a single large table, *L'Endehors* was written and produced, about six thousand copies every week. Many of its contributors also worked at *Entretiens politiques et littéraires,* whose chief editors, the poets Henri de Régnier and Francis Vielé-Griffin, wrote impassioned articles for *L'Endehors* about bourgeois "charity" and the lot of the poor: "work without bread, the slow suicide of the mines and the blast-furnaces. . . ."[11] Art and literary criticism was written by Verhaeren, Jules Christophe, Charles Saunier, and F. F., who also helped the managing editor of the review, Armand Matha, a coiffeur by trade. Matha, who had a dark rich beard which curled on his chest, "like an Assyrian prince," was a brave and dedicated man who would go through fire for a comrade in need; but letters were not his forte. It was Fénéon who proofread *L'Endehors,* crossing Paris every Thursday night after dinner to work in the little shop on Avenue Rapp where the large folio pages were typeset and printed.

He put his own name on three small pieces of art and literary criticism for the paper, in November and December 1891. Apolitical as these writings were, the police took notice, and it was about this time that they opened a dossier on F. F. But then Fénéon's signature disappeared from *L'Endehors,* and the full extent of his participation was veiled.

His clandestine social criticism was virulent. On May Day 1891, troops had fired on a crowd of workers in the textile-producing town of Fourmies, killing nine people, two of them children. Fénéon recorded the impact of this event with his customary irony:

> After Fourmies.
>
> In front of the Pépinière barracks two children are playing. It is time for the changing of the guard; soldiers step out. One of the terrified moppets cries to the other: "Let's scram—they are going to shoot!" (F, 891.)

This comment appeared in a column called "Hourras, tollés et rires maigres" (Hurrahs, outcries and thin laughter), which Zo d'Axa created and then gave over to F. F. Behind Fénéon's thin laughter lay the most extreme of anarchist opinions. True to the ideal of nonrule, F. F. ridiculed the socialists for their attempts to effect reforms through political oratory:

> Succi, the fellow famous for his fasting, announces that he will speak continuously for three days and three nights without taking any food.
>
> Socialist conventioneers invented that experiment long since, although they split it up: for three days, three nights, and as long as you want they will talk, but it is their constituency who will not eat. (F, 902)

Fénéon respected neither deputies nor the right to vote, because the whole system of government crushed the very people it was supposed to serve. He joined in the struggle for economic and social change, but he regarded political reforms as irrelevant and even counterproductive.

Anarchism appealed not only to the intellectual elite of the 1880s and 1890s, but to the many artisans who saw their independence threatened by industrialized society, and to increasing numbers of laborers. Anarchist leaders addressed themselves to the latter because, as Bakunin said, a real revolution could only be achieved by people who had nothing to lose.

Fénéon did not speak of revolution, but encouraged individuals to act according to their own conscience—to steal, if need be—rather than give up the struggle for life. It was bitterly cold in January 1893, "several degrees below the *Bourse* [Stock Exchange]," Fénéon said, adding that the whole race of down-and-outs would soon be extinct if the cold continued. He recommended that they raid the stockpiles of coal then in storage on the docks; and that they hurry (F, 907). In the summer he noted with satisfaction that burglars were managing to redistribute the wealth in small ways while the owners of rich apartments were away on vacation. But, he warned, to facilitate their investigations the police were suggesting to complainants that it could only be a dismissed servant who had pulled the job:

> Of course it is possible, it is even fair for certain of those fine people to try to compensate for the damage inflicted on them when they were unjustly let go.
>
> So we will not hesitate to tell them, "Never, never do the job yourselves!"
>
> Be satisfied with having enterprising, discreet, trustworthy—and well informed—friends. (F, 903)

On another occasion he said, "Let's be fearless and defy the five years' hard labor and three-thousand franc fine for incitement to stealing and justification for stealing; let's quote the Gospel of Mark (Chap. II, verses 23–27): 'Now it happened that he was passing through the cornfields on the sabbath, and as the disciples made their way through, they began to pick the ears of corn. . .'" (F, 935).

Fénéon had a good word to say whenever people revolted against authority:

> The Japanese, who have had such a positive influence on our painting, would that they could influence our political ways!
>
> "Yokohama, 23 May (1892). One thousand residents of Saga refused to pay their taxes. . . ."

Or when they retaliated against oppression:

> Those South-American republics—so often disparaged—sometimes set a good example:
>
> Juan Omevedo, plantation owner and general who, thanks to this double title earned the nickname of Hyena, was executed by his workers on April 18 in the streets of Las Feques, thanks to that same double title. (F, 899)

This commentary reflects a slogan launched by the anarchists after Bakunin's death in 1876, "Progaganda by Deed," by which was meant some sort of direct action to demonstrate discontent. In Italy, for example, militants burned the parish records of a little village, broke open the tax collector's safe and distributed its contents among the poor. On 25 December 1880, an anonymous article in *Le Révolté* gave a violent twist to the new tactic: "Permanent revolt in speech, writing, by the dagger and the gun, or by dynamite . . . anything suits us that is alien to legality."[12] Throughout the 1880s, anarchist publications multiplied the call for violence, with little effect. The dynamiting began, as I noted earlier, only after the arrest and conviction of anarchist workers on 1 May 1891.

Whereas most intellectuals who sympathized with the anarchists dissociated themselves from propaganda by deed, Fénéon in his offhand way defended the "explosions that awakened the bourgeois from their torpor." In order to be effective, these acts should be totally clandestine: "Too ostentatious," he said of the way Paulino Pallâs had avenged the death of four comrades by tossing a bomb at a Spanish general on parade. The horse, not the general, was killed. When 465 cases of dynamite were deliberately sunk at sea because some had exploded and killed several people, Fénéon remarked, "How dumb to lose good merchandise like that!" (F, 928). He approved more deadly, anonymous gestures, such as the bomb laid in a Barcelona theater that killed twenty members of high society. And when another bomb exploded in Paris after the police had found it and carried it back to their headquarters, Fénéon murmured, "What intimate charm in this story. . ." (F, 929).

Symbolists who had formerly applauded anarchist acts now withdrew their support. When the director of *La Plume* expressed his disapproval, Fénéon replied: "Bless my soul! How propaganda by deed is stigmatized. M. Deschamps is really ungrateful, for if a few comrades had in fact not demonstrated so well by knife and by bomb, it is not very likely he would have ever thought of writing this article" (F, 939).

Not surprisingly, while defending these illegal acts of violence, F. F. took an unorthodox stand on military violence and "discipline." The War Office provided much grist for his mill:

> In its list of condemned prisoners waiting for the president's decision, the press has omitted, of course, soldiers also condemned to death.
>
> Why should they get any attention? Their misdeeds are paltry misdeeds that a court of summary jurisdiction would have priced at a fine of sixteen francs.
>
> . . . .
>
> Ugly, such slaughter? but so useful. . . "The bullets, model 1886, after penetrating through a small cut, come out by tearing flesh over a large expanse, and perforated a stake fifteen centimeters thick."
>
> There's a report to comfort a really patriotic heart! (F, 896–97.)

Fénéon's antinationalism knew no bounds. He had equal contempt for Colonel Dodds's "pacification" of Dahomey and for Senator Déroulède's campaign to reclaim Alsace-Lorraine from Germany. Whether called colonization or revenge, war was war, and soldiers, no matter their country, were ignorant pawns. At Camille Pissarro's first retrospective (1892), Fénéon remarked that only one canvas from 1870 and no earlier ones were on display, because the soldiers occupying Pissarro's house during the Franco-Prussian War were "too ignorant to think of swiping his paintings, and destroyed them" by using them as doormats or cooks' aprons. Contradicting other reports claiming that the soldiers were Prussians,[13] Fénéon said they were French officers:

> Oh, a visit of German cavalrymen might have been just as bad, perhaps. We willingly admit as much.
>
> (With pride:) The French flag is not worth less than any other national rag. (F, 895)

When France, to celebrate a military and diplomatic alliance with czar Alexander III, enthusiastically received a shipment of Russian sailors in Toulon, Fénéon quoted from Admiral Lebourgeois's speech: "Every Russian sailor will now have his French sailor, just as every French sailor will have his Russian sailor."—"Mon dieu!" remarked F. F., "we are not Puritans; and we know that in the army those mores are allowed and in common use. And yet is it really necessary to give so much publicity to things that cannot do anything for the repopulation of France?" (F, 924–25). This "love affair" between France, which claimed to be a democracy, and the repressive regime of czarist Russia showed a total lack of principle and sensitivity. Fénéon reported on the incredible level of ignorance and the extreme poverty of Russian workers and commented wryly on the enthusiasm of the Parisian press for things Russian (F, 939–40). He observed proud fathers promenading with their children dressed up in Russian costume and drew sad conclusions about what sort of thoughts could develop in little heads used as political carnival masks (F, 921).

Fénéon satirized the press, the army, the Chamber of Deputies, and other aspects of the Third Republic, but only rarely the Church. This was because the state had preempted religion's role as the watchdog of public morality. Two deputies, Jules Simon and Frédéric Passy, had created a "French League for Rebuilding Public Morality," which concerned itself with such vital questions as the indecency of the nude figure of Hercules engraved on the five-franc coin. Fénéon made merry of their hypocrisy:

> The latest statistics show that there has been a decrease in the number of houses of ill fame playing their trade. Each day brings about another closing of one of these interesting enterprises. This datum is obviously the sign of a moral rearmament in the Nation. Faced with such a satisfactory state of affairs, the supporters of M. Simon and Passy's League will no longer be able to cry, *Where are we going?* They will have to whisper, *Where shall we go?* (F, 900)

F. F. held the judiciary, too, in contempt. He thought they would be better employed as monologists at the Follies, until they eliminated themselves.

> Dead sick of himself after reading the book by Samuel Smiles (*Know Thyself*), a judge just drowned himself at Coulange-la-Vineuse.
>
> If only this excellent book could be read throughout the magistracy . . . (F, 904)

More logical than cynical, such remarks reflected the anarchist's belief that justice really resides in the individual's capacity to act according to his own conscience. A judge, even a policeman, was free to do this:

> A policeman, Maurice Marullas, has blown out his brains. Let's save the name of this honest man from being forgotten. (F, 927)

Unlike most other anarchist publicists, Fénéon did not lampoon ordinary police, but rather their superiors.

Active anarchist as he was, F. F. laughed at the attempts of some of his symbolist colleagues to systematize anarchist thinking:

> *La Plume* (1 January 1894) opens with an article by which M. Léon Deschamps rallies his review to anarchism. The form of certain insights will make some banterers smile—this one, for example: "Anarchism denies the immortality of the soul." Doesn't it sound as if a group of comrades met in some Nicene Council to dogmatize about that? (F, 938–39)

Fénéon's social commentaries touch on nearly every aspect of anarchist thought in the early 1890s, but to codify them would be to distort them. The fragments they form pinpoint critical problems as they incite to new awareness and action.

Late in 1892 Fénéon and his parents moved from their little apartment at 85 rue Lecourbe to an equally small place at 78 rue Lepic, or from seven to twelve o'clock on the face of the map of Paris. Their new dwelling was near the top of Montmartre, still well removed from the nightclub district that would spread its way from such spots as the Moulin Rouge on the boulevard below. Behind scaffolding, on the spot where the Commune's cannon had stood, were rising the white walls of the Sacré Coeur, a monumental temple begun in 1873 after the Franco-Prussian War, in fulfillment of a national vow forswearing the wickedness of the Commune and the evils of defeat.

The rest of the hill was dotted with shacks and vegetable gardens. Beside empty lots new tenement houses offered "reasonable rents" to those who chose to live in this rather ill-famed outlying district. For 420 francs a year ($84) the Fénéons had a three-room apartment on the fifth floor of a building toward the end of rue Lepic, a narrow street twisting and climbing from place Blanche toward the crest of Montmartre hill. At the War Office, after thirteen years' service, F. F. had risen to the rank of chief clerk, third class (equivalent to second-lieutenant). His salary of 3,500 francs annually ($700) had to suffice for the whole family, since Jules Fénéon, now aged sixty-nine and seriously ill, had left his job as copyist's aid for the Bank of France. His was not a peaceful old age. Félix's habit of parting with some of his earnings before reaching home on payday was a source of constant anxiety to his father, as were the strange people who came to see Félix. The concierge noted the number of times she heard the old man berating his son for the bad company he kept. She herself thought that in spite of young Fénéon's impeccable manners he was a disgraceful sort: he received *too much mail* and too many visitors—some coming as late as two o'clock in the morning, waking her up in order to get past the locked entrance. He also went out at odd hours of the night.

Fénéon's father would have been even more unhappy had he known that he had a grandson, born on 25 July 1893. Félix had found solace and pleasure in the arms of a singularly strong-minded woman, Marie Joséphine Félicie Jacquin, who ran a laundry on rue du Moulin-Vert. For young men of Fénéon's generation the laundress was such a frequent muse that the term entered the language: "Politics must be a really boring occupation," remarked the *Revue indépendante* in 1885, "since all those who are in her clutches are frequently unfaithful to her and court their laundress, Madame Poetry."[14]

But this was no tender young literary romance. Marie-Félicie was thirty-nine that year, and Félix thirty-two. Both held the belief: *la liberté du coït est une liberté élémentaire.* She came from a long tradition of independence; her people were from Valle d'Aosta, a Celtic enclave in the alps that had long resisted assimilation by France, Switzerland, and the Crown of Piedmont. Some of Fénéon's forebears—his mother's maiden name was also Jacquin—had fled Valle d'Aosta when their independent way of life was threatened. Maternity did not lessen Félicie's independent spirit. She placed her infant son in an orphanage which she and another woman managed in the industrial suburb of Montrouge. This was partly out of necessity, for how else was she to care for him while she worked? But it was also because she believed, as Max Stirner wrote, that parental authority was more pernicious than any other kind of domination.

But the birth of the child hardened Marie-Félicie's outlook, embittered her; she was no longer a free agent. She turned away from Félix, and from any sort of tenderness. Their son bore the name Jacquin, and with it a yoke of loneliness, according to his own son, Pierre-Félix who never met F. F., and who has remarked: "Félix Fénéon was not a father. My grandfather is the non-father, that is something as positively true as the Immaculate Conception."[15] In fact, Marie Jacquin banished from her son's life the very idea of a father. Nonetheless, F. F., with his customary discretion, saw to their material welfare. Marie-Félicie soon left her work as laundress for a job in the post office, a rather surprising move for a middle-aged woman with no resources but her own intelligence and the solicitude of a former lover (whose mother had a career in the *P. T. T.*). When the child was twelve, he was sent to work in a bookstore in Berlin—the mother had never wanted him nearby—and, without ever receiving any explanation, he was thereafter offered positions in literary concerns, in Spain and Paris, although he was indifferent to letters. Presumably, these positions were found for him by Fénéon, who had international connections in the art and literary worlds.

None of Fénéon's friends was aware of these events in his personal life, at the time or later. But his activities in 1893 were nonetheless intricately involved with those of many other individuals.

At *L'Endehors,* the spacious, lamp-lit cellar room that served as the editorial office became, during the review's lifetime (5 May 1891—19 February 1893), the first, and last, anarchist salon. It was there that Fénéon met a nineteen-year-old former student, Emile Henry, who came and said he wanted to work actively for the anarchist cause. Fénéon was impressed with the youth's intelligence, the mathematical precision of his thinking, and the intense way he identified with the suffering of the people while maintaining a cool and detached exterior.

People from all walks of life used to stop and chat at *L'Endehors.* Poets, painters, bohemians and bandits alike found it a congenial place. Fencing matches occasionally

(*From left*) ***Pierre and Marie Jacquin*** with their sons, ***Jérome and Jacob.*** 1987. Saint-Cannat, France.

sprang up (foils, masks, and gloves were kept handy near the entrance). Once or twice Fénéon sparred there with an elegant stranger named Ortiz, silent and, it was rumored, marvelously light-fingered.

He befriended a young Swedish painter, Ivan Aguéli, recently introduced to anarchist circles in Paris by Maximilien Luce, who let Aguéli use his studio on rue Cortot in Montmartre, just a block or two from Fénéon's apartment. In October 1893 Aguéli wrote to a painter friend in Stockholm:

> I have made some good sketches and have finally found the key to the oscillating lines in this sea of roofs, marked by streets, towers, monuments, parks, etc. The comrades like them. Félix has two at his place. I have often caught him gazing at them. . . .[16]

Fénéon liked the "frank and handsome" young Swede, and also "the very personal style of the synthetic, nearly monochrome paintings he did in Paris." He saw a certain parallel between Gauguin's work and Aguéli's: "their palettes were very different, but the two painters had the same interest in organizing the forms in their figure studies and landscapes by simplifying them."[17]

Ivan Aguéli, for his part, was very taken with Félix, who seemed to him the epitome of the avant-garde intellectual and also the incarnation of the "new social being" on which anarchism depended. He described a meeting at Fénéon's to his friend in Stockholm—"You should know that we live a fine life of comrades here"—and continued with a long description of F. F.:

> I can't keep from talking about this fellow, with his modern French culture, hospitable, simple and moderate in manner, absolutely without snobbery or affectation. Emancipated as a social being, international to the point of anti-patriotism . . . great critical intelligence. Everyone asks for his advice, and it's really pleasing to see the high regard they all have for him. Active mind, roving skeptic, irony full of humor. He can recite a poem or a play in an incomparable manner.[18]

Aguéli would be indicted along with F. F. in the Trial of the Thirty, for the prosecution needed a sprinkling of foreigners to prove the existence of international conspiracy. A portrait Aguéli had done of Fénéon and another he painted of an actress who played Ibsen roles at the Théâtre de l'Oeuvre were claimed to be sufficient evidence of his guilt.

Meanwhile, the outcries of *L'Endehors* had not gone unnoticed by the authorities. In January 1892, Zo d'Axa was indicted for "outrages against morals"; his journal's commentaries on the army, the parliament, and the judiciary were deemed criminal. He disappeared to the British Isles, leaving *L'Endehors* in the hands of F. F., who, along with Barrucand, Bernard Lazare, Quillard, and Descaves, was to liquidate the review if he could not prolong its life.[19] It survived, however, for fully another year.

Zo d'Axa was imprisoned by the British police shortly after his arrival in February 1892, apparently on suspicion of being an undesirable entrant to England. He immediately had a cable sent to Fénéon, who traipsed to London "in the company of Antoine alias Anybody"* and extricated his friend. Thereafter Zo regularly sent Fénéon his caustic lead articles to publish in *L'Endehors,* while Fénéon took over writing all of the "Hurrahs, outcries and thin laughter." Fénéon also received and delivered messages from Zo to his wife, a Florentine remembered by her daughter as a fair, Botticellian beauty. It was not long before Zo became tormented with the thought that his elegant emissary might please his lady too well.[20] He returned to France and was promptly arrested and held incommunicado for two weeks by the Paris police. Released pending his trial, he had disappeared by the time the court ruled that the outrages committed by *L'Endehors* upon the sensibilities of the establishment were punishable by seven years and four months imprisonment and 13,150 francs in fines to be paid by Zo d'Axa and his two *gérants* (managing editors), Matha and Cholin. *L'Endehors* announced this news in the next issue (10 July 1892) and gave the name of a new managing editor, "*Le {belli}gérant: Félix Bichon*" (Félix Sweetie).

Six months later, *L'Endehors* was finally silenced, its vendors jailed, its last copies destroyed.

Fénéon brought discussion of contemporary art to the pages of anarchist reviews. In the next-to-last issue of *L'Endehors,* he reported on Toulouse-Lautrec's first "one-man" show—which he shared with an anarchist friend, Charles Maurin, who had

*Agent's report from London, Paris Police Archives BA/79 no. 215.

HENRI DE TOULOUSE-LAUTREC. ***La Goulue and La Môme Fromage at the Moulin Rouge.*** 1892. Brush and spatter lithograph printed in six colors, 45 x 35 cm. Courtesy Herbert D. Schimmel.

instructed him in printmaking. Lautrec himself professed no interest in anarchism or in any sort of politics, but his anticonformist character and art endeared him to the *libertaires.* His deformity had made him an outsider, and he had acquired a healthy distrust of most of his fellow men—he preferred animals, and, above all, women—but he had confidence in F. F. "I would be glad to let you into my studio today after 4:30," he wrote in an undated note to the critic; "I'll give you the poster and we can talk about painting."[21]

F. F. had been the first critic to notice Lautrec at the Indépendants of 1889, when he described in detail the large composition Lautrec was exhibiting, *Bal du moulin de la galette,* and concluded, "He has repudiated certain macabre elements of caricature in his women . . . He has leafed through Forain and pondered over Degas, but does not plagiarize them" (F, 168). This last remark amused Lautrec. When a reporter later asked him to describe his development, he replied, "I don't belong to any school. I work in my corner," then added, with a snicker, "I admire Degas and Forain."[22]

Fénéon appreciated the economy with which Toulouse-Lautrec "elucidated the character" of his subjects—La Goulue, for example, seen from the rear, "defined . . . with amazing precision by her hair, her cheekbone and the line of her back" (F, 213). When Lautrec began making posters, the critic was enthusiastic:

> By its starched, ferocious boldness, one such poster—let us say *Queen of Joy*—will forever be alive. (F, 220)

This merciless chronicler of Montmartre nightlife, Fénéon noted, transformed his favorite subjects: "He loves them, studies them insatiably—and soon hallucinates." The male spectators, "morose and empty creatures inclined towards senility . . . become droll . . . while the young lady dancers are sepulcral . . . malefic" (F, 217).

Lautrec's technique was totally different from that of the neo-impressionists. "His color, not at all 'pretty,' is subservient to the lines." Yet Fénéon gave him his highest praise:

> By drawing not a traced copy of reality but a set of signs suggesting it, he immobilizes life in unexpected emblems. . . . Technique, color and drawing conspire in works that have authentic originality and a stealthy, almost hostile, but indubitable beauty. (F, 217)

Shortly after his article on Lautrec for *L'Endehors,* Fénéon wrote his last pieces as an art critic, for the *Père peinard* (The Old Work Horse), an anarchist review founded in 1889 by Emile Pouget, early leader in the creation of labor unions.

Meant to express the voice of the worker, the *Père peinard* used only slang, from the first word down through the subscription rate list. Few intellectuals subscribed to it, although it was illustrated by Maximilien Luce, Camille and Lucien Pissarro, H.-G. Ibels, Willette, Steinlen, and Félix Vallotton. Its high rate of sales attested to its popularity among the masses whom Pouget addressed. In the first issue he had announced:

> SEEING AS HOW THE OLD WORK HORSE IS NOW A FUCKIN' JOURNALIST. . . . Naturally, in my capacity as *gniaff,** I don' hafta write like the dumb dodos in the Academy: y'know, those forty immortal pickles preserved in bell-jar on the other side of the Seine. . . .
>
> Am I gonna keep harpin' on the same old strings, like those eunuchs?—I don't think so, by damn! . . .
>
> The guys in the workshops, the kid in the factories, all those who sweat and

**Gniaff:* slang for cobbler, the traditional leader of popular anarchism in Lyons and Paris.

Opposite, **HENRI DE TOULOUSE-LAUTREC. *Queen of Joy.*** 1892. Brush, spatter, and transferred screen lithograph printed in four colors, 130 x 89.5 cm. Poster to announce the publication of a novel by the Polish writer Victor Joze (Dobsky). New York, Collection of Mr. and Mrs. Herbert D. Schimmel. *No one like {Lautrec} to peg the mugs of drivelling moneybags sitting over drinks with tuned-in tarts licking the old boys' kissers to make'em fork over.* (F, 230, for *Le Père peinard*).

HLautrec
Reine de Joie
par
Victor Joze
chez tous les libraires
Imp. Edw. ANCOURT & Cie PARIS

Cinquième Année. — N° 202 | DEUX RONDS | Du Dimanche 29 Janvier au 5 Février 1893

LE PÈRE PEINARD

Réflecs HEBDOMADAIRES d'un GNIAFF

ABONNEMENTS FRANCE: Un An ... 6 fr. Six Mois ... 3 fr. Trois Mois ... 1 fr. 50

BUREAUX : 4bis, rue d'Orsel, Paris
OUVERT DE 9 HEURES DU MATIN A 6 HEURES DU SOIR
Adresser toutes les Correspondances à l'Administrateur

ABONNEMENTS EXTÉRIEUR: Un An ... 8 fr. Six Mois ... 4 fr. Trois Mois ... 2 fr.

Dédié à Rothschild, Roi des Grinches.

LE CAPITALO PELOTÉ PAR MADAME FORTUNE

Le Père peinard. Title page, 29 January 1893. Headline drawing by Maximilien Luce. Cartoon of Madame Fortune and the capitalist by Félix Pissarro. Photograph G. Roche.

> slave, they'll understand me. I spout the lingo of the populo. . . . What I want is to be understood by the reg'lar fellers—as for the rest, I don't give a shit![23]

People who knew nothing of Pouget except that he wrote the *Père peinard* were always astonished when they met this courteous, gentlemanly fellow, with his slow, deliberate speech and finely chiseled features. He was a well-educated young man who came originally from comfortable circumstances but had been obliged to leave school after the successive deaths of his father and a stepfather. He got a job as a store clerk and soon discovered the misery of the working world.

The *Père peinard* grew, other writers joined the staff, but none signed his name, and all wrote in the same slang. Fénéon used the language of the "gniaff" with flair, but his articles stood out: art criticism was not the usual fare at the *Père peinard.*

Writing on the Indépendants, street posters, and the official fine arts collection, Fénéon expressed basic ideas about painting, articulated for the first time some thoughts on the relationship of the artist and art to the masses, and gave the clearest expression of his own anarchist views. He took the reader first of all on a "Jaunt through the *Artisses* [sic] *indépendants.*" After roundly (and crudely) excoriating most of the so-called Indépendants—"that quid-juice and dung-water painting of theirs is a pain in the ass"—he finally found things to admire by the neo-impressionists, Toulouse-Lautrec, and the Nabis. But, he advised,

> When you visit this room, *camaros,* don't just scrutinize the paintings, get a load of the mugs of the bourgeois. You're in, like, the lair of the *anarchos* of painting. And no mistake, what the bourgeois understand 'bout anything that's new and bold ain't worth a fart. Some hee-haw like donkeys; others grouse through their teeth; and those who like to air their views just sound like a chamber pot under a sick man's ass. (F, 228)

For that matter, Fénéon concluded, the way capitalist society treated works of art was really stupid: people hung paintings on their walls the way they stuck decorations in their lapels.

> Day'll come, Goddam, when art will fit into the life of ordinary Joes, just like steak and vino. Then, plates, spoons, chairs, beds—the whole works, what d'ya think! . . . everything, great guns, will have nifty shapes and fabulous colors. When that happens, the *artisse* won't look down his nose at the worker: they will be united. But before we get to that point, the old Union will have to get up some steam and we gotta be slap-dab in the middle of *anarcho* civilization. (F, 226)

Fénéon paid his respects to the neo-impressionists, "chock full of air and light!" but he dwelt longer on the work of younger painters and pictures likely to attract his audience, painful scenes of coal miners by Eugène Boch, for example, or prostitutes:

> Not much fun here, either, for these gals. The poor janes do some tall work on sidewalks and mattresses and get regularly messed up, exposed to the low-down tricks of the mugs and the filthy treatment of the coppers. (F, 228)

Toulouse-Lautrec was a natural winner, here:

> One who has a hell of a lot of nerve, damn it all, is Lautrec. No highfalutin' in either his color or drawing. Some white, some black, some red—in big patches, and simplified forms—that's his bag. No one like him to peg the mugs of driveling moneybags sitting over drinks with tuned-in tarts licking the old boys' kissers to make 'em fork over. . . (F, 230)

Fénéon also singled out Louis Anquetin, Dujardin's talented friend, whose work kept "circulating, looking for alibis," as F. F. had said earlier:

> A good lookin', strapping fellow, this Anquetin. Sometimes he shows us a guy sipping a snifter in a dive, sometimes a street sister makin' eyes to pivot the passerby, or just some molls struttin' their stuff in a garden. (F, 195 and 227)

ALMANACH DU PÈRE PEINARD 37

Il y a deux ans, dans ce même patelin, deux terrassiers étaient en train de creuser un puits. Mal outillés, ils travaillaient comme des lapins : creusant des pattes, creusant du pic, enlevant des terres dans un panier, — une misère quoi !

Quand je dis qu'ils étaient deux à masser dans cette taupinière, je me gourre ; y en avait qu'un : l'autre était *l'entrepreneur*, Mossieu Solive, qui surveillait son homme, un pauvre déchard nommé Martel.

Le bougre était d'attaque, taillé dans le chêne ! Il turbinait à 14 mètres de profondeur, quand le terrain se mit à souffler du gaz carbonique, kif-kif une outre dégonflée. Mossieu Solive se tire des flûtes et engage l'autre à se barrer à sa suite, — mais le gas s'acharne à la besogne, crainte de perdre sa journée. Quand il veut se fuiter il est trop tard, un vertige le prend, il tombe les quatre fers en l'air.

Solive, ne voyant rien venir, ni homme ni panier, gueule sur le bord du trou ; pris de trac, il appelle les voisins, se fait accrocher et tente d'aller reluquer ce qui se passe en bas ; mais, dès qu'il sent que l'air lui manque il crie et gigotte comme un poulet : on le remonte !

La foule s'amasse — et quelle foule ! — un tas d'andouilles ficelées, des Normands aux doigts crochus, tous plus ou moins proprios, parmi lesquels pas un n'aurait risqué sa peau pour le pauvre bougre qui râlait dans la fosse.

Au lieu de faire quéque chose, ces capons-là se foutent à courir le pays, cherchant les pompiers, le maire, le médecin et même les gendarmes.

Les autorités constipées ne bougent pas. Ça, c'était certain ! Le médecin n'était pas levé, un autre vise-au-trou avait filé à la chasse.....

Enfin, les pompiers s'amènent avec..... une pompe à incendie !

Zut, pas de veine !

—o—

Pendant ce temps, Martel cassait sa pipe, et les campluchards s'excusaient de leur lâcheté en chuchottant que ce n'était pas un grand malheur, que Martel était un propre-à-rien, un sans-le-sou, — ce qui, pour ces salops, est la dernière insulte.

Les oiseaux du ciel ont leurs nids, les fauves ont leurs tanières... seuls les prolos vagabondent dans la vie, sans feu ni lieu!

Le cadavre du pauvre bougre serait encore au fond du puits, si tout à coup un de ces tristes moineaux n'avait eu une idée :

« Allons chercher Barbieux ! » qu'il dit.

Et tous en chœur : « Tiens, nom de dieu ! allons chercher Barbieux ! On le fera descendre. Il descendra. C'est un risque-tout, un abruti : il n'a rien à perdre, il peut bien faire ça, lui Barbieux ! »

Barbieux, c'est un riche fieu qu'en temps ordinaire les campluchards proprios n'ont pas à la bonne. Il chipotte par ci, il braconne par là..., enfin il vivote comme il peut, — en chien maigre, — mais pas en porc assurément comme ces gros Normands foireux.

En voilà un qui est en coquetterie avec la gendarmerie, et avec le garde-chasse donc ! Ah jarnidieu, ce qu'il leur en a fait bouffer des kilomètres ! Il serait une gironde fille que ces marloupins ne le serreraient pas de plus près.

Heureusement, le gas se fout pas mal d'eux, bougrement plus que d'une crotte de lapin.

Pas moins le Barbieux s'amène : il traite les proprios, les culs-terreux, les épicemards, toute

LUCIEN PISSARRO. ***Illustration*** for the ***Almanach du Père peinard,*** 1896. "Birds have their nests, wild beasts have their lairs . . . only the proles must keep moving on, with no hearth or home." Oxford, The Ashmolean Museum.

He noticed the Nabis, one of whom, Ibels, was a regular contributor to anarchist sheets:

> I really gobble up the things by Ibels. Bonnard's have first-rate cooled-down colors and classily intertwined lines. Maurice Denis ain't got his head in a bag, neither. . . .
>
> One who really gives the needle to the gawkers is Vallotton: he shows us a bunch of women taking a swim, both young and old, some in the buff, others in their chemise; it will tickle you silly! (F, 227)

FÉLIX VALLOTTON. ***Summer, Women Bathing in a Brick Pool.*** 1892–93. Oil on canvas, 97 x 131 cm. Property of Gottfried Keller Foundation, Zürich, Kunsthaus.

Vallotton's painting, *Summer,* created a small scandal at the Indépendants, for he had starkly depicted the female bodies as age, pregnancy, or corsets had molded them.

In the next issue, Fénéon invited his readers to look at art in the streets. There instead of "dirty linen in gold frames" he found a kind of real-life art, colored posters. "It's an outdoor exhibition, all year long and wherever you go." Even if made by a great artist, "they don't pretend to be precious stuff; they'll be torn down in a little while and others will be put up, and so on: they don't give a damn! That's great!—and that's art, by God, and the best kind, mixed in with life, art without any bluffing or boasting and within easy reach of ordinary guys."

At the end, Fénéon offered his readers a recipe for ripping off street posters and fixing them up in their rooms, "where your bastard of a *proprio,* natch, has let the wallpaper rot away. A Lautrec or a Chéret at home, good Lord, that gives a good light!" (F, 229–31).

Art mixed in life; life mixed in art; this was the formula of Fénéon's existence. And perhaps he was right in thinking the workers could understand it better than the bourgeois. At any rate, nowhere did he express himself so directly as in the *Père peinard.* And more than once he lent a comrade a hand in carefully detaching an advertisement by Chéret or playbill by Lautrec.

He was also accomplished in plastering up less artistic posters on the walls of Paris in the dead of night. These were announcements of meetings or anarchist slogans, printed, one of his friends recalled, in flaming red, shrill yellow and hot orange, with gigantic letters to catch the eye.[24] One such manifesto, called "Panama and Dynamite," denounced the financial shenanigans of members of parliament and showed in contrast the figures of Dame Dynamite and her suitors. One winter night Fénéon and two helpers covered the walls and fences in Montmartre with this poster. They made a strange trio: a dapper Don Quixote carrying a bucket of paste and roll of posters, his Sancho Panza from across rue Lepic, the Dutch émigré Alexandre Cohen, and Cohen's sixty-year-old physician, Dr. Sallazin, whom Cohen had recently converted to anarchism. The three of them prowled the streets like young pranksters, but more stealthily. Not a word was said as Fénéon unfolded one of the sheets, smeared it with paste, and handed it to Cohen standing on the broad back of the good doctor, whose dark coat and top hat were soon splattered with white. The trick was to plaster "Panama and Dynamite" high on the walls out of reach of the gendarmes. They were successful, and Montmartre wore her new face for several days, until another poster went up.

As the government pursued and outlawed the older anarchist journals, Fénéon joined others in creating new ephemerals and served as a link with literary and theater people sympathetic to anarchism. He worked for a tiny new publication, the *Revue anarchiste,* founded in August 1893 by Charles Chatel, whom Fénéon knew from *L'Endehors.* The new review was located on rue Gabrielle in Montmartre, a stone's throw from Fénéon's apartment, where Chatel sometimes visited. He was a tall young man who wore his dark hair long and gave the impression of being an artist—"another shady character," observed Fénéon's concierge. Chatel was in fact not an artist although he had several acquaintances among painters and made a close personal frield of Ivan Aguéli. He had received little formal education but, like many attracted to anarchism, was driven by a fever to learn. Fénéon described him many years after his early death (aged twenty-eight, in 1897) as "thirsting for literature and science."[25]

At the *Revue anarchiste,* Fénéon contributed his increasingly virulent notes of social commentary, interspersed with book reviews and advice on exhibitions or new posters "on the walls." He brought some of his favorite authors into the anarchist fold, printing remarks of Stendhal and editing unpublished notes by Jules Laforgue, "who," said Fénéon, "always gave the finest, most positive example of individualist thinking." He quoted Laforgue:

> Yes, the ideal of liberty would be to live *without any habits.* Oh, what a dream! What a dream! It's enough to drive you crazy! A whole existence without a single act being generated or influenced by habit. Every act an *act in itself.*[26] (Emphasis Laforgue's)

It was this fundamental reverence for individuality that attracted so many symbolists and contemporary artists to the anarchist movement. It explains their eager interest in foreign authors and their contempt for chauvinistic attitudes. The government was not blind to this union of forces, and began prosecuting writers who were only faintly touched with anarchism: Dujardin was condemned to one month in prison for some remarks he made in *Fin de siècle,* a journal no more subversive than *Esquire.* When in December the government passed a new law limiting freedom of the press, *Entretiens politiques et littéraires* went out of business, while the *Revue anarchiste* changed its name to the not very different *Revue libertaire* and quoted Ibsen—favorite author of the anarchists: "The State is the curse of the Individual."

Ibsen's *Rosmersholm* had initiated Lugné-Poe's new theater, l'Oeuvre, on 6 October 1893. The following month *An Enemy of the People* was presented, and Fénéon performed as one of the rough crowd at the public meeting where the would-be hero is shouted down. After the scene was over and the other crowd actors had withdrawn, Fénéon stayed on alone, picking pins up off the stage boards. Some of the audience saw an "Ibsenian symbol" in this gesture, as Paul Signac laughingly reminded F. F. many years later.[27]

On 13 December 1893, the Oeuvre produced a work by the young German author, Gerhardt Hauptmann. The play, *Lonely Lives,* had been translated by Alexandre Cohen, who asked F. F. to correct and refine the French; Cohen later credited Fénéon with having given him an understanding of language and literature and for awakening his sense of beauty.[28] Hauptmann's vision of humanity was akin to Ibsen's, but according to Fénéon his style was more modern, breaking with naturalism to present a series of brilliant

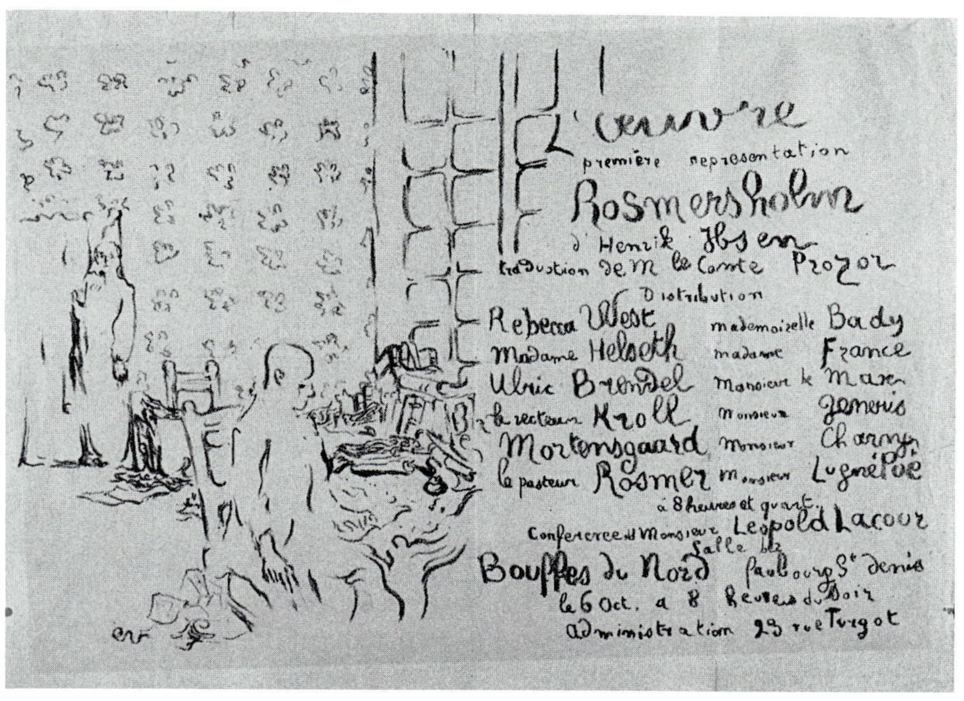

EDOUARD VUILLARD. ***Program*** for "***Rosmersholm,***" by Henrik Ibsen. Théâtre de l'Oeuvre, 6 October 1893. Lithograph, 24 x 32.5 cm. The Atlas Foundation.

le Novemb
1893
Loeuvre
deuxième soirée
un ennemi du peuple
d'Henrik Ibsen
unique représentation
traduction de M.M. Ab. Chennevière et
mise en scène conforme à celle du Théâtre
Distribution
rôles
Stokmann . M. Lugné-Poe
Madame Stokmann . M.me de Pontry
Petra . M.lle Camée
Ejlif . M.lle Royer
Morten . Ravet
Peter Stokmann . M. Ravet
Morten Kiil . M. Charny
Hovstad . M. Lagrange
Billing
Horster . M. Craveri
Aslaksen . M. Depas
Conférence de M.
Bouffes du Nord
Administration

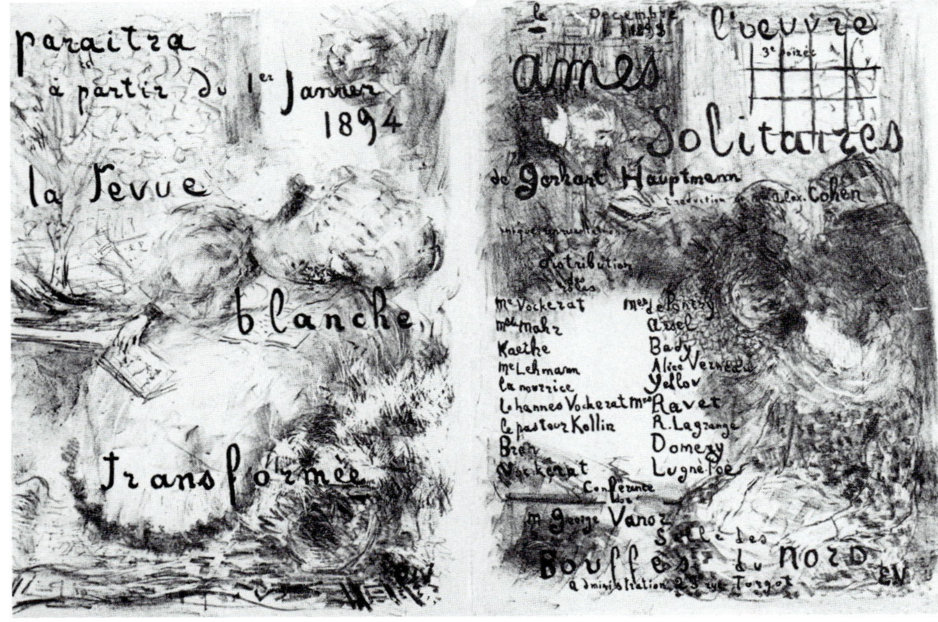
paraitra
à partir du 1er Janvier
1894
la revue
blanche
transformée
l'oeuvre
3e soirée
1893
âmes
solitaires
de Gerhart Hauptmann
Alex. Cohen
Distribution
rôles
M.e Vockerat
M.elle Mahr
Kaethe
M.e Lehmann
La nourrice
Johannes Vockerat
Le pasteur Kollin
Braun
Vockerat
Axel
Bady
Alice Verneuil
Yellow
M. Ravet
A. Lagrange
Domezy
Lugné Poe
Conférence
M. George Vanor
Salle des
Bouffes du Nord
EV

images, apparently well rendered in the free version of Cohen-Fénéon. The play was enthusiastically received by Lugné-Poe's public. Alfred Jarry said that it showed the "highest kind of Idealism, even more touching than *An Enemy of the People,* because it is closer to us."[29] Fénéon found rather that it resembled *Rosmersholm,* but with "less haughty characters, less proudly draped in their ideas," and a hero who was more alive and sensitive. The program design, he noted, contributed to the play by making its characters yet more attractive through the hazy veil of Vuillard's drawing.[30]

There was only one performance, however, and that was the dress rehearsal. *Lonely Lives* was pulled off the boards by police order even before it officially opened. Symbolists and anarchists published a protest accompanying F. F.'s review of the play in the *Revue libertaire*[31]—in vain. The Oeuvre had become suspect, and the government had decided to take draconian measures since a new act of terrorism had occurred five days before, right in the Chamber of Deputies.

The Chamber reacted immediately by passing a law against "Associations of Malefactors" (the law under which Fénéon would be brought to trial in August 1894). Shortly thereafter, the *Revue libertaire* reported, in the style of the daily press:

> At last we know the leaders of this mysterious Association. This discovery is due to a piece of good luck: a highly placed member of the Security Force, upon learning that there was a means of transmitting thought called *literature,* had the idea of directing his investigations along those lines. He discovered, in some parallelepipeds called *books,* certain signs for which, by dint of labor, he found the key, and which revealed appalling things. It was a question of nothing less, in these books, than the destruction of authority and the emancipation of men. Most of the names of those who corresponded in this manner were so bizarre that they were obviously pseudonyms, unless they were foreigners, in which case they are even less worthy of our pity. Here are some of these names: Tolstoy, Ibsen, Herbert Spencer, Nietzsche. . . . Warrants were even sent out for two of the worst, the so-called Stirner and Multatuli.* At the moment of arrest, it was found they were dead. The investigation revealed that they died in poverty. Let that serve as a lesson to those who might be tempted to imitate them.[32]

This mocking tone typified the attitude of Fénéon and his friends to conservative governmental authority. Since it had indeed become dangerous to be identified with the anarchists, they playfully indulged their taste for mystification.

*Multatuli: pseudonym of the Dutch writer Eduard Douwes Dekker (1820–87), some of whose works had been translated into French by Alexandre Cohen. Max Stirner (Kaspar Schmidt), 1806–56): German schoolteacher whose work, *Der Einzige und sein Eigentum* (The Ego and Its Own), was brought to light by anarchist thinkers of the 1890s (in *Entretiens,* for example, Aug.–Dec. 1892).

Opposite, above, EDOUARD VUILLARD. ***Program*** for ***"An Enemy of the People,"*** by Ibsen. Théâtre de l'Oeuvre, 8 November 1893. Lithograph, 24.1 x 31.9 cm. The Atlas Foundation.

Opposite, below, EDOUARD VUILLARD. ***Program*** for ***"Ames solitaires" (Lonely Lives),*** by Gerhart Hauptmann. Théâtre de l'Oeuvre, 13 December 1893. Lithograph, 33 x 23 cm. The Atlas Foundation.

No one played this role better than Fénéon, who seemed so proudly aloof, the perfect dandy—and functionary. An aesthete, a man of letters—few of his contemporaries saw behind this façade. When he was arrested and tried as an anarchist, most of the literary world expressed disbelief that he could have been involved in a violent protest against the existing social structure. Fénéon kept silent, playing his disquieting role of superior being even in the courtroom, so that in the end his involvement remained a mystery.

CHAPTER 13

Bombs, and the "Woman" in Mme Fénéon's Gown

Suddenly, in 1892, France was wracked with an epidemic of anarchist terror that lasted until the assassination of President Sadi Carnot in 1894 and the Trial of the Thirty. It was a chain reaction that began with bombs manifesting solidarity with the striking workers in Fourmies and the Clichy marchers whose demonstrations on 1 May 1891 had been brutally repressed. Fénéon was one of the last links in this chain of violence.

It began with three bombs in March 1892: one at the apartment house of the judge who had tried and sentenced the anarchists arrested at Clichy on May Day of the previous year; another at the Lobau barracks in Paris, a reminder that army troops had fired on men, women, and children with the new Lebel gun during the May 1 strike in Fourmies; a third at the home of the prosecuting attorney, Bulot, who had asked for the heads of the Clichy anarchists. The bombings killed no one, but property damage was considerable. The jails began to fill with suspected anarchists.

A man called Ravachol was arrested on March 30 and admitted to the bombings. Tried, found guilty and guillotined, he became the image of the public martyr. Victor Barrucand compared him to Christ, also executed at thirty-three, and recalled that Renan had called Jesus an anarchist.[1] Fénéon described a popular wood-engraving of Ravachol by Charles Maurin, the friend of Toulouse-Lautrec:

> Comrade Ravachol.—His head, proud, energetic and calm, and his naked chest are framed by the vertical posts and the triangular blade of the guillotine. In the distance crops are rippling, and the sun, as for a holiday ceremonial, is rising.[2]

In the meantime, the jails were kept full of other suspects. On March 31, the day after Ravachol's arrest, the police filed a report on Fénéon, warning that he was a militant anarchist. This report, however, was but one among thousands, and Fénéon was not yet put under strict surveillance.

CHARLES MAURIN. ***Ravachol Vanquishing the Guillotine.*** 1892. Woodcut reprinted from *The Anarchists* by Roderick Kedward, London: Macdonald & Co., 1971, p. 40.

L'Endehors solicited contributions "for the children of comrades in prison." For several weeks each issue carried the list of donors; among many humbler names appeared those of Camille Pissarro, Gustave Charpentier, Henri de Régnier, Jules Christophe, Tristan Bernard, Théo van Rysselberghe, Verhaeren, Fénéon, Signac, Ibels, Séverine, and others. Each gave according to his means. Camille Pissarro came up with 20 francs, and donated another 20 in the name of his son Lucien, who was in England; Signac gave 5 francs; Matha—in hiding since his conviction as managing editor of *L'Endehors*—50 centimes. Fénéon's donations were modest (2 francs, 5 francs, 0.25 francs), but regular. Printing the names and the amounts was an act of solidarity that revealed how widespread the anarchist sentiment had become. The public became more acutely aware of this when, the night before Ravachol's trial on April 26, the Restaurant Véry, where a waiter had denounced him, was shattered by an explosion that killed the owner and a customer. This gave, some anarchists said, a new meaning to the word, *vérification*.

F. F.'s friend, Emile Henry, was profoundly affected by the courage and resolve Ravachol displayed at his trial and execution. In the short time since Fénéon had met him, he had become extremely fond of Emile, seven years his junior but painfully mature. With his wide eyes, pale complexion, and close-cropped hair he looked even younger than he was. He was a brilliant student who had passed part of the difficult entrance examinations to the Ecole Polytechnique. But in the middle of 1891, when he was barely nineteen, he abandoned his studies and threw himself into the anarchist movement. His anarchist conviction stemmed from his keen sensitivity to the in-

Top, FÉLIX VALLOTTON. *The Anarchist.* 1892. Woodcut, 17.1 x 25 cm. Lausanne, Galerie Paul Vallotton.

Bottom, FÉLIX VALLOTTON. *The Attack.* 1894. Woodcut, 20 x 26 cm. Lausanne, Galerie Paul Vallotton.

justices and misery he saw around him, and from a dedication to the memory of his father, a former Communard who had died when Emile was just ten years old, of industrial poisoning contracted during his years of exile, working in a mercury mine in Spain.

Upon leaving school, Emile Henry took a job as a shop clerk and evolved rapidly toward a new militancy. He carried his beliefs to their logical conclusions. If he saw a poor wretch wasting of hunger and had nothing of his own to share with him, he stole.

Fénéon delighted in telling about one of his young friend's first exploits: spiriting away a cow and deliverying it to a starving old woman.[3] Henry soon decided that in the interest of efficiency he should learn the locksmith's trade. When Fénéon introduced him to his mother, the dear woman exclaimed when she saw the kit of tools, "Ah! You didn't tell me he was an artisan?" However, when Emile presented Félix with a fine new cane which had disappeared from a multimillionaire's vestibule, Mme Fénéon understood and accepted the situation, though not without alarm.

The worsening situation for workers soon moved Emile Henry from stealthy redistribution of wealth to propaganda by deed. In August 1892, striking miners in the coal fields of Carmaux organized a direct attack on the mine equipment, thus wounding the owners' sensitive spot, their purse. Socialist politicians intervened, offering to mediate for the workers. The result was the usual agonizing months of hunger for the miners, while the politicians gave speeches that earned them the reputation of courageous crusaders. When the strike ended early in November, Fénéon remarked in *L'Endehors:*

> Well, the strike at Carmaux is over.
>
> As in '48, the socialist Deputies have credited the Republic and universal suffrage with three months of starvation.*
>
> But it was others who did the starving. . . . (F, 904)

Emile Henry was outraged that the old pattern of useless strikes was manipulated by the socialists to serve their own purposes; he resolved to inform the miners that the anarchists, men like Ravachol, would speak for them, daring to use the loud voice of dynamite. He began to prepare for a bombing—he had been an excellent student of chemistry. Matha and Fénéon tried to dissuade him. But seeing that he was determined to carry out his beliefs, F. F. gave him one of his mother's dresses to use as a disguise.[4]

Henry made a powerful time bomb out of an old iron pot. On 8 November, three days after F. F.'s little comment appeared in *L'Endehors,* his young friend wrapped the loaded kettle in newspapers and carried it to the main offices of the Société des Mines de Carmaux, on the avenue de l'Opéra in Paris. Two witnesses saw a strange woman come in with a large bundle in a basket over her arm. After she left, the suspicious package was discovered in the staircase outside the door to the Carmaux office. The police were called, and they had the office boy carry the bomb to their headquarters on rue des Bons-Enfants, where it immediately exploded, instantly killing the boy and four

* An allusion to a speech made by Louis Blanc shortly after the Revolution of 1848 where Blanc said the people would have to suffer through three months of hard times before the Republic could get on its feet.

officers and mortally wounding a fifth. That same evening Henry went to England. He was not pursued. The police collected the names of 186 other people capable, they thought, of such a crime.

Fénéon approved Henry's act, particularly the way he avoided turning himself into a martyr. It was of this bomb that he wrote, "What intimate charm in this story. . . ." When the *Père Peinard's Almanac* for 1894 mistakenly recorded 3 November as the anniversary of the event, F. F. set the facts straight in his usual manner. "It was the 8th and not the 3rd of November 1892 that the delightful kettle of rue des Bons-Enfants exploded" (F, 866).

The following year, 1893, the government organized a general crackdown on anarchists after the bombing of the Chamber of Deputies on December 9. The perpetrator, a loner called Auguste Vaillant, was seized immediately; he had wanted, he said, to draw attention to his miserable plight. The day after Vaillant's attack, Alexandre Cohen was taken from his apartment at 59 rue Lepic and locked up. Because he was a Jew and a foreigner, the police were sure he was an agent for international anarchism. His statement that he was a man of letters and had translated a play for the Théâtre de l'Oeuvre made him even more suspect.

The attack on the Deputies bore prompt and predictable fruit. Though numerous prior bombs had produced only debate, just four days after Vaillant's bomb, parliament enacted the first of three laws, later known as "les lois scélérates"; aimed at the press, it forbade inciting or *approving* future or past criminal acts. A second law, passed on December 18, lumped both intellectuals and activists together in so-called Associations of Malefactors. It forbade any contact between persons "intending" to be "evildoers," regardless of how innocent their conduct. The third, written after the assassination of President Carnot in July 1894, prohibited anarchist propaganda "by any means whatever."

Cohen was taken in manacles to the border and deported, while Emile Zola, Arsène Alexandre, and Octave Mirbeau protested in vain that there was no evidence against him. The fact of the matter was that Cohen was persona non grata because he had publicly denounced General Dodds for massacring the people of Dahomey in his campaign of pacification. Cohen took refuge in London. His young bride, Kaya, stayed behind, hoping her factory wages could provide for them both.

Fénéon took care of some personal matters for his Dutch friend, such as giving the traditional New Year's gift to Cohen's concierge (who later reported this curious detail to the police and testified against F. F. at his trial—the voice of gratitude, noted the newspapers). Cohen had let a room on the top floor of a house further down rue Lepic, number 69, for a newlywed friend from Berlin, Bernhard Kampffmayer, who knew enough to leave France shortly after Cohen's expulsion; he had already been arrested once—for acting upon Fénéon's advice and taking a poster by Chéret off a public wall in order to brighten up his bleak room. He left the key to the room in Fénéon's care, and when he got resettled asked F. F. to send his furniture. Fénéon naturally did so, which provided the concierge at 69 rue Lepic with further information to contribute to the Trial of the Thirty.

A massive dragnet for suspected anarchists began all over France early on 1 January 1894. Countless police raids were conducted, and in the course of the next six months nearly eight hundred people were locked up and questioned—more than three hundred in Paris alone. Many were released, with no compensation for the indignity or the loss of work; others were kept. Jean Grave was one of the first to be held for formal charges and eventual trial. Emile Pouget retreated to London and continued to direct the *Père peinard* at a distance. Charles Chatel evaded the police for some time by staying with the painter Aguéli. When Chatel was finally found on 14 March, still editing the *Revue libertaire,* the police arrested Aguéli, too.

The hue and cry was taken up by the press. The dispatch room of the newspaper *Le Gaulois* offered the public a gallery of portraits, "les anarchistes intellectuels," which, as Gustave Kahn remarked, were taken from the illustrations to Vanier's series, *Hommes d'aujourd'hui.* Next to pictures of poets with genuine anarchist sympathies, such as himself and Laurent Tailhade, Kahn noticed the portrait of Jean Moréas, "who I believe never articulated the least political opinion and who steers away from any social question with all the speed of his trireme."[5]

Meanwhile, police agents were busy listening in on café discussions and gathering tidbits on such notable figures as Paul Adam, Bernard Lazare, Augustin Hamon, Fénéon, Lucien Descaves, Octave Mirbeau, and even old Dr. Letourneau, who had given a certain distinction to Fénéon's *Revue indépendante* in 1884. Many of the more active anarchists fled.

In Paris, Fénéon received the mail of a number of refugees and by ingenious methods distributed it to their friends and families. Large envelopes from England and Germany, sent by registered mail, arrived at 78 rue Lepic addressed either to F. F. or to Berthe Jacquin, a twelve-year-old niece of his mother who was living with them. Fénéon took charge especially of Emile Pouget's correspondence concerning the *Père peinard* and of his letters to his common-law wife, who was being held by the police supposedly because of her relations with Pouget (the charge was adultery, though her former husband had died several years before).

To avoid incriminating his friends and their families, Fénéon had mail and messages delivered by different, discreet individuals. However, he went himself to see more than one political prisoner, a fact which the police noted. F. F. also drew attention when Alexandre Cohen sent a series of frantic telegrams from London, inquiring after his wife, from whom he had had no word. Fénéon learned that she had written to Cohen several times, and he deduced that her correspondence was being seized. He reassured his friend, and although the content of these communications was totally apolitical, F. F.'s dossier at the Préfecture de Police was considerably fattened by them. Cohen's sense of humor was suspect to the intelligence officers. As a gesture of thanks he offered to send F. F. a "lady seal" that he had seen in a fishmonger's shop the day before. He knew it was a female (*une "phoquesse"*) because she was very big in the middle—about ready to give birth. What could this seal signify if not a bomb, ready to explode, thought the police.[6]

Through collections in London and other centers, the anarchists did what they could to provide funds for families of exiles and prisoners. Matha, traveling under the name Dubois, used to come to Paris and deliver both money and mail to F. F. for distribution. Matha was under indictment as a former editor of *L'Endehors,* and when Fénéon saw him, he treated him as a stranger, although Matha's exuberant beard and Inverness cape made him easily recognizable to the concierge. One day late in January, Matha brought a note from Cohen authorizing F. F. to give Matha the key to the room Kampffmayer had used earlier. This note, which Matha kept, forgetting the anarchist maxim, DESTROY YOUR CORRESPONDENCE, eventually became one of the pieces of evidence against F. F. in the conspiracy trial. Matha wanted to stay in Paris in spite of the danger because he had learned that Emile Henry, exasperated with the government persecution of anarchists since the first of the year, was planning another act of vengeance. Matha was determined to dissuade Henry and dogged his steps.

Fénéon's own family was undergoing a crisis. On February 12, 1894, F. F. wrote Paul Signac and his wife:

> Friends,
>
> My father has just died, after two operations, at Necker hospital. You are among the very rare persons whose sympathy would be good for me in this grief and whom I am informing. But my letter has yet another motive. I do not want to have any pomp at his funeral, sad and intimate. Yet it entails an expense of 350 to 400^{f}. To complete this sum I am lacking about a hundred francs. Is it possible for you to lend them to me? They would be given back to you before the end of the year—or even earlier, at any time you might need them. I will go see you around half past five. You can tell me your answer then. If by the force of circumstances it were negative, I would not be the less sure of your friendship.
>
> *félix*[7]

The day after the death of Jules Fénéon, a bomb exploded in a Paris café, but this time Fénéon, preoccupied with his father's last illness, death, and funeral, probably had no foreknowledge of the plan. Emile Henry had returned to the capital some time before Vaillant's trial in January 1894 and had stayed alone under an assumed name in a room in the working class district of Belleville. He associated with no one and told Matha coldly, "Your friendship is a nuisance." Vaillant's execution for the parliament bomb was the signal for him to carry on propaganda by deed.

The case of Vaillant had aroused much sympathy among the people. Raised in poverty and distressed beyond measure that he had been unable to provide a decent life for his daughter and woman companion, Vaillant had decided to commit a symbolic act to represent "the cry of a whole class which demands its rights."[8] His bomb had killed no one, but he was condemned to death,—the first time in nearly a hundred years that the death sentence was imposed on a civilian who had not actually killed anyone. A petition for clemency was circulated by one of the wounded legislators, but President Sadi Carnot refused to sign a pardon.

Vaillant's death was avenged, as was Ravachol's, more than once. Sadi Carnot himself would pay with his life in June 1894, when an Italian anarchist, Santo Jeronimo Caserio, struck him down in a merciless act against one who had shown no mercy. But before that, on February 12, exactly one week after Vaillant's execution, Emile Henry put an intricately fashioned little bomb in his overcoat pocket and went to the avenue de l'Opéra. He strolled by the fashionable restaurant Bignon, the café Américain and the café de la Paix. None of them was very crowded. He continued until he came to a café frequented by ordinary folk, the Terminus, near the Saint-Lazare railroad station. The place was full of people having a drink and listening to the band, for it had lately become the rage to listen to music as one relaxed from the cares of the world. Why not strike at them, thought Henry; in this society there are no innocents.

He sat at a small table near the door and ordered a beer, paying in advance. He watched with satisfaction as more people came in, crowding around the small stage where the musicians sat playing polkas and vaguely Wagnerian strains. At nine o'clock he ordered another beer and a cigar, again paying in advance. Out of his pocket he pulled the small cooking pot which he had loaded with explosives and 120 bullets. Unlike Vaillant, who had used nails, Henry meant not just to injure, but to kill. He touched his cigar to the end of the fuse, which he had cut to burn for fifteen seconds. He rose, went to the door, turned, and tossed the pot in the direction of the stage. It hit the electric chandelier, landed on the floor, and exploded. Flying glass and bullets created havoc and wounded twenty people, one of whom later died. Meanwhile Henry fled, thinking to escape by catching a train at the Saint Lazare station. A waiter sped after him and a hot pursuit ensued, for others soon joined in the chase. Henry emptied a revolver at his pursuers, but he was finally captured and taken to police headquarters.

The morning after the arrest, Matha and two other comrades went to Henry's lodgings and removed all incriminating material. They may have entrusted some of the bomb-making articles to Fénéon. For three days Henry resisted interrogation, refusing to give his real name and place of residence; "say that I just arrived from Peking," he mocked. But then he suddenly made a full confession. When he learned that several people were being held on suspicion of planting the bomb that exploded in the police station on rue des Bons-Enfants in November 1892, he said he had also been the author of that act.

The bombing of the café Terminus was the more terrible because it struck at innocent victims: shopkeepers, clerks, and other Parisians with modest incomes enjoying a quiet beer. "Not 'innocent,'" claimed Emile Henry: "These beer-drinkers, petty bourgeois with a steady salary in their pockets, are the ones that always line themselves up on the side of the powerful, ignoring the problems of the workers. They hate the poor more than the rich do!"[9] But Henry was repudiated by most of the anarchist community. "The act of Henry," said the militant Charles Malato, "has hurt anarchy most of all."[10] Octave Mirbeau, who had defended Ravachol, suddenly saw a distinction between criminal acts and essential anarchism, and wrote an article condemning Henry.[11]

But at least one anarchist saw in Emile Henry's deed the logical development of propaganda by deed. Félix Fénéon later said to Paul Signac: "The anarchist acts of terrorism have done a lot more for propaganda than twenty years of pamphlets by Reclus or Kropotkin." He went on to analyze the logic of the different acts: the Stock Exchange hit by Gallo, the judiciary and the army by Ravachol, the Chamber of Deputies by Vaillant, the electors by Henry, and the President of the Republic by Caserio. It was Henry's act, F. F. thought, that was "the most anarchist" because it was directed toward the voting public, more guilty in the long run, perhaps, than the representatives they elected to office.[12]

Is the uncompromising concern for humanity expressed by Fénéon consistent with the wounding or killing of human beings who see no connection between themselves and the "crimes" they die for? He argued, it seems, that the spectacular deaths of two or three victims of violence point up the death and suffering of hundreds of innocent men, women, and children exploited by the capitalist system. But to the twentieth-century mind, troubled by terrorism in our time, there is an uneasy edge to Fénéon's logic. One must question whether terrorism in fact alleviates the suffering of the dispossessed, or only hardens the hearts of the powerful.

Fénéon was motivated nonetheless by an immense concern—for a whole class of people, the workers, and also for his friend, Emile Henry. It is yet one more paradox that his concern made him commit a crime, one of the final bombings of the era.

It was rumored that Henry was not the only author of the statement that he delivered before the court sentenced him to death, and that Félix Fénéon and Victor Barrucand gave it literary form.[13] Emile Henry, however, had considerable literary talent himself, and it is impossible to verify that rumor. What is certain is that F. F. agreed with Emile Henry about the justification for random bombing: "The assassins behind the massacres of Bloody Week and Fourmies have no right to call others assassins," said Henry in his *Déclaration* to the court.

> Are these not innocent victims? Children dying slowly of anemia in the slums because bread is scarce at home? Women turning pallid in your sweatshops and wearing themselves out to earn forty *sous* a day, still lucky that poverty has not yet forced them to become prostitutes? Old people you have turned into machines for production all their lives, and then cast on the garbage dump and the workhouse when their strength is exhausted?
>
> At least have the courage of your crimes, gentlemen of the bourgeoisie, and agree that our reprisals are fully legitimate.

Henry shared Fénéon's indifference to death; or perhaps it was Henry's example that hardened Fénéon. "We inflict death," said Henry, "we will know how to endure it. . . . You have hanged men in Chicago, decapitated them in Germany, garroted them in Jerez, shot them in Barcelona, guillotined them in Montbrison and Paris, but you can never destroy Anarchism. Its roots are too deep."[14]

The government continued jailing anarchists and cracking down on the press. The *Père peinard* interrupted publication on 21 February 1894, *La Révolte* and the *Revue libertaire* both disappeared in March. One week after the Terminus bomb, two more explosions took place in Paris, the work presumably of a Belgian anarchist called Pauwels, killed on March 15 when a third bomb he was carrying into the church of the Madeleine exploded prematurely.

For Fénéon the path was clear. He repeated Emile Henry's act, but with more discretion. He fabricated a small lethal bomb from a mixture of dinitrobenzene and ammonium nitrate and packed it with bullets. The container was—not a cooking pot—a flowerpot, tightly sealed, with an opening for a fuse to hide inside a stalk of hyacinth. On Wednesday, 4 April, at about half past eight in the evening, Fénéon went to the Latin Quarter. His destination was the Foyot Hotel, whose ground floor housed a luxurious restaurant with an international reputation for fine cuisine. The Foyot sat directly across from the Palais du Luxembourg, the seat of the Senate; its clientele was composed of politicians, bankers, pretty women, and well-heeled tourists. It was a favorite spot of the Prince of Wales, who was in town that week. One sometimes saw literary and theatrical personages there—the Odéon was just behind the restaurant.

One glance told Fénéon that the dinner hour had not begun as briskly as usual. He went for a short stroll in the Luxembourg gardens, smoking impatient cigarettes. Shortly before nine, the Foyot had filled to capacity. Among the guests were Laurent Tailhade, a poet whose anarchist leanings did not inhibit his taste for fine food, and a friend, Julia Mialhe. Fénéon had returned, approaching by the little rue de Condé that passed behind the Foyot. There the four windows of the stately back room opened onto a side view of the Odéon. Fénéon touched the glowing end of his cigarette to the fuse in the hyacinth, and set the flowerpot on the first window sill. He looked at his watch and strode away toward Odéon square. An omnibus for Clichy and Batignolles was just leaving; he jumped on and climbed quickly to the open-air seats on top. He heard the bomb explode. It shattered windows, chandeliers, but injured seriously only one diner, who had risen to protect his companion—Laurent Tailhade.

It has never been generally known that Fénéon was the author of the Foyot incident. He spoke of it to no one at the time, nor for years to come. When he was old, however, he admitted to the wife of Alexandre Cohen that he had indeed set that bomb.[15]

The next morning, April 5, the police conducted a search at the Fénéon apartment. Chief inspector Bernard confiscated several visiting cards (Descaves, Tailhade, Mirbeau, Pissarro) expressing simple thanks for Fénéon's art and literary criticism, or condolences for the recent loss of his father. The inspector seized a portrait of Zo d'Axa. Finding nothing more incriminating, he said to Madame Fénéon, "This operation must be the result of some misunderstanding. However," he continued, turning to F. F., "you will oblige me by coming down to the Préfecture." Imperturbably, Fénéon went along and signed a prepared statement declaring that he repudiated the ideas of militant anarchists. Then he went to work at the War Office, where he had stored a box of detonators and some mercury that he had probably gotten while clearing a comrade's room of incriminating material, or had been given by those who did the same chore for Emile Henry.

It was Fénéon's unflappable calm that put the police off the scent. They arrested dozens of people whose dossiers were much thinner than his. Others were kept in jail simply because their names or persons resembled those of suspected anarchists; two such unfortunates were eventually tried along with Fénéon. The fact was, the police had too much information to sift through. The previous month an agent signing "Léon" had reported:

> Two former illustrators of the "Père peinard" were talking yesterday afternoon in the café du Delta about the numerous contacts anarchists have in administrative offices

> and apropos of this they said that an employee of the War Office, who had a friendly relationship with Pouget and others, was totally dedicated to the anarchist cause.[16]

This information was lost in one of the many general files on anarchists. The Foyot bomb, according to another police report, caused a real panic among the intellectuals ("les anarchistes scientifiques"), who were refusing to give reporters their opinion about it:

> They are running away. They fear the police like fire. M. Paul Adam keeps his door locked and has [his concierge] say he is in the country. M. Hamon won't say a word. M. Bernard Lazare unbuttons his lips only for those newsmen whom he knows well. Messieurs [Félix] Dubois, Natanson, etc., of the *Revue blanche* are extremely prudent.[17]

In their investigations, the police did not neglect Laurent Tailhade and went to the hospital to interrogate him twice. He had composed a much quoted (or misquoted) aphorism immediately after the Vaillant incident: "What matter the victims, if the gesture is beautiful!"—*Oh, le beau geste!* said the newspapers, reporting on the ugly wounds he had sustained. Although Tailhade lost an eye as the result of the Foyot bomb, he became yet more dedicated to the anarchist cause, as his writings and speeches testified even after the turn of the century. Faithful, however, to his image as a cynic and a dandy, he used sometimes to remove his glass eye before dinner and put it in a goblet of water on the mantlepiece: "The gesture is neither beautiful nor elegant, but allow me to present myself before you as a Cyclops, since destiny willed that I pay with an eye for the publicity Foyot received."[18]

The concierge at 78 rue Lepic was sorely disappointed that the police raid on the Fénéon apartment had borne no fruit. She complained to the proprietor that Fénéon "never stopped receiving too much mail and crowds of suspicious people." The landlord threatened F. F. and his mother with eviction, although Fénéon protested that he had no legal right to do, since they were up to date on their rent and none of their neighbors, only the concierge, had ever complained. When the concierge gloated before some of Fénéon's visitors, "The owner is going to put your fine host out on the street," they unfortunately sent the landlord an old issue of the *Père peinard* with one of the regular columns, "Mort aux proprios" (Death to Landlords) circled in red ink.[19] This was the last straw, and Félix, his mother, and young niece were obliged to move within twenty-four hours.

They found a place not far away, on passage Tourlaque, a short lane connecting rue Damrémont to rue de Maistre. There were only two buildings there, side by side, numbers 2 and 4. All the other lots were vacant, blocked from sight by muddy fences posting huge for-sale signs. On 10 April Fénéon moved his little family into number 4, a tall brick façade pierced with many windows. Their meager furnishings—and his numerous paintings—quickly filled up the three-room apartment, no larger than their last one, but 80 francs dearer. The concierge and his wife, however, were kindly, and they quickly became attached to the elegant and courteous young man who lived quietly on the fifth floor. Fénéon received few visitors at 4 passage Tourlaque, and none after ten o'clock in the evening. But registered letters from foreign places still arrived in volume, most of them addressed to twelve-year-old Berthe Jacquin. The landlord of 78 rue Lepic carried his griefs and the offending *Père peinard* to the police, claiming that his former tenant was the author of the nasty article addressed to him. Two plainclothes men were put in charge of watching F. F.'s every move. He stopped going out at night.

Emile Henry's trial was approaching. He had heard of the Foyot bomb, although he did not know of Fénéon's connection with it. He changed the end of the statement he had prepared for his day in court to say:

> I know that my head is not the last you will cut off; others still will fall, because the down-and-out are beginning to know the road to your cafés and big restaurants, Terminus and Foyot.[20]

Through an intermediary he sent his completed *Déclaration* and a private will to Fénéon. He showed them to Madame Fénéon and she took them for safekeeping. She wept when she read Emile's proud words to the jury, "I await your verdict with indifference."

CHAPTER 14

Imprisonment and Trial

Two days before Emile Henry's trial on Wednesday, 25 April 1894, Louise Fénéon heard her son's voice resounding in the stairwell, "OPEN UP, MOTHER! THE POLICE!" This gave her time to run and dispose of the one article she thought could incriminate him, Emile's manuscript. Then she opened the door. There stood Félix, hatless, coatless, surrounded by four police inspectors, including M. Clément, head of the antianarchist operations. "Don't worry, Mother dear, this is another 'misunderstanding',"[1] he said, referring to inspector Bernard's remark twenty days earlier. While Clément supervised the search, he allowed F. F. to explain matters to Madame Fénéon. He had just finished work for the day and was preparing to leave the War Office when M. Lallamant, head of his bureau, sent for him. When he reported, however, not M. Lallamant but M. Clément was waiting for him.

"Come with me," said Clément, "examining magistrate Meyer wants to see you about the Foyot restaurant affair."

"The Foyot restaurant?"

"Of course. You know Laurent Tailhade well, don't you?"

"I'll get my hat and coat."

"No, you won't!" replied Clément, and with the aid of three policemen who were waiting in the next room hustled F. F. down the stairs and into a waiting cab. Instead of taking him to the préfecture, they took him home.

"Don't be upset, Madame," said Clément, as he concluded his search, "your son will probably be back home with you tonight." He confiscated the one suspicious item he had found, a letter from the antivivisectionist, Marie Huot, inquiring after the health of the delicate lad from Sweden, Aguéli, who had been unjustly arrested the previous month. He also took F. F., clipped handcuffs on him, and subjected him to vigorous questioning in the préfecture.

Didn't Fénéon know Matha? Did he know Matha had been arrested? Matha's

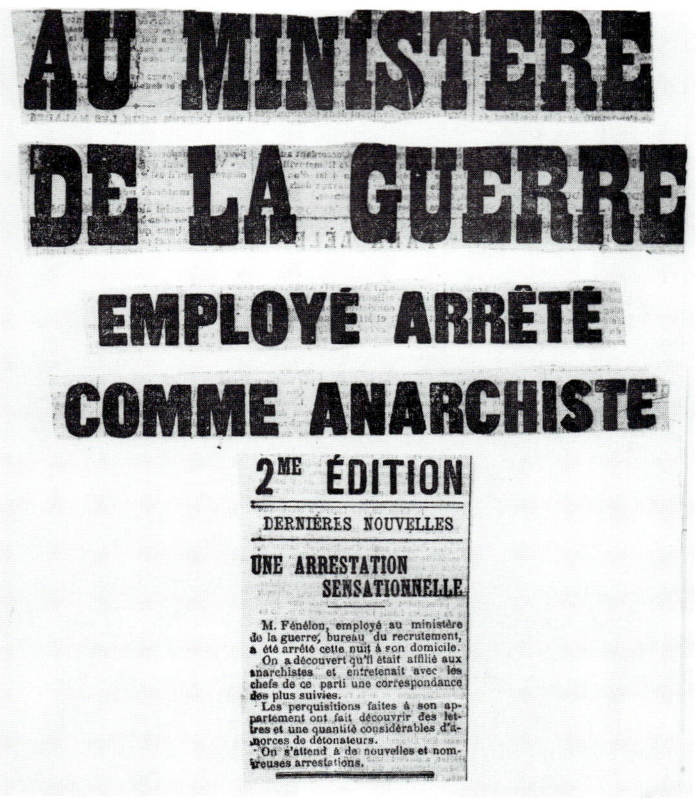

AU MINISTERE DE LA GUERRE

EMPLOYÉ ARRÊTÉ COMME ANARCHISTE

2ME ÉDITION

DERNIÈRES NOUVELLES

UNE ARRESTATION SENSATIONNELLE

M. Fénélon, employé au ministère de la guerre, bureau du recrutement, a été arrêté cette nuit à son domicile.

On a découvert qu'il était affilié aux anarchistes et entretenait avec les chefs de ce parti une correspondance des plus suivies.

Les perquisitions faites à son appartement ont fait découvrir des lettres et une quantité considérables d'amorces de détonateurs.

On s'attend à de nouvelles et nombreuses arrestations.

La Cocarde. 17 April 1894. Headlines announcing an arrest at the War Ministry (Fénéon). Clipping kept by Louise Fénéon in a dossier on the Trial of the Thirty. Paris, Bibliothèque littéraire Jacques Doucet.

room contained evidence that fully implicated Fénéon. Hadn't he entertained Matha? And also Emile Henry? Was he aware what this meant according to the law of 18 December? He had collaborated with Zo d'Axa. And who else? Wasn't he a close friend of Alexandre Cohen, of Laurent Tailhade?

Fénéon coldly denied everything or refused to answer at all.[2] They put him in a cell at the Conciergerie, after registering him on the long list of prisoners. His name came directly after Matha's. Realizing that her son was not coming home, Madame Fénéon tried to see him, but in vain.

At six o'clock the next morning, Chief Clément, accompanied by Inspectors Bernard and Lejeune, returned to the War Office and raided the area around Fénéon's desk on the second floor. They seized several cartons of papers, letters, manuscripts, and some page proofs of symbolist reviews. They probed the leather seats of the chairs and checked the contents of the inkwells. On the top shelf of a coat closet outside Fénéon's office they found a small vial of mercury and a nickel-plated matchbox containing eleven tiny capsules. These, it turned out, were detonators. The inspectors deposited their haul at the préfecture, and in the afternoon conducted a four-hour search of the Fénéon apartment, finding nothing more than some literary correspondence, which they dutifully collected.

That evening the papers were full of the ARRESTATION SENSATIONNELLE AU MINISTERE DE LA GUERRE, but most withheld the name. "The préfecture is keeping his name secret . . ." "This arrest is very important, given the quality of the accused . . ." "At the last minute, we have learned the name of the arrested anarchist," reported the *Echo de Paris,* "he is a man of letters. But since his arrest is perhaps only provisional, we prefer not to name him." But the next day the name was out, and F. F., known until then only by the happy few, became a topic of public conversation.

Reporters crowded around 4 passage Tourlaque, vying for a chance to interview Fénéon's mother. When the police inspectors had completed their search, the apartment was a shambles. A few moments later, Madame Fénéon appeared, her widow's veil shielding her face and with little Berthe's hand in hers. They found a cab, moved quickly off, and did not return that night.

Fénéon was brought before the examining magistrate, Judge Anquetil, who shared with Judge Meyer the burden of interrogating suspected anarchists. Confronted with the vial of mercury and the detonators, Fénéon remained imperturbable. But M. Anquetil was patient and subtle. He wanted to know which of Fénéon's friends had given him these articles. Surely Matha? It was known that Matha had emptied Emile Henry's room. These detonators were identical to those used by Henry. Now Matha was undoubtedly the author of the Foyot bomb . . . ?

Fénéon spoke up. The matchbox was his.

"Who gave you the detonators inside?"

"Nobody. I found them in my father's room, after he died, when we moved to a new apartment."

Anquetil smiled. Here was a tough nut to crack. He continued to probe. Fénéon became angry and declared simply: "I am an anarchist and that is my right." He was consigned to a cell in Mazas, an old prison often used to house political prisoners and located appropriately close to the Place de la Bastille. Fénéon was kept in solitary confinement, like all other anarchist suspects, following a recent order from the Minister of Justice, who did not wish the "conspiracy" to continue behind bars.

The newspapers elaborated on the story. Some exulted over the *importante capture.* It seemed somehow blasphemous that Fénéon had dared to keep the detonators in the War Office. Doubtless the confiscated correspondence would reveal the identities of the ringleaders of anarchy, including a mysterious banker of London. Other reports expressed dismay that this refined man of letters was being held in preventive detention, leaving his mother and young niece without support. The numerous articles on him highlighted his activities as editor of symbolist reviews, his unusual face and even more unusual character, "fit for the pen of Edgar Allan Poe."[3] The day after the arrest, reporters from *Le Soir* went to interview both Verlaine and Mallarmé. The former responded from his sickbed that he knew Fénéon "quite intimately" but that he had no idea of his political opinions: "All that I can tell you is that I consider Félix Fénéon very talented, a young man with rare intelligence, who writes with refinement." Mallarmé admitted he was extremely surprised at the news. "M. Fénéon is one of our most distinguished young writers and a remarkable art critic, extremely sharp in his judgments. . . . You say they are talking of detonators. Certainly, for Fénéon, there were no better detonators than his articles."[4]

Mallarmé's defense of Fénéon was sincere and convincing. "I cannot help believing that there has been an error and I refuse to accept the validity of such accusations until there is material proof of the contrary." Fénéon was simply a victim of the current wave of repression. "I was myself a victim of this mood when M. Clément conducted a search of my home following some house-to-house collections for workers' soup-and-lecture programs."

Bernard Lazare and Octave Mirbeau immediately defended their friend. Noting that Fénéon was accused of evil-doing because he had contributed to *L'Endehors,* Bernard Lazare remarked that the same was true of Jules Christophe, who was also, incidentally, deputy chief clerk at the War Office:

> I imagine that tomorrow they will also arrest M. Henri de Régnier, M. A.-Ferdinand Hérold, M. Francis Vielé-Griffin, M. Pierre Quillard, M. Lucien Descaves, M. Pierre Véber, M. Tristan Bernard and myself, for we have all contributed, along with M. Fénéon, to *l'Endehors.* We have often met and talked with him; we are his friends; he has all our affection and all our esteem.[5]

Octave Mirbeau explained that Fénéon helped the exiled Alexandre Cohen because "once he gives himself to someone, he gives himself completely, and when misfortune strikes, his charming, ingenious friendship becomes something deeper: dedication."[6]

As in any cause célèbre, Fénéon was tried in the papers long before he was tried in court. One of the chief inspectors at the préfecture, a certain M. Puybaraud, regularly supplied reporters with inside information. Actually, it was M. Puybaraud who originally conceived of a conspiracy trial, and he enjoyed orchestrating the effects. He saw to it that the public was informed of the exact size of the incriminating vial of mercury (5 cm) and the detonators (3 cm)—and their destructive potential. The papers made much of the little bottle of mercury; some called it, quite mistakenly, "fulminate of mercury." Others published a fictitious account of how Emile Henry in his prison cell recognized the bottle as once his own, "only fuller then." Puybaraud furnished the *Temps* with picturesque extracts of Fénéon's criticism, so that a description he had made of an impressionist painting by Guillaumin was made to seem subversive.[7]

Fénéon's admirers who thought he would soon be released were disappointed. "People in high places are thoroughly convinced that if Fénéon did not participate directly in anarchist terrorism, he knew all about it and became so to speak the accomplice of the militants," reported the *Presse* (28 April). His name was frequently printed along with that of the condemned man, Emile Henry, and that of the prisoner suspected of the Foyot incident, Matha. However, no further evidence against F. F. was discovered. Assiduous analysis of the four or five hundred letters seized in his home and office revealed only the names of writers and painters who regularly discussed contemporary work with the critic. The campaign in Fénéon's favor—feature articles by Arsène Alexandre, Henry Bauër, Gustave Kahn, Louise Michel, Octave Mirbeau,

Henri Rochefort, and Séverine—became increasingly bitterly critical of the impending prosecution.

The Chamber was considerably upset when Fénéon was arrested. Prime Minister Casimir-Périer called in General Mercier, who held the portfolio of War. On 2 May, a week after F. F.'s arrest, the ministry announced that he had been fired, adding: "This purely administrative measure is independent of the judicial proceedings against him."[8] This was more than three months before his trial. On the same day, Judge Anquetil interrogated Fénéon's mother and also his twelve-year-old niece.

Fénéon had an excellent lawyer, although he was not allowed to consult with him for several weeks. This was Edgar Demange, who before the end of 1894 also became the defense attorney in the case of Captain Dreyfus. The services of Demange were obtained by the director of the *Revue blanche,* Thadée Natanson, who did not yet know Fénéon personally. Natanson was a lawyer himself, and he assisted Demange in preparing Fénéon's defense.

The government had a heavy caseload on its hands. Hundreds of people—785 according to one account—were in prison suspected of the crime of Association of Malefactors. The number was gradually whittled down by the two examining magistrates to 127 and then to 56. Throughout the long weeks of preliminary examinations, Fénéon, looking somewhat detached and more than a little bored, admitted nothing more than he had on the first day.

Emile Henry was executed toward the end of Fénéon's first month of detention. Early in the morning of 21 May, the young man was led out of La Roquette prison to the place where the guillotine stood. Georges Clemenceau and Maurice Barrès were among the crowd of onlookers, some of whom presented little cards allowing them to get a good view of the beheading. Henry's face was white with effort, blindingly white, said Clemenceau. He tried to walk quickly to the guillotine, but his legs were bound too tightly, and he tottered—like a child learning to walk, observed Barrès. Before he died he shouted the traditional "Courage camarades. Vive l'Anarchie!" but in a choking hoarse cry, unlike the assured voices of the older men who had preceded him, Vaillant and Ravachol. Both Barrès and Clemenceau wrote moving accounts of the scene. The young man's ideas, they concluded, "could not be cut off" as easily as his head.[9] Marie-Louise Fénéon, who had clipped out and saved the newspaper version of the declaration Emile Henry read in court and the way he, smiling, had refused to appeal for clemency, could not bring herself to read even the sympathetic accounts of his execution.

She had begun to set aside some of the numerous articles on her own son, beginning with the interviews with Mallarmé and Verlaine, which she passed on to Attorney Demange. She also personally thanked everyone who wrote in Fénéon's favor, even anonymously, as this note to Octave Maus shows:

> Sir, you are certainly the author of the article concerning my son, Félix Fénéon, published in *l'Art moderne* of 29 April. . . . The sympathy expressed in these lines is a balm on the painful wounds of a poor mother overwhelmed—not by "the fault of her son" as the *Figaro* said on 5 May—but because she is separated from her child—her joy and her pride.[10]

Fénéon was not allowed to read newspapers or even literary reviews in prison. It was three months before he became aware that Gustave Kahn had defended him shortly after his arrest. Kahn himself was living in Brussels, and Madame Fénéon did not hear of his article, "Souvenirs sur Fénéon,"[11] until shortly before the Trial of the Thirty. When she saw it, she went to Mazas to tell her son about it, and then wrote Kahn:

> Félix dropped his fine air of impassitivity when I told him, through those horrible grilles in the visiting room, that like the great-hearted you came to him in this time of danger. I did not read your article (no one is allowed to read), but recited it to him. It was well documented, and the end deeply moved him.[12]

F. F. had been estranged from Kahn for three years, ever since Seurat's death, when Madame Kahn had ineptly divulged the contents of a confidential letter Félix had written Gustave about Seurat's mistress.[13] But the present crisis rekindled their friendship. As soon as he could (that is, after his release from prison), Félix wrote Kahn:

> Believe me, of all that was written concerning me, your article gave me the most pleasure, and I cannot have any regret about my judicial adventure since it brought us together again. Thank you for the forceful and spontaneous way you spoke up: it oriented the press right from the start and from then on "the exterior defense," as [Prosecutor] Bulot complains, worked to perfection.[14]

Fénéon never complained of his treatment in prison. Indeed, he later found that compared to conditions in the twentieth century, the penitentiary regulations of the early Third Republic were rather liberal.[15] Misia Godebska, wife of Thadée Natanson, Marie Huot, and the American poet Stuart Merrill regularly brought fruit and sweetmeats to their friends in Mazas. Chatel and Aguéli relied heavily on this aid, for both were in poor health and found they could not eat the "shapeless dog food they throw (not give, throw!) at us."[16] They spoke increasingly of the lack of fresh air. "I am slowly suffocating here," wrote Aguéli to his family in Sweden. Chatel fared worse in the dank atmosphere and contracted tuberculosis, from which he died three years later. Fénéon accommodated himself to prison conditions, and never asked for a favor. The guards habitually growled and yelled at the inmates; he seemed not to hear them. When they came to get him for interrogation, he rose and crossed his arms behind his back for them to handcuff. He preferred that his bound wrists be hidden from the examiner. He was urbane even in prison garb. When a solicitious visitor could not accept his answer, "Nothing, nothing at all," in response to urgings to tell his needs, Fénéon said: "Perhaps a bit of shoe polish; they are rather stingy with it here."[17]

Boredom was a major problem. The prison library contained little of interest; among some old school books were a few volumes of George Sand and *Northanger Abbey* by Jane Austen. Women writers, like women visitors, were considered innocuous. Stuart Merrill brought Fénéon a dictionary, and he began patiently to translate the English novel. He was soon happily involved in rendering the author's pithy style and keen insights on human nature. He was not interrupted in this pastime, unlike Chatel, whose wordy poems and philosophical treatises were confiscated by the prison director.

Preparations for the conspiracy trial ground slowly on, heightened by a new anarchist attack: on 24 June, a month after the execution of Emile Henry, a young

Above left, **MAXIMILIEN LUCE.** ***In the Cell.*** Félix Fénéon in prison. 1894. Lithograph, illustration for *A Mazas* by Jules Vallès. Photograph courtesy of the late Frédéric Luce.

Above right, **MAXIMILIEN LUCE.** ***In the Yard.*** Félix Fénéon in prison. 1894. Lithograph, illustration for *A Mazas* by Jules Vallès. Photograph courtesy of the late Frédéric Luce.

Italian worker named Caserio stabbed President Carnot to death on the streets of Lyons. The Chamber hastened to replace Carnot with Jean Casimir-Périer, a millionaire mining entrepreneur, and voted the third "loi scélérate" against anyone who "apart from any conspiracy or previous understanding commits by any means an act of anarchist propaganda." Carnot, whom the people had dubbed "Made of Zinc" because of his stilted personality, was buried in the Panthéon between Jean-Jacques Rousseau and Victor Hugo.[18]

More arrests. Among them, Fénéon's good friend Maximilien Luce, charged with painting pictures of workers and giving lithographs of them to anarchist publications which were already defunct at the time of his arrest. An agent who signed ┼ gloated over this coup. "The arrest of Luce," he reported, "has planted terror in the hearts of all the illustrators, sculptors and painters of Montmartre; even the most moderate of the anarchists talk of fleeing."[19] Indeed, not only artists but many writers left France, fearing imminent arrest. Pissarro wrote his son from Belgium that their friends Paul Adam, Bernard Lazare, and Augustin Hamon had managed to escape, as well as the illustrator Steinlen.[20] It was too late to include Luce in the present proceedings; the prosecution wanted a manageable number of conspirators and had fixed on a round thirty. Luce and scores of others were therefore kept in preventive detention at Mazas in anticipation of a second trial to follow upon the expected success of the first one.

August, vacation time. The government chose this moment to try its case against the thirty accused anarchists, while Paris was empty of its usual throngs. There would be less chance of public manifestations, less chance of a bomb planted near the "Palais de l'Injustice," as the *Père peinard* had habitually called the Hall of Justice. Apprised just three days before that the trial was finally to take place and that Félix was indeed among the thirty, Madame Fénéon sent hurried notes to professors Mallarmé and Charles Henry, both vacationing outside Paris: would they come and testify on her son's behalf? Yes, she could count on them. She approached M. Lallamant, Fénéon's chief at the War Office for the past eight years, and two family friends of long standing, M. Cahen, a Post Office clerk, and M. Magnin, a wine merchant, solid citizens all, who had nothing but good to say of Félix. They would testify.

The case was to be tried in criminal court, the first application of the law against the "Association of Malefactors." The accused were transferred to the Conciergerie prison adjacent to the Hall of Justice and, contrary to usual procedure, kept in solitary confinement. Presiding Judge Dayras interrogated each in turn two days before the trial. In the midst of the routine questioning, Fénéon interrupted. He would like to have admission cards for two lady friends interested in following the judicial proceedings. The astonished judge replied no. Fénéon queried: "So there are no complimentary tickets for actors in your theater? And yet we hold the main roles. . . ."[21]

The trial opened at the Assize Court of the Seine on Monday 6 August 1894, four days after Caserio was condemned to death in Lyons. The municipal guard was doubled both inside and outside the Paris Hall of Justice, patrolling with fixed bayonets. No one was allowed in without an entrance card and corridors were blocked so that all traffic could be monitored. Publicity was controlled: the government had authorized the distribution of ten thousand copies of a composite photograph showing the "ten principal anarchists"[22]—among them F. F. in profile, standing straight as a ramrod, his arms locked behind his back.

The prosecution was intent upon proving complicity between revolutionary thinkers and simple criminals. The jury was to decide on the guilt of nineteen "militants"—Sébastian Faure, Jean Grave, Fénéon, Matha, Chatel, and other theorists or propagandists—and eleven "thieves," including the anarchist bandit Ortiz and four women. Fénéon was accused both of belonging to an association of malefactors and possessing explosive materials and murderous devices. The prosecution had toyed with the idea of trying him separately because of the second charge, but abandoned this plan, for reasons unknown.

The defendants included several men of letters, a carpenter, a shoemaker, a typesetter, a butcher's apprentice (accused of stealing a cutlet), a tailor, a mechanic, a coffee-roaster, and a painter (Aguéli, looking wan in his velvet jacket and yellow cravat). As for the women, none was good-looking, the newsmen remarked, and one was old, the mother of an idiot son who sat among the accused, grinning and uncomprehending. In fact, the defendants numbered only twenty-five: five more, including Emile Pouget, Alexandre Cohen, and Paul Reclus, scientist nephew of the Reclus brothers, had preferred to stay abroad until "justice" was done.

In the courtroom, those accused sat sandwiched between members of the municipal guard. They occupied three long benches, normally used by the press: "a triple necklace of black coats and grey jackets, relieved by the red of the uniforms," reported the *Journal* (7 August 1894). Soberly dressed, mild in manner, the defendants did not resemble the public image of anarchists. They smiled in anticipation of seeing some familiar faces in the gallery—but alas, it was occupied mostly by lawyers in their robes, policemen, and only a sprinkling of the "public."

Two young women in the audience attracted some attention. Fénéon's request had been granted, after all; he gave a discreet sign of welcome to his guests. One was modestly but elegantly dressed and sat sideways, averting her face from the crowd—quite possibly his Belgian lover, Camille Platteel. The other, less reserved, was an actress called Denise Ahmers who had performed in symbolist drama at the Théâtre d'Art and in the May 1891 benefit performance for Verlaine and Gauguin. Just four days before, she had been Madame Fénéon's right hand in the last minute rush to assure Félix a good defense witness, and she had written Mallarmé before his mother dared to do so.

The courtroom below was filled with tables for the twenty-three defense lawyers and substitute accommodations for the journalists. There was the chair of the prosecuting magistrate, Avocat Général Bulot, infamous among the anarchists since 1892, when he had demanded the death penalty for the 1 May demonstrators of Clichy, and who had just prosecuted Emile Henry. In the middle stood a table covered with evidence: trunks and bundles filled with allegedly stolen goods, letters and pamphlets, and the little yellow vial of mercury associated with Fénéon. The accused were made to stand and identify themselves, and finally the clerk of the court read Bulot's bill of indictment:

> The accused belong to a sect which establishes among all its followers bonds of *Compagnonnage,** with the purpose of destroying society as a whole, by means of theft, pillage, arson, and murder. In this sect, each member contributes to the final purpose according to his temperament and abilities, one by committing crime, the others by aiding and abetting him. . . .[23]

The indictment went on in this vein, describing each "member" of the "sect" in detail. Charging secret relationships, it pointed out that one of the women was the mistress of Ortiz and that widow so-and-so slept with Bertani (accused of theft). The main characteristic of this gang was its "cosmopolitanism, not only by inclination, but by origin and habit." Ortiz was the son of a Mexican and a Pole; Fénéon was an intimate of foreigners Kampffmayer and Cohen.

*Many anarchists used *compagnon* ("mate" or "comrade") as a term of address, rather than *monsieur* ("milord") or *citoyen* ("citizen")—which, although associated with the Revolution, still implied that the individual was subjugated to the State. The *Compagnonnage* was historically a kind of workers' Freemasonry, organized after the degeneration of medieval guilds. Influential among the working class during the Restoration, it played an active role in the revolution of 1848. It was practically obsolete by 1870. Bulot's use of the term in 1894 reveals the government's contempt for any workers' organization, its belief that such a group was secret and conspiratorial, and its fear that organized workers would destroy the power of the bourgeoisie, just as middle-class Freemasons had destroyed the power of the Crown and the Church.

The accusation dwelt on Fénéon's alleged affiliation with all kinds of anarchists and his possession of explosive devices. Bulot drew a sinister picture of F. F.:

> He was two-faced: a solemn and silent civil servant during the day, he received Ortiz and Emile Henry at home in the evening. He wrote for anarchist papers, and in some decadent publications he had acquired real authority over certain young people with a morbid curiosity for strange literary topics.

The charge against Fénéon was the final one in the indictment.

Judge Dayras announced that the interrogation of the accused would begin. At once, Prosecutor Bulot requested that, pursuant to a new law passed on 29 July, a "gag order" be issued prohibiting the press from reporting the interrogations of Sébastien Faure and Jean Grave. Faure's attorney, Maître de Saint-Auban, vigorously objected in the name of all the accused, saying it was a question of self-defense now, and not propaganda. The order was issued, however, and the press left blanks marked "forbidden" for the remarks of Grave and Faure. Henri Rochefort reported that there was indeed a conspiracy in the Trial of the Thirty, one between Magistrate Dayras and Prosecutor Bulot.[24] Indeed, throughout the trial, whenever a defendant scored a point, Dayras inevitably replied, "That is of no consequence."

By preventing publicity on the statements of Jean Grave and Sébastien Faure, Bulot thought he had silenced the only eloquent anarchist defendants. The second day proved him wrong, for the session opened with the interrogation of "mute Fénéon." The first day had ended with an ugly scene: as the room slowly emptied, Fénéon stopped for a moment to exchange a word with his attorney, and two guards brutally pulled him away. "Go home!" they yelled at the reporters and lawyers who objected to this treatment of the defendant, and then violently pushed Fénéon through the prisoner's exit.[25]

The following day, F. F. appeared with his usual aplomb and took his place in the second row of the accused. (The court had established a certain hierarchy, with the intellectuals or "doctrinaires" in the first two rows and the bandits and women in back—all separated by uniformed bodies on each side.) The courtroom was even more cluttered than on the first day: the stolen goods had been taken from the trunks and spread out on tables and on the floor—ladies' linen, a clock, silver saltcellars, a telescope, bright silk coverlets, a complete set of burglary tools and a few knives and guns. This décor was presented to a very limited public, much smaller than on the first day. The gallery contained twice as many policemen as visitors, and Fénéon's two women friends were absent; their invitation, after all, had been only to the première.

Fénéon's presence in the courtroom turned what was essentially a sinister drama into a sophisticated comedy. His remarks were recorded with delight by the journalists, and they have been quoted frequently since. Only isolated ripostes are cited, however, creating the myth that Fénéon quipped his way to an acquittal in the Trial of the Thirty. In fact, his self-defense was infinitely more subtle. He posed as a dilettante; he had been quite interested in the work of the symbolists and the neo-impressionists, he said, and when the anarchist movement came on the scene he was curious to know the new, complex ideas it presented. Since no book contained all these ideas, he went to

L'Endehors to talk with people and get a firsthand account. But, he added, there were infinitely more artists than anarchists at *L'Endehors*. Yes, he had contributed three articles to that review in 1891, when it was "exclusively literary." No, he had nothing to do with the antimilitary remarks published in *L'Endehors*. Yes, he had run an insignificant errand or two for Zo d'Axa, but only because he was a personal friend.

Fénéon's responses as a whole exhibit an exaggerated picture of naïveté. He claimed, for example, that he did not know that the little tin tubes inside the matchbox were detonators: "I certainly would not have kept these objects if I had been aware of their exact nature," he told the judge. He appeared to answer each question fully, even volunteering small (but exculpatory) details. This apparent openness—combined with some ineptitude on the part of the judge and the public prosecutor—came close to making him seem the righteous victim of a complete slander. Physically he was impressive, "rigid as justice and straight as a soldier at arms," said the *Figaro*. His manner was icily correct, his voice cool and reserved, his lean, sharp face expressionless except for a brief smile that flashed his scorn once or twice at the court.

These selected questions and answers demonstrate how he played his dangerous game:[26]

JUDGE DAYRAS: You were the intimate friend of the German anarchist, Kampffmayer.

FÉNÉON: The intimacy could not have been very great. I do not know a word of German and he does not speak French. (Laughter)

J. Matha, under indictment for antimilitary propaganda, stopped at your house when he came to Paris.

F. Perhaps he was short of money.

J. When you were arrested, you were asked if you knew Matha. You said no!

F. Yes, systematically. I was not used to being in handcuffs, and at that moment, I wanted to have time to think.

J. Well, you knew Ortiz?

F. I had seen him two or three times in the offices of *l'Endehors*.

J. But your concierge at rue Lepic declared that she saw him going all the time to your place.

F. What I might say, in order not to use stronger language, is that she was mistaken. Her deposition was perhaps somewhat lacking in good-will.

J. You refused to give any information about Matha and Ortiz.

F. I did not care to say anything that might compromise them. I should behave in the same manner toward you, Your Honor, if the occasion arose.

The *Figaro* described Fénéon: "His lower lip falls and rises automatically without a single muscle of his face moving. Only the long American goatee of M. Félix Fénéon stands up mocking and diabolic at each movement. It is quite an extraordinary facial play."

J. It has been established that you surrounded yourself with Cohen and Ortiz.

F. (Smiling) One can hardly be surrounded by two persons; you need at least three. (Explosion of laughter)

J. You were seen speaking with them behind a lamp-post!
F. Can you tell me, Your Honor, where behind a lamp-post is?

Ordinarily, said the reporter for the *Libre parole,* Fénéon keeps his hands down along the sides of his long body. Only once or twice he makes a brief gesture, not abrupt, however—geometric rather.

J. Eleven detonators and a vial of mercury were found in your office. Where did you get them?
F. I found the mercury and the little tin tubes in my father's bedroom after he died in March.
J. When your mother was interrogated, she said your father found these detonators in the street.
F. That is possible.
J. That is not possible. One does not find detonators in the street!
F. And yet Monsieur Meyer, the examining magistrate, said to me one day: "You should have thrown those detonators out the window!" So you see one can find such objects on the public way. (Laughter)
J. That is not very likely. Your father would not have kept such things. He was an employee of the Banque de France and it is difficult to see what he could have done with them.
F. I do not actually think he would have used them any more than his son, who was employed at the War Office.

Fénéon answers the judge with a certain barely concealed contempt and a hint of impatience, said the *Temps.* Pressed for the reason why he kept the incriminating objects at the War Office, he replied that after his friend Cohen was arrested and deported, he took these things and three cartons of letters to the office, in case the police should take it into their heads to search his home. He did not want his mother upset by such a raid, and he did not want to sit in prison for several weeks while the prosecutor's office examined the letters—none of which was, by the way, from an avowed anarchist. As for the objects, he thought of them simply as curious. "They sent me an inventory of the things taken from my office; the list begins with a medal of Saint Helen and ends with a chamois skin. You would not call that dangerous, now, would you, a chamois skin?" (Laughter)

Judge Dayras asked the bailiff to show the detonators and flask of mercury to the members of the jury. Then he held up the mercury to Fénéon.

J. Here is a flask found in your office. Do you recognize it?
F. The flask is similar, certainly.
J. Do you know that Mr. Girard, head of the municipal laboratory has established that this very flask belonged to Emile Henry? And Henry admitted as much.
F. If a vat of mercury had been shown Emile Henry in his cell, he would have claimed it. His attitude—according to the papers—was not without a certain braggadocio and desire to mystify those who were judging him. (Laughter) But, to come to the point, will you read me Mr. Girard's deposition?
J. That is impossible. Mr. Girard is a witness and I cannot read his deposition before he testifies in court. The law. . .
F. (Conciliatory) Very well, very well.

J. You have said that you thought the detonators were not dangerous. Now, Mr. Girard has performed experiments which prove them to be extremely dangerous.

F. That proves that I was mistaken.

J. You know that mercury is used to make a highly explosive powder, mercuric fulminate?

F. (Coldly) It is also used to make thermometers, barometers, and other instruments. (Laughter)

J. You have nothing more to say?

F. No, nothing at all.

So ended Fénéon's interrogation, amidst laughter from the gallery and the jury box. That night a police spy assigned to the cafés "Deux Marronniers" and "La Cigale" in Montmarte, reported that the anarchists who gathered there to read the evening report on the Trial of the Thirty went gaily out to discuss the new turn of events in the open air, down little-used streets. where they could not be overheard.[27]

The hearings droned on, from eleven in the morning until seven at night. Everyone had his turn. The reputation of several lawyers was made. As the week progressed, the "association of malefactors" disintegrated before the jurors' eyes. The witnesses for the prosecution made a poor showing. A police inspector who had been in Emile Henry's cell when Mr. Girard questioned the prisoner testified that Henry said the little flask of mercury had *not* been his. Girard confirmed this testimony, but declared he was nonetheless personally convinced that the flask found in Fénéon's office had belonged to Henry. Several reporters remarked that laboratory director Girard seemed more devoted to Bulot than to the scientific method.

"The day of the five concierges," as the reporters billed the session of witnesses against Fénéon, turned out to be a disaster for Dayras-Bulot. The defendant appeared not the least interested in the parade of concierges and their husbands: Cohen's concierge, Kampffmayer's concierge, his own concierge on rue Lepic. The latter said she often saw Ortiz, as well as Matha and Cohen, go to Fénéon's. Ortiz interrupted to say that he would have felt flattered to have been invited to Fénéon's but that he had never been there. Judge Dayras called Fénéon to attention: Had he nothing to say? F. F. stood up, uncoiling like a boa, although once he was up, André Salmon later said, he had nothing of the boa about him. "It is difficult to get worked up over this testimony," he intoned. "I did not receive Ortiz in my home. However, I do not wish to insist on this detail, for that would make me seem to attach some importance to it. I might have received him, as I would anyone, hospitably. For if certain charges—about which it is not my business to worry—have been raised against him, one can hardly say that in consequence *I* am a thief! What could one conclude from such a visit?"

"That is enough," said the judge. "You may sit down; your lawyer will defend you. [Turning back to the witness] And Cohen? Did he not also often come to Fénéon's?

"Yes, Your Honor. Five or six times a day!"

Fénéon chuckled from his seat. "Come now, that is beyond all probability. I was at the War Office all day; five or six times is too much, Your Honor; let's decrease the dose."

Witnesses in Fénéon's defense were more impressive than those who testified against him. His chief at the War Office said that in the eight years he had known him, Fénéon was considered a remarkably distinguished and intelligent employee, one who could have aspired to a high position in the Ministry. The wine merchant and postal employee, friends of Fénéon's father, had known Félix for many years and spoke of him in glowing terms. The poet Mallarmé stepped forward and said:

> I know Félix Fénéon. He is beloved by all. I have pledged him my friendship because he is a gentle and an upright man, and a very fine intellect. We have met in my home, on evenings when I gather friends together to chat. There is no one who has not enjoyed meeting him. I have never, nor has any of my guests, heard Fénéon discuss a subject alien to art. I know he is above using anything, other than literature, to express his thought. I have gladly responded to a summons not so much because of the real fondness I feel for him as in the interests of truth.[28]

Charles Henry, of the Sorbonne, was announced. He testified:

> I met Fénéon in 1884. I consider him to be a very talented and a very trustworthy person. He has participated in my scientific experiments and has worked mathematical problems out for me. He has been very helpful to his friends in important, practical matters. He is a perfectly straightforward fellow and has nothing to do with anarchy.[29]

Public Prosecutor Bulot began his closing argument at the end of the third day and continued on the fourth. He was obliged to drop charges against three or four of the accused, such as the coffee-roaster Soubrier, arrested in a case of mistaken identity and kept in preventive detention for the Trial of the Thirty even after this fact was discovered. How amazing, remarked the press, that out of the hundreds of people kept in detention, the government should choose him to figure in their select group of anarchists. "I admit we have nothing against him," said Bulot. But he demanded twenty years' hard labor for the bulk of the accused. For Fénéon—only five. In his summation, Bulot dramatically ticked off the unanswered questions about Fénéon's relations with Matha, with Emile Henry, and the others, and concluded: "He was right to keep silent. In his place, I would have done as much."

Then it was the turn of the defense lawyers. Two days later, Attorney Demange spoke in Fénéon's behalf. F. F. sat with closed eyes and seemed not to hear him as he evoked with pathos the deathbed adieu between Fénéon and his father, "the best friend one ever has." But the jury paid attention, especially when Demange enumerated the events in Fénéon's private life when Emile Henry's last bomb exploded:

> The Terminus bomb was on 13 February. The eleventh, Fénéon lost his father. He buried him on the fourteenth . . . Do you suppose that on that day he cared what Matha was up to?[30]

Earlier that day, Bulot had interrupted another defense lawyer by jumping up and dramatically sniffing his fingers: "Gentlemen, this morning I received in my chambers a package of fecal matter wrapped in a copy of the *Intransigeant.* It was one of the accused, or rather, one of their friends, who sent it through the post. I beg your pardon, I must go wash my hands." And he disappeared, for about a minute. Fénéon said, in tones loud enough to be heard by all: "Since Pontius Pilate no magistrate has washed his hands so ostentatiously."[31]

Court was convened in extraordinary session the next day, Sunday, 12 August 1894. The spectacle was enlivened slightly by the bright plumes replacing the everyday pompoms on the helmets of the guards. Final arguments were heard and Judge Dayras read off sixty questions to be decided by the jury, the last of which concerned Fénéon's possession of explosives. After deliberating two-and-one-half hours, the jury returned its verdict: All Thirty NOT GUILTY of Association of Malefactors. Fénéon NOT GUILTY of possessing explosives. Eight of the eleven thieves NOT GUILTY. Fénéon dropped his icy manner and while the other defendants filed solemnly out between the guards, he rushed over to shake Attorney Demange's hand, his cheeks flushed, radiant with joy.

The liberal press later exulted: "All acquitted, except the three burglars! Poor government! A lot of good it did to arrest 350 comrades, stir up public opinion for six months and parade noisily as the exterminator of anarchy!" (*L'Eclair,* 14 August 1894). Police investigators reported another point of view: "The anarchists hardly expected this large scale acquittal . . . Fénéon, Matha and Faure were the most surprised. Fénéon has made no secret of his intention to leave France, since his life is not safe in Paris. Well, they are acquitted, but they were all accomplices and they were just lucky."[32]

The jury was closely divided. Although the vote was unanimous against Ortiz and the two other burglars, it was seven to five in favor of all the other defendants, except for Fénéon and the four women, where it was six against six. What would have been a hung jury in a British or American court resulted in a bonus for these defendants, thanks to a rule allowing the accused to benefit from a vote divided equally. According to one juror, Fénéon's quicksilver remarks had thrust home—annoying some and disposing others equally in his favor. The deliberations concerning him lasted nearly three-quarters of an hour. The defendants had generally benefited from the prosecution's lumping the intellectuals together with thieves. "Judged singly, Sébastian Faure, Jean Grave, Fénéon and the others would certainly have been convicted, for we did not mean to claim, in acquitting them, that it is lawful to preach social upheaval and approve attacks on human life and individual property!" one juror explained.[33]

Since it was Sunday, the clerk's office was closed, and the defendants were told they would have to spend another night in prison. Attorney Demange insisted that they had a right to immediate freedom, and while the lawyers argued over this, all of the male defendants, convicted and acquitted alike, were kept in the same room waiting for a ruling from the court. Most of them were happily congratulating one another on the outcome of the trial. Ortiz, who had been sentenced to fifteen years in a penal colony, stood off alone to one side. Fénéon struck up a conversation with him; they had never really spoken together before, although their names had often been linked during the trial. He was intrigued by this fellow who had allegedly been Emile Henry's accomplice in a brilliantly conceived burglary at Fiquefleur the previous year. Fénéon felt keenly that Ortiz had borne the brunt of the conspiracy trial, and expressed this freely to reporters as soon as he was released:

> In reality, he was victimized because of us, the "intellectuals," as the judge called us. . . . If Ortiz had appeared alone before the jury instead of being included with us, he would have gotten off with seven or eight years.[34]

Fénéon declared he found Ortiz to be like a character out of a novel, who was looking for adventure more than for lucre and who enjoyed danger more than gain, "which," Fénéon added, "was negligible." He admired Ortiz's courage and the proud, calm way he faced his sentence.

Later that evening Fénéon was released, along with most of the others (Jean Grave, Matha, and Paul Bernard were sent back to prison to serve previous sentences). To avoid any demonstration, the defendants were sent out at intervals from different doors in the préfecture. Fénéon was one of the last to appear. The reporters caught sight of him coming down the long corridor, walking slowly and deliberately toward them. He saluted them briefly and stopped outside the door to shake his attorney's hand. Then he jumped into a hackney cab retained for him by Thadée Natanson. But before he could get away, several bystanders ran to hold the horse's head. They all wanted to shake Fénéon's hand before letting him go. He looked into each face as if trying to recall it distinctly before he spoke. Finally his impassive features relaxed, and he said in a voice husky with emotion, *Merci . . . tous mes remerciements . . . merci.* Meanwhile Attorney Demange hastened around the building to the cab where Madame Fénéon and Denise Ahmers had been awaiting Félix's exit; he told them to join F. F. at the Natanson's for dinner. Off they went, smiling radiantly.

Not everyone's release was as joyous. Some did not possess cabfare, after months in prison, and were obliged to walk home. All—including F. F.—were followed by plainclothes men.

Anarchism. Its very name can suggest chaos, destruction, and murder. The wave of terrorist acts in the 1880s and 1890s in France and elsewhere appears to justify that association. Yet those bombs and daggers, repudiated by the vast majority of anarchists, were but a tiny, if sensational, fragment of the movement. Their shock effect reverberated through the press, in an age when the first cheap newspapers appeared, and "shook from their torpor" a good number of workers, if not the bourgeois, as Fénéon had hoped.

The Trial of the Thirty, according to the historian Jean Maitron, marked the end of the epidemic of terror in France. Maitron credits the sudden end to anarchist violence primarily to: the "generous verdict" rendered in the Trial of the Thirty (but such a verdict might also have given a green light to future violent acts); continuous, reinforced surveillance of the anarchists (though this had not deterred Emile Henry, Fénéon, Pauwels, and Caserio); most important, a "new element in the class war," trade-unionism, some of whose architects were anarchists, including Emile Pouget of the *Père peinard;* and, finally, the tactic of the general strike, which satisfied the anarchists' ideas of revolution and their need to manifest ideas through action.[35]

Fénéon never renounced his anarchist involvement. The Paris Prefecture of Police has claimed that even in 1908 he was "militating in anarchist groups and contributing to *libertaire* publications." No direct evidence of this activity has been found. But he openly embraced Communism later in the twentieth century, an evolution due in part to the anarchist involvement in the labor movement.

PART FIVE

And After . . .
1894–1910

CHAPTER 15

At the Revue blanche

The next day, reporters besieged Fénéon. What were his plans? "I do not believe I should be very welcome back at the War Office, nor would I feel at ease there," he replied. "I shall very probably go to Japan." He said he was negotiating with a London firm that would send him to Asia to look for antiques and paintings. This retort was recorded in a police file with the comment, "Fénéon is running for his life." In fact, F. F. did want to go to Japan. When the position with the London firm did not materialize, he tried to become an agent for Parisian dealers in oriental art. His friends Charles Henry and Maximilien Luce helped him approach the manager of the Bing gallery and also Marty, director of the *Estampe originale.* But they already had their own people established in Asia. Charles Henry then proposed that F. F. try to sell some scientific inventions on the Parisian market; Fénéon objected that he probably could not support himself and his family in such a venture.

During this time of forced leisure, he posed for a series of drawings by Maximilien Luce, illustrating the life of a political prisoner in solitary confinement. The charges against Luce had been dropped shortly after the Trial of the Thirty, and he was released from Mazas. A petition covered with names of artists, beginning with that of Puvis de Chavannes, had been circulated in his favor. But in fact the government had no desire to risk a second unsuccessful conspiracy trial and freed numerous prisoners they had been holding in reserve. Although Luce and Fénéon had spent weeks in the same prison, they never saw one another there. Fénéon, dressed atypically in ill-fitting clothes and wearing a shapeless felt hat, posed in the artist's studio, but the two comrades must have made at least one commemorative visit to the prison: an unpublished pen-and-ink sketch by Luce shows F. F. in top hat and dress coat speaking with workers on the prison roof! Luce used the drawings of Fénéon to make lithographs for an edition of an old text by Jules Vallès telling of the tedium, solitude, and degradation of life as a political prisoner in Mazas.

MAXIMILIEN LUCE. ***Fénéon with Workers on the Roof of Mazas Prison,*** after the Trial of the Thirty, September 1894. Private collection. Photograph courtesy of the late Frédéric Luce.

Fénéon managed somehow to eke out an existence for himself and his family (two nieces now lived in the little flat that he shared with his mother). Without a regular job, he began doing editorial work for the *Revue blanche,* publishing manuscripts of Jules Laforgue, doubtless at the invitation of Thadée Natanson, who, along with his brothers Alexandre and Alfred, had launched this exceptionally fine literary magazine in Paris three years before. Sons of a successful Jewish immigrant from Poland, the brothers shared a keen appreciation of avant-garde writing and art, and their family was connected with the intelligentsia and the *haute bourgeoisie* of Paris and other European capitals. Warm-hearted Thadée had a multifaceted mind, while the eldest brother, Alexandre, had a good head for business. Alfred, an aspiring playwright just barely out of school, had made friends with painters he met at the Théâtre de l'Oeuvre, Vuillard and his fellow Nabis, Bonnard, Maurice Denis, Vallotton, and Ranson, whom he brought to the review. When Thadée decided in 1893 to publish lithographs and other illustrations in the monthly magazine, these artists, along with Toulouse-Lautrec, became known as the "Painters of the *Revue blanche.*" The review quickly became a haven for innovative artists and writers, who were actually paid for their contributions. Fénéon fit into this milieu naturally, and in January 1895 the Natansons offered him a regular position as their "literary counsellor" and editorial secretary. So Fénéon was able at last to spend his days doing what he loved to do, and be paid for it as well, all because he had been caught and tried as an anarchist!

He was to stay with the *Revue blanche* for nearly a decade, until 1903, when it ceased to appear. Since its inception, this "White Review"—colored by no particular "-ism"—had welcomed any writer of worth, regardless of age or allegiance. This openness was complemented by Fénéon's intuition for the new and the unusual. He threw himself into the *Revue blanche* with the same dedication that he formerly brought to making known those who meant the most to him. On his first official day, he wrote Octave Mirbeau, among others, inviting contributions and announcing new editorial and production policies:

> *10 January 1895*
>
> My dear friend,
>
> If I tell you that as of this morning I am the editorial secretary of the "Revue blanche," you will not be surprised if I ask for your contribution. Starting in February, the review will come out twice a month, with just 50 pages, rather than 100. Shorter articles (3–4 pages), a more lively tone, more concern for what is happening currently, and so forth.
>
> MM. Natanson, directors of the "Revue blanche," as you know, have long wanted to ask for something from you. I told them that during your recent trip to London you had studied some of the Pre-Raphaelites, Burne-Jones and Rossetti in particular, for an article that you were going to publish in Pall Mall Gazette. Would you kindly agree to publish articles on this subject in the Revue Blanche and write generally about art in England? You can imagine how happy I would be if your entrance to the Revue blanche coincided with mine. . . .
>
> *Most cordially yours,*
> *félix fénéon*[1]

This gracious invitation, full of practical advice and information, is typical of Fénéon. Mirbeau did not come forth with the requested articles at that time, but the new editor of the *Revue blanche* was not at a loss for writers to recruit. Many years later, in an article on the youngest Natanson brother, Fénéon paid tribute to the *Revue blanche* and its contributors:

> This review . . . is perhaps even better known today than when, twice a month, its appearance provoked animated discussion. What other publication is still a topic of conversation twenty years after its disappearance? The *Revue blanche* was unique in that, far from playing to the public, each issue offered a salty surprise to its readers, for it was free of moral and social supersititons.
>
> Its literary quality is attested by the frequent appearance in its Table of Contents of Paul Adam, Claude Anet, Victor Barrucand, Tristan Bernard, Bernard Lazare, Léon Blum, Lucie Delarue-Mardrus, Robert Dreyfus, Coolus, Fagus, André Gide, Remy de Gourmont, Alfred Jarry, Gustave Kahn, Ernest La Jeunesse, Paul Leclercq, Pierre Louÿs, Pierre Veber, Maeterlinck, Mirbeau, Lucien Mühlfeld, Marcel Proust, Marcel Schwob, Jules Renard, Ch. Saunier, Verhaeren, Verlaine, [Vielé-]Griffin, Apollinaire, Benda, Claudel, Edm. Cousturier, Ed. Dujardin, P. Fort, Gorki, Jammes, Kipling, M.-A. Leblond, Marinetti, Moréas, Nau, Péguy, Ch.-L. Philippe, André Picard, Rob. Scheffer, Ed. Sée, Séverine, Strindberg, P.-J. Toulet.

Fénéon added that Thadée Natanson was the regular art critic and that Charles Henry contributed a column on contemporary science (everything from disorders of the nervous system to the dynamics of the newly invented bicycle). The names of some relatively obscure writers appear in Fénéon's long list, but he justified the whole by concluding:

> Allowing that some of these have faded with time, at least the *Revue blanche* had them in all the piquancy of their first bloom. But the name of Stéphane Mallarmé shines brighter than ever, and many a *Divagation* appeared there first. (F, 454)

He did not mention that, without his prodding, those prose pieces of Mallarmé might never have been written; that when the magazine wanted a music critic, he thought to ask Debussy (who in his column parried with an alter ego, "M. Croche"); that he invited André Gide to report on contemporary literature and Romain Coolus to write on sports; and that he launched Léon-Paul Fargue and Apollinaire through the review. He also neglected to say that he published Gauguin's manuscript *Noa Noa* and introduced Luce, Signac, Van Dongen, and Matisse to the review, thus widening the circle of artists who enriched its pages.

Along with his new responsibilities, Fénéon took up once again his life as a literary man about town, inevitably followed by his two police "shadows." He religiously attended performances at the Oeuvre, which had become even more sympathetic to anarchism during his incarceration,[2] and he freely expressed his opinions to Signac and other friends at the theater. He declared he did not like *The Father* by Strindberg at all, because of its "anti-anarchist thesis which gives the husband complete rights over the wife."[3] He was well aware that his shadows were listening. The Trial of the Thirty had also made it clear that many police informants mingled in anarchist circles. Thus, if he was outspoken about his own ideas, he was circumspect where others were concerned. He was noncommittal when an unfamiliar face made inquiries on behalf of Emile Pouget in London. Pouget, Cohen, and two others who had chosen to remain abroad rather than sit among the accused at the Trial of the Thirty, wanted to know their chances for acquittal if they should return now. Fénéon suspected, rightly, that the inquirer was a police informant who had wangled a letter of introduction through Pouget's brother.[4] But in spite of police pressure, the climate had changed enough so that the exiles soon felt safe in returning, and all were acquitted in a new jury trial. Only Paul Reclus, who as an engineer had found employment in England, preferred not to gamble on French justice and stayed abroad.

Prison had not made F. F. "sick of anarchism," as he once remarked of a former activist (F, 541). The police kept a dossier on him until he died in 1944, or at least until 1940, when his file, along with others of the Paris Préfecture, was accidentally sunk in the Seine on a barge the police had loaded with documents in order to save them from the approaching German enemy. In spite of the disappearance of this evidence, the police archives contain many references to F. F., scattered in the files of other political suspects.

If he was annoyed at being trailed by the police, he usually did not show it. "My two mute friends," he occasionally introduced them. In a contemporary roman à clef by Pierre Veber, *Une Passade,* Fénéon was depicted flanked by two silent anarchists who were, in fact, his hounds. But there were times when he wanted privacy, and he found willing assistance in gaining it. Once one of Lugné-Poe's actresses, Hedwige Morre, gave him the key to her dressing room at the Oeuvre. While the tails waited in the theater concierge's office, Lugné-Poe made sure Fénéon had joined the entering audience before ending a conversation with three policemen during which they warned him: "You have a dangerous anarchist hiding in the wings of your theater!" The next day the police raided the theater as a lesson to the director.[5] Of course, Morre was an anarchist, and she lived openly with Victor Barrucand, well known for reviving a popular issue of the Revolution, *le pain gratuit* (free bread for the people).

In January 1895 Lugné-Poe asked Fénéon to perform, reciting the prologue to a lively Hindu drama more than a thousand years old, the *Chariot de terre cuite* (Little Clay Cart), adapted by Victor Barrucand for its revolutionary idealism. In the play, Buddha is a rebel whose words inspire hatred and fear among the ruling class, while the heroine, a rich courtesan, falls in love with a pauper and shows her love by giving away all her possessions (which fill the Clay Cart). Fénéon probably helped write the final version; he published an amusing description of the play a year before it appeared on the stage (F, 604). At the performance, Fénéon stepped in front of the curtain, wearing only a white linen wrapping, and proclaimed: "May the benediction of Sambu protect you. . . ." His naked arm shot out, fingers outspread, while he rhythmically intoned verses inspired by the Sanskrit text, ending, "Be therefore gladdened and protected by the God of the Blue Neck, clasped in the brilliant arms, precious collar, of Gaori." As he moved away in measured stride, the theater burst into applause—somewhat exaggerated applause, reported one critic, "if we had not known that this strange priest was none other than Félix Fénéon, whose prestige seems not to have diminished among a certain public since his recent judicial adventure."[6] Although Fénéon's name was not on the program, his profile was clearly recognizable on it, drawn by Toulouse-Lautrec, who also helped paint the scenery for the *Chariot de terre cuite.*

The play became a milestone in the history of the Oeuvre because of its artistic appeal and its statement of the anarchist message that nobility of soul can triumph over social injustice. Gérard de Nerval's earlier translation of the play for the Odéon had been, in Nerval's own opinion, not up to the "revolutionary genius" of the Hindu author.[7] But both Barrucand and his audience at the Oeuvre believed that Barrucand's version made the propaganda of the ancient drama perfectly applicable to modern society, the only difference being that in India, privileges of caste or class were attributed to divine authority, whereas in contemporary France, they supposedly stemmed from the will of the people; "but that is perhaps just a play on words," Barrucand said.[8]

During their collaboration for the play, Fénéon invited Barrucand to join him in writing a small bimonthly column for the *Revue blanche.* Called *Passim* (Here and There), it was much like the anonymous commentaries he had made in anarchist reviews, but without the notes on art and literature. Politics was its exclusive concern, and now that Fénéon no longer earned his bread at the War Ministry, he signed with his initials, next

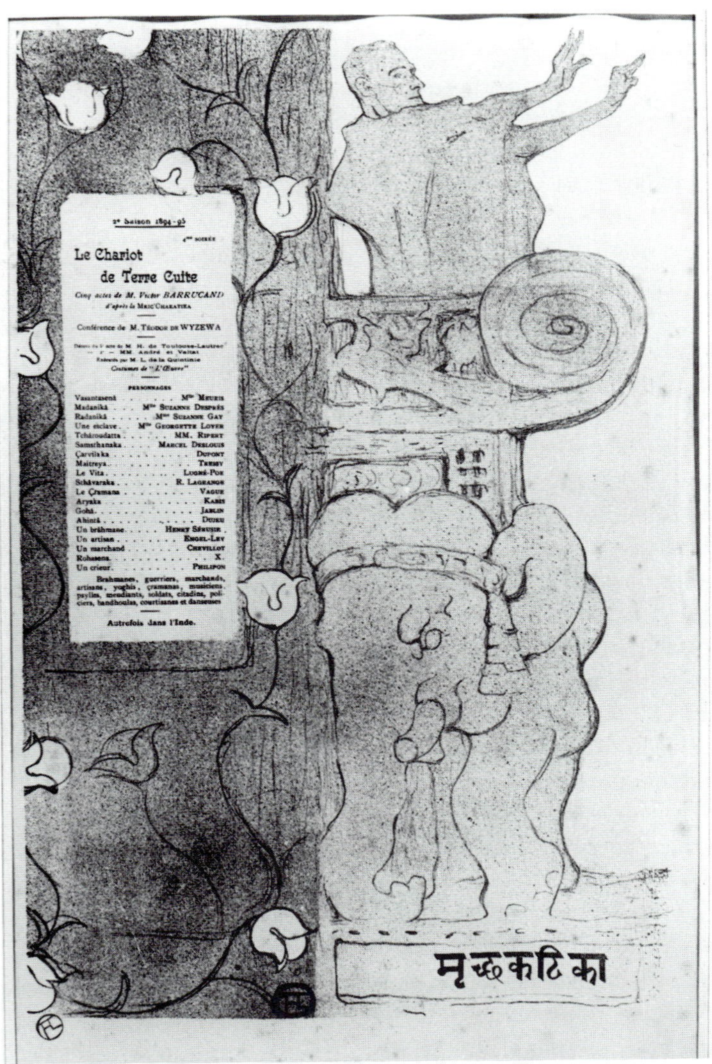

HENRI DE TOULOUSE-LAUTREC. ***Program*** for the play, ***Le Chariot de terre cuite*** at the Théâtre de l'Oeuvre, January 1895, showing Fénéon reciting the prologue. Brush, crayon, and spatter lithograph in blue with a rose tint stone, 40 x 28 cm. Albi, Musée Toulouse-Lautrec.

to the "V. B." of his friend. Fénéon's entries are readily distinguishable from Barrucand's by their sarcastic sting.

Six years had passed since the scandal over the financing of the Panama Canal had first broken into print, but the government was still trying to whitewash itself. Fénéon reported: "Various arrests (politico-financial world). Let us hope this mania for purification will end at last: people will start to think that everything will be all nice and clean afterwards" (F, 943).

The very first *Passim* carried this item:

> —On the occasion of the New Year festivities, we have had the degradation of Captain Dreyfus and, around it, the noble spectacle of some people cringing in immobility and others raging in lynching fury.

With withering irony, Fénéon added: "There is, said Renan at an awarding of the Monthyon prize,* a day in the Army when virtue is recompensed" (F, 943). In a later *Passim,* he reported:

> 7 May.—The ingenious torturers operating on Devil's Island have thought up a variant of forced labor for Captain Dreyfus—forced inactivity: in addition, pens, paper and pencils are strictly denied him. Would they tend to modify public opinion? (F, 950)

Thus, many months before the Dreyfus affair got under way, and years before most anarchists paid serious attention to it, F. F. characterized the court martial of the Jewish officer as a lynching. When Bernard Lazare approached Fénéon in 1897 to convince him of Dreyfus's innocence, he was amazed when the former clerk at the War Office said simply: "Yes, I know." Fénéon spoke softly, but true. He should have been read more closely.

F. F. and Barrucand also reported on the trial of Oscar Wilde: "7 April (1895).—The [only] time Oscar Wilde regretted having spoken out." After he was sentenced to two years hard labor, they remarked on the wave of sympathy among the French for the English poet: "France is always ready to rage in indignation over Albion's puritanical depravity, closing her eyes to her own sores. . . ." (F, 949, 955, 957). Fénéon understood that it was not Wilde's homosexuality so much as his refusal to conceal it that led to his conviction. Such blatant individualism was a threat to the political status quo: by refusing to deny his sexuality—at a time when society was growing obsessed with the relationship of sex to power, as Michel Foucault has argued[9]—Wilde posed a challenge not unlike the iconoclasm of the anarchists.

Toulouse-Lautrec, who never closed his eyes to scenes of French "depravity," saw a connection between Fénéon's extreme individualism and that of Oscar Wilde. He juxtaposed these two unusual jailbirds in a painting for his old friend, "La Goulue," who had left the Moulin Rouge and was now dancing in traveling fairs on the boulevards. She wanted the artist to paint some decorations for the collapsible walls of her booth, and he quickly complied with two large pictures done on rough canvas, one showing La Goulue's past glory, dancing the quadrille at the Moulin Rouge, and the other depicting her present status, performing on the street in the garb of an Egyptian belly dancer. Two imposing figures loom in the foreground of the second picture: Oscar Wilde and Félix Fénéon, standing elbow-to-elbow. Wilde is seen in lost-profile view, engrossed in the spectacle before him, while Fénéon, painted yellow, wears a detached, gently satanic air (pl. *19*). So Lautrec honored, after his fashion, these two quite

*The *Prix Monthyon,* the most lucrative of French literary prizes, is awarded for a work of "elevated character and moral utility."

different aesthetes, the one just released from prison and the other about to enter it. He did not ask F. F. for a sitting or tell him of his plan; fascinated by the critic's self-made mask, he had often sketched him at the *Revue*. But Lautrec had apparently never seen Wilde or observed him closely. So he went to England and visited him in jail. When the beleaguered poet refused to pose, Toulouse-Lautrec etched him in his memory and went ahead with his painting, which La Goulue gleefully used to decorate her booth. (The canvas was later cut up to be sold in pieces, but finally reassembled and put in the Jeu de Paume collection of the Louvre.)

The entires in *Passim* on Dreyfus and Wilde are few when compared to those on the progress of French imperialism in Africa, Indochina, and Madagascar. When the big newspapers reported in detail on the atrocities committed by Japanese troops invading Port Arthur in China (murder and mutilation of prisoners), Fénéon commented:

> Pooh! Not bad, if you like; but, all things considered, that Japanese army is not yet very Europeanized, and they could take some lessons from our workers in Dahomey. (F, 943)

He quoted *Le Temps* exulting over the sinking of a Chinese ship, which "justified the cost" of France's new military hardware, and he exposed the racism in this prestigious paper by simply citing the editorial: "We are not at all sorry that Asians have been the first victims of modern science" (F, 946).

He quoted also from the speeches of Ranavalo Mandjaka, Queen of Madagascar, challenging the French invasion of her country: "We do not want to take anybody else's land. We just want to protect our own." F. F. added, with bitter irony, "Quite right, Madam, but you forget there are at least two ethics involved here" (F, 948).

In succeeding weeks, he quoted wires reporting "brilliant battles" on the island of Madagascar, and concluded: "The French army is no longer invincible, it is quite literally invulnerable according to the dispatches from Madagascar: . . . one [French] dead! A suicide, perhaps. . . . In any event, everything is fine. It even appears that the natives *came over to our side*. Hmm! We would have said it was the other way around" (F, 950).

He was not without sympathy for the soldiers themselves, and analyzed the news from their perspective: "General Duchesne, head of the Madagascar expedition, telegraphs from Majunga: '*Le Carolina* arrived. State of health satisfactory. Thirty mules died in the crossing.'—These animals cost between five hundred and a thousand francs," mused F. F. "You can imagine how carefully they were tended during the voyage, and yet thirty died. Imagine the mortality rate of the soldiers, whose hides are worth nothing" (952). F. F. understood the psychological trauma inflicted upon young veterans and reported, with characteristic sarcasm:

> Over there, young Baron covered himself with glory; he was better than anyone at shooting down the natives, and he earned the Tonkin medal. On leave in Paris, the lack of action weighed on such a well-trained man, and so he seized a chance to kill a certain fellow called Geiger. Now the system of justice is going to get after this brave trooper. But really, how silly of him to have chosen the wrong theater for this new act

HENRI DE TOULOUSE-LAUTREC. ***Oscar Wilde and Romain Coolus.*** 1896. Program for the production of Wilde's *Salomé* and *Raphael* (the latter written with Coolus), at the Théâtre de l'Oeuvre, 11 February 1896, when Wilde was serving his sentence in Reading Gaol. Lithograph, 30 x 49 cm. Oscar Wilde on the right. The Atlas Foundation.

> of war! Why not go and operate in Madagascar with his comrades! He would have returned with a red ribbon and gold stripes. Such a fine military craeer ruined by a little mistake in latitude. . . . (F, 952)

For reasons unknown, *Passim* was discontinued after five months. It may be that the sardonic comments and anarchist sympathies of F. F. and V. B. irritated members of the haute bourgeoisie who supported the *Revue blanche.* Or perhaps F. F. and his friend simply became bored with writing this column. In any event, after June 1895, Fénéon's signature all but disappeared from the contents of the review.

His name or initial appeared only a half-dozen times in the next eight years: on a translation of some love letters of Edgar Allan Poe, for example, and on installments of Jane Austen's *Northanger Abbey,* which he called by the heroine's name, *Catherine Morland.*[10] This was the work he had begun in prison, and now he meticulously refined it, striving to capture the subtleties in Austen's language, aided by John Gray, who read and corrected the translation. It may seem odd that Fénéon bothered with the work of a woman who, as Stuart Merrill pointed out, "never looked at what was going on in the world" outside her narrow circle.[11] But F. F. found satisfaction in the way she crafted a microcosm of the middle class. Her subversive irony and characteristic understatement were also akin to his.

In response to a plea from Camille Pissarro ("The yap of *la Revue blanche* seems hostile to me. . . . I am going to see Fénéon. . . . Saw Fénéon, *he* at least plays fair!"),[12] the critic broke his self-imposed silence and wrote a paragraph on the artist's latest exhibition. At the same time, he published a review of the painter Léo Gausson, as if to say he would not play favorites (F, 237, 238). He made another exception for Jarry's *Ubu Roi* played in February 1898 with puppets made by Bonnard.

A single initial identified Fénéon as the interviewer of Maximilian Harden in a "Conversation about Germany," but nothing indicated that it was he who carried out two interesting *reportages:* one an extensive inquiry among people who had witnessed or taken part in the Paris Commune, and the other about the influence of Scandinavian literature on current trends in France.[13]

The topics he investigated, like the authors he picked to translate, reveal his own interests. The Commune shaped his lifelong political orientation. Around the turn of the century, his focus, like that of other anarchists, evolved from violent agitation by word and deed to syndicalism; and the labor movement subsequently led Fénéon and other friends, like Paul Signac, to join the Communists. The Russian revolution was, in Fénéon's eyes, the most significant political event of his lifetime. When, in 1939, a student of the late nineteenth century wrote him, "I, too, am a Dreyfusard!" F. F. replied, "You are a Dreyfusard, and I can say I am a Communist."[14] He planned to bequeath his large collection of paintings to the Soviet Union, but was thwarted by World War II.

His contributions to the *Revue blanche,* transmitting the work or the thoughts of others, show a particular talent he now chose to pursue, renouncing the role of critic and symbolist stylist. His "invisible work" pervaded the review. In the words of one writer, "He excelled in pointing out an unexplored path or a new way of looking at things."[15] But "he never gave instructions," said Lugné-Poe. "It was enough to meet him, to exchange a few words with him in order to understand and accept the orientation that a piece of work or an article should follow. . . . He was the keystone of the *Revue blanche,* the more so as he pretended to delight in finding his own peace and happiness by remaining in the background."[16] He could be seen at the office at all hours of the day and night, reading manuscripts or working on copy. "His accuracy," Thadée Natanson remarked, "suggested perfection and explained his taste for figures, the most concise expression of reality. . . . The noisy audience that surrounded him would have prevented any other person from doing anything."[17]

Fénéon always had a word for an aspiring author, even if he found himself obliged to reject the manuscript. One young writer reported his experience:

> Around 1902 I . . . took some of my writing to the *Revue blanche.* . . . With some trepidation, I was going to see, for the first time, that subtle and formidable Fénéon, whose legend I knew, and even his face, for many effigies of him had appeared in literary magazines.
>
> He read my poems and my short story very attentively, and then handed them back to me very kindly. Seeing my timidity and disappointment, he took pity on me

FÉLIX VALLOTTON. ***Félix Fénéon in the Offices of the Revue Blanche.*** ca. 1896. Oil on board, 52.5 x 65 cm. Josefowitz Collection.

> and said, with that unique smile of his, as he saw me to the door, "Don't be discouraged. Besides, you are not yet an old, old man."[18]

Manuscripts did not sit for long unread on this editor's desk. He responded favorably to Paul-Jean Toulet's first attempt to get into print:

> *11 Dec. 1897 {to Toulet in Pau}*
>
> Sir, I have not had the time to write you, but the very evening of the day you brought them to us, I had the time to read your poems. We are pleased to publish some of them—glad to have the honor of such a fine beginning. The date? Not certain, naturally. But it seems to me that your poems should be given priority.[19]

Several portraits of Fénéon at the *Revue blanche* show his lanky frame hunched over his desk at a thirty degree angle. A pen-and-ink sketch by Bonnard, an airy, impish cartoon, portrays the masterminds of the review calmly installed in a cloud above the narrow streets of Paris, as if dominating the intellectual life of the times. While Mirbeau engages in discussion with Régnier and the Natanson brothers confer, Fénéon, his back turned, pores over his papers.[20] A shimmering painting by Vuillard

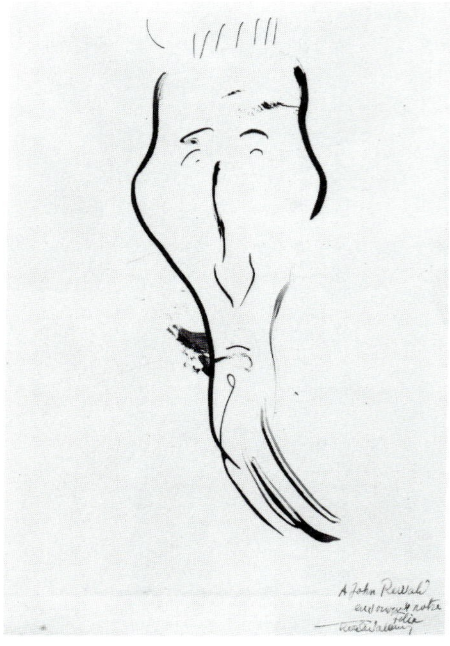

HENRI DE TOULOUSE-LAUTREC. ***Caricature of Félix Fénéon.*** ca. 1896.
Ink drawing, 28 x 20 cm. New York, Collection John Rewald.

depicts him alone, his elongated head bent in concentration over his work (pl. 20). Van Dongen sketched him in the same posture, pen in one hand, cigarette in the other. Vallotton's hyperrealistic painting reveals him working at night, the glare of the desk lamp accentuating the angles of his face. Toulouse-Lautrec did not show him at work, but captured something of the wit and enigma of Fénéon's features in an almost ethereal caricature, with a puff of cigarette smoke—or is it an inkblot?—trailing outside the wisps of his goatee.

Lautrec, Fénéon, and writers like Alfred Jarry all delighted in creating paradox and introduced a ferocious kind of humor at the *Revue blanche.* In February 1895, Lautrec organized a famous cocktail party in the mansion of Alexandre Natanson on the avenue du Bois de Boulogne (now avenue Foch). The reception was to celebrate new wall decorations for the dining room, ten elegant paintings by Vuillard. Lautrec decided to add a note of gaiety and contradiction to the sophisticated event. He had most of the furniture removed, ostensibly to show off the subtle art in the wall panels. He sent out invitations in the form of a lithograph he made with lettering in English: *American and other drinks. . . .*

More than three hundred guests arrived to find the grand piano replaced with a huge bar, presided over by the painter and a companion he had chosen for his size (more than twice his own), Maxime Dethomas, whom he called Gros n'Arbre ("humongous tree"). Even more absurd, Lautrec had his own head and chin shaved and wore a vest cut from the Stars and Stripes. The ferocity was in the drinks, made from various liqueurs poured more or less knowingly in layers, forming bands of color—a visual pun on cock('s)tail. The polychrome drinks were tantalizing and lethal; Lautrec applied all his art to destroying the dignity of the respectable crowd, the flower of French letters and arts, with his "Prairie oysters," "Love-pushers,"* and other variations on the American "*drink.*" Fénéon, weaving ever so slightly, "obstinately polite, more than ever a sphinx," was seen following Mallarmé from room to room, trying in vain to convince the poet to partake of the "excellent, innocuous libation." A friend found Bonnard at the bar, gazing through foggy glasses at a "constellation of colored goblets."—"I want a rose one," he said dreamily. The rose one proved to be the "coup de grâce for Bonnard, imprudent neophyte," out cold on the floor, teeth chattering in a way that made his frightened comrade understand the full meaning of the words, "dead drunk." Beds, thoughtfully prepared by the ingenious barman, were soon strewn with bodies, Fénéon's among them. One of the rare ones not to succumb, besides Mallarmé, was Lautrec, who completed the paradoxical reception by remaining stone sober.[21]

Fénéon recognized another genius of the absurd in Alfred Jarry and brought him to the *Revue blanche.* Jarry was marginally associated with the established voice of Symbolism, the *Mercure de France.*[22] when Fénéon wrote him, early in March 1896:

> My dear Alfred Jarry,
>
> . . . Why don't you send in a bit of copy to *La revue blanche,*—choosing, perhaps, something that you like a lot and yet that would not be too abstruse (the first time! . . .)
>
> *most cordially,*
> *félix fénéon*

Jarry responded:

> My dear Félix Fénéon,
>
> I am sending you something written especially for *La Revue blanche;* but if (for reasons of length, obscenity, or obscurity) it doesn't pass muster, that would not matter and you can just tell me. Now, if it passes, that would really make me happy. I would send you *La Baleine* (The Whale) right away.
>
> *Very cordially,*
> *Alfred Jarry*[23]

Bypassing the editorial committee, Fénéon published Jarry's contribution, *Le Vieux de la Montagne,* in the May 1 issue. He managed to print four more texts of Jarry's before the year was out, including *Paralipomènes d'Ubu,* a kind of anthology of *Ubu the Cuckold,* just in time for the roof-raising première of *Ubu Roi* at the Oeuvre (10 December 1896). But then he apparently encountered opposition. He could introduce a radical new

**L'Huître des prairies* was taken from the American euphemism for the frontier dish of bull or bison testicles, "prairie oysters," and a similarly named drink made with whole raw eggs, while *le pousse-l'amour* is a simple variant on the French expression for after-dinner drink, *le pousse-café.*

Alfred Jarry at Age Nineteen. Detail from a group photograph, Lycee Henri IV, Paris, spring 1893. In front of Jarry stands the poet Léon-Paul Fargue. France, private collection.

writer but could not maintain him at the *Revue* without the assent of the staff. Léon Blum, the review's main literary critic, reported in November 1897 that although he was among those "who feel and enjoy the beauty of Ubu," he really could not make much sense out of Jarry's latest novel, *Les Jours et les nuits,* about an army deserter: "[Jarry] is perhaps a great genius, but this time he has gone beyond the bounds, even for his friends and contemporaries."[24]

The *Revue blanche* did not mind spicing its pages with a bit of anarchism, and a man like Fénéon brought with him a certain radical chic. But Jarry's flouting all accepted laws of behavior, his mockery, in the persona of Ubu, of the laws governing the universe—man-made postulates, Jarry insisted—this was too much! Thadée Natanson turned a deaf ear when asked to take *Faustroll,* and in 1899 Bonnard pleaded with him in vain to publish Jarry's *Almanach du père Ubu,* which Bonnard had illustrated. Nonetheless, after the turn of the century, when Jarry's "phynances" were really at a low ebb, Fénéon managed to offer him a regularly paid column, *Spéculations,* from 1 July 1901 until 15 April 1903, the last issue of the *Revue.*

Jarry pushed the laws of reason (and conformity) to their logical conclusions, and from this outrageous practice reinvented humor. "Isn't the wrong way as good as the right way?" postulated Ubu, claiming that opposites were equal. Jarry dedicated the final chapter of his *Faustroll* to Fénéon, the part called "Concerning Linearity" (*De la ligne*) wherein Ubu/Jarry explores mathematically, as he had the Surface of God, nothing less than the nature of *tout art et toute science!*

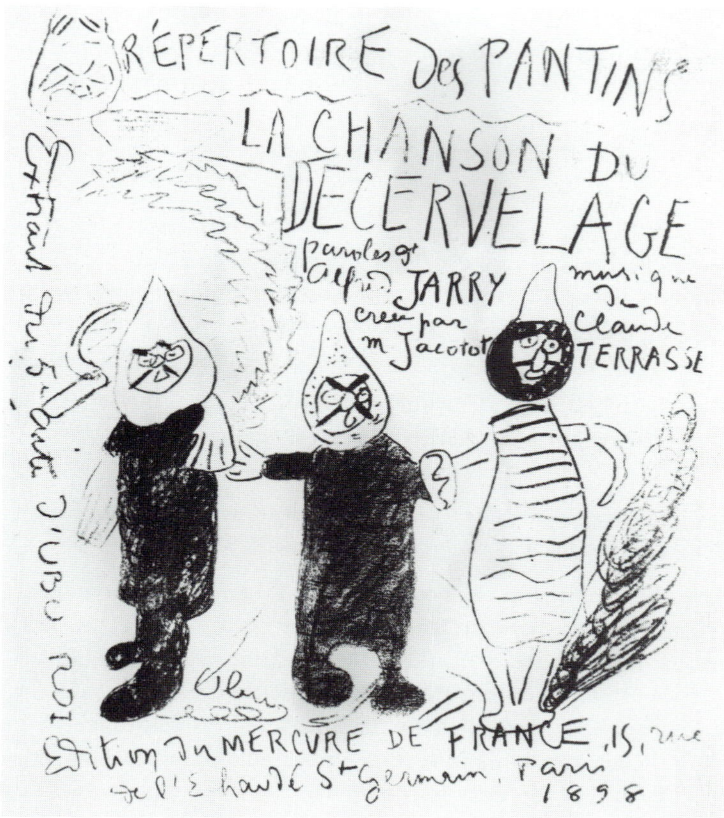

ALFRED JARRY. ***The Puppets' Repertoire.*** Three palotins holding hands. Drawing for cover of the score for the "Song of Debraining" from *Ubu Roi,* music by Claude Terrasse, 1898. Lithograph, 35 x 27 cm. France, private collection.

Fénéon sometimes extricated his friend from an awkward situation that Jarry had created by his iconoclasm. Faced once with the disagreeable prospect of a duel with a man who felt insulted by Jarry's language, the poet confided in Fénéon: "Félix, I have a problem on my hands: I absolutely do not wish to fight this man; it's stupid to risk my life—or his—over such nonsense!" The next day the Boulanger brothers, who enjoyed a good social position and a reputation for competency in dealing with quarrels of honor, were charged with representing Jarry's adversary. They were to arrive at noon at Jarry's place, a room on the top floor of a building that had a narrow, dark, and winding stairwell. Jarry spent the morning coating the handrail with feces. The witnesses, dressed in morning coats, silk top hats, and yellow kid gloves, arrived somewhat discountenanced and quite filthy. Fénéon answered the door and inquired politely:

"Monsieur X . . . has indeed done his military service, that is to say, his *volontariat,* one year instead of five?"

"Yes, that's quite exact," responded the brothers.

"Then that means he went through the military preparatory school?"

"No doubt!"

"Then, I regret, we cannot fight a *spadassin* [trained swordsman]." So the code of honor saved the day, for it was legitimate to refuse to duel with a professional man of arms. With the word, "spadassin," Fénéon had found the way to disarm the offended gentleman.[25]

As Signac's diary reveals, Fénéon often fed Jarry (who took little regular nourishment other than alcohol):

> *December 1901*
>
> Dined at Fénéon's with Jarry who is very Père Ubu, especially when he has had a few glasses of cognac, although he says he can drink with impunity and that only water is deadly for him. He told me that his lunch consisted of "three fat fish weighing two pounds each."

At this time, Jarry was living in his "Tripod," a hut on stilts on a bank of the Seine, and fed himself primarily on what he got from the river. Signac again:

> *2 May (1902)*
>
> Dined at Fénéon's with Jarry. He answers a woman who asks why he wears his hair long: "Because, Madam, I use them to haul up my fishhooks."[26]

Jarry used to take F. F. fishing and once rowed off into the reeds to show him a very big fish, which turned out to be a drowned man. In 1907, at age 34, Jarry succumbed, like Lautrec (in 1901, aged 37), to diseases complicated by alcoholism. Even as he lay dying, he appealed to Fénéon, this time to shield him from his doctor, buzzing 'round his manuscripts: "You are the only man in Paris I can ask to fend him off." Charged with this "delicate, awful mission," F. F. appeared to Jarry as "Hathi the Silent One," Kipling's elephant, who "only hurries when the right time comes" in order to exterminate Mowgli's enemies.[27]

In 1896, Fénéon was named chief editor of the *Revue blanche* and helped to create a publishing house based on the review. Although the Natansons had the final say, F. F. did all the editorial work and, as in the review itself, delighted in bringing together the work of artists and writers such as Bonnard and Jarry, Lautrec and Jules Renard. Volumes he published included Mirbeau's *Diary of a Chambermaid;* Léon Blum's first book and the first one Bonnard illustrated; Signac's *D'Eugène Delacroix au neo-impressionnisme;* novels and plays by Knut Hamsun, Gerhardt Hauptmann, and Alfred Jarry (*Messaline* and *Le Surmâle*). He printed a translation of the entire *Thousand and One Nights* by J.-C. Mardrus, who dedicated the first volume to Paul Valéry and the last to Fénéon. Claudel's *Paysages de Chine* and Tristan Bernard's *Mémoires d'un jeune homme rangé* also appeared. Foreign works included some by Max Stirner, Chekhov, Mark Twain, Tolstoy, and the Polish author Sienkiewicz, including *Quo Vadis.* The author gave Fénéon credit for having rendered that best seller into "a faithful finished form."[28] Working from a draft established by a linguist, Fénéon helped translate many books into French. His friends remembered his working long and hard, for example, on *The Idiot.* But his name appeared on only two works: *Catherine Morland* and Dostoyevsky's early novel, *Un Adolescent.*

Regarding these editions, Fénéon carried on an extensive correspondence, most of which has been lost. He gave away to young visitors or friends eager for "autographs," letters he received from many now famous authors. His own letters were generally business-like, explaining to Verlaine, for example, Alexandre Natanson's "prices for poetry: 5 francs per page, i.e., 15 francs for that printed in the November 1st [1895] issue, or 20 francs, since it was printed close"[29]—a poignant note inasmuch as it indicates that Verlaine, old and ill, was still obliged to earn his living "by the inch." Fénéon wrote Valéry concerning a line of poetry for Mardrus' *Thousand and One Nights:*

14 november 1899

My dear Paul Valéry,

Tome III of the Nights will come out at the end of this month. Would you kindly provide a line of verse and a photograph of it? So that we will not have an unpleasant surprise as to the dimensions, please write the verse out in a hand that conforms to that of the colophon and warn the photoengraver not to "reduce."

Very cordially yours,
fel. fénéon[30]

More extensive is his correspondence with Signac concerning the installments of the painter's study of color and neo-impressionism. A letter to Signac in Saint-Tropez:

Paris, 3 June 1898

My dear Paul,

I am sending you the *chronique des Arts et de la Curiosité.* Saw M. Mallarmé yesterday. Without my asking, he spoke admiringly of your study. You will soon receive, directly from the printer, page proofs of your article, which I ask you to send back with your observations. Try to find a title. I have not been able to. "The Color of Neo-Impressionism" would be a bad title, wouldn't it? What are the dimensions of Théo [van Rysselberghe]'s cover? As soon as I have the information, I can ask the printer for a page model and a cost estimate for the book.

There is an exhibition of Monet that I haven't yet seen at Boussod's and one of C. Pissarro at Durand-Ruel's (boulevard and avenue de l'Opéra). Not at all as good, I think, as preceding paintings. It's photographic, washed out and worried. But beautiful landscapes from this year and last. A room of Renoir, those from the rue de Rome transported to rue Laffitte.

Yesterday at the Drouot auction house I acquired a Seurat drawing (an old woman and an equestrian Victor Emmanuel) for thirty odd francs the lot. They also sold a Dubois-Pillet (encampment of travelling players), 8 fr., the Boilerman by Luce, 24 fr., but I couldn't dream of buying it, since it used to belong to Kahn; A Horse by Félix Pissarro, 12 fr. Sad spectacles, these sales. . . .

f. f.

Although Fénéon was now supporting, indirectly, other painters at the *Revue blanche,* his primary concern was still the neo-impressionists. His sponsorship of Signac's book would soon change the tide in their favor, for the little volume made a lasting impact on Matisse, Derain, and other artists enamoured of color. After Signac chose the title for his essay, "From Delacroix to neo-impressionism," F. F. wrote him:

Paris, 18 June 1898

I saw the Tabourier Collection sold recently at the Drouot auction house. There were some little works by Delacroix there: Fiancée d'Abydd, Lady Macbeth—paintings, or sketches of large paintings?—and a sketch of King John at the battle of Poitiers, all acquired by Durand-Ruel for sums going between 15 to 18,000 francs. . . . Also the sketches for the decorations at the Chapelle des Saints-Anges, sold to I don't know whom, or at what price.

In the same vein of painting, I thank you for the landscape where the curves of the mountains disappear in the spirals of the clouds. You have made me very happy.

Paintings of Delacroix always cast their spell on me. Yet there are hardly any that I would passionately want to see on my walls for everyday life: the anecdotes that so often make up these paintings would always give me an uneasy feeling. But I could covet, for example, *les Femmes d'Alger, l'Entrée des Croisés* (in spite of the disheveled women and the old men that fill up the corners and the foreground), etc.: those do not appear to me to be anecdotes. All that, of course, is beside the essential question. . . .

félix[31]

The "essential question," for Fénéon as for Signac, was the "primary matter of painting," the science and intuition of color.

Painting was not the only subject that Fénéon and Signac discussed: there was the news about town, and then there was bicycling! Jarry, Coolus, and Tristan Bernard had converted practically everyone at the *Revue blanche* into fanatics of the new sport. (Is it a coincidence that all three were extraordinary humorists, experts in the ridiculous?) It is hard to think of Fénéon rolling majestically along on two wheels, although many of his comrades, including Signac and Charles Henry, were adept at the sport. But he was a frequent spectator at the races run by Tristan Bernard at the "Vélodrome Buffalo," and it was rumored that he sometimes filled in for Coolus and Bernard as sports reporter for the *Revue.*

Fénéon saw the new century in by organizing the first large one-man show of Seurat. He was assisted by a young painter who had espoused the neo-impressionist method and had been studying with Signac, Lucie Brû. She later married F. F.'s friend, Edmond Cousturier. Quiet but intense, a gifted writer as well as a painter, she was a "creature quite out of the ordinary," with a critical social conscience similar to Fénéon's.[32]

The exhibition opened in January 1900, in the new premises of the *Revue blanche* on the boulevard des Italiens—offices renovated by Henri van de Velde and decorated with panels by Vuillard and Bonnard. The murals inhibited Fénéon's ability to hang Seurat's work, but the show was nonetheless a revelation: sixty-four paintings (twenty-six of which were "croquetons," as Seurat called the little studies he did directly from nature), and nearly three hundred drawings. Most of the works had been lent by members of the painter's family, who were eager to sell them; the mother had died the previous year and the others, apparently, were interested only in the money. Signac came back from the Midi in time to see the show, and jotted down his impressions to send the painter Charles Angrand, who was working in his Normandy retreat:

> *Paris, 30 April 1900*
>
> . . . Arrived still in time to see the Seurat exhibition. His works piled up pell-mell, without any selection, without taste, set on the floor against the light, [still] gloriously command attention.
>
> Not many visitors, for that matter. But quite a bit has been sold, for the family, though rolling in money, is trying to get rid of its keepsakes at a good price. Fénéon bought the *Baignade,* I the *Cirque* (500 fr.). The father of the girl who was working in my studio [Lucie Brû]: *la Grande Jatte* (800 fr.) with the portrait of Mme Seurat thrown in (their mother's portrait by their brother—they're willing to sell it!). . . .[33]

In all, Fénéon later reported, ten paintings were sold including, besides those Signac named, *The Side Show,* plus ten "croquetons" and about fifty drawings. Camille Pissarro bought ten of the drawings, and Fénéon even more. (They sold for ten francs each, or one hundred francs if framed.) Pissarro bequeathed six of his to the Luxembourg museum of modern art, which did not show them for another quarter century or more (F, 468).

Thereafter, Fénéon put himself at the service of art lovers, dealers, and buyers interested in Seurat and the other neo-impressionists. With Henri van de Velde, Count Kessler, art critic Julius Meier-Graefe, and others, he helped organize exhibitions in Germany and elsewhere on the continent. Soon Berlin, Hagen, and Weimar became centers for collections of neo-impressionism. Fénéon's anarchism is evident in this lack of care for the "national heritage," letting French art, which he knew would soon be qualified as great, flow across the borders—German borders at that! The anarchist in him was also averse to "elevating" works of art by granting them the official status of a museum collection. The enjoyment of a good painting was like a love affair, an individual matter, and Fénéon the middleman was rather like a matchmaker.

During the mid-nineties, Thadée Natanson and his young wife Misia used to invite friends from the *Revue blanche* to spend holidays with them in their little country house, "La Grangette," near Mallarmé's retreat in Valvins. It was an additional pleasure for both hosts and guests that Mallarmé himself sometimes came by to visit. In summer, Valvins became an "informal branch of *La Revue blanche,*" according to Annette Vaillant, the daughter of Alfred Natanson. "Misia, Fauré's beloved pupil, gay and whimsical, with her winning ways and her bluntness and the swagger of a low-life princess, was none the less everyone's muse. . . . On Toulouse-Lautrec's poster, Misia comes toward you with her fur scarf, her lovely little frozen face tense under her spotted veil. She personifies *La Revue blanche.* . . ."[34] Lautrec and others artists associated with the review, Vallotton, Bonnard, and Vuillard, used to make Misia's country place their second home during the summer months. Fénéon used to come, too, but not as often as

HENRI DE TOULOUSE-LAUTREC. ***La Revue blanche.*** 1895. Brush, spatter, and crayon lithograph printed in four colors. Poster to advertise the periodical, showing Misia Natanson, 130 x 95 cm. New York, Collection of Mr. and Mrs. Herbert D. Schimmel.

his friends wished: somebody had to "keep shop" in town, reading and delivering copy. An undated letter from Vuillard shows how much Fénéon's presence was desired: "I have just arrived from Valvins where I hasten to return tomorrow morning. Thadée, Misia, Mallarmé entrust me to beg you, to beseech you to come visit them. Why shouldn't you do them this favor?"[35]

Fénéon must have accepted this or a similar invitation, for there is a letter to him from Mallarmé, dated August 21, 1896: ". . . Good day, I can still see you silhouetted against the white sail [of the boat Mallarmé sailed on the Avon]. You will return from time to time, won't you, when my neighbors are back from the seashore and their little house is full of people again?"[36]

Two years later, while on a trip to Holland, Fénéon received a telegram announcing the sudden death of Mallarmé in Valvins on September 9. "It was as if the sun went out." He started back to Paris, stopping in midjourney to write Mallarmé's widow, in a poor hand pinched with emotion:

> *Lille, 11 September 1898*
>
> Madame,
>
> The terrible, sudden news brings me infinite pain. Far from Paris, with all my heart I am with you, near the body of the beloved man. . . .[37]

On reaching home, he learned that the poet (aged fifty-six) had died from an obstruction or muscle spasm in his throat, while his wife looked on helplessly and his daughter Geneviève pleaded, "Breathe, Papa! Breathe!"

Fénéon and Thadée Natanson inserted an anonymous homage in the September 15 issue of *Revue blanche:*

> Grief
>
> Stéphane Mallarmé has just died.
>
> Even were not all homage to him superfluous, none of us, in the pain of our loss, can be distracted from the tears we shed over our beloved master, time enough to weave a crown over his fresh tomb.
>
> This house was his own and is now in affliction.
>
> Death can not wipe out his goodness or the memory of his grace. The example of his life will continue to teach us wisdom and his secret of serenity; but even these higher thoughts, where our lesser strength gives out, can not free us from the bitterness of the separation.
>
> We who loved him can only sorrow in this hour, for the writer has left his own time that did not know him, to triumph in our memory.[38]

Mallarmé's death came at the height of the Dreyfus affair. In spite of Fénéon's remarks on the injustice done Dreyfus in *Passim* of January 1895, most of his colleagues at the *Revue blanche* paid little attention to the matter until Zola published *J'accuse* in January 1898 and was himself convicted of defaming the highest officers of the state. The novelist became a more prestigious martyr than the Jewish captain. The *Revue blanche* authors and staff immediately staged a special performance of *An Enemy of the People* as a protest against Zola's maltreatment, changing enough lines so that his image behind Ibsen's hero was unmistakable. The performance, given at the Oeuvre, was broken by various interruptions and much applause. Fénéon was again in the crowd scene of act four, along with comrades from the review, Romain Coolus, Octave

PAUL GAUGUIN. ***Portrait of Stéphane Mallarmé.*** 1891. Etching, 18.2 x 14.3 cm (plate). A symbolic work evoking Mallarmé's translations of Poe. In the shadows above the poet's head, one can see the image of a raven. Boston, Museum of Fine Arts. Gift of William G. Russell Allen.

Mirbeau, and Tristan Bernard. The offices of the review soon became a rallying center for the Dreyfusards. Jules Renard described the scene in his Journal:

> 18 February. This evening at the *Revue Blanche.* Everyone passionately involved in the Dreyfus affair. We would sacrifice wife, children, even our fortune for it. Thadée, who brings us the news, is really becoming somebody.[39]

By the end of 1898, the whole country had become polarized over the matter: belief in the Individual, Truth, and Justice was pitted against loyalty to the Nation, the Army, and the Church. The Affair aroused antisemitism throughout France, while awakening others to the vital need to combat racial and religious prejudice. Socialists and anarchists, many antisemitic until now, joined the Dreyfus camp. Emotions ran high, and the Affair tended to skew people's judgment in other matters. A few months after Mallarmé's death, Geneviève wrote Dujardin concerning her success in getting artist friends of the poet to participate in the tribute Dujardin was organizing:

> *29. I. 99*
>
> . . . Whistler, upon receiving my letter, very kindly sent us his sister-in-law to say that he would visit us one evening soon. He also sent a superb print of his portrait of Father with a very touching dedication.
>
> I am very hopeful as to him.
>
> But Degas! After he very nearly said yes to Mlle Manet, now he is claiming he can't, somehow mixing in his political opinions about the Dreyfus affair, saying he has to stay with those on "the right side," etc. all sorts of nonsense. It's insane. . . .[40]

Fénéon, a Dreyfusard before the term was invented, managed to keep politics and personal life separate. His name appeared in some of the pro-Dreyfus protests that were published. But his friendship for Paul Valéry and Paul Léautaud was not affected by their subscribing to a monument to Colonel Henry (who committed suicide in prison when it was learned that the letter he "discovered" affirming Dreyfus's guilt was a forgery).

In December 1900, Georges Clemenceau, leader of the Dreyfusards in parliament, sent F. F. a note:

> Dear Monsieur Fénéon,
>
> If you don't have anything better to do one of these mornings, come say hello to me. It has been quite a while since I have seen you. I won't be at all sorry to tell you *certain things*.
>
> *As ever,*
> *G Clemenceau*[41]

It seems likely that this note pertained to questions Fénéon had asked about the rehabilitation of Captain Alfred Dreyfus, which, as it turned out, would not take place until 1906.

Oscar Wilde, that other victim of prejudice for whom Fénéon had spoken, reappeared in Paris in 1898, physically and morally depleted after his two-year prison term. At the *Revue blanche,* Fénéon welcomed him back, savoring his witticisms and regularly inviting him to dine or to the theater. But Wilde, sensing that his faculties were in decline, was drawn toward thoughts of suicide. He told F. F. that one night he had decided to make an end of it and went to the Seine. He passed another rather strange-looking person, gazing down at the water from the parapet of the Pont Neuf. Thinking it was a fellow sufferer, the poet stopped and asked: "Are you also a candidate for suicide?"—"No," the other replied, "I am a hairdresser!" This non sequitur, F. F. later recounted,[42] convinced Wilde that life was still comical enough to be endured, and so he lasted until the first year of the new century.

The year 1903 was another year of endings. In May, on the island of Fatu Iwa, Gauguin died of syphilis, which he had tragically carried to his South Seas paradise. He

MAXIMILIEN LUCE. ***Portrait of Camille Pissarro.*** 1895. Conté crayon, 31 x 23 cm. France, private collection.

was fifty-five and had achieved the art, the vision he thirsted after; fame would not be long in coming. On November 13 Camille Pissaro died at age seventy-two, a master for some, ignored by more.

The *Revue blanche* put out its last issue on April 15. Some said its strong pro-Dreyfus stance was its downfall, but there were other reasons. Fénéon had been given more leeway in choosing contributors and topics since 1900. Thadée's art column was supplemented at times by a fellow called Fagus, a poet and former anarchist who wrote brilliantly of Picasso in 1901. That was the year Fénéon also called Gide and Debussy to write literary and music criticism, and when he instituted a regular slot for Jarry's extravagant prose. He welcomed newcomers soon to make their mark: Charles Péguy, Charles Louis Philippe, and Guillaume Apollinaire. Subscribers could hardly complain that the review had ceased to live up to its reputation as a purveyor of new authors of quality! But Fénéon also broadened the political spectrum, publishing many more articles on foreign policy, international affairs, and matters of social concern. The subjects of some, such as "The Labour Problem in Australia and New Zealand," or "The Communist Saga of the Banished Manchurians," must have seemed highly irrelevant to the Parisian intelligentsia.

The Natansons, who were financing all this, began to wonder how much longer they wanted to sink their money into this bottomless ocean. Production costs were extremely high, for the review offered quality prints and drawings in nearly every issue, and they continued to pay both its artists and writers relatively good sums. The *Revue blanche* had always spent much more than it brought in. Doubtless Alexandre was having second thoughts about the value to him of a family venture that now seemed to be run by the *libertaire,* F. F. Thadée was still thoroughly committed to the review but, more a dreamer than a financier, made some unwise investments through connections in eastern Europe and lost a good part of his fortune, according to Misia. Misia left him in 1902 for the millionaire newspaper magnate, Mr. Edwards, and while this defection of the "Muse" caused friends to rally round Thadée, it was too late. The era of the *Revue blanche* was over.

"There is doubtless no painter and no writer whose real worth is recognized today," said André Gide in 1946, "who does not owe a grateful tribute to the Natanson brothers and Félix Fénéon—the sure and subtle pilot of the ship. . . .

"Valiant *Revue Blanche!* We could really use her today," Gide concluded, referring to the way the review "willingly colored itself red" in attacking social and political problems.[43]

It was the last of the literary magazines with which Fénéon was involved. He used his reputation as an editor to get a job with the newspapers, working as a news writer first for the *Figaro* and then the *Matin,* where he created his famous *Nouvelles en trois lignes*. He chose the late evening or night shift, in order to leave his days free for the things and the people he loved.

CHAPTER 16

Private Life and Loves

F. F. was a devoted lover to several people at the same time, and he was loyal to his lovers as he was to his friends, admiring and nurturing them while enjoying the pleasures they shared in common. Lover of beauty and enemy of social "superstitions," he was able, in this Victorian era, to relish the sensual nature of love to the utmost.

At the same time, as one of his women biographers remarked, he could not avoid hurting some of the people he loved, particularly those who felt they had a special claim on him, such as his wife and the lifelong companion whose relationship with Fénéon predated his marriage. But for F. F. the anarchist the give and take of love had nothing to do with possession. Loving, loyalty, and caring stemmed from individual freedom and mutual trust—the anarchist basis for all human relations. For women, this was not an easy ideal to live by, especially in a society that denied them the means to personal and economic independence. Did Fénéon not recognize this contradiction?

Perhaps not, for women were not the center of his life. Indeed, the women he hurt apparently did not love him the less, and he, for his part, reportedly "arranged things so as to cause the least possible pain."[1]

Amour-propre, esteem for oneself, was a critical factor in Fénéon's intimate relations—another aspect of the dandy's "pride" explored earlier, the stance that appeared on the outside as coldness or insensitivity to the anxiety of others. That he could be loving to several people at once stemmed from a self-esteem that was independent of a lover's devotion. His sense of self derived from the anarchist belief in the worth of the individual—and from Louise Fénéon's trust and pride in her son, attested by his extraordinary devotion to her.

Fénéon did not quarrel with women over matters that involved his pride and self-respect, as he did with Gustave Kahn and Seurat. His attitude toward women was condescending. "He was indulgent toward us," one of them admitted. Yet none of his lovers seems to have objected; they, like Fénéon, had expectations shaped by their era. He treated his wife indulgently too, as this anecdote reveals: they were visiting Matisse and other friends on the Riviera, and F. F. joined the painter for a swim. The two men went out a distance and were treading water, talking, when Fanny Fénéon became alarmed. "Félix!" she cried. "Come back! You're too far out!"—"Don't worry, my dear, I can touch bottom."

Matisse, incredulous: "You can touch bottom?"

"No. But one must always reassure the women."[2]

Treating women like children enabled Fénéon to allow himself all kinds of freedom, identifying with his lover, her problems and successes, and then again turning as silly as a small child delighting in naughty puns and obscene postures. Some of his love letters are openly erotic, playful and tender at the same time. But the greater part of his known correspondence is circumspect, discreetly discussing common interests and expressing comradely concern for his lover, her family and friends.

The longest of his liaisons was with Camille Platteel, the Belgian schoolteacher whom he had met in the home of Théo and Maria van Rysselberghe. Before she encountered Félix Fénéon, Camille Platteel's passion had been her profession, teaching French literature to privileged young women in the Daschbeck School in Brussels. The students there, unlike most women in that time, were given a solid education. Many, including Maria van Rysselberghe, remained devoted to Mademoiselle Platteel long after they left school.

Platteel was small in stature, with rather ordinary features. Nonetheless she radiated refinement, and in discussions she showed strong opinions. "The face of Camille Platteel, under its apparent banality, hid a very special character that is most difficult to define," said one of her friends.[3] She might have struck other young men of Fénéon's time as a sexless bluestocking, but he was charmed by this petite, extraordinarily well-informed woman and her air of independence.

Although adored by the young women she had taught and treated with deference by the men they married, Camille had never before enjoyed the attention of a man like Félix. She gave him all her love. He responded with a devotion that was unusual in a time when the prevailing social ideal saw women as either angels or devils, and love as a lark or an impossible dream.[4]

Intelligent and discreet, Camille Platteel was a "diminutive version of F. F.," whom she loved as one might a powerful alter ego, and in whom she found a perfect companion. Born in 1854, she was several years older than Fénéon. In response to a question as to why they had not married and whether she played a mothering role to him, her friend said:

> This role of "mère chérie" that you imagine doesn't fit in the least! Perhaps she was in fact older than he; the thought never occurred to me; her lively mind and manner made one unaware of such a possibility. What is remarkable was the incredible degree to which C. P. was subjugated by her friend; she was like a reflection of F. F.—to a point that seemed almost comical at times to the very few who knew her well. . . .

> Let me add that personally I *never* saw Camille and Fénéon together, whereas I often saw them separately, those two very unusual beings.[5]

For several years, Félix and Camille saw each other only infrequently, when Fénéon was in Brussels on brief visits. As their friendship deepened, they exchanged letters almost daily, a habit that continued to their dying days. None of their correspondence has been found.

A crisis occurred for Camille Platteel in 1897. After several years of friendship with F. F., she learned that in obedience to his mother's wishes, he was marrying a woman from the Charolais, Stéphanie Goubaux, who was always called Fanny. She was a family friend who, because she was divorced, found herself in difficult circumstances. The fact that this was an arranged marriage did not lessen Camille's despair, for she felt it meant the end of the unique friendship she had with Félix. She even attempted suicide, but not without warning Maria van Rysselberghe, who arrived in time to prevent it. Mme van Rysselberghe wrote Fénéon of his friend's state of mind, and he came at once to Brussels, there to make a pact: although he would not go back on his promise to marry Fanny Goubaux, he would never abandon Camille; his relationship with his future wife had nothing to do with his abiding love for Camille, and they would see one another as often as before. Upon his return to Paris, Félix told his bride-to-be of the promise to Camille; Fanny entered the marriage with her eyes open, though she undoubtedly thought she would win out over the Belgian woman in due time.

For Camille Platteel, perhaps fearing what Fanny Goubaux hoped, the distance between Paris and Brussels suddenly became too great. She left her cherished post as professor and moved into two garret rooms at 52 rue Saint-Georges, below Montmartre. One of the rooms served as a kitchen, and the walls of the other soon became covered with drawings by Seurat and bookshelves containing first editions of the best contemporary writers. Faithful to his promise, Fénéon came to take his midday meal with her every day, bringing proofs and manuscripts which she helped him to read and correct. Platteel was now past forty, and she did not obtain a teaching position in Paris. She lived frugally, supported by the discreet and devoted attention of a small group of intimates, which included, besides the van Rysselberghes, Gustave Kahn and his wife. Fénéon's liaison with her was a secret to most of his friends, who were intrigued by this unknown lady who appeared at all the major events in the avant-garde, always alone, always up to date on the latest developments, unobtrusive and discreet, ordinary and yet elegant, dressed in sober good taste.

Marie-Louise Fénéon, mother of Félix, either did not know Camille or did not wish to know her. She had urged her son to marry Fanny, the daughter of a long-time friend. Fanny had had an unhappy first marriage, and Madame Fénéon's heart went out to her. Divorce had only recently become legally permissible, and a divorcée was generally regarded as a "fallen woman." Fanny, raised as a respectable bourgeoise, had no way of supporting herself. There was also a hidden drama behind her divorce that haunted Fanny all her life: the infant she bore her first husband died, through an accident or negligence on her part. Forty years later, she still felt that a life could be ruined by "those screaming machines given the fine name of 'babies'."[6]

Fanny's case was not unique. Ever since the defeat of 1870 and the upheaval following it, children and motherhood seemed a useless burden to many middle-class families, struggling to achieve security. As Ernest Raynaud wrote in *La Mêlée symboliste:*

> The child was an intruder in the bourgeois marriages of 1864. . . . Oh the [human] damage done by the economic situation! No sooner born, the infant is a cause of trouble and worry. Take the nuisance away![7]

Children were farmed out, first with a wet nurse and then at boarding schools. Society expected a girl like Fanny to marry and become a mother, but gave her no models to learn from and no help when she foundered. "Not everyone can be an orphan," sighed Jules Renard, one of many fin-de-siècle writers who told of uncaring parents. Félix, the much-beloved son, was both an exception and a product of the same middle class. He was able to understand the frustration, fear, and anger Fanny had experienced in her unwanted motherhood. He was glad she wanted no more children; he saw no sense in bringing a new life into the world as it was presently constituted.

Besides, Fénéon was attracted to blond women, and Fanny Goubaux was both blond and pert; "my big blond kitten," F. F. called her, late in life. They were married in the town hall of the eighteenth arrondissement on June 17, 1897, with "no preliminary contract." He was thirty-six that year, and she twenty-nine. It was the marrying season for several among the symbolists. Paul Adam made a love match that same June, while earlier Dujardin outdid himself, with the poet Mallarmé and the painter Raffaëlli as his official witnesses and lunch for all in a pump room on the Champs-Elysées. There were no guests at Fénéon's wedding, which was reported without an exact date in the July issue of the *Mercure de France.*

Soon thereafter, F. F. and his bride were invited to the Natansons' large new country home at Villeneuve on the Yonne. A photograph of them in the garden there contrasts with pictures of other people at Villeneuve—men and women lounging on the grass, playing *boules,* or sitting at tables under the trees. Wearing a gentle but diffident expression, Fénéon, cigarette in hand, stands slightly apart from his wife. She, in her pretty, Vuillardesque dress, gazes past him, her mind on something else—trying, perhaps, to maintain her own in the presence of the Natansons and their other guests. The photograph spells out "social obligation" and shows the impassive mask Fénéon maintained even among friends. Man and wife seem ill at ease to find themselves together. In spite of this inauspicious beginning, their marriage eventually grew into a warm and loving union.

Fanny moved in with her mother-in-law and Félix at 4 passage Tourlaque in Montmartre. The little apartment continued to be a meeting place for painters, poets, and other friends. "Fanny, a good soul if there ever was one," one of them recalled, "always ready to set an extra place at table, made everyone feel at home, with a humility bordering on self-effacement."[8] She worshipped Fénéon and espoused his anarchist thinking, though not necessarily all of its logical consequences. It was not easy for her to prepare dinner when kitchen funds were "robbed" for hand-outs! "We can make do

Félix Fénéon and His Bride Fanny Goubaux at the Country Home of Thadée and Misia Natanson. Villeneuve-sur-Yonne, 1898. Photograph by Alfred Natanson, courtesy Annette Vaillant.

with potatoes," her husband would reply, "whereas that fellow has growing children to feed." Later on, when she was dismayed that objects of value disappeared during a move to a new apartment, he refused to bring charges against the laborers: "Let them enjoy those things . . . they weren't aware of the monetary value."

It also became increasingly difficult for her to share Félix with Camille. "Where are you going?" she would ask, as he rose to go out at lunchtime.

Félix and Fanny Fénéon at Saint-Rafaël, 1939. Photograph courtesy André Berne-Joffroy.

"Fanny, my dear, why persist in asking a question that wants only a lie for an answer?"[9]

Camille Platteel lived for forty-five years in the little rooms on rue Saint-Georges. When the Fénéons would spend a season in the south, she would follow discreetly on the next train and settle nearby. "Old dame Platteel has arrived, I suppose?" Fanny would query.

Fénéon's genuine love for his wife can be seen in this letter that he wrote when she was in her late sixties (she had gone on a trip to Paris, leaving him and her brother Gustave in their summer home near Royan):

Sunday evening

My beautiful, tender one,

We celebrated, not without a tint of melancholy, your birthday. Because of the occasion, Gustave was curious to read your horoscope; he was particularly struck by the passage where the astrologer announced that persons born at ten o'clock in the morning between the 24th of July and the 23rd of August are voluptuous and very fond of love. I am quite disconcerted by your absence and Sunday was spent reading some reviews that had just arrived and little naps, in between thoughts of where you might be on your trip and what you might be doing. I felt so very near you, enmeshed in you. On the table was a bouquet of purple heather and the blue envelope of a letter from Gaston. The weather was nice and cool. But the coolness made me feel how stuffy the air must have been in your train compartment, so far from the sea. My thoughts follow you faithfully and I find joy in imagining your return trip already. All my kisses on your sweet heart, my Fanny, my own chosen penguin.

Your
félix[10]

However sincere his love for her, he gave himself just as heartily to others. Around the time of their marriage or within a year or two afterwards, Fénéon had an affair with a woman whose identity remains unknown, but who was reportedly a simple and very beautiful person. Like the woman who bore a son to Fénéon in 1893,* this woman, too, was a laundress, "always impeccably dressed in spite of her modest situation," recalled another of Fénéon's woman friends. In 1899, she also bore Fénéon a son, an accident, presumably. This time the mother and child remained close to the father. From the age of six on, the boy came regularly to the Fénéons' for family dinner on Sundays. Other guests credited the presence of this working-class boy to Fénéon's traditional generosity. Fanny, who perhaps never guessed his relationship to Félix, became very fond of the well-mannered child, and used to give him money for the movies. When he was fifteen, Fénéon helped him gain employment,[11] just as he did for his other son, who nonetheless remained estranged, thinking of F. F. as his "nonfather." The second son, named Gilbert Gardin, never claimed to have a father and kept his identity a secret. He became an engineer and often spent his holidays with Fénéon and his wife, who chose him at her legal executor after Félix died. He carried out their last wishes exactly, and then seems to have disappeared.

If F. F. was the *non-père,* he would never be the *mal-aimé,* nor would he ever be in danger of "dying for lack of love," as Stendhal predicted the rich would do ("just as the poor do for lack of bread"). Twenty years after Fénéon died (at age eighty-two), some of the women he loved were still alive and eager to talk about him. Only one of his lovers, the dancer Suzanne Alazet Des Meules, made his letters available, "but not the best ones—I can't part with those!" These fragments show a new side of Fénéon, part of the

*See chapter 12, p. 252.

FÉLIX FÉNÉON. ***End of a Letter to Fanny.*** Instead of a signature, drawings of a cat, a penguin ("my Fanny, my own chosen penguin") and a dog (F. F.), ca. 1934. Courtesy Gina Doveil.

total man. They are but a bit of one relationship, however, and should not necessarily be regarded as typifying the nature of other liaisons.

In loving, F. F. sometimes allowed himself to assume a female identity, an erotic game that was also a way of entering into a deeper intimacy:

> Thank you, Suzanne, for these flowers that you picked in the Forum. They were soft on my lips. I think Rome must be wondering at your presence, for its ancient soil can never have been trod by such grace. I would like to know what fine adventures led you to go there and now hold you fast. When you find the time to write me, gentle one, let me penetrate your intimacy a bit by confiding in me as woman to woman [amie à ami*e*]. But perhaps you prefer to remain a mystery. . . . I am happy that life is good to you.
>
> A garland of kisses entwine the sweet body of Noura,
>
> *félix*[12]

Other times he signed, "*ta confidente,* Félicie." Later, more astounding transmutations took place, as he gave words to lesbian love, which she, in fact, enjoyed: "Let us play at which of our tongues, yours or mine, can plunge more deeply into the wound of the other."

Fénéon helped Suzanne Des Meules choose her professional name, Noura, signifying "brilliance," from the Arabic for "(divine) light." She was indeed for him a bright light through his sixties and seventies, and was so as well for Fanny, who loved and accepted her as a buffer against a more formidable rival—a tall young woman with China blue eyes, deeply in love with Félix. But Suzanne was a devotee of Venus, the very agent of love, and more than once she pretended to be with Félix when in fact he was with the other one.

Above right, ***Suzanne Alazet Des Meules.*** Opéra de Marseilles, 1927.

Above, ***Suzanne Alazet Des Meules.*** 1927.

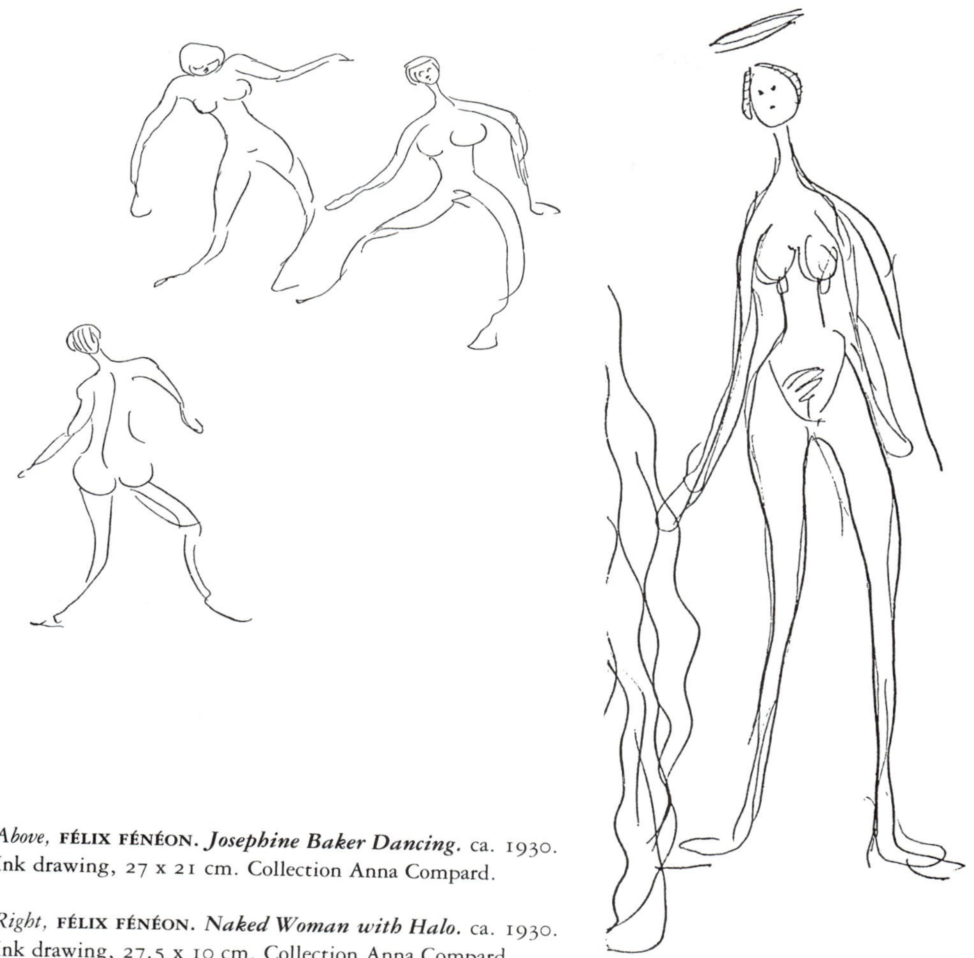

Above, FÉLIX FÉNÉON. ***Josephine Baker Dancing.*** ca. 1930. Ink drawing, 27 x 21 cm. Collection Anna Compard.

Right, FÉLIX FÉNÉON. ***Naked Woman with Halo.*** ca. 1930. Ink drawing, 27.5 x 10 cm. Collection Anna Compard.

F. F. expressed himself to Suzanne with complete openness. His playful iconoclasm and unusual sexual freedom can be seen in this letter:

the 21st

Now that Easter has come, it is meet we should approach the Holy Table. Thy belly is the altar, thy chemise the cloth. I kneel and on my tongue is placed, ever so delicately, thy clitoris—the host.

These devotions done, hear how delighted I am by your good news: first that you have your health back (nothing could please me more), and then your adventure with the virgin Blanche. Being robbed of her virginity by the tongue of Noura will leave her a far finer remembrance than if she had suffered violation by a male.

"Une puce qui me suce . . . ", as you used to hum . . . [a flea is sucking me]. You did not say if Blanche was for you that *puce.** It's understood, I guess. You

*Wordplay on the *puce* of *pucelage, pucelle,* and *dépuceler.*

prognosticate that this girl will be a volcano. I am imagining the volcano Blanche and the volcano Noura, and I see their two sexual craters boiling with love. I heartily approve the picture that you draw [. . . .] But when you put me to bed with one of your women, you are the center, the charm of the game for me, you know that, don't you, my tender little mouth-pig. . . . A propos, what has become of Charlotte? Have you had a cooling-off, you who were so hot for one another in Avignon and Tunis, giving each other such smooth caresses while I dipped into first one and then the other. Delicious moments: your breasts so pure, your cunt so delectable, your eyes so luminous. . .

And the gallant whose letter I read, one evening in Paris, have you news of him? You know, the one who told you so poetically about his long walks in the country and how he kissed the crotch of trees, excited as he was by the remembrance of you.

It's time for the mail to go . . . I diddle you, my darling; I lick you, my heart; I encunt you, tender one; I enass you, my sweet; my tart, I love you.—But I think I have overstepped my bounds! What indecorous language! I beg your pardon, Madame. Allow me, please, to lay my most respectful homage at your feet.

felix[13]

Not all the women F. F. loved were his lovers. One he prized above all, Lucie Cousturier, was simply a friend. Another artist, Louise Hervieu, allowed herself a "brief, breathless" affair with him—the only one in her life, according to those who knew her well.[14] "Valiant, weak Louise Hervieu" was born syphilitic. Fénéon saw the power of her drawing and encouraged her to illustrate Baudelaire's *Fleurs du Mal.* When her failing vision made her despair of fulfilling herself as an artist, he helped her write her autobiographical novel, *Sangs* (Bloodlines) and supported her public campaigns for the establishment of health-identity cards and measures to prevent syphilitics from bearing children. (There would be no effective control of this dread disease for another forty-odd years.) Near the second anniversary of Fénéon's death, Louise wrote Suzanne:

5 Feb. '46

Nourah, dear Nourah,

With you I can evoke our dear Departed in the deepest way. Your magnificent Firebird—of all fires!—before whom even the proudest of the proud fell silent, I believe it is the simplicity of heart in each of us that allowed us to approach his own and to know the fineness of its temper. . . . The understanding he had of my [physical] failings, my drawings, my cries—even my madness: I mean my attempt to save our insane human race. . . .[15]

Fénéon's women friends did not complain, as André Breton once did, that they could not penetrate "his rough—and slippery—outer shell." Nor did they fear that he was judging them or secretly laughing at them "from behind his mask" as did many of his male contemporaries.[16] Perhaps women's acceptance of their vulnerability, their "simpleness of heart," as Louise Hervieu said, made Fénéon drop his guard. Oddly, most of those who trusted him implicitly were people whom society classified as inferior or strange—misfits, outcasts, indigents, poets like Jarry—and women.

LUCIE COUSTURIER. *Self-Portrait.* 1919. Oil on panel, 34.9 x 26.5 cm. Indianapolis Museum of Art. Gift of Dr. and Mrs. Milton D. Ratner.

Among his male friends the artists, more than the writers, knew his capacity for love and appetite for sex; their wide-open, receptive gaze saw the playful, private side of him. Fénéon knew, too, that the libido was a main force on the artist's creative unconscious: "Go to the Louvre," he urged his twentieth-century readers, "and discover the sexual spot in some famous canvas, the part the artist treated with love. . . ."[17]

Fénéon's cloak of secrecy allowed him to cross barriers with impunity. He was Félicie and Félix, outrageous and decorous, lover and spouse. He undermined those oppositions which, as Georges Bataille has said, cripple our judgment: up/down,

Dis-moi, ton cœur parfois
s'envole-t-il Agathe,
Loin du noir Océan, de l'immonde cité
Vers un autre océan où la splendeur éclate
Bleu-clair profond ainsi que la virginité
Dis-moi, ton cœur parfois s'envole-t-il Agathe

Above left, FÉLIX FÉNÉON. ***Louise Hervieu.*** ca. 1919. Drawing on blue scratch paper, 16 x 13.8 cm. Courtesy Gilbert Gruet. "Ag." is for "Agathe," from Baudelaire's poem, *Moesta et Errabunda.*

Above right, FÉLIX FÉNÉON. ***Study of a Woman's Head.*** ca. 1916. Drawing, 27.5 x 21.5 cm. Collection Anna Compard.

man/beast, white/black, male/female—superior/inferior.[18] By eluding those distinctions—assuming an "inferior" nature—Fénéon escaped the underlying moralism of rational discourse. In love, he sought not conquest but unsettling freedom and a partnership in pleasure.

For Fénéon was no Lothario. He no more ran after women than he ran after fame.

Opposite, LOUISE HERVIEU. ***Dis-moi, ton coeur parfois s'envole-t-il Agathe. . . .*** ca. 1919. Conté crayon, charcoal, and crayon Wolf BBB, 17.7 x 11 cm, with the opening lines of Baudelaire's poem in Hervieu's hand. Illustration for Baudelaire's poem *Moesta et Errabunda* (To the Trapped and Wandering) beginning:

Tell me, does not your heart at times take flight, Agathe,
Far from the black ocean of the unclean city,
Towards another ocean ablaze in light,
As blue, deep, and bright as virginity?
Tell me, does not your heart at times take flight, Agathe?

Photograph courtesy Bernheim-Jeune Galleries, Paris.

FÉLIX FÉNÉON. ***Portrait de l'auteur*** (Self-portrait). ca. 1930. Drawing, blue crayon, 28 x 21 cm. Collection Anna Compard.

The rather raunchy roman à clef, *Une Passade,* has the heroine reply, when asked if she ever gave her favors to the Fénéonesque "Elie":

"Don't laugh. He never . . . he never asked."[19]

A great part of Fénéon's emotional life was devoted to male friends, as I have already shown in this book. As he grew older, more and more young people found a friend in him, while former comrades still remained. He and Bonnard, especially, enjoyed one another's company. The painter used to come and spend ten days or so "to relieve F. F.'s boredom" at a spa where Fanny Fénéon was taking the waters. Or F. F. would visit Bonnard at his home in Le Cannet and silently enjoy the progress of a painting. Once Fénéon told a joke on himself, saying that after several days of watching, he asked his friend how long he thought it would take him to finish that particular painting. "Why," replied Bonnard, "I finished it this morning!"[20]

Letters from Fénéon's friends reveal their fondness for him. An unpublished one

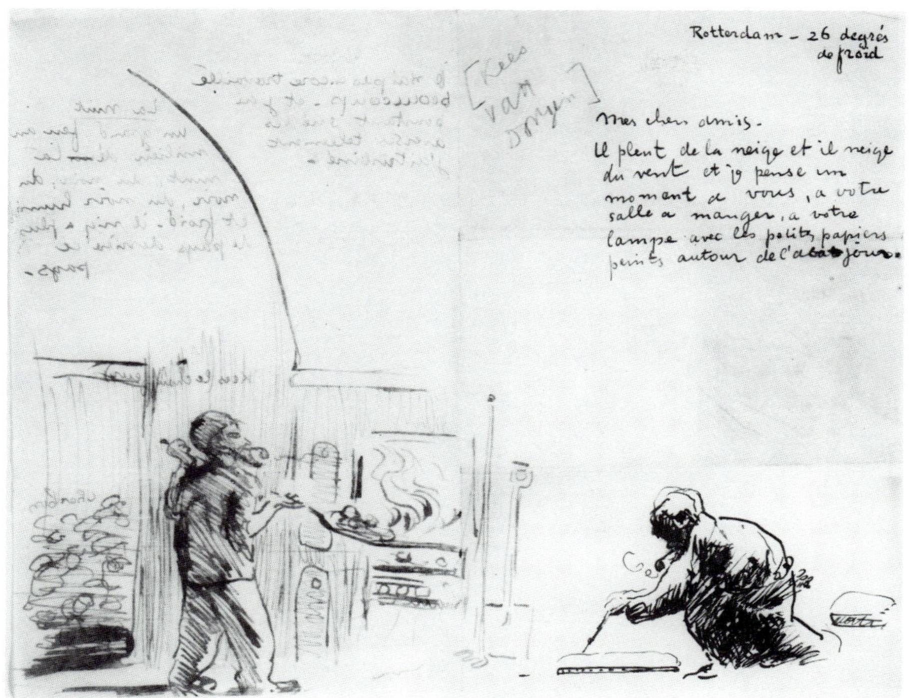
Rotterdam – 26 degrés de froid

[Kees van Dongen]

Mes chers amis.
Il pleut de la neige et il neige du vent et je pense un moment à vous, à votre salle à manger, à votre lampe avec les petits papiers peints autour de l'abat-jour.

KEES VAN DONGEN. ***Page from a Letter to Félix and Fanny Fénéon,*** dated "Rotterdam, 26 degrees of cold," with drawings of himself and his father combatting the cold. ca. 1897. The artist's name is penciled in brackets in Fénéon's hand. Paris, Paulhan archives. The image on the left shows through from the other side in reverse, which reads: *I've not yet got much work done—and yet I've lost oceans of sweat, swogging. At night a big fire in the middle of the night, blackness cold and damp—there's no more land behind this land. Kees (the stoker).*

from Kees van Dongen, who humorously sketched in scenes of an uncomfortable visit with his father in Holland, evokes the warmth of the Fénéon household:

Rotterdam

My dear friends,

It's raining snow and snowing wind here, and I stop to think a moment of you, your dining room, your lamp and the bits of painted paper you put around the shade. . . .[21]

Other artists wrote him about their work: Henri-Edmond Cross, for example, who sent him some reflections on an article Maurice Denis had written:

San Rafaël, 21 May 1905

. . . Still, I cannot accept for myself the idea of getting one's guidance from the old masters, nor can I understand how such a fine artist [as Maurice Denis] can do so. . . .

Life will always remain the only source of our emotions. . . . To assert that another period—the Venetian Renaissance, for example—is more beautiful than ours

KEES VAN DONGEN. ***Last Page of the Same Letter.*** The ghost image behind the drawing of the woman shows the drawing on the other side, Kees and his father loading coal in a "room heated to 90° by the fire below." Paris, Paulhan archives.

> seems to me to be a literary notion. How can one compare the different degrees of *artistic* beauty in different times? As I see it, ugly periods would be those when poets and painters were powerless or incapable of understanding their own times. . . .
>
> To see life around us, to be alive to our own sensations and to create, I believe that suffices for our joys as for our anguish.[22]

F. F. also served as a liaison between his friends, as can be seen, for example, in this letter to Maximilien Luce at the beginning of World War I:

> *19 August 1914*
>
> My dear Luce,
>
> Vuillard is guarding a bridge, I don't know where. Bonnard is at 29 route des Andelys, in Vernon (Eure). Roussel, probably at l'Etang.
>
> The Pankiewiczes* have been expelled from Collioure and are in Barcelona, without money.
>
> Signac is still at the hôtel des Alpins, in Saint-Julien-en-Beauchêne (Hautes-Alpes). To paint outdoors, he says, is to risk getting hit by rifle fire. So he is going to do some watercolors illustrating a dozen lines of the "Bateau ivre."

*The Polish artist, Joseph Pankiewicz and his wife Wanda. F. F. would later show his work at the Galerie Bernheim-Jeune, and identified him in one of Bonnard's paintings, "Conversation provençale," as the "giant, rather like a Chinese Sage, sitting in the foreground, a flower in his hand" (F, 328).

MAXIMILIEN LUCE. ***Portrait of F. Fénéon.*** 1903. Oil on canvas, 140.3 x 130 cm. Piled against the wall, Seurat's *Standing Model* (study in Conté crayon, ca. 1887) and a Japanese print. Musée de Nevers.

> Paris, cheerless the first two weeks, is taking on a rather lively character, quite warm and friendly. But the night life has been interrupted: cafés close at 8:30; restaurants at 9:30. The last North-South metro leaves at 8:30 [. . .].
>
> A certain General Barral claims that the war will be over by the end of October. [. . . .] Jacques Rodrigues* is conquering Alsace. His regular address is: Corporal in the 18th Company of the 352nd Line, Langres, Haute Marne. A word from you would obviously please him. May he get it! On 10 August he had been fighting for 48 hours and we have not heard from him since. [. . . .]
>
> Fanny joins me in sending fond thoughts to you; give some to Ambroisine and the children. félix.[23]

Fénéon harbored a deserter throughout the Great War, but his anarchism did not keep him from sympathizing with people caught up in the military; he wrote to many soldiers on the front and to war prisoners. When he learned that Jacques Rodrigues had been captured, he sent him news and packages but, more importantly, arranged for a

*Rodrigues-Henriques, young art dealer.

COLLECTION FÉLIX FÉNÉON

Quinze Dessins - Aquarelles - Gouaches

DE

CHAGALL — Raoul DUFY — Constantin GUYS
Louise HERVIEU — Camille PISSARRO — RAPPA
RODIN — TOULOUSE-LAUTREC et Van DONGEN

Quinze Dessins et Neuf Peintures

DE

GEORGES SEURAT

Quarante-huit Tableaux

DE

BONNARD, BRAQUE, COMPARD, Lucie COUSTURIER, H.-E. CROSS
DEGAS, Maurice DENIS, DERAIN, DUREY, Max ERNST, GOERG
GROMAIRE, Marie LAURENCIN, LOUTREUIL, LUCE, André MASSON
HENRI-MATISSE, MODIGLIANI, RENOIR, K.-X. ROUSSEL, SIGNAC
VALLOTTON et VUILLARD.

DONT LA VENTE AUX ENCHÈRES PUBLIQUES AURA LIEU A PARIS

HOTEL DROUOT, SALLE N° 6

le Jeudi 4 Décembre 1941, à quatorze heures 30 précises.

Me ALPH. BELLIER

COMMISSAIRE-PRISEUR, 30, PLACE DE LA MADELEINE, PARIS-8e

Exposition Publique le **Mercredi 3 Décembre 1941,** de **14** à **18** heures.

Title Page of the catalogue of the partial sale of Fénéon's collection on 4 December 1941, Hôtel Drouot, Paris.

monthly stipend-loan for Rodrigues' wife by the gallery with which the young man had been affiliated.

Painting was the object of much of Fénéon's love. Not that that he ever tried seriously to paint, although he often sketched or doodled. His intense involvement with art was not due to frustration over not being himself an artist. He was its lover.

He gave himself to this love with the same abandon as to other loves. His art collection, worth millions at his death, was not built for speculation, but for pure enjoyment. Once someone offered him a considerable sum for *Bathing at Asnières,* and he replied: "What could I do with all that money, except buy it back from you?"[24] (Perhaps the offer came from Lucien Pissarro. acting on behalf of the Tate Gallery in London, for whom he finally obtained it.) Fanny indulged her husband in this passion. Early in their marriage she noticed in a store window a painting by "the painter Félix loves so much" (Seurat) and managed to buy it with the little money she had.* Their

*The merchant was asking fifty francs for this painting, "Young Woman Powdering Herself." Fanny reportedly obtained it for forty-five (René Delange and Emile Compard, interview with the author, La Vallée aux Loups, 17 March 1963).

COLLECTION FENEON
Deuxième Vente

TABLEAUX MODERNES
DESSINS - AQUARELLES - GOUACHES - PASTELS

Bonnard, Braque, Compard, Lucie Cousturier, Cross, Degas, Raoul Dufy, Goerg, Gromaire, Constantin Guys, Louise Hervieu, Loutreuil, Luce, Lurçat, Matisse, Modigliani, Pascin, Pissarro, Roussel, Seurat, Signac, Van Dongen, Van Rysselberghe, Vuillard.

"LES POSEUSES"
Trois œuvres importantes par Seurat

dont la vente aux enchères publiques
après décès de Monsieur et Madame FÉNÉON

AU PROFIT de l'UNIVERSITÉ de PARIS

aura lieu

HOTEL DROUOT, Salles 9, 10 et 11 réunies
Le Vendredi 30 Mai 1947, à 14 h. 30

Me ALPH. BELLIER
Commissaire-Priseur
30, Place de la Madeleine, PARIS

Assisté de :

M. André SCHŒLLER
Expert
33, Avenue du Général-Sarrail

M. Étienne BIGNOU
Expert près les Douanes Françaises
8, Rue La Boëtie

EXPOSITIONS : HOTEL DROUOT
Salles 9, 10 et 11, de 14 à 18 heures
PARTICULIÈRE : Le Mercredi 28 Mai — PUBLIQUE : Le Jeudi 29 Mai
(Entrée particulière : Rue de la Grange-Batelière)

Title Page of the catalogue of the second of four posthumous sales of the Fénéon collection, 30 May 1947, Hôtel Drouot, Paris.

tiny apartment was encumbered with art. In 1904 they moved to a somewhat larger place at 15 rue des Grandes Carrières (now renamed Eugène Carrière, after the painter), still in the Montmartre area. Many people got to know Fénéon and his art collection there:

> It was a rather small apartment with a low ceiling, literally invaded by painting. The walls of all the rooms and even the corridors were covered from floor to ceiling. . . That is where I learned to know and love Seurat, Bonnard, Matisse, Modigliani, Vuillard, Signac, Gromaire, Gauguin, Pissaro [*sic*], and many others.[25]

Seurat's *Bathing at Asnières* "reigned in the drawing-room, a chest of drawers was bulging with his conté crayon drawings. There was the table with *art nouveau* tiles by 'daddy Luce,' as Fanny called him; and later on the African fetishes and sculptures—a tribal king's chair that Kleinmann was drooling over," Emile Compard recalled.[26] A nude by Modigliani stretched over the head of the bed. A dark narrow corridor contained various portraits of Fénéon with other pictures, "among them a Gromaire of 1924," Fénéon later wrote John Rewald, "where you might have recognized me

Three Pieces from Fénéon's Collection of African Art. Reprinted from the catalogue of the auction sale, 11 June 1947, Hôtel Drouot, Paris. Notes by Fénéon: [left to right] "Animal mask. (Ivory Coast. Baoulé.)"; "Mask-helmet with a face on either side. (Belgian Congo. Baluba group.)"; "Dog-faced baboon, mouth wide open baring its teeth. (Ivory Coast. Senufo.)."

although it was actually another friend of the painter, and a Luce from 1903 where you could have mistaken me for another, in spite of my many hours of sitting."[27] Fénéon, it seems, was hard to please; he did not see himself as others saw him.

Thus, he objected when Fanny showed a young anarchist friend the clippings his mother had saved from the Trial of the Thirty when Fénéon was away on a trip in 1935:

> I really don't approve that . . . you read him those old newspaper clippings, full of bombast and inaccuracies. Mirbeau, notably, was exaggeration itself, in praise as in blame.* When all is said and done, I really want to earn your affection by more humble, familiar, even familial and domestic deeds. If circumstances sometimes led me to parade in public, it was against my will. To love you was my joy; to be loved by you, my ambition, and you have fulfilled that wish far beyond what was my due.[28]

Fanny's very ordinariness made her dear to Félix. People who did not know them well failed to understand how he, "so trenchant, so witty," could tolerate living with her. "She was a good woman and a good wife, but a crashing bore," said a member of the Bernheim-Jeune firm, "He must have married her in a moment of forgetfulness."[29] But she took good care of her husband, and of her mother-in-law. She gave piano lessons for years in order to supplement Félix's income, though she had no particular

*Whatever reservations he expressed here, Fénéon was very fond of Octave Mirbeau and appreciated his verve.

MARCEL GROMAIRE. ***Nude with Blue Bouquet.*** 1927. Oil on canvas, 81 x 100 cm. Formerly Félix Fénéon. Photograph courtesy Bernheim-Jeune Galleries, Paris.

EMILE COMPARD. ***The Motorists, "Climbing to 80."*** 1927. Oil on canvas, 65 x 81 cm. Formerly Félix Fénéon. Collection Anna Compard.

interest in music. For her, as for generations of other well-brought-up girls, the piano was simply the only decent way to earn some money. She was also inquisitive and forward-looking, thrilled by the many new contrivances that appeared at the end of the century—the automobile and moving pictures, for instance. In 1899, Signac wrote Fénéon: "I have just ordered, under special conditions through my friend Mr. Acatène, a little motor car driven by petrol, so as to take our dear Fanny out for rides in the suburbs."[30]

When, in order to relieve his wife of the burden of giving piano lessons, Fénéon relinquished *Bathing at Asnières,* she invested first in a practical wine and coal shop and then in something she dearly loved: the cinema. She bought a movie house and went there to "supervise," no longer guilty at spending her time and money there. Then she became an antique dealer, or at least owned an antique store. One evening the Bernheim-Jeune family had their famous salesman and his wife to dinner, and Fanny spent the whole evening talking without stop. It seemed as if she had fallen into the habit of both asking and answering her own questions. Félix soberly listened to this flood of words and then suddenly exclaimed: "Fanny, you are the prettiest antique dealer in all of Paris!" Those were, according to the hosts, the only words he spoke all night.[31]

Did he mean by this ambivalent compliment to silence his wife, or rather to baffle the others? He spoke with such grace and gentility that it was often hard to tell, except upon reflection, for whom the sting was intended. In effect, he struck not at individuals but at a total situation, His basic style, the same self-patterned freedom that enabled him to love so many, also allowed him to pack a wallop in a single phrase. This was never so evident as in the *Nouvelles en trois lignes* which he wrote for the newspapers in 1906: F. F. the moralist—or, according to Jean Paulhan, the terrorist—in three lines, alive and open to the bitter comedy of life.

CHAPTER 17

The Terrorist in Three Lines

Fénéon found a diversion—and his broadest audience—with his *Nouvelles en trois lignes,* the newpaper fillers he wrote for *Le Matin* in 1906. Even today, he has been called the inventor of the "minimal" story, the forerunner of such works as *Steps* by Jerzy Kosinski and *The Very Thing That Happens* by Russell Edson.[1] Fénéon's concision, his irony and delight in the absurd, predisposed him to drawing up odd news items in less than twenty-five words—three short lines. The way he chose and placed each word made his *Nouvelles* stand out from others and startled his readers into a consideration of the terror and absurdity of everyday events.

> —The 515, at the Monthéart crossing (Sarthe),
> ran over Mme Dutertre. Accident, they say,
> although she was wretchedly poor.
>
> —It was his turn at nine-pins when a cerebral
> hemorrhage felled Mr. André, 75, of Levallois.
> While his ball was rolling, he ceased to be.

If, as John Kenneth Galbraith once said, a good journalist is obliged to find significance every week in events of absolutely no consequence, then F. F. should have won a Pulitzer prize. But rather than explicate, he requires that the readers think for themselves. Was Mme Dutertre's death a suicide? What of inanimate Mr. André's rolling ball? Mallarmé was right, after all; Fénéon's detonators were his words.

When the *Revue blanche* folded in April 1903, Fénéon was once again in search of a job. He landed one first at the establishment newspaper, *Le Figaro.* Life at a big city newspaper around the turn of the century was both elegant and lively, as André Billy has described:

> The editorial room, the writers' offices, the corridors and the waiting room were invaded by fashionable women and men of the world. The reporters themselves had a

> quite different presence and style from those of the following generation. The columnist in charge of theatre, whatever his name . . . was under constant siege by actors and authors trying to get a word printed in their favor.[2]

Ever since the 1870s, the *Figaro* had employed a brilliant stable of critics, including Léon Daudet, Maupassant, Barrès, Bourget, the politician Jules Simon, and the influential Albert Wolff, who had so staunchly opposed the impressionists. Fénéon, however, was hired simply as an anonymous writer of news bulletins.

He worked the night shift, as he indicated in this letter to the Italian artist, Severino Rappa:

> My dear friend, you would be sure to find me at the *Figaro* from 10 o'clock at night (allowing for a few minutes' tardiness) until 2:30 in the morning, every day without fail. Or, if you prefer, make a date to meet me at the *Figaro* at seven in the evening. . . .[3]

If Fénéon chose to work at night, it was to keep his days free and to avoid some of the bustle and stir of the fashionable crowd at the *Figaro*. However, he entertained his own friends there and used its stationery to write Gide, Apollinaire, and others about things that did not concern the paper at all. He wished to see Rappa, in fact, about the newly established *prix Goncourt* which, according to Edmond de Goncourt's will, was to be awarded to the year's best work of imaginative literature. Fénéon was campaigning for a novel written by John Antoine Nau, a strange postsymbolist writer whose earlier poems and stories had appeared in the *Revue blanche*. Speculating about the ballots to be cast by the members of the Académie Goncourt, Fénéon wrote Rappa:

> If they are divided equally five against five and assuming Huysmans (as President) has the deciding vote, then Nau will come out on top.[4]

Fénéon's candidate indeed won the first Goncourt prize for his novel *Force ennemie,* about a schizophrenic who recounts his imaginary and real adventures in the various voices of his split personality. Today the *prix Goncourt* assures instant fame and commercial success, but John Antoine Nau—born Eugène Torquet in San Francisco, 1860—remained as obscure as his sponsor, F. F.

The management of the *Figaro* prided itself on its businesslike approach to journalism; every line had to "pay for itself" as hidden advertising or "editorial publicity." In 1903, Theodore Zeldin reports, an outraged author claimed that in order to have a book reviewed by Albert Wolff, the author would have to pay the *Figaro* 2,000 francs. In another instance, it came out in court that the *Figaro's* chief editor had "paid his florist's bill of 4,000 francs by mentioning her in his reports of society parties."[5]

Fénéon did not play this game and declined even to solicit favors for his former literary associates. He replied to a request from Karl Boès, director of the symbolist review, *La Plume:*

> My dear Boès, I do not see anything available at the *Figaro*. For that matter, once the "City and Society," theatres, sports, advertisements and war dispatches have been placed, there's no room for anything else. . . .
>
> As for the other papers, I have no idea what goes on there.[6]

It therefore comes as a surprise that Fénéon not only managed to place a delightful piece of nonsense by Alfred Jarry in the *Figaro,* but that he also negotiated a handsome payment to Jarry for this and three more *fantaisies,* which never appeared. André Salmon, protosurrealist poet at age twenty-two and future defender of Cubism, recalled late in life that F. F. placed his earliest pieces of whimsy in the *Figaro.*[7] Reversing official policy, Fénéon exploited the newspaper for the good of these two outrageous writers.

While working at the *Figaro,* Fénéon contributed monetarily to *L'Humanité,* which the socialist Jean Jaurès had just founded. "L'Huma," as Signac and F. F. called it, was the only newspaper Fénéon thought worth reading, and he took it with him to the café during his midnight break. There, propped up in front of him, it represented a barrier to some but an invitation to others. More than one close friend of his later told me, "I met him on the terrace of a café, where he was reading *L'Humanité.*"

Also during his years at the *Figaro,* Fénéon broke his silence to write signed prefaces for the catalogues of one man shows by three close friends who were also anarchists: Maximillien Luce, Paul Signac, and Kees van Dongen. In his preface for the Signac catalogue, Fénéon described the neo-impressionist's technique much as he had in the 1880s, without regard for the new life Signac had infused into divisionism by exploding the dot into large mosaic-like patches of saturated color. Yet this new development had strongly influenced van Dongen and other artists who would become known, less than a year later, as the "Wild Beasts" of Fauvism. Young van Dongen had settled in Paris in 1897, expressing his political views by contributing illustrations to the antiestablishment paper, *L'Assiette au beurre.* Signac and Fénéon soon befriended him and he joined the group at the *Revue blanche,* where Fénéon published his drawings. The critic's remarks on the exhibition of 1904 show he was attracted to van Dongen's use of strong color and to the sexual subject matter of certain paintings, such as the painter's interpretation of the myth of Astarte descending into Hell, where the goddess is divested of a veil at every level so that "when she arrives among the multi-colored coils symbolizing her destiny, her pudendum shines forth in splendor" (F, 244). Allowing for his attraction to the erotic, Fénéon's delight in van Dongen's work nonetheless surprises, given his former objections to expressionism and literary symbolism in art. Just as for Luce and Signac, common political sympathies and friendship probably influenced his judgment.

Although he did not write about the latest developments in art, Fénéon was still very much involved in what was going on. Besides van Dongen, he took a keen interest in the work of Marquet, Derain, and Matisse, and he acquired a number of their paintings. He spent part of the summer of 1904 with Signac at the painter's villa in Saint Tropez, where Matisse was also working. His first loyalty was, however, to the memory of Seurat. He helped Signac set up a retrospective of Seurat at the Indépendants of 1905, and the previous winter lent *Bathing at Asnières* and other neo-impressionist works to a comprehensive exhibition of impressionism in Brussels.

Torn between his love of painting and the need to make a living, he began to look for a job compatible with both interests. He considered opening a gallery with a painter called Lelong, a friend of Signac's. Théo van Rysselberghe, Signac, Luce, and Henry van de Velde helped and encouraged him, although Signac cautioned that Lelong "thinks you are far too good-hearted to succeed in business." Signac offered to lend him his Pissarros for an initial show and advised him not to take a third partner: "You will [both] be much freer on your own."[8]

Fénéon was uncertain himself about what to do, as he wrote to van de Velde:

Le Figaro, 19 September 1905

My dear friend,

I am really quite touched by your readiness to answer us and the very terms named in your letter. However, I beg you not to take any further steps at this point: since Théo wrote you, a certain journalistic project—to which I had previously given my adhesion and which promises me a significant role—now appears to be looking up, after having been seemingly abandoned. So I shall have to postpone my commercial venture until the end of the year; then I should know if the promoters of this other affair will give it up, and so render me my liberty.

To tell the truth, I would rather handle paintings than a magazine.

I will keep you informed; if circumstances orient me towards painting, I would be most happy to call upon you, who have been such a friend to me and who saw right away which people were likely to take an interest in my plan. For that matter, the names you gave me are familiar to me and I have the pleasure of knowing certain ones: MM. de Kessler and de Bodenhausen. Their support, even if only moral, would be most precious to me. . . .[9]

Both plans fell through: Fénéon neither opened a gallery nor joined the new "journalistic project." At the beginning of 1906 he moved from the *Figaro* to another big newspaper, the *Matin,* where Misia Godebska had introduced him. The owner of the paper was a little man from the province of Auvergne who changed his name, Varillat, to Bunau-Varilla, suggestive of Latin American wealth and power. He fancied himself a champion of noble causes and used his paper to condemn corruption in the courts, raise money for explorations, and campaign for clean post offices (he sent in sweeping teams when the government paid no heed). At the *Matin,* he assumed the manners of a tyrant, forbidding his writers to publish under their own names—to prevent their becoming conceited.[10]

When F. F. appeared for his interview at the "Maison Rouge" (the great hall painted red at numbers 4, 6, and 8 boulevard Poissonnière) Varilla abruptly queried:

"Sir, are you still an anarchist?"

"As you please, sir," replied Fénéon.[11]

In February 1906, Fénéon wrote a hasty note to the actress Maleck, wife of the painter Albert André, and to Misia Godebska to excuse himself for not appearing at Misia's the previous Sunday: his mother had been taken suddenly ill and he had gone to be with her.[12] Marie-Louise Fénéon died soon after, aged seventy. She had spent the last twenty years living with her son, the last nine with Fanny as well. Portraits that Severino Rappa did in 1904 of each of them show the mother to be a plump, attractive person with a luminous gaze. During the vigil over his mother's body, Fénéon made

Top, SEVERINO RAPPA. ***Portrait of Marie-Louise Fénéon.*** 1904. Pencil drawing, 30 x 24 cm. Formerly F. Fénéon. Photograph courtesy Gina Doveil.

Above left, SEVERINO RAPPA. ***Portrait of Fanny Fénéon.*** 1904. Pencil drawing, 30 x 24 cm. Formerly F. Fénéon. Courtesy Gina Doveil.

Above right, SEVERINO RAPPA. ***Portrait of Félix Fénéon.*** 1904. Pencil drawing, 30 x 24 cm. Formerly F. Fénéon. Reprinted from Jean Paulhan, *F. F. ou le critique.*

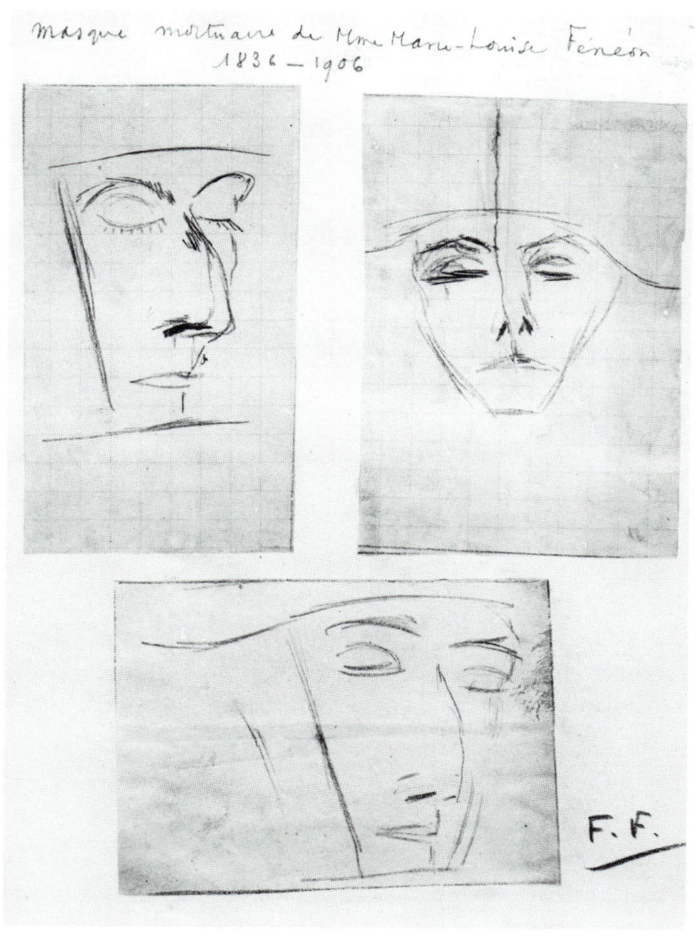

FÉLIX FÉNÉON. ***Death Mask of Marie-Louise Fénéon.*** 1906. Three pencil drawings (one torn down the center), placed by F. F. at the head of the dossier his mother had kept on the Trial of the Thirty. Paris, Bibliothèque littéraire Jacques Doucet.

three drawings of her, nun-like in her shroud. He later turned the dossier she had kept on the Trial of the Thirty into a memorial by placing this icon on top of all the papers.

Two or three months after his arrival at *Le Matin,* Fénéon took over the little column called "Les Nouvelles en trois lignes" that appeared anonymously on the third page of the six-page paper. Normally called *faits divers* ("diverse incidents") these were reports of miscellaneous accidents, petty crimes, murders, and other odd events—a category of news popular today in British tabloids and some French papers. "You wonder sometimes, reading the *faits divers,* if *France-Soir* is not a surrealist journal," a reporter for *Libération* once remarked. "Multiply the banal by the tragic, and you have a very weird effect." The same reporter also noted: "Fénéon played with such equations."[13]

Play is the right word, for it was a question, again, of style. Contrary to the opinion of most Fénéonites, F. F. did not invent the "three line short story." It was a conventional journalistic device for writing up faits divers—*chiens écrasés,* as the French like to say ("flattened dogs"). Fénéon's *brèves,* however, have a unique flavor. Almost always funny:

> —Nothing but plate! At least Saint Louis's finger had to be authentic, so the thieves of Poissy church took it.

Most often black humor:

> —On the outskirts of Noisy, Louis Delilleau, aged 70, fell down, dead, a sunstroke. Quickly, his dog, Fido,* gobbled up his head.

The laughter at times conceals a judgment:

> —Louis Lamarre had neither work nor lodging; but he did have a few coppers. He bought a quart of kerosene from a grocer in Saint Denis, and drank it.

Pathos and humor parry:

> —Vermot, the seventy-year-old beggar of Clichy, just died of hunger. His mattress hid 2,000 francs, but one should not generalize.

And pity assumes a new voice:

> —"What! all those children perched on my wall!" With eight shots, Mr. Olive, a Toulon property-owner, made them scramble down, covered with blood.

A single word (*property-owner*) or syntactic device (*blood* at the end) changes a banal event into a moral statement.

Fénéon plays on incongruity and contrast, underlining the comical in the event—here, a great deal of work for a small reward:

> —After climbing through the roof, sawing a hole in the ceiling and breaking into the house, some thieves took 800 francs from M. Gourdé, of Montainville.

As F. F. writes, numbers often point up absurdities:

> —In Essoyes (Aube), Bernard, 25, bludgeoned Mr. Dufert, who is 89, and stabbed his wife. He was jealous.
>
> —Two hundred resin tappers are on strike in Mimizan (Landes). Three detachments of gendarmes and a hundred infantry from the 34th division are watching them.

*In French, *Fidèle,* "faithful."

Events are sometimes vivified by an unexpected modifier. Thus, we learn that a gypsy avenged the eviction of her tribe from a Paris suburb by biting a *leathery* gendarme, that a train was derailed after some urchins *gaily* placed tree trunks on the tracks.

The suggestiveness and density of Fénéon's *Nouvelles,* their flexible structure and variety in perspective, make them quite different from ordinary news fillers. Compare a few that had appeared in *Le Matin* shortly before he took over the column:

> —The funeral of gendarme Refeveuille, killed by a burglar, took place yesterday, paid by the city of Evreux.
>
> —M. Jules Roche, before 600 delegates from the region, gave a lecture in Vogüé, near Aubenas, on the principles of liberty.
>
> —In Brignoles, Mme S. . . . , who had recently given birth, killed herself yesterday by jumping out a window, during a bout of fever.
>
> (12 March 1906)

Each of these news items contains the germ of a "moralité" which would make the reader reflect, if the mirror were held by a hand such as F. F.'s. Here are two similar faits divers, *one* written up by Fénéon:

> —In Bordeaux, a woman named Marie Chiron killed her lover, who was deserting her, and poisoned herself. She is in serious condition.
>
> —Deserted by Delorce, Cécile Ward refused to take him back, unless he married her. He knifed her, finding that clause quite scandalous.

In 1960, Germaine Brée recognized Fénéon's "Three-Line Stories" as highly crafted pieces of fiction and published translations of several in her anthology, *Great French Short Stories.* The word *nouvelle* itself is ambiguous, suggesting a (long) short story as well as a piece of news. Many of Fénéon's three-liners could be expanded into novellas:

> —Fleeing Poissy and their families who opposed their love, Maurice L . . . and Gabrielle R . . . , 20 and 18 years old, reached Mers and killed themselves there.

The names of the hateful families will never be known, but "Gabrielle" and "Maurice" lived on for a time, at least in the thoughts of *Le Matin* readers.

The essential nature of faits divers, as Jean Paulhan pointed out, is their pointlessness, their absurdity: "They arouse mixed, unstable feelings in us. We can't foresee them; a certain admiral who lived the life of a fool, happens to die like Caesar. What should be a farce ends up as a tragedy: we learn of the existence of M. Dupont the day this fine man falls from a moving train or gets killed by his wife. That is surely the least

Félix and Fanny Fénéon with a niece. Around 1909. Courtesy Gina Doveil.

interesting event in M. Dupont's existence. (For we die of any little thing, but it is hard to live.)"[14]

Fénéon shaped these trivial events not into novels or Shakespearian dramas but into pithy lessons on life. His *Nouvelles* have been compared by Jean Paulhan and others to the maxims of La Rochefoucauld and Saint Evremond. We might therefore call him by the French term *moraliste,* "something different from a moralist," Will Moore has pointed out, ". . . not concerned with ethical issues only but with a picture of human behaviour which shall throw into relief its paradox, its complexity, in a word which shall suggest the irony of the human condition."[15]

> —Behind the coffin, Mangin, of Verdun, trudged along.
> That day, he did not reach the cemetery. On the way,
> death caught him unawares.

In this "news," Fénéon achieves surprise and suggestiveness through paradox and compression. The word order, the careful setting of the man in his hometown, even the commas, delay comprehension of the horrible truth, revealed only in the last word, *surprendre* (to surprise).

This metallic brevity, a hallmark of F. F., gives the words a deeper resonance. The form, the very shape of the statement, matters most. "For life," Oscar Wilde said, "is terribly deficient in form. Its catastrophes happen in the wrong way and to the wrong people. There is a grotesque horror about its comedies, and its tragedies seem to culminate in farce. One is always wounded when one approaches it."[16]

Fénéon shows the wound for what it is, and makes us laugh. At the same time the reader is forced to think what is often unthinkable. Between Fénéon's words and his meaning he has left a gap, something for the reader to decipher: not Truth, but a new angle on the truth, an unsettling angle that one would not normally have considered but for the teasing laughter.

It was in the temper of the times to recognize the absurd and confront the meaningless. With values fragmented, there was a new emphasis on the importance of random thoughts over and above reason, continuity, and logic. Yet, unlike "minimalists" today, sometimes accused of making "less of less" in stories whose main point appears to be their pointlessness,[17] Fénéon remains an activist—*terrorist/moralist*—whose moral point of view is clearly stated regarding any issue, whether it be *workers' rights:*

> —The May Day celebration at Lorient was noisy, but no
> act of violence served
> as a pretext for repression;

religious superstition:

> —A dishwasher in the city of Nancy, Vital Frérotte,
> after his return from Lourdes cured forever of
> tuberculosis, died Sunday by mistake;

civil liberties:

> —The Catholic Youth Association is meeting today in
> Béthune. A hundred gendarmes will prevent them from
> marching in a group;

or politics:

> —"If my candidate is beaten, I shall kill myself," M.
> Blanchard of Ploubalzanec kept saying before the
> election. He killed himself.

Fénéon differs from other moralists in one respect, said Jean Paulhan: "He enjoys himself."[18] Some stories are just for fun:

> —Frogs plucked by the storm from Belgian ponds
> rained like cats and dogs on the hottest
> streets in Dunkirk.
> —A stranger was found painting the walls of the
> Pantin cemetery in ocher, and Dujardin* was wandering
> naked in Saint-Ouen. Insanity, it seems.

*Not Edouard, the Symbolist.

Often, he penetrates the protective word to the point of revealing the ambiguities in all behavior:

> —Love. In Mirecourt, a weaver, Colas, planted a bullet in the head of Mlle Fleckenger, then treated himself with equal severity.

Whether he is simply amused, or indignant, or moved to compassion, the *presence* of the three-line terrorist is very much felt. Because of this, his friends and lovers treasured the three-line "fillers" that appeared daily in the *Matin* between May and November 1906; Camille Plattell carefully cut out and pasted them in a notebook that totaled 1,220 entries, subsequently published by Paulhan. Fanny Fénéon apparently kept a similar notebook. Fénéon wrote twenty at a throw on some days, on others simply one or two. The material came off the wire, or from provincial newspapers, telephone calls, and even letters from readers. As Eileen M. Baldeshwiler has pointed out in her study, "Félix Fénéon and the Minimal Story," F. F. created "simultaneously both a mirror and a critique of modern life" by placing his stories on an ordinary newspaper page: "In mass media, in the daily paper, he tapped a massive and absolutely pervasive mythic system which both writer and reader shared and which did not require Fénéon either to exhume Ulysses or invent a set of lunar cycles to explain the world."[19] Had he known he would one day be cited in the same breath with Yeats and Joyce, F. F. would have heartily objected: his *Nouvelles* were not at all the fruit of his imagination, but trivial events "stranger than fiction," recorded not for posterity but simply to divert the reader of the daily news. It is piquant, nonetheless, that among the variety of texts in his *Oeuvres plus que complètes,* many modern readers prefer these "ready-mades," infused with his own spirit.

Taken separately, Fénéon's *Nouvelles en trois lignes* are simply written renditions of nasty pieces of news. Multiplied and concentrated on the page, they create "an anti-world," Michel Décaudin points out, "that destroys the order of things by an all-pervasive subversion."[20] In a distilled, yet more quintessential form, they resemble the succinct political and social commentaries Fénéon had written in symbolist and anarchist journals in the 1880s and 1890s.

Fénéon soon called a halt to these journalistic feats and left the *Matin* to pursue his first love, painting. In November 1906 he wrote Henry van de Velde to say that the Bernheim brothers, owners of a well-established gallery on the boulevard de la Madeleine, had agreed to let him take charge of a section in their stores which would be devoted to contemporary art. He had been introduced to the owners of the gallery by Thadée Natanson and the painter Félix Vallotton, who had married into the Bernheim family. "I have just taken over my duties," Fénéon wrote van de Velde, "and in this locale where Bonnard, Denis, Roussel, Vuillard have already been recognized, I can introduce Théo [van Rysselberghe], Signac, Cross, Luce, Lucie Cousturier and some other good painters. The Bernheims and I have agreed to try out the experiment for just a few months; if the results are good, we will conclude a contract associating me with the commercial fortunes of their enterprise. The financial help you so kindly offered me for an independent gallery will not be necessary now."[21]

Close friends were astounded at Fénéon's entry into this bourgeois establishment. Signac wrote to Charles Angrand:

> You know the news, Fénéon has joined Monkey-nut Bernheim. I can't work up much enthusiasm about it; I don't see our friend winning out over the boorishness of those industrialists. But the struggle will be interesting. He is suggesting I have an exhibit in January. . . .

By the end of January, however, Signac was ecstatic, writing again to Angrand:

> Félix Fénéon and I were playing for high stakes and were not a little worried—he hiding his concern better than I, for that matter.
>
> But the success (!?!) was beyond our expectations. Every day, in spite of the bad weather, more people came than to any other exhibition at this gallery. The first day there was a crowd and Félix sold 11,000 francs worth (eleven thousand!)—canvases going for 30 to 2,500, watercolors for 250.
>
> Faced with such results, Bernheims-Fénéon, who had already bought 9 canvases and 20 watercolors, took three more of my paintings.[22]

Fénéon tried to do as well by all his friends. Luce confessed, writing to Angrend, "I have even made a deal with [the Bernheims], Signac too, as well as Cross. Fénéon is going to show each of us in turn. . ."[23]

Fénéon's gallery, along the side of the Bernheim-Jeune building, opened through a small door onto the picturesquely named rue Richepanse ("Richpaunch"—later spelled *Richepance,* apparently to hide its original meaning). There the anarchist, who now declared himself a Communist, sold fortunes worth of paintings and arranged contracts for Cross (1906), Signac (1907), Matisse (1908), van Dongen (1909), and many others so that they could paint without having to "hustle" their work, as artists of Pissarro's generation had been obliged to do. He added sculptures by Rodin and a newcomer, Maillol, and built up a stock of paintings by van Gogh, Cézanne, Lautrec, Seurat, *le douanier* Rousseau, Picasso, Utrillo, Modigliani, Raoul Dufy, and others.

He was a superlative agent, looking out for the interests both of the artists and the gallery. He wrote Charles Angrand, who was pathologically shy about showing and marketing his work:

> What became of the drawings you had at the Indépendants? I am asking in the event you might consent to leave them here in trust. If so, I would also ask you what would be your minimum price if we found a taker for them. Naturally, you will name a price big enough to leave a large margin for the cupidity of the merchant.[24]

"Matisse was particularly touchy about the terms of his contract," explained Gilbert Gruet, F. F.'s successor at the gallery, "and Fénéon took particular pains to make the written document conform to the painter's demands." Matisse was paid for his paintings when he left them at Bernheim-Jeune's and also received a commission when they were resold by the gallery. A clause specified that the artist had the latitude to review the contract yearly. Matisse, who stayed with the gallery for twenty-nine years, was presumably well satisfied. "I looked for Bonnard's contract," M. Gruet also said. "He was with the house for forty years. Well, I did not find it. There never was a [written] contract. Bonnard was Fénéon's friend, and it was enough for each man to give his word. Bernheim could take what he wanted from Bonnard's studio, and Bonnard could sell the other things elsewhere if he wished."[25]

Sometimes the Bernheims objected to a work Fénéon had accepted for the gallery; so he would buy it himself, and apologize to Fanny, "I simply couldn't resist it. . . ." His fabulous collection of paintings grew apace. Along with masterpieces, it also contained works not listed in the auction catalogues after his death, works he had bought to help someone out and which the appraiser/auctioneer feared would diminish the worth of the "known values."

There is conflicting evidence concerning Fénéon's earnings at the gallery. Several close friends—Georges Besson, for example—said he took no commission and had a fixed salary of 500 francs a month, later raised to 1,000. Solange Lemaître confirmed this latter figure, and said Fénéon frequently gave half of it to a family in need.[26] On the other hand, a letter Fénéon wrote to Josse and Gaston Bernheim in 1912 gives proof that he did earn a commission and looked after the details of his own contract as conscientiously as he did the contracts of artists whose work he sold. The exact percentage of his commission is not known, but he apparently averaged about 15,000 a year after his first five years at Bernheim-Jeune. This increased in 1912, so that the 15,000 became a minimum with a drawing account of 19,000, and the obvious expectation that his commission would prove to be greater at the annual settlement. If he earned over 19,000, the excess was to be put in a reserve account for a "lean" year.[27]

He continued to live modestly in spite of this turn in his fortunes. His friends could not have learned from him how much he earned, for he never discussed money. Fanny, however, was more outspoken, and she was known to complain that Bernheim-Jeune did not pay him what he was worth. Perhaps Fénéon misled his wife as to his earnings, telling her that it was simply 1,000 a month, so as not to arouse possible desires on her part for a more elegant lifestyle. She was not deprived, however, for Fénéon saw that she had money of her own to invest, and later on a visitor to their summer home near Courlay found her happily working in the garden with diamonds on her fingers. No doubt F. F. also maintained his accustomed secrecy in order to share his new income with those in need. In this he was so successful that the gallery posted a guard outside his office for fear that their prize employee would be interrupted all day long by the stream of acquaintances coming to him for help.

From the start, Fénéon built an international clientele for the gallery, working through personal contacts and those of his artist friends. While his style led people to believe that he was lethargic, he was constantly on the move. A junior member of the Bernheim-Jeune firm later explained:

> Quite often, Fénéon traveled on behalf of the Gallery, in particular to England, Germany, and Scandinavia. Every time a transaction appeared to be in difficulty, he went on the road. His prudence and tact made him report back to us every day about his negotiations, which were facilitated by his personal charm and prestige. His

> success resided in letting people believe he was not a "businessman"—which was not the case at all.
>
> Sometimes he traveled not for business but to organize big exhibitions. Fénéon went out to open negotiations, and then once the thing was under way, quietly withdrew, letting the bosses collect the compliments and laurels—for which he had no use.[28]

Once again, F. F. merged letters and art, creating a "Bulletin" of news concerning writers and painters which he began publishing in the back of Bernheim-Jeune exhibition catalogues in 1914. Apollinaire, now an avant-garde art critic himself, hailed the venture and the "modern sound" of *bulletin.* "The false-Yankee of rue Richepance," he said, "that laconic writer who invented, so to speak, in his immortal three-line-stories for the *Matin,* the *mots en liberté* that the Futurists have adopted . . . . is combining his gifts as an art writer and reporter."[29]

Something—most likely the war—interrupted publication of Fénéon's bulletins. But in 1919, Fénéon started up a more ambitious version, the bimonthly illustrated *Bulletin de la vie artistique,* which lasted seven years, or, as F. F. pointed out in its last issue, from the death of Renoir (December 1919) to that of Claude Monet (December 1926). In the meantime, Fénéon created Editions Bernheim-Jeune, publishing books and albums on the gallery's artists, with top-notch texts, such as the one by Gustave Kahn on Seurat's drawings.

Friends who came to see Fénéon at Bernheim-Jeune's observed with amusement the salesman at work. He treated the potential buyers with cool disdain, placing the paintings before them without any comment, or leaving the room while they were contemplating a choice. If questioned, he replied in urbane monosyllables. When a customer queried, "What is *that?*", pointing a finger at a torso with wide-spread thighs sculpted by Rodin, Fénéon responded, "That is a lady, Madame." Once an adolescent from the Bernheim family fell into a trance in front of a Modigliani nude; F. F. came up and said, "How do you like those big shameless girls?" He broke the strictures of middle-class gravity by organizing an exhibition called "Fauna," purportedly to please animal lovers. Included were some pickled herring by van Gogh, and in a landscape by Théo van Rysselberghe, a double comma in the sky: a swallow. There was even a pastel of a nude in a tub by Manet. "Why?" someone inquired. "The sponge," explained F. F.[30]

Business boomed at Bernheim-Jeune's in spite of—or because of—Fénéon's impertinence. Clients trusted a man to whom it mattered more to love a painting than to sell it. He would not cheat them, or himself, they knew, because the center of his concern was the work of art itself. Matisse once told a revealing anecdote: "I had just convinced a couple who were interested in my painting to go with me to the Bernheim-Jeune Gallery where our Félix was working—the famous salesman and expert on modern art. . . . I introduced my companions to him; he had the office boy show my latest paintings, and just as the husband seemed to have made up his mind to buy certain ones, Fénéon, who up to that moment had kept his peace, raises his voice and strongly advises them not to buy, saying that it would be better to wait for some new

Direttore:
F. T. Marinetti

Milano
Via Senato, 2
Telefono: 40-81

Mon très cher Félix Fénéon,

Vous avez peut-être appris par les journaux que je viens d'être condamné à deux mois et demi de prison, avec sursis, dans un procès violent et inique contre le Futurisme. Mon roman n'a été qu'un prétexte; c'est le mouvement futuriste que l'ingénuité hargneuse des passéistes voudrait frapper mortellement.

Comme il fallait s'y attendre, cela a tourné à notre faveur. Le martyrologe futuriste commence, et la presse italienne, devenue en grande partie favorable à notre mouvement nous peint déjà avec de vagues couleurs de victimes héroïques.

Il faut néanmoins que *Mafarka* triomphe devant la Cour de Cassation. Je vais de ce pas à Rome, pour m'occuper de la chose. D'où un petit retard quant à mon retour à Paris.

J'y serai néanmoins dans la première quinzaine de février, et je viendrai immédiatement chez Bernheim Jeune pour conclure définitivement le contrat de l'Exposition futuriste.

Mes amis les peintres futuristes, qui vous connaissaient et vous admiraient depuis votre admirable et puissante *Revue Blanche*, sont enchantés d'exposer à Paris leurs oeuvres, sous votre patronnage intellectuel.

En attendant le plaisir de vous revoir, agréez mon très cher ami, une chaleureuse poignée de main de votre admirateur et ami

F. T. Marinetti

AMEDEO MODIGLIANI. ***Nude with Coral Necklace.*** 1917. Oil on canvas, 64.4 x 94.4 cm. Formerly Félix Fénéon. Allen Memorial Art Museum, Oberlin College, Oberlin, Ohio. Gift of Mr. and Mrs. Joseph Bissett.

work of mine. Well, after my two art-lovers had gone, I couldn't help telling him how astonished I was at how he had acted.

"'But, my dear friend,' he replied, 'You surely did not want your beautiful compositions to go live with those stuffy people!'

"I could hardly bear him a grudge for that," concluded Matisse. "His remarks always caught one off guard, disarmingly droll and logical. Needless to say, those fine folk that I had so diligently buttered up never bought a thing of mine: they became collectors of eighteenth-century stuff!"[31]

F. F. became something of a legend in the Bernheim family, whose many children were fascinated by the man—and his name.

> My brother, my cousins and I were convinced that *fainéant* ("do-nothing") or *Fénéon* meant the same thing . . . and this little in-joke had perhaps more truth to it than we knew.
>
> His reputation for nonchalance made him into a sort of divinity for us; he

Opposite, ***F. T. Marinetti to Félix Fénéon,*** [January 1912], saying that he had just been given a suspended prison sentence in a trial "against futurism" (because of his novel, *Mafarka*); and that he would be coming to Paris to finalize the contract for the Italian Futurist art exhibition that Fénéon was organizing at the Bernheim-Jeune Galleries, [opening 5 February 1912]. Paris, Paulhan archives.

> embodied *fainéantise* (laziness), the source of his very name, the mark of a monopoly, indeed a kind of royalty. [The children would have learned in school about the ineffectual Merovingian kings, *les rois fainéants*.]
>
> Fé-né-on! His lazy, warm voice, with timid tics and hiccoughs, exuding ennui, was for us the proof that he was the epitome of idleness.[32]

The picture of F. F. the Idler was not the least of the many paradoxes Fénéon created around himself. He worked for more than a quarter of a century for the Bernheim firm, forged their fame and a good part of their fortune, but was considered something of a lazybones who had to be coaxed into coming to the office by being fetched in a taxi.

One day in 1924 he said to the Bernheims: "I am ripe for the idle life." He was sixty-three. So he retired (or rather, pretended to retire). Friends wanted to re-edit his *Impressionnistes en 1886*. He said no. An editor asked for his mémoirs. He said no. Someone pleaded for a collection of his "Nouvelles en trois lignes." This time he said no in anger: "Je n'aspire qu'au silence."

What sort of silence could he aspire to, this man who had been so important to so many people?

"In the days when I could be impartial," he said to Paulhan, "protected by my unimportance, the 'friends of So-and-So', and So-and-So himself, whoever he was, seemed comical to me."[33] His yearning for silence, for obscurity, came from his insatiable need to be himself, simply, and his will to relate to other people simply as they were.

This desire for simplicity, in such a complex man, baffles the onlooker. The play of contradiction seems so extreme: curious how this man who was so opposed to "bombast" was not opposed to throwing bombs.

It would be easier to stop, as those who knew him did, with the word, Enigma.

> Such an enigmatic individual, who always seemed to be mocking others. A triumphant use of irony, coupled with an infinite goodness. . . . An enormous disdain for everything . . . and great indulgence. I still wonder . . . what he thought of humanity![34]

Thus wrote a member of the Bernheim family. Thadée Natanson, who also knew Fénéon for years, gave a talk about him on the radio, and concluded:

> At bottom, it is quite possible that my friend Félix Fénéon, choosing the most intimate of all intellectual pleasures and drawing nothing but food for his imagination from his sensuality, was only putting on an act—for himself more than anyone else—from dawn till dark: the most entertaining, charming, varied, and subtle of acts.[35]

Both of these portraits, though focusing on the enigma Fénéon posed, are inadequate. The inadequacy stems from the portraitists' own feelings of vulnerability. Each was, in everyday terms, Fénéon's boss, yet felt threatened by the obvious superiority of the man. "I still wonder . . . what he thought of humanity" (that is, of me). Though they fall short of the mark, both reveal the richness of F. F.'s personality. Fénéon's style, his way of being, created a distance, a "dissonance," which forbade entrance to some, as Nietzsche would have said, while inviting others in.[36]

ANDRÉ ROUVEYRE. ***Fénéon.*** ca. 1910. Ink drawing, reprinted from *Visages des contemporarains,* Paris, *Mercure de France* [1913].

What seems enigmatic, dissonant, or contradictory represents an energy central to his character. For instance, he was normally scrupulous as to such things as rights of authorship and identity, yet his anarchism left him with a certain scorn for property rights. Some of his later writings, the 1920 preface to Duranty's *La Cause du beau Guillaume,* for example, are simply copies of his earlier work or possibly even plagerized.[37]

There will always be many unanswered questions about F. F. Much about him perplexes even the closest observer. A writer who knew him well remembered his saying: "To reveal your innermost thoughts to someone else is an act of indiscretion." Emile Compard, who was present, commented, "His reticence came, I believe, from his respect for the other one's liberty."[38]

Along with unusual freedom and joy, there is an underlying sense of disillusionment in Fénéon. The causes of this can only be complex. One thinks, however, of the

EMILE COMPARD. *F. F. in 1926.* Ink wash drawing.

untimely deaths of Seurat and Laforgue, and also of the reasons that led Fénéon to prison. "He suffered," Solange Lemaître remarked, "from the wretched disparities among human beings, the rich. the poor, the brilliant, the stupid."[39] He hated to seem superior, and this may be one of the reasons for his silence and hesitations in speech. No false pride, however, prevented him from formulating razor-edged comments—to which he was also sensitive. When asked once if he had known Degas, he replied, "Not very well, I did not care to get myself cut by a tongue like his"—whereas Degas reportedly lived in fear of Fénéon's jibes![40]

Even as Fénéon achieved recognition as the creator of a new style of criticism, he seems to have decided that while he could reflect, refract the work of others in the prism of his mind, he would not, himself, create. Remy de Gourmont said of Fénéon in 1898:

> I think there are some minds satisfied as soon as they have discovered their own value; one proof is enough. Just so, some men, after proving their virility, abandon a game that for them was just a test of their own valor.[41]

Fénéon's Shadow. Photograph taken at the Fénéons' summer home, "Villa Ubu," near Royan (Charente-Maritime), ca. 1934. Courtesy André Berne-Joffroy.

Was Fénéon satisfied? By the age of twenty-five he had established the "value" of his critical writing. Earlier, he had tried writing fiction and apparently proved to his own satisfaction that he lacked that sort of talent. Surely, he "suffered from the demon, writing," one of his admirers said. He himself admitted that writing was not easy, and he took Mallarmé as his model. Cracking the shells of old formulae, he shaped new cadences, then dropped "symbolist" language when it threatened to coagulate into clichés. Adopting a newspaperman's style, he approached the "degree zero" of writing

Félix Fénéon at Age 81. Writing to a friend. Fénéon remarked: "This quatrain [of Apollinaire] concerns me":

Dans vos viviers, dans vos étangs,
Carpes, que vous vivez longtemps!
Est-ce que la mort vous oublie,
Poissons de la mélancolie?

(In your holding tanks and ponds, how long you live, O carps! Does death forget you, O fish of melancholy?) Photograph courtesy Henri d'Amfreville.

that Roland Barthes would later delineate. Never long-winded, he became progressively briefer, and never sustained any mode for long.

He was content to be a conduit for others' thoughts, a mediator, an interpreter. This interpretive writing eventually bored or fatigued him, and he chose to put forth the work of others in a more simple and direct way: editing and publishing manuscripts, selling paintings. Can this preference be taken as real, not imposed by an *échec,* or "drying-up" of talent? Hidden in Jarry's definition of Fénéon, "Celui qui silence," is the pun "s'y lance" = "Who throws himself into"—life, one necessarily concludes.

He refused, or was refused by his temperament, the commitment it takes to be an artist. His "silence" contains both a problem and the resolution of the problem. He surely aspired to creative work; his love of beauty alone assures us of that. He was also idealistic in his hopes for humanity. But strong ideals and a sense of beauty are not enough. He felt very keenly that one must have something unique to say. And his

HENRY D'AMFREVILLE. ***Death Mask of Félix Fénéon.*** Pencil drawing, 28 x 22 cm. 29 February 1944. "He kept the dandy's cult of impassivity until the end, stoically enduring the pain of a terrible illness [cancer]. His face at death was unrecognizable." (André Berne-Joffroy, "F. F.," *Confluences.* 44:33 (July 1944).

idealism was tempered with a deep pessimism, or rather, lucidity about the nature of humanity. Creating means making choices; as Paulhan said about F. F., there were many works in him, any one of which would have been valid, if it had not been annulled and contradicted by the others.[42] Any one of those choices would also have revealed his inner self—private things, however masked. To put himself on the line. Expose himself, before an ignorant, uncaring public. That is what Seurat did. Surely Fénéon did not envy that agony. He took the "I" out of his own writing altogether. This discretion can not be attributed entirely to the dandy's ideal of detachment.

He was an elitist, yet his commitment to proletarian interests was central to his life. How could he live in a growing industrial nation, one committed to capitalism and bourgeois values, without despairing, as Camus said, or renouncing his own values? With exquisite urbanity, never to compromise—*that* was the "act" he put on which intrigued or troubled his contemporaries. Never to identify with bourgeois society, but to say, "*Their* love-affairs, *their* Chamber of Deputies, *their* business affairs."[43] In 1923, a young writer rather naively asked him if he should let his work be affected by changes in contemporary society. "After a moment of silence, [Fénéon]

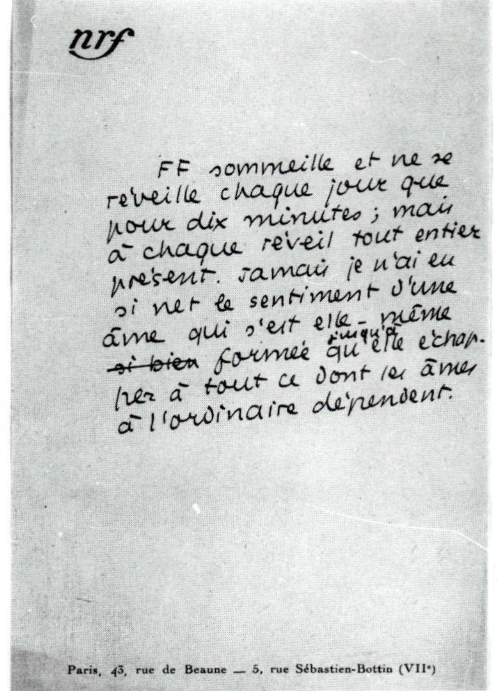

nrf

FF sommeille et ne se réveille chaque jour que pour dix minutes ; mais à chaque réveil tout entier présent. Jamais je n'ai eu si net le sentiment d'une âme qui s'est elle-même ~~si bien~~ jusqu'à formée qu'elle échappe à tout ce dont les âmes à l'ordinaire dépendent.

Paris, 43, rue de Beaune — 5, rue Sébastien-Bottin (VIIe)

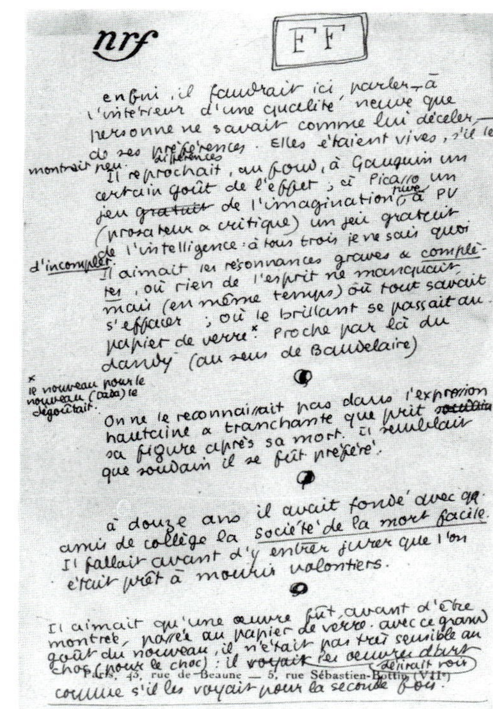

nrf

FF

enfin, il faudrait ici parler — à l'intérieur d'une qualité neuve que personne ne savait comme lui déceler — de ses préférences différences. Elles étaient vives, s'il les montrait peu.

Il reprochait, au fond, à Gauguin un certain goût de l'effet ; à Picasso un jeu ~~gratuit~~ de l'imagination pure ; à PV (prosateur & critique) un jeu gratuit de l'intelligence : à tous trois je ne sais quoi d'incomplet.

Il aimait les résonances graves & complètes, où rien de l'esprit ne manquait, mais (en même temps) où tout savait s'effacer ; où le brillant se passait au papier de verre.* Proche par là du dandy (au sens de Baudelaire)

* le nouveau pour le nouveau (Dada) le dégoûtait.

On ne le reconnaissait pas dans l'expression hautaine & tranchante que prit sa figure après sa mort. Il semblait que soudain il se fût préféré.

à douze ans il avait fondé avec un ami de collège la Société de la mort facile. Il fallait avant d'y entrer jurer que l'on était prêt à mourir volontiers.

Il aimait qu'une œuvre fût, avant d'être montrée, passée au papier de verre. avec ce grand goût du nouveau, il n'était pas très sensible au choc (pour le choc) : il ~~voyait~~ désirait voir les œuvres d'art comme s'il les voyait pour la seconde fois.

JEAN PAULHAN. ***Notes on F. F.,*** written at Fénéon's death. Paris, Paulhan archives. An extract from the note on the left: ". . . Never have I had so clear a feeling of a soul that has formed itself so completely that it escapes from everything on which souls normally depend."

went to look for a literary review, and found it, opened it, flipped through it nonchalantly and finally said: 'Here is Paul Valéry's answer to your question. . . . *The importance of the social factor is so great that it determines the value of the work of art.* No doubt he could have written, *modifies,* or, if you will, *influences.* Nonetheless, he wrote *determines.*' "[44] Typically, Fénéon reveals his innermost thought by quoting another's strong words.

Fénéon was one of those rare persons of genius content to remain in the shadow of others. Yet his role was so essential that if one were to remove him now from the history of French letters and art at the turn of the century, "the whole construction would come tumbling down," as the critic Hubert Juin has said.[45] Directly or indirectly, he shaped the taste—the values—of his and succeeding generations. He formulated a poetics—in a broad sense—for painting and writing in the post-impressionist era. And he lived a personal ethic/aesthetic that informed his critical judgment and his commitment to others—both artists and workers.

"But a man, even the greatest of all," wrote Fénéon at age sixty, "will always remain inferior to the formidable task created by each day as it passes, generating new thoughts and inclinations."[46] Because of his nineteenth-century gentility and his lifelong commitment to the artists he loved in his youth, F. F. has been characterized by his earlier biographer, Françoise Cachin, as démodé, "A man turned toward the past . . . above all a man of the past."[47] My reading of his life and his writings finds a man extraordinarily in and of the present. And I like to think that the contradiction in interpretation between his first biographer and this one would have amused him.

Notes

F Abbreviation for Félix Fénéon, *Oeuvres plus que complètes,* 2 vols., Joan U. Halperin, ed., Geneva: Droz, 1970.

Preface

1. *IIe Livre des Masques,* pp. 40 and 43.
2. "Master of postcards."

Preview

1. The Foyot restaurant was bombed on 4 April 1894. There were no fatalities; v. Jean Maîtron, *Le Syndicalisme révolutionnaire,* ch. 3: "La Bombe du restaurant Foyot"; Georges Blond, *La Grande armée du drapeau noir,* p. 234; Marius Boisson, *Les Attentats anarchistes,* pp. 156–57; André Salmon. *La Terreur noire, pp. 356–57;* André Billy, *L'Epoque 1900,* p. 435; Ernest Raynaud, *En marge de la mêlée symboliste* (Paris, 1936), pp. 130–31.

The attribution of the Foyot bomb to Fénéon is based on an accumulation of evidence; in particular, André Salmon's statement, passed on to the author, that Kaya Cohen (Alexander Cohen's wife) had said Fénéon disclosed his role in the bombing to the Cohens in his later years. This is consistent with Salmon's written description of the Foyot bomber: "a subtle man of letters." Jean Paulhan spoke with me about Fénéon's well-veiled commitment to propaganda by deed. And Fénéon's participation in a bombing is the most reasonable explanation for his possession of a box of detonators (evidence held against him in the Trial of the Thirty). How he managed to distract his accusers will be shown in chapter 14. In the absence, however, of a formal accusation for this crime or a confession in his own hand, fairness to Fénéon's memory requires that doubts as to his role in the bombing be recognized. André Berne-Joffroy has commented to the author that he believes such an act would have been completely out of character for the man he knew; and other close friends of Fénéon—Mallarmé most notably—felt the same way. In chapter 1, I show how difficult it was, even for those who knew and loved him best, to perceive the multiple, apparently conflicting personas of this man.

2. *Pensiero e Volontà,* 16 May 1925, in *Errico Malatesta, His Life & Ideas,* p. 19.

CHAPTER 1: *Burning the Effigy*

1. John Rewald, "Félix Fénéon," p. 55.

2. Jean Paulhan, *F. F. ou le critique,* p. 19.

3. Mallarmé quoted in "Arrestation d'un employé du ministére de la guerre: chez Paul Verlaine; chez M. Mallarmé," *Le Soir,* 27 April 1894.

4. Remy de Gourmont, *IIe Livre des Masques,* p. 41.

5. Paul Valéry quoted by Solange Lemaître, interview with the author, 17 Dec. 1962.

6. Paulhan, *F. F. ou le critique,* pp. 71–75.

7. Maria van Rysselberghe, under the name, M. Saint-Clair, *Galerie privée,* p. 64.

8. Emile Compard, interview with the author, 3 March 1963.

9. F, 617. "Jules Christophe. . ." *Hommes d'aujourd'hui,* no. 308 [1887].

10. Fénéon quoted by Girardet, *Ceux que j'ai connus.* p. 181.

11. John Gray to Fénéon [ca. July 1890], Paulhan archives, Paris. Fénéon's later self-portrait of his head on a hook was published in *L'Esprit français,* 4 July 1930, with the caption, "Félix Fénéon seen by himself (Portrait made at the War Office at the time of the Trial of the Thirty)." He actually was in prison before and during the trial.

12. Dauberville, *Bataille de l'impressionnisme,* pp. 151–52.

13. Paul Adam, "FENEON," *Petit bottin des lettres et des arts* (Paris, 1886), p. 45.

14. J.-H. Rosny aîné, *Torches et lumignons,* pp. 262–63.

15. *Crime and Punishment* was translated into French in 1885, and Fénéon immediately wrote a review of it (see F, 568–71). One might imagine other allusions in the pseudonym of Porphyre, to the iconoclast philosopher, for example, or the volcanic rock. But Willy, who knew Fénéon well, once called him, "This examining magistrate" (*ce juge d'instruction; Lettres de l'ouvreuse,* p. 310).

16. *Crime and Punishment,* Constance Garnett, trans. (London, 1914), p. 300.

17. F, 151. "Cercle de l'union artistique," *Revue indépendante,* May 1889. For an explanation of these mathematics, see chap. 7, p. 124. After this article appeared, Willy addressed F. F. with the algebraic form, "My dear polynomial."

18. "Elie Manéon" and "Ottocar Phellion" appeared under articles in *Art et Critique* in 1890. F. F. signed "Outagawafénéon" in a letter to Gustave Kahn [1890], Dr. Karpman-Boutet archives, Paris.

19. Willy to Fénéon, 25 May 1891, Paulham archives, Paris.

20. André Breton to Jean Paulhan, 16 July 1949, Paulhan archives, Paris. The letter continues: "What power of expression this book reveals! [that is, Paulhan's edition of Fénéon] As concerns painting, he is really the only one to have understood *everything*—well beyond Huysmans and even Baudelaire."

21. Fénéon to Solange Lemaître, 4 October [ca. 1930]. Communicated to the author by Madame Lemaître.

22. Jourdain, "Du Côté de *la Revue blanche,*" p. 166.

23. Maria van Rysselberghe, pseud. M. Saint-Clair (a friend, not a lover), *Galerie privée,* pp. 74–75.

24. F. F. to Paul Signac, 28 Sept. 1932. Remark while reading Stendhal's *Souvenirs d'égotisme,* 28 Sept. 1932, Cachin-Signac archives, Paris.

25. Francis de Miomandre, "Vingt ans après," pp. 51–52.

26. Henri de Régnier quoted by Edmond de Goncourt, *Journal,* entry on 13 May 1894.

27. Georges Besson, "En Souvenir du très singulier Félix Fénéon."

28. René Tavernier. "Félix Fénéon mon ami," p. 118.

29. F. M. [François Michel, adoptive "son" of Fénéon] to Bernard Groethuysen, 28 Jan. 1944, Paulhan archives, Paris.

30. René Tavernier, "Félix Fénéon mon ami."

31. Verhaeren quoted by van Rysselberghe, *Galerie privée,* p. 66.

32. Fénéon quoted by Joseph Jolinon, "Fénéon ou l'intelligence faite homme," *Nouvelles littéraires,* 6 May 1965. In 1892, Aristide Bruant was earning 5,000 francs a month at the café-concert Les Ambassadeurs. Two years later he was living in leisure in a château he had bought. In 1889, Seurat answered an inquiry concerning his painting, *Les Poseuses:* "I am hard put to name a price. I count one year's expenses at 7

francs a day, so you can see where that puts me. It boils down to this: the interested person can pay the difference between his price and mine." (Seurat to Octave Maus, 17 Feb. 1889, quoted by Maus, *Trente années de lutte pour l'art,* 1926, p. 87.) The painting thus would have cost well under half Bruant's monthly salary. It was not sold.

33. Solange Lemaître, interview with the author, 17 Dec. 1962.

34. Oscar Wilde, "The Critic as Artist" (1890), *Complete Works,* p. 1058.

35. René Tavernier, "Félix Fénéon mon ami."

36. Baudelaire, "Le Dandy," *The Painter of Modern Life,* p. 27.

37. Ibid. Italics Baudelaire's.

38. Ibid. p. 29.

39. G. Brummel quoted in Moers, *The Dandy, Brummel to Beerbohm* p. 18.

40. The art dealer Jacques Rodrigues-Henriques, with whom Fénéon worked for many years, said, "He had no pride; or so much one couldn't see it" (interview, 14 March 1963).

41. F, 844. "Le Pica," *La Cravache,* 14 July 1888, on the Italian critic Vittorio Pica.

42. J. Paulhan, *F. F. ou le critique,* pp. 67–68.

43. "Hombre" signature to "Patrie," a critique of chauvinism published in Fénéon's *Revue indépendante,* Sept. 1884, omitted in error from *Oeuvres plus que complètes.* Russian anarchists of the nineteenth century sometimes used the signature "man" (see "Chouettes Bouquins," *Père peinard,* 5 April 1891, no. 107, p. 7).

44. "Cher Homme," Arthur Cravan to F. Fénéon, Tossa [Barcelona], 27 Sept. 1916, letter published in A. Cravan . . . , *Trois suicidés de la société* (Paris, 1974), pp. 183–85.

45. René Tavernier, "Félix Fénéon mon ami."

46. O. Wilde, "The Critic as Artist," *Complete Works,* p. 1053.

CHAPTER 2: *Genesis of an Anarchist*

1. Baptismal names recorded (in Italian) in the parish of San Massimo, formerly Borgo Nuovo, register 325, 13 Oct. 1861.

2. Fénéon family tree, courtesy of Michel Berger-Fénéon, Lyons.

3. Reported by Jean Paulhan (conversation, 10 July 1962). Another Jules Fénéon, member of a different branch of the family, published a pamphlet, *Les Parasites de la revanche* (Paris, 1871–72), written in the backwash of exasperated patriotism and municipal pride after the siege of Paris and the repression of the Commune. He was formerly a councilman of Orléansville in Algeria and probably had no contact with the father of Félix.

4. Marginal notes by F. F. on a clipping from the *Journal des Débats,* 27 April 1894, in a dossier kept by Marie-Louise Fénéon and now at the Bibliothèque littéraire Jacques Doucet, Paris.

5. Description of F. F.'s parents in *Le Jour,* 28 April 1894.

6. Note from Cluny concerning the student Félix Fénéon in 1876, courtesy of Michel Berger-Fénéon, Lyons.

7. Incident concerning the lycée's brass band, *L'Autunois,* 6 July 1879.

8. F, 885–86, "L'Education spiritualiste," signed with a star, *Revue indépendante,* June 1884.

9. For *lycée* architecture, see Danièle Granet, "L'Ecole qui n'est plus l'école," *L'Express,* 12 April 1976, p. 58.

10. F. F. at school, Fabre des Essarts, "Un Aquitté."

11. P.-J. Proudhon, from *Amour et mariage,* 1876, reprinted in *La Femme au 19e siècle,* Nicole Priollaud ed., p. 240.

12. Georges Besson, "En souvenir du très singulier Félix Fénéon." F, 103–4, "7e Exposition annuelle des Femmes peintres et sculpteurs," *Revue indépendante,* March 1888.

13. Jules Laforgue, posthumous "Notes," published by Fénéon in the *Revue anarchiste,* 1 Nov. 1893, pp. 65 and 68.

14. Courbet, founder of realism in painting, was elected a member of the Commune. Subsequently he was accused of having given the order to pull down the Vendôme column (symbol of Napoleonic

imperialism). Henri Rochefort, a radical journalist of aristocratic origins, approved of the Commune while not actively participating in it. Jules Méline, Commune sympathizer of peasant stock, was destined to a political career in the Third Republic and became known for his stubborn resistance to change. Clemenceau, who saw himself as a partisan of justice for all, retained bitter memories of the Commune (see *Sur la démocratie* [Paris, 1930], p. 17). Interestingly, twenty-three years later, both Clemenceau and Rochefort (who reentered France after the 1880 amnesty) wrote articles supporting F. F. when he was tried for anarchism. Rochefort was exactly thirty years older than Fénéon, and Clemenceau twenty years older.

15. Ajalbert, *Mémoires en vrac au temps du symbolisme,* pp. 26 and 43.

16. Anatole France quoted by Ajalbert, ibid., p. 119.

17. Bourget, *Nouveaux essais de psychologie contemporaine,* p. vi. Fénéon reviewed this book and said that the essays themselves were not outstanding but that the preface, quoted here, was quite logical (F, 666).

18. Letter attributed to Rimbaud by Jules Mouquet, dated "Versailles, 9 September 1871," published in the *Nord-Est,* 16 Sept. 1871. See Rimbaud, *Oeuvres* (Paris: Garnier, 1960), pp. 137–41.

19. F. F.'s *Société de la mort facile* in notes on Fénéon by Jean Paulhan, Paulhan archives, Paris.

20. Fénéon's "Enquête sur la Commune," *Revue blanche* 12(1897): 249–305 and 356–88, illustrated by Manet, Maximilien Luce, Félix Vallotton, and Walter Crane.

21. F. F. and the Popular Front, information given to the author by the Paris Prefecture of Police, July 1967.

22. "Médaillon: Félix Fénéon," *Le Décadent,* 25 Sept. 1886, reprinted in F, p. v.

23. Fénéon to Paul Signac, Paris, 5 Sept. [1932?], Cachin-Signac archives, Paris. Signac, like F. F., was a Stendhal enthusiast and published an unsigned *Aide-mémoire Stendhal-Beyle* in 1914 (Antibes).

24. Remark by Emile Compard, interview, 5 March 1963.

25. Note by M. Lallemant in Fénéon's dossier at the War Office, quoted by Jean Paulhan, *F. F. ou le critique,* pp. 23–24.

26. *Echo de Paris,* 27 April 1894.

27. F, 892–93. "Hourras, tollés et rires maigres," *L'Endehors,* 24 January 1892.

28. Ibid., 7 Feb. 1892. F, 894.

29. Map in Fabre des Essarts, *Dupleix et l'Inde française* (Paris, 1883), p. 125.

30. Fabre des Essarts, "Un Aquitté."

31. J.-K. Huysmans, "Préface, écrite vingt ans aprés le roman" to *A Rebours,* edition of 1903.

32. See Eugenia W. Herbert, *The Artist and Social Reform,* ch. 2.

33. "Inédits de Laforgue," notes written ca. 1885, published by F. F. in the *Revue blanche,* 15 April 1896, pp. 371–74 and *Entretiens,* Jan. 1891, p. 10. Translation taken in part from William Jay Smith, *Selected Writings of Jules Laforgue* (New York, 1956), p. 203.

34. Régnier and Adam to Fénéon, note on a War Ministry form in Paulhan archives, Paris.

CHAPTER 3: *Young Editor and Critic*

1. Fénéon to Nadar [Félix Tournachon], Paris, Papiers Nadar XI, Bibliothèque Nationale, n.a.fr. 24996, no. 89–90.

2. *La Muselée,* F, 517. *Libre revue* 1, no. 6 (16 Dec. 1883), inside cover page, "Pour paraître prochainement."

3. F, 635. "Livres," *Libre revue,* 16 Feb. 1883.

4. F, 5–6. "Exposition nationale des Beaux-Arts," *Libre revue,* 1 Oct. 1883.

5. "Le compagnon Fénéon," p. 13.

6. F, 7. "Exposition nationale."

7. F, 44. *Les Impressionnistes en 1886,* "IIe Exposition de la Société des Artistes indépendants."

8. F, 6. "Exposition nationale." Millet's death in 1875 rekindled public interest in his work. In March 1881 the *Angélus* was sold at auction in Paris for 160 thousand francs. Fénéon, who took up his position at the War Office that same month, most probably witnessed the event. Two months later the Hartmann collection of Millet's work was sold, offering the chance to see some of the painter's most carefully conceived canvases.

9. Baudelaire on Millet, "The Salon of 1859," p. 281. J.-K. Huysmans, "L'Exposition de Millet," *Revue indépendante,* July 1887, pp. 42–47.

10. Fénéon on Puvis, F, 8. "Exposition nationale."

11. *Mes souvenirs du symbolisme,* p. 98.

12. Emile Verhaeren to Joseph Nève, 1880, in Verhaeren, *Sensations,* p. 222.

13. Huysmans on Puvis, *L'Art moderne,* p. 13, and "Salon de 1887," *Revue indépendante,* June 1887, p. 346.

14. For an explanation of "optical mixture," see chap. 5.

15. F, 20. "A l'Exposition d'Edouard Manet," *Libre revue,* 16. Jan. 1883.

16. F, 15–16. "Exposition des oeuvres de C. A. Sellier," *Libre Revue,* 16 Dec. 1883.

17. F, 18. "L'Art du xviiie siècle," *Libre revue,* 1 Jan. 1884.

18. F, 9. "Exposition nationale." Gambetta, perhaps the most dedicated architect of the Third Republic, was accepted by neither the Opportunists nor the Radicals. Briefly Premier in 1881, he died in 1882, at age forty-four, under circumstances never fully explained.

19. Fénéon to J. E. S. Jeanès, 11 Jan. 1944, Paulhan archives, Paris.

20. Huysmans to Fénéon, n. d., Houghton Library autograph file A.L.s., Cambridge, Mass.

21. "Matérialisme," *Revue indépendante,* May 1884, p. 2. Unsigned article, presumably written by both Georges Chevrier and Fénéon, not included in *Oeuvres plus que complètes.*

22. Fénéon quoted by his physician, Dr. Lesavoureux, in an interview with the author, Vallée aux Loups, 19 July 1963.

23. F, 887. "L'Education spiritualiste," signed with a star, *Revue indépendante,* June 1884. Fénéon was responding, in part, to Jules Ferry's secular education program, and in particular to Article Seven of the Ministry of Education's proposed reform, which transformed the clergy into state employees on the condition that they sign a loyalty oath to the Republic. Fénéon labeled this a totally false reform and called for a complete separation of church and state, the abrogation of the Concordat and the "dechristianization" of schools.

24. "Patrie," signed "Hombre," *Revue indépendante,* Sept. 1884, p. 400 and 412. Not included in *Oeuvres plus que complètes* (soon to be retitled The More or Less Complete Works . . .).

25. "Programme pratique," *Revue indépendante,* March 1885, pp. 361–71. Signed *la Rédaction* (the editors), not in *Oeuvres plus que complètes.* It is assumed Fénéon was not the principal author. The fifteen points were by Chevrier, who sketched them in an earlier article, "Banqueroute!"

26. Albert Pinard, "Chronique du mois," *Revue indépendante,* Dec. 1884, pp. 170–71. The same article made a curious remark about the 1884 American presidential campaign:

> The United States name a Democrat as president and the opponents squabble over a thousand votes; finally Mr. Cleveland wins. I am sorry not to know the number of votes received by the honorable candidate Miss Belva Blackwood. I don't dislike colored stockings, even blue ones; what color stockings will women politicians choose, since indigo is reserves for *femmes de lettres?*

27. See Chevrier, "Banqueroute!," *Revue indépendante,* Dec. 1884, pp. 91–98, where he speaks of the crash as the "final, fatal flowering" of the economic system set up under Napoleon I and "cultivated since by three monarchies, to be harvested at last by our pseudo-Republic in the hothouse of modern industrialism."

28. Cf. this note of Fénéon, returning a manuscript to Edouard Dujardin, 23 Mar. 1885, Bibliothèque littéraire Jacques Doucet, Paris.

> Sudden decision on the part of Georges Chevrier, proprietor-director of the *Revue indépendante:* the periodical is becoming . . . almost exclusively *political* . . . I find myself obliged to send you back this article on the *Meistersingers,* which would have been one of the good pages in the review.

29. Parts of Wilde's chronicle (signed O. W.) appear to have been co-authored by F. F. and were printed in F, 653–54.

30. Emile Hennequin, esteemed by his colleagues, translated Edgar Allan Poe's tales of mystery

and horror and published works on Dickens, Heine, Turgenev, Dostoyevsky, and Tolstoy as well as studies of contemporary French authors. He is little known because of his early death in 1889, by accidental drowning in the Seine on his way to visit the artist Odilon Redon.

31. "Sur Diderot," F. 559–65, signed with a star, *Revue indépendante,* Aug. 1884.

32. On Poictevin, see Verlaine, "Francis Poictevin," *Hommes d'aujourd'hui,* no. 424, n.d.; Maurice Barrès, "La Sensation en littérature," *Taches d'encre,* Nov.–Dec. 1884; Henri de Régnier, "Francis Poictevin," *Entretiens politiques et littéraires,* Mar. 1891, pp. 91–95.

33. Aragon, *Je n'ai jamais appris à écrire ou les incipit,* p. 62.

34. F, 554–57. "Les Romans de M. Francis Poictevin," *Revue indépendante,* Nov. 1884.

35. Francis Poictevin, *Ludine* (Bruxelles, 1883), quoted by Fénéon, "Les Romans de Poictevin," F, 553. For the resemblance to F. F., see "Lettres inédites de Jean Lorrain à Charles Buet," *Esprit français,* 4 July 1930.

36. Henri Céard to Zola, 10 Nov. 1884, Paris, Bibliothèque nationale, n.a.fr. 24516, no. 228.

37. André de Fontainas, *Mes souvenirs du symbolisme,* p. 189.

38. "Elie-Félix-Fénéon," *Le Décadent,* 25 Sept. 1886, also in F, p. v.

39. Verlaine to Mallarmé, 29 Oct. 1883, in Mallarmé, *Correspondance,* vol. 2, p. 248, n. 1. Mallarmé to Morice, Nov. 1883, in Guy Michaud, *Mallarmé,* p. 101.

40. Rhymed envelopes, excerpts printed by Joseph Jolinon, "Fénéon ou l'intelligence faite homme," p. 7.

41. Verlaine reading, and his room, from Gustave Kahn, "La Vogue," *Vogue,* Jan. 1889, p. 7.

42. Verlaine reciting from under the table at Fénéon's, Jolinon, "Fénéon on l'intelligence faite homme," p. 7. (Jolinon, who heard the anecdote from Fénéon's wife Fanny, understood that it was she, not Fénéon's mother, in the story; but F. F. didn't marry until after Verlaine died.)

43. P. de Katow, *Gil Blas,* 17 May 1884.

44. F, 487. "Sur Georges Seurat," *Bulletin de la vie artistique,* 15 Nov. 1926.

45. Léopold S. Senghor, *Liberté I, Négritude et Humanisme* (Paris: Editions du Seuil, 1964), p. 232.

46. Fénéon to John Rewald, Marseilles, 8 May 1940, in Rewald and Dorra, *Seurat,* pp. x and xi.

47. Clark, *The Painting of Modern Life,* p. 163.

48. Fénéon to Rewald, 8 May 1940: ". . . I cannot bring to mind the contribution of Seurat to the first exhibition (10 December 1884–January 1885) of the 'Société des Artistes indépendants'."

49. Roger Marx, *Le Voltaire,* 10 Dec. 1884. Jean Le Fustec, in the *Journal des Artistes* (20 Dec. 1884) also gave a detailed, if less laudatory, description of Seurat's contribution.

50. Teodor de Wyzewa to Dujardin, 7 Jan. 1885, formerly in the collection of Mme Edouard Dujardin, Carrières-sous-bois.

51. Lecomte, *Pissarro,* 1922.

52. F, 654. Signed O. W. [Oscar Wilde and F. F.], "Chronique de janvier," *Revue indépendante,* Feb. 1885, pp. 347–51.

53. F, 656, *Revue indépendante,* Feb. 1885. The novelist was Louis Desprez. See further on, chapter 9, p. 192. "The purpose of all government . . . ": unsigned, quoting a statement made in 1811 by someone at the University of Berlin, "Livres," *Revue indépendante,* Aug. 1884, p. 352. Not in *Oeuvres plus que complètes.*

CHAPTER 4: *Midwife of Symbolism, 1886*

1. A. Charpentier, quoted by R. de Bury, "Revue de la 15e," *Mercure de France,* 16 July 1917, pp. 333–34.

2. Ch. Henry to Fénéon, Luxeuil-les-Bains, 8 Oct. 1886, Bibliothèque de la Sorbonne, ms. 1768, Paris.

3. Jules Christophe, "Symbolisme," *La Cravache,* 16 June 1888.

4. Fénéon to John Rewald, 12 March 1940, courtesy of John Rewald, New York.

5. Extracts from *Petit bottin,* F, 537–49.

6. *Revue moderniste,* not to be confused with the better known *Moderniste illustré* of 1889, publishing Saint-Pol-Roux, Albert Aurier, Dubus, Charles Morice, and Gauguin, authors of a "mystical" symbolism at odds with the theories of Fénéon, Gustave Kahn, Seurat, and the "scientific" impressionists.

7. Jean Moréas, "Peintures," *Le Symboliste,* 22 Oct. 1886. The original text reads: *Le hourt fut impétueux au son des orthies et des épinices; Bibliques pauvresses à la chair atramantée, Abrahams tintalorisés, Jésus à barboire de droguiste (. . .) Titans halbrenés, Vénus napieuses, Nymphes tapides, Napoléons de banlieues, tous les carêmes-prenants du quai Malaquais, de Bleu de Prusse et de bitume et de terre de Sienne crousteleurs (. . .) s'en furent. Malgré les bêlements niais du public et les imprécations des morosophes clavés au lieu commun, les novateurs s'imposèrent.*

Hourt is a medieval word corresponding to the Old English, *hoarding,* a defensive palisade (here rendered freely as "the lists"). Moréas invented *orthie* from a Greek word for shouting or high-pitched singing, and *épinices* from the Greek for songs of triumph. He glued *atra* (Latin for "black") onto the Old French *mante* to mean "coated with black" (I think). *Tintalorisés* is anybody's guess, perhaps related to the Italian word for "dye", *tinta. Barboire* is another medieval word, "bearded mask." The Renaissance word *halbrené* referred only to falcons whose wings were injured in hunting the *halbran,* a young wild duck (shades of Ibsen!); as applied to Titans, it suggests their no longer celestial state. Vénus *napieuses,* if one looks to the Greek, means "of a wooded vale." *Nymphes tapides* suggests "hidden," from *tapi,* as an animal crouching in its hole (in the translation, *latitant* is an obscure English word for "lying hid"). The Beaux-Arts gallery on quai Malaquais sold works by Salon artists. *Crousteleurs* ("daubers") does not have a dictionary existence, but is obviously related to *croûte,* slang for bad painting. *Morosophes* ("foolosophers") was coined by Erasmus in his *Praise of Folly.* I took license in translating *clavés* as "nailed" (from Old French, *clavel*); it could also come from *clavis,* "key." Enough of keys!

8. Plowert (Paul Adam), "Parenthèses et incidences," *Le Symboliste,* 30 Oct. 1886.

9. Fénéon's remarks repeated in the Symbolist manifesto, see Robert A. Jouanny, *Jean Moréas,* p. 293.

10. F, 605. "Skillful and forbidding poems . . . ": F, 544 and 607. "Jean Moréas," *Hommes d'aujourd'hui,* no. 268 [June 1886].

11. Henri de Régnier, *Figures et caractères.* pp. 333–34.

12. Mallarmé to Léo d'Orfer, 27 June, 1884, in response to a request for a definition of poetry, first printed in *Vogue,* 18 April 1886, p. 70–71. In reply to the same request, Jean Moréas had sent twelve question marks, and Sully Prudhomme an essay.

13. F, 606. "Jean Moréas." *Hommes d'aujourd'hui.*

14. Laforgue to Kahn, Paris, Feb. 1881, *Lettres à un ami,* p. 39.

15. Kahn, "Souvenirs sur Fénéon," *Le Soir,* 30 April 1894.

16. F, 625. "Kahn," *Hommes d'aujourd'hui,* no. 360 [1890].

17. Signac, journal entry 14 Dec. 1894, in "Extraits du journal inédit," ed. John Rewald, *Gazette des Beaux-Arts,* ser. 6 36(July–Dec. 1949): 112–13. In 1881 Jules Laforgue wrote this portrait-poem, whose opening line is an echo from La Fontaine "The Heron" (*Fables,* book 7):

[Charles Henry]

Bound for the Sorbonne one evening, on his long legs,
  His fat-bellied briefcase under his arm,
Henry! Grimy guttersnipes poked fun at him,
  But he—so tall—didn't see them!
Hurrying along, he smiled up at the dismal chimneys
  —Hearts of gold in tin-plate tubes—
And these ladies of the evening, consumed with a sooty spleen,
  Saluted this noctambulist.

(*Poésies complètes,* p. 467).

18. Henry to Fénéon, correspondance in 1884–85, Bibliothèque de la Sorbonne, Paris. "Why chain ourselves down?" 12 Oct. 1885, italics in original. The others not dated. Théophile Ysaÿe, pianist and brother of the gifted violist Eugène Ysaÿe, was a close friend of Jules Laforgue.

19. Henry to Fénéon, n.d., Bibliothèque de la Sorbonne, Paris.

20. Kahn, *Symbolistes et décadents,* p. 56.

21. Fénéon to Henri de Bouillane de Lacoste, Valescure, 30 April 1939, extract printed in Rimbaud, *Illuminations, Painted Plates,* p. 139.

22. Fénéon to Bouillane de Lacoste, 14 May 1939, same edition, p. 146.

23. Anatole France, "La Vie à Paris," *Le Temps,* 24 Oct. 1886.

24. The drawing of Rimbaud by Manet has apparently been lost. There is a sketch of a young man with the face of Rimbaud in an edition of Manet's sketchbooks whose authenticity has been questioned. "Bust of a man," number 3 in vol. 2 of the disputed sketchbooks, *Graphisme de Manet,* Jacques Mathey, ed. (Paris, 1963).

25. F, 572–75 (mistakenly dated 1887). "Arthur Rimbaud—*Les Illuminations,*" *Le Symboliste,* 7 Oct. 1886.

26. Fénéon to Henri de Bouillane de Lacoste, 27 June 1939, Bibliothèque littéraire Jacques Doucet, Paris.

CHAPTER 5: *Catching up with Seurat*

Nearly all the quotations from Fénéon in this chapter are from two articles in *La Vogue:* "VIIIe Exposition Impressionniste" (13 June 1886) and "Ve Exposition Internationale" (28 June 1886), both reprinted with some changes in *Les Impressionnistes en 1886.*

1. For F. F. and painters at Robert Caze's, see Jean Ajalbert, *Mémoires en vrac,* chap. 7, (p. 117 in particular). Camille Pissarro also appeared there at least once (Feb. 4, 1886), in the company of Cézanne; see Pissarro, *Letters to His Son Lucien,* p. 93.

2. Duel between Caze and Vignier, Ajalbert, *Mémoires en vrac,* pp. 131–36.

3. Paul Adam, *Soi.* I want to thank Mr. Paul Smith for suggesting I take this novel into account. The duty copy of *Soi* was deposited for copyright in May 1886. In September, at the Indépendants, Dubois-Pillet showed the paintings Adam had described as "Vibrac's." Compare pp. 418–20 of *Soi* with Adam's review, "Les Artistes Indépendants," *La Vogue,* 2: 8 (6–13 Sept. 1886), 264–65. In his novel, Adam also speaks *directly* of Raffaëlli, Forain, Seurat (Bathing scene), Signac, Pissaro [*sic*], Guillaumin—and Dubois-Pillet.

4. F, 44 and 49. "M. Albert Dubois-Pillet," *Les Impressionnistes en 1886* and variants from "VIIIe Exposition Impressioniste."

5. This idea has been developed by John House, "Meaning in Seurat's Figure Painting." Cf. Richard Thomson, *Seurat,* pp. 117–19, who points out a stronger contrast between Asnières, a relatively nice suburb, and Clichy on the Parisian bank of the Seine, with heavy industries, soot-blackened docks, and slums or shantytowns.

6. F, 56.

7. From Emile Verhaeren, "Georges Seurat," *p. 200.*

8. *Ogden N. Rood, Modern Chromatics.* See also Seurat's copy of Rood's Contrast-Diagram in Homer, *Seurat and the Science of Painting,* pp. 40–41. Seurat later returned to the more traditional oppositions because he has found that pigments did not in fact act like colors in transmitted light; it is not primary but reflected light that reaches the eye from a painting.

9. From F, 35–36: "VIIIe Exposition Impressionniste."

10. Fénéon described the disintegration of colors in *La Grande Jatte* the year after Seurat's untimely death: "This painting, an historic landmark, has lost its luminous charm: if the blues and pinks have held firm, the Veronese greens are now olive-green, and the bright oranges that used to represent the sunlight are now nothing but holes" (F, 212, *Chat noir,* 2 April 1892).

11. Paul Signac, *Le néo-impressionnisme, Documents,* p. 148.

12. J.-K. Huysmans, *Certains,* p. 23.

13. See, on this passage, the brilliant analysis by J. P. Guillerm, "Sur quelques lignes de Félix Fénéon."

14. F, 30: "VIIIe Exposition Impressionniste."

15. F, 33.

16. André Du Bouchet, "Félix Fénéon or the Mute Critic," p. 79.

17. Paul Adam, "Peintres impressionnistes," p. 545.

18. Fénéon on *La Grande, Jatte,* F, 35–37.

19. F, 202.

20. Rood's experiment with Maxwell's disks and the equations quoted by F. F. are in Rood, *Modern Chromatics,* p. 146–49.

21. "La peinture au point" is a pun, as is, earlier in the sentence, "sabrée et torchonnée, which both mean "botched" as well as "scumbled." *La peinture au point,* besides indicating the use of the dot, calls to mind such expressions as *technique au point,* "perfected technique," or the colloquial *c'est au point,* "it's just exactly right" (not as Linda Nochlin suggested in translating it as "well-done (cooked) painting," which would have been *à point*). Puns not being translatable, I have put an admittedly inferior one in the English version, where none existed in French: "give 'virtuoso painting' points" (*soutenir les avantages de la "belle facture"*).

22. Degas quoted by Pissarro, March 1886, *Letters,* p. 74.

23. *Confessions of a Young Man.* p. 32. First published in French by Kahn and Fénéon in the *Revue indépendante,* March 1888.

24. "Sur Georges Seurat," F, 487–88, *Bulletin de la vie artistique,* 15 Nov. 1926.

25. Heinrich Wilhelm Dove (1803–79), German physicist whose writings on optical mixture had not been translated into French in 1886. Seurat and Fénéon knew of Dove's explanation of the luster created by the use of small lines or dots of color through Ogden Rood, who described Dove's experiments in *Modern Chromatics.*

26. F, 37.

27. O. N. Rood (F. F. mistakenly says *N. O.* Rood), *Modern Chromatics,* p. 280.

28. F, 74. "Le Néo-impressionnisme," *Art Moderne de Bruxelles,* 1 May 1887.

29. Rood on the brillancy of separated colored particles, *Modern Chromatics,* pp. 279–80.

30. Signac, *Le sujet en peinture,* in *D'Eugène Delacroix au néo-impressionnisme,* p. 154.

31. P. Adam under the pseudonym B. de Monconys, *La Vie moderne,* December 1886, pp. 779*ff.*

32. Dinner at lake Saint-Fargeau, Gustave Kahn. "Au temps du pointillisme," pp. 16–17.

33. Auguste Renoir, draft of a letter to the dealer Durand-Ruel, Feb. 1883, translated in Loevgren, *The Genesis of Modernism,* p. 34: "To exhibit with Pissarro, Gauguin, and Guillaumin would be like showing my work with some socialistic group. A little more and Pissarro would invite the Russian Lavrof [anarchist philosopher Petr Lavrovich Lavrov, 1823–1900, a refugee from czarist Russia] or some other revolutionary. The public doesn't like what smells of revolution, and I have no wish, at my age, to be a revolutionary. To remain with the Jew Pissarro, that would be the revolution."

34. F, 40. "Ve Exposition Internationale," 15 June–15 July 1886; F, 126. "Quelques Impressionnistes," *La Cravache,* 2 June 1888.

35. F, 41.

36. Degas quoted by Coquiot, *Les Indépendants,* p. 49.

37. Seurat to Signac, 16 June 1886, quoted by Rewald, *Seurat,* p. xlix.

38. F, 37. As Robert L. Herbert pointed out in the catalogue to the Guggenheim exhibition in 1968, this painting has been confused with a similar one, *Le Passage du Puits-Bertin à Clichy,* because F. F. inverted their names in this review.

39. Fénéon to John Rewald, 26 April 1940, in *Georges Seurat,* p. 47.

40. Henri de Régnier, *Vestigia Flammae.* This is the first of three stanzas.

41. Quoted by F. F. (*L'Art moderne,* 10 July 1887, F, 81) and incorrectly identified as "Préceptes: du *Livre des Métiers,* de l'Hindou Wehli Zunbul Zadé." Apparently Seurat as well as Fénéon was misinformed about the source.

42. Jules Christophe, "Georges Seurat," *La Plume,* September 1891, p. 292.

43. See chap. 1, n. 5.

44. "Georges Seurat," p. 202.

45. Emile Compard, interview with the author, 5 March 1963.

46. "Ve Exposition Internationale de Peinture et de Sculpture," *La Vogue,* 28 June 1886, in a section eliminated by F. F. from *Les Impressionnistes en 1886.* See variants in F, 50.

CHAPTER 6: *Inventing Neo-Impressionism*

1. *Le Figaro,* 16 May 1886. For the press, "intransigents" was another name for the impressionists or the independents. Cf. J.-K. Huysmans writing on the Salon of 1879: "I nevertheless had to separate these painters from the official painters. So I have called them by any one of the well-known, understandable words in common use: impressionists, intransigents or independents." (*L'Art moderne,* footnote on p. 7.)

2. Paul Signac, "Le Néo-impressionnisme—Documents."

3. F, 56 and 55. "L'Impressionnisme aux Tuileries," *Art moderne,* 19 September 1886.

4. Pissarro to Signac, [April 1887], extract published by Dorra and Rewald, *Seurat,* p. xix.

5. Pissarro to Fénéon, Paris, 15 September 1886, published by Pierre Descarges in *Lettres françaises,* 8 October 1953.

6. F, 55, "L'Impressionnisme aux Tuileries."

7. Robert L. Herbert, "Seurat's Theories," p. 29.

8. C. Pissarro, Paris [15 Sept. 1886], *Letters to His Son Lucien,* p. 81.

9. C. Pissarro, Eragny, 25 Feb. 1887, Bailly-Herzberg, *Correspondance,* t. 2, p. 133.

10. F, 58. "L'Impressionnisme aux Tuileries."

11. Fénéon to C. Pissarro, 6 September 1886, Fondation Jacques Doucet, Universités de Paris, Bibliothèque d'Art et d'Archéologie. Pissarro's reply, Eragny, 8 September, Bailly-Herzberg, *Correspondance,* t. 2, pp. 67–68.

12. A. Retaux to F. Fénéon, Abbeville, 25 August 1886, Paulhan archives, Paris.

13. Fénéon to G. Kahn [ca. 20 September 1886], Dr. Karpman-Boutet archives, Paris.

14. *Les Impressionnistes en 1886* at the Bibliothèque nationale, Paris, 8°V. Pièce. 6159.

15. F, 15. "Exposition des oeuvres de C. A. Sellier, Ecole des Beaux-Arts," *La Libre revue,* 6 Dec. 1883.

16. Solange Lemaître, interview with the author, 17 Dec. 1962.

17. F, 157. "Autre groupe impressionniste," *La Cravache,* 6 July 1889.

18. F, 65. Cf. F, 36 on *La Grande Jatte:* "Tout cela: trop évidemment en cette écriture—indications brutales; mais, dans le cadre—dosages complexes et délicats" (All this: too obvious in this description—blunt indications; but, within the frame—delicately, complexly measured out).

19. F, 56. "L'Impressionnisme aux Tuileries."

20. Teodor de Wyzewa, "*Les Impressionnistes en 1886* de Félix Fénéon," pp. 148–49.

21. F, 34. *Les Impressionnistes en 1886.*

22. F, 44. Ibid.

23. Fénéon concerning *Soi,* F, 44: "And it might very well be that the sensibility of this Marthe Grellou of Paul Adam was moved by one of Dubois-Pillet's paintings: 'Coming closer, she marveled at the extreme color division obtained by these flecks of pigment. Each hue consisted of tiny drops of pigment juxtaposed with others, much like the individual threads of an intricate tapestry; and the overall impression came from the perfect harmony of this orchestral multitude of little spots'." (From *Soi,* p. 420.)

24. Remy de Gourmont, *Le IIe Livre des masques,* p. 42.

25. Paul Adam under the pseudonym B. de Monconys, *La Vie moderne,* December 1886, p. 779*f.*

26. Jean Moréas, "Peintures," *Le Symboliste,* 22 October 1886.

27. Teodor de Wyzewa, "Les Livres," *Revue indépendante,* Feb. 1887, pp. 148–49.

28. Arsène Alexandre, "Critique décadente."

29. Hennequin to Fénéon, 11 Dec. 1886, Paulhan archives, Paris.

30. Charles Henry to Fénéon, 12 Oct. 1885, Bibliothèque de la Sorbonne, Paris.

31. Note on a piece of paper accompanying a letter of Seurat to Signac, 26 Aug. 1888. See Rewald, "Artists' Quarrels," pp. 104–5; originally in Rewald, *Georges Seurat,* pp. 114–15.

32. F, 64. "L'Impressionnisme," *Emancipation sociale.* 3 April 1887.

33. See F, 65.

34. Ibid.

35. Paris [20 May 1887], *Letters to His Son Lucien,* Rewald, ed., p. 112.

36. F, 66.

37. F, 73–74. "Le Néo-impressionnisme," *Art moderne,* 1 May 1887.

38. Extract of a letter from Pissarro to Signac, quoted in *Seurat* by Dorra and Rewald, p. xix, n. 15.

39. F, 74. "Le Néo-impressionnisme," *Art moderne,* 1 May 1887.

40. F, 152. "Le Salon de 1889," *Revue indépendante,* June 1889.

41. F, 182. "Artistes indépendants: sténographie par Willy," *Chat noir,* 21 March 1891.

42. F, 176. "Signac," *Hommes d'aujourd'hui,* no. 373 [June 1890].

43. F, 177. Ibid.

44. F, 58. "L'Impressionnisme aux Tuileries," *Art moderne,* 19 Sept. 1886.

45. Paris [6 Dec. 1886], *Letters to His Son Lucien,* Rewald, ed., p. 84.

46. F, 82. "Le Néo-impressionnisme," *Art moderne,* 15 April 1888.

47. Martha Ward, "Félix Fénéon and the Interpretation of Neo-impressionism," unpublished paper delivered at the John Hopkins symposium, 6 March, 1981, "Theory, Critics and the Practice of Painting."

48. F, 162. "Tableaux: Exposition de M. Claude Monet," *La Vogue,* September 1889.

49. F, 117. "Calendrier de septembre," *Revue indépendante,* October 1888.

50. F, 83. "Le Néo-impressionnisme à la IVe Exposition des Artistes indépendants," *Art moderne,* 15 April 1888.

51. F, passim: *versicolores gouttes; semis de menues touches colorantes; ocellures; tourbillonnante cohue de menues macules; une tavelure de bleu; un semis d'orangé clair; menue tache pullulante; un fourmillement de paillettes prismatiques en concurrence vitale pour une harmonie d'ensemble.*

52. F, 116. "Calendrier de septembre," *Revue indépendante,* October 1888. Cf. Schapiro's discussion of the dot in "New Light on Seurat."

53. F, 74. "Le Néo-impressionnisme," *Art moderne.* 1 May 1887.

54. F, 84. "Le Néo-impressionnisme," *Art moderne,* 15 April 1888.

55. F, 165. "Tableaux: 5 Expositions de la Société des Artistes indépendants," *La Vogue,* Sept. 1889.

56. F, 163. Ibid.

57. F, 83. "Le Néo-impressionnisme," *Art moderne,* 15 April 1888.

58. F, 180. "Albert Dubois-Pillet Mort," *Art moderne,* 24 Aug. 1890.

Fénéon's judgment concerning Dubois-Pillet proved faulty years later, when a friend asked him to verify the authorship of a pointillist gouache. Fénéon thought at first that it might be a "modest study" by Seurat which a skillful counterfeiter would have "studded with a thousand tiny gems to make it appetizing.—I hadn't thought of Dubois-Pillet," he wrote Signac, who had apparently set him straight, "He was so stiff, and this gouache sparkles, scintillates." (F. F. to Paul Signac, 17 March 1925, Cachin-Signac archives, Paris.)

59. Pissarro to Fénéon, 21 Feb. 1889, *Lettres à son fils Lucien,* Rewald, ed., footnote on p. 181. Fénéon's letter to Pissarro, 18 Feb. 1889, in the Bibliothèque d'art et d'Archéologie (Fondation Jacques Doucet), is printed in part in Bailly-Herzberg, *Correspondance,* vol. 2, p. 266.

60. F, 166. "Tableaux . . . ," *La Vogue,* Sept. 1889.

61. Camille to Lucien Pissarro, Eragny, 27 May 1887, Bailly-Herzberg, ed., *Correspondance,* 2, p. 175.

62. Pissarro to O. Mirbeau, 22 Nov. 1892, Musée du Louvre, Cabinet des Dessins, Musée du Louvre, Paris; courtesy of J. Bailly-Herzberg.

63. Camille to Lucien Pissarro, Paris, 22 Jan. 1887, Bailly-Herzberg, ed., *Correspondance,* vol. 2, pp. 118–19. Lucien's story, about a doll who sneezed, was never published. However, Fénéon continued

to encourage Lucien and suggested other tales for him to illustrate. In gratitude, Camille told Fénéon to choose one of his works that he had left in Signac's keeping. Fénéon hesitated, then finally picked out the pastel, *Peasant Woman Kneeling.* (Fénéon to Pissarro, 3 May 1887, Bibliothéque d'Art et d'Archéologie, Paris: *J'ai enlevé à Signac votre paysanne à la gerbe. Je me complaisais à cette sensation de retarder un choix entre des oeuvres également admirées et aimées. Enfin, et ce m'est une joie, je détiens ce très beau pastel, et je vous remercie, mon cher maître, de votre amitié et de cette gracieuse attention.*)

64. Fénéon to C. Pissarro, 18 Feb. 1889, Universités de Paris, Bibliothèque d'Art et d'Archéologie.

65. Camille to Lucien Pissarro, 8 April 1891, extract of an unpublished letter (Ashmolean Museum) in Thomson, "Camille Pissarro and Symbolism," p. 19.

66. F, 185. "Cassatt, Pissarro," *Chat noir,* 11 April 1891.

67. F, 209. "Exposition Camille Pissarro," *Art moderne,* 14 Feb. 1892.

68. F, 186. "Cassatt, Pissarro." Fénéon reprinted this statement at the end of his last article on Pissarro, in the *Revue blanche,* 15 May 1896 (F, 238).

69. F, 68. "L'Impressionnisme," *Emancipation sociale,* 3 April 1887.

70. Concerning Maximilien Luce, interview with Frédéric Luce by the author, 11 May 1963. See also Jean Sutter. "Maximilien Luce, 1858–1841," *Les Néo-Impressionnistes,* pp. 153–64.

71. F, 82–83. "Le Néo-impressionnisme," *Art moderne,* 15 April 1888.

72. F, 177. "Calendrier de septembre," *Revue indépendante,* Oct. 1888.

73. F, 166. "Tableaux," *La Vogue,* Sept. 1889.

74. F, 241–42. "Maximilien Luce," preface to the catalogue of the Luce Exhibition, Druet Gallery, March 1904.

75. F, 74–75. "Le Néo-impressionnisme," *Art moderne,* 1 May 1887. Fénéon lifted some of these remarks directly out of Rood's *Modern Chromatics,* p. 154: "If we are immersed in this light, it will appear to us white, and our judgment of all colours will be more or less disturbed . . . . we have practically rendered ourselves colour-blind."

76. F, 84. "Le Néo-impressionnisme," *Art moderne,* 15 April 1888.

77. F, 165. "Tableaux," *La Vogue,* Sept. 1889.

78. F, 134. "Catalogue des 33," *La Cravache,* 19 Jan. 1889.

79. F, 481. "Charles Angrand," *Bulletin de la vie artistique,* 15 April 1926. In these remarks, made upon the painter's death, F. F. noted that Angrand's correspondence with Signac, Luce, and Cross was "a mine of documents for a future history of impressionism. In such a history, his place would be more significant than has been thought."

80. F, 227. "Balade chez les artisses [*sic*] indépendants," *Père peinard,* 16 April 1893.

81. F, 182. "Artistes indépendants: Sténographie par Willy," *Chat noir,* 21 March 1891.

82. F, 213. "Au Pavillon de la Ville de Paris," *Chat noir,* 2 April 1893.

83. H.-E. Cross to Fénéon, (Paris) rue de Siam, April 1892, John Rewald Collection, New York.

84. Cross's notebook published by F. F.: "Le dernier carnet d'Henri-Edmond Cross," *Bulletin de la vie artistique* 3:10–20 (15 May–15 Oct. 1922).

85. Théo van Rysselberghe and his plan to live in a gypsy caravan, Fénéon to Paul Signac, Paris, 3–4 August 1891, Cachin-Signac archives, Paris.

86. F, 325. "Dialogue sur l'eau," *Cahiers d'aujourd'hui,* Sept. 1921.

87. Fénéon to Jean Paulhan, 2 Jan. 1943, Paulhan archives, Paris. The association of Signac with Claude de Lorrain came from the artist's own interest in this painter. See F, p. 246, and Françoise Cachin, *Signac,* p. 77.

88. See R. L. Herbert's exhibition catalogue, *Neo-Impressionism.* At the end of 1889, Fénéon named the following: "Belgians of 'optical painting': Anna Bosch (*sic* for Boch), Frantz Charlet, Willy Finch, Georges Lemmen, Dario de Regoyos, Jan Toorap, Henry Van de Velde, Théo Van Rysselberghe, Guillaume Vogels. And let us add MM. Hayet, Filliger, and Perrot to the French." (F, note on p. 172.)

89. See: 1) Lindzey, Hall, and Thompson, *Psychology* (New York: Worth, 1975, 1978); "*A Sunday Afternoon on the Island of La Grande Jatte,*" explains Rudolph Arnheim in a note about the cover, "seems an appropriate choice to introduce a psychology textbook because Seurat deliberately applied scientific

principles of visual perception to his color relations. . . . [and his] human figures [reflect] the social isolation of urban man. . . ." 2) *Playboy* cover, May 1976. 3) *A Sunday in the Park with George,* music and lyrics by Stephen Sondheim, book and direction by James Lepine, Booth Theatre, New York, opening April 29, 1984.

CHAPTER 7: *Lines and Loyalties*

1. Charles Henry to Félix Fénéon, 11 May 1889, ms. doc. no. 1768, Bibliothèque de la Sorbonne, Paris. I wish to thank Robert L. Herbert for directing me to these papers. My thanks also to Michael Zimmerman for the extracts from his dissertation, "Seurat, eine theoretische Monographie. Sein Werk, der Diskurs über Kunst in den 1880er Jahren und die 'wissenschaftliche' Ästhetik Charles Henrys" (University of Cologne, 1984).

2. F, 148. "Une esthétique scientifique," a review of Charles Henry's work, *La Cravache,* 18 May 1889.

3. F, 147–48. In quoting Gauss's theorem, F. F. left out a word which I have reinserted and set in boldface in the quotation below. Fénéon explains—or does he?

> [One should] create only those angles that intercept the side of a regular polygon constructible with a compass. Such polygons, according to the beautiful theorem of Gauss, have a number of sides equal to a power of 2, or to a prime number of the form $2^n + 1$, or the product of a power of 2 by one or several [**different**] prime numbers of this form. It is not possible for the compass—and therefore for a living creature—rationally to divide the circumference in any other way. More or less consciously, that living being will thus be inhibited or impeded from executing expressive movements [that follow different angles].

Gauss's theorem is sometimes misprinted in *Oeuvres plus que complètes* as 2n instead of 2^n—a typographer's error not imputable to Fénéon.

4. Charles Henry, "Introduction à une esthétique scientifique," *Revue contemporaine,* Aug. 1885, pp. 450 and 451–52. My thanks to Jane Sangwine-Yager and Steven Cortright for certain clarifications regarding Henry's text and for the sketch showing an angle determined by the arc of a circle.

5. On Henry's influence, F, 489. "Les disparus. Charles Henry" (obituary), *Bulletin de la vie artistique,* 15 Nov. 1926.

6. F, 178. "Signac," *Les Hommes d'aujourd'hui,* no. 373 [June 1890]. F, 118. "L'Affiche de M. Paul Signac," Calendrier de septembre, *La Revue indépendante,* Oct. 1888.

7. Henry, *Essai de généralisation de la théorie du rayonnement,* p. 196, quoted by Arguëlles, *Charles Henry,* p. 155.

8. F, 42. "Ve Exposition internationale," *La Vogue,* 28 June 1886, reprinted in *Les Impressionnistes en 1886.*

9. F, 32. "VIIIe Exposition impressionniste," *La Vogue,* 13 June 1886, reprinted in *Les Impressionnistes en 1886.*

10. F, 167. ". . . 5e Exposition de la Société des Artistes indépendants," *La Vogue,* Sept. 1889 and *Art moderne,* 17 Oct. 1889. See "Portrait of Jeanne," No. 29 in Thorold, *A Catalogue of the Oil Paintings of Lucien Pissarro,* with a quotation from Camille Pissarro also criticizing the folds of the cloth in the background (letter to Lucien, 9 Sept. 1889).

11. F, 165. Ibid.

12. F, 212. "Au Pavillon de la Ville de Paris," report on the eighth Independants' exposition with its memorial exhibition of Seurat's work, *Chat noir,* 2 April 1892.

13. F, 198. "Paul Signac," La Plume, special issue dedicated to contemporary painters, *1* Sept. 1891.

14. F, 76. "Le Néo-impressionnisme," Art moderne, 1 May 1887.

15. F, 85. "Le Néo-impressionnisme," *Art moderne.* 15 April 1888.

16. Cf. paragraphs 2 and 3 in Fénéon's "Paul Signac" (F, 197–98) and Hermann von Helmholtz, *L'Optique et la peinture,* pp. 192ff. (Paris, 1878, in the second part of a volume containing Brüke's *Principes*

scientifiques des beaux-arts). Without citing Helmholtz, Fénéon drew from his interpretation of Fechner's law on the relationship of stimulus intensity to sensation intensity and how it pertains to painting.

17. Henry van de Velde, "Notes sur l'art," *La Wallonie,* May 1890, p. 123. Van de Velde seems to be speaking partly in jest. Later in 1890 he left painting altogether for architecture and the decorative arts. According to a letter he wrote Jean Rewald many years later, he was troubled by Seurat's "distrustfulness and meanness" and came to doubt the value of the neo-impressionist method (letter of 17 Jan. 1950, quoted in *Post-Impressionism* by Rewald, p. 418).

18. G. Kahn on *Chahut,* "Seurat," *Art moderne,* 5 April 1891 (. . . *cette beauté n'a de signification complète que dans cet acte principal de cette cervelle féminine, danser ainsi* . . .).

19. Fénéon quoted by Parmelin, *Picasso dit,* p. 37. Picasso's response: "Fénéon, c'était pourtant quelqu'un" (and yet Fénéon was somebody). In talking of the event later, Picasso "remarked that [Fénéon's advice] was not so stupid since all good portraits are in some degree caricatures" (Penrose, *Picasso,* p. 126).

20. F, 75. "Le Néo-impressionnisme," *Art moderne,* 1 May 1887.

21. F, 84–85. "Le Néo-impressionnisme," *Art moderne,* 15 April 1888.

22. Fénéon to Jean Paulhan, 6 Jan. 1944, Paulhan archives, Paris.

23. F, 75. *Art moderne,* 1 May 1887. The first Seurat Fénéon owned was one of the Honfleur seascapes, *Entrée du port, Honfleur (1886),* which was given him by the painter in 1887.

24. F, 164–65. "5e Exposition de la Société des Artistes indépendants," *La Vogue,* Sept. 1889. These paintings are now known as *Vue du Crotoy, Amont, Vue du Crotoy, Aval,* and *Port-en-Bessin, les ponts et les quais.*

25. F. F. to John Rewald, 24 June 1940, courtesy of Mr. Rewald. Fénéon continues: "Perhaps [Seurat] was also contemplating the nuances in the flat tints of the old poster-artist."

26. Charles Henry to Félix Fénéon, [March/April 1890], Bibliothèque de la Sorbonne, Paris.

27. Note by Fénéon to Signac, [April 1890], Cachin-Signac archives, Paris. Musschenbroek, an eighteenth-century Dutch natural philosopher, was cited in Rood's *Modern Chromatics* (p. 132) as having "rediscovered . . . in 1762" Ptolemy's method of mixing colors on disks. Charles Henry probably encouraged Signac and Fénéon to look into the work of Musschenbroek, who died in 1761, rendering Rood's date problematical. Musschenbroek is remembered today for inventing the Leyden jar and other instruments but not the disks mentioned by Rood. Fénéon made a reference to them again the following year in another article on Signac (F, 197. "Paul Signac," *La Plume,* 1 Sept. 1891). It is curious that he should name these disks instead of Maxwell's, which were a great improvement, according to Rood.

28. Signac to Fénéon, 29 April 1890, Cachin-Signac archives, Paris, published in part by John Rewald, *Post-Impressionism,* p. 421.

29. Fénéon to Signac, n.d., Cachin-Signac archives, Paris.

30. F, 179. "Signac," *Les Hommes d'aujourd'hui,* (1890).

31. Note by Fénéon to Signac, [April 1890], Cachin-Signac archives, Paris.

32. Ibid.

33. Ibid., and F, 177. "Signac," *Hommes d'aujourd'hui.*

34. Signac to Fénéon, 29 April 1890 and the reply, "That is why . . . ," n.d., Cachin-Signac archives, Paris. Signac gave Fénéon a study for one of the paintings he most admired, *La Seine à Herblay,* cardboard, 27 × 35.5 cm. (no. 109 in *2e Vente,* Fénéon Collection, 30 May 1947).

35. F, 177. Cf. a similar, previous statement, quoted in chap. 6, note 39.

36. Fénéon to John Rewald, 9 Oct. 1937, courtesy John Rewald, New York.

37. Seurat to Fénéon, facsimile in César M. de Hauke and Paul Brame, *Seurat et son oeuvre,* p. xxi; text printed in F, 507–9.

38. Fénéon to Seurat, 23 June [1890], facsimile in *Seurat et son oeuvre,* text in F, 509, where the three "indecipherable lines" read: *ni directment ni sous la forme à laquelle je serais inhabile de l'insinuation* (heavily crossed out).

39. See F, 212. "Au Pavillon de la Ville de Paris," *Chat noir,* 2 April 1892.

40. Seurat to Fénéon, 24 June 1890, cited in note 7, p. xxiii and F, 510. In regard to the postscriptum, Seurat did go near Calais, to Gravelines, where he painted, as it turned out, his last series of seascapes.

41. Fénéon to Paul Signac, Paris, 25 June [1890], Cachin-Signac archives, Paris; published by Françoise Cachin, "Le portrait de Fénéon par Signac," p. 90.

42. Signac to Fénéon, Saint Briac, 21 July (1890), ibid.

43. Fénéon to Signac, Paris, 30 July [1890], ibid.

44. Fénéon to Kahn, Dr. Karpman-Boutet archives, Paris.

45. See Françoise Cachin, "Le portrait de Fénéon par Signac," and "Les Neo-Impressionnistes et le Japonisme," esp. pp. 231–32. For "Utagawafénéon," see chap. 1.

46. *Charles Henry and the Formation of a Psychophysical Aesthetic,* p. 131.

47. Camille Pissarro negative on Fénéon portrait: *Lettres à son fils Lucien,* Rewald, ed., 30 March 1891, p. 222. Delaunay influenced by portrait, see Gilles de la Tourette, *Robert Delaunay,* and P. Francastel, *Du cubisme à l'art abstrait.*

48. Emile Verhaeren, "mais la fleur qu'il tient dans la main . . . indique en le contrariant ses qualités de grâce et de politesse souriante. Ce porrait froid et sec ne nous sourit guère. . ." *Art moderne,* 5 April 1891, p. 111.

49. van Rysselberghe, *Galerie privée, pp. 75 and 76.*

50. Fénéon to Maria van Rysselberghe, in *Galerie privée,* p. 76.

51. Fénéon to Jean Paulhan, "Monday evening," [1943], Paulhan archives, Paris. Paulhan was looking for works to illustrate his essay, "F. F. ou le Critique."

52. Fénéon to Signac, 3–4 August [1891], Signac archives, Paris.

CHAPTER 8: *Working Behind the Scenes*

1. B. de Monconys [Paul Adam], "Symbolistes et Décadents—Les Personnalités symbolistes," *Vie moderne,* Dec. 1886, p. 779.

2. Dujardin to Fénéon, [Mar. or April 1886]. Correspondence in the Bibliothèque littéraire Jacques Doucet, Paris, locus of all letters between F. F. and Dujardin or Wyzewa in this chapter, unless otherwise indicated.

3. Fénéon to Dujardin and Wyzewa, [Ministère de la] Guerre, 19 March 1886.

4. F. F. to Dujardin, 17 Oct. 1885.

5. F. F. to Wyzewa, Feb. 1886.

6. Rhymed envelope of F. F. to Wyzewa, 10 March 1886. This "obelisk of Luxor"—normally spelled *Louksor* or *Louqsor* in French—stands in the middle of the Place de la Concorde in Paris: Fénéon's spelling evokes another word, *luxure* (lust).

7. F. F. to Dujardin, 30 March 1886.

8. F. F. to Dujardin, 17 March 1888.

9. F. F. to Dujardin, 17 June 1886.

10. Laforgue to Teodor de Wyzewa, 14 July 1886, *Oeuvres complètes,* vol. 5, Paris, 1925, p. 198, misdated "1887." In another letter to Kahn, Laforgue spoke of owing Fénéon 330 francs (Berlin, 23 Sept. 1886, *Lettres à un ami,* p. 223).

11. Dujardin to Fénéon, 12 June 1886.

12. Fénéon to Dujardin, 6 Oct. 1886.

13. F, 483–84. "Questions d'origine," *Bulletin de la vie artistique,* 15 May 1926. The quotation, "refabricated out of several old words . . "is from Mallarmé's "Avant-dire au *Traité du verbe* de René Ghil."

14. C. Pissarro to Lucien, Paris, 10 Dec. 1886, *Letters to His Son Lucien,* Rewald, ed., p. 85.

15. Dujardin to Théodore Bovet, 16 Jan. 1887, formerly in the collection of André Vasseur, Paris.

16. G. Kahn, "Souvenirs sur Fénéon," *Le Soir,* 30 April 1894.

17. F. F. to Dujardin and Wyzewa, 16–17 Dec. 1886.

18. F. F. to Dujardin, 10 Aug. 1887.

19. F. F. to Henri de Bouillane de Lacoste, 17 June 1939, Bibliothèque littéraire Jacques Doucet, Paris.

20. F, 712. "M. Joseph Caraguel," *L'Emancipation sociale de Narbonne,* 28 July 1887.

21. F, 63. "Le Musée du Luxembourg," *Symboliste,* 15 Oct. 1886.

22. F. F. to Dujardin, 13 Jan. 1888.

23. F. F. to "M. l'organisateur de l'exposition Willette," 4 Feb. 1888, Bibliothèque littéraire Jacques Doucet, Paris.

24. Paul Alexis, "Visite à la *Revue indépendante,*" *Cri du peuple,* 14 April 1888.

25. F. F. to Dujardin, [12 Dec. 1888].

26. F. F. to Dujardin, 6 Sept. 1888.

27. F. F. to Dujardin, 8 Feb. 1887.

28. F, 580. "Les Poèmes de Jules Laforgue," *Art moderne,* 9 Oct. 1887.

29. Fénéon's "obituary" of Laforgue, *Art moderne,* 28 Aug. 1887. See F, 579, n. 1.

30. F, 578. "Jules Laforgue," *Portraits du prochain siècle* (Paris: E. Girard, 1894).

31. F. F. to Dujardin, 8 July 1890. In the last sentence, "And from a literary point of view," Fénéon crossed out "literary" and put in "practical."

32. F. F. to Dujardin, 31 Oct. 1890.

33. Emile Verhaeren, "*Les Derniers Vers* de Jules Laforgue," p. 377.

34. Fénéon to Octave Maus, 24 Nov. 1887, Albert Vanderlinden archives, Brussels. Laforgue had said, in "L'Imitation de Notre Dame la lune, Pierrots (scène courte mais typique)," *Bref, le violet gros deuil est ma couleur locale.* (Wordplay in *gros* rather than *grand deuil: gros* normally used in mundane expressions, *gros rouge,* coarse wine, *gros sel,* cooking salt.)

35. F. F., description of ms., "Inédits de Laforgue: Notes," *Entretiens politiques et littéraires,* April 1891, p. 97.

36. Francis Vielé-Griffin, *Entretiens,* Jan. 1892, p. 13.

37. (Illegible signature), Conservateur, Bagneux, to Fénéon, 6 Jan. 1891, Paulhan archives, Paris.

38. Laforgue, verses in the tale, "Hamlet," "Moralités légendaires," *Vogue,* Nov. 1886.

39. Reported by Solange Lemaître, interview, 17 Dec. 1962. A similar remark can be found in a letter from F. F. to Jean Paulhan, "mardi" [1943], Paulhan archives, Paris.

40. P. Pia, preface to Jules Laforgue, *Poésies complètes,* p. 12.

41. Lecomte quoted by G. Kahn, "Souvenirs sur Fénéon," *Le Soir,* 30 April 1894.

42. Signac to Fénéon, published in *La Cravache,* 22 Sept. 1888; and Fénéon to Signac, 30 Sept. 1888, Signac archives, Paris.

43. *Voyages* de Balthasar de Monconys, Ch. Henry ed. (Paris: Publications *Vogue,* 1887), note on p. 17. Balthasar, a seventeenth-century French scholar and scientist, was approaching Portugal by sea when "gay Gil de Bache from Dunkirk" attacked his ship; all the voyagers were "captured, robbed, and stripped of their clothes, then dressed in old rags, some without hats, others without hose or shoes," and finally put ashore. Balthasar continued his voyage on foot.

44. F, 846–47. "Poe et Mallarmé," *Cravache,* 22 Sept. 1888.

45. Mallarmé to Fénéon, 15 Oct. (1888), *Correspondance,* vol. 3, Mondor and Austin, eds., p. 267.

46. Retté, *Le Symbolisme,* p. 18.

47. G. Kahn, "Souvenirs sur Fénéon."

48. Fénéon to Dujardin, 20 Nov. 1888.

49. Willy [H. Gauthier-Villars] to Fénéon, [Dec. 1890], Paulhan archives, Paris.

50. On John Gray, see Brocard Sewell, *In the Dorian Mode;* G. A. Cevasco, *John Gray:* Campbell, ed., *A Friendship of the Nineties.*

51. John Gray, *Silverpoints,* p. ix. The intensity of Gray's feelings can be seen in the rest of the poem:

Men, women, call thee so or so,
 I do not know.
 Thou hast no name
For me, but in my heart a flame

Burns tireless, neath a silver vine,
 And round entwine

Its purple girth
All things of fragrance and of worth.

Thou shout! thou burst of light! thou throb
Of pain! thou sob!
Thou like a bar
Of some sonata, heard from far

Through blue-hue'd veils! When in these wise,
To my soul's eyes,
Thy shape appears,
My aching hands are full of tears.

52. Gray to Fénéon, London, 20 Nov. [1890], Paulhan archives, Paris.

53. Comte de Lautréamont (Isidore Ducasse), *Les Chants de Maldoror.* Fénéon edited the text anonymously. Léon Genonceaux wrote the preface, which mentions the use of the original manuscript.

54. Gray to Fénéon, London, 2 Jan. 1891, Paulhan archives, Paris.

55. *Chants de Maldoror,* Paris, Editions de la Sirène, where F. F. also brought out a new edition of Lautréamont's *Préface à un livre futur* [1922].

56. F, 946. F. F. and V. B. (Victor Barrucand), "Passim," *Revue blanche,* 15 March 1895.

CHAPTER 9: *New Consciousness and New Voices*

1. André Berne-Joffroy, "Le Problème de la critique d'art."

2. "Kahn," manuscript for *Les Hommes d'aujourd'hui,* No. 360, [1890], formerly in the André Vasseur Collection, Paris.

3. F, 558. Review of Poictevin's novel *Double* (1889), *Art et Critique,* 16 Nov. 1889.

4. F, 865. Review of Léon Bloy, *Sueur de sang,* in *Revue anarchiste,* 15 Nov. 1893.

5. Georges Vanor, *L'Art symboliste,* pp. 32–33.

6. F, 705. "Le Fétichisme obligatoire," *Emancipation sociale de Narbonne,* 10 April 1887.

7. F, 626–27. "Les *Palais nomades* de Gustave Kahn." *Emancipation sociale,* 22 May 1887.

8. Peter Amacher, *Freud's Neurological Education,* pp. 51–52.

9. F, 580. "Les Poèmes de Jules Laforgue," *Art moderne,* 9 Oct. 1887.

10. On Marie Krysinska: F.-A. Casals, *Encres-de-Chine,* extract published in *Art et critique,* 23 Aug. 1890. Verses quoted by Fénéon (without naming an author), in "Exposition du cercle artistique de la Seine," *Libre revue,* 16 Jan. 1884, F, 22.

11. F, 835. "Au Théâtre d'Art," *La Paix,* 15 Dec. 1891, signed Willy. The poems of Laforgue in *Vogue,* 16 Aug. 1886, were "L'Hiver qui vient," and "Le Mystère des trois cors" (under the title, "La Légende des trois cors"). Arthur Rimbaud had recently had a leg amputated, hence the rather flippant epithet "peg-legged poet."

12. F, 607. "Jean Moréas," *Hommes d'aujourd'hui,* no. 268, (June 1886).

13. G. Kahn, *The Drawings of Seurat,* pp. vii–viii: "We were attuned to the mathematics of his art. Very possibly the fire of youth inspired us with the near-certainty that his research on line and color presented definite analogies to our theories on the verse and the phrase. . . ."

14. F, 189. "Exposition Carrière," *Chat noir,* 2 May 1891.

15. Both quotations from unsigned "Notes et notules," *Entretiens politiques et littéraires,* April 1891, pp. 143–44 (among which also F. F.'s unsigned announcement of Seurat's death). Not in *Oeuvres plus que complètes.*

16. F, 74. "Le Néo-impressionnisme," *Art moderne,* 1 May 1887.

17. Mallarmé, from the sonnet, "Le Tombeau d'Edgar Poe," translation by Joseph Frank, Notes to Introduction of Paul Valéry, *Masters and Friends* (Princeton, 1968), p. 355.

18. F, 555. "Francis Poictevin," *Revue indépendante,* Nov. 1884.

19. F, 607. "Jean Moréas," *Hommes d'aujourd'hui.*

20. Paul Adam, "Peintres impressionnistes," p. 542.

21. Fénéon, "*Les Lauriers sont coupés,* de M. Edouard Dujardin," *Vie moderne,* 27 May 1888, not in *Oeuvres plus que complètes.* A copy of *Ulysses* dedicated to Dujardin by James Joyce, signing "le grand larron" (the big robber), was kept in the collection of Marie Dujardin, Carrières-sous-bois.

22. Mallarmé, response to Jules Huret, *Enquête sur l'évolution littéraire,* 1891, in Mallarmé, *Oeuvres complètes,* p. 869.

23. Poictevin was appreciated in the twentieth century by Paul Eluard, André Breton, and Louis Aragon; in his own time by Verlaine, who wrote a sonnet-portrait of him, "A Francis Poictevin," *Revue blanche* 5:24 (Oct. 1893): 227. Here it is in translation:

> Always discontent with his work
> All the more exquisitely nebulous for that.
> And duly mad for the love of art,
> Where the slug and the snake
>
> Can do nothing but use up their teeth
> And their spit—isn't that true, literary
> Press in general? Who
> Is this ineffable, imprudent soul
>
> Who does not write for the average
> Public and never responds
> To the hue and cry except by the halo
>
> Of a spirit in the hands of fortune,
> Mysterious as the Moon,
> Clear and winding as Water?

24. J. Ajalbert, "Théâtres," p. 172. The story: "An escaped prisoner, before a sleeping, newly-married couple, whom he must kill if he is to remain free, gives way to pity and finally gets himself arrested."

25. Reported by Lugné-Poe, *La Parade,* vol. 1, p. 105.

26. F, 798. "Calendrier d'octobre," *Revue indépendante,* Nov. 1888. Read *cladélienne,* not "caldélienne." Léon *Cladel* was a novelist described in the *Petit bottin:* ". . . rigged out like the ragged villain of a melodrama, perspiring fumes of alcaline caproates [ammonia of old goat] . . . the sight of him is not recommended for pregnant women" (F, 540). "Rollinatesque, richepinesque. . ." refers to poets Maurice Rollinat and Jean Richepin, who recited their works at the Chat Noir cabaret, Rollinat acclaimed for his morbid, fin-de-siècle poems, *Névroses* (1883), and Richepin for his *Blasphèmes* (1884).

27. Lugné-Poe, *La Parade,* vol. 1, p. 189.

28. Audience reaction to the adaptation from Laforgue, Retté, *Le Symbolisme, anecdotes et souvenirs,* p. 200.

29. Henry to Fénéon, 2 Feb. 1891, Bibliothèque de la Sorbonne, Paris.

30. Henry to Fénéon, 11 May 1891. ibid.

31. Fénéon, "Notes et notules," unsigned, *Entretiens politiques et littéraires,* June 1891, p. 31. Not in *Oeuvres plus que complètes.*

32. Arsène Alexandre, "Signalement d'un accusé."

33. Unsigned "Notes et notules," *Entretiens,* April 1891, p. 144.

CHAPTER 10: *Transitions*

1. Edouard Dujardin to his parents [1889], formerly in the collection of Mme Marie Dujardin, Carrières-sous-bois.

2. Allais to Fénéon [late 1890 or early 1891], Paulhan archives, Paris.

3. *Le Symbolisme,* p. 160.

4. F, 143. "Couleurs à l'eau," *Cravache,* 9 Feb. 1889.

5. Joseph M. Dongarra to the author, 18 Oct. 1977: "Went in search of the 'lac St Fargeau.' At Père Lachaise, I chatted with the gatekeeper, a man between fifty and sixty, about this lake. And he remembered it, but as a child, and as a lake that at a certain moment, in his childhood, literally disappeared. He said I would look in vain for it. Then I asked him if the lake might not have become a reservoir. He knew indeed about the reservoir but was in doubts as to whether it was a transformation of the waters of the vanished lake."

6. Fénéon to Maria van Rysselberghe, [1943] in M. Saint-Clair, *Galerie privée,* p. 67.

7. Jean Ajalbert, "A travers mes souvenirs—Félix Fénéon."

8. Fénéon to Paul Signac, 30 July 1890, Cachin-Signac archives, Paris, extract published by Françoise Cachin, "Le portrait de Fénéon par Signac," p. 90. Fénéon to Theo van Gogh, 31 July 1890, in the exhibition catalogue, *Van Gogh à Paris* (Musée d'Orsay, 1988), p. 262; letter in Amsterdam, Rijksmuseum Vincent van Gogh.

9. F, 182. "Artistes indépendants: sténographie par Willy," *Chat noir,* 21 Mar. 1891. F, 247. "Van Gogh," preface to Van Gogh exhibition catalogue, Bernheim-Jeune Gallery, Jan. 1908.

10. F, 168. ". . . 5e Exposition de la Société des Artistes indépendants," *Vogue,"* Sept. 1889.

11. Vincent to Theo van Gogh, Arles, Sept. 1888, *The Complete Letters of Vincent van Gogh,* p. 56, no. 543. Theo telling Vincent that one could not see the painting from a sufficient distance, *Letters,* p. 550, no. T16.

12. F, 488. "Sur Georges Seurat," *Bulletin de la vie artistique,* 15 Nov. 1926.

13. F. F. quoted by Joseph Jolinon, "Fénéon ou l'intelligence faite homme," F, 720. "Cirques, théâtres, politique." *Revue indépendante,* Jan. 1888.

14. Fénéon to Benedict Nicolson, 1939, extract published by Dorra and Rewald, *Seurat,* pp. 279–80.

15. F, 183. "Notes et notules," unsigned, *Entretiens politiques et littéraires,* April 1891. Fénéon omitted *La Parade* and *Jeune Femme se poudrant* from the list of principal canvases, perhaps because they were smaller than the others. He misnamed *Une Baignade* (Seurat cared whether one said *La* or *Une*); and he wrote *Posender* for *Poseuses.* Perhaps this was a typographical error: *n* an inverted *u;* a gracefully written *s* seen as a *d;* a terminal *s* taken for an *r?*

16. Verhaeren, "Georges Seurat," pp. 197–203.

17. Kahn, "Seurat," pp. 107–10. Jules Christophe, "Georges Seurat," *La Plume, 1* Sept. *1891.* Wyzewa, "Georges Seurat," *L'Art dans les deux mondes,* 18 April 1891.

18. F, 248. Unsigned preface to the exhibition catalogue, *Seurat,* Bernheim-Jeune Gallery, 14 Dec. 1908–9 Jan. 1909.

19. Fénéon to Dujardin [15 or 16 April 1891], Bibliothèque littéraire Jacques Doucet, Paris.

20. Kahn, *Symbolistes et décadents,* p. 67.

21. Willy to Fénéon, (1891), Paulhan archives, Paris: "Dear F. F., In this morning's *Echo,* it was pointed out, finally! that F. F. has been piously passed over by the churls who have been interviewed. Let me add that after I insulted Huret for not having wrung a conversation out of you, he defended himself, pleading that your absurd, unpardonable, and n + 1 accusable modesty and indolence had refused. What a naughty boy!"

CHAPTER 11: *Speaking of Symbolist Painting*

1. Camille Pissarro, Paris, 13 May 1891, *Lettres à son fils Lucien,* p. 246.

2. Loevgren, *The Genesis of Modernism,* pp. 143–44.

3. Jean Paulhan, notes on Fénéon, [1943], Paulhan archives, Paris.

4. "Moi j'adorais le rouge: où trouver un vermillon parfait?" Gauguin, "Natures mortes," *Essais d'art libre,* Jan. 1894.

5. Gauguin to Emile Bernard, Le Pouldu [June 1890], *Lettres de Gauguin à sa femme et à ses amis,* Malingue, ed., p. 194.

6. Gauguin to Schuffenecker, 26 March 1888, Malingue, ed., p. 128.

7. The Littré dictionary Fénéon used says of *grièche:* Used only in compound words and meaning

"painful, unpleasant, spiteful," as in *ortie-grièche* (Greek nettle), *pie-grièche* (Orn. shrike, or F. shrew—for woman). "Some dictionaries," Littré added, "give the meaning of 'gaudy, splashed with color' (*bariolé*)—for some unknown reason."

8. Gauguin to Schuffenecker, Arles, 23 Nov. 1888, in Arsène Alexandre, *Paul Gauguin, sa vie et le sens de son oeuvre* p. 89. The word stuck in Gauguin's craw. He later wrote Emile Bernard about his lack of success: "Well, it was in the cards. It seems I was cut out for that, no heart, bad tempered, *grièche.*" [November 1889], Malingue, p. 175.

9. "Bars et brasseries à l'Exposition."

10. Jules Antoine, "Impressionnistes et Synthétistes," *Art et critique,* 9 Nov. 1889. A. Aurier, "Concurrence," *Le moderniste,* 27 June 1889.

11. Loevgren, *The Genesis of Modernism,* p. 144.

12. Gauguin to Bernard, La Pouldu [Nov. 1889], Malingue, p. 172.

13. Gauguin to Emile Schuffenecker, [Brittany, 1890], in A. Alexandre, *Paul Gauguin,* p. 154.

14. O. Mirbeau, "Chronique—Paul Gauguin," pp. 92–94. See p. 93, second column for extract quoted here.

15. A. Aurier, "Le Symbolisme en peinture," pp. 215–16 and 211.

16. Ibid., p. 213.

17. Aurier's article annotated by C. Pissarro, *Mercure de France,* March 1891, copy in Ashmolean Museum, Oxford, quoted and discussed by Thomson, "Camille Pissarro and Symbolism," pp. 14–23. See p. 18 for extract used here.

18. Gauguin not a seer. Pissarro, 20 April 1891, *Lettres à son fils Lucien,* Rewald, ed., p. 235.

19. Mallarmé's toast, quoted in the *Mercure de France,* May 1891, p. 318.

20. Signac to Fénéon, Brussels, 10 Feb. 1891, Cachin-Signac archives, Paris, published in *Le Post-impressionnisme* by John Rewald, p. 286. The first three "Be's . . . " were the titles of Gauguin's bas-relief carvings, "Soyez amoureuses . . . " and "Soyez mystérieuses . . . ," and a portrait of Jean Moréas, "Soyez Symboliste," on display at the *XX.*

21. Fénéon on Gauguin, according to François Michel, notes to Bernard Groethuysen, Paulhan archives, Paris.

22. Fénéon quoted by André Berne-Joffroy in an interview with the author, 14 Feb. 1963.

23. Fénéon to John Rewald, Valescure, 15 Oct. 1938. courtesy John Rewald, New York.

24. For example, F, 74 and 626.

25. F, 213. "Au Pavillon de la Ville de Paris," *Chat noir,* 2 April 1892. Bonnard later said in a letter to Mme Hahnloser: "In my youth I was excited by the magnificent gaudiness of Japanese crepon—a sort of wove paper, used for popular art. Much later I learned to appreciate the beauty of the great Japanese engravers . . . Fénéon called me *Bonnard très japonard.*" (Le Cannet, 4 Jan. 1946, in Hahnloser, Notes to *Bonnard* by Annette Vaillant, p. 182.)

26. See Colta Feller Ives on Mary Cassatt in *The Great Wave.*

27. See F, 92. In preparation for this article, F. F. wrote Camille Pissarro, 20 Dec. 1887:

> *By return mail,* send me, I beg you, some information on the way you made the etchings exhibited at the Revue indépendante. . . . It is not always easy to distinguish [the method used] in these plates where the technique seems to me rather complicated. So I am asking you to point out some of the intimate tricks of the trade concerning these plates.
>
> *Respectfully and affectionately,*
> *félix fénéon*

(Universités de Paris, Bibliothèque d'Art et d'Archéologie, Fondation Jacques Doucet, Paris.)

28. Remy de Gourmont, *Ile Livre des Masques,* p. 42.

29. A. Aurier, "Claude Monet," pp. 223–24.

CHAPTER 12: *Move Toward End Game*

1. For widespread contemporary views, including those of Mallarmé, Verlaine, and Zola: see "Un Référendum artistique et social," *l'Ermitage,* 1893, No. 7, pp. 1–24 and no. 11, pp. 257–65. See also

Eugenia W. Herbert, *The Artist and Social Reform:* Robert L. Herbert and Eugenia W. Herbert, "Artists and Anarchism"; Jacques Monférier, "Symbolisme et Anarchie"; John Rewald, *Post-Impressionism,* pp. 154–56 and passim.

2. Peter Kropotkin, *Paroles d'un révolté,* pp. 66*ff.*

3. See *La Révolte,* 22–28 July 1893, p. 3, on Vielé- Griffin's "bourgeois" poems.

4. Fénéon, "Notes et Notules," *Entretiens,* April 1891, p. 150. Not in *Oeuvres plus que complètes.*

5. Fénéon, "Notes et Notules," unsigned, in *Entretiens politiques et littéraires,* April 1891, p. 142. Not in *Oeuvres plus que complètes.*

6. Editors' notes in *Entretiens,* 1 Oct. 1890. p. 239, and 1 Nov. 1890, p. 288.

7. Camus, *The Rebel,* pp. 200–201.

8. J. Huret quoted in *L'Endehors,* 10 Jan. 1892.

9. Fénéon to Paul Signac, Paris, 3–4 August [1891], Cachin-Signac archives, Paris. The novel F. F. refers to, *Bas les coeurs!* (Keep your hearts out of it!) was about the war of 1870–71 seen by a street urchin of Versailles.

10. L. Descaves, *Souvenirs d'un ours,* p. 116.

11. F. Vielé-Griffin, "Epitaphe pour un enfant," *L'Endehors,* 28 Feb. 1892.

12. [Carlo Cafiero], "L'Action," *Le Révolté,* No. 22. 25 Dec. 1880. Cafiero was identified as the author by Nattlau, *Errico Malatesta,* pp. 177–78.

13. Individuals who wrote to Pissarro describing the damage to his house in Louvenciennes assumed that it was done by Prussians, and this has been the evidence accepted by the painter's biographers. Fénéon said it was done by French officers and doubtless got his information directly from Pissarro, who also told Jean Grave that when he returned to Louvenciennes, he found several washerwomen wearing magnificent canvas aprons as they worked at the public laundry—the remains of some of his paintings (anecdote printed by Fénéon in *Bulletin de la vie artistique,* 1 April 1921). A number of paintings actually survived. But Fénéon's point was that German soldiers did not have a monopoly on ignorance and brutality.

14. Léo d'Orfer, "La Grande Marotte," *Revue indépendante,* April 1885, p. 523. See also Eunice Lipton, "The Laundress in Late Nineteenth-Century French Culture."

15. Pierre Jacquin, letter to the author, Saint-Cannat, 2 July 1975.

16. Ivan Aguéli to Richard Bergh, translated from the Swedish into French and quoted in part to Félix Fénéon by Axel Gauffin, Aguéli's biographer, on 9 July 1939, Nationalmuseum archives, Stockholm.

17. Concerning Aguéli, Fénéon to Axel Gauffin, Valescure-St. Raphaël (Var), 22 July and 22 Aug. 1939, National museum archives, Stockholm.

18. Aguéli to Richard Bergh, Oct. 1893, Nationalmuseum archives, Stockholm.

19. L. Descaves, *Souvenirs d'un ours,* p. 123.

20. Reported by the daughter of Zo d'Axa, Mme Marcel Arnac, in an interview with the author.

21. Toulouse-Lautrec to Fénéon, n. d., Dr. Karpman-Boutet archives, Paris.

22. Lautrec quoted by Jacques Daurelle, "Chez les jeunes peintres," *Echo de Paris,* 28 Dec. 1891.

23. Emile Pouget, *Père peinard,* no. 1, Sunday, 24 Feb. 1889.

24. Cohen, *In Opstand* pp. 215–17.

25. Concerning Chatel, Fénéon to Axel Gauffin, 13 Aug. 1939, Nationalmuseum archives, Stockholm.

26. "Inédits de Laforgue," *Revue anarchiste,* 1 Nov. 1893, p. 65.

27. Signac to Fénéon, 18 Feb. 1934, courtesy of John Rewald, New York.

28. Cohen, *In Opstand,* pp. 187–88.

29. Alfred Jarry, "Ames solitaires," pp. 21–25.

30. Fénéon, signing "Gaston Dubois," "Ames solitaires," *Revue libertaire,* no. 1, 15 Dec. 1893, p. 13. Not in *Oeuvres plus que complètes.*

31. Ibid. Among the signatures were those of: Georges Auriol, Henry Bauër, Louis Capazza, Charles Chatel, F.-A. Cazals, Rodolphe Darzens, Léon-Paul Fargue, A. Hamon, L.-W. Hawkins, André Ibels, Alfred Jarry, Julien Leclercq, Stuart Merrill, Gabriel Mourez, P.-N. Roinard, Saint-Pol-Roux, Paul Sérusier, and Georges Vanor.

32. C. C. and H. G. [Charles Chatel and "Henri Gauche," pseud. of René Chaughi], "Des Faits," *Revue libertaire,* 1 Jan. 1894, pp. 22–23.

CHAPTER 13: *Bombs, and the "Woman" in Mme Fénéon's Gown*

1. V. Barrucand on Ravachol, *L'Endehors,* no. 64, 24 July 1892.

2. F, 217. "Peintures: Henri de Toulouse-Lautrec et Charles Maurin chez Boussod et Valadon," unsigned article in *L'Endehors,* 12 Feb. 1893.

3. Henry's theft of a cow, told by Fénéon to Suzanne Alazet Des Meules, who reported it to the author, interview 16–17 July 1966.

4. Reported by Jean Paulhan, Emile Compard, and Suzanne Alazet Des Meules in separate interviews with the author, 1962 and 1966. At the time, the police believed a woman, Marie Puget, laid the bomb (Police Archives B/A 1.115).

5. G. Kahn, *Symbolistes et décadents,* p. 59.

6. A. Cohen, incident of the "lady seal," reported in *La Patrie,* 19 July 1894, after a telephone interview with Cohen, residing in London.

7. Fénéon to Signac, [12 Feb. 1894], Bibliothéque littéraire Jacques Doucet, Paris.

8. Statement read to the court by Vaillant to explain his action, reprinted in Bouchardon, *Ravachol et Cie,* p. 216.

9. Paraphrased from Emile Henry's "Déclaration" addressed to the Assize Court of the Seine, 28 April 1894, reprinted in Maitron, *Histoire du mouvement anarchiste en France,* 1st edition only, pp. 528–34.

10. Charles Malato interviewed in London and quoted in *Le Matin,* 28 Feb. 1894.

11. Octave Mirbeau, *Le Journal,* 19 Feb. 1894. Cf. his laudatory "Ravachol!", *L'Endehors,* 1 May 1892.

12. Fénéon, conversation recorded in Paul Signac's journal on 26 Dec. 1895. Rewald, ed., "Extraits du journal inédit de Paul Signac," p. 113.

13. See Maitron. *Histoire du mouvement anarchiste en France,* p. 534, n.1.

14. Emile Henry, "Déclaration" to the court, Maitron, *Histoire du mouvement anarchiste en France,* 1st edition, p. 533.

15. Information told by André Salmon to François Sullerot, 1964, according to a memo sent by M. Sullerot to the author. See also André Salmon, *La Terreur noire,* pp. 356–67 and p. 407: for "un subtil homme de lettres" read Félix Fénéon and for "un très vieux témoin," Alexandre Cohen.

16. Paris Police Archives, BA/79, no. 89, report dated 10 March 1894.

17. Ibid., BA/79, no. 138 (ca. 10 April 1894), signed "Legrand."

18. Tailhade quoted by André Billy, *L'Epoque 1900,* p. 437.

19. "Les Anarchistes," *L'Eclair,* 28 April 1894; "Le Procès des Trente," *Gazette des Tribunaux,* 9 Aug. 1894.

20. E. Henry, in Maitron, *Histoire du mouvement anarchiste en France,* 1st edition, p. 534.

CHAPTER 14: *Imprisonment and Trial*

In this chapter, most of the quotations from newspaper articles on Fénéon's arrest and the Trial of the Thirty are from a dossier Madame Fénéon *mère* kept in 1894 and which F. F. annotated after her death in 1906: 112 pages of press clippings, trial notes taken by Thadée Natanson, notes and drawings by Fénéon. Paris, Bibliothèque littéraire Jacques Doucet, B[1]–111–13, Ms. 6920.

1. Details on arrest of F. F., including dialogue, from "Arrestation de M. Félix Fénon [*sic*].—Interview de Mme Fénon . . . " *Le Jour,* 28 April 1894.

2. Details on the questioning of F. F. up to and including "I am an anarchist and that is my right" (p. 281, above), as reported in: (1) *Le Temps,* 28 April 1894, "L'Arrestation de M. Félix Fénéon" (information leaked to the press by M. Puybaraud, police inspector); (2) *Le Figaro,* from *La Gazette des Tribunaux,* 8 August 1894, "Le Procès des Trente (seconde audience)."

3. Fénéon described in *L'Eclair*, 7 Aug. 1894.

4. Verlaine and Mallarmé quoted in "Arrestation d'un employé du ministère de la guerre: chez Paul Verlaine; chez M. Mallarmé," *Le Soir*, 27 April 1894.

5. B. Lazare, "Félix Fénéon," *Le Journal*, 27 April 1894.

6. O. Mirbeau, "Félix Fénéon, *Le Journal*, 29 April 1894.

7. "Arrestation de M. Félix Fénéon," *Le Temps*, 28 April 1894. Inspector Puybaraud quoted this description of a painting by Guillaumin in Fénéon's *Impressionnistes en 1886:* "In the shadow of frutescent tangles of brushwood the moirés of the little stream expand into ellipses swept off by the water, then form again . . . " (F, 33). To show how skewed F. F.'s judgment was, he then juxtaposed another extract about an officially accepted artist (Mr. Protais), whose paintings of bloody battles hung in the Luxembourg Museum of contemporary art: "For many years his malarial eye will dampen his canvases, patiotic handkerchiefs . . . " (F, 62).

8. F. F. fired from the War Office, *Le Jour*, 2 May 1894.

9. Barrès writing on execution of Emile Henry, *Le Journal*, 22 May 1894, and Clemenceau, "La Guillotine," *La Justice*, 23 May 1894.

10. Marie-Louise Fénéon to Octave Maus, 17 May 1894, Albert Vanderlinden archives, Brussels.

11. G. Kahn in *Le Soir*, 30 April 1894.

12. Marie-Louise Fénéon to Gustave Kahn, 5 Aug. 1894, Dr. Karpman-Boutet archives, Paris.

13. See chap. 10, "Transitions," p. 211.

14. Fénéon to G. Kahn, [August 1894], Dr. Karpman-Boutet archives, Paris.

15. Fénéon to Axel Gauffin, 8 July 1939, Nationalmuseum archives, Stockholm.

16. "Après le verdict . . . le régime de Mazas," interview with Chatel and Aguéli, *L'Eclair*, 15 Aug. 1894.

17. Reported by Thadée Natanson, "Ceux de la *Revue blanche:* Félix Fénéon," radio broadcast, Paris, 25 Nov. 1938, quoted by Rewald, "Félix Fénéon," pp. 107–08.

18. See Georges Blond, *La Grande Armée du drapeau noir*, p. 238.

19. Paris Police Archives, BA/79, no. 500, report dated 27 July 1894.

20. C. Pissarro to Lucien, Knocke near Bruges, 30 July 1894, *Letters to His Son Lucien*, p. 245.

21. Fénéon quoted in *Le Gaulois*, 9 Aug. 1894.

22. Paris Police Archives, report signed "contrôle général" and dated 6 Aug. 1894.

23. This extract and the following one are from "Justice criminelle, première audience du Procès des trente: l'acte d'accusation," *Gazette des Tribunaux*, 6–7 Aug. 1894.

24. H. Rochefort, "Les Hommes aux masques de fer," *L'Intransigeant*, 9 Aug. 1894.

25. Reported by E. Cravoisier in the *Libre parole*, 7 Aug. 1894.

26. Extracts from the *Gazette des Tribunaux, Libre parole, Petit Parisien, Temps, Intransigeant, Presse, Figaro, Journal, Eclair, Petite République, Soir, Echo de Paris*, week of 6–14 Aug. 1894. Although the news reports are in substantial agreement, they differ sufficiently in detail so that none can be accepted as verbatim.

27. Police report on conversations in Montmartre bars, Paris Police Archives, BA/79 No. 528, report signed ╂, 8 Aug. 1894.

28. Mallarmé, "Citation à témoigner," quoted by Henri Mondor, *Vie de Mallarmé* (Paris, 1941), pp. 688–89. This text, copied from Mallarmé's original manuscript, is more accurate than the newspaper versions.

29. Charles Henry, quoted in *Gazette des Tribunaux*, 9 Aug. 1894.

30. E. Demange, quoted by Henri Varenne, "Plaidoirie de Me Demange," *L'Intransigeant*, 13 Aug. 1894.

31. Reported by Henri Varennes, "Incident de cabinet," *L'Intransigeant*, 13 Aug. 1894, and in several other newspapers.

32. Paris Police Archives, reports dated 13 and 18 Aug. 1894 by agents signing ╂ and "Z.I." (BA/79, nos. 531 and 537).

33. *La Presse*, 14 Aug. 1894.

34. Fénéon quoted in "Après le verdict," *L'Eclair*, 15 Aug. 1894. Note the judge's (pejorative?)

use of the noun, "intellectuals." Historians have thought that this word, used as a noun, came into existence only later in the decade, at the time of the Dreyfus affair. Here is evidence that it was used earlier for the anarchist writers in the Trial of the Thirty. Cf. this extract from the *Libre Parole,* 8 Aug. 1894, reporting on the second day of the trial:

> Il y a trente-neuf témoins à charge: tous parleront des vols commis par Ortiz et sa bande. Les *intellectuels* semblent, dès à présent, n'être que des spectateurs. (*Italics in the text.*)

35. Maitron, *Le Mouvement anarchiste en France,* vol. 1, pp. 258–59.

CHAPTER 15: *At the* Revue blanche

1. Fénéon to Octave Mirbeau, 10 Jan. 1895, Bibliothèque nationale, Paris, ms. n.a.fr. 14687: 69–70.

2. A month after Fénéon's arrest in April 1894, a police agent reported that Alfred Jarry, Léon-Paul Fargue, Louis Lormel, and other writers at the Oeuvre were planning to launch an anarchist publication like the defunct *Revue libertaire* (Paris Police Archives BA/79 No. 376, dated 25 May 1894, signed ╪).

3. Remarks by Fénéon recorded on 16 Dec. 1894, Rewald, ed., "Extraits du journal inédit de Paul Signac," p. 113.

4. Police informant, Paris Police Archives, report dated 28 Nov. 1894, BA/79, No. 719, signed "Cottance."

5. Lugné-Poe, *La Parade,* vol. 2, *Acrobaties,* p. 132.

6. In "La Vie contemporaine," *Revue contemporaine,* 8th year, vol. 1 (1895), p. 321.

7. Gérard de Nerval to Jules Janin, 1 June 1850, *Oeuvres* (Paris, 1966), vol. 1, pp. 995–96. Nerval's version played at the Odéon between 13 May and 2 June 1850. The name of the mythical king-author, Sudraka, means "low-casteling."

8. Victor Barrucand, preface to *Chariot de terre cuite,* quoted by Lugné-Poe, *La Parade,* vol. 2, *Acrobaties,* p. 272.

9. *The History of Sexuality,* 1978.

10. *Catherine Morland, Revue blanche* July–Dec. 1898, and in book form, 1899, published by the review.

11. Stuart Merrill, "Quelques livres anglais," *La Vogue,* May 1899, pp. 129–30.

12. C. Pissarro, *Letters to his Son Lucien,* Rewald, ed., letters dated 16 and 25 April 1896.

13. "Enquête sur l'influence des lettres scandinaves" and "La Commune."

14. F. F. to Henri de Bouillane de Lacoste, Valescure, 18 May 1939, Bibliothèque littéraire Jacques Doucet, Paris.

15. Edouard Deverin, "Fénéon l'énigmatique," *Mercure de France,* 15 Feb. 1931, p. 80.

16. Lugné-Poe, *La Parade,* vol. 3, *Sous les Etoiles,* p. 37.

17. Th. Natanson, "Ceux de la *Revue blanche,*" radio broadcast, Paris, 25 Nov. 1938, quoted by Rewald, "Félix Fénéon," p. 114.

18. Francis de Miomandre, quoted by Ed. Deverin, "Fénéon l'énigmatique," p. 78.

19. F. F. to Paul-Jean Toulet, Paris, 11 Dec. 1897, Archives of the Bibliothèque de la ville de Pau. Toulet's poems, "Entr'Actes, Epigrammes," appeared in the March 1898 issue of the *Revue blanche.*

20. Bonnard's ink drawing, *The Life of the Painter: the "Revue blanche,"* was published by John Rewald, *Gazette des Beaux-Arts,* Feb. 1948, p. 119. Van Dongen's pastel of F. F. at the *Revue blanche* was published by Jean Paulhan in *F. F. ou le critique,* p. 61.

21. Toulouse-Lautrec's "Bar" at Alexandre Natanson's, Francis Jourdain, *Né en 76,* pp. 172–74. Cf. Henri Perruchot, *La Vie de Toulouse-Lautrec* (Paris; 1958), pp. 162, 240–242.

22. Regarding the *Mercure,* F. F., indulging in a bit of rivalry, wrote a note to Dujardin about his listing of reviews for *L'Agence Universelle de journaux et publications illustrées:* "Shouldn't you put the names of the two reviews in alphabetical order? *L* (La revue blanche) comes before *M* (Mercure de France). . . . This is a purely personal observation." (F. F. to Ed. Dujardin, 18 Feb. 1899, Paris, Bibliothèque littéraire Jacques Doucet, fonds Mondor.)

23. F. F. to Alfred Jarry, Paris, 7 March 1896, and Jarry to Fénéon, 15 March, published by Maurice Saillet, "Petite Histoire," introduction to Jarry, *La Chandelle verte,* pp. 15–16.

24. Léon Blum, "Les Romans," *Revue blanche,* 15 Nov. 1897.

25. Dauberville, *Bataille de l'impressionnisme,* pp. 157–58. Fénéon's use of *spadassin* had a double barb, for it really meant a swashbuckler or—in commedia dell'arte and Molière—a hired assassin.

26. P. Signac, "Fragments de Journal," (extraits par Georges Besson), *Arts de France,* 1947, Nos. 11–12, p. 102, and nos. 17–18, p. 75.

27. Jarry to Fénéon, Laval, 6 June 1906; also, Jarry to Vallette, in "Petite Histoire" by Maurice Saillet, ed., Jarry, *La Chandelle verte,* p. 25.

28. Henryk Sienkiewicz to F. Fénéon, Warsaw, 14 Dec. 1901, Paulhan archives, Paris.

29. F. F. to Verlaine, 30 Oct. 1895, Bibliothèque littéraire Jacques Doucet, Paris, ms. 7203.33.

30. F. F. to Paul Valéry, 14 Nov. 1899, courtesy Mme Paul Rouart.

31. F. F. to Paul Signac, 3 and 18 June 1898, Cachin-Signac archives, Paris.

32. Fénéon's admiration for Lucie Cousturier can be seen in the article he wrote after her death in 1925 (F, 477). See also Thadée Natanson, *Peints à leur tour,* pp. 128–29.

33. Signac to Angrand, 30 April 1900, courtesy Pierre Angrand.

34. Vaillant, "Les amitiés de la *Revue Blanche,*" p. 119.

35. Vuillard to Fénéon, "Monday," [ca. 1896], Paulhan archives, Paris.

36. Mallarmé to Fénéon, Valvins, Friday [21 Aug. 1896], Mallarmé, *Correspondance,* Mondor and Austin, eds., pp. 211–12.

37. Fénéon to Madame Stéphane Mallarmé, Lille, 11 Sept. 1898, Mallarmé, *Correspondance,* Vol. 10, p. 289.

38. Homage to Mallarmé, "Deuil," reprinted in F, 849.

39. Jules Renard, *Journal 1898,* Paris, 1927, p. 461.

40. Geneviève Mallarmé to Edouard Dujardin, 29 Jan. 1899, courtesy Mme Marie Dujardin.

41. Georges Clemenceau to F. Fénéon, Paris, 26 Dec. 1900, Paulhan archives, Paris.

42. In Dauberville, *Bataille de l'impressionnisme,* pp. 163–64.

43. André Gide, *Feuillets d'automne,* "La Revue blanche," dated October 1946, pp. 139–41.

CHAPTER 16: *Private Life and Loves*

1. Maria van Rysselberghe, under the name, M. Saint-Clair, *Galerie privée,* pp. 74–75.

2. Reported by Mme M. Duthuit, daughter of Matisse, interview, March 1963.

3. Letter to the author by a person who wishes to remain anonymous.

4. See "L'Expression de l'amour chez les poètes symbolistes," in Raynaud, *Mêlée symboliste,* vol. 2, pp. 57–90.

5. Letter cited in note 3 above.

6. Fanny Fénéon to John Rewald, 24 Aug. 1938, courtesy Mr. Rewald.

7. Raynaud, *Mêlée symboliste,* vol. 2. p. 38.

8. Philippe Girardet to Jean Paulhan, 2 Oct. 1949, Paulhan archives, Paris, and Joseph Jolinon, "Fénéon ou l'intelligence faite homme," p. 7.

9. Reported by Emile Compard, interview, 5 March 1963.

10. F. F. to his wife, Royan (Charente Maritime), ca. 1935. Fanny's birthday, mentioned in the letter, was August 2d. If the year 1935 is right, it was her sixty-seventh. Courtesy Gina Doveil.

11. Fénéon wrote his own employers, Josse and Gaston Bernheim, on 12 Nov. 1914, asking for a recommendation for Gilbert Gardein, aged 15, who was seeking employment at the Crédit Lyonnais. "Indeed, we have known the applicant since his infancy, and we have always taken an interest, rightly, in him and his mother" (Archives of the Bernheim-Jeune Gallery, Paris, courtesy Gilbert Gruet).

12. Fénéon to Suzanne des Meules, n. d. except "Vendredi." They met around 1910, and the friendship continued until Fénéon's death.

13. Fénéon to Suzanne des Meules, n.d. except "the 21st."

14. Vaillant, *Bonnard,* p. 132. Thadée Natanson, *Peints à leur tour,* pp. 113–120.

15. Louise Hervieu to Suzanne des Meules, communicated to the author by S. des Meules.

16. André Breton to Jean Paulhan. 16 July 1949, Paulhan archives, Paris. See chap. 1.

17. F, 336. "Exposition de 50 tableaux et de 100 dessins d'Emile Compard," preface for the exhibition catalogue, the Renaissance, 1–14 Feb. 1930. Cf. Fénéon's inquiry among artists and writers on the sexual origins of art. "Enquête sur l'origine de lart," *Bulletin de la vie artistique,* IV: 14 (15 July 1923), p. 291 ff.

18. Bataille, "Informe."

19. Pierre Veber and Willy, *Une Passade,* pp. 53–54.

20. Fénéon quoted by Albert Charpentier, in *Bonnard, Laprade, Bouche,* p. 3. Translation in Rewald, *Pierre Bonnard,* p. 51.

21. Kees van Dongen to Félix and Fanny Fénéon, Rotterdam, [ca. 1897], Paulhan archives, Paris.

22. Henri-Edmond Cross to Fénéon, Saint Rafaël, 21 May 1905, John Rewald Collection, New York. According to a note that F. F. penciled in the margin of the letter, the article by Maurice Denis to which Cross was reacting was "La Réaction nationaliste," *Ermitage,* 15 March 1905, reprinted in Maurice Denis, *Théories* (Paris, Bibliothèque de l'Occident, 1912).

23. Fénéon to Maximilien Luce (in Brittany), Paris, 19 Aug. 1914, courtesy of the late Frédéric Luce.

24. Fénéon quoted by John Rewald, "Félix Fénéon," p. 117.

25. Fénéon's apartment on Grandes Carrières described by Philippe Girardet, *Ceux que j'ai connus,* p. 174. See also Ernest Millard, "Le Commerce de la peinture," p. 286.

26. Emile Compard to J. U. Halperin, Paris, 10 June 1973.

27. Fénéon to John Rewald, Marseille, 17 May 1940, courtesy Mr. Rewald.

28. Félix to Fanny Fénéon, "Jeudi 26" [1935?], courtesy Gina Doveil.

29. Dauberville, *Bataille de l'impressionnisme,* pp. 156–57.

30. Paul Signac to F. Fénéon, Saint Tropez, [1899], Cachin-Signac archives, Paris.

31. Dauberville, *Bataille de l'impressionnisme,* p. 157.

CHAPTER 17: *The Terrorist in Three Lines*

1. Baldeshwiler, "Félix Fénéon and the Minimal Story."

2. Billy, *L'Epoque 1900,* p. 357.

3. Fénéon to Severino Rappa, on a card from the *Figaro,* [Dec. 1903]. Bibliothèque littéraire Jacques Doucet, Paris.

4. Idem.

5. Zeldin, *France,* vol. 2, p. 520.

6. Fénéon to Karl Boès, 1st March [1904?]. Bibliothèque littéraire Jacques Doucet, Paris.

7. *Souvenirs sans fin,* vol. 1 p. 352.

8. Three letters of Signac to Fénéon, 16 Aug. 1905. Sept. 1905, and a third, undated. Cachin-Signac archives, Paris.

9. Fénéon to Henry van de Velde, Paris, 19 Sept. 1905. Bibliothèque Royale, ms. F.S.X. 393/1, Brussels.

10. Concerning *Le Matin,* see F. I. Mouthon, *Du Bluff au chantage,* pp. 50–61.

11. Bunau-Varilla's question and Fénéon's response, reported in separate interviews with René Delange (La Vallée aux Loups, 12 July 1962) and Jacques Rodrigues-Henriques (Paris, 8 Oct. 1963).

12. Fénéon to Mme Albert André, postcard, Méréville, 6 Feb. 1906. Courtesy Mme G. Besson.

13. *Libération,* 30 Sept. 1976.

14. Paulhan, *F. F. ou le critique,* p. 56.

15. Moore, *La Rochefoucauld, His Mind and Art,* p. 7.

16. O. Wilde, "The Critic as Artist," (1891), *Complete Works,* p. 1034.

17. Madison Bell, "Less is Less, The dwindling American short story," *Harper's* 272 (April 1986): 64–69.

18. Paulhan, *F. F. ou le critique,* p. 67.

19. Baldeshwiler, "Félix Fénéon and the Minimal Story," p. 66.

20. Décaudin, "Celui qui silence."

21. Fénéon to Henry van de Velde, Paris, Bernheim-Jeune stationery, 4 Nov. 1906. Bruxelles, Bibliothèque Royale, ms. F.S.X. No. X393/3.

22. Signac to Charles Angrand, Paris, 21 Nov. 1906, and Paris, 21 Nov. 1906. Courtesy Pierre Angrand.

23. Maximilien Luce to Angrand, 7 Dec. 1906. Courtesy Pierre Angrand.

24. Fénéon to Charles Angrand, Paris, Bernheim-Jeune stationery with a new FF logo, 3 May 1907. Bernheim-Jeune archives, Paris.

25. Gilbert Gruet, interview with the author, Paris, 7 March 1963.

26. Georges Besson, "En souvenir du très singulier Félix Fénéon." Solange Lemaître, interview with the author, 17 Dec. 1962.

27. Fénéon to Josse and Gaston Bernheim, Hamburg, 3 Jan. 1913, on Hotel Atlantic "Der Kaiserhof" stationery. Bernheim-Jeune archives, Paris.

28. Gilbert Gruet, letter to J. U. Halperin, Paris, 28 Dec. 1966.

29. G. Apollinaire, "M. Félix Fénéon." p. 431.

30. "La Faune" exhibition at Bernheim Jeune, Dec. 1910. See Francis Jourdain, "Du Côté de la *Revue blanche*." Cf. this letter from Luce to Charles Angrand (who was doing a series of pastels on farm animals):

> *Paris 17 Oct. 1910*
>
> I saw Fénéon yesterday. The Fauna exhibition will probably take place in November. This exhibition, which I thought was earmarked exclusively for animals, is a huge joke, I see. Thus . . . there will be a work by Manet—a woman in the tub—since the sponge is an "animal." A woman looking for a flea will also be a pretext. A painting by Van Gogh—pickled herrings, etc. On the whole, there won't be much place for Fauna. (Courtesy Pierre Angrand)

31. Anecdote told by Matisse, quoted by Dauberville, *Bataille de l'impressionnisme,* pp. 153–54.

32. "Fénéon-fainéant," Henry Dauberville, pp. 161–62. The pun was made by others than the Bernheim children, but Fénéon himself claimed not to have noticed it until the year before he died. In a letter to Jean Paulhan, F. F. remarked on an article by Jacques Lemarchand in *La Gerbe* (6 May 1943): "He also uses my supposed nickname, 'le roi Fénéon." Surely this joke, whose Merovingian sting I missed on the first hearing, only dates from April, invented by the reporters of rue Gaillon. Moreover, it matters little to the Republic." (Fénéon to Paulhan, La Vallée aux Loups, 11 June 1943, Paulhan archives. Paris.)

33. Fénéon to Jean Paulhan, 17 Nov. [1943], Paulhan archives, Paris.

34. Claude Dauberville to J. U. Halperin, 13 Jan. 1973.

35. Thadée Natanson, "Félix Fénéon," talk on Radio-Paris, 25 Nov. 1938, extracts printed in César M. de Hauke, *Seurat et son oeuvre,* Vol. 1, p. xix.

36. Nietzsche, *The Gay Science,* No. 381, "On the question of being understandable."

37. Much in Fénéon's preface to Duranty's *Cause du beau Guillaume* (F, 589–93) resembles an article by Jules Christophe in Fénéon's *Revue indépendante* of April 1885, pp. 494–513. It is impossible to determine now whether Christophe's material was originally furnished him by Fénéon, who all his life was intrigued by Duranty, or whether F. F. later copied Christophe.

38. Fénéon quoted by René Delange and comment by Emile Compard, interview with the author, La Vallée aux Loups, 10 March 1963.

39. Solange Lemaître, interview, Paris, 17 Dec. 1962.

40. Fénéon's and Degas's mutual fear of being wounded by the other's wit, reported by Jacques Rodriques-Henriques, interview with the author, Paris, 14 March 1963.

41. Remy de Gourmont, *Le IIe livre des Masques,* p. 40.

42. J. Paulhan, *F. F. ou le critique,* pp. 67–68.

43. Fénéon quoted by Bernard Groethuysen in a note by Paulhan: "Bernard Groeth. me fait

observer l'intransigeance sociale de F. F. que j'aurias dû mieux marquer. Très précisément, l'honnête homme était à ses yeux celui qui ne se mêlait pas à la société bourgeoise; celui qui "n'en était pas" mais qui disait à son propos *leur* (leurs amours, leur Chambre des Députés, leurs commerces). Il n'a jam[ais] pardonné à Gide, pour qui il avait eu longt[emps] une vive affection, son *Retour de l'URSS*." Paulhan archives, Paris.

44. Fénéon quoted by Joseph Jolinon, "Fénéon ou l'Intelligence faite homme," p. 7.

45. Hubert Juin, "Félix Fénéon, le gentleman des lettres," p. 103.

46. Unsigned obituary, "Raymond Cox," *Bulletin de la vie artistique,* 1 Jan. 1921, p. 11. Not included in *Oeuvres plus que complètes.*

47. Françoise Cachin, Introduction to Félix Fénéon, *Au-delà de l'impressionnisme,* pp. 27 and 28.

Bibliography

Abric, L. "Félix Fénéon," *Le Monde illustré,* 21 May 1938.

Adam, Paul. *Soi.* Paris, 1886.

———. "Peintres impressionnistes." *Revue contemporaine* (April–May 1886): 541–51.

——— [Plowert, pseud.]. "Parenthèses et incidences." *Le Symboliste,* 30 Oct. 1886.

——— [B. de Monconys, pseud.]. On Fénéon's *Impressionnistes en 1886. La Vie moderne* (Dec. 1886): 779.

——— [Jacques Plowert, pseud.]. *Petit glossaire pour servir à l'intelligence des auteurs décadents et symbolistes.* Paris, 1888.

Ajalbert, Jean. "Théâtres." *Revue indépendante,* Dec. 1887.

———. "A travers mes souvenirs—Félix Fénéon." *L'Esprit français,* 6 Dec. 1929.

———. *Mémoires en vrac au temps du symbolisme, 1880–1890.* Paris, 1938.

Alexandre, Arsène. "Critique décadente: *Les Impressionnistes en 1886.*" *L'Evénement,* 10 Dec. 1886.

———. "Signalement d'un accusè [Félix Fénéon]." *L'Eclair, 4 May 1894.*

———. *Paul Gauguin, sa vie et le sens de son oeuvre.* Paris, 1930.

Alexis, Paul. "Visite à la *Revue indépendante.*" *Cri du peuple,* 14 April 1888.

Amacher, Peter. *Freud's Neurological Education and Its Influence on Psychoanalytic Theory.* New York, 1965.

Angrand, Pierre. *Naissance des Artistes indépendants, 1884.* Paris, 1965.

Anonymous [Carlo Cafiero?]. "L'Action." *Le Révolté,* No. 22 (25 Dec. 1880).

Anonymous [Paul Adam, Félix Fénéon, Oscar Méténier, Jean Moréas]. *Petit bottin des lettres et des arts.* Paris, 1886.

Anonymous. "Médaillon: Elie-Félix-Fénéon." *Le Décadent,* 25 Sept. 1886.

Anonymous. "Un Référendum artistique et social." *L'Ermitage* 1893, no. 7: 1–24 and no. 11: 257–65.

Anonymous. "Arrestation de M. Félix Fénéon," *Le Temps,* 28 April 1894, information leaked to the press by Mr. Puybaraud, police inspector.

Anonymous. "Arrestation de M. Félix Fénon [sic].—Interview de Mme Fénon . . . " *Le Jour,* 28 April 1894.

Anonymous. Newspaper reports on the "Procès des Trente," 6–14 August 1894. In the *Gazette des Tribunaux, Libre parole, Petit Parisien, Gaulois, Temps, Intransigeant, Presse, Figaro, Journal. Eclair, Petite République, Soir, Echo de Paris.*

Anonymous. "Après le verdict . . . le régime de Mazas." Interview with Charles Chatel and Ivan Aguéli. *L'Eclair,* 15 Aug. 1894.

Anonymous. Report on "Le Chariot de terre cuite," "La Vie contemporaine." *Revue contemporaine,* 8th year, 1(1895):321.

Anonymous. "Zo d'Axa." *Revue anarchiste,* July–Oct. 1930.

Antoine, Jules. "Impressionnistes et Synthétistes." *Art et critique,* 9 Nov. 1889.

Apollinaire, Guillaume. "M. Félix Fénéon." *Mercure de France,* 14 Feb. 1914, p. 431.

Aragon, Louis. *Je n'ai jamais appris à écrire ou les incipit.* Geneva, 1969.

Arguëlles, José. *Charles Henry and the Formation of a Psychophysical Aesthetic.* Chicago, 1972.

Arlin, J. "F. Fénéon." *Arts,* 12 March 1948.

Astruc, A. "Félix Fénéon ou la vocation." *Confluences* (April–May 1944): 372–76.

Aurier, Albert. "Concurrence." *Le Moderniste,* 27 June 1889.

———. "Le Symbolisme en peinture: Paul Gauguin." *Mercure de France,* March 1891, reprinted in *Oeuvres posthumes.* Paris. 1893.

———. "Claude Monet" (March, 1892). *Oeuvres posthumes.* Paris, 1893.

Austin, Lloyd James, and Mondor, Henri, eds., *Stéphane Mallarmé, Correspondance,* Paris, vols. 2–9. Paris, 1965–83.

Bachrach, Susan D. "The Feminization of the French Postal Service." Ph.D. diss., University of Wisconsin, 1981.

Baedeker, Karl. *Paris and Environs.* Paris, 1888.

Bailly-Herzberg, Janine, ed. *Correspondance de Camille Pissarro,* vols. 2 and 3. Paris, 1985–87.

Bakunin, Mikhail A. *La Commune de Paris et la notion d'état.* Paris, 1871.

———. *Etatisme et anarchie.* Paris 1873.

Baldeshwiler, Eileen M. "Félix Fénéon and the Minimal Story." *Critique* [Studies in Modern fiction, 14] 1(1972): 63–75.

Barrès, Maurice. Report on the execution of Emile Henry. *Le Journal,* 22 May 1894.

Barrucand, Victor. On Ravachol. *L'Endehors,* no. 64, 24 July 1892.

———. "Le Chariot de Terre cuite." Drama adapted from the Sanskrit. Paris, 1895.

Barrucand, Victor, and Fénéon, Félix. "Passím," *Revue blanche,* Feb.–June 1895.

Bataille, Georges. "Informe." *Documents* 1, No. 7 (December 1929).

Baudelaire, Charles. "The Salon of 1859." In *The Mirror of Art,* ed. and trans. Jonathan Mayne. Garden City, 1956.

Baudelaire, Charles. "Le Dandy," trans. Jonathan Mayne. *The Painter of Modern Life and Other Essays.* London, 1965.

Benjamin, Walter. "Paris, capitale du xixe siècle" (1935). *Essais 2,* trans. M. de Gandillac. Paris, 1983.

Béraud, Henri [Urbain Dhère, pseud.]. "Félix Fénéon." *Les Hommes du Jour,* no. 35 (12 Nov. 1921).

Berne-Joffroy, André. "F. F." *Confluences,* July 1944, p. 69.

———. "Le Problème de la critique d'art." Exposé given at a meeting of the International Association of Art Critics, Paris, (A.I.C.A.), 14 March 1963.

———. *Jean Paulhan à travers ses peintres.* Exhibition catalogue, Grand Palais, Paris, 1974. Letters and other documents concerning F. Fénéon.

Bernier, Georges. *La revue blanche, Paris in the days of Post-Impressionism and Symbolism.* Exhibition catalogue, New York, Wildenstein, 1983.

Berthier, Philippe. Review of J. U. Halperin, *Félix Fénéon and the Language of Art Criticism* (Ann Arbor, 1980). *Revue d'histoire littéraire de la France* 82(1982): 945–46.

Besson, Georges. "En Souvenir du très singulier Félix Fénéon." *Lettres françaises,* 18–25 Feb. 1954.

Billy, André. *L'Epoque 1900 (1885–1905).* Paris, 1951.

Blond, Georges. *La Grande armée du drapeau noir.* Paris, 1972.

Blum, Léon, "Les Romans." *Revue blanche,* 15 Nov. 1897.

———. *Souvenirs sur l'Affaire.* Paris, 1935.

Boisson, Marius. *Les Attentats anarchistes sous la Troisième République.* Paris, 1931.

Bouchardon, Pierre. *Ravachol et Cie.* Paris, 1931.

Bouillane de Lacoste, Henri de, ed. Rimbaud, *Illuminations, Painted Plates.* Paris, 1949, with extracts from letters of F. Fénéon.

Bourget, Paul. *Nouveaux essais de psychologie contemporaine.* Paris, 1885.

Brame, Paul, and de Hauke, César M. *Seurat et son oeuvre, etudes et documents.* 2 vols. Paris, 1961. Catalogue prepared in large part by Félix Fénéon.

Brée, Germaine, ed. *Great French Short Stories.* New York, 1960.

Bruchard, H. de. *Petits mémoires du temps de la ligue avec haine et sans crainte.* Paris, Nouvelle Librairie Nationale, no date [ca. 1896]. Chapter 2, on Fénéon: "one of the men who have done the most in corrupting the minds of their young contemporaries with cowardly dilettantism and aimless irony."

Cachin, Françoise, ed. Paul Signac, *D'Eugène Delacroix au neo-impressionnisme.* Paris, 1964.

———. "Le portrait de Fénéon par Signac: une source inédite." *Revue de l'art,* no. 6 (1969).

———. *Paul Signac,* trans. Michael Bullock. Greenwich, Conn., 1971.

———. "Les Neo-Impressionnistes et le Japonisme, 1885–1893." In *Japonisme in Art, an International Symposium.* Tokyo, 1980.

———, ed. Félix Fénéon, *Au-delà de l'impressionnisme.* Paris, 1966.

Campbell, A. W., ed. *A Friendship of the Nineties: Letters between John Gray & Pierre Louÿs.* Edinburgh, 1984.

Camus, Albert. *The Rebel* [*L'Homme révolté*], trans. A. Bower. New York, 1961.

Carr, Reg. *Anarchism in France: The Case of Octave Mirbeau.* Montreal, 1977.

Cevasco, G. A. *John Gray.* Boston, 1982.

Charpentier, Armand. *Le Roman d'un singe.* Paris, 1895.

Charpentier, Albert. Introduction to the exhibition catalogue, *Bonnard, Laprade, Bouche.* Paris: Durand-Ruel, May 1939.

Chastel, André. "Seurat-Fénéon." *Le Monde,* 30 Dec. 1970, p. 9.

Chatel, Charles, and Chaughi, René, signing C. C. and H. G. ["Henri Gauche," pseud. of René Chaughi]. "Des Faits." *Revue libertaire,* 1 Jan. 1894, pp. 22–23.

Christophe, Jules. "Symbolisme." *La Cravache,* 16 June 1888.

———. "Seurat." *Les Hommes d'aujourd'hui,* vol. 8, no. 368, Paris, 1890.

———. "Georges Seurat." *La Plume,* September 1891.

Clark, T. J. *The Painting of Modern Life, Paris in the Art of Manet and His Followers.* New York, 1985.

Clemenceau, Georges. "La Guillotine" [execution of Emile Henry]. *La Justice,* 23 May 1894.

———. *La Mêlée sociale.* Paris, 1919.

Cohen, Alexandre. *In Opstand.* Amsterdam, 1932, repr. ed., G. A. van Oorschot Uitgever, 1967.

Colette. *L'Etoile Vesper, Souvenirs.* Paris, 1946.

Coquiot, Gustave. *Les Indépendants.* Paris, 1920.
Cornell, Kenneth. Review of F. F., *Oeuvres plus que complètes. French Review* 44 (1970–71): 1128–29.
Cravoisier, E., reporting on the Procès des Trente, *Libre parole,* 7 Aug. 1894.
Dauberville, Henry. *Bataille de l'impressionnisme.* Paris, 1968.
Daurelle, Jacques. "Chez les jeunes peintres." *Echo de Paris,* 28 Dec. 1891.
Décaudin, Michel. "Celui qui silence." *La Quinzaine littéraire* 102(16 Sept. 1970): 9–10.
———. "Félix Fénéon, Soft Spoken Anarchist." *Evergreen Review* 4, no. 13 (May–June 1960): 103.
Delange, René. "Fénéon sous les feux de l'actualité." *Culture française* 11(1964): 185–86.
Demange, Edgar, quoted by Henri Varennes. "Plaidoirie de Maître Demange." *L'Intransigeant,* 13 Aug. 1894.
Denis, Maurice. "La Réaction nationaliste." *Ermitage,* 15 March 1905. Reprinted in M. Denis. *Théories.* Paris, 1912.
Descaves, Lucien. *Souvenirs d'un ours.* Paris, 1946.
Deverin, Edouard. "Fénéon l'énigmatique." *Mercure de France,* 15 Feb. 1931, p. 80.
Dorra, Henri, and Rewald, John. *Seurat.* Paris, 1959.
Douwes Dekker, Eduard [Multatuli]. *The Oyster & the Eagle, Selected Aphorisms and Parables of Multatuli.* Ed. and Trans. E. M. Beekman. Amherst. 1974.
Drumont, Edouard A. *La Fin d'un monde.* Paris, 1889.
Du Bouchet, André. "Félix Fénéon or the Mute Critic." *Transition* 49, no. 5 (Dec. 1949): 79.
Dubois, Félix. *Le Péril anarchiste.* Paris, 1894.
Duranty, Louis Edmond. *La Nouvelle Peinture.* Paris, 1876.
Duret, Théodore. *La Critique d'avant-garde.* Paris, 1885.
Edwards, Stewart. *The Paris Commune, 1871.* New York, 1971.
Fabre des Essarts. "Un Aquitté" [F. Fénéon]. *La Méditerranée,* 25 August 1894.
Fénéon, Félix [Hombre, pseud.]. "Patrie." *Revue indépendante,* Sept. 1884, pp. 400–412.*
———. *Les Impressionnistes en 1886.* Editions de *Vogue.* Paris, 1886.
———. "*Les Lauriers sont coupés,* de M. Edouard Dujardin." *Vie moderne,* 27 May 1888.*
——— [unsigned]. "Notes et notules." *Entretiens politiques et littéraires,* April and June 1891.*
———[Gaston Dubois, pseud.]. "Ames solitaries." *Revue libertaire,* no. 1 (15 Dec. 1893): 13.*
———. trans. "Lettres d'Edgar Poe." *Revue blanche,* Feb. and Nov. 1895.*
———. ed. "Enquête sur l'influences des lettres scandinaves." *Revue blanche,* 12 (1897): 153–66; "La Commune," ibid.: 249–305 and 357–88.*
———. trans. Jane Austen, *Catherine Morland* [*Northanger Abbey*]. *Revue blanche* July–Dec. 1898, and in book form, 1899.*
———. Unsigned obituary, "Raymond Cox." *Bulletin de la vie artistique,* 1 Jan. 1921, p. 11.*
———. *Oeuvres.* Ed. Jean Paulhan. Paris, 1948.
———. *Au-delà de l'impressionnisme.* Ed. Françoise Cachin. Paris, 1966.
———. *Oeuvres plus que complètes.* Vol. 1, *Chroniques d'art.* Vol. 2, *Les Lettres, les Moeurs.* Ed. Joan U. Halperin. Geneva, 1970.
———. *Nouvelles en trois lignes.* Extracts illustrated with 10 color lithographs by Roland Topor. Monte-Carlo, 1975.
Fleming, Marie. *The Anarchist Way to Socialism, Elisée Reclus and Nineteenth-Century European Anarchism.* Totowa, N.J., 1979.

*Not in *Oeuvres plus que complètes.*

Fontainas, André de. *Mes souvenirs du symbolisme.* Paris, 1928.

Foucault, Michel. *The History of Sexuality,* Vol. 1. Trans. Robert Hurley. New York, 1978.

Francastel, P. *Du cubisme à l'art abstrait.* Paris, 1957.

France, Anatole. "La Vie à Paris." *Le Temps,* 24 Oct. 1886.

Gauguin, Paul. "Natures Mortes." *Essais d'art libre,* Jan. 1894.

———. *Lettres de Gauguin à sa femme et à ses amis.* Ed. Maurice Malingue. New edition. Paris, 1949.

———. *Noa-Noa.* Facsimile edition by Sagot-Le Garrec. Paris, 1954.

Gauthiers-Villars, Henry. *See* "Willy."

Gide, André. *Feuillets d'automne.* Paris, 1949.

Girardet, Philippe. *Ceux que j'ai connus.* Paris, 1952.

Goldwater, Robert J. *Symbolism.* New York, 1979.

Goncourt, Ed. de. *Journal, vol. 9 (1892–95). Paris, 1896.*

Goncourt, Edmond et Jules de. *Etudes d'art.* Paris, 1893.

Gourmont, Remy de. *Le IIe Livre des Masques.* Paris, 1898.

Gray, Christopher. *Sculpture and Ceramics of Paul Gauguin.* Baltimore, 1963.

Gray, John. *Silverpoints.* 1893; repr. ed., London, 1973.

Guillerm, J.-P. "Sur quelques lignes de Fénéon. Peinture et description." In *La Description.* Paris, 1974, pp. 167–79.

Hackett, C. A. Review of F. F., *Oeuvres plus que complètes. French Studies* 130 (1976): 85–87.

Hahnloser, H. R. Notes to *Bonnard* by Annette Vaillant. Trans. David Britt. Greenwich, Conn., 1966.

Halperin, Joan Ungersma, ed. Félix Fénéon, *Oeuvres plus que complétes.* 2 vols. Geneva, 1970.

———. *Félix Fénéon and the Language of Art Criticism.* Ann Arbor, 1980.

———. "*Jamais qu'unique:* Paradoxes in a Critic's View of Monet." In *Le Gai Savoir, Essays in Linguistics, Philology, and Criticism, in Memory of Manfred Sandmann,* pp. 168–87, ed. Mechthild Cranston. Potomac, Md., 1983.

Hamon, Augustin. *Psychologie de l'anarchiste-socialiste.* Paris, 1895.

Hauke, César M. de, and Brame, Paul. *Seurat et son oeuvre, etudes et documents.* 2 vols. Paris, 1961. Catalogue prepared in large part by F. Fénéon.

Helmholtz, Hermann von. *L'Optique et la peinture.* Fr. trsl. Paris, 1878, in the second part of a volume containing Brücke's *Principes scientifiques des beaux-arts.*

Henry, Charles. "Introduction à une esthétique scientifique." *Revue contemporaine,* Aug. 1885.

———. *Essai de Généralisation de la théorie du rayonnement.* Paris, 1924.

Herbert, Eugenia W. *The Artist and Social Reform, France and Belgium, 1885–1898.* New Haven, 1961.

Herbert, Robert L. *Seurat's Drawings.* New York, 1962.

———. *Neo-Impressionism.* Exhibition catalogue, Solomon R. Guggenheim Museum. New York, 1968.

———. "Seurat's Theories." *The Neo-Impressionists.* Ed. Jean Sutter. Greenwich, Conn., 1970.

———. "Master of Postcards [Félix Fénéon]." *Times Literary Supplement,* 10 August 1971.

———. " 'Parade de Cirque' de Seurat et l'esthétique scientifique de Charles Henry." *Revue de l'Art,* no. 50 (1981).

Herbert, Robert L. and Herbert, Eugenia W. "Artists and Anarchism. Unpublished Letters of Pissarro, Signac and Others." *Burlington Magazine* 102, no. 692 (Nov. 1960): 473–82, and no. 693 (Dec. 1960): 517–22.

Hoffstätter, H. H. "Félix Fénéon, Kritiker der avant-garde." *Kunstwerk* 19(Nov. 1965): 51–52.

Homer, W. I. *Seurat and the Science of Painting*. Cambridge, Mass., 1964.

House, John. "Meaning in Seurat's Figure Painting." *Art History* 3, no. 3 (Sept. 1980): 345–56.

Huret, Jules. *Enquête sur l'evolution littéraire*. Paris, 1891.

Hutton, Patrick H., Bourque, Amanda S., and Staples, Amy J., eds. *Historical Dictionary of the Third French Republic, 1870–1940*. 2 vols. New York, 1986.

Huysmans, Joris-Karl. *L'Art moderne*. Paris, 1883.

———. *A Rebours* (1884) and "Préface, écrite vingt ans après le roman," edition of 1903.

———. "Salon de 1887." *Revue indépendante*, June 1887.

———. "L'Exposition de Millet." *Revue indépendante*, July 1887, pp. 42–47.

———. *Certains*. Paris, 1889.

Ireson, J. C. *L'Oeuvre poétique de Gustave Kahn*. Paris, 1962.

Ives, Colta Feller. *The Great Wave: The Influence of Japanese Woodcuts on French Prints*. New York, 1979.

Jackson, A. B. *La Revue blanche (1889–1903), Origine, influence, bibliographie*. Paris, 1960.

Jankélévitch, Vladimir. *L'Ironie ou la bonne conscience*. Paris, 1950.

Jarry, Alfred. *Tout Ubu*. Paris, 1962.

———. *La Chandelle verte*. Ed. M. Saillet. Paris, 1969. Correspondence between Fénéon and Jarry, pp. 15–16, and 25.

———. *Gestes et opinions du docteur Faustroll* (1911). Paris, 1955.

———. "Ames solitaires." *Art littéraire*, 1894, nos. 1–2: 21–25.

———. *Selected Works*. Eds. R. Shattuck and S. W. Taylor. New York, 1965.

Jaulme, A., and Moncel, H. *Cinquantenaire du symbolisme*. Exhibition catalogue, Bibliothèque nationale. Paris, 1936.

Jeanson, Francis. "*Oeuvres* de Félix Fénéon." *Temps Modernes* 4, no. 40 (Feb. 1949): 355–56.

Jelenski, K. A. "Fénéon, le critique et l'amateur." *Preuves* 191 (Jan. 1967): 86–89.

Jolinon, Joseph. "Fénéon ou l'intelligence faite homme." *Nouvelles littéraires*, 6 May 1965.

Jouanny, Robert A. *Jean Moréas*. Paris, 1969.

———. Review of F. F., *Oeuvres plus que complètes* (1970). *Revue d'histoire littéraire de la France* 74 (1974): 132–33.

Jourdain, Francis. *Né en 76*. Paris, 1951.

———. "Du Côté de la *Revue blanche*." *Europe* 33, no. 112–13 (April–May 1955): 154–69.

———. *De mon temps*. Paris, 1963.

Juin, Hubert. "Félix Fénéon, le gentleman des lettres." *Ecrivains de l'avant-siècle*. Paris, 1972, pp. 101–9.

Kahn, Gustave. *Les Palais nomades*. Paris, 1887.

———. "Seurat." *Art moderne*, 5 April 1891.

———. "Souvenirs sur Fénéon." *Le Soir*, 30 April 1894.

———. *Symbolistes et décadents*. Paris, 1902. First printed as "Les Origines du symbolisme." *Revue blanche*, vol. 26, no. 202.

———. "Au temps du pointillisme." *Mercure de France* 171 (1 April 1924): 5–22.

———. *The Drawings of Seurat* (Paris, 1928). Trans. Stanley Applebaum. New York, 1971.

Kapferer, Simone. "Le vrai Fénéon—réponse à l'article de J. Arlin." *Arts*, 2 April 1948.

Kedward, Roderick. *The Anarchists*. London, 1971.

Kropotkin, Peter. *Paroles d'un révolté*. Paris, 1885.

———. *Les Bases scientifiques de l'anarchie; l'Anarchie future*. London, 1887.

Kuhn, Thomas S. *The Structure of Scientific Revolutions*. 2d ed. Chicago, 1970.

Laforgue, Jules. *Les Derniers Vers*. E. Dujardin and F. Fénéon, eds. Paris, 1890.

———. "Inédits de Laforgue." F. Fénéon, ed. *Revue anarchiste,* 1 Nov. 1893.

———. *Mélanges posthumes.* Paris, 1903.

———. *Oeuvres complètes,* vol. 5. Paris, 1925.

———. *Lettres à un ami* [Gustave Kahn]. Ed. G. Jean-Aubry. Paris, 1941.

———. *Poésies complètes.* Ed. Pascal Pia. Paris, 1970.

Lautréamont, Comte de [Isidore Ducasse]. *Les Chants de Maldoror.* Ed. F. Fénéon, preface by Léon Genonceaux. Paris, 1890.

Lazare, Bernard. "Félix Fénéon" (protesting Fénéon's arrest). *Le Journal,* 27 April 1894.

Lecomte, Georges. "Camille Pissarro." *Les Hommes d'aujourd'hui* 8, no. 366 (Paris, 1890).

———. *Pissarro.* Paris, 1922.

Lee, Ellen Wardwell. *The Aura of Neo-Impressionism.* Indianapolis, 1983.

Lemoyne de Forges, Marie-Thérèse. *Catalogue de l'exposition du centenaire de Paul Signac.* Musée du Louvre. Paris, 1963–64.

Levin, Miriam R. *Republican Art and Ideology in Late Nineteenth-Century France.* Ann Arbor, Mich., 1986.

Lipton, Eunice. "The Laundress in Late Nineteenth-Century French Culture." *Art History,* 3, no. 3 (September 1980): 295–313.

Lissagaray, P. O. *L'Histoire de la Commune de Paris.* Paris, 1876.

Lloyd, Christopher. *Pissarro.* Geneva, New York, 1981.

———. *Camille Pissarro.* Exhibition catalogue. London, Paris, Boston. Paris, Musées nationaux, 1981.

———, ed. *Studies on Camille Pissarro.* London, New York, 1986.

Loevgren, Sven. *The Genesis of Modernism.* New ed. Bloomington, Indiana, 1971.

Longhi, R. "Proposte per una critica d'arte." *Paragone,* Jan. 1950, p. 14.

Longoni, Joseph C. *Four Patients of Dr. Deibler.* London, 1970.

Lugné-Poe [Aurélien Lugné]. *La Parade,* vol. 1, *Le Sot du tremplin.* Paris, 1931; vol. 2, *Acrobaties.* Paris, 1932; vol. 3, *Sous les etoiles, souvenirs de théâtre (1902–1912).* Paris, 1933.

Maitron, Jean. *Le Mouvement anarchiste en France (1880–1914).* 2 vols. New ed. Paris, 1983. See the first edition, Paris, 1951, for appendixes not printed on subsequent editions.

———. *Le Syndicalisme révolutionnaire. Paul Delesalle.* Paris, 1952.

———. *Ravachol et les anarchistes.* Paris, 1964.

Malatesta, Errico. *Pensiero e Volontà* (16 May 1925). Trans. Vernon Richards, *Errico Malatesta, His Life & Ideas.* London, 1965.

Malingue, Maurice, ed. *Lettres de Gauguin à sa femme et à ses amis.* New ed. Paris, 1949.

Mallarmé, Stéphane. Quoted in "Arrestation d'un employé du ministère de la guerre: chez Paul Verlaine; chez M. Mallarmé." *Le Soir,* 27 April 1894.

———. "Citation à témoigner." Quoted by Henri Mondor, *Vie de Mallarmé.* Paris, 1941, pp. 688–89.

———. *Oeuvres complètes.* Paris, 1945.

———. *Correspondance,* ed. Henri Mondor and Lloyd James Austin. Vols. 2–9. Paris, 1965–83.

Martin, Elisabeth Puckett. "The Symbolist Criticism of Painting, France, 1880–1895." Ph.D. diss. Bryn Mawr College, 1948; University Microfilms no. 3576, Ann Arbor, Michigan.

Maus, M. Octave. *Trente années de lutte pour l'art, 1884–1914.* Brussels, 1906.

Merrill, Stuart. Review of Fénéon's translation of Jane Austen, *Catherine Morland* [*Northanger Abbey*]. *La Vogue,* May 1899, pp. 128–29.

Michaud, Guy. *Mallarmé.* Trans. M. Collins and B. Humez. New York, 1965.

Michel, François. *Par coeur.* Paris, 1985.

Michel, Jacques. "Le critique d'art" (review of F. F., *Oeuvres plus que complètes*). *Le Monde,* 8 Aug. 1970, pp. 9 and 11.

Millard, Ernest. "Le Commerce de la peinture." *Les Lettres nouvelles,* 1. 3(May 1953): 286.

Miomondre, Francis de. "Vingt ans après." *Bulletin de la vie artistique,* 15 Feb. 1926, pp. 51–52.

Mirbeau, Octave. "Chronique—Paul Gauguin." *Echo de Paris,* 16 Feb. 1891. Reprinted in *Art moderne,* 22 March 1891, pp. 92–94.

———. "Ravachol!" *L'Endehors,* 1 May 1892.

———. On Charles Henry. *Le Journal,* 19 Feb. 1894.

———. "Félix Fénéon" (protesting Fénéon's arrest). *Le Journal,* 29 April 1894.

———. "Potins!" (in defense of Fénéon). *Le Journal.* 7 May 1894.

Moers, Ellen. *The Dandy, Brummel to Beerbohm.* Lincoln, Nebraska, 1978.

Moffett, Charles S., with the assistance of Ruth Berson, Barbara Lee Williams, and Fronia E. Wissman. *The New Painting, Impressionism 1874–1886.* Exhibition catalogue. Fine Arts Museums of San Francisco, 1986.

Mombello, G. Review of F. F. *Oeuvres plus que complètes* (1970). *Studi francesi* 17(1973): 176–77.

Mondor, Henri. *Vie de Mallarmé.* 2 vols. Paris, 1941–42.

Monférier, Jacques. "Symbolisme et Anarchie." *Revue d'histoire littéraire de la France,* April–June 1965, pp. 233–38.

———. "La Revue Indépendante." Ph.D. diss. Université de Lille III, 1973.

Moore, George. *Confessions of a Young Man.* New York, 1917.

Moore, Will G. *La Rochefoucauld, His Mind and Art.* Oxford, 1969.

Moréas, Jean. *Les Syrtes* and *Cantilènes.* Paris, 1884 and 1886.

———. "Le Symbolisme." *Le Figaro,* 18 Sept. 1886.

———. "Peintures—les articles de Fénéon." *Le Symboliste,* 22 Oct. 1886.

Morelle, Paul. "Félix Fénéon dans ses *Oeuvres plus que complètes.*" *Le Monde,* 8 Aug. 1970, pp. 9 and 11.

Mouthon, F. I. *Du Bluff au chantage. Les Grandes Campagnes du Matin. Comment on fait l'opinion en France.* Paris, n.d.

Multatuli. See Douwes Dekker, Eduard.

Nadeau, Maurice. "*Oeuvres* de Félix Fénéon." *Mercure de France* 305(1 Feb. 1949): 312–16.

Natanson, Thadée. "Ceux de la *Revue blanche:* Félix Fénéon." Radio broadcast, Paris, 25 Nov. 1938. Extract in John Rewald, "Félix Fénéon," *Gazette des Beaux-Arts,* Feb. 1948, pp. 107–8. Other extracts in *Seurat et son oeuvre,* "Portrait de Félix Fénéon," by César M. de Hauke, Paris, 1961, p. xix.

———. *Peints à leur tour.* Paris, 1948.

Nettlau, Max. *Bibliographie de l'anarchie.* Paris and Brussels, 1897.

———. *Errico Malatesta.* New York, 1922.

Nietzsche, Friedrich. *The Gay Science* (1883–1887). Trans. Walter Kaufmann. New York, 1974.

Nochlin, Linda. *Impressionism and Post-Impressionism, 1874–1904. Sources and Documents.* Englewood Cliffs, N.J., 1966.

Parmelin, Hélène. *Picasso dit.* Paris, 1966.

Paulhan, Jean. *F. F. ou le critique.* Paris, 1945. Reprinted as Introduction to Fénéon, *Oeuvres,* Paulhan ed., Paris, 1948.

Penrose, Roland. *Picasso, His Life and Work.* London, 1958.

Perros, Georges [Georges Poulot]. "Oeuvres de Fénéon." In *Lectures*. Cognac, 1981, pp. 7–8.

Pia, Pascal. "Le compagnon Fénéon." *La Quinzaine Littéraire,* no. 9 (15 July 1966): 13–14.

———, ed. Jules Laforgue, *Poésies complètes*. Paris, 1970.

Pissarro, Camille. *Lettres à son fils Lucien*. Ed. John Rewald. Paris, 1950. *Letters to His Son Lucien*. ed. John Rewald. 2d ed. Mamaroneck, N.Y., 1972.

———. *Correspondance*. Ed. Janine Bailly-Herzberg. Vols. 2 and 3. Paris, 1985–87.

Pouget, Emile. *Père peinard,* no. 1 (Sunday, 24 Feb. 1889).

Pouilliart, R. Review of F. F., *Oeuvres plus que complètes* (1970). *Les Lettres romanes* 24(1970): 409–10.

Priollaud, Nicole, ed. *La Femme au 19e siècle*. Paris, 1983.

Proudhon, Pierre-Joseph. *Qu'est-ce que la propriété?* Paris, 1840.

———. *De la justice dans la révolution et dans l'église,* 3 vols. Paris, 1858.

———. *Du principe de l'art et de sa destination sociale*. Paris, 1865.

———. *La Pornocratie ou les femmes dans les temps modernes*. *Oeuvres posthumes,* vol. 2. Paris, n.d.

Raynaud, Ernest. *La Mêlée symboliste*. 3 vols. Paris, 1920.

Régnier, Henri de. *Figures et caractères*. Paris, 1900.

———. *Vestigia Flammae*. Paris, 1921.

Renard, Jules. *Journal 1898*. Paris. 1927.

Retté, Adolphe. "Bars et brasseries à l'Exposition." *Vogue,* Aug. 1889.

———. *Le Symbolisme, anecdotes et souvenirs*. Paris, 1903.

Rewald, John. *Georges Seurat*. New York, 1942.

———. "Félix Fénéon." *Gazette des Beaux-Arts,* ser. 6, 32(July–August 1947): 45–62 and 34(Feb. 1948): 107–26.

———. *Pierre Bonnard*. New York, 1948.

———. "Artists' Quarrels." *Seurat in Perspective,* ed. Norma Broude (Englewood Cliffs, N.J., 1978), pp. 104–5; originally in Rewald, *Georges Seurat,* Paris, 1948, pp. 114–15.

———, ed. "Extraits du journal inédit de Paul Signac." *Gazette des Beaux-Arts,* ser. 6, 36 (July–Dec. 1949).

———, ed. Camille Pissarro, *Letters to His Son Lucien*. Rev. ed. Mamaroneck, 1972; *Lettres à son fils Lucien*. Paris, 1950.

———. *The History of Impressionism*. 4th ed. New York, 1973.

———. *Post-Impressionism from van Gogh to Gauguin*. 2d ed. New York, 1962.

———, and Dorra, Henri. *Seurat. Paris, 1959.*

Rimbaud, Arthur. *Illuminations, Painted Plates*. H. de Bouillane de Lacoste, ed. Paris, 1949, with extracts from letters of F. Fénéon.

Rochefort, Henri. "Les Hommes aux masques de fer." *L'Intransigeant,* 9 Aug. 1894.

———. "L'Avenir d'un acquitté." *L'Intransigeant,* 17 Aug. 1894.

Rood, Ogden N. *Modern Chromatics, with Applications to Art and Industry*. New York, 1879. French trans. *Théorie scientifique des couleurs*. Paris, 1881.

Rosny aîné, J.-H. [J.-H. Boëx]. *Torches et lumignons, souvenirs de la vie littéraire*. Paris, 1921.

Ruchon, François. *Jules Laforgue*. Geneva, 1924.

Russell, John. *Vuillard*. Greenwich, Conn., 1971.

Rysselberghe, Maria van [M. Saint-Clair, pseud.]. *Galerie privée*. Paris, 1947.

Saillet, Maurice. "Petite Histoire." Introduction to Alfred Jarry, *La Chandelle verte*. Paris, 1969. Correspondence between F. Fénéon and Jarry, pp. 15–16 and 25.

Salmon, André. *Souvenirs sans fin,* vol. 1 (1903–1908). Paris, 1955.

———. *La Terreur noire*. Paris, 1959.

Schapiro, Meyer. "New Light on Seurat." *Art News* 57(April 1958):22–24, 44–45, 52.

Schmidt, J. Kaspar. *See* Stirner, Max.

Séverine [pseud. of Caroline Rémy]. "Que faire?" (protesting Fénéon's arrest). *Le Journal,* 8 May 1894.

Sewell, Brocard. *In the Dorian Mode: A Life of John Gray, 1866–1934.* Padstow, Cornwall, 1983.

Shattuck, Roger. *The Banquet Years.* New York, 1955.

Shiff, Richard. *Cézanne and the End of Impressionism.* Chicago, 1984.

Shikes, Ralph E., and Harper, Paula. *Pissarro, His Life and Work.* New York, 1980.

Signac, Paul. *Le Néo-impressionnisme, Documents* (1934). In *D'Eugène Delacroix au neo-impressionnisme* (1899). Ed. F. Cachin. Paris, 1966.

———. "Fragments de Journal." Ed. Georges Besson. *Arts de France* (1947), nos. 11–12: 102, and nos. 17–18:75.

———. "Extraits du journal inédit de Paul Signac." Ed. John Rewald. *Gazette des Beaux-Arts,* ser. 6, 36(July–Dec. 1949).

Stirner, Max [pseud. of J. Kaspar Schmidt]. *Der Einzige und sein Eigentum.* Berlin, 1845.

Sutter, Jean, ed. *The Neo-Impressionists.* English ed. Greenwich, Conn., 1970. Essays by R. L. Herbert (Seurat), I. Compin (H.-E. Cross), L. Bazalgette (Dubois-Pillet and H. Petitjean), Alan Fern (Lucien Pissarro), P. Eberhart (Cavallo-Peduzzi and Léo Gausson), F. Cl. Legrand, H. Thévenin and M.-J. Chartrain-Hebbellinck (Belgian Neo-Impressionists), and H. Certigny.

Tavernier, René. "Félix Fénéon mon ami." *Poésie* 44, no. 19 (May–June 1949): 117–19.

———. "Petit Journal de Vacances." *Cahiers des Saisons,* no. 48 (Winter 1967): 335.

Texier, J. "Félix Fénéon, curieux homme." *Le Populaire-dimanche,* 9 Jan. 1949.

Thomson, Belinda. "Camille Pissarro and Symbolism." *Burlington Magazine* 124 (Jan. 1982): 14–23.

———. *The Post-Impressionists.* Secausus, N.J., 1983.

Thomson, Richard. *Seurat.* Oxford, 1985.

Thorold, Anne. *A Catalogue of the Oil Paintings of Lucien Pissarro.* Boston, 1983.

Tourette, Gilles de la. *Robert Delaunay.* Paris, 1950.

Vaillant, Annette. "Les amitiés de la *Revue Blanche.*" *Derrière le miroir,* no. 158–59 (April–May 1966). Catalogue of the exhibition "Autour de *la Revue Blanche,*" Galerie Maeght. Paris, 1966.

———. *Bonnard.* Greenwich, Conn., 1965.

———. *Le Pain polka. Au Pays d'avant-hier.* Paris. 1974.

Valéry, Paul. *Variété II.* Paris, 1930.

van Gogh, Vincent. *The Complete Letters of Vincent van Gogh,* vol. 3. Greenwich, Conn., 1958.

Vanor, Georges. *L'Art symboliste.* Paris, 1889.

Varennes, Henri. "Incident de cabinet." *L'Intransigeant,* 13 Aug. 1894.

———. "Plaidoirie de Maître Demange." *L'Intransigeant,* 13 Aug. 1894.

Veber, Pierre and Willy. *Une Passade.* Paris, n.d.

Velde, Henri van de. "Notes sur l'art." *La Wallonie, May 1890.*

Verhaeren, Emile. "*Les Derniers Vers* de Jules Laforgue." *Art moderne,* 30 Nov. 1890.

———. On the Salon des Indépendants, 1891. *L'Art moderne de Bruxelles,* 5 April 1891.

———. "Georges Seurat." *Société nouvelle,* April 1891. Reprinted in *Sensations.* Paris, 1927, pp. 197–203.

Verlaine, Paul. Sonnet "To Francis Poictevin." *Revue blanche,* 5, no. 24 (Oct. 1893): 227.

———. Quoted in "Arrestation d'un employé du ministére de la guerre: chez Paul Verlaine; chez M. Mallarmé." *Le Soir,* 27 April 1894.

Vielé-Griffin, Francis. "Epitaphe pour un enfant." *L'Endehors,* 28 Feb. 1892.

Vuarnet, Jean-Noël. "Féneon ou: le critique." *Europe* 501 (Jan. 1971): 166–69.

Ward, Martha. "Félix Fénéon and the Interpretation of Neo-impressionism." Paper delivered at the John Hopkins symposium, 6 Mar 1981, "Theory, Critics and the Practice of Painting."

———. "The Rhetoric of Independence and Innovation, the Eighth Impressionist Exhibition 1886." In Charles S. Moffett, *The New Painting, Impressionism 1874–1886.* Exhibition catalogue. The Fine Arts Museums of San Francisco, 1986.

Welsh-Ovcharov, Bogomila. *Van Gogh in Perspective.* Englewood Cliffs, N.J., 1974.

———. *Van Gogh à Paris.* Exhibition catalogue. Paris, Musée d'Orsay, 1988.

Whelan, Richard. " 'Le Roi' Fénéon and the Neo-Impressionists." *Portfolio* 3, no. 2 (March–April 1981): 46–55.

Wilde, Oscar. "The Critic as Artist" (1890). From *Intentions* (1891). *Complete Works.* London, 1948.

Williams, Raymond. *The Long Revolution.* New York, 1961.

Willy [Henry Gauthiers-Villars and A. Ernst]. *Lettres de l'ouvreuse.* Paris, 1890.

Woodcock, George. *Anarchism.* New York, 1962.

Wright, Gordon. *France in Modern Times.* New York, 1981.

Wyzewa, Teodor de. "*Les Impressionnistes en 1886* de Félix Fénéon." *Revue indépendante* (Feb. 1887): 148–49.

———. "Georges Seurat." *L'Art dans les deux mondes,* 18 April 1891.

Zeldin, Theodore. *France,* 1848–1945. 2 vols. Oxford, 1973, 1977.

Zimmermann, Michael. "Seurat, eine theoretische Monographie. Sein Werk, der Diskurs über Kunst in den 1880er Jahren und die 'wissenschaftliche' Ästhetik Charles Henrys." Ph.D. diss., University of Cologne, 1984.

Zola, Emile. *Paris, 1898. Oeuvres complètes,* vol. 7. Paris, 1968.

ARCHIVES

Documents and manuscripts were consulted in the following public collections:

Ashmolean Museum, Oxford.
Archives Nationales, Paris.
Archives and Museum of the Préfecture de Police, Paris.
Archives of the Department of the Seine, Paris.
Archives of the Department of Saône-et-Loire, Mâcon.
Archives of the Bibliothèque de la ville de Pau.
Archives Albert Vanderlinden, Brussels.
Archives of the Nationalmuseum, Stockholm.
Beineke Library, Yale University, New Haven, Conn.
Bibliothèque d'Art et d'Archéologie, Fondation Jacques Doucet, Paris.
Bibliothèque Littéraire, Fondation Jacques Doucet, Paris.
Bibliothèque de la Sorbonne, Paris.
Bibliothèque Nationale, Salle des Manuscrits, Paris.
Bibliothèque Royale, Brussels.
Houghton Library, Harvard University Cambridge, Mass.
Institut français d'histoire sociale, Fonds Jean Grave, Paris.

In addition, many private collections and archives, named in the notes, contributed to this study.

Index